AUSTIN'S
TOPICAL HISTORY
of
CHRISTIANITY

AUSTIN'S
TOPICAL
HISTORY
of
CHRISTIANITY

Bill R. Austin

TYNDALE HOUSE PUBLISHERS, INC.   WHEATON, ILLINOIS

First printing, September 1983
Library of Congress Catalog Card Number 83-50142
ISBN 0-8423-0096-1
Copyright © 1983 by Bill R. Austin
Printed in the United States of America

C O N T E N T S

INTRODUCTION   7

I
THE FULLNESS OF TIME:
THE COMING OF JESUS CHRIST (4 BC-AD 100)   11

I I
THE MARTYRS' FAITH:
PERSECUTIONS AND FOUNDATIONS (100-313)   57

I I I
THE OVERCOMERS: AN IMPERIAL CHURCH (313-590)   83

I V
THE STORMS AND THE ROCK:
CONFLICTS AND CONTROVERSIES (590-800)   121

V
FRIEND OR FOE?: THE EAST-WEST SCHISM (800-1054)   139

V I
MASTERS AND SERVANTS:
THE POWER STRUGGLE (1054-1305)   161

V I I
A HOUSE DIVIDED: DISRUPTION AND DECLINE (1305-1517)   197

V I I I
CLEANSING THE TEMPLE: THE REFORM CRISIS (1517-1648)   *225*

I X
THE FOOLISHNESS OF GOD AND THE WISDOM OF MEN:
FAITH AND REASON (1648-1776)   *311*

X
THE WORLD-SHAKERS:
REVOLUTIONS AND REPERCUSSIONS (1776-1900)   *353*

X I
THE WITNESSES: MISSIONS AND MOVEMENTS (1792-1914)   *395*

X I I
ABOUNDING SIN, ABOUNDING GRACE:
THE PARADOX OF RECESSION AND ADVANCE (1914-1981)   *451*

INDEX   *519*

INTRODUCTION

EMERSON once said, "I have no expectation that any man will read history aright who thinks that what was done in a remote age, by men whose names have resounded far, has any deeper sense than what he is doing today." Accordingly, this account of the history of Christianity is presented in the hope that the reader will feel that he or she is a vital part of the continuing story and current episode of Christianity.

However, in order to have that sense of involvement, one must have a perspective before and beyond the immediate situation. Unless one knows where he has come from, he cannot understand where he is, nor foresee where he is going. This volume is written to help explain the present religious situation (especially in America) by looking at those events which brought us to this place.

Alexander Miller very cogently says, "We are inexplicable to ourselves without reference to our history: and this is true both of our individual and of our social life. If I want to know what makes me tick morally, I shall find more illumination from a study of the Puritans than from the most diligent discipline of introspection. And the character of American society is similarly inexplicable without proper attention to the rock from which it was hewn."

So, the study of history is not merely the learning of ancient facts and dates. It is the learning of oneself. It is learning what has made us what we are, and why we believe what we do. Learning the past is really the exciting adventure of learning what the present is all about. To this end and purpose this book has been written.

The beginning student of church history is faced with the formidable task of comprehending the major issues, personalities, and move-ments in the history of Christianity. The vast amount of material in Christianity's two-thousand-year history is overwhelming and confusing. Names, dates, and issues are caught up in a swirling mass of information. It is difficult to organize and remember which names belong in which century, and what issues produced what movements.

This book is one more attempt to assimilate the best-known data in such a way as to help the student sort out and retain the facts which have had the most general influence on Christianity. I believe that this can best be done by arranging the material in topical outlines which suggest causes, relationships, and results.

A topical history has both advantages and disadvantages. It is very advantageous for the student to be able to see a topical outline which immediately identifies certain people under certain headings. Otherwise, one has to wade through many pages, gathering names and trying to see where they fit into the scheme of things. It is also helpful to have a movement or issue discussed thoroughly in one setting rather than trying to trace the continuing story and outcome in later pages. The ability to set one movement against another or to make a comparative study of conflicting ideas is also facilitated by topical outlining.

On the other hand, an obvious disadvantage of a topical history is its interference with the natural flow of chronological events. For example, the crusades span three centuries and affect many lives and situations. By listing them all together, it is easier to learn and memorize the crusades as such. But it is also necessary to skip over and postpone discussion of some important people and events during those three hundred years, because those people and events belong more appropriately under a topic other than the crusades. Another disadvantage of a topical history is the problem of deciding where some people belong, because many Christian leaders were involved in several issues and movements.

I believe, however, that the advantages of a topical study outweigh the disadvantages for the beginning student who needs to have some definitive "handles" to grasp. I hope that this topical grouping of issues, movements, theologians, and events will give the student a visual learning tool to help sort out and categorize the huge amount of material in church history.

This is not a history of Christian theology, but, of course, the history of Christianity has most definitely been shaped by theological concerns and parties. I have tried to review the most critical theological issues as they affected the outcome of history. Naturally, selection has been a serious limitation at this point. Some periods may seem heavier in theology than necessary and some may appear to need wider and more thorough treatment of theological factors. As with any volume of church history, the student and teacher will need to augment practically every period with additional research in related theology.

Geographically, Christianity covers the whole earth; but what follows is not an exhaustive study of worldwide Christianity. It would be impossible to compile in one volume even the barest amount of data from every region to which Christianity has spread, but I have tried to indicate the major thrusts of missions and expansion. This volume is essentially concerned with European and American Christianity, with only scant mention of the work in Africa and the Orient. The South American scene appears only briefly in the early developments, and the vast enterprise of Brazilian Christianity is not even attempted. Obviously, every historian must limit himself somewhere, and I have chosen to limit myself to those areas which I feel are the most pertinent for a survey study of the beginnings of Christianity and the development of the American situation. I have tried to treat those men and movements which had an unquestionable bearing on the historical outcome, or who represent a specific period or issue. I have also approached every subject as though it were being introduced to the reader for the first time, rather than assuming he would recognize certain names or movements.

There is no "original" history. All of our information comes from some source, and the sources of Christian history are manifold. I have made no attempt to rewrite history through my own interpretation. Naturally, my personal biases will occasionally show through, but my intention has been to be a compiler of history, not a creator. I am indebted to many sources, both primary and secondary. I have roamed freely through dozens of textbooks to see how others have done it. I have tried to learn from a wide variety of approaches and styles. Then I have taken the familiar information of conventional church history and arranged it in a format which I believe will help the beginning student more easily learn the data involved.

After several discussions, the publisher and I decided not to hamper the flow of reading with footnotes. As I have just acknowledged, all of the material is gleaned from other sources, and every historical fact has been passed on from someone. I have cited the source of quotations, but I have done this in the text rather than in footnotes.

The outlines at the beginning of each major section were carefully planned to aid the student in mentally organizing the material during that period, and should be referred to often while reading and reviewing.

For assistance in making this volume a reality, my appreciation goes to Wendell Hawley, vice-president and editor-in-chief of Tyndale House Publishers, who suggested the project to me, encouraged and prodded me for some four years, and demonstrated a genuine Christian attitude toward the whole purpose of our endeavor. I am also indebted to the several professors across the country who read and critiqued the embryonic manuscript. I am embarrassed to think how many mistakes would have appeared had it not been for their sharp eyes and astute knowledge. My very personal and warmest gratitude goes to my wife, Margie, who would not let me give up, and who tirelessly and cheerfully typed almost the entire manuscript. No man can create history on his own, and certainly no one can compile it without the help of many hands and hearts.

I

THE FULLNESS
OF TIME:
THE COMING OF
JESUS CHRIST
(4 BC-AD 100)

When the fulness of time had come,
God sent forth his Son. . . .

GALATIANS 4 : 4

Jesus came into Galilee, preaching
the gospel of the kingdom of God,
And saying, The time is fulfilled,
and the kingdom of God is at hand:
repent ye, and believe the gospel.

MARK 1 : 14 , 15

A. Preparation: "The Time Is Fulfilled"
  1. Religious and Historical Judaism
     a. Old Testament Background
        (1) The Patriarchs
        (2) Egyptian Bondage
        (3) Exodus and Sinai
        (4) Conquest and Monarchy
        (5) Exile and Restoration
     b. Interbiblical Period
        (1) Expansion of Hellenism
        (2) Maccabean Revolt
        (3) Religious Parties
  2. Political and Social Palestine
     a. The Roman Period and the Herodian Dynasty
        (1) The Roman Empire
        (2) The Herodian Dynasty
     b. The Greco-Roman Civilization
        (1) Citizenship and Culture
        (2) Philosophy and Religion
B. Revelation: "The Kingdom of God Is at Hand"
  1. The Birth of Jesus
  2. The Childhood of Jesus
  3. Chosen and Proven
  4. Teaching and Healing
     a. Message and Methods
     b. Miracles and Signs
  5. The Question of Authority
     a. Personhood and Authority
     b. Religion and Authority
     c. Politics and Authority
  6. Rejection and Crucifixion
  7. Resurrection and Commission
C. Proclamation: "Repent and Believe in the Gospel"
  1. Pentecost and Proclamation
  2. Gathered and Scattered
  3. Paul and the Gentile Mission
     a. Conversion and Commencement
     b. The Jerusalem Conference
     c. Missionary Journeys Continued
     d. Arrest and Imprisonment
  4. Literature and Canonization
  5. Close of the Apostolic Age

THE CITY OF ROME was approximately 780 years old, and in the Greco-Roman world, the calendars of men counted time from the founding of that colossal capital of the empire (AUC—*ab urbe condita*). But along the northwest coast of the Sea of Galilee, in the small province of Palestine, lay an average-sized city called Capernaum, from which was about to be launched such startling ideas and world-shaking events that in centuries to come people would date their calendars not by AUC but by AD—*Anno Domini*, "in the year of the Lord." Thus, the year AUC 780 would be more easily recognized as the year AD 27. "The Lord" to which the new dating referred was a thirty-year-old carpenter from the village of Nazareth who was named Jesus!

The reason for Jesus being thirty years old rather than 27 in the year AD 27 (as would be supposed if the Christian era dates from his birth) rests in an error of calculation by Dionysius, a Scythian monk who started the Christian calendar in the first half of the sixth century. The biblical record informs us that Jesus was born during the last few months of the reign of Herod the Great. (Roman records indicate that Herod died in AUC 750, not in AUC 754, as Dionysius miscalculated. The birth of Jesus was, therefore, sometime prior to 4 BC. There is no year 0, so from 1 BC to AD 1 is one civil year, and from 4 BC to AD 4 is seven years. Thus, Jesus began his ministry at the age of thirty in the year AD 27.)

In a few short weeks, this Jesus had startled the whole region of Galilee with teachings and actions which clearly set him apart from other men. He taught religious doctrines with an authority which superseded even the scribes. He cast an "unclean spirit" out of a man in the synagogue of Capernaum. He healed the mother-in-law of Simon, one of his earliest followers. The masses came to him with their sick and afflicted, and he healed many, including such serious ailments as leprosy and palsy. The people were amazed and excited. They were certain that a prophet had come among them.

The scribes and Pharisees, however, accused him of violating Jewish religious laws and of being in league with the devil himself. Confusion erupted: Was it possible for one to do the works of God while breaking the laws of God?

A half century later, a learned Jewish convert to the Jesus movement by the name of Paul explained what was happening: "When the fulness of time was come, God sent forth his Son, made of a woman, made under the law, to redeem them that were under the law, that we might receive the adoption of sons" (Galatians 4:4, 5). Paul seemed to be echoing the very words of Jesus himself in those early days of his Galilean ministry: "The time is fulfilled, and the kingdom of God is at hand: repent ye, and believe the gospel" (Mark 1:15).

This is the first message of Jesus which Mark recorded, and its three distinct emphases of preparation, revelation, and proclamation form the outline for the biblical period of church history. The appearance of Jesus Christ on the stage of history culminated a long period of political, religious, and cultural *preparation*. The New Testament account of his appearance and the consequent results present Jesus of Nazareth as the ultimate *revelation* of God. The activity and witness of the early church clearly marked *proclamation* of that revelation as the first priority of Christianity.

A. PREPARATION

"The Time Is Fulfilled." Christianity was not born in a vacuum. Ancient cultures influenced and shaped its character. Powerful governments stood poised to regulate its activities and punish its defections. Established religions surrounded its camp, infiltrated its ranks, and challenged its right to exist. Further, the people who became known as Christians were not aliens who had invaded the small territory of Palestine. They were people of the land. They were products of and participants in these ancient customs, powerful governments, and established religions.

1. RELIGIOUS AND HISTORICAL JUDAISM

The critics who attacked Jesus at Capernaum were the teachers and leaders of his own religious faith. The synagogue where he preached his first sermon and cast out the unclean spirit was a tangible part of the legacy of Judaism. The teachings of Jesus came from and expanded upon the ancient laws and instructions of his people, the Israelites. Jesus was a Jew, and as such his religious and cultural heritage was Jewish to the core. Christian history cannot be properly understood apart from the history of Judaism, the people and the religion which produced Jesus of Nazareth.

a. Old Testament Background. The "Bible" which Jesus and his contemporaries studied comprised the Jewish history, poetry, law, and prophecy, which is known today as the Old Testament. This rich literary heritage not

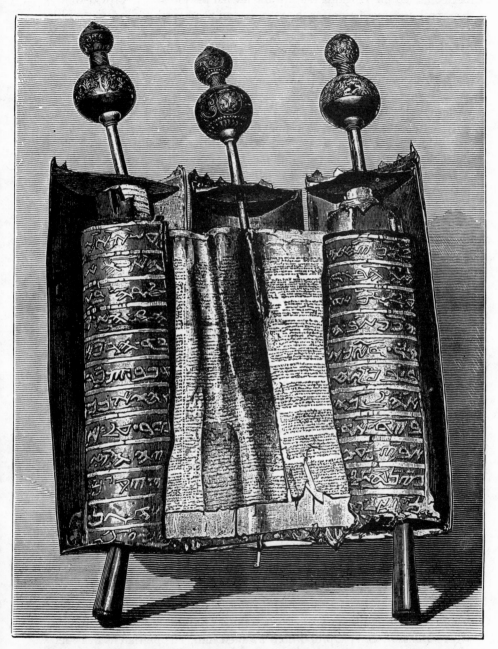

A copy of the Torah, a leather or parchment scroll of the Pentateuch and other Old Testament Scriptures, as it may have stood in the synagogue of Jesus' day. (Historical Pictures Service, Chicago)

only outlined the religious faith of the Jewish people; it also provided historical documentation for their origin and development. Today it enables Christians to know their spiritual forebears and to understand the setting in which their own odyssey began.

(1) The Patriarchs. Two thousand years before Jesus was born, a prosperous clan chieftain by the name of Abraham moved from northwestern Mesopotamia into a narrow strip of land located at the eastern extremity of the great Mediterranean Sea. Known as Canaan, and later to become known as Palestine, this small territory comprised approximately 10,000 square miles, was about 150 miles long, and 40 to 75 miles wide. Although only slightly larger than the American state of Vermont, this compact area was destined to become the stage for international interest and conflict for centuries to come. One reason for its critical importance in world affairs is its strategic location between the continents of Asia and Africa, forming a veritable land bridge, and establishing it as the crossroads of the world.

Another reason lay within the purpose and motivation of the original migration by Abraham, who reported that God himself had called him out of his homeland, "unto a land that I will show thee" (Genesis 12:1). The divine call had included a threefold promise that would become known as the Abrahamic Covenant. Abraham was promised that he would become the father of a great nation, which would become a blessing to all nations, and that his descendants would possess this land. This promise of seed, land, and universal blessing became the keystone of Jewish politics and religion for succeeding generations.

The promise of the seed, that Abraham would become a great nation, seemed unlikely as he and his wife advanced into old age childless. However, in a dramatic fulfillment of the promise, they were given a son, Isaac, when Abraham was 100 years old and Sarah was 90. The covenant was passed on to Isaac, a stable businessman of personal integrity. By *primogeniture* (the inheritance right of the firstborn) the covenant should have passed from Isaac to Esau, the firstborn of Isaac's twin sons. By connivance and deceit, Esau's brother, Jacob, wrested the birthright and the covenant blessing from him, and set in motion the whole future identity of the descendants of Abraham.

In a cataclysmic encounter with God, Jacob's nature and name were changed. The deceiver became the believer; Jacob became Israel, the name by which all the Jews are known to this day. To him were born twelve sons, who became the ancestors of the twelve tribes of Israel. Jacob's favorite son, Joseph, was sold by his jealous brothers into slavery in Egypt, where a destiny of epic proportions awaited him. The patriarchs of Israel are usually identified as Abraham, Isaac, and Jacob. But, because of his significant role in preserving his people, Joseph surely must rank as one of the ancient fathers.

(2) Egyptian Bondage. Through an unexpected rise to prominence, Joseph, the former slave, became the prime minister of Egypt and the wise administrator who saved the land from disaster during a severe famine. He brought his father Jacob (Israel) and his brothers and their families into Egypt to provide for them. They were settled in the fertile and productive region of Goshen and were treated cordially by the Egyptians. This initial hospitality was undoubtedly due to two facts: Joseph's position and favor among the people, and the Egyptian government being under the domination of the Hyksos, an Asiatic people who had invaded the land and overthrown the Semitic dynasty around 1710 BC. Similar Semitic backgrounds caused the Hyksos to deal favorably with the Israelites who entered Egypt about 1700 BC. An Egyptian revolution in 1570 BC, however, brought the Hyksos regime to an end.

The favored sons of Jacob and their growing descendants were gradually degraded and eventually pressed into abject slavery, a deplorable condition which lasted some four hundred years. To several generations of Israelites it appeared that God had forgotten his covenant with the patriarchs. When all hope of deliverance seemed gone, God raised up from among the people a deliverer, Moses. After forty years of training in the courts of Pharaoh, and forty more years of maturing in the desert, Moses was sent on divine commission to deliver his oppressed kinsmen.

(3) Exodus and Sinai. The unfolding drama of Israel's deliverance included warnings to Pharaoh, plagues upon the land, the horror of the death angel's visit, and the supernatural crossing of the sea. The Exodus became, for all time, the greatest event in history for the Jewish people. It was there that God vindicated himself and openly identified this poor helpless people as his own. The Passover feast, still devoutly observed to this day, commemorates this intervention of God on behalf of Israel.

Emerging from the banks of the sea, strewn with the bodies of drowned Egyptians, the Israelites were free at last, and a nation was born in a day. Accomplishing the monumental task of organizing and providing for the people, Moses marched them across the desert to keep their appointment with God at Mt. Sinai. At Horeb, the holy mountain where Moses had first encountered God at the burning bush, Moses now received the Ten Commandments, the covenant code, and instructions for constructing the tabernacle and formulating the religion of Israel.

With the revelation finished at Sinai, the great host struck out for the Promised Land, Canaan, which God had promised Abraham. Through fear and lack of faith, the people were not willing to invade Canaan and were sentenced to forty years of wandering in the wilderness. Moses was called home to God, and Joshua was appointed to lead the people into the Promised Land.

(4) Conquest and Monarchy. With lightning swift military strategy, Joshua swept through the central highlands, subdued the southern city-states, and

then swung north to conquer the whole of the land which Israel considered theirs by divine decree. Without a formal government, the Israelites were held together by an ingenious *amphictyony* (a religious confederation united around worship at a central sanctuary). The league of tribes thus functioned under this common religious commitment for about two hundred years, inspired and led by gifted personalities known as "judges."

Through the influence of neighboring nations and because of growing national affairs, the people began to demand a monarchial form of government, and Saul became the first king of Israel. He was followed by David, the most renowned and beloved of all Israel's kings. After bringing the kingdom to great power and religious fervor, David passed from the scene and his son Solomon ascended the throne. Wealth and wisdom were the two descriptions of Solomon's magnificent reign until he began to deteriorate morally and politically. Only three kings served the united kingdom of Israel—Saul, David, and Solomon—and then the nation was divided.

The divided kingdom consisted of Israel in the north and Judah in the south, with the former retaining ten tribes and the latter only two. The northern kingdom continued for approximately two centuries after the death of Solomon before it was destroyed in 722/721 BC by the rising power of Assyria. Judah existed almost twice as long before it fell to the Babylonians, climaxed by the destruction of Jerusalem in 587 BC.

(5) Exile and Restoration. Large numbers of Judeans were deported into Babylon, including most of the social, political, and religious leaders. The exile, which was never slavery as was the Egyptian bondage, lasted for almost seventy years. The people of the covenant retained their identity in the strange land of their captors, and out of the exile came significant additions to their culture and religion.

It was in Babylon that the Aramaic language began to replace Hebrew as the popular language of the Jews, and this Aramaic was the language used by Jesus and the New Testament people. Technically speaking, it is also the exile which dates the use of the term "Jew" for the Israelites. A contraction of the name Judah, the term was used because most of those in exile and later the majority of the returnees to Palestine were from the prominent tribe of Judah.

Religiously, the practice of sacrifice was discontinued for a time, but sabbath observance and circumcision continued to be strongly enforced. During this period the synagogue came into existence, supplying the people with a temporary place of meeting in a strange land. Perhaps the most lasting and influential result of the exile was the collecting and editing of Israel's vast literature of faith. The people of God had lost their amphictyonic structure, their nationalistic institutions, and their temple cult. They no longer had Jerusalem, the Davidic monarchy, or the great temple, which had been leveled. The one thing they still had was the revealed

Word of God. In the years of exile the Jews began to organize and codify their literature of faith, and the Torah ("instruction") formed the basis of the community's life.

After the death of Nebuchadnezzar, the Babylonian emperor who had conquered Judah and destroyed Jerusalem, the empire began to decline, and in a few years was overthrown by Cyrus of Persia. The Persians reversed the previous policy of repression, humiliation, and destruction. Subject peoples were allowed to return to their homelands, and a dedicated core of Jews returned to Palestine to rebuild their temple and the walls of Jerusalem. The postexilic religion of Israel became known as Judaism. Ezra is generally recognized as the father of Judaism, for his diligent scribal work with the Torah and his fervent efforts toward a national revival after the Jews returned to their homeland. Sporadic attempts to organize the people, as well as the intermittent ascendency of new leaders, raised hopes of a restored kingdom; but it never materialized into the grandeur that once was Israel's. Judea was annexed to the district of Coele-Syria, subject to the control of the Syrian governor.

Under nearly two centuries of Persian rule, the Jews enjoyed a relative peace and saw great developments in Judaism. The high priest became the political, social, and religious leader of the people. Monotheism became prominent in the world of religion. Jewish exclusiveness resulted in strong nationalism and a sense of aloofness and separateness. The law of Moses became the standard of holiness and the symbol of nationality. Ceremonial law and ritualism were the measure of piety.

b. Interbiblical Period. Between the writing of the Old Testament and the New Testament, momentous events occurred which had worldwide repercussions. The Hebrews of Judea were also affected and the course of their destiny changed.

(1) Expansion of Hellenism. The Persian Empire began to disintegrate and fell to the rising power of the Greek states. In 336 Alexander the Great assumed control of all Hellas; and in his march to conquer the Near East, he crossed the Hellespont in 334, signaling the entry of Greek culture into Asia. In 331 Persia fell to Alexander; and since Judea was under Persian rule, it also became a vassal state of the Greek empire.

Upon Alexander's death, his empire was divided among his five generals, two of whom became important to Jewish history. Ptolemy gained Egypt and Seleucus won Babylonia, including Syria. Between them lay Phoenicia and Palestine and for more than a century and a half the two rulers and their successors fought for possession of the "neutral" territory. The Seleucids finally gained undisputed control in 198 BC and the benevolent Antiochus III (Antiochus the Great), improved the standing of Hellenism with the Jews. His improvements were reversed, however, under the tyrannical reign of Antiochus IV (Epiphanes, 175-163), who outlawed the practice of

Judaism, ransacked the temple, destroyed the fortifications of Jerusalem, and slaughtered many devout Jews.

(2) Maccabean Revolt. Rebellion against the Seleucid oppression began with an aged priest Mattathias and his five sons. Upon the death of Mattathias, his son Judas became head of the growing guerrilla band. Called "Maccabee" (hammer) because of his lightning ability to strike devastating blows to the organized Seleucid garrisons, Judas led his untrained soldiers into phenomenal victory after victory. By 165 BC the Maccabean revolt had gained religious freedom for the Jews. The Jerusalem temple, which had been dedicated to the pagan god Zeus three years earlier, was purged by the Jews and rededicated to their God, Jehovah. This religious emancipation is still celebrated annually by the Jews in the Feast of Hanukkah (rededication).

Two of Judas' brothers, Jonathan and Simon, followed him as priest-rulers, and the Maccabean dynasty established an independent rule in Palestine which lasted almost one hundred years. John Hyrcanus, grandson of Mattathias, ruled for thirty turbulent years, followed by brief and inglorious administrations of corruption and intrigue. Civil war erupted and so weakened the country that Pompey, the Roman general, literally walked in and took over Jerusalem in the name of the Roman Republic in 63 BC. By the time Jesus was born, Roman rule was in full force and Herod was ruler of the Jews by the authority granted him from Rome.

(3) Religious Parties. Three major religious sects emerged during this period: the Pharisees, the Sadducees, and the Essenes. There were two minor groups of considerable influence: the Herodians and the Zealots. All of these parties impinged in one way or another upon the life and ministry of Jesus and his Church.

The word *Pharisee* means "separated ones." This small but powerful sect sought moral and theological separation. They were very scrupulous in the observance of all Jewish laws; they upheld the strictest forms of Jewish worship; they advocated reverence for oral tradition; they believed in the resurrection, punishment and rewards in the afterlife, angels, supremacy of the Pentateuch, and divine sovereignty over history.

The Sadducees were more interested in politics than religion. They were associated with the aristocrats and ruling classes. They accepted only the Pentateuch as inspired, resisted oral tradition, and did not believe in angels or the resurrection.

The Essenes, although not mentioned in the New Testament, are widely discussed by Philo, Josephus, and Pliny. They devoted themselves to simple communal life, practiced ritual washings, baptisms, and periods of prayer, and were dedicated to the study of the Old Testament. John the Baptist is thought by many to have been influenced by the Essenes.

The Herodians were Jews of influence and standing who supported the Herodian rule, which was maintained by the Romans. Most Palestinians were opposed to the Romans and Herodians, putting the Herodian party in a despised minority. They are mentioned in the Gospels as being enemies of Jesus (Matthew 22:16; Mark 3:6; 12:13).

The Zealots were founded by Judas the Galilean, who stirred up a rebellion against the Romans in AD 6 (Acts 5:37). They advocated Jewish nationalism and zealously (hence "Zealots") sought the violent overthrow of Rome. Jesus had a Zealot in his apostolic group (Luke 6:15; Acts 1:13).

The majority of Palestinian Jews (perhaps as many as 90 percent) did not belong to any of these religious sects or groups. These multitudes were known as the common people, and it was to these that Jesus showed a distinct compassion (Matthew 9:36). From them he also received a gracious hearing (Mark 12:37).

2. POLITICAL AND SOCIAL PALESTINE
The life of Christ and the history of Christianity cannot be told and interpreted only in religious language. The political forces and social structures of the day were extremely influential on the outcome of the unfolding story.

a. The Roman Period and the Herodian Dynasty. From 63 BC to AD 39, Palestine was under complex and shifting administrations of Jews, Romans, and Herods. When Pompey conquered Jerusalem, the Hasmonean kingdom became part of the Roman province of Syria. Pompey appointed Hyrcanus II (a Maccabean descendant) as high priest and ethnarch over Judea, Idumea, and Perea. The territory was subject to Rome, and Hyrcanus was personally responsible to the Roman governor. This arrangement lasted from 63 to 37 BC, when the Herodian dynasty began. An understanding of Roman rule is essential to an account of the beginnings of Christianity.

(1) The Roman Empire. According to tradition, Rome was founded on seven small hills by the banks of the River Tiber in 753 BC. Eight hundred years later it had become the center of the largest empire the world had ever known, embracing between 75 and 100 million people. In its early humble beginnings, Rome was governed by a series of Etruscan chieftains who were cruel rulers. In 509 BC the Romans revolted, expelled the Etruscans, and set up a republican system of government.

By the fourth century BC, Rome had built up a series of vassal states and had secured alliances with potential rivals, which made them masters of Italy. Expanding trade and commerce made Rome an international power and precipitated a confrontation with the North African merchant state of Carthage, a superpower which had colonies, great wealth, and a large fleet. For more than a hundred years Rome was involved in three Punic wars (so called because Carthage was founded by the Phoenicians, in Latin *Poeni*), finally destroying and burning Carthage to the ground in 146 BC. The Carthaginian African territories were annexed to Rome, being added to the previous conquests of Sicily, Sardinia, Corsica, and southern Spain. The Romans turned east across the Adriatic to gain Illyria and a foothold in Asia. Macedonia and parts of Greece were also conquered, and in 133 BC Attalus III, the last king of Pergamum in Asia Minor, relinquished his kingdom to Rome. By 50 BC the entire Mediterranean area was Roman property and Julius Caesar had conquered Gaul (France) and made his first landing on the coast of Britain.

Caesar desired supreme power for himself, rejected the constitution of the republic, and marched against Pompey (who had occupied Jerusalem in 63 BC), the champion of the republican rule by the Roman senate. The civil war which followed was fought over a vast battlefield which included Spain, North Africa, Greece, and Asia Minor. Pompey was finally defeated, betrayed, and stabbed to death, leaving Caesar a one-man dictator over all of Rome.

Opposition and conspiracy led to Caesar's assassination by Brutus and others in 44 BC. The assassins were hunted down and killed by Mark Anthony, who seized power after Caesar's murder. Octavian, Caesar's great-nephew, at first joined and then opposed Anthony, defeating him in the last battle of the civil wars in 31 BC. This date marks the beginning of the Roman Empire as such, for the republic was forever vanquished, and Octavian was proclaimed the first Roman emperor, calling himself Augustus, "the revered one" (in 27 BC). During his reign, the imperial boundaries were pushed north to the Danube, while to the east Judea and Egypt became provinces. He ruled until AD 14 and was the reigning Caesar at the time Jesus was born: "And it came to pass in those days, that there went out a decree from Caesar Augustus, that all the world should be taxed" (Luke 2:1).

(2) The Herodian Dynasty. The rise of Herod the Great began when he was appointed governor of Galilee (at the age of twenty-five) by his father Antipater. About three years later (44 BC) Julius Caesar was assassinated and Cassius, one of the conspirators, fled to Syria. Herod aided and abetted Cassius, who rewarded him by confirming him as governor of Syria also. Cassius rejoined his fellow conspirator Brutus and marched against the combined forces of Anthony and Octavian (Augustus) who crushed them, and divided the empire, with Octavian taking the West and Anthony the East. Herod became immediately loyal to Anthony, and in spite of his previous friendship with Cassius, was given full political power in Syria, Galilee, and Judea. When Octavian opposed and defeated Anthony at Actium in 31 BC, Herod switched his allegiance to Octavian, who complimented him for his earlier loyalty to Anthony and confirmed him in his rank, which now appeared to be "King of the Jews."

Herod was a descendant of the Idumeans who had been conquered by John Hyrcanus and had been compelled to adopt a semblance of Judaism. He was never a Jew, ethnically or spiritually, but was determined to rule the

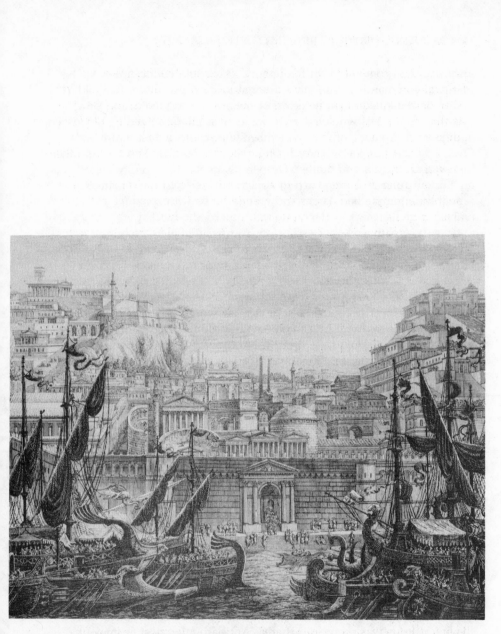

The port of ancient Rome. (The Bettmann Archive)

Jews who had conquered his forefathers. This could count in part for his maniacal command that all male children in Bethlehem two years old and under be killed when he heard of the birth of a "king of the Jews" (Matthew 2:16). His whole reign, however, was characterized by bloodshed, and he even disposed of family members who were a threat to his rule. Over the years he killed two of his ten wives, at least three sons, a brother-in-law, and a wife's grandfather. Despite his unabashed cruelty, Herod was an efficient ruler and even tried to appease the Jews in some matters. He rebuilt their temple on a larger and grander scale with ornate embellishments (Mark 13:1).

Upon his death in 4 BC, Herod's kingdom was divided, according to his will, among his sons. Archelaus inherited the southern portion of Palestine, embracing Samaria, Judea, and Idumea. In the early days of his reign Archelaus was forced to put down a rebellion in Jerusalem during the Passover season, killing over three thousand persons, many of whom were religious pilgrims during the feast days. This would account for Joseph's concern for the safety of Mary and the infant Jesus and his subsequent retreat to Egypt: "When he [Joseph] heard that Archelaus reigned over Judea in place of his father Herod, he was afraid to go there, and being warned in a dream he withdrew to the district of Galilee" (Matthew 2:22). In the ninth year of his reign (AD 6), Archelaus was deposed and banished for his tyrannical cruelty. Judea, Samaria, and Idumea were put under the jurisdiction of Roman governors, one of whom (Pontius Pilate) later condemned Jesus to be crucified.

Philip, another son of Herod the Great, inherited the northern and northeastern parts of Palestine. A mild and peaceful ruler, Philip rebuilt the ancient city of Panias and named it Caesarea in honor of Caesar Augustus. Other cities were similarly named, so this one was usually called Caesarea Philippi (that is, Caesarea of Philip). This city figured prominently in the life of Jesus as the site of the great confession of Peter and Jesus' definitive statement about the establishment of his Church (Matthew 16:13-20). This is the only record of Jesus traveling north from Galilee into the territory of Philip.

Another son of Herod the Great, Herod Antipas, called simply Herod in the New Testament, became tetrarch of Galilee and Perea. Since most of the life of Jesus was spent in this area, Antipas is the most prominent Herod of the Gospel accounts. It was he who beheaded John the Baptist for opposing his unlawful marriage to his sister-in-law Herodias (Mark 6:17-29). An uneasy conscience caused Herod later to fear that Jesus was John the Baptist returned from the dead (Matthew 14:1, 2). Jesus warned against the leaven of Herod (Mark 8:15) and openly defied "the fox" (Luke 13:31). This was the Herod who was in Jerusalem at the time of Jesus' trial and crucifixion. Pilate tried to escape the responsibility of deciding Jesus' fate by sending him to Herod because Jesus was from Galilee and therefore under

Herod's jurisdiction. When Jesus refused to perform any miracles for Herod, he was treated with contempt and mockery and sent back to Pilate (Luke 23:6-12).

Herod Antipas was banished to Gaul in AD 39 by the Emperor Caligula, and his domain given to Herod Agrippa I, brother of Herodias and son of Aristobulus who had been executed by his father Herod the Great. Already king over the territory once ruled by his late half-uncle Philip, he now became ruler also of Galilee and Perea. Two years later the Emperor Claudius added Judea and Samaria to Agrippa's domain which now equaled that of his grandfather, Herod the Great (all of Palestine). Aggressively persecuting the early Christians, Agrippa I executed James and imprisoned Peter (Acts 12:1-3). His sudden death in AD 44 was seen as a punishment for his pride and cruelty (Acts 12:21-23). Since he was only seventeen years old at the time of his father's death, Agrippa II was not permitted total rule. Palestine was placed under the rule of governors until about AD 53 when Herod Agrippa II acquired the tetrarchy of Philip, and a few years later Nero added Galilee and Perea to his rule. It was before this Herod Agrippa II that the Apostle Paul pled his cause in Acts 25:13— 26:32. Thus, the Roman Empire and the Herodian dynasty both influenced and were influenced by the characters and events of the New Testament. The political machinations of the first century cannot be easily discounted in an effort to understand and interpret the religious events of ancient Judaism and the embryonic faith of Christianity.

b. The Greco-Roman Civilization. The birth of the Christian Church occurred within a world submerged under the dual influences of Greek and Roman conquests. The Macedonian Empire had left its indelible stamp of intellectual achievements on the world, and the Roman Empire consolidated the world in political and military accomplishments. Intertwined in shaping the destinies of all men, these two great forces naturally affected the shape of the emerging church.

(1) Citizenship and Culture. The Greeks had not been able to hold what they had won under the conquests of Alexander the Great. Their vast empire was absorbed by the Romans, who in the course of five hundred years (31 BC —AD 476) united practically all the civilized nations of the known world. Under the Roman Empire, the world was fused into one great mass of humanity with one emperor, one government, one military organization, a common body of laws, a common language, a common coinage, a central mail and transportation system, and one recognized citizenship.

Roman citizenship was bestowed upon the provincials and eventually included all freeborn subjects. Roman law and protection applied to all citizens wherever they might be in the world. Rome treated her subjects as friends, not as conquered peoples, and permitted them to take part in local governments according to their own traditions through their own officials. Consequently, even though there was chafing under the strong bit of Rome, there was virtually universal peace throughout the first Christian century. Sporadic revolts were quickly and decisively extinguished.

Although Latin was the official language of the Roman courts, Greek was the universal cultural language. This precise and matchless language was utilized as the first written medium to tell the story of Jesus and the message of his Church. A splendid Roman highway system and well-developed sea routes greatly facilitated the work of the government, private enterprise, and the spread of the gospel. The education, literature, art, philosophy, and science of Greece had flourished, creating a fertile climate for the planting of new ideas and religions. While there were many hardships and disadvantages for the first Christians, the gospel itself appeared to benefit from the advantages of an advanced civilization and a universal government.

Decadent paganism, however, remained at the heart of Greco-Roman morality and ethics. In the amphitheater animals and humans were slaughtered for amusement. Fights were staged between professional gladiators, or between dwarfs and women. Slavery was an accepted feature of Roman life. Corruption of public officials was encouraged by the common practice of buying and selling positions of power. While the Roman Empire appeared to enjoy a Golden Age up until about AD 100, the outward splendor failed to mask the moral decadence and personal misery throughout the empire.

(2) Philosophy and Religion. The early Greeks created mythological divinities which personified and deified the forces of nature. These deities envied rather than loved man, whom they resembled in their own passions and morality. The Greeks had no clear conception of sin, equating it more or less with ignorance. Beauty, not holiness, was their supreme ideal.

Conversely, the Roman gods were mysterious, abstract, impersonal kings, without human power or feelings. They were oppressive beings that constantly interfered with human affairs. Hence, there was the need to obtain the favors of the gods as a means of getting on in the world through elaborate religious ceremonies which the Romans performed with minute exactness. There were gods for all occasions, and they were all tolerated by Rome as long as everyone paid the proper respect on the appointed festival days to the official worship of the emperor. The practice of giving divine titles to Roman emperors originated when Julius Caesar was pronounced a *divus Julius* after his death. Emperor worship became a central part of Roman religion, and it provides a vital link to understanding the charges of treason and atheism against the early Christians. The Christians were Romans who worshiped the "Jewish god," and the Romans could neither comprehend nor tolerate that.

Numerous schools of philosophy flourished in the Greco-Roman world, influencing the thought patterns of the first Christian century. A dominant philosophy was Platonism, named after Plato (427-347 BC), a pupil of Socrates. Following the method of dialectic, the questioning of common assumptions, Platonism held that true reality is found, not in the objects of sense, but in the "idea" or "form" which lies behind each class of objects. The soul's real and eternal home is in the world beyond the senses, and man fulfills his destiny by escaping the hold of the material world and becoming one with the divine by searching for the good, the true, and the beautiful.

Epicureanism was a philosophy based on a teacher named Epicurus (342-270 BC) who opposed Platonism, and taught that sensation, rather than abstract ideas, is the standard of truth. Epicureanism held that man's wisdom lies in the pursuit of genuine happiness. While Epicureanism tended to promote atheism and self-indulgence, another philosophy, Stoicism, encouraged the development of religious and moral strength. The Stoics taught that the universe is pervaded by divine Reason; that the human soul is a spark or seed of that Reason; and that man can rise above his physical adverse circumstances and maintain a dignified tranquility. Another group of philosophers, the Cynics, taught a simplicity of life, extreme frugality, and a return to nature. Man should be independent of externals and live like the beasts (the word Cynic means "like a dog").

Other philosophical schools included the Skeptics, who exercised cautious suspension of judgment in all things, since true knowledge is unattainable because of the contradictions in perceptions and opinions. The Eclectics selected the features they liked best from various systems and developed an amalgamated philosophy. The Pythagoreans mixed philosophy, religion, and mysticism, communicating through elaborate symbolism, teaching the transmigration of souls, and practicing severe examination of conscience. Many aspects of Pythagoreanism were included in the Gnosticism of the early Christian period.

Many people who could not find satisfaction in the traditional Greco-Roman gods and goddesses or in the schools of philosophy were drawn to the mystery cults imported from the East. In fact, the mystery religions so effectively infiltrated the culture that the early Christians were often accused of borrowing from them. The Eleusinian cult was located at Eleusis, a small town near Athens, and was built around the Demeter myth, which explained the cycle of changing seasons and the growing of crops. Eleusinian rites included baptism in the sea and sprinkling with the blood of a sacrificial pig.

The Mithraic cult worshiped Mithra, a Zoroastrian mediator between man and the god of light. Mithra was depicted as overcoming evil in the symbolic slaying of a bull, and as bringing life and vegetation to man. He is also seen as rising out of a rock and riding to heaven in a four-horse chariot with the sun god. The rituals of Mithraism included a ceremony of baptism, a sacramental communion of bread and water, and a blood bath from a slaughtered bull.

The Isiac cult celebrated the myth of Isis and Osiris, which revered Isis as the giver of security and happiness in this life and the next. After Osiris was hacked to pieces by his brother Set, Isis, wife and sister of Osiris, recovered and reassembled the pieces of Osiris' dismembered body and revived him by means of a ceremonial lament over the corpse. The Isiac cult performed funerary rites over the body of deceased persons, conferring the benefits of spiritual rebirth.

The Dionysiac cult revolved around Dionysus (also called Bacchantes), the god of wine and of animal life. Orgiastic rites, called Bacchanalia, included total intoxication by wine and the feast of raw flesh. The cult of Cybele or Magna Mater ("the Great Mother") was built on the myth of the goddess Cybele and her young shepherd consort Attis. After the death of Attis, Cybele restored him to life, and her cult emphasized the annual dying of vegetation in the autumn and its coming to life again in the spring. During the annual rites, devotees gashed their arms and sprinkled their blood on the altar. Some priests went so far as to emasculate themselves.

As indicated earlier, Christians were often accused of borrowing many of their doctrines and rituals from the mystery religions. The observance of the Lord's Supper and the idea of a dying and rising god were especially pointed out as obvious borrowings from contemporary mystery cults. Christians, however, insist that the Lord's Supper had its origin in the last meal which Jesus had with his followers at the Passover season. As to the charge that the story of Jesus was patterned after the savior-gods of the mystery cults, Christians point out that Jesus was a known historical figure of very recent existence before the first Gospel was written, whereas the mystery gods were mythological figures of a dim antiquity.

Also, Jesus' death is different in that he died by choice, not compulsion, from the motive of redeeming love. The mystery religions feature a dying and rising deity to represent the recurring seasons and the vegetative cycle. The death and resurrection of Jesus Christ are proclaimed by Christians as an unrepeatable, once-for-all event in history, which will be climaxed by Christ's return in glory.

Thus, while the religions, philosophies, and mystery cults had an undeniable influence in the contemporary culture of Jesus and his followers, there was a distinct uniqueness in Jesus' life and message which set him apart from the whole religious and philosophical milieu. That uniqueness rests in the Christian claim that Jesus did not come to give another religion which tells *about* God, but to reveal God himself in human form.

B. REVELATION: "THE KINGDOM OF GOD IS AT HAND"

The self-revelation of God is the key theme of both the Old and New Testaments. Both Jewish and Christian theology teach that God reveals himself and that we are dependent on this revelation for all our knowledge of God. Efforts to obtain knowledge of God by human wisdom are futile (1 Corinthians 1:21). The knowledge of God must be given to us by God himself, for God is transcendent and is not accessible to us in the categories at our disposal. Revelation cannot be procured from God by any technique, but is to be received only by waiting upon God.

The biblical message is that God reveals himself in his acts in the realm of human history. The creed of Israel consists of a rehearsal of the mighty acts of God within history (Psalm 106:2; Deuteronomy 3:24, 11:2-7). The greatest act of God in Israel's history was the Exodus, the liberation of Israel from Egypt. The greatest act of God in Christian history is the Incarnation, when God appeared on earth in the person of Jesus of Nazareth (John 1:14). The Christian message contends that the self-revelation of God achieves its culmination in Jesus Christ. The history of Christianity cannot be properly appraised without understanding that the followers of Christ believe him to be the full and final revelation of God, "born of a woman, born under the law, to redeem those who were under the law."

1. THE BIRTH OF JESUS

The Gospel of Matthew and the Gospel of Luke provide the only sources for the account of Jesus' birth and childhood. The Gospel of Mark begins with his baptism and public ministry. After a brief prologue on the divinity of Christ (the Word), the Gospel of John begins with the appearance of John the Baptist and the subsequent baptism and ministry of Jesus. Matthew and Luke, however, give detailed accounts of the birth and childhood of Jesus. Matthew's narrative appears to be told from the viewpoint of Joseph, and Luke's story reflects the personal experiences of Mary.

Matthew's infancy narrative begins with a genealogy (1:1-17) which contains forty-six names of individuals from Abraham to Jesus. The most significant names are Abraham and David. It was Abraham who had received the promise that in him all the families of the earth would be blessed, and the Messiah of Jewish expectation was to be the "son of David," the greatest king of Israel. Matthew's clear intention is to present the message that God's promises to Israel have been fulfilled in Jesus. Also, Matthew purposes to prove that Jesus is the rightful Messiah according to Jewish law by showing his descent from Abraham, from David and the kings of Judah, and from Zerubbabel, head of the Jewish community in the postexilic period.

Luke's genealogy (3:23-38) traces the ancestry of Jesus back to Adam rather than to Abraham, as does Matthew. Also, the line goes not through kings, but through David's son Nathan and many obscure people. The obvious purpose of Luke is to establish Jesus' connection to the whole human race and to God himself. Both genealogies attempt to trace the lineage of Joseph, although both Matthew and Luke present the supernatural conception of Jesus. This would not have been inconsistent with the purpose of the genealogies, because ancestry was commonly traced through the father, and the validity of Jesus' claim to Davidic descent would need to be established by his ancestry through Joseph.

According to Luke, the birth of Jesus occurred during the reign of Caesar Augustus when Quirinius was governor of Syria (which may refer to a position of military authority before he actually became governor, since other records do not list him as governor before 4 BC, when Herod the Great died). In response to an imperial edict that all Roman subjects should return to their ancestral homelands for a census, Joseph, a descendant of David, went with Mary to Bethlehem, the city of David. The influx of travelers had left no room in the common inn, and thus they were required to seek shelter in the stable. It was there, in the most humble circumstances, that Jesus Christ, the founder of Christianity, made his entrance into the world. The first cradle to hold him was a manger, a feeding trough.

Luke also records that shepherds in nearby fields received an angelic announcement of the birth. The shepherds immediately went to Bethlehem and were apparently the first to adore and worship the Christ. They broadcast their experience far and wide, but there is no record of the response to their witnessing. Luke does note that Mary pondered and kept all these things in her heart, which leads to the natural inference that Mary herself was the source for Luke's infancy narratives, giving more credibility to the stories than if they were merely myths or legends retained in the church's later *kerygma* (preaching) or liturgy.

The ceremonial presentation of the infant Jesus took place in two stages. First, he was circumcised and officially named at the end of eight days. The rite of circumcision indicates that Jesus was a true child of the covenant community. The giving of the chosen name testified that the child had a divinely preordained destiny.

Then, thirty-three days later, Jesus was presented in the temple in Jerusalem for the purification rituals according to Leviticus 12. A devout Israelite named Simeon rejoiced at the sight of the child, declared him to be the promise of "consolation for Israel," and warned Mary of the crisis and suffering that would come to Jesus and to her. A prophetess named Anna added her witness of praise to him who would become the "redemption of Israel."

According to Matthew, Jesus was worshiped by magi, eastern astrologers who ascertained important earthly events from heavenly signs. This episode is full of theological importance to Matthew, whose purpose was to depict Jesus as the eschatological king of Israel. The visit of the magi places the birth of Jesus in Bethlehem in fulfillment of Micah's prophecy, dates the birth in the time of Herod, and introduces Jesus as "King of the Jews." Herod's concern is further evidence of the child's significance.

As the story unfolds, the magi are warned in a dream not to return to Herod as he had requested, and in another dream Joseph is told to flee into Egypt with Mary and Jesus to escape the treacherous Herod. The accounts of the flight to Egypt and the subsequent return suggest that Matthew saw Jesus as a second and greater Moses. The Gospel writer even quotes Hosea 11:1, "Out of Egypt have I called my son" (which originally referred to Israel's exodus), as being fulfilled in the infant Jesus. Because of the flight to Egypt, Jesus escaped the slaughter of the children ordered by Herod. After the death of the brutal king, Joseph took his little family back to Israel, but upon hearing that Herod's son Archelaus was reigning in Judea with brutality, he turned to Galilee and settled in a town called Nazareth, where Jesus was reared.

2. THE CHILDHOOD OF JESUS

The records are almost totally silent about the years between the infancy of Jesus and the beginning of his ministry. The only mention of those days comes from the pen of Luke, another clue that Mary was his primary source of information.

Although Luke gives no account of the flight into Egypt, as does Matthew, he locates the hometown as Nazareth in Galilee. Jesus obviously spent all his childhood and adolescent years in Nazareth, where he "grew and became strong, filled with wisdom; and the favor of God was upon him" (2:40). He is later identified as a carpenter, apparently following the vocation of Joseph. Every indication is that it was a devout home and that Jesus grew up in a typical Jewish family, learning the Scriptures and obeying the laws. All of the Lucan accounts affirm the Jewishness of Jesus' environment and training. Five times the statement is made that an act was performed "according to the law."

The last look we have at Jesus before he begins his ministry at age thirty is the story of his visit in the temple when he was only twelve. Mosaic law required every male to participate in the feasts of Passover, Pentecost, and Tabernacles, and residents of Palestine made an effort to be in Jerusalem for at least one of the feasts each year. At puberty the Jewish boy became a son of the law, a responsible member of the covenant community, and Jesus appropriately joined his elders in their annual pilgrimage. When he was found to be missing in the caravan on the homeward journey, Jesus was discovered in the temple, deeply involved in theological discussions with the learned scholars there. His response to his parents was that he must be about his Father's business. However, the temple experience did not alter the status of Jesus in the home, and he continued to lead the normal, obedient life of a child. Since nothing more is said of Joseph after the temple episode, tradition has held that he died while Jesus was still fairly young. However, other children were born to Joseph and Mary (Matthew 12:46; 13:55, 56).

Eighteen years later, Jesus stepped onto the stage of the Greco-Roman world, ready to end the years of silence and inaugurate a new kind of faith that would turn the world upside down.

3. CHOSEN AND PROVEN

The beginning of Jesus' ministry, probably early in AD 27, was marked by two distinctive events, one openly public and the other intensely private. The first attested to his Messianic identity and the second affirmed the direction of his Messianic mission. The first was his baptism by John, and the second was his temptation in the wilderness.

The "special gift" child of Elisabeth, Mary's cousin, had grown to be a forceful preacher of righteousness, attracting crowds from towns and cities to the banks of the Jordan River where he baptized sincere penitents. After living like a hermit in the wilderness, John had returned to preach against social injustices and to call the entire nation, every class and every individual, to repentance. John also identified himself as "the voice of one crying in the wilderness, 'Make straight the way of the Lord' " (John 1:23; Isaiah 40:3, RSV). He indicated that the promised Messiah was already among them and would soon be revealed.

The day that Jesus stepped out of the crowd and moved toward John, the Baptist proclaimed him to be "the Lamb of God who takes away the sin of the world." Although John hesitated to baptize Jesus because of his own unworthiness, Jesus insisted that he wanted to be identified with those who were taking their stand for a kingdom of righteousness. In his baptism, Jesus publicly dedicated himself to the work of God which John had announced. The Synoptic Gospels (Matthew, Mark, and Luke) record that when Jesus emerged from the water, the Spirit of God, in the form of a dove, descended upon him and a voice from above acknowledged Jesus to be God's beloved Son. The heavenly proclamation appears to be a compiled quotation of Psalm 2:7 and Isaiah 42:1, which would constitute an ordination rite of Jesus as the Suffering Servant Messiah. Thus, the baptism of Jesus served to authenticate the ministry of John the Baptist as God's chosen vehicle through which to proclaim the coming of the kingdom, and to identify Jesus of Nazareth as the promised Messiah who had come to establish his kingdom.

Immediately after his baptism, Jesus was led by the Spirit into the wilderness to be tempted by the devil. The clash between Jesus and Satan represented a power struggle between two kingdoms, the kingdom of God and the kingdom of evil. Three distinct temptations were presented to

Jesus: to use his supernatural powers for his own advantage, to win a large following by means of miracle and magic, and to acquire power over secular kingdoms by temporizing with evil, all of which Jesus rejected.

The significance of the temptation episode lay in the response of Jesus to decide what kind of Messiah he would be, the strategy by which he would accomplish his work, and his posture toward the evil of his day. Since no one else was present, the account of the temptations had to come directly from Jesus to his disciples. The remembered and repeated story contributed greatly to the early church's understanding of the person and work of Jesus.

4. TEACHING AND HEALING
The public ministry of Jesus included approximately three years, from AD 27 to 30. The first year was spent in relative obscurity, the second in public favor, and the third in open opposition. Jesus' activities consisted basically of a preaching-teaching and caring-healing ministry. The former involved the content of his message and the latter the authority of his person.

a. Message and Methods. Immediately following his baptism and temptation, Jesus revealed his deep concern for hurting humanity, and used practically every incident as an occasion to preach and to teach the kingdom of God. We have no record of his receiving formal theological training, yet his teaching was of such authority that even members of the Sanhedrin called him "Rabbi." He did not set up a school to enroll and instruct students, yet eager disciples followed him everywhere, making a school of every journey and a pulpit of every rest stop.

The content of his message was not built around philosophical theses in abstract thought. What he said always related to real life situations, and spiritual principles came alive as tangible realities. His material was not arranged in a systematic fashion. He did not discuss doctrines in clearly defined categories. His proclamations sprang spontaneously in the midst of a need or were hammered out in direct confrontation with opposition.

The picturesque style of Jesus' expressions reflected the culture of the Near East. As did his contemporaries, Jesus used sharp contrasts and extreme statements. His colorful teaching sometimes employed puns: "Ye strain at gnats and swallow camels." Often he punctuated his lessons with proverbs: "Judge not that ye be not judged." Sometimes he almost broke into song with eloquent poetry: "Love your enemies, do good to those who hate you, bless those who curse you, pray for those who abuse you."

Perhaps his best known method of teaching was the parable, of which we have about sixty preserved in the Gospels. Employing some real life setting, Jesus would weave a story which inevitably portrayed a type of human character and revealed a principle of God's government. Each parable either taught a certain kind of conduct the hearers were supposed to practice or avoid, or it revealed something of the character of God. A few of the parables included both ethics and theology, such as the story of the prodigal son.

Although Jesus' methodology was not systematic and his presentation appears extemporaneous, there was a consistency of content which gave a cohesiveness to the overall message. Thus, it is possible to formulate and categorize the teachings of Jesus, assimilating the vast material into recognizable patterns and applicable principles. In fact, in their original contexts, his teachings called for application and response. He was intent upon eliciting reaction to and acceptance of his truths. Often employing dialogue, discussion, and question and answer methods, he repeatedly called for response or action. "Who was his neighbor?" "Go, thou, and do likewise." "Sell all, and follow me." "Go call thy husband." "Who do you say that I am?" These calls for response followed pertinent ethical or theological teachings, making religious maxims relevant and contemporary. Jesus expected to be taken seriously; if these words reveal the way God is and the way that men should be, then acknowledgment and action are expected by the hearers.

Jesus did not teach about God in abstract terms as did the Greek philosophers. Rather, he presented God vividly, as a caring Father actively involved in the lives of all creatures. In his sovereignty, God is in control of the world he created. In his omniscience he knows all about everything in his universe. In his benevolence he is generous, merciful, and forgiving. God was always presented in such living reality as to demand emulation from man. "Be ye perfect as your Father in heaven is perfect." "If you do not forgive others, neither will your Father forgive you."

The kingdom of God was a unifying theme in Jesus' teaching, flowing through a great variety of intellectual and theological terrain to unite numerous odds and ends and bits and pieces into one strong stream of spiritual experience. All that Jesus taught by word and example was to enlist men into a relationship with God which would acknowledge his sovereignty and kingship. The kingdom of God is his domain, the sphere of his reign and rule. While Jesus obviously anticipated the future glory of the kingdom, he also insisted that kingdom principles could begin immediately with a relationship of obedience to God. His parables, therefore, were often urgent appeals for men to prepare for the future kingdom by knowing and serving the King in the present.

Man is presented in Jesus' teachings as a sinner who needs forgiveness, a prodigal who is called home by a waiting father, and an immortal soul who faces the choice of the double destiny of heaven or hell. To enable man to make that choice, Jesus offered himself as the open door to the Father, a door which can be entered only by a "new birth" of the Spirit. To enrich man's relationship with the Father, Jesus taught his disciples how to pray and how to interpret the Scriptures. To strengthen man in his earthly pilgrimage Jesus revitalized the ethical and moral codes of his day with the

Art has gone through various periods of acceptance and rejection on religious grounds throughout the ages of church history. (The Bettmann Archive)

dynamics of a demonstrative life-style. Without attempting to legislate or politicize his positions, he made it clear that all of society would be revolutionized if his teachings were applied seriously on a personal basis and a universal level.

b. *Miracles and Signs.* Perhaps that which restrained Jesus' enemies from persecuting and executing him sooner than they did was the overwhelming evidence of supernatural power by which he accomplished many "mighty works" and "signs." Even Jesus' opponents acknowledged that he possessed more than human power, but they attributed that to his being in league with the devil.

The four Gospels record thirty-seven miracles of Jesus. The Synoptic Gospels (Matthew, Mark, and Luke) refer to the miracles as "mighty works," a designation which signifies acts of power. The Gospel of John describes the miracles as "signs," calling attention to their spiritual significance or theological message. Jesus clearly considered his miraculous power to be an integral part of his messianic ministry. When John sent inquirers to ask Jesus to say plainly whether he was the promised Messiah, he replied, "Go and tell John what you hear and see: the blind receive their sight and the lame walk, lepers are cleansed and the deaf hear, and the dead are raised up, and the poor have good news preached to them. And blessed is he who takes no offense at me" (Matthew 11:4-6, RSV).

Jesus, however, refused to perform miracles merely for a spectacle or to entertain or attract a following. In fact, he frequently told those who were healed to say nothing about it. His mighty works were performed to meet human need and to serve as a sign of the new age which would be ushered in by the realized kingdom of God. Most of his miracles were acts of healing, with even a few resurrections from the dead. On occasion he performed mighty works on inanimate objects of nature, changing water to wine, feeding the five thousand, or calming the storm.

To Jesus himself, the miracles had a twofold meaning. They attested to the power of God in his person and ministry, and they were signs that the kingdom of God had been inaugurated in and through him. "But if it is by the spirit of God that I cast out demons, then the kingdom of God has come upon you" (Matthew 12:28, RSV). The miracles multiplied Jesus' popularity with the crowds and intensified the opposition of the establishment. A winsome teacher was difficult enough to oppose, but a miracle worker with God-power was an insoluble problem which could not be allowed to continue.

5. THE QUESTION OF AUTHORITY
The Jews were actually quite tolerant in their attitude toward new teachers and fresh ideas. This is evidenced by early deference shown Jesus in synagogue gatherings and in the abundant opportunities the Apostle Paul

was later given to expound in the synagogues. The issue with the Jews was the matter of authority. They carefully scrutinized a person's credentials and watched for any signs of counterfeit authority.

a. Personhood and Authority. In his own self-identity, Jesus considered himself to be the inauguration of the kingdom of God, often proclaiming, "The kingdom of God is at hand." Although rarely using the term Messiah in referring to himself, he did acknowledge that identification when pressed to it by Peter (Mark 8:29) and Caiaphas (Mark 14:61). He more often referred to himself as the Son of Man, identifying with humanity in general with the apocalyptic figure in particular. In the book of Daniel and various apocryphal writings, there is portrayed a "Son of Man" who was destined to appear as the messianic ruler of the kingdom of God. Jesus also referred to himself as the Son of God, in fact, the "only begotten Son of God" (John 3:16). There is no question as to whether he considered himself merely *a* son of God or *the* Son of God. He emphasized his singular unshared sonship: "All things have been delivered to me by my Father; and no one knows the Son except the Father, and no one knows the Father except the Son and anyone to whom the Son chooses to reveal him" (Matthew 11:27, RSV). Besides his teachings and his miracles, the other authenticating factor of Jesus was his own purity. So free was he of any sin, that his accusers finally had to resort to paying false witnesses at his trial. His threefold right of authority—teachings, miracles, and personal righteousness—was not enough to stop those determined to stop him.

b. Religion and Authority. The Pharisees considered themselves to be the custodians of divine law and were very punctilious in performing every minute detail of both law and tradition. Not only did Jesus refuse to acknowledge the Pharisees' role as divine custodians, he called them blind leaders of the blind and brushed aside many of their cherished customs and prohibitions. He accused the Pharisees of pride, the deadliest of all sins, and indicated that they were only after place and position. He painted graphic word pictures of the contrast between sincere worship and the prevalent temple hypocrisy. He challenged the Sadducees, the politically influential group which controlled the temple, and in a moment of righteous indignation "cleansed the temple" of money changers. Jesus refused to submit to the authority of the Pharisees and Sadducees and even placed his own teaching above that of Moses. He claimed a priority to Abraham and found himself deadlocked with the Jews on the fundamental question of authority.

While much of Jesus' teaching could have been accepted by normative Judaism, two glaring aspects kept the Jewish leaders incensed against him. One was his open charge of hypocrisy. On a personal and professional level, this was not easily digested nor lightly taken. The other unacceptable aspect of his teaching was Jesus' claim to deity and ultimate authority. It was one thing to accept his popular ministry and even admit that he had some good things to say. It was quite different, however, to allow him to place himself above Moses (and thus the Torah) and even to equate himself with God, the blasphemy of all blasphemies. Regardless of how sound his teachings may have appeared, his charge of hypocrisy upon the religious leaders and his claim for unlimited authority for himself marked him as one who must be silenced.

c. Politics and Authority. Jesus lived as a Jewish subject in a Roman world. As such, he accepted the authority of the secular government. He paid taxes like any other citizen, on one occasion performing a miraculous retrieving of money from a fish in order to pay taxes. When his adversaries tried to trap him with a devious question about who should receive our money, God or the state, Jesus gave his famous reply, "Render unto Caesar that which is Caesar's, and unto God that which is God's." When Jesus was brought before Pilate for trial, the charge was changed from blasphemy to insurrection, the religious leaders hoping to convince the governor that Jesus was leading the nation astray and had claimed himself to be a king. When questioned by Pilate, Jesus insisted that his kingdom was not of this world. In the end, Pilate affixed the inscription, "King of the Jews" over the crucified Jesus. His crown was a crown of thorns and his throne was a Roman cross of execution.

Jesus had repeatedly rejected efforts to make him a political leader and had insisted that the kingdom of God which he proclaimed was an inward reign of righteousness in the human heart. Although he envisioned a day when the Son of Man would return to judge and rule the world in righteousness, he gave no indication of advocating the overthrow of the present political system. He assumed a role above political intrigue, addressing himself to all men in all circumstances of every kind of political system to allow the kingdom of God to reign in their hearts and rule their interaction with each other.

6. REJECTION AND CRUCIFIXION

The last year of Jesus' ministry was one of open opposition. The occasional displays of hostility by the scribes and Pharisees became daily attacks, increasing in number and intensity. This outward and official opposition by the Jewish rulers began to scare off the thronging mobs who had followed Jesus for almost two years. Also, his popularity began to wane more when his strict demands for discipleship were understood more clearly. When Jesus refused to conform to popular ideas of a Messiah who would fulfill material needs and national aspirations, many of his followers "drew back and no longer went about with him" (John 6:66, RSV).

During the early days of his ministry, Jesus had selected twelve disciples who left their vocations and homes and became the constant companions of Jesus. As traveling evangelists, they went everywhere Jesus went, both learning from him and assisting him in his ministry. They were distinctly different individuals from a wide variety of backgrounds. There were two pairs of brothers, Simon Peter and Andrew, and James and John. The group also included Philip, Bartholomew, Matthew, Thomas, James the son of Alphaeus, Thaddaeus, Simon the Zealot, and Judas Iscariot.

Jesus also had other disciples close to him. On one occasion he sent out seventy on a special ministry of preaching. There were a number of women among the followers of Jesus, including Mary Magdalene, the converted woman of the streets, and the sisters Mary and Martha. But, although Jesus had a substantial following, and although his fame was spread abroad, the eventual reaction to his ministry was characterized by rejection and defection. The Zealots rejected him because he would not join and support their efforts to overthrow Rome. The Sadducees rejected him because of his emphasis on the spiritual as opposed to the secular. The Pharisees rejected him because of his attacks upon their hypocrisy and his undermining of the temple and the Law as the two pillars of Jewish life. Decent ordinary people, not particularly associated with the religious parties, were offended because Jesus associated with publicans and sinners, even prostitutes.

Although the rejection by the parties and populace had its devastating effect upon Jesus' ministry, that which hurt the most was defection from within the very ranks of his closest disciples, the twelve apostles. Judas Iscariot, bribed with thirty pieces of silver, became the informer who led the soldiers to Jesus in the Garden of Gethsemane. Upon the arrest of their Master, the other disciples fled for their lives. Later that night around a campfire, Peter, who had so recently pledged his undying loyalty, denied that he even knew Jesus, let alone that he was his disciple. Thus, of the first group assembled to be companions and students of Jesus, one betrayed him, another denied him, and all forsook him. From the very outset, the Christian enterprise appeared destined to hold its treasure "in earthen vessels."

Jesus was tried by the Jewish religious authorities and by the Roman procurator, Pilate. First Jesus was taken before Caiaphas, the high priest, who accused him of blasphemy when he confirmed the messianic claim. Then the official plenary session of the Sanhedrin condemned Jesus, but since it did not possess the power of life and death, its findings had to be ratified by Pilate, the Roman governor. Pilate soon became embroiled in a conflict between conscience and expediency. He personally could find no fault in Jesus, but the crowds demanded he dispose of the troublemaker. Learning that Jesus was from Galilee, he sent him to be examined by Herod Antipas, the tetrarch of Galilee, who was in Jerusalem for the feast of the Passover. Herod refused to exercise jurisdiction and returned the prisoner to Pilate, who finally condemned Jesus to be crucified.

Before the execution, Jesus was cruelly scourged and mocked by the Roman soldiers. He had already suffered the humiliation of being selected to die in the place of a common criminal named Barabbas. Now he was further humiliated by the mock subservience of the soldiers who plaited a crown of thorns, gave him a reed for a scepter, threw a robe about his shoulders, and hailed him as "king of the Jews." After being beaten, he was compelled to bear the heavy wooden beam on which he was to die.

The execution took place a short distance outside the city of Jerusalem on a hill called Calvary, also known as Golgotha, which means "skull." Jesus was crucified on a cross between two criminals who were crucified on either side of him. The Gospel accounts record various details of the day of crucifixion which serve to point out the auspiciousness of the event. A great crowd was gathered for the spectacle of the famous preacher's final destiny, and the religious leaders taunted him as he hung on the cross. While the soldiers gambled over his garments, his disciples and family mourned deeply. In his well-known "seven last words" from the cross, Jesus expressed forgiveness for his executioners, concern for his mother's welfare, physical thirst in his torment, anguish over being forsaken by God, compassion for the penitent thief dying beside him, satisfaction that his mission was completed, and final commitment of himself into the providence of God. The death of Jesus was accompanied by a great darkness over the land for several hours, a rock-splitting earthquake, and the rending of the temple curtain separating the holy place and the holy of holies. The early church readily saw the torn curtain as symbolic of direct access to the presence of God accomplished by the death of Jesus, which is generally believed to have occurred on April 7, AD 30.

The death of Christ upon the cross eventually became the central message of Christianity (1 Corinthians 2:22). The gospel could very well have been described as the word of the cross (1 Corinthians 1:18). It was in Jesus' death upon the cross that believers realized the depth of Christ's love for men (Ephesians 3:18, 19). They saw his death as a voluntary submission to the demands of the law on behalf of sinners (Philippians 2:8). As a willing victim, Christ bore the curse of the law, and took away that curse as he was nailed to the cross (Galatians 3:13; Colossians 2:14). So, the cross became the redemptive symbol of the saving work of Christ in reconciling God and man (Colossians 1:20; 2 Corinthians 5:19).

Jesus was buried in the tomb of Joseph of Arimathea, a respected and pious Jew. The burial was late Friday afternoon. The body of Jesus was wrapped in a linen shroud and laid in the hewn rock tomb. A large stone was rolled over the mouth of the tomb and a guard was set at the tomb for several days. Thus it appeared that the brief flurry created by the whirlwind ministry of Jesus had ended. Doubtless, the political and religious communities hoped that things would settle back down into the normalcy of the pre-Jesus days, a hope that was never to be realized in the history of men.

To all observers, the mission of Jesus Christ appeared to be over. Even his closest disciples believed the dream was ended and that the enemies of truth and righteousness had won. The history of Christianity, however, had not ended, but was, in fact, about to begin. The validity of the Christian message and mission has always rested on the foundation of what God did after Good Friday. If Easter had never occurred, the life and work of Jesus would have been meaningless and powerless (see 1 Corinthians 15:1-20).

Christian theology and Christian history derive from and focus upon the claim that Jesus of Nazareth came back from the dead. Regardless of scientific or philosophical debates on the subject, historically speaking, it is certain that the disciples believed that after being crucified, dead, and buried, Christ rose again from the tomb on the third day, and that he met and conversed with them several times thereafter. The primary elements of the resurrection faith are these: (1) Jesus died, not in appearance but in reality. (2) His body was buried in a tomb as other corpses are buried. (3) On the morning of the third day he arose from the dead. (4) He appeared repeatedly during forty days to the apostles and other witnesses. (5) Afterward he ascended to the right hand of the Father.

Through the centuries many theories have been suggested to explain the "alleged" resurrection of Jesus. The first, occurring in the scriptural account, was that the body of Jesus had been stolen by his disciples (Matthew 28:13-15). Others have suggested that the followers of Jesus experienced hallucinations, or that God granted objective visions to the disciples. Some insist that the resurrection was a spiritual experience for the disciples, emphasizing that it is the spirit of Christ which lives on. We repeat, however, that explanations and theories are not the purview of history, and the historical data irrefutably establishes that, regardless of what others thought, the disciples themselves believed that the resurrection was corporeal, tangible, empirical, and thus historically verifiable. The Christian doctrine of the resurrection, based upon the disciples' reports, is simply that the grave of Jesus was emptied of its contents. It was not merely a resurrection of the spirit of Christ. What was laid in the grave dead came forth therefrom alive. This and nothing less is the Christian claim.

The claim is substantiated by the visible appearances of Jesus after the resurrection. In the various accounts of the Gospels, Christ appears to Mary Magdalene, to the other women, to Peter, to two disciples walking to Emmaus, to the apostles without Thomas, to the apostles with Thomas, to seven of the apostles by the Sea of Galilee, to five hundred on a mountain in Galilee, to James, and to the eleven preceding the ascension. In these reports, Christ appeared ten times after his resurrection, not counting the later appearance to Paul. The appearances were under a great variety of circumstances and conditions. The witnesses on these occasions reported that their eyes had seen his familiar form, that their ears had heard his familiar voice, that their minds recognized the same authority and substance of his teaching, that their hearts were stirred with the same feelings of love and devotion. There was no question in their minds that this was the same Jesus they had seen dead and buried.

Were these credible witnesses? It is generally held that the credibility of a witness depends on several conditions: that the fact fell within the reach of his senses; that he observed or attended to it; that he possesses a fair amount of intelligence and memory; that he is free from any ulterior purpose; and that he is a person of veracity. The cited witnesses appear to qualify on all accounts. It is often pointed out, even by those who are not believers, that so pure an ethical movement as Christianity could not have originated in a deliberate fraud by the disciples. Also, it is obvious that the psychological disposition necessary for hallucinations was not present. The disciples were not intensely preoccupied with expectations of Jesus' resurrection. In fact, they were amazed and even skeptical when it was first announced. The history of the Christian church, one of the most conclusive proofs of the resurrection, could not have been accomplished by lies, fraud, hallucinations, and sick minds. Those brave and clear-minded saints were willing to die for what they believed because they knew it to be real and eternal.

Christianity stands or falls with the resurrection of Jesus. "If Christ be not risen, then is our preaching vain, and your faith is also vain. Yea, and we are found false witnesses of God; because we have testified of God that he raised up Christ: whom he raised not up, if so be that the dead rise not. For if the dead rise not, then is not Christ raised: and if Christ be not raised, your faith is vain; ye are yet in your sins" (1 Corinthians 15:14-17).

Jesus remained with his disciples for forty days after his resurrection, giving instruction to them concerning the continuity of his work, and explaining the fulfillment of Old Testament Scripture in his life, death, and resurrection. Then, after the forty days, he ascended out of their sight. The forty days served as a transition period during which the disciples were trained for future ministry, and accustomed to thinking of their Lord as absent and yet living, as invisible and yet near them. The strange episode of the ascension provided a definitive end to the transition period. Such a dramatic rising from their midst demonstrated to the disciples that the transition period was ended, that there would be no more appearances, that it was time for them to carry on without his physical presence, but with the assurance of his royal power and divine rule.

Immediately before his ascension, Jesus delivered to his disciples a mandate for missions, commonly known as the Great Commission. The history of Christianity cannot be appreciated, let alone understood, without a thorough awareness of the impact this commission has had and continues to have upon the disciples of Jesus Christ. Considered the marching orders for the church, the Great Commission has literally molded religious and social patterns for two thousand years. It cradles the inherent concepts of divine authority, world evangelization, church fellowship,

Christian education, ethical and moral responsibility, assurance of divine presence, and anticipation of the consummation of the age. The most widely known version of the commission is found in Matthew 28:18-20, "And Jesus came and spake unto them, saying, All power is given unto me in heaven and in earth. Go ye therefore, and teach all nations, baptizing them in the name of the Father, and of the Son, and of the Holy Ghost: Teaching them to observe all things whatsoever I have commanded you: and, lo, I am with you alway, even unto the end of the world."

Since it was first pronounced, the church has taken the commission seriously. The programs of the commission have proven to be broad and general enough to allow for an infinite variety of implementation and organization through the centuries. The principles, however, have remained intact as to the singularity and uniqueness of the claims of Christ, the urgency of mission, and the expectations of discipleship. The early disciples had been told by their Master that they would continue his work after he was gone. Now the promise had been fortified with a program, and they were as committed to carrying it out as they had been to Jesus himself.

C. PROCLAMATION: "REPENT AND BELIEVE IN THE GOSPEL"

With the joy of the resurrected Christ burning within their hearts (Luke 24:32) and the urgency of the Great Commission crowding their minds, the little band of disciples was eager to be about the assigned task of witnessing to the world. Jesus, however, had instructed them to wait in Jerusalem until they received the promised power from the Father (Acts 1:4). He explained that this power would be theirs after the Holy Spirit came upon them, and then they would be witnesses unto him "in Jerusalem, and in all Judea, and in Samaria, and unto the uttermost part of the earth" (Acts 1:8).

1. PENTECOST AND PROCLAMATION

The disciples must have known the essence of what they were waiting for but not the exact form it would take. Jesus had promised before his crucifixion that his own person would be replaced with that of the Comforter ("Paraclete"—one who stands alongside). At the conclusion of the Great Commission, just before his ascension, he had promised to be with them always. So the disciples were expecting an experience which would so nearly duplicate the presence of their beloved Lord, that they would feel that he was, indeed, still with them always.

On the first Pentecost after the resurrection of Jesus, one hundred and twenty of his disciples were gathered in one place to pray and wait for God's promise. Pentecost was observed on the fiftieth day after the first day of the Passover, and had evolved from an agricultural festival to one of historical meaning, related especially to the giving of the covenant at Sinai. (The church came to see the significance of the day in much the same way as they had surmised the symbolic importance of the Passover transformation. For Christians, the Passover, commemorating the deliverance of Israel from Egypt, was replaced by the Lord's Supper, commemorating the deliverance from sin by the blood of the Lamb of God. Now, the coming of the Holy Spirit on Pentecost suggested to them that the covenant of Torah was to be replaced by the covenant of Spirit. Whereas the Jewish community had received its impetus and direction from the Torah, the church would receive its power and chart its course according to the presence of the Spirit.)

During the hour of prayer, at nine o'clock in the morning, the praying band of disciples was suddenly immersed in an unusual and ecstatic experience understood by them as being the outpouring of the Holy Spirit, the fulfillment of the promise for which they had waited. The experience was accompanied by the sound of a rushing mighty wind, the appearance of cloven tongues of fire, and the ability to speak in other tongues. The entire city was stirred by the news of this phenomenal experience and multitudes gathered to hear the apostles proclaiming the gospel of Jesus Christ. Although the people were from many different countries and spoke a variety of languages, each one understood the message clearly in his own language.

Peter became the chief spokesman for the group and stood to proclaim, in an extremely cogent fashion, the first complete Christian sermon. The immediate result was the conversion of some three thousand men. The long-range result was to launch the Christian movement on its great odyssey. The early church believed thoroughly that their little community of faith had been invaded by the presence of God himself in an obvious power known as the Holy Spirit. Early Christianity thrived in a strong consciousness of being under the power and direction of the Spirit. Now the Christians knew what Jesus meant about being with them always.

It became immediately clear that the giving of the Spirit was accompanied by the proclamation of the gospel. The new power was available for the express purpose of proclaiming the new covenant of Jesus Christ. Although Peter and John were given special powers by the Spirit to heal a lame man, the occasion was immediately seized as an opportunity for Peter to preach Christ again, this time alluding to Abraham, Moses, and the prophets.

When the high priest commanded Peter and the other apostles to refrain from preaching Jesus, they replied, "We ought to obey God rather than men. The God of our fathers raised up Jesus, whom ye slew and hanged on a tree. Him hath God exalted with his right hand to be a Prince and a Saviour, for to give repentance to Israel, and forgiveness of sins. And we are his witnesses of these things; and so is also the Holy Ghost, whom God hath given to them that obey him" (Acts 5:29-32). This became the format of their proclamation: Jesus of Nazareth was the Messiah promised by Israel's prophets; the Jewish leaders were guilty of killing him; but God had vindicated and exalted him in the resurrection, and salvation was offered to all who would believe in him.

The two new emphases of the disciples of Jesus were clearly defined: (1) their authority, motivation, and power were derived from a supernatural presence recognized as the Holy Spirit of God; and (2) their religious experience and beliefs were expressed primarily in the public proclamation of the gospel claims rather than by ritual and meditation. When these latter expressions were employed, they were always secondary and symbolic. Primary and essential was the presence of the Spirit and the preaching of the good news.

2. GATHERED AND SCATTERED

From the outset, the new community of faith depended upon—literally thrived upon—fellowship. The gathering at Pentecost was a foretaste of the untold millions of gatherings that would occur in the unfolding centuries. Christianity is not a solitary religion. It lives or dies on the strength of its togetherness with other believers. Christians are called participating and responsible members of the same body (1 Corinthians 12). The church is seen as a family, the household of faith, and members are urged to "assemble themselves together."

Immediately after Pentecost, "they continued stedfastly in the apostles' doctrine and fellowship" (Acts 2:42). When pressure came to bear because of their acceptance of Jesus as the Messiah, the believers united and met each others' needs. "And all that believed were together, and had all things common" (Acts 2:44). Their fellowship extended beyond the stated meetings for prayer and proclamation, finding them "breaking bread from house to house" (Acts 2:46). The communal life of the apostolic church is an underlying factor in assessing the solidarity of the Christian community through the ages. Although there seemed to be no conscious or overt organizational structure at the beginning, there was obvious harmony, unity, and acceptance of responsibility.

A significant event for the history of Christianity occurred within the early days of the church's communal life. The burgeoning growth of the infant church multiplied the welfare needs of the membership, and the apostles asked the church to set aside wise and spiritual men to oversee the administration of the physical needs of the fellowship. This event is usually understood as the ordination of the first deacons. The first "deacon" thus set aside was Stephen, who also became the first Christian martyr. Accused of blaspheming against Moses and God, Stephen's defense before the Sanhedrin was a masterpiece in historical theology, tracing the divine plan all the way from Abraham in Mesopotamia to Jesus of Nazareth. Following the aforementioned format of proclamation, Stephen accused the Jewish leaders of murdering the Son of God, and then he himself was condemned and stoned to death.

Stephen's martyrdom signaled the beginning of open persecution against the followers of Christ, "and they were all scattered abroad throughout the regions of Judaea and Samaria, except the apostles. . . . Therefore they that were scattered abroad went every where preaching the word" (Acts 8:1, 4). Thus, the gathered church became the scattered church, and these two activities express the overall program of the church to this very day. The church gathers as a fellowship to worship, strengthen, heal, and refuel. It scatters abroad, by choice or by coercion, to spread its message and enlarge its fellowship wherever it goes.

Another of the first "deacons" was Philip, the catalyst for the first missionary enterprise of the scattered church. Fleeing the persecution in Jerusalem, Philip took the gospel to Samaria, where his preaching and ministry of healing were well received, "and there was great joy in that city" (Acts 8:8). Among those converted was a notable sorcerer by the name of Simon. Continuing his flight from Jerusalem, Philip met, converted, and baptized an Ethiopian eunuch in the desert of Gaza. The missionary significance of this event was that one who was ceremonially unacceptable to Judaism was accepted as a believer in Jesus.

3. PAUL AND THE GENTILE MISSION

The greatest sphere of missionary expansion, however, was to be the Gentile world to the west, and the apostle to this region became one known as Paul, a devout Jew of the tribe of Benjamin. First encountered as Saul of Tarsus, he was a zealous Pharisee and a persecutor of Christians. It was he who had been the consenting official at the stoning of Stephen. It was also he who was destined to become the great theologian of the early church, a figure second only to Jesus in the history of Christianity. An educated and cosmopolitan man before he became a Christian, Paul was uniquely equipped for the task awaiting him. Although a Jew, he had been born in the Greek city of Tarsus in Cilicia, in Asia Minor. He could address a mob in Jerusalem in Aramaic, the language of Jesus, or he could speak to the Gentiles in Greek, the language he used in writing his letters. He was a Roman citizen, entitled to all the privileges of Roman jurisprudence, even the right of appeal to Caesar himself. As a young theological student, Paul had studied at the feet of Gamaliel, one of the outstanding teachers in Pharisaic circles. Prepared and capable of becoming one of Judaism's most outstanding leaders, he became its most infamous defector.

a. Conversion and Commencement. After the death of Stephen, Paul seemed to be on a personal crusade to stamp out the Christian heresy. He proceeded on a mission to Damascus to arrest followers of Jesus and to bring them to

More than any other man in the first century, the Apostle Paul was most responsible for the spread of Christianity throughout the Gentile world. (Historical Pictures Service, Chicago)

Jerusalem for trial (these would be the scattered ones who fled at the onset of persecution). Paul's mission was interrupted by the famous Damascus road experience in which a great light struck him down and a voice asked why Paul was persecuting the Lord, who was none other than Jesus of Nazareth. This identification of Christ with his followers was to serve as the seminal idea of Paul's later doctrine of the church.

Paul at once accepted and submitted to the call to Christian discipleship. He was baptized by Ananias in Damascus, and then departed to Arabia ostensibly to prepare himself by solitude and prayer for his future ministry (this excursion into Arabia is not told in Acts, but is mentioned by Paul in Galatians 1:17). Three years later he returned to Damascus, from whence he was forced to make a secret escape from Aretas, the Nabataean king. Going to Jerusalem, he was initially received by the disciples with great suspicion and fear because of his notorious persecutions of their number. He was eventually supported and sponsored by Barnabas, who became a devoted friend and missionary colleague.

Because of Jewish threats against his life, Paul returned to Tarsus for some ten years, about which little is known. He obviously established a reputation of leadership among the Christians there, for when the Jerusalem church sent Barnabas to visit the church in Antioch, Barnabas summoned Paul from Tarsus to join him. For more than a year Paul and Barnabas taught and trained the new believers in Antioch, where, incidentally, "the disciples were called Christians first in Antioch" (Acts 11:26).

The focus of the Acts account began to move from Jerusalem to Antioch. Whereas Jerusalem had been the center from which the gospel had moved out into Samaria and Syria, now the center of the Christian mission became Antioch. The church there sent Paul and Barnabas back to Judea with relief money for those in the midst of a great famine. Upon their return to Antioch, the church commissioned them to begin their vast missionary enterprise.

Paul and Barnabas were joined on their first missionary journey by Barnabas' cousin, John Mark, who soon left them and returned to Jerusalem. His leaving thus became the issue of a dispute which separated Paul and Barnabas on their second missionary journey. (John Mark eventually wrote the Gospel of Mark.) The first missionary effort took them through the island of Cyprus and across to the southern coast of Asia Minor. In the province of Galatia, they visited Pisidian Antioch, Iconium, Lystra, and Derbe. Paul established a practice of speaking first in the synagogue in each city. Following a masterful sermon by Paul in Antioch, the entire city was stirred, with many new believers coming forth. Strong hostility by the Jewish leaders caused Paul to make his life-changing commitment to the Gentile mission. The rest of Christian history was forever shaped by those famous words spoken to the Jews in Antioch of Pisidia: "It was necessary that the word of God should be spoken first to you. Since you thrust it from you, and judge yourselves unworthy of eternal life, behold, we turn to the Gentiles. For so the Lord has commanded us, saying, 'I have set you to be a light for the Gentiles, that you may bring salvation to the uttermost parts of the earth' " (Acts 13:46, 47, RSV). The result was the conversion of great numbers of Gentiles and the intensified hatred of the Jews, who followed Paul and Barnabas into Iconium and Lystra, where they persuaded the mobs to stone Paul, leaving him for dead. Recovering from his brush with death, Paul and Barnabas briefly visited Derbe and then circled back to encourage the new converts in all the places they had visited in South Galatia. Then they sailed for Antioch in Syria to report the efforts of their first mission activity.

b. *The Jerusalem Conference.* When the missionaries arrived in Antioch with the exciting news of the many Gentile conversions throughout Galatia, they discovered that their news added to a growing controversy within the church. Men from Judea had come to Antioch teaching that Gentile converts had to be circumcised after the manner of Moses before they could be saved. The dispute grew to such proportions that a conference of church leaders to settle the issue was convened at Jerusalem. Paul and Barnabas represented the Antioch congregation and met in Jerusalem with the apostles and elders. It was about the middle of the first century AD, probably in the year 49, about sixteen years after the crucifixion of Jesus of Nazareth, that the conference was convened. Known as the Apostolic Conference or the Council of Jerusalem, this was the first political act in the history of Christianity and marks the first effort of organized ecclesiastical authority to preserve doctrinal orthodoxy.

The question before the Jerusalem conference was the status of Gentiles within Christianity. The problem focused on two issues: (1) should circumcision be required of Gentiles when they became Christians? and (2) what should be the personal relationships between Jewish and Gentile Christians? The "Judaizers" insisted upon absolute allegiance to Judaism as prerequisite to being members of the Body of Christ, who was, after all, the Jewish Messiah.

Three strong voices against the Judaizers were Peter, Paul, and James. Peter recounted his experience in being sent by God to the Gentile centurion Cornelius, and the resulting conversion and outpouring of the Holy Spirit. Paul told of the recent mission successes he and Barnabas had witnessed among the Gentiles in Galatia. James reminded the gathering of prophetic instances in the Scriptures which foresaw the inclusion of the Gentiles in God's plan of redemption.

The Judaizers were soundly defeated and the council stated once and for all that Gentile converts were not required to accept the rituals of Judaism. However, upon the suggestion of James, the brother of Jesus, the Gentiles were requested to make some concessions so as not to offend the more traditional Jewish elements in the church. They were especially admonished to abstain from eating food that had been sacrificed to idols, then used for human consumption; from eating blood or meat that had been slaughtered without draining out the blood; and from sexual immorality (Acts 15:29).

The Jerusalem conference was, thus, a compromise in the first crisis faced by the infant church. Gentiles were relieved from strict Jewish legal requirements, but were asked to refrain from practices which might offend their Jewish brothers. The account of the conference in the book of Acts presents a unity and harmony among the leaders. Paul, however, in his letter to the Galatians, emphasized the differences and reasserted his insistence upon absolute liberty for all believers. The Jerusalem conference established precedence for two key issues in Christianity: (1) the scope of the gospel includes all races and not just Jews, and (2) the method of salvation is by faith only and not by Jewish works of law.

c. Missionary Journeys Continued. The Jerusalem conference was a significant step in the progress of Christianity. Not only did it acknowledge the freedom of Gentiles from Mosaic law, but it also heartily commended and endorsed the missionary policies of Paul and Barnabas. After returning to Antioch, Paul proposed another visit to the new churches they had established in Galatia. Barnabas was also eager to go, but when he insisted on taking John Mark again, Paul refused. Thus the two parted company, with Barnabas taking John Mark with him and Paul taking Silas with him. While Barnabas sailed again to Cyprus, Paul went overland through Syria and Cilicia. He thus entered the Galatian mission territory backward from his first journey there, beginning at Derbe and working toward Antioch of Pisidia. At Lystra he found the youthful Timothy and persuaded him to accompany them.

Proceeding from Antioch, Paul, Silas, and Timothy went to Troas, a seaport near the mouth of the Hellespont, where another momentous step was taken in the history of the expansion of Christianity. At Troas, Paul had a vision of a man beseeching him to, "Come over into Macedonia and help us." Macedonia was across the Aegean Sea and was a district of the continent of Europe. The decision to heed the Macedonian call was the initial move which spread Christianity from Asia Minor to Europe. The first church established on European soil was at Philippi, the leading city of the district of Macedonia. The first European convert was a prominent merchant woman named Lydia. The Philippian church became Paul's favorite and most beloved. It was during this first visit that he was imprisoned, miraculously freed by an earthquake, and added the Philippian jailer to his growing list of converts.

Traveling about one hundred miles west of Philippi, Paul visited the city of Thessalonica where he established a church within a few weeks. During his Thessalonican stay he plied his trade of tentmaking in order to pay his way. Persecution from local Jews drove him from the city to Berea, where he was warmly welcomed. Agitation from his Thessalonican enemies made it necessary for him to go to Athens, where he preached in the philosophers' court of the areopagus. His famous sermon on Mars Hill dealt with "the Unknown God" worshiped by the Athenians. He called for them to acknowledge the God of Jesus Christ as creator, preserver, and redeemer of mankind. His mention of Christ's resurrection caused division and resistance among his hearers. And, although he had a few converts, he was not able to establish a church in Athens.

Paul's next stop was at Corinth, the capital of the Roman province of Achaia (Greece). Corinth was a great commercial metropolis, notorious as a center for immorality. However, Paul's mission in Corinth was one of the most fruitful in the history of the early church. Congregations were established in Corinth and in adjacent towns. Several distinguished citizens were converted, including the ruler of the Jewish synagogue. After about eighteen months in Corinth, Paul sailed eastward to Ephesus, where he left Aquila and his wife Priscilla who had come with him from Corinth. He then sailed from Ephesus to Caesarea, visited Jerusalem briefly, and went north to give his second mission report to the church at Antioch.

Within several months after his return to Antioch, Paul began his third mission, probably in AD 54. He went again throughout Galatia and Phrygia, strengthening the disciples, and then settled in Ephesus, the capital of the Roman province of Asia. Working from a hired lecture hall, Paul continued his ministry in Ephesus for two years, penetrating the entire province of Asia. He had notable success in combating the ignorance and superstition that was perpetrated by the black arts.

While in Ephesus, Paul wrote his Galatian letter, in which he set forth the first formal statement and discussion of the doctrines of grace and of justification by faith. He also wrote letters to the Corinthian church when he heard of their many internal problems. From Ephesus, Paul went to Troas, sailed again to Macedonia, and on to Corinth, where he personally worked with the Corinthian problems for some three months. While in Corinth he wrote his monumental letter to the Roman Christians, a systematic dissertation of Christianity as the way of salvation. From Corinth, he swung back through Macedonia and struck out from Philippi to go to Jerusalem. Stopping off at Tyre and Caesarea, he was warned about antagonistic Jews and Jewish Christians who were lying in wait for him in Jerusalem. Nevertheless, he persisted in going to Jerusalem, thus completing his third missionary journey, which extended from about AD 54 to 58.

d. Arrest and Imprisonment. In Jerusalem fanatical Jews caused a riot, accusing Paul of bringing Gentiles into the temple. Paul was arrested as the obvious cause of the disturbance and would have been scourged if he had not appealed to the protection of his Roman citizenship. Tried before the Sanhedrin, Paul ingeniously divided that august group on the subject of the resurrection. Upon the rumor of a plot to assassinate Paul, he was taken to Caesarea, where he remained in prison for two years under the custody of Felix, the Roman procurator. When Felix was replaced by Festus, the latter attempted to get Paul to return to Jerusalem to be tried, whereupon Paul made his dramatic appeal as a Roman citizen to the emperor's court in Rome. Before leaving for Rome, Paul had the opportunity of witnessing to Festus and the visiting King Herod Agrippa II, delivering his famous apologia and personal testimony.

The voyage to carry the prisoner Paul to Rome began from Caesarea in the early autumn of AD 60, but the ship was wrecked in a fierce storm near the island of Malta, and another voyage was launched the next spring. They landed in the bay of Naples and delegations from the Roman Christians greeted Paul as he approached the capital of the empire along the Appian Way. Paul was kept in custody under house arrest, but he was free to receive visitors. As an "ambassador in chains" (Ephesians 6:20) he continued to instruct, admonish, and encourage congregations and individuals in Macedonia and Asia Minor. He wrote letters to the churches at Ephesus, Colossae, and Philippi. He penned personal epistles to Philemon, Timothy, and Titus.

Appeals to Caesar were slow processes, and for at least two years Paul waited the disposition of his case. The narrative in Acts ends with Paul still waiting. Several traditions have suggested that Paul was released and went to Spain, and that he continued his evangelistic work in the eastern Mediterranean world. Some traditions hold that he was rearrested about AD 67, sent back to Rome, and beheaded by the order of Emperor Nero.

Although there is uncertainty about the conclusion of his life, there is no doubt about the importance of his contribution to Christianity. Through his ardent missionary activity and powerful preaching, he opened up Asia Minor, Europe, Asia, and indeed the whole Mediterranean world to the influence of the gospel. He established churches, drew the blueprint for ecclesiastical organization, set qualifications for church officers, and determined the whole pattern of church growth, evangelism, missions, and doctrine. In his writings he laid the foundation upon which all subsequent Christian theology was to be built. The Apostle Paul remains today the most powerful personality in the history of the church, other than Jesus Christ.

4. LITERATURE AND CANONIZATION

The reception and influence of Paul's letters soon established the written word as powerful and authoritative as the preached word. Since the days of the Babylonian exile, the Jews had been a "people of the book," with profound veneration for the sacred Scriptures. However, there was no official canon in the time of Jesus, although the Torah (the first five books of the Old Testament), the Prophets, and the writings were held in highest esteem by all orthodox Jews. The Palestinian Jewish canon was not closed until AD 90 at the Synod of Jamnia. One contributing factor to the decision to close the canon was the proliferation of so much Christian literature. Fearful that some of it might be accorded sacred stature, the Jewish community at last ended the official pages of their Scriptures with what we now know as the Old Testament.

By the end of the first century, all of the material that was to become known as the New Testament had already been written. The earliest writings were the letters of Paul, written mainly in the decade AD 50-60. These thirteen letters include Romans, 1 Corinthians, 2 Corinthians, Galatians, Ephesians, Philippians, Colossians, 1 Thessalonians, 2 Thessalonians, 1 Timothy, 2 Timothy, Titus, and Philemon. This is not the order in which they were written. But they were probably arranged in the canon according to length, with the longest first and shortest last.

The first Gospel to be written was probably John Mark's around AD 65. Matthew and Luke obviously had much of the same source material as Mark and these three are known as the "synoptics" (see together). The fourth Gospel was written by John toward the end of the century and is drastically different from the other three in story, style, and theological intent.

Ten other writings complete the New Testament canon. The Book of Acts describes the expansion of the early churches from the time of Jesus' resurrection to Paul's imprisonment in Rome. Six of the remaining nine writings are in letter form (James, 1 Peter, 2 Peter, 2 John, 3 John, and Jude), and two of them are seen as theological treatises (Hebrews and 1 John). One apocalyptic ("uncovered; revealed") book appears in the New Testament, the Book of Revelation, written in the last of the first century to Christians who were under persecution. Elaborate symbols and imagery are employed in Revelation to show how God will act on behalf of his suffering people until and including the consummation of the age.

The New Testament canon was not fixed until the fourth century. By then, the various lists, changes, additions, and deletions had settled into the New Testament as we have it today. In his Easter letter of AD 367, Athanasius, bishop of Alexandria, named the canon of both the Old and New Testaments as we now know them. He not only named the books which the church had accepted, but also those rejected, and some books for use in the church although they were not canonical.

5. CLOSE OF THE APOSTOLIC AGE

The first century AD is commonly known as the Apostolic Age because the church was led and directed by the apostles themselves. Because they had been the intimates of Jesus during his entire ministry and had been personally commissioned by him, what the apostles taught and instituted became the authoritative model for all subsequent teaching and practice. Places where the apostles labored also became centers for church activity.

There were three chief centers during the Apostolic Age. From AD 30-44, Jerusalem was the great church center, with all of the original apostles headquartered there. It was in Jerusalem that the Holy Spirit was given for the church's enduement. It was from Jerusalem that the first mission efforts extended into Samaria and Syria. It was in Jerusalem that the critical apostolic council was convened to deal with the problem of the Judaizers. Jerusalem would always be considered the "mother church" of early Christianity.

The next center of Christianity was Antioch, where the church launched the mission enterprises of Paul and Barnabas, began relief programs for distant churches, and became the center for Gentile Christianity as Jerusalem had been for Jewish Christianity. The leaders of the Antioch church led the battle against the Judaizers, and from AD 44-68, Antioch was the base for expansion and mission work.

Persistent tradition has held that from AD 68-100 the Apostle John made Ephesus the center of the Christian world. John had probably moved to Ephesus because of the Jewish War, which had Jerusalem locked under siege for four years (66-70). The tactlessness and misgovernment of the Roman procurator in Palestine had provoked a general revolt among the Jews there. The long and savage war resulted in the destruction of Jerusalem, the burning of the temple, and the cessation of Jewish sacrifices forever. The Christians in Palestine had decided not to join the Jewish nationalists and remained neutral in the war. This one act alone served notice to Rome that Christianity was not a sect of Judaism but a viable religious force in its own right. Christians left Jerusalem while there was yet time and established themselves in Pella, a Greek city in Decapolis.

According to ancient tradition, the church which Paul had so thoroughly established in Ephesus became the outpost for Christian orthodoxy and the scene of John's encounter with the heretic Cerinthus. Because of Cerinthus' attacks upon the doctrines of Christ's deity, supernatural birth, and resurrection, it has been supposed that John wrote his Gospel in conscious opposition to these heresies, firmly establishing the believers in their orthodox doctrines. The Gospel is thought to have been written, however, on his second residence in Ephesus. He was banished to Patmos during the reign of Domitian (AD 81-96), where he wrote the Book of Revelation. He returned to Ephesus under Nerva, wrote the Gospel and his epistles in his old age, and died soon after AD 98.

The final ministries and deaths of the remaining apostles are known only through traditions of varying degrees of credibility. The notable exception is that of James, the brother of John, whose martyrdom in AD 44 is recorded in Acts 12:2. According to rather unreliable tradition, Peter is generally connected with the church at Rome where Eusebius says that he was crucified head downward. Andrew is believed to have labored and died in Scythia (hence the Russians venerate him as their apostle). Bartholomew is said to have taken the Gospel according to Matthew into India. Thomas is often identified as the apostle to Parthia and India, although many historians find this doubtful. Matthew preached to the Hebrews and then went on foreign missions, and is reported to have been martyred in either Ethiopia or Persia. James Alphaeus is said to have worked in Egypt, Thaddeus in Persia, and Simon Zelotes in Egypt and Britain. The evangelist John Mark is usually credited with founding the church at Alexandria, and the evangelist Philip spent his last years in Hierapolis in Phrygia.

Jesus had proposed to send his disciples forth, had indeed commanded them to go into all the world, promising his abiding presence. That presence had become realized in the outpouring of the Holy Spirit. The mission to the world had begun immediately with the first church at Jerusalem, spread through the mission vision of the Antioch congregation, and been made permanent through the preservation of inspired writings. The venture of the new humanity in Christ had begun. The enterprise was started, the foundations were laid. The church was growing, the Holy Spirit was moving among the followers of Christ, and a new kind of history was being written.

11

THE MARTYRS' FAITH: PERSECUTIONS AND FOUNDATIONS (100–313)

And the God of all grace, who called you
to his eternal glory in Christ,
after you have suffered a little while,
will himself restore you and
make you strong, firm and steadfast.

1 PETER 5:10, NIV

A. Persecuted Servants
   1. Causes for Persecution
   2. Periods of Persecution
     a. Nero
     b. Domitian
     c. Trajan
     d. Marcus Aurelius
     e. Septimius Severus
     f. Maximinus Thrax
     g. Decius
     h. Valerian
     i. Aurelian
     j. Diocletian
B. Persevering Believers
   1. The Apostolic Fathers
     a. Clement of Rome
     b. Ignatius of Antioch
     c. Polycarp of Smyrna
     d. Hermas of Rome
     e. Papias
     f. Epistle of Barnabas
     g. Epistle to Diognetus
     h. The Didache
   2. The Apologists
     a. Aristides
     b. Justin Martyr
     c. Tatian
     d. Athenagoras
     e. Theophilus
     f. Minucius Felix
   3. Heresies and Schisms
     a. Judaistic Heresies
       (1) The Ebionites
       (2) Cerinthus
       (3) The Elchasaites
       (4) The Pseudoclementines
     b. Gnosticism
       (1) Dualism
       (2) Emanation
       (3) Docetism
     c. Marcionism
     d. Montanism
     e. Monarchianism
   4. Early Catholic Theologians
     a. Irenaeus
     b. Tertullian
     c. Clement of Alexandria
     d. Origen
   5. The Monarchial Episcopate
     a. Bishops and Mother Churches
     b. Callistus and Rome
     c. Cyprian and Novatian

n his *Apologeticum,* Tertullian wrote to those who were persecuting the Christians, "We multiply whenever we are mown down by you; the blood of Christians is seed." This affirmation of ultimate victory is often rendered as: The blood of the martyrs is the seed of the church. Jerome wrote that "the church of Christ has been founded by shedding its own blood, not that of others; by enduring outrage, not by inflicting it. Persecutions have made it grow; martyrdoms have crowned it." In the seventeenth century *Church History of Britain,* Thomas Fuller referred to "the seed of the church, I mean the blood of primitive martyrs." In the twentieth century Miguel de Unamuno noted that "Martyrs create faith."

Thus, through the ages it has been consistently recognized that rather than being extinguished by persecution, faith has often been strengthened and established in martyrdom. The "firm foundation" which Peter envisions is to follow a time of suffering (1 Peter 5:10). Thus it is appropriate that the dark night of the persecutions be linked together with the dawning of new strength and hope for survival.

A. PERSECUTED SERVANTS

The first Christians should not have been surprised that they were persecuted, if they remembered the words of Christ: "The servant is not greater than his lord. If they have persecuted me, they will also persecute you" (John 15:20). Exactly as he had predicted, the servants of Christ followed their Lord through the fires of persecution. For the first three hundred years of its existence, Christianity was bathed in the blood of martyrs.

The crucifixion of Jesus Christ, instigated by Jewish authorities and ratified by the Roman governor, was a foretaste of the double-edged sword of Jews and Romans lifted against the Christians. The New Testament records the violent reaction of Judaism toward the blasphemous defectors of the Jesus sect, but by the close of the New Testament the persecutions were taken over entirely by the Roman Empire.

We have already seen rather clearly why the Jews were inexorably drawn to reject the new wine that tried to force itself into old wineskins, but why should the Romans have opposed the Christians so forcefully?

1. CAUSES FOR PERSECUTION

The Roman government generally tolerated foreign religions that were no danger to morality and discipline. Since national religions were respected, Christianity at first received shelter under Jewish privileges, but after the fall of Jerusalem in AD 70, it became clear that Christianity was a distinct religion from Judaism and was judged by Rome on its own merits or demerits.

Chief among the charges was that the Christians refused emperor worship, which undermined the religious foundations of the state and was therefore treasonous. Of course, they also renounced and opposed all heathen worship. Since they had no images, and did not believe in the Roman gods, they were charged with being atheists. They preached "foolish and unreasonable" doctrines, such as the incarnation, resurrection, and worship of a crucified Jew. Thus they injured certain trades that were dependent on idolatry. They earned dislike and mistrust by their aloofness from society. Because of a misunderstanding among non-Christians about "Agape," they were accused of promiscuous immorality. Because of a similar misunderstanding about the Lord's Supper, they were accused of cannibalism. They were often blamed for natural disasters such as earthquakes, floods, famines, and pestilence. They were criticized for professing to know more of life and reality than the learned philosophers.

The Christian claim of uniqueness was one of the gravest problems. Every new religion was required to be licensed, and Christianity was never licensed, causing suspicion and mistrust. Dissolving and recasting society and government wherever it went, Christianity was frequently causing unrest and uproars. Christians held secret meetings thought to be politically dangerous, and most Christians avoided civil and military service. Added to all of this, there must have been the inescapable animosity and antipathy of sinful hearts to a cleansing gospel. It was obvious that wherever Christianity prevailed, men and society changed. The equally obvious way to stop unwanted change was to extinguish the source; thus the official arm of Rome was raised to strike down the followers of the new faith called Christianity.

Non-Christian society expressed its opposition to the Christians through social ostracism, oral discussions, injury to position and business, literary attacks, and personal persecution. The persecutions, carried out by various officers of the Roman government, involved confiscation of property, banishment, imprisonment, labor in the mines, torture, execution by fire and wild beasts. Those who were Roman citizens were executed by the sword.

Christian reactions to the persecutions fell into several categories. Those who suffered death were called *martyrs*. Those who survived great punishments and remained true to the faith were called *confessors*. Many, however, renounced Christ, some permanently and some temporarily, to escape torture; they were known as the *lapsed*. Those who bribed officers or purchased certificates stating they had sacrificed to gods were called *libellatici*. Some delivered up copies of Scriptures and came to be scornfully identified as *traditores*. The persecutions began almost accidentally, at least spontaneously, but soon became a planned and legal policy of the state. From local situations, the persecutions spread out to include the vast territory of the empire, affecting Christians wherever they were found.

2. PERIODS OF PERSECUTION

Orosius, a church historian of the fifth century, listed ten periods of persecution. Actually, that number is too large for the general persecutions, and too small for the provincial and local. Some of the persecuting emperors, such as Nero, Domitian, and Galerius, were monstrous tyrants, and others, like Trajan, Marcus Aurelius, Decius, and Diocletian, were not motivated by hatred of Christianity but by a determination to maintain law and the power of the government. Some of the ineffective and inconspicuous emperors of this period, Commodus, Caracalla, and Heliogabalus, were relatively favorable to the Christians. One thing that all the emperors had in common was a basic ignorance of the true nature and character of the new religion. The ten traditional periods of persecution are the following:

a. Nero, Roman emperor from 54 to 68, began a reign of great prosperity and enterprise, but soon became decadent and ruthless. His unchecked extravagances brought grave financial difficulties to the empire. He executed his nobles who opposed him, and was suspected of causing the fire which destroyed a large part of Rome in 64. He sought to fix the responsibility for the fire on the Christians at Rome and severely punished them, not only for the fire, but also for their "hatred of the human race."

Nero was the Caesar to whom Paul appealed (Acts 25:10), but it is unknown whether he took any part in Paul's trial. Tradition has insisted that both Paul and Peter suffered martyrdom at Rome during Nero's reign.

Increasing unpopularity, revolts throughout the empire, and desertion by the Praetorians caused Nero to commit suicide in June of 68. After his death there was a widespread belief that the tyrant would return ("Nero redivivus") and this myth is sometimes considered the basis for the reference to the Beast in Revelation 13:11-18, especially since the "number of the Beast," 666, corresponds to "Neron Caesar" in Greek notation. Nero's persecution of the Christians set a precedent for treating them as criminals and condemning them "for the Name" (of Christ) by summary magisterial jurisdiction.

b. *Domitian* served as emperor in the years 81-96. He gradually assumed despotic powers and demanded that public worship would be given to him as *Dominus et Deus*. Toward the end of his reign, he declared a widespread persecution of Christians and Jews. He executed Flavius Clemens and Glabrio and banished Domitilla for Atheism, all of which were personally related to Domitian but suspected of being Christians. Tradition holds it was during the Domitian persecutions that the Apostle John was banished to Patmos, where he received the revelations recorded in the Apocalypse.

c. *Trajan* (98-117) was one of the best emperors, but when he revived the rigid laws against secret societies, his provincial officers applied them to Christians because of their frequent meetings for worship. In 112, Trajan issued regulations which made Christianity formally an illegal religion, and which formed the basis of all subsequent state persecutions. These regulations stated that (1) Christians as such were not to be sought out by officials, but (2) when accused and convicted, they were to be executed; (3) those who denied being Christians and those who renounced Christianity were to be freed; and (4) anonymous accusations against Christians were not to be considered. Overall, Trajan left the matter of carrying out these regulations in the hands of provincial governors, resulting in a wide variety of intensity in the persecutions.

Following Trajan, the emperor Hadrian tended toward toleration rather than repression. Churches were even allowed to hold property, but by grace, not by law. He is said to have decreed that Christians should be executed only if they had committed specific crimes. It was during Hadrian's reign that the Christian Apologists did most of their writing, several of them addressing their pleas directly to the emperor, perhaps influencing his policy of leniency.

d. *Marcus Aurelius* (emperor 161-180) was deeply concerned for the moral strength and material prosperity of the empire. He felt that the Christians were in conflict with his avowed purposes because their ethic was irreconcilable with his extreme Stoicism. They also resisted the official state religion and recognized Romans and barbarians as equals since neither were Christians. Marcus Aurelius sanctioned severe persecutions at Lyons. The leading apologist, Justin Martyr, was beheaded at Rome during these widespread persecutions.

e. *Septimius Severus* was not an active persecutor, but was responsible for some notable martyrdoms. In 202, he forbade conversion to Christianity,

One of the miracles of the New Testament church in the Roman Empire was its survival and growth despite 250 years of severe persecution under ten emperors, most of whom were openly hostile to Christianity. (Historical Pictures Service, Chicago)

and a spiritual woman in the African church, Perpetua, was imprisoned and condemned to execution in the arena at Carthage. Tertullian, who records Perpetua's martyrdom, made a strong appeal to Severus for toleration, which obviously had some effect on the emperor. Following the death of Severus in 211, a long period of peace ensued under his successor Alexander Severus, who appeared well disposed toward the Christians.

f. *Maximus Thrax* (235-238) resorted again to persecution, some think out of mere opposition to his predecessor. He gave free course to the popular fury against Christians, called the "enemies of the gods," and accused them of causing a devastating earthquake. He is credited with ordering bishops especially to be executed, and some records indicate his order included the entire clergy. A legend which arose in the tenth century accused this emperor of the martyrdom of Ursula, a British princess, and her company of eleven thousand virgins. The legend is generally disregarded as being highly exaggerated, but the facts of history fix Maximus Thrax as a rude barbarian who slaughtered Christians and plundered heathen temples.

g. *Decius* was emperor for only two short years (249-251), but he had a lasting effect upon the status, and even the theology, of Christianity. His was the first systematic persecution of the Christians, beginning with the execution of Fabian, Bishop of Rome, in January, 250. Decius had decreed that all citizens of the empire were required to furnish proof of having offered sacrifice to the emperor and state gods under pain of death. This obvious move against Christianity reveals how seriously the new religion was considered a threat to the state. Many Christians were put to death, but many others denied the faith (the "lapsed") or escaped through bribery (the "libellatici"), which led to the controversy over penance, rebaptism, and reconciliation. The conflict and resulting theological disputes between Cyprian, Novatian, and Cornelius set precedents for the developing episcopate. The persecutions by Decius were ended when he was killed in battle with the Goths in 253.

h. *Valerian* (253-260) was at first mild toward Christianity, but changed in 257, making an effort to stop the progress of Christianity without bloodshed. He banished ministers and prominent laymen, confiscated their property, and prohibited religious assembly. When these measures failed, he brought the death penalty back, ordering the execution of all clergy and laymen of high rank who would not recant. The most distinguished martyrs of this persecution were the bishops Sixtus II of Rome and Cyprian of Carthage.

i. *Aurelian* (270-275) is listed by Orosius as one of the persecutors, but in fact he did not seriously trouble the church. His predecessor, Gallienus

(260-268) had given peace to the church, even recognizing Christianity as a legitimate religion. Aurelian, warlike and energetic, sought to overthrow Gallienus' policies and issued an edict of persecution, which was made void by his assassination. The six emperors who rapidly followed from 275 to 284 did not bother the Christians. Thus, for some forty long years Christianity enjoyed a calm and a great season of growth and prosperity. Large and splendid houses of worship were erected in the chief cities. The churches amassed wealth, collections of sacred books, and vessels of silver and gold for administering the sacraments. The period was also, however, filled with quarrels, intrigues, factions, and worldiness in the church. While they had grown spiritually during persecutions, the Christians now appeared to grow physically and diminish spiritually during prosperity. Yet their greatest and last persecution was looming on the horizon.

j. Diocletian (emperor from 284-305) made his main purpose to stabilize and reform the empire. He created an absolute monarchy, centering all power in himself as the semidivine ruler, and making his palace the "domus divina" and his own person sacred. He divided the empire into East and West for administration, strengthening the power of Rome in areas where it had been weak.

At first, Christians continued in the policy of toleration and the atmosphere of calm. However, in 303 the Great Persecution broke out when Diocletian issued an edict ordering the demolition of all Christian churches and the burning of Christian books. Incidents which followed (fires and unrest) led to further edicts, solely against the clergy, inflicting imprisonment, torture, and death for the crime of resistance. A fourth edict issued in 304 extended these penalties to the laity also. The persecution resulted in a large number of martyrdoms, and continued for several years even after Diocletian abdicated. His nephew Maximin Daza, who had been given supreme command of Egypt and Syria, issued a fifth edict in 308. He commanded all Christians to sacrifice and eat the accursed offerings, ordering that all food in the markets be sprinkled with sacrificial wine. The Christians were left with no alternative but apostasy or starvation. During the ten years of the Diocletian persecutions, Christians throughout the empire were barbarously mutilated, condemned to lingering deaths in prisons and mines, and slaughtered by beasts in the arenas. The church historian Eusebius lived during this period, witnessed the persecutions in Caesarea, Tyre, and Egypt, and was himself imprisoned but released. He vividly describes the atrocities of the persecutors and the heroics of the persecuted. At last, he said, the bloody swords became dull and shattered, the executioners became weary, but the Christians sang hymns of praise and thanksgiving in honor of their God, even to their last breath.

During these dark and bloody days, the persecuted Christians had reason again and again to recall the words of their Lord: "Behold, I send you forth as lambs among wolves" (Matthew 10:16), and his warning that "they shall deliver you up to councils; and in the synagogues ye shall be beaten: and ye shall be brought before rulers and kings for my sake, for a testimony against them . . . brother shall betray the brother to death, and the father the son; and children shall rise up against their parents, and shall cause them to be put to death. And, ye shall be hated of all men for my name's sake; but he that shall endure unto the end, the same shall be saved" (Mark 13:9-13).

B. PERSEVERING BELIEVERS

As severe as the persecutions were, the believers endured, and Christianity flourished even as Rome tried to extinguish it. We have traced the periods of persecution from New Testament times to the beginning of the fourth century. Now, we must go back and see what was happening inside the church during those turbulent years. The Christian faith did not survive accidentally or easily. Strong hearts and strident voices appeared when needed the most, and their perseverance more than matched their foes' persecution.

By the end of the first century, thriving Christian communities could be found throughout the eastern, southern, and western parts of the Roman Empire. Christianity had begun its worldwide conquest, but its expansion had been dependent upon the vision and leadership of the apostles, who were now all gone. New leaders and new thinkers were needed for the new kind of encounters the church faced. Persecutions had already begun, heresies were springing up repeatedly, and intellectual challenges were demanding response. To meet each crisis, the new faith remarkably produced the right persons for the time.

Most of the available information on the postapostolic era comes from the *Ecclesiastical History* of Eusebius, written sometime before AD 325. Eusebius was bishop of Caesarea, personal friend of the emperor Constantine, and a respected leader of the church at the Council of Nicaea and the Synod of Jerusalem. He had access to the Christian libraries of Caesarea and Jerusalem which he used in his attempt to write an orderly account of church history. His work is our principal source for Christian history of that period, and has earned Eusebius the title of "Father of Church History." Other valuable writings of the period were produced by the leaders and thinkers who were combating the adversaries of the church, and were the actors as well as the preservers of church history.

1. THE APOSTOLIC FATHERS
Since the late seventeenth century, the title "Apostolic Fathers" has been given to a group of church fathers who immediately succeeded the New Testament period. These writers were thus named because it was long

Polycarp, Bishop of Smyrna (A.D. 69-155). One of the leading defenders of the Christian faith. He was burned at the stake during a pagan festival because he refused to renounce Christ. (The Bettmann Archive)

believed that they were personal disciples of the apostles. This erroneous idea has long since died, but the title has remained. There are eight or nine works of these writers, some of which hovered for a time on the edge of being included in the New Testament canon.

a. Clement of Rome (fl. c. 96). The earliest of the Apostolic Fathers was Clement, probably the third bishop of Rome, and even possibly the Clement referred to in Philippians 4:3. The *Epistle of Clement* (commonly designated as 1 Clement) was written from Rome to Corinth to deal with strife in the Corinthian church over certain presbyters who had been deposed. Clement gives valuable information as to the state of the ministry in his time, on the history of the Roman church, and the martyrdoms of Peter and Paul. The *Second Epistle of Clement* is a homily, the earliest surviving Christian sermon, setting out in general terms the character of the Christian life and the duty of repentance. Because of the different style, it is generally considered to be by a separate author.

b. Ignatius of Antioch (c. 35-107). Early in the second century, Ignatius, the bishop of Antioch, was seized in a persecution and taken to Rome to be thrown to wild beasts in the arena. On the way to martyrdom he wrote at least seven epistles. From Smyrna he wrote to the churches in Ephesus, Magnesia, Tralles, and Rome; from Troas he wrote to Smyrna and Philadelphia and to Polycarp, the bishop of Smyrna. These epistles are the most important Christian documents of the period. They reveal that the writer was a man passionately devoted to Christ and that he had a consuming desire for martyrdom. With unusual insight into controversies yet to come in the church, he insisted on the reality of both the divinity and humanity of Christ, and upheld the office of bishop as the best hope for unity in Christianity. Ignatius may have been the first to use the threefold order of bishop, elder, and deacon.

c. Polycarp of Smyrna (c. 69-155). The leading Christian figure in Roman Asia in the middle of the second century was Polycarp, bishop of Smyrna. His long life was an important link between the Apostolic Age and the great Christian writers at the end of the second century, one of whom (Irenaeus) said that Polycarp had talked with John and the rest of those who had seen the Lord. Polycarp was a staunch defender of orthodoxy, combating such heretics as the Marcionites and Valentinians. A letter addressed to him by Ignatius survives, as does his own *Epistle to the Philippians*. He was arrested during a pagan festival in Smyrna and ordered to renounce Christ. Proclaiming that he had served Christ for eighty-six years, he refused to recant his faith and was burned to death.

d. Hermas of Rome (c. 100-140). Initially a Christian slave, Hermas was sold to a woman called Rhoda, who set him free. He married and became a wealthy merchant. In a persecution, he lost all his property, was denounced by his own children, and went through a long period of penance. His book *The Shepherd* upholds the necessity of penance, and suggests the possibility of the forgiveness of sins at least once after baptism (a doctrine which causes Tertullian to call it the "Shepherd of the Adulterers"). It was, however, greatly esteemed for its teachings on Christian behavior and virtues and served as an early textbook for catechumens.

e. Papias (c. 60-130). This little-known bishop of Hierapolis in Asia Minor is said by Irenaeus to have been a disciple of John and a companion of Polycarp. His work in five books survives only in quotations in Irenaeus and Eusebius. It contained many oral traditions, legendary accounts, and Gospel material. He did leave some valuable and original insights into the origin of the Gospels of Matthew and Mark. He states, on the authority of the Elder (John?), that Mark, having become the interpreter of Peter, set down accurately, though not in order, everything that he remembered of the words and actions of Jesus. He holds that Matthew composed his work in Hebrew and everyone translated it as best as he could. He was one of the first Millenarians, believing that there would be a period of a thousand years after the general resurrection during which the kingdom of Christ would be set up on earth in a material form.

f. The Epistle of Barnabas is an epistle of early Christian times ascribed by Clement of Alexandria to the Barnabas who accompanied Paul. This is very unlikely, and the author was probably a Christian of Alexandria who wrote between AD 70 and 100. The work contains a strong attack against Judaism, explaining animal sacrifices and the temple as mistakes due to Jewish blindness which were never God's will. It also interprets the Old Testament in an esoteric (typical) sense in order to build the case for Christianity against Judaism.

g. The Epistle to Diognetus was a letter written by an unknown Christian to an unknown inquirer. The author explains why paganism and Judaism cannot be tolerated, describes Christians as the soul of the world, and insists that Christianity is the unique revelation of God, whose love works man's salvation.

h. The Didache (Teaching of the Twelve Apostles) was a short early Christian manual on morals and church practice. The first section describes the "Two Ways" of life and death. The second section contains instructions on baptism, fasting, prayer, the Eucharist, and how to treat prophets, bishops, and deacons. The third section contains prophecies of the Anti-christ and the second advent of Christ. The treatise is of special interest to the student of early Christian liturgy. The author, date, and place of origin are unknown. It was thought for many years to have been written during the time of the emperor Trajan (d. 117), but recent opinion has put it later. Its significance rests in the fact that it is the earliest of "church orders" and formed the basis of the Seventh Book of the Apostolical Constitutions.

Thus, the writing of Christian literature continued, furnishing the churches with instruction and inspiration. This literature, however, tended to be moralistic and considerably below the spiritual level of the New Testament. The vast world of non-Christians did not understand this literature nor the message of the church. To address the questions and oppositions of unbelievers, another important group of Christian thinkers developed.

2. THE APOLOGISTS

Those Christian writers who first addressed themselves (c. 120-220) to the task of making a reasoned defense and recommendation of their faith to outsiders are known as the Apologists. They met head on pagan philosophy and Jewish objections. They applied Old Testament prophecy to Christianity and defended the divinity of Christ in relation to monotheism. The Apologists were not primarily theologians. They were devoted thinkers who desired to present Christianity to emperors and to the public as politically harmless, and to defend Christian morality which was under attack.

a. Aristides was a philosopher of Athens who sought to defend the existence and eternity of God. He endeavored to show that Christians had a fuller understanding of God than either the barbarians, the Greeks, or the Jews. He emphasized the nature of Christian love as evidence of the Christians' superiority. According to Eusebius, Aristides delivered his Apology to the emperor Hadrian in 124, but later arguments insist that it was addressed to Antoninus Pius (d. 161) early in his reign.

b. Justin Martyr (c. 100-165). After a long search for truth in pagan philosophy, Justin embraced Christianity about AD 130. For a time he taught at Ephesus where he engaged in his famous disputation with Trypho the Jew (c. 135). Later he moved to Rome and opened a Christian school, where he wrote his "First Apology" (c. 155) addressed to the Emperor Antonius Pius. Soon afterward he issued his "Dialogue with Trypho." His "Second Apology," addressed to the Roman senate, was written shortly after the accession of Marcus Aurelius (161). Justin and some of his disciples were denounced as Christians, and on refusing to sacrifice they were scourged and beheaded.

Justin was the most outstanding of the Apologists, being the first Christian thinker to seek to reconcile the claims of faith and reason. He held that although traces of truth could be found in pagan thinkers, Christianity alone was the truly rational creed. In his "First Apology" he stressed the transcendence of God, the incarnation of the Word, and millenarianism. In his "Second Apology" he rebutted certain specific charges against Christians. In the "Dialogue with Trypho," he developed the ideas of the transitoriness of the Old Covenant, the identity of the Logos with the God of the Old Testament, and the vocation of the Gentiles to take the place of Israel.

c. *Tatian* (c. 160) was a native of Assyria, educated in Greek rhetoric and philosophy. He became a Christian in Rome between 150 and 165 and was a pupil of Justin Martyr. He soon showed leanings toward heresy, and in 172 he founded the Gnostic sect of Encratites. He is the author of an apology called *"Oratio ad Graecos,"* a passionate defense of the venerable age and divine purity of Christianity combined with a violent attack on Greek civilization. His chief claim to fame is the *Diatessaron,* a history of the life of Christ compiled from the four Gospels, which was used in the Syriac Church until the fifth century. Among Tatian's literary opponents were Irenaeus, Tertullian, Clement of Alexandria, Hippolytus, and Origen.

d. *Athenagoras,* described as "the Christian Philosopher of Athens," delivered his "Apology" or "Supplication" to Marcus Aurelius in 177, seeking to rebut current charges against the Christians, such as atheism because they refused to participate in pagan ceremonies, and immorality because both sexes met together at night. Later he wrote "On the Resurrection of the Dead" to refute erroneous objections and defend the Christian belief in the resurrection. Athenagoras was one of the ablest and most gifted of the Apologists, and was the first to give a philosophical defense of the Christian doctrine of God as "three in one."

e. *Theophilus,* Bishop of Antioch, wrote his "Apology" to Autolycus for the purpose of setting before the pagan world the Christian idea of God and the superiority of the doctrine of creation over the immoral myths of the Olympian religion. He developed the doctrine of the Logos further than any of his Christian predecessors, being the first to use the word "Triad" of the Godhead.

f. *Minucius Felix,* an African, wrote in Latin an elegant defense of Christianity in the form of a conversation between Octavius, a Christian, and Caecilius, a pagan, who was converted by the argument. The book, called *Octavius,* refutes the current charges against Christians, argues for monotheism and providence, and attacks pagan mythology. It is not clear whether the work was before or after Tertullian's day, but it definitely reflects the latter's interests.

3. HERESIES AND SCHISMS
All of the literary work during the second and third century was not constructive in the progress of the church. All of the doctrine was not orthodox, for already the church was experiencing extreme tensions from

heretical teachings which reflected perversions of Christianity, leading to schisms within the faith. In fact, heresy was a problem even during the development of the New Testament. 1 John, 2 Peter, Jude, and the pastoral epistles denounce teachings which were obviously related to later Gnosticism. But the earliest heretic appeared even in the early chapters of Acts.

Simon Magus, "the patriarch of heretics," was a sorcerer who professed Christianity, but attempted to obtain spiritual powers from the apostles for money (Acts 8:9-24). Centuries later, the term "Simony" was applied to the purchase or sale of spiritual offices. A Gnostic sect in the second and third centuries traced its origins to this Simon, who was said to have come from Gitta in Samaria to Rome in the time of Emperor Claudius (AD 41-54). This sect held to Phoenician mythology and oriental syncretism and exhibited the earliest signs of speculation clearly defined in later Gnosticism. While it is generally doubted that Simon of Gitta and Simon Magus were the same person, it is certain that the latter was the first to attempt to pervert the gospel and selfishly control the Holy Spirit.

The heresies and schisms in the early ancient church can generally be divided into five classifications: (1) Judaizing Christianity, (b) Gnosticism, (c) Marcionism, (d) Montanism, and (e) Monarchianism.

a. *Judaistic Heresies.* The earliest confrontation with the Judaizers resulted in the Jerusalem Conference (Acts 15) and the church's firm stand against those who stubbornly insisted upon adherence to Mosaic law, even for Gentile converts. This mind-set, however, continued to be a thorn in the side of the early church, producing some rather influential sects.

(1) The Ebionites. A sect flourishing east of the Jordan who called themselves Ebionites ("poor men") adopted a severe ascetic mode of life. They continued to emphasize the binding character of the Mosaic law and said that Jesus was the human son of Mary and Joseph. They used only the Gospel of Matthew, rejecting the Pauline espistles. To them, Paul was an apostate and enemy of the Mosaic law.

(2) Cerinthus. Already mentioned under our discussion of the Apostle John, the heretic Cerinthus taught that the world was not created by God, but by an angelic being (demiurge), and that Jesus was a mere man. He had connections with both the Ebionites and Alexandrine Gnosticism. Irenaeus asserts that John wrote his Gospel to refute Cerinthus.

(3) The Elchasaites. This strange group traced their origins to one named Elchasai ("sacred power") who lived east of the Jordan during the reign of Trajan (AD 98-117). They observed the Mosaic law (circumcision, Sabbath, ceremonial), but without the blood sacrifices. They believed in baptism for the remission of sins, and in Chaldean astrology and magic, abstaining from meat and wine, and ritualistic ablutions. They preached that the Redeemer Christ was the first ambassador of the most high God, and that he was a

spirit of fantastic proportions who appeared in various forms, but first of all in Adam.

(4) The Pseudoclementines. The works from this group include twenty books called the "Preaching of the Apostle Peter" and probably originated around AD 220-230 in Syria. They taught that Christianity is nothing more than Judaism purged of all ambiguity and error. Jesus was a prophet greater than Moses, but not the Redeemer, and neither true God nor true man. They also taught that believers should abstain from meat, marry early, and practice poverty. Thus, Jewish Christianity in various forms continued as a disturbing factor until almost the fifth century.

b. Gnosticism. One of the most insidious dangers to early Christianity was the movement known as Gnosticism. Strictly speaking, Gnosticism was not a Christian heresy but a religion in its own right. The main tenets of Gnosticism came from the syncretism of oriental religions and Hellenic mysticism, and were already well established before the Christian era. The term Gnosticism derived from the Greek word *gnosis* (knowledge), and claimed a superior revealed knowledge of God and of the origin and destiny of mankind. Upon confronting Christianity, Gnostic teachings attempted to satisfy the longing of the pagan world for salvation by reconciling the religion of Christ with the culture and philosophy of Babylonia, Syria, Asia Minor, Persia, India, and the Judaism of Philo. Because they believed, as did the Christians, in salvation, a supreme deity, and heavenly beings, the Gnostics often became associated with the Christian churches. But, while maintaining the centrality of Christ in human history and a divine plan of salvation, the Gnostics claimed higher knowledge than was offered in the simple truths of the Gospels. The source of this special *gnosis* was held to be that of the apostles themselves (handed down by the secret tradition) or a direct revelation given to the founder of a particular sect. Although embracing a great variety of forms and philosophies, basic Gnosticism supported the following tenets:

(1) Dualism. With the background of Persian dualism, which viewed light and darkness as two antagonistic principles, Gnosticism developed a metaphysical dualism of spirit and matter. The world of matter is under the governance of the evil principle, and is from all eternity in violent opposition to the world of spirit, which is ruled by the good god. In this eternal conflict, some of the spiritual elements became imprisoned in the world of matter, producing the world, man, sin, and misery. The ethical problem which dualism presented was twofold. If the physical body is of the principle of evil, then it must be subjugated, denied, disciplined, and punished. On the other hand, if the body was entirely separated from the spirit world, then what the body did would not affect the status of the soul. This second point led to all sorts of promiscuous moral anarchy.

(2) Emanation. This theory served to explain how the world and man

came into existence. From the hidden God there emanated a long series of divine essences *(aeons)* whose inherent power diminished as the distance from the original divine source increased. This process continued until the spiritual element came into contact with matter and was imprisoned in a material body. Thus man and the world were created by the demiurge ("the middle god"), an angelic being who was inferior to and ignorant of the good god, and had unwittingly brought the world and man into existence.

(3) Docetism. The central doctrine of Christianity is the incarnation, which Gnosticism rejected, declaring that Christ could not possibly have a real human body. This docetic view was based on the ideas that the absolute cannot enter into a real union with the finite, and that matter is evil and the spiritual world is ever in conflict with it. The word *docetism* comes from a Greek verb meaning "to seem." The Gnostics taught that Christ was not really a man, but only "seemed" to live and suffer for mankind's sins, simply joining himself for a brief time with the body of a good man called Jesus. This union was accomplished either at the birth or baptism of Jesus, and was dissolved shortly before the crucifixion so that Christ was not really crucified. Although Gnosticism clearly derived its Christology from pagan philosophy, the issue of docetism was to have a profound effect on the Christological councils in years to come.

These basic tenets of Gnosticism were articulated most clearly in the works of Valentinus, founder of the Gnostic sect of the Valentinians. He was a native of Egypt, but lived at Rome from around 136 to 165, where he seceded from the church. His system was founded on the platonic conception of a parallelism between the world of ideas and the world of phenomena. Valentinus taught that the demiurge who created the world was the God of the Old Testament, and that redemption was accomplished by the *aeon* Christ who united himself to the man Jesus at his baptism to bring men the *Gnosis*.

Another, although somewhat less influential, Gnostic leader was Basilides, who taught at Alexandria in the second quarter of the second century. He claimed to have a secret tradition transmitted from Peter, which spoke of a supreme God separated from the world by many heavens and grades of spiritual beings. The God of the Jews was the creator God of the lowest rank who tried to subject men to himself. In order to free man, the supreme God sent his *nous* (mind) into the world to dwell in the man Jesus (who suffered in appearance only). In order to gain freedom and rise to the supreme God, man must follow the *nous* as revealed in Jesus.

Because Gnosticism posed a serious threat to Christian orthodoxy and unity, much of the development of early Christian doctrine was to a large extent a reaction against Gnosticism. To counteract docetism, which negated the humanity of Christ and denied the reality and necessity of atonement, the Fathers of the church, especially Irenaeus, underscored the reality of the incarnation and stressed the importance of the work of Christ. When the

Gnostics rejected the Old Testament and denied the reality of creation as the arena for God's activity, the Fathers developed a theology of history, strongly identifying God as both Creator and Savior. When Gnosticism denied the unity of human beings and divided them into spiritual, psychic, and material categories, the Fathers developed the doctrine of free will and emphasized the personal responsibility of each individual.

One reason that Gnosticism appealed to so many Christians was its central concern for answering the problem of evil. Serious Christians wanted to know the nature of evil and how man can be redeemed from it. Gnosticism held that men are essentially spiritual and that redemption is the freeing of the pure human spirit from the impure, evil, physical world. Through special revelation man becomes conscious of his origin, essence, and transcendent destiny. This revelation, however, is not on the same plane as Christian revelation, which is rooted in history and transmitted by Scripture. Neither is it to be equated with philosophical enlightenment, for it cannot be acquired by the forces of reason. Gnostic revelation was the intuition of the mystery of the self. Throughout the centuries, those who have claimed special knowledge beyond the revelations of history, Scripture, and reason have reflected Gnostic tendencies and concepts.

c. *Marcionism.* Although Marcion stood in the tradition of current Gnosticism, his influence was so great that his teachings and followers were the chief danger to orthodox Christianity in the latter half of the second century, and thus his heresiarchy is usually listed separately in its own unique category. Marcion was a native of Sinope in Pontus and a wealthy shipowner. In 144 he was formally excommunicated from the orthodox church by his own father, a bishop, on the grounds of immorality. He organized a systematic philosophy of Christianity which he propagated in established compact communities throughout a large part of the empire. He was widely opposed by some of the great minds and voices of early Christian theology, including Dionysius of Corinth, Irenaeus of Lyons, Theophilus of Antioch, Philip of Gortyna, Tertullian of Carthage, Hippolytus and Rhodo at Rome, and Bardesanes at Edessa. This imposing list of his avowed enemies attests to Marcion's success and danger to the church.

Marcion's central thesis was that the Christian gospel was wholly a gospel of love to the absolute exclusion of law. Thus he rejected completely the Old Testament. He said that the creator God, or demiurge, revealed in the Old Testament, had nothing in common with the God of Jesus Christ. The Old Testament God was fickle, capricious, ignorant, despotic, and cruel. The supreme God of love whom Jesus came to reveal was entirely different, and it was his purpose to overthrow the demiurge. Marcion believed that only Paul understood the contrast of law and spirit, and that the apostles and Gospel writers were blinded by the remnants of Jewish influence. Hence, for Marcion the only acceptable Scriptures were ten of the epistles of Paul (he rejected the pastorals) and an edited version of the Gospel of Luke. His rejection of the other three Gospels influenced the church to differentiate between true and spurious works and to begin serious construction of the canon. In the main line of Gnosticism, Marcion's Christology was docetic, making the passion and death of Christ the work of the old creator God, not the supreme God of love. Marcion invoked a severe morality upon his followers, many of whom suffered in the persecutions.

By the end of the third century, most of the Marcionite communities had been absorbed in *Manichaeism,* a highly ascetic philosophy developed by Manichaeus (Mani), in the capital city of the Persian Empire. Mani (c. 215-275) based his eclectic teachings on the supposed primeval conflict between light and darkness. He taught that Satan had stolen particles of light from the world of light and imprisoned them in man's brain, and that Jesus, Buddha, the prophets, and Mani had been sent to help release these particles of light. Although the theology of Manichaeism was never a threat to orthodox Christianity, its ascetic standard of austere morality is believed to have influenced several branches of Christian thought.

d. Montanism. About the year 156 (according to Epiphanius) or 172 (according to Eusebius), Montanus, a recently converted pagan priest, appeared on the scene to mark the transition from the extra-Christian heresies to the reactionary and reformatory movements within Christianity. Montanism has often been called the first movement of any distinction that was called forth by the problem of the church's worldliness. Montanus protested against the secularization of the church and sought to restore it to its original status. Montanism was an attempt to preserve the eschatological mood of early Christianity which was disappearing at the end of the second century, but a brief look at its main tenets will reveal the sad story of a good idea gone bad.

Montanus claimed to possess the spirit of prophecy, and, in fact, he declared himself to be the manifestation of the Paraclete promised in John 14. The period of revelation was closing, and with its conclusion would come the end. "After me there will be no further prophecy; then shall the end be." Montanism recognized the stages of revelation in the Old and New Testaments, but the new revelation was to be in the area of ethics and ecclesiology, with the sternest discipline being emphasized. It prohibited second marriages, condemned the existing regulations on fasting as being too lax, forbade flight in persecution, and condemned the penitential discipline in Rome as being too lenient. Only those Christians who met the stringent demands of the Paraclete were the true Christians, the communion of saints. Montanus proclaimed that the heavenly Jerusalem would soon descend near Pepuza in Phrygia, and his goal was to prepare a called out people to be ready for that eschatological event.

About the year 207, Tertullian became the most famous follower of Montanism. He was particularly attracted by the disciplined life-style and the idea that only the pure church of the true saints, not the externally organized church, possessed the power of absolution. Tertullian wrote: "Therefore the Church will indeed forgive sins; but only the Church of the Spirit can do this through Spirit-filled people, and not the Church which consists of a number of bishops." Thus, Montanism was one of the first manifestations of an ecclesiastical reaction as well as a reform movement.

e. Monarchianism. A theological movement of the second and third centuries attempted to safeguard monotheism and the unity (hence "monarchy") of the Godhead. However, in failing to do justice to the independent subsistence of the Son, the movement became heretical. There were two distinct groups of Monarchian theologians, the Adoptionist or Dynamic Monarchians, and the Modalists or Sabellians.

The Adoptionists maintained that Jesus was God only in the sense that a power or influence from the Father rested upon his human person. A leading proponent of adoptionism was Paul of Samosata, bishop of Antioch, who was condemned for his heretical teachings and deposed in 268. His controversial Christology taught that Christ differed only in degree from the prophets, and his adoptionist views laid the foundation for Nestorianism and the basic issue of the later Christological councils. Other leading adoptionist Monarchians were Theodotus and Artemon.

The modalistic Monarchians held that in the Godhead the only differentiation was a mere succession of modes or operations. They were also called "Patripassians," indicating that the Father suffered as the Son. An alternative title for the Modalist form of Monarchianism is Sabellianism, named for Sabellius, an early third century theologian of Roman origin. Other notable Modalists were Noetus and Praxeaus.

Thus, the Trinitarian controversy stirred by the Monarchians presented a double-edged heresy. The Adoptionists overemphasized the unity of God, denying the divinity of persons, and the Modalists contended that the Father merely appeared in different modes or ways, thus denying the distinction of persons. In order to challenge and correct these heresies, as well as the host of others already mentioned, unprecedented attention was given to developing orthodox theology in this critical period.

4. EARLY CATHOLIC THEOLOGIANS

The word "catholic" is derived from a Greek word meaning general or universal. One of its earliest appearances is in the writings of Ignatius of Antioch (c. 115). To combat the growing heresies of the second and third centuries, the term became widely used in making the distinction between orthodoxy and heterodoxy. Doctrine which agreed with the Holy Scriptures and the faith of the church was received as catholic, or universal; and every departure from the general sentiment of the church was considered heresy. The concern of the church to preserve apostolic tradition and teaching resulted in the emergence of some great scholars and theologians.

a. Irenaeus (c. 130-c. 200). The first great catholic theologian is generally conceded to be Irenaeus, bishop of Lyons, who opposed Gnosticism by emphasizing the traditional elements of the church, especially the episcopate and the canon of Scripture. In his most famous work *Against Heresies,* he refuted the teachings of Valentinus and other Gnostics, contending that God is the creator of both matter and its form and that all creation is dependent on God. He does not reject the world as evil, but sees God involved in his world. In fact, in the incarnation of Jesus Christ, God took on full human nature and exhibited what perfect man was intended to be at every level of life. Irenaeus developed a doctrine of "recapitulation," or summary, of human development in the humanity of the incarnate Christ. He laid great stress on the coordinated authority of all four Gospels, strengthened the unity of the teachings of the church, and substantiated the written records of the church. As the first great Latin theologian, he furnished much of the theological thought of the great western theologian, Quintus Septimus Florens Tertullian.

b. Tertullian (c. 160-220), the African Church Father, ranks beside Augustine as one of the greatest western theologians of the patristic period. A native of Carthage, he received a pagan education, became a lawyer, and moved to Rome where he became a Christian in 195 or 196. He returned to Carthage and became a priest. He joined the apocalyptic movement of Montanism, especially because of its ascetic traits and rigorous discipline. He soon, however, broke away and formed his own party, the Tertullians, who survived until the fourth century.

Tertullian was the author of many apologetic, theological, controversial, and ascetic works in Latin, and some in Greek. His renowned defense of Christianity, the *Apologeticum* (c. 197) deals with the absurdity of the accusations brought against the Christians; it maintains that Christians are good citizens who refuse to give divine honors to the emperor because of their monotheistic religion. He gives a vivid description of life in Christian communities and warns that persecution only multiplies Christianity. He wrote definitive works against heresies within the church, such as *Against Marcion* and *Against Praxeaus.* In his attack against Patripassianism, he elaborated the orthodox doctrine of the Trinity. In fact, this is the first time that the term "Trinity" is applied in Christianity to the three divine Persons. His *De Anima* was probably the first Christian writing on psychology. In it he stresses the unity of the soul and body. More than anyone else, Tertullian created the language of western theology, which owes its characteristic precision to his legally trained mind.

c. Clement of Alexandria (c. 150-215). An Athenian by birth, Clement studied Christianity and philosophy in several cities, became a pupil of Pantaenus, and succeeded him in 190 as head of the catechetical school at Alexandria. He was succeeded in turn by his pupil Origen. Clement fled in 202 to escape the persecution of Severus and possibly suffered a martyr's death in 215. Clement agreed with the Gnostics in holding that *gnosis*, religious knowledge or illumination is the chief element in Christianity. But for him the only true *gnosis* was that which presupposed the faith of the church. He saw ignorance and error as more fundamental evils than sin, and he had an optimistic view of the ultimate destiny of even the most erring. By making Christianity philosophical, Clement made it acceptable to Alexandria's cultured society, but unfortunately he left the impression that Christianity should cater to the intellectual superior.

d. Origen (c. 184-254). The brilliant young pupil of Clement succeeded him and became one of the most controversial figures in all of church history. Origen was a biblical critic, exegete, theologian, and spiritual writer. His principal work, *De Principiis*, is a systematic explanation of Christian thought about God, man, the world, and Scripture. His *Exhortation to Martyrdom* was written during the persecutions of Maximinus in 235 and presents Origen's ascetic austerity. *On Prayer*, a treatise on the communion of the soul with God, was widely read in his day. Origen saw a triple sense in Scripture: the literal, the moral, and the allegorical, of which he preferred the last. He believed that God was perfect Being, expressing himself eternally in three hypostases as Father, Son, and Holy Spirit. Although he attempted to keep the Father and Son coequal, Origen ended with the Son being subordinate because he cannot precede the Father. In prayer, petitions are to be addressed to God and presented by Christ. The Holy Spirit is definitely subordinate, brought into being through the Son. To the Father, Origen ascribed existence, to the Son rationality, and to the Holy Spirit sanctity.

His teachings on souls created perhaps the greatest controversy. He taught that all spirits were created equal, but that they developed in hierarchical order (through their own free will), and some fell into sin and became demons or souls imprisoned in bodies. Death does not finally decide the fate of a soul; it may turn into a demon or an angel. This process of ascent and descent goes on until the final "Apokatastasis" when all creatures, even the devil, will be saved. Origen's mystical theology— that one advances from purgation to illumination to union—is the foundation of all later mysticism in the church. Three hundred years after his work, Origen was condemned as a heretic at the First Council of Constantinople in 543 and again at the Second Council of Constantinople in 553.

The period from Apostolic Fathers through the early Catholic theologians was one of doctrinal development and systematic defense of the faith.

Intellectual activity, however, was not the only pursuit of the church during this period. Political machinations were at work, and the structure of church government was taking shape.

5. THE MONARCHICAL EPISCOPATE

The notion of one bishop at the head of the church has a hazy and spotted beginning, but accelerates into a well-documented movement relatively early in church history.

a. Bishops and Mother Churches. As already noted, Ignatius of Antioch (d. 115) was the first to employ the term "catholic." He was also the first to speak of one bishop at the head of the presbyters and deacons in each congregation. (The term bishop is analogous to the modern term pastor.) He insisted upon the monarchical episcopate as a necessity for the church. Yet he was speaking of local congregations only, with no thought of one bishop for all of Christendom. The idea for the episcopate was traced back to Acts 15 where James presided over the council of Jerusalem. Eusebius reports in his church history that James was succeeded by Simeon, also a relative of Jesus. So, a kind of episcopacy was seen as a tradition in Jerusalem and then carried to Antioch. The bishops of individual churches cooperated in keeping the churches in the unity of the faith during the assaults of persecutions and heresies. This solidarity was accomplished by appealing to the authority of the "mother churches" where the apostles themselves had labored, such as Smyrna, Ephesus, Jerusalem, Corinth, Philippi, Thessalonica, and especially Rome.

b. Callistus and Rome. Among the mother churches, Rome was regarded as preeminent. Tradition held that the apostles Peter and Paul had both taught and died there. Also, the Roman church was in possession of a confession of faith, the Roman symbol, which was accepted by other churches in the West. Heretics were kept out of the Roman church with better success than in Alexandria and Constantinople, and Rome soon came to be looked upon as a guardian of the unity of Christianity. Rome was also the political center of the empire.

Callistus was bishop of Rome from 217-222, and in this short time established a precedent for the idea of the superiority of Roman bishops. He claimed such titles for himself as *Pontifex Maximus* ("highest pontiff") and *Episcopus episcoporum* ("bishop of bishops"). Tertullian furiously rejected such claims and insisted upon the equality of the various churches. Callistus took the position that the church is subject to the control of the bishop who pardons or retains sin by divine authority, and that the bishop is, therefore, lord over the faith and life of the people by virtue of divinely bestowed supremacy. He further argued that the regulation of repentance belonged to the council of bishops, that the power of the keys had been given to Peter as representative of the bishops, and that since Peter was generally conceded to be the first bishop of Rome, the obvious conclusion was the monarchical episcopate with its ultimate authority in the Roman See.

c. *Cyprian and Novatian.* Cyprian, the Bishop of Carthage (248-258), laid the foundation for the development of the church into the Roman hierarchy. He believed that Rome represented the unity of the Church universal as Peter represented that unity among the apostles. His most important work, *On the Unity of the Church,* was occasioned by the conflict over the regulation of repentance. During the Decian persecution (AD 250), large numbers of Christians had lapsed from their faith. The *confessors,* those who had stood firm, were reconciling the lapsed on easy terms by virtue of the merits of the martyrs. Cyprian strongly opposed this practice and led councils to decide that the lapsed should be reconciled only after suitable penance and delay. Meanwhile, Novatian, a Roman presbyter, opposed Cornelius, the Bishop of Rome, for the latter's lenient policy toward the lapsed. Novatian insisted on a pure congregation, requiring excommunication for such sins as homicide, idolatry, fraud, blasphemy, adultery, fornication, and denial of the faith in times of persecution. He organized a rigorist party and was consecrated rival Bishop of Rome. He insisted upon the rebaptism of all who joined him, and called for the appointment of likeminded bishops in other places.

Cyprian sided with Cornelius against Novatian, especially in the matters of rebaptism and the appointment of new bishops. While he opposed leniency toward the lapsed, he felt even stronger about presbyters judging bishops. He said that the church was established upon bishops, that they could be judged by no one except God, and that to criticize a bishop was rebellion. He further supported the college of bishops (the episcopate) as the authority of the church. Indicating that the Bishop of Rome was the "first among equals," he openly recognized the preeminence of Rome, especially when Rome agreed with him. Although Cyprian did not suggest or favor the papal system, his leadership and attitude laid the foundation for establishing the Bishop of Rome as the head of the Catholic Church.

In summary, the events of the first three hundred years of Christianity lie along two tracks which appear headed in different directions but which keep crossing and interacting with each other. On one track, the Roman persecutions seem determined to extinguish the new flame. On the other track, courageous spirits keep the flame aglow and brilliant minds construct strong foundations.

When Diocletian launched his great persecution in the early part of the fourth century, he collided with a force which had grown stronger instead of weaker during the long siege of persecutions. That strength had accrued from the Christians' capable and articulate defense of their faith, the movement of their churches toward ecclesiastical unity, and the increasing influence of their testimony among their non-Christian neighbors.

Diocletian not only miscalculated the strength of the Christians; he also misread the attitude of the citizenry. Christianity had not only become an established force within the Roman Empire; it was about to take over the empire itself.

I I I

THE OVERCOMERS: AN IMPERIAL CHURCH (313-590)

He that overcometh,
and keepeth my works unto the end,
to him will I give power over the nations.
REVELATION 2:26

A. Victims Become Victors
  1. The First Christian Emperor
    a. The Rise of Constantine
    b. The Conversion of Constantine
    c. The Tenacity of Paganism
    d. The Threat of Controversy
      (1) Monasticism
      (2) Donatism
      (3) Arianism
  2. The Byzantine Empire
    a. Constantinople, The New Rome
    b. Division, Defection, and Renewal
    c. The Fall of Rome
    d. Justinian the Great
B. Theologians Become Activists
  1. Athanasius
  2. Ambrose
  3. Jerome
  4. John Chrysostom
  5. Augustine
    a. The Conversion of Augustine
    b. The Controversies of Augustine
    c. The Contributions of Augustine
C. Bishops Become Popes
  1. Political and Church Organizations
  2. Presumed Basis for the Papacy
  3. The Preeminence of Rome
  4. The Earliest Popes
    a. Victor I
    b. Stephen I
    c. Sylvester
    d. Damascus
    e. Innocent I
    f. Leo I
    g. Gelasius
D. Monks Become Missionaries
  1. Monasticism
  2. Missions
    a. Ulphilas
    b. Martin of Tours
    c. Patrick
    d. Columba
    e. Benedict of Nursia
E. Beliefs Become Creeds
  1. Nicaea
  2. Constantinople
  3. Ephesus
  4. Chalcedon

n *The Story of Civilization* Will Durant wrote: "There is no greater drama in human record than the sight of a few Christians, scorned or oppressed by a succession of emperors, bearing all trials with a fierce tenacity, multiplying quietly, building order while their enemies generated chaos, fighting the sword with the Word, brutality with hope, and at last defeating the strongest state that history has known. Caesar and Christ had met in the Arena, and Christ had won!"

A. VICTIMS BECOME VICTORS

The incredible irony of the Diocletian persecution, which was intended to stamp out Christianity once and for all, became instead the catalyst for the Christian takeover of the Roman Empire. Heroic martyrs strengthened the faith of the wavering and won new converts. As the brutalities of the persecution increased, the citizens of the empire were themselves repulsed and became openly critical of their government for the unjustified oppression. Many of them risked death to hide and protect Christians.

Throughout the empire the cry went up for the persecutions to cease. The wife of Emperor Galerius begged him to make peace with the undefeated God of the Christians, and in 311 he issued an edict of toleration, recognizing Christianity as a lawful religion.

1. THE FIRST CHRISTIAN EMPEROR
Standing in the wings, ready to assume his spectacular role on the stage of human history, was brave and energetic young soldier-politician, Flavius Valerius Constantinus, who would become known as Constantine the Great.

a. The Rise of Constantine. Born around 272 or 274, Constantine was the illegitimate son of Constantius by his legal concubine, Helena. When Constantius became a "Caesar," he was required by Diocletian to put away Helena and to take Maximian's stepdaughter Theodora as his wife. His son

Constantine, however, remained deeply devoted to his natural mother, Helena, who figured largely in his accomplishments as a Christian emperor.

Constantine became emperor through a long chain of complicated and controversial events. Diocletian had retired as emperor in 305 and had set up an intricate organizational scheme in an effort to avoid civil war. He decentralized the government by dividing the empire into two great districts, East and West. Each was to be administered by an official called an Augustus, assisted by a subordinate called a Caesar. The Augusti were to retire at a specified time, to be succeeded by their Caesars. Diocletian was the first Augustus in the East and Maximian was the first Augustus in the West. The Augusti were not exactly equal, since Diocletian retained supreme control. When he and Maximian retired as planned, their Caesars succeeded them, Galerius in the East and Constantius Chlorus (the father of Constantine) in the West. New Caesars were appointed to replace them, Severus in the West and Maximines Daza in the East.

Diocletian's scheme appeared to be working as planned until the death of Constantius. His troops had been deeply loyal to him and now acclaimed his son Constantine not merely as "Caesar" but as Augustus, emperor. Galerius, too distant to intervene, reluctantly consented to recognize him as a Caesar. Since Constantine had successfully succeeded his father without the due process of appointment, Maxentius, the son of Maximian, undertook to succeed his retired father. He killed Severus, entrenched himself in Rome, and demanded recognition. Galerius refused and instead appointed Licinius to succeed the slain Severus. These events brought Maximian out of retirement to reclaim the title of Augustus. Now there were six men claiming to be the ruler of the empire. Civil war, the very disaster that Diocletian had sought to avert, was upon the empire.

b. The Conversion of Constantine. In the struggle for supremacy in the West, Constantine had to defeat Maxentius, still entrenched in Rome. Constantine invaded Italy from Gaul (France) and descended upon Rome. Until now he had been an adherent of the religion of Helios, the sun god, and had placed the image of the sun upon his coins. Just before his encounter with Maxentius he made the astonishing announcement of his conversion to Christianity.

According to Eusebius (the "Father of Church History," c. 260-c. 340), on the afternoon before the battle with Maxentius, Constantine saw a flaming cross in the sky, with the words "in this sign conquer." To confirm the vision, Eusebius says that early the next morning Constantine dreamed that a voice commanded him to have his soldiers mark their shields with the letter X with a line drawn through it and curled around the top, the symbol of Christ. That morning Constantine marched to the forefront of the battle behind a standard (called the *labarum*) carrying the initials of Christ interwoven with a cross.

Flavius Valerius Constantinus (Constantine). The first Christian emperor of the Roman Empire. (The Bettmann Archive)

Maxentius left the protection of the walls of Rome, and clashed with Constantine while crossing the Tiber River over the Mulvian Bridge. Maxentius and thousands of his troops were defeated and drowned in the Tiber. His father, Maximian, who had conspired against Constantine, was captured and granted the courtesy of suicide. Thus, in 312, Constantine entered Rome the undisputed master of the West.

Early in 313 Constantine met with Licinius, whom Galerius had appointed to succeed the slain Severus. They both desired to coordinate their rule and to consolidate Christian support throughout the empire. Meeting at Milan, they issued the famous "Edict of Milan," which confirmed the religious toleration previously proclaimed by Galerius. In addition, the edict extended freedom to all religions, and ordered restoration of Christian properties seized during the recent persecutions.

Historians and theologians continue to debate to this day over the sincerity and motive of Constantine's conversion. Undoubtedly many influences converged upon that fateful day across from the Mulvian Bridge. His mother, Helena, had converted to Christianity when Constantius divorced her, and she surely acquainted her son with the positive aspects of Christian teaching. Also, Constantine had observed the failure of three persecutions during his lifetime, and had noted that Christianity had grown in spite of them. He had been impressed with the order and morality of Christian conduct. In spite of the bitter persecutions, the Christians had rarely revolted against the state and even taught submission to civil powers and the divine rights of kings. Constantine doubtless speculated as to how these attitudes and doctrines could be used effectively to purify Roman morals and solidify the empire.

Subsequent decisions and actions by Constantine would cause many to question the validity of his conversion; but, for the time, the Christian world rejoiced over the unbelievable news that the Roman Empire had a Christian upon the throne. The emperor declined, however, to be baptized until he was almost dead, at the age of sixty-four. He wanted to be sure that baptism would come late enough to cleanse away all the sins of his crowded life.

c. The Tenacity of Paganism. Although Constantine had openly embraced Christianity, he found it difficult to completely extricate pagan religion and culture. His world was still predominantly pagan; and being a man-of-the-world politician, Constantine used a gradual plan of supplanting paganism. He restored pagan temples, used pagan magic formulas to protect crops and heal diseases, and used pagan as well as Christian rites in dedicating Constantinople. It was not until 317 that his coins dropped the use of pagan images.

As a former worshiper of the Unconquered Sun, Constantine obviously continued to identify the sun with the Christian God in some way. In 321 he made the first day of the week a holiday and called it "the venerable day of the Sun" (Sunday). The celebration of Christ's birth on the twenty-fifth of December appears to be related to the annual sun festival. The Philocalian calendar, representing Roman practices in the year 336, is the earliest mention of the observance on December 25. Some historians contend that the date was chosen to oppose, others that it was chosen to coordinate, the feast of the *Natalis Solis Invicti* (the birth of the Unconquered Sun). Regardless of the original intention, the date was definitely influenced by the sun festival, and Christian records of that time repeatedly refer to Christ as the "Sun of Righteousness."

As Constantine's reign grew more secure, he favored Christianity more openly. Although he never made Christianity the official religion of the empire, he encouraged all his subjects to become Christians. He gave Christian bishops the authority of judges in their dioceses, he exempted church realty from taxation, gave money to needy congregations, built several churches in Constantinople and throughout the empire, and forbade the worship of images in the new capital. In the Edict of Milan he had proclaimed toleration and freedom for all religions. He now revoked that freedom as it applied to heretical sects and ordered the destruction of their meeting places. He gave his sons a Christian education and financed his mother's many Christian philanthropies. He ordered a church of the Holy Sepulcher to be built over the alleged tomb of Christ in Jerusalem, and Helena built a chapel over the traditional site of Jesus' birth at Bethlehem (both edifices remain today).

When Eusebius wrote his *Life of Constantine* he used eight chapters to extol the virtues of the emperor's piety and good works, telling how he "governed his empire in a godly manner for more than thirty years." He somehow neglected to mention that during this time Constantine executed his son, his nephew, and his second wife. The reasons for the executions have never been clear, but the fact of them indicates that the first Christian emperor had a difficult time being thoroughly Christian.

d. The Threat of Controversy. Three clouds darkened the bright new day of the Christian world, all of them theological and terribly frustrating to Constantine. He was a man of politics and war, not religion. Yet he had become the champion of Christianity and therefore was also its defender. Christianity was a means, not an end, for Constantine. He was a statesman, not a theologian. Agitated by the theological issues that threatened his empire's peace, he summoned the bishops to be his political aides, presided over their councils, and enforced their decisions.

(1) Monasticism. A secluded life-style which has continued as one minor expression of Christianity began as early as the late third and early fourth centuries. Monastic asceticism was a reaction against the growing worldliness of the church. Even before Constantine united the church and

the empire, the general toleration of Christianity had brought in many new members to the churches, and a corresponding lowering of standards.

Between the Decian and Diocletian persecutions, the church had become the richest religious organization in the empire. Parishioners were obsessed with gaining wealth; bishops held lucrative offices of state, made fortunes, and lent money at usurious interest. A devout minority feared for the direction Christianity was taking and sought a return to absorption in spiritual matters. They believed that the only hope was to renounce all possessions and retreat to the desert. Thus hermits and monks became a permanent expression of piety. The word *hermit* comes from the Greek word meaning "desert," and the word *monk* comes from the Greek meaning "alone."

Anthony, a Coptic peasant from Egypt, was the first famous hermit. About 275, he began a quarter-century of isolated existence, and is said to have battled demons in the desert. His reputation for sanctity filled all Christendom, and peopled the desert with disciples who tried to emulate him. About 305 Anthony came out of solitude to organize his followers. He retired to solitude again in 310, but remained influential in support of the Nicene party in the Arian controversy.

After the conversion of Constantine, the church received another invasion of worldliness. While Christianity converted the world, the world also converted Christianity. The natural impulses of pagan humanity were openly displayed among professing Christians. Doubtless tens of thousands had followed their emperor into the fold of the church without ever experiencing true regeneration or new birth. What had at first appeared to be the gift of an entire empire to the church became an albatross around the necks of spiritual Christians. Monks retreating to desert solitude again became a familiar sight.

In 325, a converted soldier named Pachomius accepted the principle of monasticism but rejected extremism. Believing that absolute solitude was selfish, he established the first monastic community where spiritual brothers could retreat together to renounce the world and devote their time to Scripture and meditation. This was the first example of monasticism known as *cenobitic*, so called from the Greek words *koinos bios*, meaning "the life in common."

Martyrdom had died out, and whereas martyrs had once been the spiritual elite of the faith, that position now went to the monks. Yet these spiritual recluses began to exhibit some of the very traits of humanity they had sought to flee. While they were critical of the worldly competition of the marketplace, they became competitive in their religious devotions. They competed to see who could stand longest on one leg without food or sleep, or who could remain the longest time on the highest pillar. Those who had sought to call the church back to the fundamentals of the faith often became engrossed with trivia themselves.

Constantine did not understand the emphasis of the ascetics, and their retreat from society reflected negatively against the culture he was attempting to build. He turned to the church fathers for answers and assistance, and at first many bishops opposed the monastic movement. However, they gradually began to accept it as a necessary balance to the church's increasing involvement with commerce and government, and because the sincerity of the monks' piety could not be ignored.

Basil the Great (330-79) contributed the most to a harmonious relationship between orthodox Christianity and monastic asceticism. Highly educated at Constantinople and Athens, and made a bishop of Caesarea in Cappadocia, he nonetheless believed that monasticism was a valid expression of normative Christianity. He integrated the monastic communities more closely with the church and insisted that the bishop should have ultimate authority over a monastery. He began the first outward-looking concerns of monasticism, providing education and medical treatment for the poor. Basil's important theological works, his stand against the Arian party in the Christological controversies, his extensive organization of benevolent work, and his sincere personal holiness have ranked him in Christian history as one of the three great Cappadocian Fathers. The other two are Gregory, Bishop of Nazianzus, and Gregory, Bishop of Nyssa. These three, all Cappadocians by birth, were the chief influence which led to the final defeat of Arianism at the Council of Constantinople in 381.

Rather than splitting the church and damaging the empire, monasticism was allowed to express itself somewhat in the same manner that the party out of office in England operates as "the loyal opposition." The monks were opposed to the worldliness of the church, but still recognized it as the legitimate Body of Christ on earth.

(2) Donatism. Another cloud which threatened Constantine's clear sky was the Donatist schism which traced its grievances back to the severe Diocletian persecutions. One edict of the persecution was that all copies of the Scripture be surrendered to the state upon threat of death for the entire congregation. Many clergy had complied with the edict in order not to imperil the lives of their flock. Rigorists who had refused called these *traditores* ("handers over" of the Scriptures, obviously carrying the sense also of traitor), and insisted that they should not be restored to communion, let alone to ecclesiastical office.

A large contingency of rigorists in North Africa refused to accept Caecilian as Bishop of Carthage because his consecrator, Felix of Aptunga, had allegedly been a *traditore*. The African bishops consecrated Majorinus as a rival to Caecilian, and he was soon afterward succeeded by Donatus, from whom the schism was named.

Donatus insisted that clergy who had surrendered the Scriptures to the pagan police during the persecution had forfeited their office and powers.

He held that baptisms or ordinations performed by such clergy were null and void. This led naturally to the position that the validity of sacraments depends in large part upon the spiritual state of the administrator. "Donatism" remains the designation for such a position. The church refused to approve this stringent creed, and the Donatists set up rival bishops wherever existing ones did not meet their tests.

Constantine had thought that Christianity would be the one great unifying force that the empire needed, and now it threatened that empire with divisiveness and chaos. The emperor became personally involved when the issue evolved into legal claims over property. In the Edict of Milan he had decreed the restitution of church buildings confiscated in the persecution. But, in light of the Donatist schism, which party had the rightful claim to these buildings?

Constantine referred the matter to the bishop of Rome, who decided against the Donatists, a decision confirmed by the Council of Arles in 314. The rigorists still refused to submit, violence erupted, the Donatists appealed directly to the emperor, and Constantine grudgingly gave them a semblance of toleration. A century later the Donatists outnumbered the orthodox in North Africa, where they received their greatest theological blow from the brilliant mind of Augustine. They continued, however, to exist and oppose the orthodox until both were overthrown by the Saracens (Moslems) in the seventh and eighth centuries.

(3) Arianism. If Constantine had been out of his element in trying to understand the holiness of ascetics and in trying to unravel the ecclesiastical disputes of rival bishops, he was completely at sea when the peace of his empire was threatened by theological debate about the person and nature of Jesus Christ. The Christological controversy which was to embroil all of Christendom until 451 was ignited by a priest in Alexandria named Arius. Because his teachings were branded as heresy, Arius went down in history as one of Christianity's first and most famous heresiarchs.

Arius denied the true divinity of Jesus Christ. He maintained that the Son of God was not eternal but created by the Father, that he was therefore not God by nature, but a changeable creature. His dignity as the Son of God was bestowed upon Jesus by the Father because of his righteous life. Christ was not "consubstantial" with the Father, and the Holy Spirit was begotten by the Logos (Christ), which makes him still less of God than the Logos. The philosophical ideas from Plato through the Stoics, Philo, Plotinus, and Origen to Arius were obviously at work. Platonism, which had so deeply influenced Christian theology, was now fomenting conflict in the church.

Arius' bishop, Alexander, condemned the heretical teachings and called a council which defrocked Arius and his followers. Many priests sympathized with Arius; and throughout the empire, clergy as well as laity were divided on the issue. Eusebius recorded that there was such "tumult and disorder that the Christian religion afforded a subject of profane merriment to the pagans, even in their theaters." The year was 318 and Constantine was still trying to stabilize the empire, having just returned from overthrowing Licinius. He was extremely agitated with both Arius and Alexander and wrote a scathing letter to them. He stated that he was about the business of leading the people back to a single idea of the Deity, and they were causing dissension and strife among believers. To them both, he said, "There was no need to make these questions public . . . since they are problems that idleness alone raises, and whose only use is to sharpen men's wits . . . these are silly actions worthy of inexperienced children, and not of priests or reasonable men."

The letter reflected the political purpose of Constantine's religious policy and his vast lack of knowledge of theology and its importance. To the church, the question was vital both theologically and politically. If Christ was not God, the whole structure of Christian doctrine was in question. Furthermore, if division were permitted on this issue, confusion of belief might destroy the unity and authority of the church, and therefore its usefulness to the state. When Constantine began to see the serious implications, he called the first ecumenical (universal) council of the church.

Meeting at Nicaea in 325, the summoned bishops debated from May 20 to July 25 on the nature of the person of Jesus Christ. Arius reaffirmed his view that Christ was a creature, not equal to the Father, but "divine only by participation." He was opposed by the eloquent archdeacon Athanasius from Alexandria. Athanasius won the first great Christological debate, and the council issued the famous creed of Nicaea which firmly presents Christ as "being one essence [homos-ousios] with the Father." Arius and other heretical bishops were banished, but the empire had not seen the last of them, nor of the issue of Arianism. Constantine was at first an ardent promoter of the Nicene faith, but he soon began to waver, probably due to the influences of his sister Constantia, who favored Arianism. In 328 several of the banished priests were allowed to return and they immediately began intrigue against the Nicene party. They were so successful in gaining support that in 335 Athanasius, who had been made bishop of Alexandria in 328, had to go into exile. Arius gained recognition as being orthodox and was scheduled for reinstatement in the church when he died suddenly in 336. But the controversy did not die, and subsequent councils and creeds would testify to the poor judgment of Constantine when he tried to dismiss the issue as trivial squabbling.

Aside from the theological issues involved, the council at Nicaea must have had a profound impact upon the participants. The gathering of the leaders of the church was impressive in itself, but the unbelievable fact was that the council had been summoned and presided over by none other than the Roman emperor. Every bishop present was old enough to remember the persecutions, and now they were all discussing with the emperor, a fellow Christian, the nature of Christ and the doctrine of the Trinity. Even the most optimistic could not have hoped for this phenomenal turn of events. The victims had become victors.

2. THE BYZANTINE EMPIRE

Religion was not the sole concern of the emperor; after all, he had an empire to run and a civilization to maintain. Even if Constantine had not turned the course of world history because of his Christian conversion, he would have been renowned for his impact on culture and civilization. His legacy in this area was the magnificent Byzantine Empire.

a. Constantinople, The New Rome. In 330 Constantine moved the capital of the empire from Rome to a new city he called *Nova Roma* (New Rome), which had been built upon the ruins of the ancient fortress town of Byzantium, from which the term "Byzantine" is derived. Strategically located on the Bosphorus, the gateway between the Mediterranean Sea and the Black Sea, the new capital established a bulwark to withstand enemies from the East and positioned the government close to the main focus of the empire's trade. New Rome soon became known as Constantinople, the city of Constantine. The modern city of Istanbul, Turkey, occupies the site made famous by Constantinople.

During its long and illustrious history, Constantinople was the center of the thriving Byzantine civilization and the seat of economic and political power. It remained the capital of the Eastern Empire for more than a thousand years, becoming the Turkish capital in 1453.

In his new capital, Constantine surrounded himself with the pomp and pageantry of an oriental court. He improved the status of the army, issued humane decrees, and gave his support to letters and the arts. He strengthened the schools at Athens and founded a new university at Constantinople. He improved the posture and privileges of physicians and teachers, and decreed that artists were exempt from civic obligations in order to pursue and teach their art. From across the empire, great art treasures were brought in to make Constantinople an elegant capital.

Although the move from Rome to Constantinople was not intended to affect the church directly, it had far reaching implications and influences. The bishop of Rome became for all practical purposes the heir to the authority of the Caesars in the West. As a counterbalance, Constantine elevated the Bishop of Constantinople to a position equal to that of the Bishop of Rome. The result was a divided empire and a divided church, although Constantine tried to make the new government the real center of Christianity.

b. Division, Defection, and Renewal. In 337, at the age of sixty-four, the tired ruler of empire and church laid aside his purple robes of royalty, put on the white garb of Christian neophyte, finally received baptism, and passed away. Upon his death, Constantine's empire was divided among his three sons, Constantine II, Constantius, and Constans.

Constantine II received the provinces of the West; Constantius had the

East; and Constans held the middle, Africa, Greece, and Italy (including Rome). Each ruler supported the religious view that prevailed in his respective territory. The East was predominantly Arian, so Constantius backed the reaction against Nicaea. Constantine II and Constans were both pro-Nicene, but a rivalry between them flamed into a war in which Constantine II was killed in 340. Constans unified the Nicene areas and thereby reversed the predominance against the Arians. Ten years later, however, Constans was assassinated by a usurper, Magnentius, who in turn was defeated by Constantius two years later. Now, Constantius ruled over the whole empire, and since he was increasingly inclined toward Arianism, Jerome later observed, "The whole world groaned and was amazed to find itself Arian."

From 354 to 360, Constantius held a series of councils in various parts of the empire in an attempt to solidify the position of Arianism. He succeeded in forcing an anti-Nicene creed on reluctant bishops and in securing the condemnation of Athanasius, leader to the Nicene party. In 358, Athanasius issued his famous statement which was the first open break of the church with the state since the beginning of the Constantine era. Athanasius asked, "When did a judgment of the church receive its validity from the emperor?" Hosius of Cardova, who had helped shape Constantine's policy toward the church, now reversed and even quoted Jesus against the emperor. He said, "Do not intrude yourself into church matters, nor give commands to us concerning them. . . . God has put into your hands the kingdom; to us he has entrusted the affairs of his church. . . . It is written, 'Render unto Caesar the things that are Caesar's and unto God the things that are God's.' " For their opposing efforts, Constantius banished Athanasius and Hosius along with Liberius, the bishop of Rome.

Upon the death of Constantius in 361, his cousin Julian (nephew of Constantine) became emperor, his infamous reign lasting for only two years. Yet in this brief time he so thoroughly shattered the empire with his return to paganism that he went down in history as Julian the Apostate. A Platonist in philosophy, Julian attempted to lead the empire into a new religion he called Hellenism. He restored pagan worship and revoked the special privileges of Christian clergy. Yet there was no open persecution of Christians, and, in fact, toleration was decreed for all religions. He even allowed the banished bishops to return. He thus became the unwitting instrument of securing the Nicene position, since the orthodox resumed their offices. Although Julian believed that Constantine had made a great mistake in adopting Christianity, he exhorted his pagan priests to imitate the sobriety, hospitality, and philanthropy of the Christians. Julian died in 363, and with him the zeal of paganism. Athanasius had rightly predicted, "Be of good courage; it is but a cloud which will quickly pass away."

All succeeding emperors placed themselves on the side of Christianity.

Jovian followed Julian in 363 and proclaimed universal religious toleration. He was soon succeeded by Valentinian I (364-75) who extended the toleration to include Arians although he was personally of the Nicene faith. Valentinian appointed the younger brother Valens to rule the East (364-78), and he vigorously opposed the Nicene party. Attempting to withstand the invading Germanic tribe of Visigoths, Valens was killed in the battle of Adrianople in 378. All subsequent emperors, in the East as well as in the West, were orthodox (Nicene).

When Valentinian died, his son Gratian became emperor in the West (375-83), and when Valens was killed, he became ruler of the East also. He soon realized, however, that he could not govern the whole empire alone, and he appointed Theodosius, an experienced Spanish soldier, to rule the East (379-95). Gratian was killed in a rebellion by another Spanish officer, Magnus Maximus, in 383. This usurper became the first Christian emperor to inflict the death penalty upon a heretic, Pricillian of Spain.

Meanwhile, in the East, Theodosius I was striking a mortal blow against paganism, prohibiting all sacrifices and closing pagan temples. Heretics were forbidden to worship, their churches were confiscated, and they lost their right to inherit property. In Christian history, Theodosius I is perhaps best known for convening the Second Ecumenical Council at Constantinople in 381. This was a concerted effort to unite the eastern church at the end of the long Arian controversy on the basis of the Nicene faith. The Creed of Nicaea was reaffirmed with slight modifications.

While Theodosius was seeing the actualization of a full Christian state, he was also realizing the dramatic increase in the power of the church. When the people of Thessalonica murdered the military commander of the city, Theodosius avenged his death by the massacre of 7,000 citizens, both guilty and innocent. Ambrose, Bishop of Milan (where Theodosius held court), excommunicated the emperor until he did penance, publicly asking forgiveness in the church. To the popular question of the day, "What has the emperor to do with the church?" Ambrose had given a ringing answer: the emperor was within the church, not above it.

c. *The Fall of Rome.* After the death of Theodosius (395), the empire was ruled by his two sons, Arcadius in the East, and Honorius in the West. Tension between them developed into hostility, and Alaric, the new king of the Visigoths, took advantage of the breach. On the night of August 24, 410, Alaric stormed the walls of Rome in a surprise attack, and for the first time in 800 years Rome was taken by a foreign enemy. Jerome, from his monastery in faroff Bethlehem, wept: "The city which has taken the whole world is itself taken!" Augustine of Hippo, the great North African bishop and theologian, wrote a monumental defense of the Christian's position in the fall of Rome, titled *The City of God.*

The sack of Rome had done more psychological than actual damage.

Honorius had already moved his court to the coastal city of Ravenna, and after Alaric's sudden death, the Visigoths returned to Gaul. In 452 Attila the Hun invaded Italy and purposed to destroy Rome, but was persuaded to withdraw (according to tradition) by Pope Leo I. In 455, another Germanic tribe, the Vandals, led by Gaiseric, attacked Rome. It is reported that Leo again saved the city by his personal pleading.

The next two decades witnessed wars against the Vandals and complicated intrigues, in which puppet emperors were set up and deposed by barbarian generals. Eventually, the barbarian army revolted, and elected as their king Odoacer, a barbarian officer of the imperial guard. In 476 Odoacer deposed the last Roman emperor in the West, the weak usurper Romulus Augustulus, who had been set up by General Crestes against the legitimate Augustus, Julius Nepos. The eastern emperor in Constantinople grudgingly recognized Odoacer after the death of Nepos in 480. Odoacer was overthrown by Theodoric in 493 and Italy became a Gothic kingdom. After the death of Theodoric in 526, the eastern emperor Justinian temporarily reconquered Italy, but the imperial army was unable to hold Italy against the Lombard invasions after Justinian's death. Italy was once more dominated by barbarians, and Rome itself was governed by her bishop.

d. Justinian the Great. The decline and fall of Rome served to emphasize the strength and dominance of Constantinople, which was soaring toward the zenith of the Byzantine era. While his brother Honorius was ruling in Rome, Arcadius was emperor in the East from 395-408. He was followed by his son, Theodosius II (408-450), who summoned the Council of Ephesus in 431, and enacted the highly influential Theodosian Code. Issued in 438, the Theodosian Code inflicted the death penalty on those who denied the Trinity (the Arians) and on those who repeated baptism (the Donatists). It also banned paganism, regulated the position of the clergy, and determined the relation between church and state.

When Theodosius II was killed in a fall from his horse in 450, his brother-in-law Marcian became emperor (450-457), and stabilized his reign with financial reforms. His theological contribution was the successful repression of Monophysitism at the Council of Chalcedon in 451.

Over the next seventy years the eastern empire was threatened politically by the invading Germans and theologically by the Monophysite controversy. "Monophysite" comes from the Greek word meaning "one nature," and the controversy centered around the doctrine that in the person of the incarnate Christ there was but a single nature, and it was divine. This drastically opposed the orthodox view that Christ was "fully God and fully man." (This issue is discussed more fully in the later section, "Beliefs Become Creeds.") Emperor Zeno (474-91) caused a bitter schism between Greek and Latin Christianity when he favored Monophysitism. Anastasius (491-518) was an able administrator, but lost the following of the people when he also showed Monophysite tendencies. An illiterate senator named Justin (518-27) usurped the throne when Anastasius died, but he was quite old and left the management of the empire to his brilliant nephew Justinian, who then succeeded him as emperor in 527.

The West had been lost to the barbarians, and much of the East—Egypt, Syria, Armenia—was torn by religious strife. Justinian pursued the high and holy ambition of restoring the political and religious unity of the empire. He reconquered North Africa from the Vandals and Italy from the Goths. He ended the schism of the eastern church from the western church on papal terms, and dreamed of bringing Arians, Monophysites, and other heretics into one great spiritual fold. Obsessed with the dream of unification, he sought to unify many diverse arts in his own person. He studied to become a musician, an architect, a poet, a lawyer, a philosopher, and a theologian. The last pursuit was integral to his passion to be defender of the faith as well as emperor. He became embroiled in the Monophysite controversy, removed a pope, set up a pope, and exiled a pope whenever the papal winds were not blowing favorably upon his unification efforts. No emperor had ever made such an open attempt to dominate the papacy. Justinian issued a document of imperial theology known as the *Three Chapters* in an effort to reconcile the Monophysites. It was eventually condemned by the orthodox and ignored by the Monophysites.

Justinian had inherited an unwieldy accumulation of legal codes, and in his unifying characteristics determined to produce one great code of law. The result was the *Codex Justinianus,* the Code of Justinian, which survived for centuries as the Roman law in East and West alike. Like the Theodosian Code a century earlier, the Justinian Code enacted Christianity into law. It began with a strong section favoring the Trinity, and condemning a long list of heresies, some to be punishable by death. It gave qualifications for bishops and ecclesiastical officers, and proclaimed the authority of the Roman church over all Christians. At the same time, it clearly stipulated that all church matters were subject to the state. The emperor had dominion over the church, and all ecclesiastical law had to come from the throne. Pagan sacrifice was declared a capital offense, as was the lapsing of any Christian into paganism. Jews were forbidden to convert Christians or hold Christian slaves. Detailed laws dealing with such matters as property, courts of law, military service, and the status of women presented some innovative and far-reaching judicial precedents.

In effect, the characteristic element of this Byzantine church-state pattern was harmony, *symphonia,* in which the spiritual and civil authorities supported each other. Some have called the whole system *Caesaropapism.* Other historians resent this term, pointing out that the emperor was not a priest and that he himself could be excommunicated. At the same time, however, the emperor did control the election of the patriarch, and not even the decision of a church council was valid without his consent.

Overall, Justinian's greatest contribution was that he gave a definitive form to Byzantine culture. It was a mixture of Roman law, Christian faith, and Hellenistic philosophy. Personally, he deserved the title which historians have given him, Justinian the Great. He was a great conqueror, a great lawgiver, a great diplomat, and a great builder (the building of Hagia Sophia, the magnificent church of Constantinople, would have been the achievement of a lifetime for most men). In many ways, however, he fell far short of greatness. He was fickle, easily influenced, pompous, egotistical, and constantly wanting to be liked by everyone. He was not physically brave and never took the field in any of his many wars. At the last, the great defender of the faith became a heretic, and announced that the body of Christ was incorruptible and never knew the indignities of mortal flesh. He refused to repent of the heresy and died (565) at the age of eighty-three after reigning as emperor for thirty-eight years.

B. THEOLOGIANS BECOME ACTIVISTS

The second half of the fourth century witnessed the flowering of the golden age of the Church Fathers. This was the period of the greatest writers and thinkers of Christian antiquity. They were not, however, only thinkers and writers. They were actively involved in shaping the destiny of both state and church. They considered practically every issue, whether local or universal, a theological issue, and scriptural expositions were brought into the midst of social, political, and ecclesiastical controversies.

The listing of their names is an impressive array of luminaries: Athanasius of Alexandria, Basil of Caesarea, Gregory of Nazianzus, Gregory of Nyssa, Evagrius the Pontic, John Chrysostom, Theodore of Mopuestia, John Cassian, Augustine of Hippo, Jerome, Ambrose of Milan, Martin of Tours, Damasus of Rome, Hilary of Potiers. It is even more impressive when one considers that all of these great theologians were contemporaries and many had direct relations one with another or exercised mutual influence wielded by this group of Church Fathers.

1. ATHANASIUS (c. 296-373)

Athanasius was, by the force of his resolute character and his clear theology, the outstanding obstacle to the triumph of Arianism in the East. He had a stormy, mercurial career which began when, as secretary to Alexander, Bishop of Alexandria, he attended the Council of Nicaea in 325. He succeeded Alexander as bishop in 328 and refused to compromise with Arianism. For this obstinance he was deposed and exiled to Trier in 336. He returned on the death of Constantine in 337, but in 339 he was forced to flee to Rome. He was restored in 346 through the influence of Constans, the western emperor, against the will of Constantius, who drove him out again in 356. He remained in hiding until the accession of Julian (361), who exiled him again in 362. He returned on Julian's death in 363, and after another brief exile (356-66), he worked the rest of his life to build up the new Nicene party, which triumphed over Arianism at the Council of Constantinople in 381. He died in Alexandria in May of 373.

Athanasius is remembered in church history for his influential role in preserving orthodoxy in the church's trinitarian theology. While still in his twenties he had written the masterful *De Incarnatione*, in which he shows how God the Word, by his union with manhood, restored fallen man to the image of God, and by his death and resurrection met and overcame death, the consequence of sin. He was the greatest and most consistent theological opponent of Arianism, against which he wrote a series of works from 339 to 359. He also upheld the deity of the Holy Spirit and the full manhood of Christ against Macedonian and Apollinarian tendencies. He aided the ascetic movement of monasticism, and generally strengthened the spirituality as well as the orthodoxy of the church.

2. AMBROSE (c. 339-97)

Ambrose was a practicing lawyer when he was appointed governor of Aemilia-Liguria, with his seat at Milan. When Auxentius, the Arian bishop of Milan, died in 374, the laity demanded that Ambrose succeed him. As bishop, he was famous as a preacher and renowned as an upholder of orthodoxy. He is credited mainly with the conversion of Augustine (386). Political and church events involved him personally with the rulers of the western empire, and he had great influence with Gratian, Maximus, Justina, and Theodosius I. He fought paganism and Arianism, maintained the independence of the church from civil power, and championed morality. His most notable work was *De Officiis Ministrorum*, a treatise on Christian ethics with special reference to the clergy. He wrote on ascetical subjects, encouraged monasticism, wrote several well-known Latin hymns, and through his knowledge of Greek, introduced much eastern theology into the West. Ambrose is one of the four traditional doctors of the Latin church, the other three being Jerome, Augustine, and Gregory the Great.

3. JEROME (c. 342-420)

Jerome was one of the greatest biblical scholars of the early church. He originally devoted himself to an ascetic life, settled as a hermit into the Syrian desert, and learned Hebrew. On his return to Antioch, he was ordained a priest, spent some time in Constantinople, and eventually became secretary to Pope Damasus. After Damasus' death, he visited Antioch, Egypt, and Palestine. In 386 he finally settled in Bethlehem, where he ruled the men's monastery and devoted the rest of his life to study and writing. His greatest achievement was his translation of the Bible into Latin from the original languages. Known as the *Vulgate*, this work was completed around 404, established by the Council of Trent in the mid-sixteenth century as the official Roman Catholic version of the Bible and remains so today. Jerome also wrote three revisions of the psalter, many biblical commentaries, a bibliography of ecclesiastical writers, translated the works of Origen and Didymus into Latin, developed the relationship of the Apocrypha to the Hebrew canon, and translated and continued Eusebius' *Chronicle of Church History*. Although he advocated extreme asceticism, he was personally involved in many passionate attacks against Arianism, Pelagianism, and Origenism. Jerome's scholarship and dedication were unsurpassed in the early church and set models for all succeeding theological writers.

4. JOHN CHRYSOSTOM (c. 347-407)

Chrysostom was bishop of Constantinople and a renowned preacher. His great powers of oratory earned him the name of Chrysostom, "the golden-mouth." However, he combined his preaching ability with dedicated scholarship and his series of "homilies" on various books of the Bible established him as the greatest Christian expositor of his day. He had an unusual facility of seeing the spiritual meaning of Scripture and at the same time making practical application. He was made patriarch of Constantinople in 398, and set about reforming the city from its corruption of court, clergy, and society. His honesty, asceticism, and tactlessness won him many enemies. Chief among these were Theophilus, the unworthy patriarch of Alexandria, and the Empress Eudoxia, who took all attempts at moral reform as a censure of herself. They succeeded in having him removed from his see and banished. Although he was supported by the people of Constantinople, Pope Innocent I, and indeed the entire western church, he was exiled to Antioch, moved to Pontus, and finally deliberately killed by enforced traveling on foot in severe weather. He has been remembered for his personal holiness, his matchless preaching, his scholarly exegesis, and his liturgical reforms. His work *On the Priesthood* is a splendid description of the responsibilities of the Christian minister.

5. AUGUSTINE (354-430)

The theological development of this period reached its zenith in the person of Aurelius Augustine, bishop of Hippo, whom many rank as second only to the Apostle Paul in the development of western Christian theology. The medieval theologians, Aquinas, Luther, Calvin, and Pascal, drew heavily on him. Contemporary theologians and philosophers, such as Kant, Hegel, Marx, and Whitehead, trace many of their ideas to the seminal work of Augustine.

(a) The Conversion of Augustine. He was born in North Africa of a pagan father and a Christian mother (Monica). He received a Christian education,

studied to become a lawyer, but decided instead on literary pursuits. He abandoned Christianity and took a mistress, to whom he was faithful for fifteen years, having a son by her. The writings of Cicero awakened in him an intense interest in philosophy, and he soon became a Manichaean, which he remained for nine years. Disillusioned by the all-too-simple Manichaean explanation of evil in terms of matter, he left them and Africa. He went to Rome and opened a school of rhetoric, where he became disgusted by the behavior of his pupils, and left for a professorship at Milan. By the time he arrived in Milan, he was embracing the philosophy of the "Academics," which denied the possibility of attaining absolute truths. A little later he became a Neo-Platonist and drew nearer to Christianity. He was attracted to the preaching of Ambrose, bishop of Milan, for the literary quality of his sermons and for the biblical answers given to many of his objections. When he heard of the conversion of the Neo-Platonist philosopher Victorinus to Christianity, Augustine turned in earnest to search the New Testament. One thing which appeared as an obstacle to his becoming a Christian was his moral incontinence. Although he had dismissed his concubine at the insistence of his mother, he had entered another illicit affair. Another obstacle was his concern about "inconsistencies" in the Bible.

With great heaviness of heart, which he describes as a "sickness unto death," Augustine went alone one day to a garden, where he tore his hair and beat his breast. He had been deeply moved and shamed by the story of Anthony and the Egyptian hermits, and how they withstood temptation. From next door he heard the voice of a child crooning *"Tolle, lege"* (take up and read). He then saw a copy of the New Testament on a bench, and opening it to Romans 13:13, he read: "Not in reveling and drunkenness, not in debauchery and licentiousness, not in quarreling and jealousy. But put on the Lord Jesus Christ and make no provision for the flesh to gratify its desires." This verse enabled him to surrender his heart and life completely to Christ, resulting in a conversion experience which he said was comparable to that of Paul on the road to Damascus. Several months later, he and his son Adeodatus were baptized by Ambrose. With his mother and son, he set out to return to Africa, but his mother died enroute, and his son died shortly after arriving in Africa. After losing the people he loved the most, he entered the monastery at Tagaste. He became a priest in 391, but continued to live the monastic life until he was consecrated coadjutor bishop to Valerius, bishop of Hippo, and after 396 he served as the sole bishop of the see. At Hippo he commenced his mighty career as administrator, pastor, and theologian.

(b) The Controversies of Augustine. During his episcopate Augustine was confronted with four major controversial issues, and it was mainly through his struggles with these issues that his own theology was formed.

Perhaps second only to the Apostle Paul, Augustine of Hippo provided the strongest foundation to Christian theology for the early church. Many of his beliefs were shaped as a result of the numerous heresies which arose during his day. (Historical Pictures Service, Chicago)

Manichaeism was the first and least dangerous heresy with which Augustine contended (we have already referred briefly to Manichaeism under the Marcionite heresy). Augustine, who embraced Manichaeism for nine years before his conversion, had become thoroughly opposed to its simplistic concepts of light and dark and good and evil. Now he opposed the Manichaean attempt to solve the problem of evil by positing an evil agency eternally opposed to the good God. Augustine maintained that God was the sole creator and sustainer of all things, that evil is the privation of some good which ought to be had, and that moral evil springs from free will.

The Donatist controversy was more urgent because of the deep divisions it had caused in the African church. The Donatist issue was almost a century old, dating from the *traditore* controversy of the persecution era. The issue was raised as to whether or not the sacraments were valid if administered by unholy men. The Donatists insisted that sacraments administered by *traditores* (those who had given up the Scriptures in the Diocletian persecution), unholy men, or heretics, were invalid. And since theirs was the only church which maintained its purity on this issue, the Donatists claimed to be the one true church. Augustine refuted this claim and taught that the sacraments are Christ's, and the validity of the sacraments rests in the sacrament itself and not the administrator. He acknowledged that unholy persons are in the church, as the parable of the wheat and tares indicates; and he said that the Donatists were wrong in trying to claim final blessedness now. This led Augustine to define a sacrament as a sign of the invisible grace of God in which God forgives sin. He finally urged the state to force the Donatists back into the fold of orthodoxy, quoting Luke 14:23, "Compel them to come in." Since he believed the church is superior to the state, he believed that the state should execute the commandments of God, as instructed by the church.

Augustine's later years were taken up with the Pelagian controversy. Pelagius was a very moral and learned lay monk who came to Rome from the British Isles about 385. Shocked by the low morality of Rome, Pelagius devoted his preaching and writing to the issues of morality and sin. He denied the idea of inherited sin, stating that Adam's sin was a bad example which men have chosen to follow, that sin is really self-generated. Actually, man could be sinless if he so desired, thus placing salvation in the hands of man himself. Pelagius was condemned for his teaching by two African councils and then excommunicated by Pope Innocent in 417. The chief heresies with which Pelagians were charged were: (1) that Adam would have died even if he had not sinned; (2) that the sin of Adam injured himself alone and not the whole human race; (3) that newborn children are in the same condition as Adam was before he fell; (4) that the whole human race does not die because of Adam's death or sin, nor will it rise again because of Christ's resurrection; (5) that the law as well as the gospel offers entrance to heaven; and (6) that even before the coming of Christ there were men wholly without sin.

Pelagius developed much of his theology as a reaction to Augustine's often quoted prayer in his *Confessions:* "Grant what Thou commandest and command what Thou wilt." Pelagius inferred this to mean that man is not responsible for good or evil deeds, that it is all in the hands of God. If this is so, man's entire moral structure was imperiled, for it served as an invitation to indulge in sin. In refuting Pelagius, Augustine maintained that man was created with certain supernatural gifts which were lost by the fall of Adam; and, as a result, man suffers from a hereditary moral disease, is subject to the inherited legal liability of Adam's sin, and can be saved from these evils solely by the grace of God. Pelagianism drove Augustine to a belief in predestination, irresistible grace, and divine control of all that happens. In fact, most of Augustine's theology on sin and salvation was worked out as a reaction to Pelagianism, which he refuted with minute exegesis of the biblical text.

Paganism became another major adversary for Augustine with the fall of Rome to Alaric in 410. This event caused great consternation throughout the civilized world, and pagans blamed the fall on the Christians who had abolished heathen worship. They contended that the pagan gods were at last venting their wrath. Augustine took it upon himself to reply to the pagan charge, producing in his reply the monumental twenty-two-book work called *The City of God.*

For Augustine, there were two major questions concerning the fall of Rome: (1) Why had God allowed this to happen? (2) Should Christians have recourse to war to repulse the barbarians? In answer to the first question, Augustine emphatically rejected the notion that Christians were to blame, and demonstrated how Rome, through the sovereign will of God, had fallen because of her own crimes. In answer to the second question, he was emphatic again in justifying the right of Christians to take arms against the barbarians under these conditions: if the object is to vindicate justice and restore peace, if the motive is love, and if the war is just (which means that one side must be unjust). Augustine envisioned a world in which the state, through its power of government (even war if necessary), made society a safe and stable place where the church could apply its teachings and principles.

(c) The Contributions of Augustine. The literary contributions of Augustine are overwhelming in their volume alone. His best known works are *The Confessions, The City of God,* and *The Enchiridion,* but he also wrote fourteen treatises against the Manichaeans, six against the Donatists, and fourteen against the Pelagians, in addition to a number of philosophical works, and numerous sermons, letters, and commentaries.

The City of God volumes follow a clear and purposeful outline. The first five books refute the charge that Rome was destroyed because of the Christian ban on pagan worship. The next five books demonstrate the worthlessness of worshiping pagan deities. Books 11-14 trace the rise of the divine and earthly cities; Books 15-18 show the growth of these cities; Books 19-22 demonstrate their proper ends. The analysis of the two cities is always set against the backdrop of God's action in history. For Augustine, history had its beginning in creation, its climax in the coming of Christ, and its conclusion in the day of judgment.

The Confessions was written shortly before 400 and is the story of Augustine's life before and including his conversion. It is the world's first spiritual autobiography, tracing his tortuous course in searching for meaning and happiness. In describing his own search, he sees himself as representing all mankind, as an example of man's corruption, redemption, and continuing imperfection. The culmination of his search is the famous conclusion that man is restless and cannot find rest until he rests in God.

Augustine's formative theological contributions are bearing fruit to this day. His doctrines of original sin and salvation by grace alone were highly influential upon Luther. His conclusions about predestination led Calvin in further elaborations on this theme. His concepts of society, especially the relationship of church and state, continue to influence politics and ecclesiology. His support of just wars stamped him as the father of the war-guilt theory. He is credited with giving definitive shape to the Catholic teaching against birth control, maintaining that the primary purpose of marriage is procreation. He firmly entrenched infant baptism by insisting that babies who die unbaptized go into everlasting perdition. He drew guidelines for ecclesiastical and theological authority which are still in use. His influence on the sacraments and ecclesiology of the Roman Catholic Church has been profound and lasting. The views of Augustine on grace and predestination, church and state, war and peace, sex and marriage, and tolerance and constraint, continue to make their impact on each succeeding generation in the western church, whether Catholic or Protestant.

C. BISHOPS BECOME POPES

In addition to the rise of the state-church and the development of formative theology, this extremely important period of history also produced the unmistakable patterns of ecclesiastical organization, including the papal hierarchy.

1. POLITICAL AND CHURCH ORGANIZATION
After Theodosius made Christianity the official religion of the state, the bishops organized the church on the basis of the political organization of the empire. The city territory was the smallest unit in the political administration; and the diocese, embracing that city territory, was the

simplest unit in ecclesiastical administration. It was headed by a bishop. Over the city territory was the province with its provincial governor, and the corresponding church office was that of the metropolitan (archbishop), held by the bishop of the provincial city. Several provinces were governed by an imperial governor (vicarius); and the church's corresponding officer was the patriarch (cardinal). The imperial council (senate) had its counterpart in the assembly of patriarchs (college of cardinals). Eventually the emperor found his ecclesiastical counterpart in the pope.

When the first Catholic (universal or ecumenical) Council met in Nicaea in 324, very distinct characteristics surfaced which permanently shaped a great portion of Christendom. These included: (1) the idea of a visible universal church composed of the bishops; (2) the belief that the sacraments (as they were now called) carried a supernatural power of transforming grace; (3) the employment of a special priesthood, the clergy, which had sole authority to administer the sacraments; and (4) the recognition of the bishops as the ruling officers (episcopal government). All of these characteristics are still observed by Roman Catholics, Greek Catholics, and Anglo-Catholics.

2. PRESUMED BASIS FOR THE PAPACY

It is impossible to document a precise date for the beginning of the papacy. While the Catholic Church insists that Peter was the first pope, others look to Leo the Great or perhaps Damasus, but hardly ever anyone earlier than Stephen of Rome. Toward the end of the second century, Irenaeus stated the case for apostolic succession clearly and forcefully. Irenaeus had known Polycarp, bishop of Smyrna, who claimed to have been instructed by the apostles and to have talked with many who had seen Christ. Irenaeus was convinced that the apostles had transmitted faithfully and accurately what had been taught them by Christ; and furthermore, he believed they had appointed as their successors bishops to whom they had committed the churches. These bishops had been followed by others in unbroken line.

In the first quarter of the fourth century, Eusebius, the church historian, gave the lists of the bishops of several churches, indicating the importance of the succession theory. When Christianity was troubled by heresy and schism, the bishops began meeting together for consultation and common action. In this fashion it dealt with the heresies of Gnosticism, Marcionism, and Montanism, and in the process developed an administrative system centered around its bishops. Thus, the idea of papal primacy—among other things—evolved from the notion of apostolic succession, which applied to all bishops.

Tertullian also strengthened the concept of apostolic succession by insisting that only those churches were valid which agreed in their teaching with those founded by the apostles and where the faith had been kept pure by a succession of bishops going back to the apostles. Cyprian, bishop of

Carthage in the third century, held that there was only one true church, authenticated by the presence of the episcopate, and that anyone who was not with the bishop was not in the church, and therefore not a Christian. Cyprian regarded all bishops as equal, but esteemed the bishop of Rome as the first among equals.

3. THE PREEMINENCE OF ROME

The Council of Nicaea in 325 had designated the bishops of Rome, Alexandria, and Antioch as "superior" metropolitans (patriarchs), but the bishop of Rome refused to be listed as equal, insisting that it had always held primacy. Between this first ecumenical council and the fourth held in Chalcedon in 451, the Roman bishops laid the foundation for the ecclesiastical monarchy, which exists to this day. The Roman church claimed not only human but divine right for supremacy, claiming that Christ assigned Peter the eminent position in founding the church. It was claimed that this gave Peter a supremacy of authority over the other apostles, that this supremacy was official, hereditary, and transferable. It was believed that Peter was bishop of Rome until his martyrdom, that he appointed his successor, and that all bishops of Rome, as successors of Peter, have enjoyed and exercised universal jurisdiction over all other churches. These claims were, and continue to be, disputed throughout Christendom; but the practical and political (if not the scriptural and spiritual) supremacy of Rome prevailed.

The first example of a papal attitude on the part of the Roman church is found in Clement (d. 102), who wrote a beautiful epistle of consolation and love to the distressed church of Corinth. Dealing with the issue of deposed presbyters in the Corinthian church, Clement called for repentance, insisting that God required due order in all things and that the deposed presbyters must be reinstated and legitimate superiors obeyed.

Ignatius (c. 35-107), bishop of Antioch, in his Epistle to the Romans, ascribes laudatory titles to that congregation although he does not mention Clement or any other bishop. Irenaeus (c. 130-200), bishop of Lyons, called Rome the greatest church, acknowledged by all and founded by Peter and Paul. However, Irenaeus rebuked Victor, bishop of Rome, in 190 for forcing uniformity on the churches of Asia Minor. Tertullian (c. 160-220), in confrontation with the heretics, pointed to the apostolic mother churches as the repositories of pure doctrine, with special commendation for the church at Rome. Later, however, he opposed Rome for its loose penitential discipline. Cyprian (d. 258) called the Roman church the chair of Peter, the foundation of priestly unity, and mother of the Catholic Church. He still insisted, however, on the equality of the other bishops and opposed Stephen of Rome in the controversy over heretical baptism. Thus, it was becoming obvious that the growing influence of the Roman see was rooted in the need for unity in the early church.

Historical and practical reasons also contributed to the ascendency of Rome. Located in the geographical and political center of the world, the Roman bishop enjoyed a unique prestige. Since AD 100, the congregation in Rome was probably the largest in Christendom. It was wealthy, hospitable to strangers, and generous to the poor. Successful resistance to Gnosticism, Arianism, and Montanism gave added strength and prestige to the Roman church. The fact that Paul wrote the longest and most profound of his epistles to Rome, and the tradition that he was martyred there, had given additional apostolic weight, along with the traditions of Peter's ministry and death there. The many missionaries sent out by the Roman church caused new churches to have a great feeling of affection and loyalty to the mother church. During the barbarian invasions, when the emperors failed to defend Rome, the popes saved the city through their intercession. Pope Leo the Great is credited with stopping both Attila (452) and Gaiseric (455). When Constantine moved to Constantinople, the Roman bishop became the most important person in Rome, and when the western empire fell in 476, the Roman popes became the most important figures of western Europe, gradually taking over the power of the state. During the later Mohammedan conquests, the cities of Antioch, Jerusalem, and Alexandria fell to the Moslems, eliminating them forever as candidates for church supremacy. Whether it can be supported by scriptural injunction or accepted by universal allegiance, the ascendency of Rome to papal primacy has been an obvious and permanent fact of history.

4. THE EARLIEST POPES

Without question, the church at Rome has always maintained a list of her bishops which far surpasses the list of any other church in age, completeness, integrity of succession, and consistency of doctrine and policy. While the Protestant world recognizes the historical worth of such a list, it does not acquiesce to the Roman Catholic tradition of calling each of these bishops a pope. Many Protestants also have difficulty in accepting at face value the claim of Peter's episcopate in Rome, which has no verifiable evidence in Scripture or history. Assuming, however, the accuracy of the claim, the successor to Peter is variously designated as Clement (according to Tertullian) or Linus (according to Irenaeus, Eusebius). Then follows Anacletus, Alexander, Sixtus I, etc. Several "popes" during the first five hundred years of Christianity exercised authority which shaped church history and wielded influence in secular history.

a. Victor I. An important step in the history of papal supremacy occurred when Victor, bishop at Rome from 189 to 198, assembled a council at Rome to excommunicate churches which did not subscribe to the Roman church's dating of Easter, and later excommunicated Theodotus for denying the divinity of Christ.

b. Stephen I (254-257) intervened in theological disputes in South Gaul and Spain, and became involved in a long and bitter controversy with Cyprian over the validity of baptism by heretics. During this controversy he invoked Matthew 16:18, implying his supremacy as Peter's successor.

c. Sylvester (314-335) baptized Emperor Constantine, and established the Lateran church as the cathedral of Rome on territory given him by the emperor. It was claimed that he received the Donation of Constantine, which provided him with wide temporal rights over the church. The Donation of Constantine was exposed as a forgery in the fifteenth century.

d. Damasus (366-384) was the first to seriously and staunchly employ the Petrine passage of Matthew 16:18 as a biblical basis for primacy. He also commissioned Jerome to prepare the Vulgate version of the Bible, promulgated a canon of scriptural books, and indicated that the Council of Nicaea was valid only because it had been approved by his predecessor, Sylvester.

e. Innocent I (402-417) made more substantial claims for the papacy than any of his predecessors at Rome. He insisted that major cases of dispute should be brought to the judgment of the Roman see. Innocent claimed that the Roman church had sole custody of apostolic tradition and primacy over all bishops because of Peter's primacy among the apostles. He also exhibited determination and ability to exercise authority in the East as well as the West. He was a powerful influence with the civil powers, and it was through his influence that Emperor Honorius issued his decree against the Donatists in 404.

f. Leo I (440-461) sealed the Roman claim to the papacy. In fact, if there could be a universally accepted date for the official recognition of the papacy, Leo would be named as "the first pope." He advanced and consolidated the influence of the Roman see to a remarkable degree. He strengthened the church by an energetic central government, claiming that his see was of divine and scriptural authority. He pressed his claims to jurisdiction to Africa, Spain, and Gaul. Emperor Valentian III recognized his jurisdiction over all the western provinces. Without reservation or hesitation, Leo proclaimed that anyone who does not acknowledge the Roman bishop as the head of the church is not of the body of the church. His legates presided over the Council of Chalcedon (451) where his personal Tome to Chalcedon was accepted as the standard for Christology. (Orthodox Christians dispute this decision.) In the political arena, he increased papal prestige by persuading the Huns to withdraw beyond the Danube (452) and secured concessions when the Vandals took Rome (455). History has named him "Leo the Great"; and for his unparalleled contributions to the strength and permanence of the papacy, he has deserved the name.

g. Gelasius (492-96) must be mentioned in this list of early popes for his effectiveness in establishing claims that priestly power is above kingly power and that there can be no legitimate appeal from the chair of Peter. In civil affairs, he declared, clergy are to submit to the emperor, but in ecclesiastical affairs, the emperor is to submit to the pope. He personally and tenaciously upheld the primacy of the Roman see against Constantinople during the Acacian Schism.

The conquests of Justin and Justinian reversed things and rendered the papacy subservient to the eastern emperor for a short time. However, Leo and Gelasius had already laid the unshakable foundations for the expansion of the papacy in the Middle Ages. The popes had a firm grasp on the keys which they claimed had been given them by Christ himself.

D. MONKS BECOME MISSIONARIES

While the politically minded bishops were debating supremacy and consolidating power, another segment of Christianity was proceeding down an entirely different path. The humble and selfless monks were keeping their vows of poverty, chastity, and obedience, going about their daily activities of prayer and work. Their quiet influence, however, thoroughly penetrated the corridors of Christendom, and some of them even eventually left their monasteries for evangelistic preaching and foreign missions.

1. MONASTICISM

As we have seen earlier, Constantine was confronted with the challenge of monasticism, believing that the retreat from society reflected on the society he was building. Thanks to Basil, the movement was brought into line with normative Christianity and church organization. Jerome successfully united the movement with scholarship and service. Monasticism became a massive movement that attracted thousands in the fourth and fifth centuries. It was essentially a lay counterculture of withdrawal that developed into a powerful social force within a century.

a. Ulphilas (311-383) was known as the Apostle of the Goths because of his ministry among his people. He had been consecrated bishop at Constantinople, but retreated to his native Cappadocia where he spent isolated years translating the Bible into the Gothic language. He spent much of his life as a dedicated missionary beyond the confines of the empire. Although never identified with monasticism as such, his personal spiritual habits certainly anticipated the rudiments of monasticism to come. Because he was an Arian, Ulphilas' influence on the Goths caused them to embrace Arianism for several centuries.

b. Martin of Tours (335-397) was the son of a pagan, served in the Roman army, and after becoming a Christian founded the monastery of Liguge, the first in Gaul (France). Becoming bishop of Tours in 372, he encouraged the spread of monasticism in Gaul. He himself set out to evangelize the hitherto neglected countryside, and introduced a rudimentary parochial system.

c. *Patrick* (389-461), the "Apostle of the Irish," was born in Roman Britain, the son of a deacon and magistrate. At the age of sixteen he was seized on his father's farm by raiders and sold as a slave in Ireland. After six years of service as a shepherd, he escaped and eventually reached home again. During his captivity his faith had deepened, and he felt compelled to return to evangelize Ireland. He studied in the monastery of Lerins and was ordained a deacon in 417. He was sent to assist Palladius in Ireland, and upon the latter's death he was consecrated a bishop in 432. After founding a church in Sabal Patraic, he went to the court of High King Laoghaire, where he gained toleration for Christianity and converted several members of the royal family. He preached extensively throughout the land and established numerous churches. He founded the Cathedral Church of Armagh, which became the educational and administrative center of the Irish church. He emphasized the ascetic life and monasticism throughout his ministry, but continued his evangelistic efforts. He taught the priority of mission to Celtic Christianity, which produced great numbers of monks who evangelized western Europe during the sixth and seventh centuries. Patrick organized the scattered Christian communities in Northern Ireland and brought the country into much closer relations with the rest of the western church. He encouraged the study of Latin, and tried to raise the general standards of scholarship. Patrick is a classic example of spiritual monasticism going forth to the world in love and dedication.

d. *Columba* (521-597) is credited with turning the religious, political, and social life of Scotland to Christianity. He came from a noble Irish family, was trained in Irish monasteries, and founded several churches and monasteries in his country. Compelled by missionary zeal, he left his home in 563 and settled with twelve companions on the island of Iona on the west coast of Scotland. There he established a monastery which served as a base for evangelism among the Scots and Picts. He preached forcefully to people who were under the influence of the Druids, dread opponents of Christianity. Brude, king of the Picts, was converted under his preaching, many churches were founded, and practically all of Scotland was Christianized. He was a man of deep visionary piety, who practiced effective involvement in the affairs of kings and chiefs and had concern for Christian scholarship.

e. *Benedict of Nursia* (480-542) is known as the "Patriarch of western monasticism." Benedict was educated in Rome, where the immorality of

Patrick, patron saint of Ireland, according to some tradition not only brought Christianity but was supposed to have rid the island kingdom of snakes. (Historical Pictures Service, Chicago)

society led him to withdraw from the world and retire to a cave at Subiaco. A community grew up around him, and he established twelve monasteries with twelve monks each, with abbots appointed by himself. In 525 he established the famous monastery at Monte Cassino, south of Rome. Here he elaborated his plans for the reform of monasticism and composed his celebrated Rule of St. Benedict, which became the universal monastic rule in the Middle Ages. Benedict did not stress poverty, nor discourage possessions, which enabled his monks to do works of mercy. The sick and guests received special treatment in Benedictine monasteries, which became centers of hospitality, learning, worship, and liturgical art. The church found the Benedictine monasteries especially effective in transmitting culture to the barbarians during the Dark Ages.

E. BELIEFS BECOME CREEDS

The joy of Christianity's victory over the Roman Empire had been shattered by an internal Christological dispute which Constantine was determined to settle once and for all. This issue was not settled finally, however, until a century and a quarter later. Four ecumenical councils were called during this time as the controversy raged back and forth and threatened to split Christianity irreparably. The councils, their dates, and the chief subjects dealt with were: (1) Nicaea, 325, Arianism; (2) Constantinople, 381, Apollinarianism; (3) Ephesus, 431, Nestorianism; (4) Chalcedon, 451, Eutychianism.

Although each of the councils dealt with many matters pertinent to the life and organization of the church, the main issue was that of Christology, the doctrine of the person of Christ. From the very beginning, the centrality of Christianity resided not in functions, liturgies, and mystical experiences, but in rationally held doctrines or beliefs, which were expressed in worship and witness. The beliefs about Jesus Christ were absolutely fundamental to the very existence of the church. The prolonged controversies of the fourth and fifth centuries were about the person of Christ: How Christ, the Son of God, was actually himself God (the doctrine of the Trinity), and how he was both man and God (the doctrine of Christology).

1. NICAEA
The Emperor Constantine personally convened and opened the first ecumenical council at Nicaea in Bithynia in the early summer of 325. His main interest was to secure unity rather than any predetermined theological verdict.

The controversy which culminated in the council had begun in 319 when Arius, a priest in one of the churches at Alexandria, had clashed with his bishop, Alexander. Arius had been teaching that the Father alone was really God and that the Son was essentially different from the Father. He believed that the dignity of Jesus as Son of God was bestowed upon him by the Father on account of his foreseen righteousness. Arianism maintained that the Son was not eternal but was created by the Father as an instrument for creating the world.

For his subordinationist teachings, Arius was excommunicated by Alexander, but not before he had gained a strong following, including Eusebius of Nicomedia (causing the sympathizers of Arius to be known as Eusebians). When Constantine could not achieve reconciliation through a personal envoy to Alexandria, he convened the Council of Nicaea in 325 to settle the matter. Arius was rather quickly condemned by his own words, and Athanasius, assistant to Alexander, emerged as the champion of orthodoxy. Eusebius of Caesarea (the historian) was present and laid before the council the baptismal creed of his own church. The council revised his creed and adopted it as its official statement. This creed became known as the Nicene Creed, and with four anti-Arian anathemas attached, was subscribed to by all the bishops present, except for two who were deposed and banished.

2. CONSTANTINOPLE
The Council of Nicaea was followed by more than half a century of discord and disorder in the eastern church, which also affected the stability of the West. Arianism both ascended and descended, Athanasius was alternately praised and banned. Councils called at Antioch (341) and Sardica (342) did more harm than good toward reconciliation.

The Nicene Creed remained officially in force until Constantine's death, but when his son Constantius died, Arianism was practically dominant in the East. Constantius forced the western bishops to condemn and banish Athanasius, and encouraged the writing of anti-Nicene creeds. The situation caused Jerome to write, "The whole world groaned in astonishment at finding itself Arian."

A decisive step toward repairing the damage was taken by Basil the Great, who had so strongly influenced eastern monasticism and other Cappadocians (Gregory of Nyssa and Gregory of Nazianzus). Their complex doctrine of the Trinity served to demonstrate that it was possible to accept both Nicaea *(homousios)* and the distinct persons *(hypostaseis)* of Father, Son, and Spirit at the same time. By giving precise meanings to the terms used in talking about the Trinity, Basil paved the way for the work of the Council of Constantinople in 381.

Theodosius, a westerner and strong supporter of Nicaea, became eastern emperor in 379 and summoned the Council of Constantinople to reaffirm the faith of Nicaea. The creed of Nicaea was upheld and thence became known as the Nicene-Constantinopolitan Creed. This council marked the end of Arianism within the empire.

There was, however, another controversy raging over the Christological question precipitated by Apollarius, bishop of Laodicea in Syria. Thus, Apollinarianism became the central issue at Constantinople rather than Arianism.

Beginning as a staunch theologian in the Nicene tradition, Apollinarius had carried the unity of the Father and Son to such extremes as to deny the complete manhood of Christ, and thus to make Apollinarianism the first great Christological heresy. In emphasizing the deity of Christ, Apollinarius rejected the idea of moral development in Christ's life, and asserted that while Christ had a human body and soul, the human spirit, or rational soul, had been replaced with the divine Logos. God in Christ was transmuted into flesh, and this flesh was then transmuted into something by nature divine. Christ did not receive his human nature from Mary. He brought with him from heaven a heavenly kind of flesh. The womb of Mary simply served as a passageway.

The fundamental objection to Apollinarius' teaching was that if there is no complete manhood in Christ, he is not a perfect example for us, nor does he redeem the whole of human nature but only its spiritual elements. The Council of Constantinople explicitly and conclusively condemned Apollinarianism, striking down the possibility of docetism gaining a foothold in Christian theology.

Because of its important place in determining the future of orthodoxy in Christian dogma, it is worthwhile to observe the Nicene-Constantinople Creed in its entirety:

We believe in one God the Father all-sovereign, maker of heaven and earth, and of all things visible and invisible: And in one Lord Jesus Christ, the only-begotten Son of God. Begotten of the Father before all ages, Light of Light, true God of true God, begotten not made, of one substance with the Father, through whom all things were made, who for us men and our salvation came down from the heavens, and was made flesh of the Holy Spirit and the Virgin Mary, and became man, and was crucified for us under Pontius Pilate, and suffered and was buried, and rose again on the third day according to the Scriptures, and ascended into the heavens, and sits on the right hand of the Father, and comes again with glory to judge living and dead, of whose kingdom there shall be no end: And in the Holy Spirit, the Lord and the Life-giver, that proceeds from the Father, who with the Son is worshiped together and glorified together, who spoke through the prophets: In one holy catholic and apostolic church: We acknowledge one baptism unto remission of sins. We look for a resurrection of the dead and the life of the age to come.

3. EPHESUS

Following the Council of Constantinople, Christological disputes continued to disrupt the East. The question of how one was to conceive of the human-divine in the historical Christ had obviously not been settled to everyone's satisfaction. Adding to the controversy was a growing devotion to Mary, the mother of Jesus. If Jesus were truly God, did not this imply that Mary was also the mother of God? Nestorius, the bishop of Constantinople, rejected and attacked this notion which was expressed in the term "Theotokos" (God bearer), and proposed instead the term "Christotokos." Strongly opposing both Apollinarianism and the growing popularity of "Theotokos," Nestorius worked out a Christology which came to be interpreted as saying that Christ was constituted of two natures. He did not deny the deity of Christ, but he spoke of a "conjunction" rather than a union of the two natures. He never divided Christ into two sons, the Son of God and the Son of Mary (as he was accused of doing), but he refused to attribute to the divine nature the human acts and sufferings of the man Jesus. He insisted that to call Mary the mother of God was to declare that the divine nature could be born of a woman, or that God could be two days old. Apparently, especially to his critics, Nestorius believed in two different natures and two different persons in Christ, which was directly opposed to the orthodox doctrine that the incarnate Christ was a single person.

Cyril of Alexandria and Egyptian monks began severe attacks on Nestorius in 428. Both sides appealed to Rome, where Pope Celestine decided against Nestorius. In 431, Emperor Theodosius II called the Council of Ephesus to dispose of the matter, which it did by disposing of Nestorius. Overwhelmingly defeated by Cyril and others, Nestorius was deposed from his see of Constantinople and excommunicated, his doctrines condemned, and the Creed of Nicaea reaffirmed. In its rejection of Nestorianism, the council also gave formal approval to the concept of "Theotokos." After the Council of Ephesus, the eastern bishops who refused to accept the decision of the council, constituted themselves into a separate Nestorian church. It had its center in Persia, and survived centuries of hostility, Moslem conquests, and pagan influences. A remnant still remains today, sometimes called Assyrian Christians.

4. CHALCEDON
In the early 440s a new generation took over. Leo I became bishop of Rome in 440, Dioscorus succeeded Cyril in Alexandria in 444, and Flavian was made patriarch of Constantinople in 446. There was, however, an aged monastic superior in Constantinople, named Eutyches, who continued to attack the doctrine of "two natures after the union." In the terms of a "single-nature" doctrine he suggested that Christ's humanity was absorbed by his divinity like a drop of wine in the sea. Thus, in his livid opposition to the Nestorian heresy, he developed his own heresy of maintaining that there were "two natures before, but only one after, the union" in the incarnate Christ.

Eutyches was condemned by his patriarch Flavian in 448 but strangely supported by the ruthless and undisciplined Dioscorus. Countercharges, intrigues, and disorder caused Theodosius II to summon another council at Ephesus in 449. Leo, opposing Eutyches, sent a statement of doctrine (Tome) for the bishops to approve, but it was refused a hearing. Dominated by Dioscorus, the council deposed Flavian, reinstated Eutyches, and banned the two-nature doctrine of Constantinople. Leo labeled the council, or synod, a "robber band." After the death of Theodosius II, his sister Pulcheria reigned with her husband Marcian, and Leo persuaded them to call the great Council of Chalcedon in late 451. Located across the Bosphorus from Constantinople, Chalcedon became the site of the last major Christological council.

The actions of the "robber synod" were rescinded, Dioscorus was deposed, and Eutyches condemned. The council put out a composite Definition which consisted of the Creeds of 325 and 381, two letters of Cyril refuting Nestorius, Leo's Tome, and a new confession. The Christological formula of the Definition of Chalcedon became and remains to this day the orthodox statement about the person of Jesus Christ: "We all with one voice confess our Lord Jesus Christ one and the same Son, at once complete in Godhead, and complete in manhood, *truly God and truly man*, consisting of a reasonable soul and body; of one substance with the Father as regards his Godhead, of one substance with us as regards his manhood, like us in all things, apart from sin; begotten of the Father before the ages as regards his Godhead, the same in the last days, for us and for our salvation, born from the Virgin Mary, the God-bearer *(Theotokos)*, as regards his manhood; one and the same Christ, Son, Lord, Only-begotten, to be acknowledged in two natures, without confusion, without change, without division, or without separation; the distinction of natures being in no way abolished because of the union, but rather the characteristic property of each nature being preserved, and coming together to form one person *(prosopon)* and one entity *(hypostasis)*, not as if Christ were parted or divided into two persons. . . ."

It had been almost five hundred years since Jesus of Nazareth had walked on the earth, and his followers had been successful in subduing empires and making converts in every land. But still they had not given to the world a definitive statement as to who this Jesus really was. It seemed now, at last, that a consensus had been reached. The church had rejected adoptionism, which emphasized the humanity of Christ to the neglect (or denial) of his divinity, and it had rejected the opposite heresy of docetism, which emphasized the divinity of Christ to the neglect of his humanity. As Chalcedon so succinctly put it, Jesus was held to be both "truly God and truly man." It is obvious from the ambiguities of the creeds that they were intended to be statements of faith and not science. It is not the business of the church to understand or explain the incarnation, but to accept it and proclaim it.

In its first three hundred years, Christianity had survived the fire of persecution. The next two hundred years had seen the radical reversal of the church's posture. Whole empires were converted, great theologians emerged, the power of the papacy developed, the missionary enterprise expanded, and generally held beliefs became orthodox creeds. For a while it appeared that the earthen vessels had been hewn from indestructible rock, but that rock was yet to face the endless tests of endurance in the centuries ahead.

I V

THE STORMS
AND THE ROCK:
CONFLICTS AND
CONTROVERSIES
(590-800)

And the rain descended, and the
floods came, and the winds blew,
and beat upon that house; and it fell not:
for it was founded upon a rock.
MATTHEW 7 : 2 5

A. The Barbarians
   1. From Invasion to Conversion
   2. Gregory the Great
      a. Peace with the Lombards
      b. Conversion of Britain
      c. Gregory's Contributions
   3. Missions on the Continent
      a. Willibrord in the Netherlands
      b. Boniface in Germany
      c. Scandinavian Missions
      d. Slavic Missions
B. The Moslems
   1. Mohammed the Prophet
   2. The Religion of Islam
   3. The Moslem Conquests
   4. Effect on Christianity
      a. The Consolidation of the Church
      b. The Iconoclastic Controversy
         (1) Leo the Iconoclast
         (2) John of Damascus

The glory of Christianity's phenomenal success seemed to be continually tarnished by controversy from within and conflict from without. Since Constantine, the issue of church and state featured both internal and external confrontations. There were, however, other issues that were more clearly defined along the lines of disputes within the family or attacks from outside the family. From both sources came storms to test the foundations and batter the structure of the church. No longer an infant church, it was reaching for maturity and stability as it braced to withstand the storms.

A. THE BARBARIANS

The conversion of Europe, and indeed the Christianizing of the whole western world, very likely owes its accomplishment to what appeared at first as a disaster to both Christianity and the empire: the invasion of vast hordes of barbarians.

1. FROM INVASION TO CONVERSION

We have already noted that a force of Visigoths led by Alaric took and sacked the eternal city of Rome in 410. While Augustine was dying in 430, the Vandals were besieging Hippo. The barbarian invasions were to last for six hundred years.

Any account of history (church or secular) must take into consideration the fact that for more than half a millennium Europe was in a virtual state of siege. It had begun shortly after Christianity was firmly established in the empire, when the great "Human Gateway" between the Caspian Sea and the Ural Mountains opened wide, and great numbers of people moved swiftly into Europe. These invading tribes broke the boundaries of Europe, and as we have previously seen, one of the barbaric chiefs, Odoacer of the Ostrogoths, dethroned the last of the western emperors in 476. In rapid succession a number of barbaric kingdoms were set up: The Kingdom of the Visigoths (415-711) in Spain and southern Gaul; the Kingdom of the Ostrogoths (493-554) in Italy; the Kingdom of the Burgundians (443-543) in southeastern Gaul; the Kingdom of the Vandals (429-533) in North Africa; the Kingdom of the Franks under the Merovingians (486-752); the Kingdom of the Lombards (586-774) in northern Italy. Between 443-485 the Angles, the Saxons, and the Jutes left Denmark and north Germany and settled in south Britain. Slavic tribes also moved into the eastern empire.

Culturally, the invaders were not savages; neither were they nomads. They were agricultural people who sought new lands because of overcrowded conditions in the East. In the arts they were not primitive. The Visigoths, for instance, introduced into Europe artistic techniques, motifs, designs, and geometric forms. The Ostrogoths quickly appropriated classical and Byzantine art, building splendid churches and public edifices. The Germanic people brought precise principles of law which later furnished the basis for the ecclesiastical practice of penance and indulgences. Salvian, a Christian in the fifth century, claimed that the barbarians were morally more chaste than the nobility of the empire, and he especially commended Gaiseric, the Vandal, for closing the brothels of Carthage.

Religiously, the barbarians were of two backgrounds. There were the pagans who were to be introduced for the first time to the gospel of Christ and the ministry of the church. But many of the barbarians already claimed to be Christian, although of the Arian variety, having embraced Christianity when Arianism was dominant in the empire. These barbaric Arians were not as interested in the theological issues as they were in the structure of the church. The Arians had no ecclesiastical center, and even after their conversion to orthodoxy, they were reluctant to accept centralization through Rome. Most of the Goths had come to embrace Arian Christianity under Ulphilas, the apostle of the Goths, who had given them an alphabet and translated the Bible into their tongue. All of the Teutonic tribes were eventually converted to Christianity. From the Visigoths Christianity came to the Ostrogoths, the Vandals, and the Lombards.

One of the most notable conversions of this period was that of Clovis, King of the Franks (Gaul). Upon the repeated insistence of his wife, Queen Clotilde, a Catholic Burgundian princess, Clovis finally embraced Christianity, was baptized, and compelled his entire army to be baptized. Using his new religion as a powerful political weapon, Clovis overthrew the Arian king of the Visigoths, Alaric II, and consolidated his dominions with the aid of the Catholic bishops and Roman officials. His codification of the Salic law and his efforts to fuse the Romans and the Teutons laid the foundations of the modern French nation.

The example of Clovis was repeated throughout all of Europe. Kings embraced the faith and their people followed suit by acclamation. Naturally, there was little evidence of individual conversion in these national mass

The overextention of the Roman Empire, which was plagued by internal corruption, made it unable to defend itself against the hordes of Goths, Visigoths, and others from northern Europe. (The Bettmann Archive)

conversions, and the people brought their old beliefs and mores into the church. For Clovis himself, Jesus was a tribal war god. The people saw Christ as the heavenly ruler, rather than the suffering redeemer. The archangel Michael of the flaming sword became a spiritual champion and his name was given to the citadel of Mont St. Michel. Churches and monasteries were built in great numbers throughout Europe, but the people and their rulers fell far short of the Christian standards of the New Testament.

After the Arian Visigoths had been defeated by Clovis, they settled in Spain where they persevered in Arianism until the King of Spain, Recared, was converted to orthodox Christianity in 587 and led the Third Council of Toledo to declare Spain for Christianity in 589. The Burgundians, who had settled in Savoy, had spread to include the territories of the Rhone and Saone rivers to the Alps and Sarine River. They were the first barbarians to give up Arianism for Catholicism and to substitute a vulgarized Latin for their rough Germanic dialect. They codified their exemplary human laws in Latin, and provided the pagan Clovis with his Christian queen.

The Arian Ostrogoths in Italy were obstinate in capitulating to Catholicism, and did so only after several defeats at the hands of Justinian in 553. The barbarian states were established because they had the military might and brute force to subdue the Roman Empire, but they did not have the education or experience to govern it. Everywhere they ruled, the barbarians were a minority, with the majority being Roman and Catholic. With a culture inferior to the conquered, the conquerors could not endure. Besides the Anglo-Saxons in England, the only barbarian kingdoms which survived at the close of the sixth century were the Franks in Gaul and the Visigoths in Spain, and they were both vigorously Catholic.

2. GREGORY THE GREAT

The barbarian invasions provided the setting for the ascendancy of one of Catholicism's most famous spiritual leaders. He was Gregory I (546-604), the fourth and last of the traditional Latin "Doctors of the Church" (the other three were Ambrose, Augustine, and Jerome). Gregory served as Pope from 590 to his death, and became the father of the medieval papacy. Of the 180 bishops of Rome between Constantine and the Reformation, none was more influential than Gregory the Great, and his place in history was hammered out in the demanding circumstances of barbarian invasions, expansion of the empire, and ecclesiastical division.

As we have already recalled, Justinian had reconquered Italy from the Goths and North Africa from the Vandals. After the death of the illustrious eastern emperor, the last of the Germanic tribes to enter the Roman Empire, the Arian Lombards, invaded Italy in 568. The ineffective imperial governor (exarch) at Ravenna was unable to combat them, and once again Italy was under the rule of barbarians. This had a positive rather than a negative effect on the position of the church at Rome. The Roman bishop became the leader and protector of the people. After the death of Justinian, three men served as Roman bishop before Gregory was elected in 590. They were John III (561-574), Benedict I (575-579), and Pelagius II (579-590).

Gregory was the son of a Roman nobleman, and at first sought a career in civil administration. After serving as prefect of Rome, he entered monasticism in 574, selling his family estates, founding seven monasteries, and distributing the rest to the poor. He was appointed by the pope to be an envoy seeking aid from the court of Constantinople. He returned to Rome in 585 to become abbot of his monastery. When Pelagius II died, one of the first victims of the bubonic plague epidemic, the people of Rome unanimously chose Gregory to be bishop. He was the first pope who had been a monk, and from this time Benedictine monasticism was closely allied with the papacy. These two institutions gave medieval Catholicism its distinctive character.

a. Peace with the Lombards. Upon consecration to the episcopate at Rome, Gregory found Italy in an alarming state. The land was devastated by inundations, famine, pestilence, and the invasion of the Lombards. Gregory set about to correct all of these evils. According to legend, the bubonic plague was miraculously ended. Then Gregory set the civil affairs of Rome in order, collected taxes, provided for welfare, repaired buildings and streets, and raised and trained an army to repel the Lombards. Although he was technically under the emperor, he acted independently, garrisoned his army, sent orders to generals in the field, and negotiated with the Lombards. No bishop or pope before Gregory had dared half as much. He appointed governors over certain areas and increased his own papal authority until the papacy was the largest, wealthiest, and most powerful institution in Italy.

b. Conversion of Britain. While still a monk in Rome, Gregory had been deeply moved by the sight of some attractive young children in the slave market. When he found out they were "Angli" from England, and that they were pagans, he determined in his heart to be a missionary to that land. He never went personally, but after he became pope, he commissioned Augustine, prior of Gregory's own monastery in Rome, to accomplish this mission for him.

Augustine and his companions arrived in England just before Easter, 597. Ethelbert, king of the Jutes in Kent, was one of Augustine's first and most notable converts. He and ten thousand of his subjects were baptized on Christmas Day, 597. Since Ethelbert was also overlord of the neighboring Anglo-Saxon kingdoms of Essex and East Anglia, Catholic Christianity came to three of the twelve Anglo-Saxon kingdoms. Gregory appointed

Augustine archbishop of the church in England, and King Ethelbert gave the new archbishop his own palace in Canterbury, which became the first episcopal center in England. Augustine of Canterbury knew very little success beyond his early accomplishments, and he met with severe opposition from the Celtic church.

Founded in the second or third centuries by missions from Rome on Gaul, the Celtic church was limited, weak, and impoverished. But it was a proud group of Christians which resented the intrusion of Augustine and his monks. They were offended when the archbishop refused to stand to greet their bishops, they would not adopt the Roman tradition of baptism, and they would not accept the Roman method of arriving at the date of Easter. When Augustine died in 605, a few months after the death of Gregory, his mission in England was still small and troubled.

The British church (Celtics) finally fused with Roman Catholicism during the course of the following century. The Celtics and Romans combined their efforts in a successful mission among the pagan Anglo-Saxons, and, thereafter, leaders of both groups sought unification. The accomplishment of this unification is usually credited to Wilfrid, bishop of York, a Celt who had become convinced of Roman superiority. Wilfrid persuaded the Northumbrian king, Oswy, to declare himself for the Latin expression of the faith. At the *Synod of Whitby*, in 664, the controversial question of the date of Easter was settled in favor of Rome by King Oswy, who was afraid to oppose Peter, the keeper of the keys to the kingdom of heaven. Thus, England severed her connection with the old Iro-Celtic church in favor of Rome.

c. Gregory's Contributions. In addition to his rescue of the land from devastation, effecting peace with the Lombards, and sending missionaries to England, Gregory left an indelible imprint on ecclesiastical and theological issues. As a theologian, he was not original, building mainly on the works of Augustine of Hippo. He did, however, initiate several enduring practices. He established the mass as a repetition of the sacrifice of Christ that would benefit either the living or the dead. He formulated the doctrine of purgatory, which played so large a part in the religion of the Middle Ages. He was interested in liturgy and popularized the Gregorian chants.

His contributions to the medieval papacy were even more noteworthy. He repudiated the Patriarch of Constantinople when the latter used the title of "Ecumenical Patriarch" (universal bishop). Gregory called this a flagrant violation of the primacy of Rome, and referred to himself as "the Servant of the Servants of God."

While Leo I is often recognized as "the first pope" by virtue of his actions, Gregory is unquestionably known as the first pope to exercise universal authority, and openly declare himself to be pope. In deed as well as name, he was patriarch of the West. He ordered the African bishops to oppose the

Donatists and punished those who had fallen into Manichaeism (thereby setting the precedent for the subsequent inquisitions). He brought Spain from Arianism into orthodoxy, directed the mission campaign in Britain, and took the Emperor Maurice to task over his restrictions on soldiers entering sacred orders. Anywhere and everywhere he did whatever he deemed necessary to govern the entire church.

Gregory's period as pope, by its extension of the pope's authority, marks the transition from the ancient world of imperial Rome to medieval Christendom united by the Roman Catholic Church. The Medieval Period (Middle Ages) is so called because of its chronological position between ancient and modern times. It forms the transition from Greco-Roman civilization to the Romano-Germanic civilization which was to control the future of the western world. Pope Gregory the Great stood on the threshold between the old and the new order of things. He was the last Church Father as well as the first medieval theologian. He was the last Roman bishop and the first medieval pope.

3. MISSIONS ON THE CONTINENT
The missionary campaign of Gregory and Augustine to the British Isles reflected a dual reaction of the church to the barbarian invasions. The Christians within the Roman Empire immediately saw and met the challenge of converting the barbarians who had come to them. But there were some with wider vision who were awakened to the possibility of Christian missions in the homelands of the invaders and beyond. They realized that if these representatives of pagan peoples needed the gospel, how much greater was the need among the untold thousands of their people they had left behind. The British mission had planted the seed, and as is usually the case, the mission spawned missionaries itself. Now the gospel would be carried from England back to the northern lands of the continent.

a. Willibrord in the Netherlands (658-739). Wilfrid, the successful champion of Romanism at the Synod of Whitby, began the missionizing of Europe with a brief preaching tour in Frisia (the northern part of the Netherlands) on a trip to Rome. When he returned to England, he spread the call for missionaries to go to Frisia, and monks literally swarmed over north-western Europe. The most successful of these was one of Wilfrid's proteges, Willibrord of Saxon Northumbria, whom history has labeled "Apostle to the Netherlands." In 690, Willibrord and a dozen companions went to West Frisia to begin missionary work there. In 693, he secured papal support for his mission, and in 695, he was consecrated archbishop of the Frisians by Pope Sergius. He was granted a seat for his cathedral outside Utrecht, and in 698 he founded the monastery of Echternach in Luxembourg, which became an important missionary center. By the time of his death, at age eighty-one, he had firmly established the archiepiscopal see of Utrecht, gained the support of the powerful Franks for his Frisian mission, and by his personal labors had brought about the conversion of most of the people in the southern part of the Low Countries.

b. Boniface in Germany (680-754). Willibrord's younger co-laborer and assistant for three years was a tireless young monk-missionary by the name of Winifrid (or Wynfrith) who became known as Boniface, "doer of good," and whom history has labeled as "The Apostle of Germany." Disappointed in his lack of success in the Frisia mission, Boniface went to Rome, where he was delegated by the pope to be his personal agent among the savage peoples of Germany. He was so successful in that appointment that Pope Gregory II ordained him a missionary bishop to Germany in 722. Generations before, Christianity had already been introduced in what is now Switzerland, southern Germany, and western Austria. But its growth had not been uniform, and the churches were scattered, disorganized, and uncooperative with each other and with the main body of Christendom. One of Boniface's major achievements was the consolidation of existing churches into one ecclesiastical body.

He was also, however, extremely popular and successful among the pagans. He single-handedly demolished their superstitions, nature divinations, and ritual incantations. They rallied to his demonstration of both physical and spiritual strength, and before he was sixty years of age, he had converted practically the whole territory of Thuringia and Hesse, that part of Germany which lay east of the Rhine and north of the Danube. Boniface was a relentless missionary, and a compassionate friend. A man of many talents and drives, he was also the paragon of Christian tenderness. He is often called the greatest missionary since the Apostle Paul. Never satisfied with his early failures in the Frisian mission, he returned there thirty years later for a second attempt, and was tragically killed by a band of robbers in 754.

c. Scandinavian Missions. Although we must return later to the chronological sequence of events in the history and structure of the church, this discussion of missions on the continent naturally leads us to mention two other significant inroads for Christianity in this area (though actually accomplished many years later). Anskar (801-865), the "Apostle of the North," was a native of Picardy, and a monk at Corbie (in France). From there he went to Westphalia, and later to Denmark, whose king had been recently converted. He established a school in Schleswig, and when he was expelled by the local heathen, he went to Sweden where he built the first Christian church. In 832 he was appointed by Gregory IV as bishop of Hamburg and in 848 he became the first archbishop of Bremen. In 854 he returned to Denmark, converted Erik, King of Jutland, and had outstanding success in suppressing the slave trade. Christianity, however, did not enjoy real success in Denmark until the reign of Canute the Great (1014-25).

Norway was Christianized from England through the efforts of two Norwegian kings, Olaf Tryggvason (995-1000) and Olaf Haraldson (1015-30). In Sweden the first Christian king, Olaf Lapking, was baptized in 1007. From the Scandinavian countries Christianity spread to Iceland, Finland, and Greenland.

d. Slavic Missions. "The Apostles of the Slavs" were two brothers from a Greek family in Thessalonica, Cyril and Methodius. After being ordained, they went to Constantinople to serve in the library of the church of St. Sophia. In 862, the Emperor Michael III sent them as missionaries to what is now Moravia. Cyril invented an alphabet for the people there, called Glagolithic (also Cyrillic), and became the founder of Slavonic literature.

A few years later Cyril died in a monastery in Rome, and Methodius was consecrated a bishop and returned to Moravia, where he was opposed by the German bishops and imprisoned for two years. Pope John VIII secured his release, but forbade him to teach in the vernacular (Slavonic language) any more.

A Christian princess brought Christianity to Bohemia, and from there it spread to Poland and Hungary. Although the Slavic peoples were Christianized mostly by Greek missionaries, all of them, except the Bulgarians, turned from the Greek to the Roman Catholic Church, and acknowledged the pope of Rome as the supreme head of their churches.

B. THE MOSLEMS

While Christianity was making great gains among the barbarian tribes of western Europe, a new storm was swirling down upon the empire from the deserts of Arabia. The emperor Heraclius (610-41) had just barely thrown back the Persian invasions and had begun to stabilize New Rome when the ferocious warriors from Arabia, fired by a fanatical faith, struck with devastating power. Marching under the banner of a new theocracy called Islam, they posed the greatest external threat yet to both empire and Christendom.

1. MOHAMMED THE PROPHET

The religion of Islam was the product of the mind and spirit of a single individual, Mohammed, its prophet (570-632). Orphaned at the age of six, Mohammed grew up under the guardianship of an uncle in the Quraysh tribe, which had control of the Kaaba, the national religious shrine of the Arabs. The Kaaba contained the sacred Black Stone and the well reputedly kicked up by the infant Ishmael when Hagar left him to search for water (Genesis 21:8-21). Mohammed became disillusioned by the idolatrous worship and degenerate behavior he observed in connection with Arabian religion, and when he began making caravan trips to Syria and Palestine, his religious feelings increased. He became the business manager of a rich widow, Khadijah, whom he married. His two sons by Khadijah died in childhood, and only one of four daughters, Fatima, survived. His wealthy status enabled him to have wider religious contacts and more leisure time for long periods of reflection on religion. One night in the hills near Mecca, in a cave on Mt. Hira, he said that he had a vision of the angel Gabriel telling him to recite. He went home and produced the entire ninety-sixth sura of the Koran. In a second appearance, Gabriel commissioned him a prophet of the Lord, and subsequent revelations that constitute the Koran came frequently.

Mohammed began proclaiming the Day of the Lord in the marketplace. The day he proclaimed was to be one of resurrection, final judgment, and everlasting fire. Although people were impressed with his poetic oratory, after four years he had only forty converts. Because of his attacks on the Kaaba, the Quraysh disturbed his meetings with violence, and he feared for his life. Three hundred miles to the north, six men left the city of Medina to seek out Mohammed as the leader who might bring the tribes of Medina and Mecca together. They arrived in Mecca just in time to help him escape assassination. Thus, in the year 622, Mohammed and his followers made their great Hegira flight to Medina, marking the beginning of the Islamic calendar. In Medina he became the undisputed leader of a religious theocracy, ingeniously defended the city against Meccan attacks, and in a bold counterattack captured Mecca itself. Within eight short years Mohammed had become the strongest chieftain in all Arabia. He stripped the Kaaba of its idols and images, but continued to pay tribute to the Black Stone. By 632, Mohammed was dead at the age of sixty-two, but he had instituted a new religion that would unify the Arabian people into one brotherhood. The strict monotheistic faith of Islam made rigid moral and spiritual demands on the people which they eagerly accepted, for Mohammed had convinced them that they were divinely appointed to bring all peoples into submission to the will of God.

2. THE RELIGION OF ISLAM

The word *Islam* implies "resignation or submission to the will of God," and means "the submitters." The religion of Islam must be understood in order to evaluate the historical developments of wars, conquests, and expansion. The fanatical followers of Mohammed have always been on a holy crusade to capture and convert the world for their God (Allah).

Islam is built around five basic doctrines: (1) There is no God but Allah, and Mohammed is his prophet; (2) God's work is carried on among men by angels, the mediating spirits of God; (3) the will of Allah is written down in the Koran, which contains all a Moslem needs to know to obtain salvation; (4) the great figures of Judaism and Christianity are revered by Islam, but its own prophet Mohammed surpasses them all. There are six great prophets: Adam, Noah, Abraham, Moses, Jesus, and Mohammed, the greatest of them all; and (5) there will be a resurrection day and a final judgment for every individual. The followers of Mohammed will cross into the Gardens of Paradise, and infidels (non-Moslems) and sinful Moslems will fall into the abyss of hell. There are four religious practices to which every Moslem is bound: (1) prayer, five times a day, facing Mecca in the bodily position described in the Koran; (2) almsgiving, including both the Jewish tithe and additional charity; (3) fasting from all gratifications of the senses during the entire month of Ramadan; and (4) pilgrimage to Mecca during the course of his lifetime, either personally or by proxy. The spiritual aspirations of Islam have found expression mainly in Sufism, a movement aspiring to union with God by renouncing one's personality and practicing an ascetic technique.

3. THE MOSLEM CONQUESTS

Believing that they were divinely commissioned to subdue all people to God's will, Moslems did not hesitate to organize, train, and give military expression to their missionary call. In developing Arabian unity around Islam, Mohammed used violent as well as nonviolent means with his own people. Then he personally led them in their first military conquests of Christianity in 629. It was not, however, until after his death that Islam spread like a devouring fire over the East. Armed with the belief that death in combat on behalf of Allah would ensure entrance into paradise, the terrifying Moslems swept down on Damascus in 635, conquering it almost instantly. Jerusalem held out longer under the heroic leadership of its patriarch Sophronius, finally falling to the bloody siege in 637. The next year saw the fall of Antioch, Tripolis, Tyre, Caesarea, and fifteen other cities along the Mediterranean coast. By the end of 639 nothing of the eastern empire was left in Syria. Mesopotamia surrendered, by 641 all of Egypt had been conquered, and the advance across North Africa had begun. To the east the Moslems conquered Iraq in 637, and by 649 had subdued all of Persia. By 652 (after only twelve years) the Moslems controlled most of Asia Minor.

When they turned their efforts to the supreme goal of capturing Constantinople, they were turned back by the awesome Taurus Mountains. Determined to take the capital of the eastern empire, they organized a navy, and with it they took Cyprus (648), destroyed Aradus (649), and ravaged Cos and Rhodes (654). They defeated the Emperor Constans II in a naval battle at Phoenix (655), but the Moslems were spread too thin and stretched too far. For five years (673-678) they tried to take Constantinople by land and sea, but were repeatedly driven back by courageous defenders and destructive fire. Then the Moslem fleet was caught in a storm off the coast of Pamphylia, which decimated the navy to the point that Constantine IV wiped out the remaining forces of the enemy. A peace of sorts was affected in 679, but it was short-lived, and hostilities resumed in 695.

In 732, Charles Martel, ruler of the Franks, turned the tide in the West by his decisive victory over the "Saracens" (a word used by medieval writers of Arabs generally and later applied to the Mohammedan nations against whom the crusaders fought). Martel had been the mayor of the palace to the Merovingian kings, had brought the Neustrians and Burgundy under his rule, and had made himself master of Normandy. But the greatest event of his career was his victory over the Saracens at the Battle of Tours in 732. If the invading Arabs had not been turned back at Tours, they might well have engulfed all of Europe. Although they had finally been stopped, the Moslems in forty-five years (633-678) had torn from the eastern empire some of its richest and most populous provinces, and had left it only a shadow of its former self. The occupation of the Holy Land by the Moslems was especially offensive to Christians throughout the world, and centuries later, the Crusades of the eleventh, twelfth, amd thirteenth centuries were undertaken to recover the Holy Land from the clutches of Islam.

4. EFFECT ON CHRISTIANITY

Even as the empire had been sorely contracted by the Moslem invasions, so had the church been depleted. The extraordinary gains of Christianity in the West were counterbalanced by excessive losses in the East, and the vulnerability of the eastern church to heretical and pagan influences.

a. The Consolidation of the Church. Three of the patriarchs were now in Moslem territory. Rome was gaining political autonomy, and Constantinople was enjoying imperial patronage, but Alexandria, Antioch, and Jerusalem had been humiliated and crushed by the ruthless infidels. The patriarchs of Alexandria and Antioch lived abroad in exile, but Sophronius stubbornly remained in Jerusalem. Multitudes of Christians found it more expedient to exchange Christianity for Islam, and within a generation, the majority of the population of North Africa, Egypt, Syria, Mesopotamia, and even Palestine became Moslem. The Christianity that survived was greatly modified, and faithful Christians found themselves cut off from the rest of Christendom for centuries to come.

That which appeared to be conclusively disastrous, however, turned out to be beneficial for the consolidation of the church. The patriarch of Constantinople, which had been one among four equals, became the head of eastern Catholicism. Together, the patriarch and the emperor denigrated the authority of the papacy in Rome. The 424 dioceses throughout the Balkan peninsula and Asia Minor came under the direct rule of the see of Constantinople. The loyalty and integrity of the clergy were strengthened with new and stringent requirements, with the exception of monasticism,

The Moslem conquest of Europe ended at the Battle of Tours, turned back by Charles Martel (A.D. 732). (Historical Pictures Service, Chicago)

where the restrictions were strangely relaxed. Society in general appeared to be intensely religious during this period. Attendance at church was large and regular. Worship developed into an exquisitely beautiful art, with sacramental worship, rather than preaching, becoming central. Baptism was universally and officially conferred upon infants. Penance was not obligatory, but it was encouraged. Marriage was regulated and controlled by the church. Fasting before communion was required. Theological writings were few and inconsequential. There seemed to be an abnormal desire to spurn the spiritual and intellectual, and to fix religion in concrete terms. This was especially expressed in the compulsion of people everywhere to see, handle, and kiss relics and icons. This widespread practice precipitated one of the greatest controversies in the eastern church, which has had worldwide repercussions in Christianity to this very day.

b. The Iconoclastic Controversy. Icons, technically speaking, are flat pictures, usually painted in oil on wood, but also wrought in mosaic, ivory, and other materials, used to represent Christ, the Virgin Mary, or some saint. Iconoclasm, which is used in our general vocabulary today as a synonym for destruction, means the shattering of something established to make room for something new and different. In church history iconoclasm refers to the effort to abolish images, pictures, or any material likenesses of any sacred personage or event. The iconoclasts, therefore, were the destroyers of icons or sacred images. The iconoclasts called the people who worshiped or venerated images the iconolaters.

(1) Leo the Iconoclast. In 726, the Emperor Leo III published an edict declaring all images idols and ordering their destruction, thus becoming known as Leo the Iconoclast. Leo believed that the use of icons was a chief obstacle to the conversion of Jews and Moslems. The Jews were offended by icons because of the second commandment which forbids the making of graven images. As a soldier on the eastern frontier of the empire, Leo had been impressed with the Moslem rejection of idolatry in any form. Serving as governor-general of western Asia Minor, he heard several bishops preach against the icons. Constantine, bishop of Nacolia, persuaded him that the veneration of images was a stupid superstition and a violation of the second commandment. When he became emperor, Leo accepted iconoclasm as a divine mission he was ordained of God to perform and set about to eliminate image worship from his empire.

The bishop of Rome condemned Leo for his iconoclastic decree, and in retaliation the emperor reapportioned Sicily, southern Italy, and the entire western part of the Balkans and Greece from the patriarchate of Rome and into the patriarchate of Constantinople. Disturbances erupted throughout the empire, and a systematic persecution was unleashed against the more ardent defenders of the icons. John of Damascus wrote his famous apologies against the iconoclasts, and Pope Gregory III held two synods at

Rome condemning Leo's supporters. In 741, Leo was succeeded by his son Constantine V who continued his father's policies. In 753, he called the Synod of Hieria, which neither the patriarchs of Antioch, Jerusalem, and Alexandria, nor the pope attended. The synod held that by representing only the humanity of Christ, the icon worshipers either divided his unity as the Nestorians or confounded the two natures as the Monophysites. The synod also declared that the icons of the Virgin Mary and the saints were idols and decreed the destruction of all of them. Opposition and persecution raged more fiercely than ever.

(2) John of Damascus (675-749). The era of the iconoclastic disputes produced the greatest medieval theologian of the eastern church. Born of a rich Christian family of Damascus, John Mansour entered the monastery at Jerusalem where he became a priest, and the ablest defender of images in the early days of the iconoclastic controversy. He wrote three discourses on the subject between 726 and 730. John appealed to the images mentioned in the Bible, the brazen serpent in the wilderness, and the lions in Solomon's temple, but his primary argument was from the incarnation and the Eucharist. If God himself became flesh, then physical things cannot be evil, and if Christ is bodily present in the bread and wine, then sensory aids to religion are not wrong. On an educational level, he argued from Plato's notion that everything we sense in this world is really an imitation of the eternal, original "form"; and while it is wrong to worship icons themselves, they could instruct and assist the believer in the worship of the true Christ. He suggested that icons should be honored in much the same way as the Bible or the symbol of the cross. He insisted that it was permissible to use icons of Mary, the apostles, saints, and angels to help the faithful give proper respect and reverence. The work of John of Damascus greatly influenced the 787 council at Nicaea where the images were sanctioned again.

Under Constantine's son, Leo IV (775-80), the persecution subsided. Then, after his death, the Empress Irene, acting as regent for her young son Constantine, reversed the policy of her predecessors. Working with Tarasius, patriarch of Constantinople, and with Pope Hadrian I, Empress Irene called the Seventh General Council at Nicaea in 787. This Council completely undid the work of the Synod of Hieria, set limits to icon veneration, and decreed their restoration throughout the country. Iconoclasm, however, retained a strong following, especially in the army. In 814, the "Second Iconoclastic Controversy" took place under Leo V the Armenian, a general elected emperor by the army. Again icons were removed from churches and public buildings, and defenders of icons were exiled, imprisoned, and martyred. Leo was assassinated in 820 and Michael II, his successor, mildly continued his policies. But Michael's son Theophilus, succeeding him in 829, brought back the violence of Leo. The persecutions ended after Theophilus' death in 842, and his widow Theodora, like Irene, acting as regent for her son, had the monk Methodius elected patriarch in 843. On the first Sunday of Lent a great feast was celebrated in honor of the icons, a feast which has been solemnly kept ever since in the eastern church as the "Feast of Orthodoxy." The long controversy was over. The icons had persevered and won.

The iconoclastic controversy in the East had very little theological repercussions in the West, but it did have a profound practical effect. This particular controversy is usually considered the last step toward the great schism between East and West, before the actual breach. The iconoclastic issue was a showcase example of Caesaropapism, the system whereby an absolute monarch has supreme control over the church within his dominions and exercises it even in doctrinal matters normally reserved to ecclesiastical authority. The popes in Rome viewed the flagrant Caesaropapism of the eastern empire during the icon dispute with growing apprehension. The unity achieved by imperial decree at Nicaea in 787 and again in 843 proved artificial. And with the development of the temporal power of the papacy, the way was prepared for the final separation between the independent church of the West and the church of the Byzantine Empire.

V

FRIEND OR FOE?: THE EAST-WEST SCHISM (800-1054)

And John answered and said, Master,
we saw one casting out devils in thy name;
and we forbade him,
because he followeth not with us.
And Jesus said unto him, forbid him not:
for he that is not against us is for us.

LUKE 9:49,50

A. The Holy Roman Empire
   1. The Donation of Pepin
   2. The Reign of Charlemagne
      a. The State of Religion
      b. The Carolingian Renaissance
   3. Nicholas and the Papacy
   4. Alfred and Britain
   5. The Dark Ages
      a. From Theocracy to Pornocracy
      b. The Otto Regimes
B. The Eastern Church
   1. Political Background
      a. The Move to Constantinople
      b. The Rule of Caesaropapism
      c. The Mohammedan Crisis
   2. Theological Background
      a. The "Mono" Christology
      b. The Iconoclast Controversy
      c. The Filioque Clause
   3. Eastern Orthodoxy at Its Zenith
      a. Suppressing Heresy
         (1) Paulicians
         (2) Bogomiles
         (3) Messalians
      b. Surviving Caesaropapism
         (1) Nicholas Mysticus and Leo VI
         (2) Nicephorus Phocas and Athanasius
      c. Expanding Byzantium
      d. Converting Russia
   4. The Great Schism

Division has always been the scandal of Christianity. Wherever it occurs it saddens the true follower of Christ; but it should not surprise him. Even in the presence of the living Christ, James and John sought preeminence with him in his coming kingdom. "And when the ten heard it, they were moved with indignation against the two brethren" (Matthew 20:24). The book of Acts, in its objective reporting, reveals the human weaknesses which produce a divided fellowship. The Council of Jerusalem was called because the brethren could not agree on doctrinal matters; and Paul and Barnabas severed their great missionary team over John Mark. Thus it has been the burden of Christianity to endure the countless divisions which have occurred through the centuries.

Characteristic of the divisive tendency and its results are the three great schisms: The Eastern Schism, the Papal Schism, and the Protestant Schism. In this section we will consider the first of these.

A. THE HOLY ROMAN EMPIRE

As previously noted, the papacy had vigorously opposed the iconoclastic efforts of Emperor Leo III and, in retaliation, the emperor had reapportioned large portions of Italy and Sicily from papal jurisdiction to the see of Constantinople. The papacy and the imperial rulers at Constantinople were now in a state of mutual antagonism. But it had come at a bad time for Rome. The Lombards were again threatening to overthrow Rome. But if Rome were to maintain any semblance of independence from Constantinople, it would have to look for protection from some other source than the emperor.

1. THE DONATION OF PEPIN

In 739 Gregory III appealed to Charles Martel, the hero of Tours, for aid against the Lombards, but in vain. When Charles Martel died in 741, his authority was divided between his sons Carloman and Pepin the Short.

Carloman soon retired from power to become a monk, and Pepin became virtual ruler of the Franks. He was much more ecclesiastically minded and ambitious than his father and quickly saw that he and the papacy could be of mutual assistance to each other. He desired the kingly title as well as the kingly power in France. He needed and sought the moral sanction of the church for a revolution that relegated the last of the Merovingians to a monastery and put Pepin on the throne. He received this approval from Pope Zacharias, and before the close of 751, Pepin was formally made king of France, being crowned by no less than Boniface, the great missionary and apostle to the Germans. In exchange for papal assistance in achieving his ambition, Pepin had agreed to drive the Lombards from Italy, which he did in 755 and 756.

The fame of Pepin has been eclipsed by his greater son (Charlemagne), but he must be remembered for establishing two critically important precedents. The first was the acquiring of the throne by the sanction of the pope. Charlemagne's coronation is much more famous, but Pepin's was actually the first demonstration of the papacy's power in setting up governments, which would lead to the reestablishment of the empire in the West. The second precedent was the granting of territory positions to the pope. After defeating the Lombards, Pepin created the papal states, consisting of twenty-two cities and their environs, stretching across Italy from Rome to Ravenna. In this action, known as the "Donation of Pepin" (756), he gave outright to the Roman church and its bishops all the cities won by him from the Lombards. This act was justified by the precedent of a fabled document called "The Donation of Constantine," in which Constantine the Great was supposed to have donated grants of land to Pope Sylvester for curing him of leprosy. In this spurious account, Constantine gave Sylvester and all succeeding popes all the cities of Italy and the western regions. Thus, in donating the papal states, Pepin appeared to be merely returning lands to their "rightful" overlord. The "Donation of Constantine" was generally accepted as authentic throughout the Middle Ages, until its forgery was conclusively exposed by Nicholas of Cusa in 1433 and Lorenzo Valla in 1440. The important result of the "Donation of Pepin" was the establishment of an entirely new commonwealth on the map of Europe, a commonwealth which was to continue in existence from 756 until the unification of Italy in 1870. Pepin had laid the foundation of the church-states and constituted himself and his successors as protectors of the Holy See.

2. THE REIGN OF CHARLEMAGNE
Pepin the Short died in 768 and his kingdom was divided between his two sons, Charles and Carloman. When Carloman died in 771, Charles became sole ruler and began the legendary reign, which so completely fused his

Charlemagne (Charles the Great), King of the Franks and the first medieval Roman emperor. According to some tradition, he was, on Christmas Day 800, while praying at the altar at St. Peter's Church in Rome, crowned emperor by Pope Leo III. (Historical Pictures Service, Chicago)

name with greatness that he became known as Charlemagne (Charles the Great).

His first conquest was that of Lombardy (774-777). The dreaded Lombards were at last and permanently defeated, their kingdom extinguished, and Charlemagne assumed the Lombard crown. Then followed a long series of campaigns against the Saxons (772-785). In 778 Bavaria was conquered, and between 791 and 796 the Avar kingdom and Pannonia fell. The systematic conquest of northern Spain began in 785, and in 801 Barcelona was captured. Everywhere that Charlemagne marched and conquered, he took the message and organization of Roman Christianity. He planted bishoprics and monasteries throughout Saxon lands, encouraged the continuing support of missions through Germanic and Bavarian regions, and extended Christianity into what is now Austria.

Charlemagne's great military conquests and accompanying missionary efforts were especially appreciated by Rome, where he was received in love and joy by the pope. He ratified the donation of his father Pepin, made a sacred compact with the pope, extended the territories of the states of the church, and promised his protection always. He made good on his promise when Pope Leo III sought his protection and support from his enemies. A council, set up in Rome by Charlemagne to give Leo a fair hearing, declared that "the Apostolic See has the right to judge everyone but can itself be judged by no one." The accused pope claimed innocence from all crimes with which he had been charged, and the resulting acclamation of the crowd of dignitaries attested to the wisdom and influence of Charlemagne in the affair.

Two days later, on Christmas Day in the year 800, while Charlemagne was kneeling at the altar in St. Peter's, Pope Leo III, evidently with no warning to Charlemagne, placed an imperial crown on his head. The assembled nobility and prelates of Rome cried aloud: "To Charles Augustus, crowned by God, great and peaceful emperor of the Romans, long life and victory." The coronation of Charlemagne signaled that he was more than the king of France; that he was, in fact, the supreme ruler of the western world. It also signaled to Constantinople that the center of the empire had returned to Rome. This constituted a challenge to the East, with whom relations were strained for the rest of Charlemagne's life. More importantly, for the church, it announced that the new emperor was dependent for his authority upon the pope who had voluntarily conferred it upon him.

a. *The State of Religion.* Charlemagne was devout, concerned, and involved in affairs of the church. Every morning he went to mass and every evening to vespers. He took an active part in the life of the church, summoning councils and interfering with their decisions. The church was virtually a department of state, but Charlemagne never ascribed to himself any religious designation. Instead, he preferred the role of David, who with his sword defended the Ark of the Lord. Because the church had so recently come into possession of lands and cities, great wealth and its attending problems had accumulated. Charlemagne set about the task of managing church business affairs, correcting oppressive practices against the poor and equally distributing the church's resources. He insisted new ecclesiastical disciplines be designed to give the people better and more helpful service from the clergy. There was outward reformation and inward revival of monasticism under Charlemagne's pursuit of genuine and spiritual Christianity. New church buildings were erected, and a new architecture emerged which proved to be the forerunner of the later Gothic style. Liturgy was enhanced, and because of his personal preference, the Gregorian chant experienced a real revival under Charlemagne. Baptism by immersion was replaced by baptism by pouring, and the baptistry gave way to the font. The one abiding contribution which the West made to theology during this period was the addition of the *filioque* to the Nicene-Constantinople creed. The word *filioque* means "from the Son," and was added to the creed as an affirmation that the Holy Spirit proceeds equally from the Father and the Son. Although generally adopted in the West, the East refused the addition, preferring to say the Holy Spirit proceeds from the Father by the Son.

b. The Carolingian Renaissance. Charlemagne inaugurated a revitalizing of culture and learning by inviting to his court the most renowned scholars of his time to form the nucleus of a palace school where administrators for the state and the church could be trained. These learned men included the Lombard known as Paul the Deacon; the Frank, Einhard, who became Charlemagne's biographer; and the Visigoth, Theodulf. The Anglo-Saxon Alcuin (735-804) was the head of the cathedral school at York when called to Charlemagne's court. As royal tutor he established a palace library; and he became Abbot of Tours where he set up an important school and library. Among his more famous pupils were Amalarius of Metz and Rabanus Maurus. His chief subjects of study were Boethius and Augustine, and his works consist of educational manuals, poetry, history, theological apologetics, and valuable letters which give unusual insight into Carolingian society.

Alcuin was the principal intellect and architect of the Carolingian Renaissance. He revived the ancient disciplines of grammar, rhetoric, and dialectic. Classical Christian culture itself was revived, mainly through the efforts of Alcuin, who dreamed of "a new Athens enriched by the sevenfold fullness of the Holy Spirit." Religiously, Alcuin was both practical and spiritual. He protested against Charlemagne's imposition of baptism by force on the Saxons. He, in fact, informed Charlemagne that he was not to use his sword, the political power of the state, to impose religion. He thus became the first to use the figure of the two swords with reference to the roles of church and state. Through Alcuin and other scholars, Charlemagne promoted the revival of classical Christian culture, and people were taught to read and write and appreciate books.

Perhaps more than any other sovereign in history, Charlemagne was head over all things in his day. He was a warrior of great gifts, a patron of learning, the kindly master of the church, and the preserver of order. When he died, he ruled all of modern France, Belgium, Holland, nearly half of modern Germany and Austria-Hungary, more than half of Italy, and northeastern Spain. He expanded his kingdom as conqueror, but stabilized it as benefactor and educator.

3. NICHOLAS AND THE PAPACY

Upon his death in 814, Charlemagne left his empire to his son, Louis the Pious (814-40), a weak and indecisive person, whose reign was marked by growing political disturbance, caused chiefly by his struggles with his sons, who divided the kingdom at his death. Charles the Bald got what is now France, Louis the German got what is now Germany, and Lothair got the section in between, Lorraine. Divided and weakened, western Europe was easy prey to constant raids from Vikings, Mohammedans, and Magyars. It soon became obvious that the greatness of Charlemagne's empire had been due to his own personal powers. The weakening of the empire, however, meant the strengthening of the papacy. Under the domineering personality of Charlemagne, the popes were relatively weak, and constantly embroiled in petty Italian politics. With the diminishing of power under Charlemagne's son and grandsons, the role of the pope became increasingly strong and vital.

In 858 a remarkable man, Nicholas I, was consecrated pope, and there ensued nine of the most formative years for the medieval papacy. His brief rule was so characterized by accomplishment and prestige that one could say that what Gregory the Great had done for the church in Italy, Nicholas I did for the church in western Europe. He definitely formulated the medieval concept of the papacy and pushed the papal claim to world supremacy in every direction. He deposed and excommunicated Photius, Patriarch of Constantinople. He humbled Archbishop John of Ravenna to complete submission to the papacy. He ordered King Lothair II to take back his divorced queen. As a missionary organizer, he has been compared again to Gregory the Great. He established the Hamburg-Bremen archbishopric and gained dominance over the Moravian church through the support of Cyril and Methodius. He furthered the cause of great literature and devised a plan for clerical censorship of books. His contemporaries hailed him as a "second Elijah," and Nicholas I is generally regarded as the last great link in the development of papacy from Gregory I (the Great) to Gregory VII.

4. ALFRED AND BRITAIN

The great Carolingian Renaissance had been fueled with the discipline of British monasticism and Irish intellect. Alcuin had come from the school of the venerable Bede, the great biblical scholar and "Father of English History." Yet, during the years when Alcuin labored with Charlemagne on the continent, the intellectual and spiritual achievements of Bede and his followers were dissipated by marauding bands of invading Scandinavians. Lands were conquered, people were slaughtered, schools and churches were destroyed. The result was rampant fear, superstition, ignorance, and immorality.

Into this deplorable state of affairs came a twenty-three-year-old sovereign by the name of Alfred. When his brother Ethelred was slain in battle with the Danes at Merton (871), Alfred ascended the throne of Wessex. He ruled twenty-eight years, dying at the age of fifty-two in 899, and is today still considered by the British as their greatest Saxon leader. He is the only sovereign in English history to have been given the title "great." This accolade is due to two outstanding accomplishments. First, he drove the Danes from England's shores, solidified the English people, and created a nation. His other accomplishment was cultural and spiritual. In the same vein as the Carolingian Renaissance, he revived learning and scholarship among his people, reformed the clergy, and restored ecclesiastical organization and discipline. Originally untutored and ignorant, he became a man of considerable learning himself. He gathered around him some of the great scholars of England, Wales, and the continent, and with their help translated numerous Latin works. He founded monastic societies, divided Wessex into manageable dioceses, and left a rich legacy of literary works, including the "Anglo-Saxon Chronicle." What Charlemagne was to the continent, Alfred the Great was to England.

5. THE DARK AGES

In the sixteenth century, Caesar Baronius coined the designation *saeculum obscurum,* meaning "dark age," for the period 880-1046 (from the end of the Carolingian empire to the beginning of the Gregorian reform). During these years men were occupied with the elemental business of keeping alive. The reason was the wave of invasions which we have already mentioned in connection with Alfred in England and Charlemagne's grandsons on the continent. The Vikings and Magyars had wrecked the churches and monasteries of France. The once splendid Carolingian Empire was a shambles. Anarchy was rampant, tempered only by the restraints of an emerging feudalism, which bound people together for mutual protection through mutual obligation, thus sowing the seeds of constitutional government. Amid the disorders of the day and the impotence of the government, men looked to the papacy for order and guidance only to find that the sickness was there also.

a. From Theocracy to Pornocracy. The Carolingian era had been called a royal theocracy (ruled by God). The period of the Dark Ages saw the papacy sink to such a level of disrepute as to be labeled by some historians a "pornocracy" (ruled by harlots). The Roman see declined to the level of an ordinary local bishopric, and like so many other bishoprics of the time, became the object of political struggles of unruly and tyrannical nobility. Forty-eight popes served during this period. Only a few were honorable men, and some suffered unimaginable crimes and indignities. Pope John VIII (872-82) was beaten to death with a hammer by his own relatives when the poison they had given him did not work fast enough. Three inconsequential popes followed in rapid succession over the next nine years. Pope Formosus (891-96) was a dangerous schemer, capable of treachery and sedition. His followers were thieves and assassins, and in his ecclesiastical affairs, he behaved as if the ends justified the means. He crowned Lambert of Spoleto as Holy Roman Emperor in 894, but repudiated his own choice and crowned Arnulf of Germany in 896. After Formosus died, the mother of the deposed Lambert had the body of Formosus exhumed, clothed again in the papal robes, and tried in public court. He was found guilty of treachery, and the royal orders conferred on him and all the decrees he had issued were declared null and void. The three fingers he used to bestow the papal blessing were cut off, his vestments and insignia were stripped from his dead body, and his corpse was dragged through the streets of Rome and thrown into the river Tiber.

From 896 to 904 there were ten popes, one of whom ruled four months, one only one month, and still another only twenty days. Then began the so-called "pornocracy," during which Theodora and her two daughters, Theodora the Younger and Marozia, virtually controlled Rome and the church itself. Enticing harlots, these women had sold their bodies for positions, titles, and land, giving them widespread power. Marozia had an illicit affair with Pope Sergius III, from which was born a son who later became Pope John XI. When Marozia sought to have herself crowned empress, her younger son Alberic kidnapped and imprisoned his mother, incarcerated his half brother, the pope, and became emperor himself. He reigned from 932 to 954, exercising absolute control over the papacy. After Alberic's death, his son Octavian was elected as Pope John XII, and proved to be the most odious member of this depraved family.

b. The Otto Regimes. In 962, the wicked John XII crowned the German king Otto I as emperor of the Holy Roman Empire. Thinking he had an ally in depravity, John soon found the new emperor to be a man of character and devoted to restoring the papacy to decency and honor. When Otto assembled a synod to discuss deposing John, the pope threatened them all with excommunication, but they deposed him anyway. Three months later John called another synod which rescinded what Otto's synod had done.

Therefore, Otto decided upon force to rid the papacy of its evil ruler. But as he prepared to attack Rome, John XII died suddenly, presumably assassinated by someone he had wronged. Otto I served as a welcome relief from papal abuses, and proved himself an able ruler and a dedicated Christian. The popes who served during his reign were at least dignified and respectable, if not outstanding. Otto I, designated by history as Otto the Great, was the founder of the German nation, a strong protector of Christianity, and the patron of its institutions and culture.

Otto II reigned after his father for ten years, and with the assistance of Pope Benedict VII, provided stability and progress in Roman ecclesiastical affairs. When Otto II died, his son and heir, Otto III, was only three years old. After a regency of eleven years, the younger ruler began an auspicious reign which had far-reaching consequences for ecclesiastical history. He made the papacy an international institution. Heretofore, only Italians had held the office; but Otto opened the way for an ecumenical papacy by nominating his youthful cousin Bruno as pope (although only twenty-three years old, he was still seven years older that Otto). Taking the name of Gregory V, Bruno became the first German pope. Afterward, there would be many nationalities represented in the papacy during the Middle Ages: Germans, Frenchmen, Greeks, Spaniards, Italians, Romans, and one Englishman.

At the death of Gregory V, the first German pope was followed by the first French pope, Gerbert of Aurillac, who became Sylvester II. He governed the church only four years, but his work was monumental. A brilliant strategist and statesman, he was also a scientist far ahead of his time. Artistic and musical, he revived the arts and culture of civilization as to remind one of Charlemagne and Alcuin. Great schools and soaring architecture were introduced by him. He and Otto III worked harmoniously in combining the powers of church and state. He commissioned Otto to go to Poland in 1000 to venerate some sacred relics. In that state visit, the emperor also freed Poland from all terms of vassalage, thereby creating the Polish nation. Though Otto and Sylvester covenanted together to restore the Roman Empire to all its majesty with a Christian Caesar at its head, neither of them was appreciated by the people. Wasted in disease and broken in spirit by the people's rejection, Otto died in 1002 at the age of twenty-one. Less than two years later Sylvester joined his friend and pupil in death.

The next forty-two years of papal history were filled with intense rivalry, expedient mediocrity, spiritual impotence, vice, and corruption. It seemed to reach its lowest depth with the election of a degenerate twelve-year-old boy, Pope Benedict IX (1032-1045), who after shameful debauchery and erratic administration, sold the holy tiara to the highest bidder. He was known as Gregory VI (1045-1046), and in the end was forced to abdicate because of his simony. Clement II followed him for one year; he was succeeded by Damasus II, who lasted only a few months. In two short years, five popes occupied the Roman see. In every sense—religiously, politically, and culturally—the West was undeniably suffering through a horrible period properly named the Dark Ages. Yet in the East it was during this very period in the Middle Ages that the empire reached its zenith.

B. THE EASTERN CHURCH

Most Christians in the West, in our twentieth-century perspective, hardly ever think of the Eastern Orthodox Church when they consider the worldwide family of Christendom. When they are reminded of the eastern church, that stange-sounding orthodoxy still seems alien to normative Christianity. Yet that branch of the family tree of Christendom includes about one-sixth of the Christian world, and has had the longest continuous Christian tradition. It has also never gone through a breach such as the Protestant Reformation was to the western church. It has, indeed, through the centuries considered itself the true expression of the continuing Body of Christ on earth. When western churchmen speak of the East breaking away, eastern churchmen reply that it is the West which broke away from the "orthodox" church.

The historical fact remains that the first great schism in Christianity was not the Protestant Reformation of the sixteenth century, but rather the schism between the East and West which climaxed in definitive action in the year 1054. The break had been coming for a long time, and can best be understood in terms of the political and theological issues which divided East and West. Our recounting of history to this point has included men and events from both East and West, with observations as to how they affected the overall progress and scheme of Christianity. At this point, we need to recapitulate briefly some of those background issues which became fundamental causes in the widening division and eventual schism.

1. POLITICAL BACKGROUND

In any history of either the western or eastern church, it is impossible to delineate specifically the affairs of state from the affairs of church, but there are some rather clear issues which, for purposes of facilitating study, can fit into one or the other category.

a. The Move to Constantinople. In 330, the Roman Emperor Constantine had moved the capital of the empire from Rome to the mouth of the Bosporus (the gateway between the Black Sea and the Mediterranean Sea) on the site of the ancient fortress town of Byzantium, and laid the foundations for the magnificent Byzantine Empire. Commercially, it was an expeditious move, for it placed the capital in the heart of imperial trade routes. Militarily, it

The fortified city of Constantinople as it appeared during the Byzantine era. The emperor Constantine, for whom the city was named, moved the capital of the empire from Rome to the mouth of the Bosporus on the site of the ancient fortress town of Byzantium. (Historical Pictures Service, Chicago)

was an ingenious location, affording the best of natural protection from invading barbarians. But politically it was the beginning of divided and diminished power. Rome, of course, lost her political importance as capital of the empire; but, on the other hand, the power vacuum left by the removal of the government immediately elevated the bishop of Rome to an unprecedented position of influence in temporal as well as spiritual matters. Gradually, the bishops, and then the popes of Rome achieved enormous political authority.

The papal office came into rivalry with secular rulers throughout the medieval period, while continuing its long-standing rivalry with the see of Constantinople. For all practical purposes, the church from Constantine's move in 330 to the final schism in 1054, had two competing centers. The competition was heightened and the relations strained almost to the breaking point when Charlemagne was crowned in 800. There were now two emperors vying for power in the political arena, and the pope of Rome and the patriarch of Constantinople vying for power in the religious arena.

b. The Rule of Caesaropapism. In the East, the patriarch did not have the rivalry with secular rulers such as the pope had to contend with at Rome. From the very outset, the eastern church enjoyed a close working relationship with the emperors who ruled from Constantinople. The relationship was so close, in fact, that western churchmen and historians have often called the arrangement Caesaropapism, which means the subordination of ecclesiastical affairs to monarchical control. The church becomes a virtual department of state in the government. Byzantine historians often refute the charge of Caesaropapism, pointing out that the emperor was never a priest and that he could be excommunicated by the patriarch. The term which is preferred by proorthodox theologians is *symphonia* (harmony), rather than Caesaropapism. In the concept of *symphonia,* the spiritual and civil authorities support each other, the church leaves civil administration in the hands of Christian rulers of state. But all of society is under the patronage of God, and the emperor is the Lord's anointed. Regardless of which term is used, the emperor did control the election of the patriarch, and even the council decisions of the church were not valid without the emperor's consent.

When one understands the concept of Caesaropapism, and/or symphonia, it is easier to understand the acquiescence of the Russian Orthodox Church (the eventual heir of Byzantine Christianity), even to the rule of the communist Soviet government. The charge of Caesaropapism was a critical issue in the growing rift between the East and West, the latter having contended for centuries for the supremacy of church over state.

c. The Mohammedan Crisis. The invasion of the Moslem Arabs affected the Mediterranean world decisively. For thousands of years the Mediterranean

Sea had served as a unifying element for the bordering peoples, a dividing barrier between the Islamic world on the one side and the Christian West on the other. Byzantium (the eastern empire) became the outpost of the Christian faith, with the difficult task of protecting eastern Europe against the incursions of Islam. Constantinople found itself constantly posed between the two fronts. The Byzantine Empire was not able to withstand the powerful Arabian drive for expansion, and lost vast holdings throughout the empire. Constantinople itself was successfully defended against two mighty sieges (674-678 and 717-718), but the East could no longer protect the West. Pope Gregory the Great (590-604) saved Rome from the Lombards, and Charles Martel stopped the Arabs at Tours in 732. The West was never ravaged like the East by the barbarians and Arabs, but neither had they been able to depend on the emperor to protect them. Another wedge of suspicion and distrust drove the two worlds farther apart.

2. THEOLOGICAL BACKGROUND
Most of the ecclesiastical issues were also intertwined with politics, such as the Caesaropapism issue. Even those issues which would ordinarily be considered exclusively theological had their involvements with and repercussions from the political machinery.

a. The "Mono" Christology. The Council of Chalcedon (451) had obstensibly ended the long Christological controversy which had begun with Arianism and the Council of Nicaea in 325. There were, however, two lingering expressions of Eutycheanism, which denied the real manhood of Christ and maintained that there were two natures before but only one after the union of the incarnation. Monophysitism was the surviving (beyond Chalcedon) notion of the single divine nature in Christ. Monothelitism was the ethical teaching which spoke of one will or one mode of activity in the God-man. Justinian I (527-565) earnestly sought to win the "mono" heretics back into orthodoxy. The effort was futile, and monophysitism consolidated itself in three great churches: the Copts and Abyssinians, the Syrian Jacobites, and the Armenians.

The theological tendencies of the "mono" heresies had left indelible impressions on Byzantine Christianity, which continued to elevate Christ's divinity above his humanity; and even the divinity was considered less than the Father's. On the other hand, the western church has always upheld faithfully the Chalcedon Definition, wherein Christ is "truly God and truly man." This was and still is a critical distinction in Christology. If Christ was not fully divine, then Christians have no ultimate revelation; but if Christ did not fully assume human flesh, we are left with a savior who belongs more to the world of spirits than to the world of history. A Christology which is not quite human restricts the activity of the church, thus in

Eastern Orthodoxy the church is viewed as a "department of state." One can readily see how this theological difference with the West invariably became a political difference.

b. The Iconoclast Controversy. At first sight the dispute over whether Christians should use icons or images in worship appears to be patently a religious issue only. And, in the strictly religious solution to the dispute, the East and the West were agreed. The West never did go along with the iconoclasts and the East ultimately repudiated them, with both areas maintaining a place and regulations for icons. There was, however, a church-state furor raised over the issue which severely damaged the relationships of East and West. When the Emperor Leo III published his edict against icons (726), the bishop (pope) in Rome condemned him, and in retaliation the emperor removed a large territory from the jurisdiction of Rome. Besides the loss of the valuable territory, a circumstance that recurringly affected events in that part of Rome's dominion, the controversy again pointed up the East's proclivity toward Caesaropapism. The emperor was meddling in purely religious affairs which ought to be the province of the church. The West also misunderstood a part of the Acts of the Second Council of Nicaea (787) to enjoin an adoration of images to be equal to that due the divine Trinity. Several western synods condemned the Acts as going too far in an attempt to restore the use of icons. Even in trying to preserve something they both believed in and eventually retained, the East and West could not agree nor cooperate.

c. The Filioque Clause. What seems a minor doctrinal matter was escalated to international proportions. During the Carolingian Renaissance, the church in the West added the word *filioque* to the Christological formula of the Nicene-Constantinople Creed. It was inserted immediately after the words "the Holy Ghost who proceedeth from the Father." The word *filioque* means "and the Son," making the statement read that the Holy Ghost proceeds from both the Father and the Son. The Emperor Leo III had no problem with the idea itself, but he staunchly opposed any effort to change the original creed in any way. There were, however, eastern theologians who disagreed with the filioque clause on theological rather than practical or traditional bases.

Photius (810-895) was the most outstanding opponent of the *filioque.* Patriarch of Constantinople, Photius was also one of the most brilliant scholars and powerful personalities ever produced by the East. Photius' objections to the filioque clause are spelled out in his theological masterpiece, "Treatise on the Mystagogia of the Holy Spirit," which gives with precision and finality the eastern church's understanding of the procession of the Holy Spirit. It is an explicit statement of the primacy, if not the superiority, of the Father in the Trinity. He contended that to say the

Holy Spirit is the product of the Son is to destroy the unity of the Godhead. He insisted that the *filioque* was a heretical innovation.

Photius was also the instigator of the first portents of schism between Rome and Constantinople over the question of whether Ignatius or Photius was the legitimate patriarch of Constantinople. Pope Nicholas I anathematized Photius, and in retaliation Photius excommunicated the pope (867). Following Nicholas, Pope John VIII was willing to recognize Photius' legitimacy and to drop the *filioque* from the creed; but in return he wanted Constantinople to recognize his supremacy and return the ecclesiastical jurisdiction of Bulgaria to Rome. The East could not accept the terms of the pope and in the Eighth Ecumenical Council (869-870) affirmed the autonomy of the see of Constantinople and raised its patriarch to an equality with the pope. Photius was reinstated as patriarch and ruled for eight years as if he were pope himself. It was 163 years from the death of Photius to the great schism of 1054, but already the precedent had been set and the guidelines drawn.

3. EASTERN ORTHODOXY AT ITS ZENITH

Our last observations of the western church had seen it in what was perhaps its deepest humiliation. Ironically, at the same period of time, the eastern church was at the pinnacle of success. It seemed that everything it attempted succeeded, whether dealing with doctrinal heresies, or juggling the balance of power between church and state, or expanding its culture and borders.

a. Suppressing Heresy. The East had survived the internal strife fomented by heresy since the early days of its existence. Monasticism had strengthened, rather than weakened, the church as many had feared. Donatism, though roundly defeated, had given the church an opportunity to form official positions on the issues of unholy clergy and rebaptism. Arianism, while defeated in the ecumenical councils, had maintained a friendly footing in the East. The "mono" churches had developed cordial relations with Constantinopolitan orthodoxy. The Armenian church supplied the empire with its best soldiers. The Jacobites of Syria were variously ignored and proselytized. The Coptic church in Egypt was tolerated and it prospered. The Nestorians of Persia, though outside the empire, won twenty thousand Turks and Mongols to Christianity. There were also a few lesser known heresies and sects which were suppressed by the larger Byzantine orthodoxy.

(1) Paulicians. One such sect was that of the Paulicians, named after either the Apostle Paul whom they held in great veneration, or Paul of Samosata, with whom they agreed in many things. They believed in a dualistic doctrine of a good God and an evil God, held that all matter was evil, and therefore denied the reality of Christ's body. They rejected the

cross and all images, probably having an influence on the iconoclastic mission of Leo III. The Paulicians were severely persecuted in the seventh and ninth centuries. When Empress Theodora tried to exterminate them, many of them adopted Mohammedanism and assisted the Saracens in the raids. Most of the Paulicians were thereafter deported to Bulgaria, where they fused with another sect, the Bogomiles, in the tenth century.

(2) Bogomiles. This sect took its name from its founder, Bogomile (the Bulgarian translation of Theophilus), who taught between 927 and 950. They were also dualistic in their doctrine of God, which extended to a dualism of the Son. The first son of God, Satanael, revolted and was driven from heaven, then created the world and Adam. Since the soul of Adam belonged to God, and his body to man, the Father sent his second Son, Jesus, to earth as a man. After conquering Satanael, Jesus returned to heaven, leaving on earth his creature, the Holy Spirit, to carry on his work among the Bogomiles, the only true Christians. The Bogomiles had a rigid ascetic life-style, and rejected baptism and communion as satanic rites. Constantinople tolerated the Bogomiles until Emperor Alexis Comnenus had their leader burned in 1118, and a synod ordered the destruction of their books in 1140. When the Turks destroyed the Bulgarian Empire in 1393, the sect of the Bogomiles disappeared.

(3) Messalians, also known as Euchites, had survived in the eastern empire from the fourth to the seventh century. They were condemned at the Council of Ephesus in 431. They believed that because of Adam's sin everyone had a demon united with his soul. This demon was not expelled by baptism, and could be destroyed only by concentrated and ceaseless prayer, the aim of which was to eliminate all passion and desire. The name of the sect means "the praying people." Eastern monasticism satisfied the craving for piety and asceticism, and rendered the Messalians impotent and unnecessary. In fact, Eastern Orthodoxy made it very hard for any sects to exist by covering such a wide spectrum in its own theology and ecclesiology. Why, for example, would one need the "mono" churches when Eastern Orthodoxy provided a strong and satisfying emphasis on the divinity of Christ? In addition, the cause of Christianity was as much at the heart of the rulers of state as it was with the prelates of the church. All of which resulted in orthodoxy as the only legitimate expression of Christianity.

b. Surviving Caesaropapism. The eastern emperors molded the policies of the church more than the patriarchs of Constantinople. This would have been disastrous in the West, but it was merely a fact of life that had to be adjusted to in the East. One example of ecclesiastical independence and one of subservience will serve to demonstrate how both church and state adjust to each other.

(1) Nicholas Mysticus and Leo VI. The ablest patriarch between Photius and Michael Cerularius was Nicholas Mysticus (895-906). He was faced

with the unwelcome task of refusing to allow the Emperor Leo VI to marry a fourth time, forbidden by canon law even though his three previous wives had died. Leo then took a concubine who bore him a son, who became Constantine VII. Later Leo married his concubine, but Nicholas refused to crown her as empress, and forbade the emperor to enter the church. Nicholas was deposed by the emperor and Euthymius made patriarch (906-911). Two strong ecclesiastical parties developed, the Nicolaitans and the Euthymites. So much dissension arose, that Leo finally deposed Euthymius, who served for nearly fourteen more years. This was a classic example of ecclesiastical independence prevailing over the emperor.

(2) Nicephorus Phocas and Athanasius. Some years later, in the reign of Nicephorus Phocas (963-969), Caesaropapism was seen in its complete application. Nicephorus was a devout Christian who had even considered becoming a monk, but after his marriage to the widow of his predecessor, he imposed stringent laws against charity to hospitals, metropolitans, and bishops. He issued a decree forbidding the founding of new monasteries or giving endowments for the upkeep of old ones. He imposed many innovations and prohibitions on the church as though he were its bishop.

There was, however, in the holy mountain of Athos, a dedicated monk who reminded Nicephorus that he had once promised him that he would become a monk if Athanasius would pray for his victory in a battle with the Saracens on Crete. Although he did win the battle, Nicephorus had failed to keep his promise, and now he sought to buy release from that vow by providing Athanasius with resources to build the Great Lavra monastery on the holy mountain (963).

Even the opposition of hermits (who appealed to Nicephorus' successor, John Tzimisces) could not halt the building nor prevail against the government. When Athanasius died in 1000, there were more than three thousand monks on Athos. On the surface, it was a triumph for the emperor, who proved he could set up and pull down rules for the church. But underneath, one notes that the wisdom for getting facilities for the church lay with the shrewd and patient Athanasius. Repeatedly, it seemed that the church would let the state have its way, knowing all the while that "the will of God" would prevail.

c. *Expanding Byzantium.* During the tenth century the Byzantine state flexed its newly developed military muscle and reconquered much of the land which had been taken by the Saracens. It regained control of the Mediterranean Sea, and most of its ancient territory in Asia Minor. It entered into favorable alliances with important principalities, and reduced Bulgaria to vassalage. During the long reign of Basil II (976-1025), Byzantine political and military power reached its zenith. A heightened sense of social responsibility accompanied this physical success. Charity and humanitarianism reached new heights, art flourished, literature abounded, and an unusual interest in history and geography emerged. Expanding its curriculum beyond the customary disciplines to include advanced law and philosophy, the school at Constantinople paved the way for the great universities of the thirteenth century. It was Byzantine's finest hour, and the church both contributed to and benefited from it.

d. *Converting Russia.* The greatest achievement of Greek Christianity during these days of glory was the conversion of Russia, and from 989 until the Bolshevik Revolution of 1917, Russia was the daughter of Byzantium in religion, alphabet, and art. The dowager Queen Olga embraced Christianity after the death of her husband Igor (945), primarily because of the impression made on her by the little Christian community of Kiev. At her request the western emperor Otto I sent missionaries to Kiev, but they had no success. Olga's grandson, Vladimir, was the real founder of Russian Christianity. Wanting his people to embrace a common religion, he invited representatives of Islam, Judaism, Roman Catholicism, and Greek Catholicism to Kiev to demonstrate the worth of their respective faiths. He was not impressed with Islam or Judaism, and he could not decide between eastern and western Christianity. He sent emissaries to both Rome and Constantinople to see the religions at work. The visitors to Constantinople were overwhelmed with the grandeur and splendor of the services at the majestic church of St. Sophia, and highly recommended Eastern Orthodoxy. After marrying the eastern emperor's sister (who was also the sister-in-law of Otto II), Vladimir was baptized in 988. His twelve sons followed his example, and the Russian people accepted Christianity en masse. When enough priests could not be found to baptize them, thousands lined up at the River Kiev and immersed themselves. Russia thus entered Christendom in 989, and Vladimir began an extensive educational program for the new religion. His son Yaroslav continued his work, having the Scriptures translated into Slavic. Slowly Russia began to lift itself out of its barbarism to establish the beginnings of a great civilization which stood for nearly a thousand years.

4. THE GREAT SCHISM

The year 1054 is a pivotal year in the history of Christianity. Prior to that time, most Christians considered themselves to be in the same ecclesiastical family. Divisions and differences had been local and/or temporary. Decisions of doctrine and church polity had been arrived at jointly through ecumenical councils, convened by the eastern emperor and approved by the western pope. After 1054, all of that changed, and East and West went their separate ways, treating each other as enemies or as heathen who needed to be converted. The differences which eventually separated them had been building for centuries, and were theological, cultural, geographical, political, and economic (to say nothing of the personality clashes involved).

The principals who affected the final schism were Pope Leo IX of Rome and Patriarch Michael Cerularius of Constantinople. Both were strong personalities, determined to accomplish their respective goals. Leo IX was a strong leader of men, intimidating the Norman army in southern Italy as he led his own troops. He persuaded Edward the Confessor of England to build Westminster Abbey, and campaigned for moral reform throughout Italy, Germany, France, England, and Spain. In fact, his reform measures were a precipitating factor in the East's final rejection of Roman supremacy.

Michael Cerularius was a learned professor and government official before becoming patriarch. He had two consuming objectives for his reign: to free the eastern church from subservience to the imperial government, and to elevate the patriarchate of Constantinople to equality with the pope of Rome. He methodically set out to achieve these goals. First, he deliberately agitated Rome with charges of serious errors, telling the pope he should be reforming himself instead of trying to reform the people. These "serious" errors included the use of unleavened bread in the Eucharist, fasting on Saturday, using meat of strangled animals, and forbidding the singing of the Alleluia during Lent. A monk by the name of Nicetas Stethatos added fuel to the fire by reminding the Greeks of the Latin error of adding "filioque" to the creed, and the despised western rule of celibacy for priests.

Michael Cerularius closed the doors of Latin churches in Constantinople, threw out the unleavened bread of the Eucharist, and ordered Latin monasteries to adopt Greek rites. Leo IX protested loudly, averring that Rome was the only church which deserved supreme respect and obedience. He offered to be lenient with Greek churches in regard to their own customs, but insisted that the Roman church would never change its doctrines. The emperor called a conciliatory session in Constantinople to settle the differences, but the papal legates were received in rude insolence, and Cerularius ordered the pope's name removed from the diptychs, tablets which contained the names for whom prayers and masses were to be said. In retaliation, on July 16, 1054, the papal legates formally laid on the altar of St. Sophia's church a sentence of anathema against Michael Cerularius and his followers. Four days later, at the same place, Michael Cerularius responded in kind and excommunicated the pope and his followers. The Great Schism had finally occurred.

In the aftermath, both East and West went their separate ways, and became involved in their own concerns. Cerularius attempted to accomplish his other ambition, to lift the government yoke from the church, but his brazen attempts to do so caused him to be deposed by the emperor and to die in bitterness and disillusionment. However, the eastern church lists Michael Cerularius with Photius as the two greatest patriarchs in medieval history. It is interesting that they are also the two "schism patriarchs." Leo

IX did not live to receive his legates back from Constantinople, and died without knowing about his excommunication by Cerularius and the attending schism. Waiting in the wings in Rome was Hildebrand, Leo's chief counselor, who would eventually become Gregory VII and usher in a golden age for Rome through the Gregorian reformation.

V I

MASTERS AND SERVANTS: THE POWER STRUGGLE (1054-1305)

But he that is greatest among you
shall be your servant. And whosoever
shall exalt himself shall be abased;
and he that shall humble himself
shall be exalted.

MATTHEW 23:11, 12

A. Spiritual and Intellectual Renewal
   1. The Gregorian Reformers
      a. The Rise of Hildebrand
      b. The Investiture Controversy
      c. The Influence of Cluny
   2. Flourishing Monasticism
      a. Ascetic Orders
         (1) The Carthusians
         (2) The Cistercians
      b. Mendicant Orders
         (1) The Franciscans
         (2) The Dominicans
         (3) The Carmelites
         (4) The Augustinians
      c. Military Orders
         (1) The Knights Hospitalers
         (2) The Knights Templars
   3. Developing Scholasticism
      a. John Scotus Erigina
      b. Anselm
      c. Peter Abelard
      d. Hugo of St. Victor
      e. Peter Lombard
      f. Thomas Aquinas
      g. Duns Scotus
      h. Roger Bacon
      i. William of Occam
B. Holy and Unholy Crusades
   1. Background of the Crusades
      a. Political
      b. Ecclesiastical
      c. Devotional
   2. Development of the Crusades
      a. The First Crusade
      b. The Second Crusade
      c. The Third Crusade
      d. The Fourth Crusade
      e. Other Crusades
   3. Consequences of the Crusades
C. Noble and Ignoble Power
   1. Papacy at Its Height
      a. Great Popes of the Twelfth Century
      b. Innocent III
   2. Dissent in the Open
      a. The Cathari
      b. The Waldenses
   3. Inquisition on the Rampage

he first half of the Middle Ages saw the church struggling to survive invasions from without and controversies from within. The second half witnessed the theological, ecclesiastical, and intellectual power struggles perpetrated by the church hierarchy. The motivation was to excel, and the compulsion was to rule. In fulfillment, some pursued noble and worthy causes, some sought to drive out evil forces, some espoused personal and universal reform, and some were determined to gain ascendancy and power over others. The intertwining results often leave a confusing picture as to the true nature and motives of the participants; but the retrospective eyes of history can often discern those who sought mastery and those who were of the servant spirit.

A. SPIRITUAL AND INTELLECTUAL RENEWAL

Leo IX was pope at the time of the Eastern Schism in 1054 and will perhaps be remembered for that above all else. He was, however, involved in leading another movement for which he deserves high recognition. The papal reforms of the eleventh century owed much to the impetus of Leo IX, who did much to restore the prestige of the papacy through his extensive travels, his stand against simony, his insistence upon the election of bishops by clergy and people, his firm position on celibacy, and his broadening of the cardinalate to include others outside Rome. When he died suddenly in 1054, Leo IX did not know of the Eastern Schism, but he did know that the tide of reform was sweeping through the western church.

1. THE GREGORIAN REFORMERS

The papacy, and indeed the entire clergy, was in need of universal reform. Problems which reflect the decadent state of the church included untrained clergy, simony (purchase of church posts), sexual laxity, and lay investiture (control of the appointment and allegiance of abbots, bishops, and popes by the lay civil authorities). The papal reforms of the eleventh century which dealt with all these problems came to be known as the Gregorian reforms, so-called after Pope Gregory VII, who was such a powerful leader before his election to the papacy, that he is generally better known by his earlier name of Hildebrand.

a. *The Rise of Hildebrand.* Born about 1025 and reared in Rome, where he would someday be the chief actor in the papal scene for nearly three decades, Hildebrand was educated in a monastery and in his early twenties became a monk, probably at Cluny. He returned to Rome in the service of Leo IX, who admitted him to minor orders. He became a close friend of Peter Damian, the Cardinal-Bishop of Ostia, and one of the most intense churchmen calling for reform. Although his rise to prominence was slow compared to others, Hildebrand laid his ground work well, worked in the inner circles of power, maintained his dedication, and by the time he was thirty-five he was being noticed as a leader of men.

In 1058, Hildebrand was presented with the opportunity to display his real power. Leo IX, who had died in 1054, was followed in death in 1056 by the Emperor Henry III. The latter's six-year-old son came to the throne as Henry IV under the regency. After the brief reigns of popes Victor II and Stephen IX, the royal regency elected Benedict X to the papacy. Hildebrand was in Germany when he received the news of this blatant determination of the nobility to retain control over the papacy. He raised an army, expelled Benedict, and seated Nicholas II on the papal throne. Nicholas' reign lasted only two years (1059-61) but was distinguished by the establishment of the College of Cardinals to elect future popes. This papal decree of 1059 is still the principal basis for governing the papal elections. The guiding hands behind Nicholas' decree were those of Hildebrand and Humbert, a cardinal-bishop from Toul.

Two years later Humbert, a strong exponent of reform, and Nicholas died within a few weeks of each other, depriving the reformers of two outstanding leaders. Again, it was Hildebrand who stepped into the breach. He convened the cardinals in Rome and led them to elect Alexander II to the papacy. The Roman nobility still had not acquiesced to this reform method of electing popes, and convinced the regent of Henry IV (still a child of eleven years) to appoint an Italian bishop, Cadalus, as pope. Although Cadalus was an annoying rival during Alexander's entire pontificate, the strong influence and skillful administration of Hildebrand kept Alexander securely in control. Alexander was an able pope and served from 1061 to 1073, when he died while in conflict with Henry IV over the appointment of the Archbishop of Milan. With the death of Alexander, Hildebrand was the sole survivor of the band of reformers who had started together with Leo IX, and the people immediately and loudly acclaimed him as their choice for Alexander's successor. The cardinals, abbots, monks, and laity all agreed, and Hildebrand, while only a deacon, was elected to the papacy. He had to be ordained a priest before he could ascend to the throne, where he took the title of Gregory VII. His reign lasted from 1073 to 1085 and was one of the most outstanding pontificates in history.

As Pope Gregory VII, Hildebrand wielded sweeping powers of clerical reform but without unanimous acceptance. He enforced clerical celibacy with a strong determination to free the church from the world; but priests and their families were thrown into such turmoil and controversy that the issue was still raging at the time of the Reformation four hundred years later. The decree for celibacy, however, did eliminate the offensive practice of holding church office by heredity, and it definitely strengthened the authority of the pope over the clergy.

In fact, the absolute authority of the papal office was the central theme of Gregory VII. In his famous *Dictatus Papae*, he forthrightly declared that, "The Roman Church was founded by God alone; the Roman pope alone can with right be called universal; he alone may use the imperial insignia; his feet only shall be kissed by all princes; he alone may depose the emperors; he himself may be judged by no one; the Roman Church has never erred, nor will it err in all eternity." Gregory also advocated that all Christian states should form a world empire with the pope at its head as God's representative on earth. Most of the claims to supremacy were well established, at least in theory, before Gregory, but no one had ever expressed them so dogmatically and enforced them so successfully. He held frequent councils in Rome to enforce his measures, with tenacious attention to stamping out simony, clerical marriage, and concubinage. He instituted a thorough and permanent chain of command, but the bishops were totally dependent on the pope, for he was determined to destroy the practice of lay investiture which became the chief issue of his reign.

b. The Investiture Controversy. In 1059 Pope Nicholas II had articulated the reform position on the selection of important clergymen, which was to be henceforth by the authority of clergy and people and not civil rulers. The pope himself was to be elected by a college of cardinals. As we have already noted, this attitude and action was opposed by the civil authorities with varying degrees of hostility rising and falling. Gregory VII brought the whole issue to a head by decreeing through the Lateran Synod of 1075 that all clergy were forbidden to receive a bishopric or abbey or church from the hands of a secular prince or lord, even from the king or emperor. His unrelenting position that investiture of clergy should be received only from the pope as God's supreme representative in the world was a radical revolution within the medieval legal and political world.

As an immediate example for implementing the investiture decree, Gregory suspended some bishops in Germany who had been appointed by civil authorities. Henry IV retaliated in anger by appointing some bishops to sees in Italy itself. When Gregory threatened to excommunicate Henry for this sort of action, the emperor put together the Synod of Worms in 1076, attended by disgruntled bishops who were easily convinced to declare Gregory unfit to be pope. Armed with the synod's verdict, Henry demanded that Gregory resign the papacy. The following month, Gregory deposed Henry for his "unheard-of arrogance and iniquities," placed him under anathema, and relieved his subjects of allegiance to him. In a swift stroke of power, Gregory swung the German political factions behind him, and Henry found himself without followers. The emperor, following the line of political expediency, asked the pope for forgiveness and restoration. In the well-known and often-told incident of absolution, Henry and Gregory met at Canossa in 1077 where the pope had taken refuge in a fortress while journeying to Augsburg. Gregory would not at first receive the penitent Henry who stood in the snow for three days, barefooted and thinly clad, seeking an audience. Gregory finally received him, and after exacting specific promises from the emperor, he absolved him. This remains one of the most vivid demonstrations of papal power in history.

Subsequently, however, both Gregory and Henry broke their vows to each other, shattering the accord of Canossa. When Henry's enemies in Germany elected a rival sovereign, Gregory supported them and declared Henry deposed again in 1080. This time the people felt that Gregory had been unfair to Henry and supported the emperor when he invaded Rome and called a synod to pronounce Gregory deposed. The synod had elected another pope, Wibert, in Gregory's place; Wibert proceeded to crown Henry of the Holy Roman Empire. Gregory retreated to the safety of the castle of San Angelo in Rome until he was liberated by his loyal Normans from the South. The Normans savagely retook Rome and reinstated Gregory as pope. Within the year, however, Gregory died a disillusioned and bitter refugee in Salerno. He died with his dream of absolute supremacy crumbling around him. He had wanted too much. He was not interested in separation of church and state, but wanted absolute control of church over state.

Gregory's struggle in the investiture controversy did eventually culminate in formal settlements. In 1122, Emperor Henry V of Germany agreed to the Concordat of Worms, in which the emperor relinquished the right of selection and investiture of the spiritual office of bishop; but the bishop was to be answerable to the civil ruler in temporal matters. A similar settlement had been reached at the Council of London in 1107, where the investiture controversy had been especially acute between Anselm and Henry I. The compromise solutions reflected the offsetting powers of church and state, and stabilized the balance of power for centuries to come.

c. The Influence of Cluny. The sweeping papal reform of the eleventh century, which came to be called the "Hildebrandine" or "Gregorian" reform, owed its instigation, in great part, to the influence of a monastic reform movement which originated in the monastery of Cluny. So powerful in fact was the impact of this monastery, that all the reforms of the tenth, eleventh, and twelfth centuries are often referred to as the Cluniac Reformation. In 910, William, Duke of Aquitaine designated the town and manor of Cluny, in southern Burgundy, for the erection of a Benedictine monastery. The religious order received not only the lands, waters, and revenues in the donation, but also the serfs, the workers on the land. Thus, with the serfs supplying the essential physical labor, the monks were free to give themselves to spiritual pursuits. They were also free, according to the conditions of the grant, from interference from the patron, his successors, or the king. The monks were to retain their own possessions and elect their own abbot. The monks of Cluny were directly responsible only to the papacy.

A deep sense of piety resulted from the long hours of attention to prayer and study, and soon a conviction for reform began to prevail. The program of Cluny involved, first of all, a call for clerical reform, especially as related to simony, celibacy, and concubinage. But it also spread to include all of society—monastic, civil, and ecclesiastical. The goal was to permeate society with Christian ideals. To implement this goal, the monks dedicated themselves to prayer, education, and hospitality. The monasteries of the Cluny chain became the inns of the Middle Ages where Christian teachings were imposed on the travelers. Many new monasteries were erected in the Cluny tradition and many older monasteries became affiliated, until there were more than three hundred houses in the Cluniac movement, with all of them subject to the mother house at Cluny.

The cluniac reformers worked to eliminate feudal warfare, teaching that nobles should use their arms only to vindicate the weak and protect the church. They inaugurated the "Truce of God" which restricted the times for fighting, and the "Peace of God" which restricted the combatants. Under the Truce of God, there could be no hostilities from sunset Wednesday to Monday morning or on holy days. Under the Peace of God, there were to be no attacks upon priests, nuns, pilgrims, merchants, farmers, their animals, tools, or properties. These efforts often did more harm than good, with princes breaking their vows to keep the "Truce" and "Peace." The bishops began organizing armies to punish the oathbreakers, and then the kings raised armies to suppress the church's armies. The Cluniacs were extremely influential in the fight to free the church from the control of secular powers. Since Cluny had been founded upon independence from the local bishop and civil authorities, it would naturally tend to support the independence movement. Pope Gregory VII, who waged the great investiture controversy with Henry IV, received his training in the monastery at Cluny.

Cluny appears to have achieved its stated objects, which were: return to strict Benedictine rule, cultivation of the personal spiritual life, reduction of manual labor, expansion of the splendor of worship, foundation of a sound economical organization, and independence from lay control. The success of the Cluniac monasteries, however, brought a backlash of concern about worldly success within monasticism. The wealth of the Cluny houses, their easy relations with the secular world, and their emphasis on worship services led some reformers to seek a more austere and primitive path.

2. FLOURISHING MONASTICISM

Both the advocates of Cluny and those who desired a new direction supplied new fervor for the monastic life-style. In fact, during this period, monastic orders multiplied so rapidly that the pope was forced to prohibit additional orders at the Fourth Lateran Council in 1215. Later, an exception was made in the case of some Mendicant Orders, but the issue reflects the intensity with which medieval piety had plunged into asceticism, the renouncing of the world to search for holiness.

a. Ascetic Orders. There were some orders which retreated to remote regions, practicing severe discipline and constant contemplation. These "Knights of Asceticism" were determined to reverse the Cluniac trend of involving Christianity in the affairs of the world.

(1) The Carthusians. In 1004, Bruno, a German from Cologne, resigned his teaching position in the cathedral school of Rheims and established an extremely strict, contemplative order of monks near Cartusia at the Grande Chartreuse. The emphasis of this order was renunciation of the world and mortification of the flesh. To attain these goals, the monks lived in austerity and self-denial, vowed to silence and committed to solitude. Each monk had his own private cell and private garden and prepared his own food, eating with his brothers only on feast days. Some of the Carthusians became scholars, mystics, and writers of devotional works; but they had limited influence on society. Their main achievement was spiritual separation and anonymity through cultivated silence. Because of their isolation and extreme asceticism, the Carthusians were the least affected by the decline of monasticism in the later Middle Ages. During the Reformation, numbers of them were put to death by Henry VIII, and even more were killed during the French Revolution. Most of them found refuge in Spain and were not able to return to Grande Chartreuse until 1940.

(2) The Cistercians. The most celebrated order of ascetic monks was founded at Citeaux in 1098 by Robert of Molesme, who sought to establish a form of Benedictism stricter and more primitive than any existing. As a reaction to the Cluniac style of monasticism, the Cistercians emphasized the spirit of prophecy rather than the spirit of power. Whereas the Cluniacs were free from manual labor, the Cistercians stressed labor instead of scholarship, believing that "to work is to pray." They became proficient in

the tasks of farming, cooking, weaving, carpentry, and sheep raising. They became important agricultural pioneers, and played a notable part in English sheep farming. Their life-style, characterized by simplicity, discipline, manual labor, vegetarianism, and spiritual contemplation, was very appealing to the medieval mind. Thus the order spread rapidly, and before the end of the twelfth century, 530 Cistercian abbeys had been established, and 150 more in the next hundred years.

The most famous Cistercian monk, Bernard of Clairvaux (1090-1153) bridged the age of feudal values and the rise of towns and universities. He was the first of the great medieval mystics. He entered the monastery at Citeaux when he was twenty-one, but soon led a group to found a new house of Clairvaux in the Champagne region. Bernard became the most extreme Cistercian of them all, emaciating his body through deprivation; lashing out at the worldly tendencies of the church, and denouncing pride, injustice, and greed wherever found. Because of his moral integrity, knowledge of the Bible, devotion to love, and fearless attacks on evil, he was often referred to as the conscience of Europe. Bernard's spiritual and intellectual pursuits centered in mysticism and produced the concept of Christian love being the imitation of Christ, especially as one contemplates the wounds of Christ. He wielded great power throughout Christendom, with at least two popes (Innocent II and Eugenius III) being elected on the strength of Bernard's support. Christians today still sing some of his beautiful hymns, such as "Jesus, The Very Thought of Thee," and "Jesus, Thou Joy of Loving Hearts."

Cistercian observances widely influenced those of other medieval orders, until after the thirteenth century when the Cistercian fame waned considerably. During the seventeenth century the Cistercians enjoyed a revival of interest and a flurry of new congregations.

b. *Mendicant Orders.* The Carthusians and Cistercians were representatives of a group of monastic orders which could have been known as the "working monks" because of their devotion to manual labor and contemplation. Another popular group could have been called the "preaching monks" because they went out from their monasteries into the world to preach among the ordinary population. They became known as "the friars" (brothers) rather than monks, and exist to the present. When the friars left their monasteries, they had no financial support or physical provisions. They depended on the alms or charity of the people, and thus became known as the mendicant (to beg) orders.

(1) The Franciscans. The Order of Friars Minor (lesser brothers) was founded in 1209 by Francis of Assisi, the son of a rich cloth merchant of Assisi. Rejecting his father's wealth and renouncing his earlier life of carefree gaiety, Francis resolved to devote his life to the ideals of "lady poverty." On a pilgrimage to Rome, he dumped all his money at St. Peter's,

exchanged clothes with a beggar, and begged himself.

Returning to Assisi, Francis devoted himself to serving lepers and repairing chapels and churches in the area. He took the words of Matthew 10:7-19 to be a personal commission to him and began preaching that the kingdom of heaven is at hand. Crowds and disciples began to follow the barefoot, impoverished, intense, and gentle Francis.

The growing number of brothers necessitated organization and rules, and Francis reluctantly drew up a simple rule of life for himself and his associates ("Regula Primitiva"). In 1210 Francis obtained approval from Pope Innocent III for his simple rule devoted to apostolic poverty. The Franciscans followed their founder in preaching and caring for the poor and sick. A society for women, the "Poor Clares," began in 1212 when Clare, an heiress of Assisi, was converted and commissioned.

Francis was constantly afraid that the order would succumb to the attachments of the world, and in 1221 he drew up a Second Rule which was stricter and more definite concerning vows of poverty, obedience, chastity, prayer, and regulations for organizations. The Third Rule was confirmed by Pope Honorius III in 1223, three years before Francis' death. The basic requirements for Franciscans included absolute poverty, for they were to possess nothing and to trust the Lord to provide. They were to guard against pride, vainglory, envy, avarice, and were to love their enemies. They were not to preach in a diocese without the consent of the bishop and none could preach without examination and approval by the minister general. They were to discuss, not theology, but penitence and forgiveness. They became renowned for the reconciliation of feuds, and practically every village, town, and farm was visited by these preaching, singing troubadours of God.

The popularity and growth of the order meant serious problems on the matter of possessions. How could so many live by working or begging for enough for only one day's provisions (one of the rules of the order)? Eventually disruption came when the Spirituals insisted on adhering to all the original rules of poverty, and the Conventuals advocated reasonable compromise, with the church owning and the brothers using necessary property. This became the divisive issue of the order, with violent discussions endangering the whole venture. Papal bulls permitted corporate ownership for the order in 1317-18, causing many Spirituals to become schismatics. With material prosperity came spiritual laxity, and a new group called the Observants took up the banner of the old Spirituals. They opposed the lax Conventuals more than a hundred years until they finally won and were declared the true Order of St. Francis in 1517.

At the beginning the rule did not encourage learning, and Francis strongly opposed any effort to start a house of study. After his death, however, the general rise of education prevailed in Europe and permeated the order. Seventy new universities were established in Europe between

Francis of Assisi, founder of the Order of Friars Minor, later called the Order of St. Francis or Franciscans. Despite the legends that surround his life, he left a reputation of contagious piety and goodness arising from a dreary period of medieval history. (Historical Pictures Service, Chicago)

1200 and 1250, and by 1234 the Franciscans themselves had a flourishing seminary. Some of the celebrated scholars of Christendom who were Franciscans were Bonaventure, Duns Scotus, and William of Occam. Much of the work of the Franciscans today is carried on in the universities of the world.

Besides the legacy of the order named for him, Francis left the personal example of contagious piety and unaffected goodness. This gentle lover of people and all of God's creation was especially at home in the wilderness among the animals and birds. He went through frequent and long periods of fasting and praying, receiving ecstatic visions. He was reported to have performed numerous miracles, and one legend says that he received the *stigmata*, bleeding wounds on his body at the places where the wounds were on the crucified body of Jesus. Francis of Assisi was beloved by everyone from lepers to leaders and was perhaps the brightest personality in the dreary medieval period of history.

(2) The Dominicans. Another mendicant order differed drastically from the Franciscans in their emphases and results. The Franciscan movement symbolized reform, redirection, and rededication; but the Dominican movement symbolized ecclesiastical orthodoxy. The Dominican order was founded by the Spaniard Domingo (Dominic) de Guzman (1170-1221), who was deeply concerned over converting the Albigenses. He believed, however, that that group of ascetic heretics could only be reached by one who lived in poverty and simplicity. He gathered around him a group of men dedicated to winning heretics and heathen by preaching and poverty. To accomplish their task, they became especially interested in study and were the first monastic order to abandon manual labor and put intellectual work in the forefront. Because they also practiced both individual and corporate poverty, they, like the Franciscans, were compelled to beg for their support from the populace.

The Fourth Lateran Council denied recognition to Dominic and his mendicant friars, but late in 1216 Honorius III sanctioned their mission, and in 1220 their rule was confirmed. In 1217, they laid plans for expanding world missions, and within four years had organized work in eight countries. Because they were devoted to learning from the outset, the Dominicans readily established themselves in the fast-growing universities and gained renown for their scholarship. Since they were also dedicated to combat heresy and heathenism, they became the watchdogs of the church's Inquisition. The popes also used them extensively in the preaching of the Crusades, the collecting of monetary levies, and the carrying-out of diplomatic missions. The leading medieval theologians produced by the Dominicans were Albert the Great and Thomas Aquinas. Although the Dominicans have contributed much in the fields of devotional books, scriptural paraphrases, religious poetry, and popular fables, their main interest has always been, and continues to be, that of education.

(3) The Carmelites. The Order of Our Lady of Mount Carmel was

founded in Palestine in 1154 by Berthold, and established by the primitive rule as laid down in 1209 by Albert of Vercelli, Latin Patriarch of Jerusalem. This rule was one of extreme asceticism, prescribing absolute poverty, solitude, and vegetarianism. After the failure of the crusades, many of the Carmelites migrated to Europe and organized on the lines of the mendicant friars. An Order of Carmelite Sisters was founded in 1452, and spread rapidly through France, Italy, and Spain. In the latter part of the sixteenth century, the mystical Teresa of Avila led in a reform of the Carmelite orders, which had grown lax and weak. Her disciple, John of the Cross, led in a similar reform among the friars. Thus the so-called "Teresian Reform" set the Carmelites again on the course of contemplation, missionary work, and theology.

(4) The Augustinians. In the middle of the eleventh century, several communities of clerks in northern Italy and southern France sought to live the common life of poverty, celibacy, and obedience, in accordance with what they believed to be the example of the early Christians. They adopted the Rule of St. Augustine, which laid down precise monastic observances. The sanity of the rule, its adaptability, and the repute of its supposed author led to its adoption by several monastic orders, including the Dominicans, the Augustinian Hermits, the Servites, and the Visitation nuns. The flexibility of the rule allowed members to follow various vocations, active and contemplative. The Augustinians had special connections with hospitals. Some of the more influential Augustinian congregations were the Victorines and the Premonstratensians; and the most notable Augustinian monk was none other than Martin Luther.

c. Military Orders. The most peculiar outcome of the monastic movement was the combination of the ascetic ideal with that of chivalry in the formation of knightly or military orders.

(1) The Knights Hospitalers. The beginnings of this order are uncertain, but by the end of the eleventh century, it was headquartered in a hospital at Jerusalem. Its original duties were to care for the sick, and to provide hospitality for pilgrims and crusaders. It established an armed guard of knights for the defense of pilgrims, which developed into a regular army. In 1099, Master Gerard obtained papal sanction for the order, and his successor Raymond of Provence greatly developed the organization. During the twelfth century the order spread to Europe, and the knights participated in the crusades. After the fall of Acre (1291), they escaped to Cyprus and conquered Rhodes, which became the center of their activities for 200 years; they then became known as the Knights of Rhodes. The order received the sovereignty of Malta from Charles V in 1530 and became known as the Knights of Malta. The surrender of Malta to Napoleon in 1798 placed the hospitalers in a precarious position which they have maintained to the present.

(2) The Knights Templars. The "Poor Knights of Christ," a military order

founded in 1118 to defend Jerusalem against the Moslems, soon had to drop their name for they had become the wealthiest of all monastic orders. Their influence spread quickly, and in a few short years they had settlements in nearly every country in Christendom. They introduced solemn forms of initiation and elaborate organization. They built several castles which served as both monasteries and cavalry barracks, of which notable ruins still remain. Their supporters loaded them with great wealth, which was deposited in their "temples" in Paris and London. Thus they developed a reputation as trusted bankers. The Templars carried on an unceasing rivalry with the Hospitalers. The Templars were suppressed by Clement V at the Council of Vienne in 1312 under charges of immorality, superstition, and heresy. Their guilt or innocence was argued for centuries, but most historians now feel the suppression was in order to get hold of the Templars' great wealth.

So monasticism thrived in various forms of expression, but always there was the testimony of dedicated men and women withdrawing from the normal intercourse of society to devote themselves to an area of spirituality which they felt deserved their entire lives. This had a profound effect on the rest of Christendom, which was called upon to evaluate its own spirituality by the standards of monasticism.

3. DEVELOPING SCHOLASTICISM

While spirituality was being revived through monasticism, the medieval period saw also the revival of learning through a movement known as Scholasticism, so called because it arose from the schools of the period and revolved around the works of the school men. This was a new kind of intellectualism, concerned with the relation between faith and reason, between realism and nominalism. A distinguishing characteristic of Scholasticism was its use of the dialectical method of philosophy. Theological problems were skillfully and energetically studied with the tools of logic and metaphysics. The Scholastic method of teaching involved the *lectio,* the public lecture in which the master explained the text, and the *disputatio,* in which a view was expounded and objections to it proposed and answered in syllogistic form. The Scholastic method of writing was typically in the form of commentaries which gave systematic expositions over the whole field of theology and were known as "Summae."

The growth of medieval Scholasticism is usually divided into three stages, a formative period (eleventh and twelfth centuries), a period of consolidation (thirteenth century), and one of criticism (fourteenth and fifteenth centuries). In the first period Scholastic thought was influenced by Platonism derived from Augustine. Aristotelian dialectic became important in the twelfth century, largely through the works of Abelard. This period was dominated by the controversy about the nature of universals, but there was also Anselm's ontological argument for the existence of God.

The thirteenth century saw the culmination and consolidation of medieval

Scholasticism as evidenced in the works of Albertus Magnus, Thomas Aquinas, Bonaventura, and Duns Scotus. This period was especially enhanced by the acquisition of Aristotle's works in Latin translations and commentaries, and by the coming of the Franciscan and Dominican orders to the universities. The final period of medieval Scholasticism was one of criticism and decline. The critical attitude is found early in the works of Duns Scotus, then in Roger Bacon, and more explicitly in William of Occam. The chief philosopher of the fifteenth century, Nicholas of Cusa, is sometimes considered a medieval Scholastic while others regard him as a Renaissance philosopher.

The Scholastics can also be grouped according to schools of thought as well as by chronological periods. The schools were lined up according to their position on the relation between universal conceptions and external reality. The question was whether thought can supply a true account of the external world. One answer was known as *extreme realism*, which asserted that mental conceptions such as goodness, justice, or equality exist independently of the particular sense objects that exhibit such qualities. Erigena and Anselm fall into this group. Another solution was called *moderate realism*, which emphasized that particular things are the most real to us but universals are most real in themselves. For example, humanity exists as realized in just men and just actions. Albertus Magnus and Thomas Aquinas were the leading proponents of this position. Another approach known as *conceptualism* acknowledged the existence of universal ideas but attributed their formation to the activity of the mind. This approach is related closely to *nominalism*, the view that universal concepts (man, tree, etc.) have no separate and independent reality but are simply names used by the mind to organize individual things with similar characteristics into one class. Scholastics of this persuasion were Abelard, Duns Scotus, and William of Occam.

The emphases and results of Scholasticism are best understood through the lives and works of the scholars, which we will now review in chronological order.

a. John Scotus Erigena (810-77). Although he lived more than a hundred years earlier, John Scotus Erigena must be listed as the first great figure in theological Scholasticism. He was one of the first to put Augustine's teaching into practice by stating clearly the distinction between *auctoriatas* (Holy Scripture) and *ratio* (reason). He revived interest in Boethius' translations of the logical treatises of Aristotle and the pseudo-Dionysian corpus, thus playing a leading role in molding medieval thought. In his major work on the division of nature, there are strong overtones of pantheism, which caused the work to be condemned at Paris in 1210 and again by Honorius III at Senes in 1225. Although constantly involved in controversy, Erigena was a deeply original thinker and a great scholar, paving the way for others to come.

b. Anselm (1033-1109). Scholasticism is often seen as the independent treatment of the doctrines inherited from the past, and the man responsible for this view more than any other was Anselm of Canterbury. The son of a Lombard landowner, Anselm led several years of undisciplined life before he crossed the Alps into France and entered the monastic school at Bec in Normandy in 1059. By 1063 he had become prior and was already gaining a reputation for his teaching ability and spiritual intensity. He became abbot of Bec in 1078, and made several visits to England, where he was eventually named Archbishop of Canterbury in 1093. His time as archbishop was marked by deep conflict with King William Rufus and his successor Henry I over the issue of the lay control of the church. When Anselm refused to compromise the spiritual independence of his office he was forced into exile by Rufus, and was returned to office upon the death of the king. When Henry I, the new king, continued to practice lay investiture, consecrating bishops rather than deferring to clergy, Anselm went into exile again (1103). He was restored again in 1107 and spent the last years of his life introducing many reforms, encouraging regular synods, enforcing clerical celibacy, and suppressing the slave trade.

Anselm is listed in the camp of the realists because he maintained that reason must be employed to apprehend revealed truth. In the demonstration of his realist methodology, he is best remembered for his arguments on the existence of God and the atonement. In *Monologium* (a Soliloquy), he engaged in a meditation on the being of God, which he contended could be proved solely from the consideration of truth and goodness as intellectual concepts, without appeal to empirical fact.

In *Proslogium* (a Discourse), he developed fully his ontological argument for the existence of God. The basic premise of this argument is that God is that of which nothing greater can be conceived. However, that which is the highest conceivable cannot exist only in the intellect, for then conceiving of God as existing would be greater than not existing. Therefore, it follows that there is a highest being (God) in both intellect and reality. Sometimes Anselm is accused of contradicting his rational arguments with his orthodox Christian faith. He would respond, however, that it is faith that leads to the right use of reason. Following Augustine, who said that understanding is the reward of faith, Anselm gave his famous *credo ut intelligam*, "I believe in order that I may understand." To square this with his ontological argument for the existence of God, he would insist that it is faith in the first place that conceives of God as the highest and most perfect being.

In *Cur Deus Homo?* (Why God-Man?), Anselm dealt with the incarnation of Christ, and formulated his well-known theory of atonement by satisfaction. He rejected the ransom theories of atonement which had prevailed since the days of Gregory I. He insisted that man's sin is a debt to God, not to the devil, and that Christ's death alone has satisfied God's offended honor. As the title of the work suggests, he asks the fuller question: "On what basis or for which urgent reasons did God become man so that by His death, as we believe and confess, He thereby gave life to the world?" His answer is that (1) the honor of God demands that satisfaction or punishment follow sin; that (2) the satisfaction must be commensurate with the sin; that (3) God alone is able to render such adequate satisfaction; that (4) man ought to render the satisfaction; and that, therefore, (5) it can be done only by one who is both God and man. Since Christ did not sin, death was not required, so his death was an offering of his free will, not of debt, an offering which God accepted for the redemption of all men.

Although Anselm never developed a systematic theology, his ideas have stimulated philosophers and theologians for centuries. He has been especially influential in efforts to link faith and reason. His basis for intellectual understanding was held to be a living, experiential faith: "Whoever has not believed will not understand. For whoever has not gained experience will not understand."

c. *Peter Abelard* (1079-1142). One of the first great scholastics to blend philosophy with theology was Peter Abelard (or Abailard), who was about thirty years old when the great Anselm died. He was born in Brittany of aristocratic parents, and became a brilliant student at a very young age. He eventually became the most popular lecturer at Paris, first in philosophy and later in theology. His brilliant academic career was almost destroyed by his famous love affair with Heloise, the young niece of Fulbert, a canon of Notre Dame Cathedral in Paris. While serving as private tutor for the beautiful and educated Heloise, Abelard fathered a child by her, and afterward, to pacify her angry uncle, secretly married her. When ugly rumors continued to circulate, Heloise retired to a local convent to become a nun at Abelard's insistence. Fulbert was infuriated by what he considered Abelard's evasion of responsibility and hired a band of thugs to break in on him and emasculate him. Trying to retreat from all his personal problems and this most recent humiliation, Abelard became a Benedictine monk, but was soon teaching large groups of students again and embroiled in theological and ecclesiastical controversies. He was condemned for heresy at a council at Soissons in 1121 for his views on the Trinity; and again in 1140 at a council in Sens, he was condemned for his teachings on the Trinity, the atonement, free will, and original sin. Abelard's strongest opponent was the mystical and popular Bernard of Clairvaux, who regarded Abelard as a dangerous rationalist. When Abelard appealed to Rome, the pope upheld his condemnation and he was excommunicated. He found refuge at the monastery of Cluny, he and Bernard were reconciled, and he spent his last months praying and reading.

One of Abelard's most famous books was *Sic et Non* (Yes and No), in which he sought to answer questions on science, ethics, and theology from the Scriptures and the early church fathers. As a nominalist, Abelard held that universals are mere names; but he insisted that the universal's function is logical, enabling man to think. He believed in man's rational ability to arrive at truth. In fact, true faith is reached through knowledge and understanding. He rejected the concept of original sin as developed by Augustine, and stressed the motive behind the sin. Abelard's controversial view of the atonement is called the moral influence theory. In rejecting Anselm's satisfaction theory of atonement, he held that God is love and awakens in men gratitude and love for God, which results in a response of devotion and right conduct. Although highly controversial, both in his own day and succeeding generations, Abelard was the major Christian thinker of his period, and his views on faith and reason set the stage for the work of Thomas Aquinas in the thirteenth century.

d. *Hugo (Hugh) of St. Victor* (1096-1141). While less popular as a teacher, one of Abelard's contemporaries, Hugo of St. Victor, also correlated philosophy and theology, and left a permanent influence on the church's doctrine of the sacraments. The son of a Saxon count, Hugo was educated in Germany and became an Augustinian canon of St. Victor in Paris. His academic contributions included commentaries on several books of the Bible, treatises on the moral life, mysticism, and theology. His largest work was *De Sacramentis Fidei Christianae*, a comprehensive survey of theology which features his famous treatment of the sacraments. He contended that a sacrament is not only a sign or a symbol of a sacred thing, but it is the physical medium through which grace operates, thus leading to a strong doctrine of transubstantiation. Although the doctrine was already being vigorously debated, Hugo is credited wih solidifying its position, which led to making it an official doctrine of the Catholic Church at the Fourth Lateran Council less than a hundred years after Hugo's death.

e. *Peter Lombard* (1100-1164). A contemporary of Abelard, Bernard of Clairvaux, and Hugo of St. Victor, Peter Lombard was less original than any of the others, and yet he exercised influence on Catholic theology for centuries by producing the standard textbook of Catholic theology during the Middle Ages. Born in Novara (near Milan) in Lombardy, he was educated at Bologna and Reims, and went to Paris to teach in the cathedral school. For a brief time before his death he served as Archbishop of Paris. His major work was *Quatuor Libri Sententiarum* (the Sentences), which was arranged in four books on God and the Trinity, Creation and Sin, Incarnation and Redemption, and the Sacraments and Eschatology. Rather than being an original work, the Sentences was a compilation of the pertinent quotations of the fathers revered by the Catholic Church. It was, however, a masterpiece of skill and comprehensive treatment. Employing the dialectic method of question and answer, Lombard supplied students with a helpful aid to learning, and his work became the leading textbook for orthodox theology. In fact, it was deemed that the Bible and Peter Lombard's Sentences were the essentials for a theological education. Although his book was superseded by the *Summa* of Thomas Aquinas, it remained a basic text even to the Reformation. Lombard is also credited with being the first major figure to insist on the number seven in identifying the sacraments, a major development in the first teachings on the sacraments.

f. Thomas Aquinas (1225-1274). The intellectual giant who dominated the thirteenth century, the prince of the school men, and the theologian destined to wield unequaled influence over the theology of Roman Catholicism was Thomas Aquinas. Born at Roccasecca in Italy, Thomas was the youngest son of Count Landulf of Aquino, who was related to the emperor and king of France. At the age of five, Thomas was sent to the Benedictine school at Monte Cassino and from there to Naples, where he was impressed to seek admission to the recently founded Dominican Order. His family strongly opposed his intentions, and held him prisoner for fifteen months at Roccasecca. He refused to weaken, however, and in 1244 he joined the Dominican Order. He studied at Paris from 1245 to 1248 under the powerful influence of Albertus Magnus, who introduced him to the philosophy of Aristotle. In 1252 he became lecturer at the Dominican Convent of St. Jacques, where he wrote an outstanding defense of the mendicant orders. He became a Master of Theology in 1256 and subsequently taught at Anagni, Orvieto, Rome, Viterbo, Paris, and Naples. Several of his years in Italy were spent as a member of the papal court. When offered the post of Archbishop of Naples, he refused on the ground that he considered himself to be a scholar, teacher, and writer. He was deeply committed to his studies and writing, and drove himself relentlessly in the pursuit of truth. He was unusually tall and bulky, but his health was frail, and he was unable to stand up under the strain of his devotion to study. He died when he was only forty-nine years of age, but he left an enormous legacy of literary output.

During his lifetime, Thomas Aquinas wrote sixty books and many hymns, commentaries, and devotions. His two greatest works were *Summa Contra Gentiles*, designed to equip missionaries to the Moslems, and *Summa Theologica*, which crowned his theological thought, and formed the basis for subsequent Catholicism. The *Summa Theologica* (written over a period of nine years and still unfinished at his death) deals with the subjects of God, creation, the destiny of man, Christ as the way of man to God, the sacraments, and last things. The incarnation and the sacraments claimed Aquinas' special attention. In refuting the Franciscans, he maintained that the incarnation would not have taken place apart from the fall of man, and that the Virgin Mary was not immaculately conceived (he was eventually overthrown on this issue when, by the Papal Bull of Pius IX in 1854, Mary was declared to have been kept free from all stain of original sin from the first moment of her conception). Aquinas led the way for the doctrine of papal infallibility (which became official dogma in 1870) by insisting that the pope had been given the supreme authority for defending the faith.

In the matter of the sacraments, Aquinas held that all seven were instituted by Christ, one for each of the major happenings of a person's life: baptism, the Lord's Supper, penance, confirmation, marriage, ordination, and extreme unction. The sacraments were given as God's ordered means of conveying grace to man. Grace is a central theme and vital key in Aquinas' thought. He taught that there is no salvation apart from grace, and that it is only the infusion of grace which brings forgiveness. He insisted that the church is the vehicle of grace through the sacraments. After receiving grace, however, man cooperates with God, and merits eternal life through righteous works.

One of Aquinas' greatest achievements was the uniting of faith and reason so effectively that those who followed Aristotelian philosophy felt they could remain Christians. In fact, the goal of his life seemed to be the reconciliation of Aristotle and the Christian faith. Much of his philosophy, as well as theology, was hammered out as a rebuttal to Averroes (1126-98), a Mohammedan philosopher who had become an Aristotelian authority. The Averroists taught both a truth of reason and a truth of revelation (double truth). Aquinas rejected this, claiming that there is but one truth, which can be arrived at by different ways. He would not accept that faith and reason, or revelation and reason, are inherently antithetical. He believed, for instance, that through the observable data of the effects of God's activity in the world, reason can point to the existence of God and both produce and justify faith. His famous analogical arguments for God's existence are based on inferential knowledge: (1) Since things in this world move, necessitating an unmoved Mover, we can infer that God exists. (2) Since we can observe in the world the operation of cause and effect, which calls for a first Cause, we infer that God exists. (3) Since contingency is obvious in all creation, there must be something that is noncontingent, which is God himself. (4) Since we make value judgments, there must be a supreme value which we infer to be God. (5) Since there appears to be a purpose in nature, we can infer the highest purpose as God. Aquinas also spoke of God as *actus purus* (pure act) since in him every possible perfection was wholly realized. He portrayed God as self-subsistent but full of justice and mercy for his creatures. Aquinas himself, however, was rather short on mercy for the creatures known as heretics. He not only promoted their excommunication, but even approved their execution, holding that leading men's souls astray was a much greater evil than forgery or robbery.

In 1278 the Dominicans officially adopted Aquinas' teachings, and in

A woodcut engraving which documents many interesting points of the life and times of Thomas Aquinas, one of the most brilliant minds known in Christian history. The costumes and decor are extracted from the Works and Commentaries of St. Thomas Aquinas, *Venetian editions (1496, 1497).* (Historical Pictures Service, Chicago)

1323 he was canonized. In 1567 he was pronounced a Doctor of the Church, and in 1879 his writings were made required reading for all Catholic students of theology and philosophy. In 1880 he was made patron of all Catholic universities; and in 1923, his authority as a teacher was reiterated by Pope Pius XI. But even at his untimely death, Thomas Aquinas was already shaping the thinking of future theologians, and churchmen were already realizing that all who followed Aquinas would be obliged to work in regard and in reaction to his vast catalogue of ideas and systems.

g. *Duns Scotus* (1264-1308). One of those who built his theological system in reaction against much of what Aquinas taught was Duns Scotus, a medieval philosopher and Franciscan monk. He studied theology under William de Ware at Oxford and later taught there himself. He also taught at Paris and Cologne where he died suddenly at the age of forty-four. Duns Scotus agreed with Thomas Aquinas in asserting that revelation does not contradict reason, but many of his theological conclusions drastically opposed Thomism. The primary difference was that in the Thomist system, knowledge and reason held first place, whereas Duns Scotus gave the primacy to love and the will. He was the first great theologian to defend the Immaculate Conception, a doctrine opposed by Thomas. He also held that the incarnation would have taken place even if there had been no fall. The Scotist system was accepted by the Franciscans as their doctrinal guide, and exercised a profound influence during the Middle Ages. A strange testimony to its popularity was the practice of the humanists and the Reformers in using the word "dunce" to ridicule the subtleties of the schools based on Duns Scotus.

h. *Roger Bacon* (1214-1292). A Franciscan philosopher of the thirteenth century became the forerunner of modern science. Roger Bacon studied at Oxford and was one of the first to lecture on Aristotle in Paris. But whereas interest in Aristotle turned Aquinas deeper into theology, it caused Bacon to resign his chair of philosophy and devote himself to science and experimentation. While in his middle sixties, he was ordered by Pope Clement IV to present an account of his doctrines to him personally. Excited with the possibilities, Bacon expounded his system on an ambitious scale, dealing with such diverse subjects as the relation between philosophy and theology, grammar, mathematics, geography, perspective, physiology, and experimental science. His three major works are known as *Opus Majus*, *Opus Minus*, and *Opus Tertium*. Unfortunately, he did not receive the papal commendation he had anticipated because Clement died before the dispatch reached him.

Bacon was an extremely original writer, and a man of exceptional learning. He was, however, constantly embroiled in controversy because of his independent views, his rash temperament, his criticism of many medieval assumptions, and his continuing challenge to conventionalism. One evidence that he was ahead of his time was his stress on the need for a knowledge of Greek and Hebrew to accurately understand Scripture. The extent of his scientific experiments is uncertain, but there are good reasons to believe that he invented the telescope, the thermometer, and gunpowder. Theology and philosophy were becoming involved in the physical world of science.

i. William of Occam (1300-1349). The historical symbol of the decline of scholasticism was also a decisive contributor to that decline. William of Occam (or Ockham) was born at Ockham in Surrey, attended Oxford, and there became a Franciscan. He took the side of the Spirituals in the order and vigorously opposed the pope on the question of poverty. He also championed the cause of the emperor as against the pope, denied the pope all temporal authority, and advocated a radical separation of the church from the world.

William of Occam was a vigorous, critical, and independent thinker. He was the chief advocate of nominalism in the fourteenth century. One of his main principles (known as "Occam's razor") was that one should not assume the presence of more entities than is necessary. He denied all reality to universals apart from our thoughts. All that we can know, he insisted, are individual things. He maintained that Christian beliefs cannot be proved by reason, but must be accepted by faith. He rejected all of Aquinas' arguments for the existence of God because they appealed to reason, not faith. This was a complete divorce between reason and faith. Scholasticism had risen on the hopes and attempts of its brilliant school men to demonstrate that reason and faith are not antithetical. At the peak of scholasticism, Aquinas employed the best tools of Aristotelianism and Christianity to propound that some Christian beliefs can be affirmed by reason, and that even those which must be accepted by faith are not inconsistent with reason. William of Occam taught that none of the essential beliefs of Christianity could be proved to the satisfaction of man's reason, but they must be accepted on the authority of the church and of the Scriptures.

B. HOLY AND UNHOLY CRUSADES

While some leaders of the western church were devoted to improving and expanding Christianity along spiritual and intellectual lines, others were relentlessly pursuing expansion and solidification through the military crusades. In fact, the monastic reforms were concomitant with the crusades, which actually started a few years before the founding of the Cistercian Order. The crusades are generally identified as the military expeditions undertaken by Christians of the eleventh, twelfth, and thirteenth centuries for the recovery of the Holy Land from Islam. The name "crusades" comes from the Latin word for cross, as all crusaders bore the insignia of the cross on their clothing.

1. BACKGROUND OF THE CRUSADES
Several reasons have been given for the appearance of the crusades in this particular time frame of history. Some suggest that simple wanderlust or thirst for adventure was on the upswing in Europe, and others point to commercial aspects, such as the search for new trade routes to the East. There are, however, three distinct causes which belong particularly in church history.

a. Political. The original impetus for the crusades came from the request of the Byzantine emperors for aid against the Moslem Seljuk Turks. Since the early part of the eleventh century, the Byzantine Empire had been rocked by internal dissensions and foreign invasions. In the West the Normans conquered southern Italy, which had been a Byzantine possession since Leo III had wrested it from the West during the iconoclastic controversy. The most ominous threat came from the Seljuk Turks of Central Asia, who had overrun the Near East, destroyed a Byzantine army in Armenia, and threatened the existence of Constantinople itself. Responding to an appeal for help from the eastern emperor, Gregory VII (the great Hildebrand) raised an army of 50,000 in 1074 to send to Constantinople, but his investiture controversy with Henry IV made it impossible to organize the enterprise. Gregory's immediate successor lived only a year, and he was followed by Urban II, who became the leader of the First Crusade.

b. Ecclesiastical. Besides the political and territorial conflicts, the church was still anguishing over the breach between East and West which had been formally finalized in the Great Schism of 1054. There was always present the desire to heal this breach of the Catholic Church and to restore universal unity. Relations between East and West had greatly deteriorated, and contact was practically nonexistent. With the crusades, commerce and communication were reopened, and the western pope's hope for religious reconciliation as well. This hope was never realized, and in most cases the crusaders did more harm than good in effecting a reconciliation.

c. Devotional. The most often announced reason for the crusades was that of personal devotion to the religious pilgrimages to the Holy Land. For centuries Christians from the West had been making pilgrimages to the sacred cities and sites of Palestine as well as sites in continental Europe. The Cluny reform had increased the desire of the common people to visit the land which had given birth to their faith. Such pilgrimages had become

Six major crusades came out of medieval Europe during the years 1074 to 1270, attempting to regain the Holy Land and its sacred sites from the Moslems. (Historical Pictures Service, Chicago)

part of the penitential system, a means of expiating sin, which included such acts a fasting, recitation of psalms, religious journeys, prayers, and alms. It was sincerely believed that arduous pilgrimages to sacred places obtained unusual and long-lasting satisfaction for sins. An historian of that period, Leo Cassinensis, attributed the First Crusade directly to the fervor of penitents.

The Seljuk Turks, however, were not tolerant of Christian pilgrimages. As long as they occupied the Holy Land, there was repression and persecution of the pilgrimages. Thus, a chief factor in the crusades was to free Palestine from the Moslem Turks, return the sacred cities to Christian control, and secure the safety of the pilgrims. As previously noted, some of the monastic orders (Knights Hospitalers and Knights Templars) were organized for the purpose of protecting Christian pilgrims from the Turks.

2. DEVELOPMENT OF THE CRUSADES

The first crusade was the most successful of all, even though the twelfth and thirteenth centuries saw a strong development of the theology and organization of crusades. From the very beginning, the papacy was prominently involved in the crusades, issuing incentives to go on crusades, such as immunity from taxes and debts, protection of crusaders' property and families, and indulgences, which guaranteed the crusader's entry into heaven and reduced or eliminated his time in purgatory. The popes sent out crusade preachers, organized financial support, and provided transportation. The number of crusades is usually given as seven or eight, but actually it was a continuous movement, featuring many small expeditions as well as the large ones. In fact, after 1150 there was a steady stream of soldiers, pilgrims, and merchants from Europe to Syria.

a. The First Crusade (1096-1099). Responding to the appeal for aid from the Byzantine emperor, Alexius Comnenus, Pope Urban II convened the Council of Clermont (in southern France) in 1095. Speaking to both church dignitaries and common people, Urban delivered one of the most outwardly successful sermons of all time. He vividly portrayed the destruction and desecration of the Holy Land by the infidels. He avowed that Christ himself would lead the army that went to the rescue of such sacred places as Jerusalem. He promised the cancellation of debts, exemption from taxes, and a crown of eternal life to all participants. He urged them to return to the greatness of Charlemagne, to cease their intramural squabbles, and to unite in driving the "wicked race" from the Holy Land. At the conclusion of his sermon, the crowd shouted, *"Deus Vult! Deus Vult!"* (God wills it), which Urban made the battlecry of the crusades. The cross was designated the symbol of the crusades, with every participant sewing a cross on his garments, and some burning the cross into their flesh.

Before an official crusade could be organized, huge groups of excited pilgrims struck out for the East. Many of them raided and pillaged as they went, meeting with disaster in the Hungarian forests. Only one group, led by Peter the Hermit, reached Constantinople. The Emperor Alexius was appalled. He had looked for a mercenary army from Urban, and a religious horde of 50,000 had descended on his city. He provisioned them, extracted oaths of allegiance from them, and rushed them through the Bosphorus into Asia Minor, where the Turks ruthlessly butchered some 7,000 of them and piled their bodies in a heap to rot.

The first official crusade in 1096 was predominantly French. Its leaders were Godfrey of Lorraine, Hugh of Vermandois, Bohemund of Tarentum, Robert of Normandy, and Raymond of Toulouse. Their poorly organized followers drifted into Constantinople from different routes. The leaders argued with Comnenus about the disposition of the lands they planned to conquer, and finally invaded the Holy Land. In June of 1098 Antioch was captured and the discovery of the "Holy Lance" encouraged the crusaders. Quarrels broke out over the possession of the city, delaying further progress. At last Jerusalem itself was besieged and captured on July 15, 1099. The streets ran with blood in a massacre that did not spare even women and children. Godfrey of Bouillon (Lorraine) was appointed Governor of Jerusalem and "Defender of the Holy Sepulchre." Upon his death in 1100, his brother, Baldwin, established the Latin kingdom of Jerusalem and was crowned its king on Christmas Day, 1100.

b. The Second Crusade (1147-1149). The Latin kingdom of Jerusalem flourished for almost fifty years, but in 1144, Edessa was recaptured by the Emir Zengi. Pope Eugenius III charged the preaching of a new crusade to Bernard of Clairvaux in 1146, and Bernard, fearing that the infidels might recapture everything, trumpeted the call. This Second Crusade was led by Louis VII of France, who was doing penance for burning a church with 1,200 people in it, and by the Emperor Conrad III of Germany. Mainly because of quarrels between Louis and Conrad, the expedition was a failure, and most of the crusaders never reached the Holy Land at all. Conrad returned to Germany in 1148 and Louis to France the following year. A crusade preached by the man with the greatest name for sanctity in Europe, and led by royalty, had failed. Medieval Christians were astounded and angered, and sought for an explanation. The treachery of the Greeks appeared as a plausible reason for the defeats, and Bernard suggested that a campaign should be made against Constantinople, which eventually happened as the Fourth Crusade.

c. The Third Crusade (1188-1192). Through a consolidation of Mohammedan forces and the unification of various sections under Saladin, this powerful Moslem leader recaptured Jerusalem in 1187. Emperor Frederick

Barbarossa swore at the Diet of Mainz (1188) to undertake a new crusade to free Jerusalem from Saladin. He was joined by Philip Augustus of France and Henry II of England, but Frederick was drowned in 1190, and the rivalry between the kings of France and England practically disintegrated the crusade. Later, Richard I, who had succeeded his father as king of England, made a three-year peace with Saladin (1192), and small groups of crusaders were allowed to visit the Holy Sepulchre.

d. *The Fourth Crusade* (1202-1204). Pope Innocent III envisioned the papacy at the head of a great religious conquest, and inspired a crusade to accomplish his vision. The whole enterprise, however, became ensnared in a nightmare of crusaders fighting other Christians. The deposed emperor of Constantinople persuaded the crusaders to attack Constantinople and put him back on the throne. The rape of Constantinople left a bitter impression on the Orthodox people, and whatever ties may have still existed between them and Rome were severed. The son of the dethroned emperor had been established on the throne, but when he would not reward his benefactors, the crusaders stormed the city, deposed him, and set up Baldwin of Flanders as the first Latin Emperor of Constantinople. This Latin empire lasted from 1204 to 1261, and a Latin patriarch was appointed; but the western church made little impression on the eastern church. The Fourth Crusade, rather than being a success, had destroyed the bulwark which the eastern empire had formed against Islam, and further embittered the relations of eastern and western Christendom.

e. *Other Crusades.* After the disastrous results of the Fourth Crusade, there occurred the pathetic spectacle of the Children's Crusade. With the intention of "recapturing Jerusalem," great numbers of children gathered from France and West Germany to march on the Holy Land. Few of them ever got as far as actually leaving the south of France and Italy, and those who did soon perished. The historical basis for the "Pied Piper of Hamelin" is thought to be located in this sad development. At the Fourth Lateran Council of 1215, Innocent III proclaimed a fresh crusade for 1217. The military operation of this fifth official crusade took place mainly in Egypt, and is said to have resulted in the surrender of the "Holy Cross" to the Christians in 1221. The so-called Sixth Crusade was led by Emperor Frederick II, who secured through treaty the possession of Nazareth, Bethlehem, and Jerusalem, where he crowned himself king in 1229. For fifteen years Jerusalem was in the possession of Christians, but in 1244 it fell to the Moslems again. In 1245, at the Council of Lyons, Pope Innocent III preached a crusade against the heathen and against Frederick II (who had been excommunicated). The only response was an expedition by Louis of France, who was routed and captured in Egypt in 1250. After his release, he went on to the Holy Land, but being unable to do anything for the kingdom of Jerusalem, he returned home in 1254. The last crusade was also undertaken by Louis, with the aid of his brother, Charles of Anjou. Louis died in an attack on Tunis in 1270, and Charles concluded the crusade by negotiation. Soon thereafter the entire former kingdom of Jerusalem passed into the hands of the Moslems.

3. CONSEQUENCES OF THE CRUSADES

While it may appear that the crusades were totally ineffective, they did produce many changes in that part of the world, and even left indelible imprints on theology and sociology. For instance, a new concept of war emerged. Augustine had required that war be conducted by the state; now it was carried out by the laity with the blessing of the church. According to Augustine, the object of a just war was the vindication of justice as in the defense of life and property; now war was for the defense of the faith, and the right to exercise the faith. Augustine's code of just war had called for considerate treatment of the enemy, especially noncombatants, hostages and prisoners; but now such restraints were abandoned and wholesale massacre was justified by such biblical accounts as the conquest of Canaan by Joshua. What little territory had been gained by the crusaders could never offset the losses in the respect of non-Christians and the critical judgment of world history.

On the positive side, the crusades did unify Christendom for a while into an international community in a common purpose to expel the Turks. There was a revival of trade, commerce, manufacturing, and industry, which in turn promoted the rise of cities and the new classes of merchants, bankers, and craftsmen. The extensive travel and geographical exploration of the period contributed greatly to the rising intellectual life in the new universities of Europe. Campaigning for the crusades stimulated a spirit of devotion and a new style of fervent, imaginative preaching.

Within the structure of the church, the crusades left a profound impact. The pope had become the supreme ruler of western Europe, the head of armed Christendom. Financial contributions to the crusades became the basis for a regular tax claimed by the pope. Interest was stimulated in relics and sacred places; and when Palestine was again lost to Christendom, people developed other sacred places and relics. For example, it was during the thirteenth century that the use of the rosary came into prominence, influenced perhaps by the Moslem ritual known as *tasbih*. The Crusades influenced the system of absolution. In the beginning, absolution was granted only to those who personally participated in a crusade. Pope Celestine III (1191-1198) granted a partial absolution to those who contributed money toward a crusade, and Pope Innocent III (1198-1216) granted complete absolution for those who sent a substitute to the field. The crusades promoted a spirit of religious intolerance and set the stage for the Inquisition. Popes proclaimed crusades, not only against Moslems, but also against heretics and dissenters within Christendom.

From the standpoint of the history of Christianity, the crusades are significant because through them western Christianity was projected into the eastern Mediterranean, because of the negative effects on relations between the western and eastern divisions of the Catholic Church, and because of the repercussions on Latin Christianity, as suggested above. Obviously, the crusades were neither a clear evil nor a pure benefit to the church and to the world.

C. NOBLE AND IGNOBLE POWER

In the thirteenth century the church reached its pinnacle of power in western Europe. Never before had the church exercised so much authority and influence over so many aspects of culture and society. The spiritual awakenings of monasticism and scholasticism had enlarged the vision of churchmen as to the possibilities for claiming the souls and minds of men. The dubious benefits of the crusades contributed to the growing strength of the papacy. With the pope acting as the head of armed Christendom, princes had become accustomed to following his leadership and obeying his orders. The dream of the church as the agent of God in directing all earthly affairs had become almost a complete reality. When compared with the church under persecution in the dark days of the Roman Empire, the medieval church was the sovereign mistress of society. Would she be able to maintain that posture, and was it the proper posture in the first place for the servant-church of the humble Christ? These questions persisted until they forced the answers painfully from the unfolding drama.

1. PAPACY AT ITS HEIGHT

When Hildebrand launched the Gregorian reforms of the eleventh century, he restored integrity to the papacy and began a long period of ascending respect which could not be abated even by less worthy pontiffs. In addition, the following century produced several outstanding popes who continued to build toward the apex of papal power in the thirteenth century.

a. Great Popes of the Twelfth Century. Brief mention should be made of some of those outstanding figures in this formative period. Innocent II (1130-1143) was successful in opposing the Holy Roman emperors of his reign and overcoming two rivals who claimed the papacy. He compared the relationship of bishops to the pope to that of serfs to their sovereign, confirming the hold of Rome over all other sees. Eugenius III (1145-1153) was a dedicated pupil of Bernard of Clairvaux. As pope, Eugenius appointed Bernard, his former teacher, to preach the Second Crusade. He encouraged an intellectual revival and improved the educational standards in the church. He demonstrated the power of pope over bishops, which Innocent I had articulated by deposing the powerful archbishops of York, Mainz, and Rheims for disobedience. Ironically, Eugenius spent most of his pontificate outside Rome because Arnold of Brescia, one of Abelard's disciples, had denounced the temporal power of the papacy and aided a civic revolt which set up a rival government for some ten years. Adrian IV (1154-1159), the only Englishman to ever serve as pope, expelled Arnold from Rome and had him executed in 1155. He demanded full homage from Frederick I (Barbarossa) before consenting to crown him. His quarrel with Barbarossa over the emperor holding his crown as a *beneficium* from the pope became acute in the papacy of Alexander III. Adrian exercised overt authority in dealing with the royalty of Sicily, France, and Burgundy. He is credited with granting to Henry II of England the overlordship of Ireland.

Alexander III (1159-1181) was an expert in canon law who further extended the papal power over secular princes. He was bitterly opposed by Barbarossa who set up a rival pope, precipitating a schism which lasted for seventeen years, until Barbarossa was decisively defeated at Venice in 1177 and knelt to kiss Alexander's feet. During his pontificate, Thomas Becket, Archbishop of Canterbury, was engaged in a heated controversy with England's King Henry II over the issue of the independence of church courts. Becket was driven into exile in France, and returned to Canterbury for Christmas in 1170, where he was murdered before his own high altar. Christian society was outraged, and Alexander enforced severe penance on Henry and exacted strong recognition from him. Alexander also canonized Becket in 1173, and established a rule that all future canonizations should be only with the authority of the pope. Alexander convened the third Lateran Council in 1179, where further measures were taken for reform.

b. Innocent III. The papacy reached its highest point of influence in the political life of Europe during the pontificate of Innocent III, who reigned from 1198 to 1216. Of aristocratic lineage on his father's side, and Roman nobility on his mother's side, Innocent III was one of the most learned and powerful men of his day. He was a cardinal-deacon by the time he was twenty-nine, and elected pope before he was forty and before he had even been ordained a priest. While his great diplomatic skills enabled him to wield power over kings and princes, he was also blessed with the fortune of well-timed events. When the formidable Frederick I Barbarossa died, his son Henry VI became emperor and began a power play to diminish the papacy. But he died in his early thirties, leaving his three-year-old son Frederick II. The boy's mother also died the year Innocent became pope, and she had designated the pope as guardian of her son and regent of Sicily. Innocent became and remained virtual ruler throughout western Europe, Spain, Norway, and England.

It was Innocent who preached and organized the Fourth Crusade of 1204. This was the crusade which was diverted from its original purpose of taking Jerusalem, and ended up capturing Constantinople. As we have already noted, this led to the setting up of the first Latin government and patriarch in Constantinople. This enabled Innocent to extend the control of Rome over large territories which had been previously committed to the Byzantine wing of the church. These gains in the East proved to be temporary, but the fact that they were made at all was significant.

The peak achievement of Innocent's reign was the convening of the highly influential Fourth Lateran Council in 1215. It would be three hundred and fifty years later, at Trent, before such a comprehensive work would be done. The Fourth Lateran Council established new reforms, improvement of life in the Christian community, better education for the clergy, precise doctrines such as a formula on the Trinity, transubstantiation, and annual confession to a priest. This council symbolized the mastery of the papacy over every feature of society, even confirming the shameful isolation of Jews from general society, requiring them to wear special badges, which began the sad saga of the Jewish people living in isolated ghettos.

Innocent III was the first to use the title "Vicar of Christ." He declared that Peter and all his successors were "left the governance not only of the church but of the whole world." He thought of the papal office as semidivine, "set in the midst between God and man, below God but above man." He affirmed himself as Melchizedek, the priest-king who would bring a centralized Christian society into being. The theories of papal supremacy over all human spiritual and secular affairs were actualized in Innocent III. He made kings his vassals, created the Inquisition, promoted the Fourth Crusade, and engineered the Fourth Lateran Council. His Christian society, ruled over by the pope, was short-lived, but an active reality nonetheless. His awesome success, however, bore an even more awesome price. More blood was shed during Innocent III's reign than at any time in papal history. Dissenters could not be tolerated and were dealt with in great severity.

2. DISSENT IN THE OPEN

While Innocent appeared to be controling all of Christendom, there were those who began to raise their voices against the worldliness of the church. One of the earliest dissenters was Arnold of Brescia, whom we have already recognized as having engineered the ousting of Pope Eugenius III from Rome. Papal worldliness and obsession for dominion brought overt and covert protests. Also, the development of national, sovereign states, and the rise of the universities contributed to new allegiances and new thought.

a. The Cathari. A widespread protest against Roman Catholicism was organized by the Cathari, also called Albigenses because of their large settlement near Albi, France. Ecclesiastically, the Cathari said that the true church endures, and does not have to persecute in order to do so.

Philosophically, they believed in a dualism of body and soul, material and spiritual worlds, evil and good; and thus they practiced severe asceticism in order to rid the soul of all impurities (Cathari stood for "pure"). Sociologically, they rejected marriage, reproduction, war, property, and oaths. The lower class of Cathari were not required to adhere strictly and were able to propagate the sect. Theologically, they believed that Christ was an angel, not a human, and that he neither died nor rose from the dead. They rejected the cross and the sacraments, and anticipated reincarnation.

Obviously, the Cathari were outside the mainstream of Christianity, even though they avidly read the New Testament, preached its morality and emphasis on love, and made vernacular translations. In line with their dualistic concepts, they maintained that there were two churches, the true one being their own, and the evil one being Rome. Their open and blatant criticism of Rome was destined to bring them to a tragic confrontation.

b. The Waldenses. Another influential group of dissenters were the Waldenses, named after their founder Peter Waldo (or some contend they were so-called after the *vallis densa*, shaded valley, in which they long existed). Peter Waldo (d. 1217) was a wealthy merchant of Lyons who took literally the injunction of Jesus to the rich young ruler to sell all, give to the poor, and follow him. Waldo paid all his creditors, provided for his wife and family, gave away all that remained, and began a career of itinerant preaching. He tried to imitate Christ in everything, even in his manner of dress and life-style.

Preaching in both city and country, Waldo soon attracted a large following, which came to be known as the "Poor Men of Lyons." At first they resembled the movement which Francis of Assisi was to begin some three decades later. When the archbishop of Lyons forbade them to preach, Peter Waldo went to Rome during the Third Lateran Council to appeal to the pope for permission to preach. He was praised for his poverty by Pope Alexander III, but told that he could preach only when approved by local clergy. He was also placed under suspicion of being an Arian because he said that Mary was the mother of Christ, not the mother of God. When local clergy refused permission for them to preach, the Waldenses affirmed that they ought to obey God rather than man and continued to preach. In 1184 they were excommunicated by the Council of Verona, and were soon lumped with the Cathari in the inquisitions and persecutions.

The beliefs of the Waldenses were based on simple adherence to the Bible above all man-made creeds. They refused to recognize either pope or bishop and taught that the church of Rome could not be the head of the Catholic Church since it was corrupt. They held to the right of laymen to preach, but did have their own organized clergy. They rejected prayers for the dead, the doctrine of purgatory, Latin prayers, church music, mandatory confession, and all of the sacraments except baptism and the Lord's Supper.

They upheld the Bible as the symbol of Christianity rather than the cross, they refused to say the Apostle's Creed, to venerate saints, images, or relics, and they opposed tithes, indulgences, and capital punishment.

The main thrust of the Waldenses was to purify the church by a return to simplicity. Confrontation with the papacy was inevitable, for it was unthinkable that the Roman church would annul its sacraments, void its priesthood, and admit that faith in God could come through some means other than the prescribed way of Rome. Thus the Waldenses were branded as heretics, and the Catholic Church and civil authorities sought to eliminate them, either by persuasion or force. They were virtually annihilated in France and Spain, and those who survived found refuge in the Italian Alps, where they surfaced again during the Reformation, and indeed, where some persist to the present time.

The Waldenses and Cathari constituted the main bodies of protest in the Middle Ages, but other protests were also expressed by the free-thinking Beghards, Bogomiles, Humiliati, Runcarii, and Amalricians. A strong apocalyptic dissenter by the name of Joachim caused considerable agitation and laid the foundation for apocalyptic criticism of the worldly church, and inspired the later Spiritual Franciscans, who were also victims of the dread Inquisition.

3. INQUISITION ON THE RAMPAGE

When the Catharist heresy began to threaten not only religion but all the institutions of contemporary society, Innocent III inaugurated the era of the Inquisition, although it was not officially instituted until 1233 under Gregory IX. Technically speaking, *inquisition* denotes the juridical persecution of heresy by special ecclesiastical courts. In the early days of the church, punishment for heresy was simply excommunication. Physical punishment was generally disapproved by the early Fathers, but after Christianity became the official religion of the empire, secular princes viewed heresy as a crime against the state, for which confiscation or even death could be inflicted.

The recorded cruelties against the Cathari date from 1145 when several were burned to death in Cologne. In 1161 thirty of them were branded and flogged at Oxford. In England, Henry II blinded and castrated all suspected of being Cathari. The Councils of Rheims (1148), Third Lateran (1179), and Verona (1184) condemned the Cathari, and directed princes to take action against them. In 1199 Pope Innocent III declared heresy a capital crime, and launched a crusade against the Cathari that lasted from 1207 until 1244.

The bloody warfare was climaxed by the massacre at Beziers, where the papal legate, upon being asked if Catholics should be spared, replied, "Kill them all, for God knows his own," resulting in the slaughter of 20,000 men, women, and children. At Minerve, 140 Cathari were burned and hundreds had their ears and noses cut off. Such violence continued throughout the thirteenth century, with Innocent III granting absolution of all sins (plenary indulgence) and acquisition of new lands to those crusading against the heretics. In 1215, the Fourth Lateran Council provided for the secular punishment of heretics, the confiscation of their property, excommunication for sympathizers, and complete forgiveness of sins for those cooperating.

Pope Honorius III, successor to Innocent III, continued the crusade against the Cathari. In 1224, Emperor Frederick II ordered the burning of heretics, an order that was approved and upheld by Pope Gregory IX in 1231. Under Gregory IX the holy office of the Inquisition was instituted and systematized inquisitorial rules were set up, with the Dominicans being given the official administration of those rules. The *Inquisitor's Manual* of 1300 discloses that the inquisitor was not subject to the law, but only to the papacy; that the accused heretic could have no counsel, and was not allowed to know his accusers; that testimony of children and criminals could be used against the accused but not for him; that the accused was always considered guilty until proven innocent; that confession could possibly reduce the death penalty to life imprisonment; that even then he would lose his tongue for having spoken against the church; and that any witnesses speaking for the accused were guilty of abetting heresy and would also be persecuted. The Synod of Toulouse which legitimized these rules also denounced all vernacular translations, and forbade the laity to possess the Scriptures.

In 1233 Pope Gregory IX ordered the Dominicans to exterminate the Cathari, and by the end of the fourteenth century this sect had disappeared. In 1252 Pope Innocent IV authorized torture as a means of getting information and confessions. The inquisition as a means of stamping out heresy and dissent continued to flourish and reached its peak in the Spanish Inquisition at the end of the fifteenth century under the tyrannical Grand Inquisitor Torquemada. This version of the Inquisition was originally directed against converts from Judaism and Islam, but was also used against Protestants. In fact, there was a general resurgence of the Inquisition to curb Protestantism in 1542, and Inquisition as a tool of the Catholic Church was not officially ended until 1834. During these seven hundred years of cruel oppression the church had left a dark stain in the pages of history. One is strained to find a resemblance between the oppressing Christians of the Middle Ages and the oppressed Christians in the earlier Roman Empire.

VII

A HOUSE DIVIDED: DISRUPTION AND DECLINE (1305-1517)

*Every kingdom divided against itself
is brought to desolation; and every city or
house divided against itself shall not stand.*

MATTHEW 12:25

A. The Eastern Orthodox Movement
B. The Nationalist Movement
    1. The Clash Between Church and Crown
    2. The Babylonian Captivity
    3. The Papal Schism
C. The Conciliar Movement
    1. The Council of Constance
    2. The Council of Basel
D. The Critical-Reform Movement
    1. John Wycliffe
    2. John Hus
    3. Mysticism
E. The Renaissance Movement
    1. Humanism in Literature
        a. Lovato Lavati
        b. Dante Alighieri
        c. Francesco Petrarch
        d. Giovanni Boccaccio
        e. Leonardo Bruni
        f. Lorenzo Valla and Nicholas of Cusa
        g. Johann Reuchlin
        h. Desiderius Erasmus
    2. Realism in Culture
        a. Renaissance Art
        b. Renaissance Architecture
        c. Renaissance Expansion
    3. Monopolism in Religion
        a. Pope Nicholas V
        b. Pope Calixtus III
        c. Pope Pius II
        d. Pope Paul II
        e. Pope Sixtus IV
        f. Pope Innocent VIII
        g. Pope Alexander VI
        h. Pope Julius II
        i. Pope Leo X

The fourteenth and fifteenth centuries are usually considered in church history as the period of great decline. Yet this should not be taken to indicate a spiritual sterility, an intellectual vacuum, or a social passivity. On the contrary, this was a period of vitality, creativity, and fanatical dedication. The syndrome of decline is applied to the declining prestige and power of the papacy, the waning quality and influence of the monastic orders, and the disintegration of the unity of church and state. Various factors and many individuals contributed to both the decline and the vitality of the period. Most of the story of these two centuries can be told under the discussion of five major movements.

A. THE EASTERN ORTHODOX MOVEMENT

As we recall, the eastern schism of 1054 had dissolved what little communion there had been with the West. In 1204 the western crusaders had captured and looted Constantinople in the diverted Fourth Crusade. For much of the thirteenth century the power of the Greek emperor was replaced by the Latin kingdom of Constantinople, making the rift between East and West even wider. By 1261, however, the Greeks had retaken their capital city and ousted the uncouth westerners. Clement V, the first Avignon pope, attempted a crusade to recapture Constantinople, but with no success. In the middle of the fourteenth century, both East and West grew closer together for mutual protection against the "savage hordes" of the Ottoman Turks. An ecumenical council was proposed to consider the union of Greek Orthodox and Roman Catholic Christianity, but the rivalry between popes and councils in the West prevented such an occurrence. Repeated efforts finally culminated in a decree of union, but it came too late. Within the year (1453), Constantinople, the ancient capital of Byzantium, the stronghold of Orthodox Christianity, was captured by the Muslim Turks. The conflict between Roman and Greek Christianity became a moot issue.

Ivan III (the Great) of Moscow is regarded as the first national sovereign of Moscow. Soon after the fall of Constantinople, Ivan married the niece of the last Byzantine emperor who had been killed at Constantinople. This union established the claim of the Russian rulers to be the successors of the Byzantine emperors and the protectors of Orthodox Christianity. Ivan took the title of tsar (Caesar) and made Moscow the capital of the eastern empire.

The Russian diocese was the only eastern diocese now free of alien control, and Moscow was the only major city ruled by a Christian prince. Profound theological significance was seen in these unfolding events, and Russian church theorists developed the claim of Moscow as "The Third Rome." The first Rome had fallen because of heresy, and the second Rome (Constantinople) had fallen because it had conspired with the papacy; but the third Rome (Moscow) would defend and discipline the life of faith until the end of history. The holy mission had passed from Byzantium to Moscow, and the tsar was declared to be God's vicar on earth, the supreme head of the state and the church. With renewed vitality and a revival of monasticism, the Orthodox Church made great gains throughout Russia, and the hope of the West to regain the eastern wing of the church was shattered again. The popes and councils had thoroughly mishandled the reunion efforts and had come too late to the defense of Constantinople. In 1472 a synod in Constantinople speaking for the Orthodox church formally repudiated the decree of union which had come from the Council of Florence in 1452 and anathematized those who had adhered to it. The house of Christendom remained divided, and the mutual strength which each needed from the other was never forthcoming.

B. THE NATIONALIST MOVEMENT

The "house" of medieval Christianity had built its roof over all of society. If its foundations could be said to have rested on the Scriptures and the church, then its columns or walls of support were made from the laws and powers of the state. In the thirteenth and fourteenth centuries, the state columns began to pull loose and to assert themselves as rivals to the church foundations. The rise of nations and the claim to state sovereignty challenged and defied the authority and power of the papacy, and the house tottered and swayed.

1. THE CLASH BETWEEN CHURCH AND CROWN

The entity of nations as we know them today was not prevalent at the beginning of the thirteenth century. Although they were separated geographically, philosophically, culturally, and linguistically, the peoples of what we know as Europe (a term that came into being in the fifteenth century) were bound in their allegiance to the two great universal powers of the Middle Ages, the empire and the church. An emerging national consciousness, however, began to consolidate the populace of the respective lands in common traditions, common language, centralized government, and naturally defensible borders.

The three most powerful western monarchies evolved along identical lines, and by the end of the fifteenth century all had solidified their form. In England the new monarchy dates from 1485, in France from 1491, and in Spain from 1492. In the developing process, the kings took over the roles of the emperors. In fact, the open slogan was *Rex est imperator in regno suo* (The king is the emperor in his own domain). At the same time, the sovereigns sought to control the church in their territories. In the sixteenth century the king of England came very close to saying that he was the pope in his own domain.

England's quarrel with the papacy went back many years and involved many issues. In 1277, Robert Kilwardby, Archbishop of Canterbury, had condemned some of Aquinas' teachings, and again in 1284, John Pecham, Archbishop of Canterbury, did the same. Also, there was the chafing matter of feudal tribute to which King John had committed the country by making England a fief of the papacy in 1213. This tribute was no longer being paid, to the displeasure of the papacy; and in 1279, legacies of land to the church were forbidden by law. In 1351, England enacted the Statute of Provisors which denied the papacy the right to fill English sees, a move primarily to keep foreigners from settling in lucrative English bishoprics. Then the Statute of Praemunire in 1353 forbade appeals to the courts of Rome, and in 1366 parliament declared that the king could not give the kingdom to the pope as a fief. John Wycliffe and other Englishmen who were to rebel against Rome were not innovators working in a vacuum. The atmosphere of independence was pregnant with the seeds of rebellion and reform.

It was in France, however, where the church and crown came to its most heated contest. Because much of its territory had been lost to the Moslems, and because the resources of Italy were not sufficient to finance the papacy's international program, the church imposed tithes on all local churches throughout Europe. The crusade tax had also been continued, although the crusades had long ceased. Kings in turn began to appropriate the wealth of the churches within their territories for their own national interests. King Philip of France levied taxes on the French clergy for one-half their annual income. In 1296, Pope Boniface VIII replied with his famous *Clericis Laicos* in which he forbade the clergy to pay taxes to secular powers, threatening with excommunication any layman who exacted and any churchman who paid such taxes. In England, King Edward reacted by outlawing the clergy in England; and in France, King Philip prohibited the export of money from France, blocking the flow of revenue to Rome. Parliament backed Edward, and the Estates-General backed Philip.

Unable to assess adequately the nationalistic movement, Boniface completely polarized the situation in 1302 by issuing his bull, *Unam Sanctam*, the most extravagant claim to universal temporal sovereignty to come out of the Middle Ages. He declared that since Christ was king as well as priest, he had given two keys and two swords to Peter. He asserted that all temporal power should be directed by a priest, and that resisting the pope was the same as resisting an ordinance of God. It is this bull which declares that no one can be saved without allegiance to the pope: "We therefore declare, say, and affirm that submission on the part of every person to the bishop of Rome is altogether necessary for salvation."

Philip responded by summoning an assembly which condemned Boniface and called for a general council to try him for heresy and immorality. Boniface replied by preparing a bull of excommunication against Philip, but the king enlisted a band of mercenaries to capture and torture the pope at his summer residence of Anagni near Rome. Friendly Italian forces freed him, but he died a month later. The fervor of a rising nationalism and the obstinance of a diminishing papacy had come to a desperate confrontation on a personal and physical level.

2. THE BABYLONIAN CAPTIVITY

Boniface's successor, Pope Benedict XI, wanted to make peace with Philip; but he felt morally obligated to issue a bull against the outrage inflicted upon Boniface at Anagni. Benedict died one month later under mysterious circumstances, and it was eleven months before his successor, Pope Clement V, was chosen. The cardinals at Rome had elected Clement, but he was crowned at Lyon, and never returned to Italy. Because Clement was completely dominated by France, and because Rome had become unstable and unsafe for the popes, the seat of the papacy was moved in 1309 to Avignon, a little principality in the south of France. This city was the papal residency for almost seventy years, a period which became known as the Babylonian Captivity, harking back to the seventy-year captivity of the Jews.

The first Avignon pope, Clement V, condemned Boniface, was subservient to Philip, and led the papacy in becoming a French institution rather than a universal power. All seven of the Avignon popes were French. Clement assisted Philip in using the Inquisition as a tool of the state, tried the Knights Templars in France for heresy, and executed sixty-nine of them. With the French crown supporting the papacy, the Avignon popes became the most powerful potentates in western Europe, and Avignon itself the most cosmopolitan city in fourteenth-century Europe.

The church continued to decline morally, however, and general unrest abounded. Many clergy practiced pluralism (holding two paying offices at once), and absenteeism (not living in the post from which their income came). There was also a growing distress over the papacy's prolonged absence from Rome. The popes were being constantly urged to return to their proper place; and Pope Urban V went to Rome in 1367, but was so distressed over the deplorable state of the churches that he returned to Avignon after less than three years. His successor, Pope Gregory XI, was dedicated from the outset of his reign to move the papacy back to Rome, which he accomplished in 1377. The "Babylonian Captivity" had ended, yet that move precipitated an almost fatal crisis for the Catholic Church.

3. THE PAPAL SCHISM

There are three great schisms in Christian history: the East-West Schism of 1054, the Protestant Schism of the sixteenth century, and the Papal Schism in the latter part of the fourteenth century. The papal schism began soon after the death of Gregory XI in 1378. The people of Rome were still rejoicing that the papacy had been moved back to their city, and they insisted that Gregory's successor should be a Roman, or at least an Italian. Although most of the cardinals were French, they yielded to the pressure and elected a native of Naples, who took the title of Urban VI. The cardinals soon became unhappy with their choice, for Urban VI was tactless, obstinate, and severe. He rebuked the cardinals for their worldliness, pluralism, simony, and absenteeism. He refused even to consider their suggestion of returning to the luxury of Avignon, so they returned without him. Back in Avignon, the cardinals declared Urban an illegal pope since they had elected him under duress. When he refused to resign, they elected another pope—a prince related to the king of France, who took the title of Clement VII. Urban rejected this action and appointed a new group of cardinals.

The nations of Europe were forced to decide where their allegiance lay. Spain, France, Scotland, and part of Germany lined up behind the Avignon pope. Italy, most of Germany, England, Scandinavia, Bohemia, Poland, Flanders, and Portugal supported Urban in Rome. The rising nationalism began to assert its importance in the life of the church more than ever. When Urban VI died, another Roman was chosen to succeed him, and Clement VII continued on in Avignon for another sixteen years. Neither Clement's personal life nor his public service were admirable, but he was succeeded by a more capable and upright Benedict XIII, who served for twenty-three years.

Many efforts were made, especially by the university leaders, to convince both popes to resign and let a new one be elected who could reunite the church. Both popes eventually agreed, but neither followed through. Finally, the cardinals from both Rome and Avignon met in a council at Pisa in 1409, deposed both popes and elected a new one. To their surprise, neither the Roman nor Avignon pontiff would recognize their action. Thus, the Catholic Church had three popes ruling concurrently, each supported by the different states of Europe. This intolerable situation created an uproar among the intellectuals as well as the grass roots populace.

C. THE CONCILIAR MOVEMENT

Since the first great ecumenical council at Nicaea in 325, the church had intermittently held general councils to express the mind of the church and take appropriate action. Indeed, the precedent for calling general councils went back to the Jerusalem council in the fifteenth chapter of Acts. Now, as the church was faced with a humiliating impasse in the spectacle of three reigning popes, strident voices throughout Christendom called for the convening of councils to untangle the confusion. The Council of Pisa was forerunner of the conciliar movement, although it is not officially recognized as representative of the entire church. In the first place, it was not summoned by a pope, and in the second place it widened the schism rather than healing it. A council which would be accepted as authority would need to be convened by both a pope and an emperor, and it had to be strong enough to accomplish its purpose.

1. THE COUNCIL OF CONSTANCE
The first pope to be appointed by the Council of Pisa was Alexander V, who died shortly after and was replaced by John XXIII. This pope so disgraced the name of John that it was not taken again by a pope until the middle of the twentieth century. Nevertheless, John XXIII and Emperor Sigismund managed to put together a dual summons to a general council, which was convened in Constance (in what is now Switzerland) in 1414. The Council of Constance was the most widely representative of the church that had ever met in western Europe, and is counted by the Roman Catholic Church as the sixteenth official ecumenical council. It was designed to end the papal schism, to bring about the reform of the church, and to deal with various heresies. In the four years that the council lasted all of these issues were addressed vigorously.

At the outset, the council called for the abdication of all three popes: John XXIII of Pisa, Gregory XII of Rome, and Benedict XIII of Avignon. Gregory promised to abdicate if John would. When John saw that the sentiment of the council was against him, and when he learned that his enemies were about to expose his "evils," he fled in disguise from Constance to Austria. Some felt that the absence of a pope (the other two never attended) deprived the council of its authority, but the Emperor Sigismund stepped in and enforced its continuance. Then a dramatic and far-reaching step was taken by the issuance of the "Articles of Constance" in which the council was declared to derive its authority directly from God, and every Christian, even the pope, was bound to obey its decisions under pain of ecclesiastical punishment.

John XXIII was brought back to Constance as a prisoner, and deposed for simony, abetting of schism, and a scandalous life. The pope who had convoked the council was its first casualty. Next Gregory XII resigned, and he was made a cardinal, dying two years later at the age of ninety, honored and respected. Benedict XIII refused to abdicate, although Emperor Sigismund journeyed to Avignon himself to implore him to comply. So the council declared him a perjurer, a heretic, an obstacle to union, and deposed him. Benedict, however, insisted until his death (1423) that he was the rightful pope. He was succeeded by two more who tried to maintain the Avignon line; but they had such a meager following, that the venture soon died. All of the Avignon popes after Gregory XI are officially listed as antipopes by the Roman Catholic Church.

The importance of the rise of nationalism was clearly manifested at the Council of Constance. When difficulties developed at the beginning with John's lack of cooperation, the council changed the usual method of the personal vote (which would have given his supporters a majority) to the vote by nations. The council was divided into five nations for the purpose of voting: England, Germany, France, Italy, and Spain. Deputies from these nations joined with the cardinals in electing a new pope, Cardinal Oddone Colonna, from an old Roman family. He took the title of Martin V and presided over the remaining sessions of the council. The papal schism had ended, but the conciliar movement was not over.

2. THE COUNCIL OF BASEL

By declaring itself the supreme governing body in Christendom, the Council of Constance had changed the papacy from an absolute to a constitutional monarchy. This change did not last long, but it did set a precedent for Vatican II of the twentieth century. The constitution adopted at Constance provided that another council should be held in five years, another in seven years, and one every ten years "forever after." Accordingly, Martin V called a general council at Pavia in 1423, which had to be moved to Siena because of an outbreak of the plague, and then had to be terminated for lack of interest and attendance.

Seven years later, Martin V reluctantly called the Council of Basel, but he died before it convened in 1431. The new pope, Eugenius IV, immediately involved the council in a confrontation of papal versus conciliar authority. Unhappy with the attitude of the council, the pope ordered it dissolved. Emperor Sigismund told the council to continue. The council did continue, ordering the pope to submit or be held in contempt. Eugenius capitulated, revoked his bull of dissolution, and gave the council his support. An ugly antipapal mood caused Eugenius to flee the city of Rome that year. Papal prestige, at a low ebb, was dealt another blow when the eminent scholars Nicholas of Cusa and Lorenzo of Valla demonstrated conclusively the forgery of the Donation of Constantine, the foundation on which claims for papal civil sovereignty had been built.

Nicholas of Cusa gave strong support for conciliar authority over papal authority, stating that the pope was just one member of the church; that the church (not the pope) was infallible and could transfer that infallibility to a general council; and that the council was superior to the pope and could depose him. Armed with such strong antipapal support, the Council of Basel made sweeping declarations, abolishing many of the sources of revenue for the papacy, filling high posts of clergy by election rather than by papal appointment, regulating the age and number of cardinals, and claiming the right to grant indulgences. The council had gone too far, and many of its strongest supporters, including Nicholas of Cusa, began to criticize its excessive overreach of power and to swing back to the support of the papacy.

The major crisis which facilitated the decline and demise of the conciliar movement was the effort to reunite the western and eastern wings of the church. In our section on the Eastern Orthodox movement, we noted that both East and West sought reconciliation for mutual defense against the Ottoman Turks, but that the western squabble between pope and council prevented an effective union. It was the Council of Basel and Pope Eugenius IV which produced this sad state. The Greek delegation preferred to meet the Latins in an Italian city which would be more convenient than Avignon in France, which the council suggested. Eugenius deferred to the Greeks, setting Ferrara and later Florence as the site for reunion discussions. A portion of the cardinals compiled, accompanied Eugenius, and worked out a reconciliation decree with the Greeks. Although it came too late to save Constantinople, it gave a decided boost to the prestige of the pope. The dissident portion of the council, however, remained in Basel, decreed conciliar authority to be a matter of faith, deposed Eugenius as a heretic, and elected Felix V in his place. Eugenius, of course, refused to step down, and his new prestige because of the successful Greek accord caused the nations to come over to him. In 1448 the council was driven from Basel and moved to Lausanne, where Felix V abdicated. Soon after Eugenius died and was succeeded in Rome by Nicholas V. The council voted to recognize him as the true pope, and this act of capitulation marked the virtual end of the conciliar movement. The purpose for the movement, in the first place, had been to restore respect and prestige to the papacy. By finally accomplishing this, it had brought about its own destruction. The pope was back in power, and although there would be many more efforts to reform the church through the conciliar theory, its days of power were over.

D. THE CRITICAL-REFORM MOVEMENT

Although our discussion of the conciliar movement has thus far centered on the papal controversy, that was not the only interest or purpose of the councils. They were also convened to attempt reform within the church and to deal with heresy and dissent. In reform efforts, the councils were very weak and ineffective; but in dealing with heretics and dissenters, they were severe and definitive. While the political and ecclesiastical battles of popes versus councils were being fought, the house of western Christendom was being further divided by deep theological and moral issues. The forerunners of the Protestant Reformation were desperately trying to save the church and turn it around, which brought about defensive reaction from the councils of this period.

1. JOHN WYCLIFFE (1328-84)

"The Morning Star of the Reformation" was an English philosopher, theologian, and reformer from Yorkshire. Educated at Oxford, John Wycliffe became an outstanding scholar and popular teacher of scholastic philosophy and theology. He was an outspoken realist who opposed the nominalism of Duns Scotus and William of Occam. His only pastorate was at Lutterworth, an appointment he received from King Edward III. The son of Edward, John of Gaunt, the virtual ruler of England, became one of Wycliffe's closest friends and strongest supporters. In turn, Wycliffe supported the British crown in its dispute with the pope over ownership and stewardship of property. In his 1375 work *On Divine Lordship* and his 1376 work, *On Civil Lordship*, he developed his views of righteous stewardship. Simply stated, he maintained that everything belongs to God; that every creature is his servant; that no man has permanent or unlimited lordship; that lordship is by the grace of God; and if any person, especially a priest, is immoral or unfit, he should be replaced. Also kings and princes are servants, not masters, and they, too, can and should be replaced if unfit.

During the scandal of the papal schism, Wycliffe argued that the true Church is invisible and made up only of those elected by God. Salvation does not depend upon membership in a visible church or mediation by a priest, but upon election by God. He further held that everyone truly elected of God is a priest, breaking ground for the doctrine of the priesthood of the believer. He insisted, however, that true and pure priests should be honored; but he condemned the cult of saints, relics, and pilgrimages. He attacked the doctrine of transubstantiation, holding rather to the doctrine of remanence, in which Christ is in the sacrament, along with the bread and wine, just as a king is everywhere present in his kingdom. Although he appealed to the works of Ambrose, Augustine, Anselm and Nicholas II, his rejection of transubstantiation caused many of his friends to reject him. He repudiated indulgences and masses for the dead but did continue to believe in purgatory. He believed that the Bible should be available for all men to read, and translated it from the Vulgate into the English vernacular. To distribute Bibles and spread the gospel, Wycliffe sent out traveling preachers known as Lollards (so-called out of derision, meaning "mumblers"). These itinerant preachers were accused of stirring up the Peasants' Revolt in 1381.

Although Wycliffe's teachings and methods created a stir throughout the church (some of his views were condemned at a synod at Blackfriars in

1382), he remained a devout Catholic and died in peace in 1384. Shortly thereafter in 1401, a strong act against heretics, clearly aimed at the Lollards, was passed by Parliament; and in 1406 a clear anti-Lollard measure was enacted. In 1407 the Archbishop of Canterbury condemned them, and in 1409 a synod in London upheld the archbishop, condemned the doctrines of Wycliffe, the unauthorized translation of the Bible, and unlicensed preachers. Some Lollards were burned at the stake. Henry V (1413-1422) was vigorously anti-Lollard and took strong measures to exterminate them. Then came the Council of Constance, which we have already discussed; and in its fervor to heal the papal schism and strengthen the church, it determined to suppress heresy. Although Wycliffe had been dead thirty-one years, the Council of Constance condemned him on 260 different counts, ordered his writings to be burned, and his bones to be exhumed and cast out of consecrated ground. By papal command, the remains of Wycliffe were dug up and burned and the ashes thrown into a nearby stream in 1428. Lollardy continued in spite of heavy persecution, and became one of the significant sources of English Protestantism.

2. JOHN HUS (1369-1415)

While the Lollards were being suppressed in England, another reformer was emerging in far off Bohemia, whose work was directly influenced by the life and writings of Wycliffe. John Hus was born of a peasant family at Husinec (hence the name "Hus"). He entered Prague University in 1390. By 1401 he had become dean of the philosophical faculty, and by 1409 was rector of the university. He was a popular preacher in Czech at the Bethlehem chapel of Prague. Despite the fact that the university condemned forty-five of Wycliffe's propositions, Hus translated many of the Englishman's works into Czech. This action and his persistent sermons on the morals of the clergy provoked hostility.

Hus did not merely parrot Wycliffe, for he was his own man and had some original views. He advocated the New Testament as the law of the church, Christlike poverty as the Christian ideal, reform of abuses such as pilgrimages, Christ as the head of the church rather than the pope, and a predestinated church of the elect. He did not agree with Wycliffe on the doctrine of remanence, but he did champion the Czech demand that laymen be allowed to receive the cup. The church had recently restricted the cup to the priest, lest the clumsy laity should spill any of the "blood of Christ." The chalice became the symbol of the Hussite movement which restored the cup of the Mass to the laity.

In 1407, the Roman papacy ordered the burning of Wycliffe's writings and the silencing of Hus. When Hus refused to comply he was excommunicated by the Archbishop of Prague. In 1409, the Council of Pisa elected a third pope to replace the schism popes. Hus supported the Pisan pope, Alexander V, but a year later Alexander also ordered Hus to cease

Numerous attempts were made to translate the Scriptures from Hebrew, Greek, and Latin, into English. One of the most notable efforts was by John Wycliffe, a page of whose work appears here. (Historical Pictures Service, Chicago) preaching. When Alexander died in a few months, Hus appealed to his successor John XXIII, but since Hus had denounced a papal crusade against the King of Naples and the indulgences sold in Prague to finance the crusade, John replied by excommunicating Hus and issuing an interdict against Prague. Hus left the city, preached from place to place throughout the country, and became a national hero. During this time Hus wrote many of his famous essays, denouncing the pope as Antichrist.

The Emperor Sigismund, a brother of the King of Bohemia, sought to remedy the situation by having Hus present his case to the Council of Constance, which Sigismund had helped convene. Although Hus went to Constance under imperial safe conduct, he was arrested, imprisoned, convicted as "a manifest heretic," and sentenced to burn. Hus protested that he was being accused of heresies he did not himself believe, that he desired to present his beliefs to the council, and that he would abide by its judgment if it did not offend God and his conscience. Hus never received his "day in court" and was burned at the stake on July 6, 1415. When news of Hus' execution reached Prague, the country erupted in revolt. Czech and Moravian nobles pledged to defend the reforms for which Hus died, and the common people attacked monasteries and churches. By February of 1416, all the Prague churches were in the hands of reform clergy and the revolt spread, abetting the rising nationalism that was challenging the sovereignty of the papacy. The sentiments of the Hussite movement were characterized by the famous Four Prague Articles: freedom of preaching, the sacrament in both kinds to all Christians, exemplary living and no secular power for priests, and punishment of all mortal sins. The conciliar movement may have healed the papal schism, but it caused an irrevocable split with a great segment of the church crying for reform.

3. MYSTICISM

Another expression of the critical-reform movement, known as mysticism, was less drastic and thoroughly nonpolitical, but still created problems for a church struggling for unity. Although the mystics did not directly challenge the papacy and priesthood, they did weaken ecclesiastical power by advocating direct contact with God. This constituted an indirect criticism of the formal sacerdotalism of the church. If man can have direct unification and identification with God, then ecclesiastical machinery, sacraments, satisfactions, and even prayer can be unnecessary.

Meister Eckhart (1260-1327) was the most dynamic force in the religious life of Germany before the Reformation. A Dominican mystic, Eckhart studied and taught at Paris but returned to Germany, first to Strasbourg and then Cologne, where he became one of the most famous preachers of his time. He held that the only reality in man and in nature is the divine spark of God, which is in everything. Because of this strong emphasis, Eckhart has often been accused of pantheism. He insisted that what he was striving for was the individual's immersion and identification with God: "Feet and hands, and mouth and eyes, the heart, and all a man is and has, become God's own." In 1326 Eckhart was accused of heretical teachings, tried before the court of the Archbishop of Cologne, appealed to the pope, and died during the proceedings. In 1329 Pope John XXII condemned twenty-eight of his teachings as heretical or dangerous. The work of Eckhart is believed to have influenced Luther's emphasis on faith, Kant's critical idealism, and Hegel's pantheism.

Two of Eckhart's most renowned disciples were Johann Tauler and Henry Suso. Tauler was also a Dominican mystic who gained great popularity throughout Germany for his preaching skill and devoted care of the sick during the Black Death of 1348. His teaching was grounded in Thomist doctrine and was strongly practical. While he reflected Eckhart's influence by stressing union with God, he made it clear that such union is not for its own sake but to produce benevolent and charitable service in the world. The Mystic Way, which he described in detail, conceived chiefly of the virtues of humility and abandonment to the will of God. Henry Suso (also Heinrich Seuse) was a pupil of Eckhart in Cologne, and became a prominent spiritual director in many women's convents in the Dominican order. His life as a mystic began at the age of eighteen, when he made himself "Servant of the Eternal Wisdom." He extolled suffering as the way to the exquisite love of God. Some of the followers of Eckhart, Tauler, and Suso called themselves the Friends of God and remained within the church, but formed loosely organized societies to promote personal transformation and union with God.

John Ruysbroeck, a Flemish priest also influenced by Eckhart, wrote in Flemish, popularizing mystic contemplation. Gerhard Groot, a Carthusian monk, was influenced by Ruysbroeck, and founded the Brethren of the Common Life. Groot was the outstanding developer of a rising new movement called the *Devotio Moderna* (the modern way of serving God). This was a spiritual revival within the Catholic Church, which emphasized personal devotion, social involvement, and education. The Brethren of the Common Life was a semimonastic group which observed the rule of poverty, chastity, and obedience, but they did not beg for alms like the mendicant friars, and they were free to quit and return to secular life. When Groot died, his associate Florens Radewijns took over leadership of the *Devotio Moderna* movement, which became increasingly influential. Many of the Brethren of the Common Life left their mark on Christianity, including such notables as Nicholas of Cusa and Erasmus the humanist.

The man who best sums up the faith of the *Devotio Moderna* is Thomas à Kempis, the author of the *Imitation of Christ*, which has been translated into more languages than any book in the world except the Bible. Thomas à Kempis attended the school founded by Gerhard Groot at Deventer, where he studied under Florens Radewijns. He lived to be ninety-one and spent his entire life in contemplating and living the devoted mysticism of *Devotio Moderna*. As the title suggests, the purpose of his *Imitation of Christ* is to teach the way of perfection through following Christ's example. The work is searching, scriptural, and thoroughly centered on Christ. It is only toward the end that it even mentions the sacrament-based Catholicism from which it came. The life and works of Thomas à Kempis are the epitome of the deep spirituality seeking to reform the church in the late medieval period.

E. THE RENAISSANCE MOVEMENT

The disruption of the medieval church was part of the larger movement known as the Renaissance, spanning roughly the years 1300 to 1600, and bringing the world out of the Middle Ages into the modern period. The word "Renaissance" means revival and describes the reviving of the values of classical Greek and Roman civilization in the arts, literature, and politics. The important motifs of the period were individualism, secularism, and rationalism. Formative developments were nationalism, urbanization, and industrialization. Most of what the world today calls modern had its roots or growth in the Renaissance.

1. HUMANISM IN LITERATURE

The Renaissance began with the revival of classical learning by scholars known as "humanists." Originally, a humanist was someone who taught Latin grammar, but it eventually came to mean those who studied classical writings and molded their lives on what they read. Most of the early humanists were Christians who called for reform of education and morality. Many of the later Renaissance thinkers, however, either rejected or ignored Christianity, which had a profound effect on a church struggling to maintain a cohesive unity.

a. Lovato Lovati (1241-1309), the first known humanist, was a judge in Padua, Italy. He composed Latin verse, cultivated literary friendships, and discovered manuscripts of forgotten classics in the library of the Benedictine abbey of Pomposa. The search for hidden treasures of antiquity became one of the characteristics of humanism, and Italy became the home of humanism.

b. Dante Alighieri (1265-1321) spanned the transition from theological to secular interests. Italy's greatest poet began his public life very unpromisingly, having his property confiscated and himself exiled from Florence after his involvement in antipapal politics. He spent a great part of his life wandering from one Italian city to another. He remained an orthodox Catholic, but in his *On Monarchy,* he rejects the notion of papal supremacy and upholds the concept of a universal emperor. In his most famous work, *The Divine Comedy,* Dante makes an imaginary, allegorical trip through hell, purgatory, and paradise. Foretastes of humanism are seen in his emphasis on contemporary life. The ultimate horror of Dante's inferno is not that man burns in hell, but that sin freezes, and man remains for all eternity what he once was. The blasphemer says, "Such as I was when living, that I am now." When Dante so forcefully demonstrates that nothing is so terrible as to be forever what one was, his reader is compelled to reevaluate his present life and circumstances.

c. *Francesco Petrarch* (1304-74) was the Italian with whom humanism came of age. Petrarch was the child of adverse social change. The Hundred Years' War between France and England had begun, the Black Death ravaged Europe, the papacy had moved from Rome to Avignon, the kingdom of Naples was ruined, the Lombard cities were in decline, and the Netherlands and lower Germany were in ashes. It began to dawn on Petrarch that the terrible woes befalling Christendom might be the result of concentrating too much on eternal life instead of appreciating and rightly using the present world. He studied law at Montpellier and Bologna, but received minor orders of the clergy at Avignon. Exiled from Florence for his family's political activities, he wandered through Europe discovering and copying classical manuscripts, thus preserving some of our only copies of ancient literature. He fell in love with Laura, a married woman, who inspired the writing of three hundred beautiful Italian sonnets. He finally settled down to a life of solitude at Vaucluse in 1337, and began writing his most important works. As a Christian humanist, Petrarch was constantly in tension between Augustine and Cicero. He was not a speculative thinker and he rejected the Aristotelian form of the medieval Scholastics, polarizing Christian opinion between the old Scholasticism and the new humanism. In many ways, he has been called "the first modern man." His graceful Latin verse and zest for learning inspired other Italians in bringing about the renaissance.

d. *Giovanni Boccaccio* (1313-75) was a close friend and admirer of Petrarch, and was the author of Europe's first novels. He was the forerunner of modern writers who ignore Christianity and write of the joys of nature, love, and the flesh. Boccaccio's famous *Decameron* is a collection of tales written against the backdrop of the Black Death, and reflects themes that are immoral, ironic, amusing, tragic, and earthy, giving vivid pictures of medieval people (in much the same style as Chaucer's *Canterbury Tales* of this same period). However, he continued the quest for hidden manuscripts, and authored Latin works which were modeled on the classics.

e. *Leonardo Bruni* (1370-1444) believed ethics to be more important than speculative knowledge, and promoted a "civic humanism." He attempted to place the study of the humanities in the service of historical and political consciousness. This was approached by developing the political implications of the great classics. Bruni eventually left Florence and found work in the papal chancery at Rome, helping that city to become the most important center of humanism in Italy after Martin V was elected to the papacy in 1417.

f. Lorenzo Valla (1406-57) and *Nicholas of Cusa* (1400-64) exemplify the critical and scholarly spirit of the Renaissance. In 1440, Valla, employing historical and form criticism, proved that the *Donation of Constantine* was spurious. He believed that all literature was subject to scholarly investigation, including Jerome's *Vulgate*. He rejected the method of Scholasticism which was based on the medieval tradition of authority, and insisted on comparing text with text. He deserves to be called the father of historical criticism. Nicholas of Cusa also demonstrated the falsity of the *Donation of Constantine*, but worked from within the church to try to reform it. He taught that reason is relational, accomplished by comparing that which is unknown to that which is known. His interest in reconciling opposites led him to examine the comparisons of the Koran and the Bible, and to seek the reunion of the Greek and Roman branches of Catholicism.

g. Johann Reuchlin (1455-1522) was the outstanding humanist of Germany, who marshalled strong support for the freedom of scholarship. In a day of anti-Jewish feelings, Reuchlin's interest in Hebrew cabalistic literature led him to promote a study of the language. When the Dominicans struck out with orders from Emperor Maximilian to destroy any Jewish literature that opposed Christianity, Reuchlin countered with the shocking proposal that chairs of Hebrew should be established in Christian universities. For this he received scathing attacks, and he defended himself with *Letters of Renowned Men*, a collection of supportive testimonies from famous people. Pope Leo X condemned most of Reuchlin's work, especially *Augenspiegel*. Broken in health, finances, and energy, Reuchlin made his peace with the church before he died. A demonstration of his loyalty to the church was his estrangement from his beloved grandnephew, Philip Melanchthon, colleague and ally of Luther.

h. Desiderius Erasmus (1466-1536) stands in history as the acknowledged prince of humanists. He reached a level of unparalleled fame among his contemporaries, and the advent of the printing press multiplied his audience by the thousands. The crowning glory of Christian humanism, however, began in extremely humble circumstances. Erasmus was born out of wedlock in Rotterdam, his father being a wayward priest. When his mother and father both died in the plague, the child was put in the school at Deventer where he was educated by the Brethren of the Common Life. He was ordained to the priesthood, but soon decided that that calling was not for him. He studied at Paris and became intensely attracted to books and close friends. These two proclivities opened up many lasting associations, such as those with John Colet, Thomas Linacre, and Thomas More in England, where the universities of Oxford and Cambridge conferred degrees on him and Cambridge gave him a professorship in Greek and Theology. But he was destined to wander until he settled permanently at Basel. In order to maintain his freedom he declined many honors and posts which would have obligated him.

Erasmus longed for and worked for reformation of the church. He never broke from the church, but he spoke against monasticism, Scholasticism, and formalism. He wanted to purge the church of superstition through intelligence and the ethical teachings of Christ. He was consumed with a conviction that faith and reason, and religion and culture, could and should harmonize and synthesize. In his personal life, writings, and teachings, he endeavored to fuse culture with piety. In 1503, he wrote *Handbook of the Christian Soldier,* a guide to Christian living which deprecates formalism and ceremonies and emphasizes morals. In 1509, he wrote his famous *In Praise of Folly,* a satirical description of all strata of contemporary life, revealing the hypocrisy, greed, ineptness, and ignorance in popes, cardinals, kings, nobles, monks, preachers, philosophers, merchants, and commoners. In 1516, he published his popular Greek New Testament, with a fresh translation into Latin, severely correcting the Vulgate. That same year he wrote *On the Education of a Christian Prince* for the future Emperor Charles V, lauding biblical and classical education as the proper training for rulers. In his *Familiar Colloquies,* he ridiculed the corruptions of the church and the monasteries and helped prepare the way for the Reformation.

At times Erasmus seemed to approve of Luther's ideas and work, but they clashed sharply over the question of free will, Erasmus basing his arguments on reason and the goodness of man, and Luther basing his on faith and the depths of sin. Erasmus had reached an unbelievable level of influence, and justifiably thought that he had rescued humanism from paganism. He earnestly believed that reform from within was possible and that he had begun that which would work if it had been allowed to continue. But it was not to be, for as he himself wrote, "While I was fighting a fairly equal battle, lo! suddenly Luther arose and threw the apple of discord into the world."

2. REALISM IN CULTURE
The Renaissance is generally understood to be that period of time when the church began to lose control over society. Earth came to be more valued than heaven, fame was more important than immortality of the soul, self-

cultivation more to be sought than self-denial, the delights of the flesh attracted more attention than asceticism, and intellectual freedom was more sacred than orthodox authority.

a. Renaissance Art. Realism appealed to and promoted the human urge to fulfillment and expression. The great artists of this period reflected that urge. Giotto (1276-1337) was one of the first to give his paintings a realistic, dramatic, human quality in contrast to the stereotyped religious art of medieval style. His subject matter showed a shocking interest in solid human beings rather than ethereal visions of heaven. Other significant artists who followed Giotto's example included Fra Angelico (1387-1455), Donatello (1383-1466), Filippo Lippi (1406-69), Sandro Botticelli (1444-1510), Donato Bramante (1444-1514), Giorgioni (1477-1510), Raphael Sanzio (1483-1520), Leonardo da Vinci (1452-1519), Michelangelo Buonarroti (1475-1564), Titian (1477-1576), and Albrecht Durer (1471-1528).

Leonardo da Vinci was the true embodiment of "the Renaissance Man." He was a many-sided genius—engineer, inventor, painter, sculptor, and natural scientist far ahead of his time. His two most famous paintings, the "Mona Lisa" and "Last Supper," demonstrate his application of realism and psychological insight to religious themes. The renowned Michelangelo was also of this same caliber, a sculptor, painter, architect, and poet. He portrayed human emotions on a monumental scale in his ceiling frescoes, "Creation of Man" and "The Last Judgment" in the Sistine Chapel. His magnificent sculptured works, such as "David," "Moses," and "La Pieta" gave anatomical realism and human strength to biblical characters. Raphael initiated the application of sensitivity and passion to such sacred themes as Madonna and Child. He also succeeded the famous Bramante as chief architect of St. Peter's basilica. Albrecht Durer, the celebrated German artist and engraver, was unexcelled in his realistic woodcuts and engravings. Supreme among the developments of the late Gothic style, his work was marked by rugged strength and vital action. Although he never left the Catholic Church, Durer was sympathetic to the Reformation, and was eulogized by Luther. Renaissance art was a perfect vehicle for the burgeoning genius of the day, but it also threatened medieval authoritarianism and cultural solidarity.

b. Renaissance Architecture. The spirit and religion of men are often expressed in their buildings. The Gothic style of pointed arch and soaring vault had expressed medieval man's aspiration of turning from the laborious soil to the exalted sky. But in the rebirth of the Renaissance, men sought to beautify life, not to escape it, and earth was to be embellished as though it were heaven. In 1450, Antonio Filarete cried, "Cursed be the man who invented this wretched Gothic architecture. Only a barbarous people could

From the works of Albrecht Durer, one of the notable Rennaissance artists. This age of realism appealed to and promoted the human urge to fulfillment and expression, ideals that were carried out in the works of Durer, Angelico, Raphael, Donatello, Lippi, da Vinci, and Michelangelo. (The Bettmann Archive)

have brought it to Italy." Believing as they did that architecture should undergo a revival of the classical and utilization of the contemporary, architects of this period created a new physical environment for worshipers and churchmen. The Gothic church was cruciform; the Renaissance church was circular. The Gothic church used the spire; the Renaissance featured the dome. Outstanding Renaissance architects were Filippo Brunellesco, Michelozzo di Bartolemmo, Alberti, Donatello, Benedetto da Maiano, Michelangelo, and Raphael.

The Renaissance architects organized their work on a system of proportions, for they considered proper proportion to be the very essence of beauty. The great Italian architect Leon Battista Alberti defined beauty in architecture as "a harmony of all the parts in whatsoever subject it appears, fitted together with such proportion and connection, that nothing could be added, diminished, or altered, but for the worse." The classic forms of architecture were Tuscan, Doric, Ionic, Corinthian, and Composite, but every kind of style and influence found expression somewhere during the fourteenth and fifteenth centuries.

This was the period of the great papal schism, and although Rome would have been the natural setting for a revival of classical architecture, the political situation there was not favorable for artistic endeavor. Florence, however, under the leadership of the Medici family, was economically prosperous and politically stable and became the capital of Renaissance art. It was not until Pope Julius II (1503-1513) that the center of the Renaissance moved from Florence to Rome. He financed hundreds of promising artists, especially Raphael, Michelangelo, and Donato Bramante, usually considered the greatest architect of this age. It was Bramante whom Julius commissioned to design a new St. Peter's, and in 1506, the cornerstone was laid for the Basilica of St. Peter. In order to finance the rebuilding of St. Peter's, Julius instituted the sale of indulgences, which was the proverbial straw that broke the camel's back and motivated Luther to proceed with posting his Ninety-Five Theses. It seems ironical that the enterprise to build more elegant houses of worship became a contributing factor to dividing further the house of Christendom.

c. Renaissance Expansion. At first the Renaissance was almost entirely an Italian movement, but gradually it spread and extended its influence through the sixteenth century. Geographical exploration became an important facet of the Renaissance times. The crusades had revived western trade and commerce, leading to travel, exploration, and discovery. Marco Polo and Sir John Mandeville traveled extensively in the Orient, astonishing Europe with their reports.

By the beginning of the fourteenth century, the compass had been perfected in Naples, ushering in a new era of exploration. The Canary Islands were discovered in 1402, the Madeira Islands in 1419, and the

Cape of Verde Islands in 1460. And in 1487 Vasco de Gama sailed around the southern point of Africa. In an effort to discover a new trade route to India, Christopher Columbus sailed westward in 1492 and discovered America. Magellan sailed around the earth in 1519-1522, proving conclusively that the world was round.

Man's agelong concepts of the physical world had changed suddenly and completely. The impact of such expansion was real upon the unstable church. Martin Luther was nine years old when Columbus discovered America, and the further voyages of Cabot, Cortes, Magellan, and Pizarro all came within the lifetime of Luther. Practically every year some new horizon was disclosed, and it was inevitable that new religious horizons would also appear.

It was also inevitable that there should be a transformation in economic, social, and cultural life. City population was rapidly increasing, industry was revolutionized, and the banking system was developed, marking the beginning of modern capitalism. A new class, known as "citizens" began to emerge in the mushrooming cities, organizing city governments, establishing public schools, and creating a new social order of merchants, bankers, tradesmen, artisans, and craftsmen.

New inventions spurred the secular as well as the religious pursuits of the period. In addition to the compass, came the invention of gunpowder and the manufacture of paper. The invention of moveable type for use with the printing press by Johann Gutenburg in 1450 marked a momentous turning point in the entire history of civilization. Significantly, the first complete book known to have been printed in the Christian world was the Bible, in 1456. By the time Luther was born in 1483, printing was well established throughout Europe.

It seemed that the whole world was vibrating with the exulting discoveries and expressions of the Renaissance, and it would appear that the church had been given new and forceful tools to implement its tasks. On the contrary, church leaders misunderstood and mishandled the opportunities of the Renaissance, and brought the church closer to self-destruction.

3. MONOPOLISM IN RELIGION

Medieval Christianity had become a kingdom in this world. Many pagan and worldly elements exerted strong influence on the church, and its leaders stoutly resisted any reform. When the Renaissance opened new doors and windows, the church retreated further into its already divided house. This does not mean that the Renaissance was not recognized or accepted. Indeed, some of the Renaissance popes were great patrons of the arts. Often, however, the benefits of the Renaissance were used to buttress the antiquated systems of the church. Power and control are not easy to relinquish, and when the church perceived it was losing its hold on Europe, it sought means to monopolize the forces of the Renaissance movement to make itself more stable and powerful.

Nicholas V succeeded Eugenius IV in 1447. The Council of Basel broke up when Felix V abdicated, and the papacy was restored to its absolute monarchical rule. Just as the Renaissance was initially an Italian movement, so also the papacy became almost an exclusively Italian power with Italian interests. Thus the age of the "Renaissance Popes" began.

a. Pope Nicholas V (1397-1455). The first and probably the best of the Renaissance popes was this same Nicholas, who set about to reform certain abuses in the church. He crowned Frederick III of Hapsburg as German emperor, the last imperial coronation in Rome. After the fall of Constantinople in 1453, he tried in vain to organize a crusade against the Turks. Nicholas was an enthusiastic lover of arts and science, a promoter of humanism and the restoration of the study of Greek. He restored many ruined churches, laid the plans for rebuilding the Vatican and St. Peter's, and founded the Vatican library. Unlike many of his successors, Nicholas lived a blameless personal life, remained free from practicing nepotism, and was eager to reconcile religion with the new spirit abroad in the land. If the spirit of Nicholas V had continued throughout the Renaissance, history would have written a different outcome.

b. Pope Calixtus III (1455-58). Alfonso Borgia of Valencia followed Nicholas as pope, and actually engineered a crusade against the Turks, but after a sputtering start, it soon died. His pontificate was scandalized by the news of his illegitimate son and his flagrant nepotism in appointing two of his nephews as cardinals and another as a duke. The most interesting event of his reign was his revision of the trial of Joan of Arc, the annulment of her sentence, and a declaration of her innocence. The tragedy of this action was the same as with many of Calixtus' actions—it had come too late. Joan of Arc had been burned at the stake as a heretic in 1431, and Calixtus' declaration of her innocence came in 1456.

c. Pope Pius II (1458-64). One of the more interesting figures of the Renaissance was Pius II, a strong humanist churchman who traveled widely in his papal affairs and business of the empire. He also tried unsuccessfully to mount a crusade against the Turks. Renaissance Europe was more interested in affairs at hand than recapturing the Holy Land. Although Pius had once been a strong advocate of the conciliar movement, in 1460 he issued the famous bull excommunicating anyone who appealed to a general council over the papacy.

d. Pope Paul II (1464-71). Unlike his predecessor, Paul II was not on friendly terms with the humanists. He was interested in lavish processions, pompous display, and enhancing his own reputation. Although the functions of his office did not interest him, he was able to strengthen the power of the papacy in its rivalry with other Italian states.

e. *Pope Sixtus IV* (1471-84). It is often said that the papacy reached a new low with the pontificate of Sixtus IV. After failing, as his predecessors had, in getting up a crusade against the Turks, he turned his interests almost exclusively to Italian politics and promotion of his own family. The nepotism of the Renaissance popes was at its worst expression in Sixtus IV, who elevated no less than six of his own nephews to be cardinals, one of whom later became Pope Julius II. He became deeply involved in Italian politics, was implicated in the murder of two de Medicis, and figured in a war with Florence.

He was a great protector of arts and scholarship. He founded the Sistine Choir, built the Sistine Chapel, and enriched the Vatican Library. In his bull of 1476, he made belief in the availability of indulgences for souls in purgatory an article of faith, and he furthered the cult of the Virgin Mary. A complex man, Sixtus IV was personally a moral man and an acceptable theologian, but he was consumed with a passion for politics and a determination to make the papacy supreme everywhere.

f. *Pope Innocent VIII* (1484-92). A weak worldling, Innocent VIII was the father of several children and worked openly to advance them. His shocking nepotism pulled down the entire moral tone of the church. His extravagant tastes led him to engage the church's energies and funds in elaborate building programs at a time when voices everywhere were crying for reform. His rule was an open example of the papacy misunderstanding and misusing the great artistic and architectural advancements of the Renaissance. An indication of his superficial theology was his bull of 1484, declaring Germany to be full of witches.

g. *Pope Alexander VI* (1492-1503). The successor to Innocent VIII, was the most notoriously immoral pope of all time: Rodrigo Borgia, who took the title of Alexander VI. He had many children who were all provided for from church revenues, before and after their father became pope. The most notorious of his illegitimate children were Lucrezia Borgia and Cesare Borgia, the latter becoming ruthless and corrupt in political intrigue and struggles for power. Alexander, however, was a skillful administrator who advanced education, patronized the arts, beautified Rome, and showed kindness to the Jews. In his desire to keep the papal states free from foreign entanglements, he used Turkish help against the French. He served as mediator between Spain and Portugal, dividing the "new world" between them.

One of Alexander's most memorable acts was the prosecution and execution of Girolamo Savonarola, who became a hero to many of the early Protestants. Savonarola was a Dominican friar who passionately denounced the immorality of the Florentines and the contemporary clergy. Believing himself directly inspired by God, he prophesied on the future of the church and other subjects, often in apocalyptic language. With the support of Charles VIII of France, he established a theocratic democracy in Florence, and instituted a radical moral reform of the city. When he refused a papal summons to Rome to give an account of his prophecies, Alexander excommunicated him. In retaliation, Savonarola demanded a general council to depose the pope. The people in general turned against Savonarola, and the Franciscans especially opposed him. He was finally imprisoned, then hanged as a schismatic and heretic on the market place of Florence in 1498.

h. *Pope Julius II* (1503-13). The most warlike pope was Julius II, who led his own troops to regain the estates of the church, actually scaling the walls of Bologna himself. Erasmus was more shocked by the vulgarity of a pope in armor than by the carnality of the Borgia. Julius restored and enlarged the temporal power of the papacy, in the process of which he drove Cesare Borgia from Italy. He formed a Holy League with England, Spain, Venice, and Switzerland with the purpose of defeating and containing France. Louis XII of France called a council to depose the pope, which Julius refused to acknowledge, calling a Lateran council himself, which won the support of Emperor Maximilian and isolated France.

Though he was essentially a statesman and a military leader, Julius was also a patron of Renaissance art, supporting the genius of Raphael, Michelangelo, and Bramante. His generosity made possible Michelangelo's statue of Moses, his paintings in the Sistine Chapel, and Raphael's frescoes in the Vatican. His selling of indulgences to finance the rebuilding of St. Peter's was a contributing factor to the final outbreak of the Protestant Reformation.

i. *Pope Leo X* (1513-21). A wealthy, pleasure-loving, easy-going member of the famed de Medici family assumed the papacy at a time when exactly the opposite was needed. When he accepted the office, he said, "Now we have the papacy; let us enjoy it." His most distinctive ability was to make impromptu speeches in Latin. He spent more on gambling than on artists, and complained about having to leave his hunting lodge to go to Rome to have his toe kissed. Excessively liberal with money, within two years he had squandered the fortune left by Julius II. His reign was characterized by trifles and a sordid series of intrigues and conspiracies. The most pathetic note of his pontificate was that he never comprehended the meaning of Martin Luther, whom he excommunicated in 1520. He was, in fact, completely blind to what was involved, or the seriousness of the fomenting revolt.

None of the Renaissance popes seemed able to understand the nature of the widespread discontent with the papacy and the whole system of ecclesiastical control. Neither did they grasp the significance of the forces of change in the Renaissance era. The medieval synthesis had been broken, the authority of the papacy had been eroded, the popes personally had lost respect and honor, and the severely divided house of western Christianity was about to come falling upon their heads.

Although the clergy, and most noticeably the papacy, was at a nadir in morality and spirituality, the rank and file of Christians were moving toward a religious awakening. The sordid portrayal of the "earthen vessels" of official Christendom should not obscure the bright hope of the rising demand for reform sweeping in from the grass roots. Luther did not initiate the cry for reform; he responded to it, for in every sense of the word, by the year 1517, the Reformation was an idea whose time had come.

VIII

CLEANSING THE TEMPLE: THE REFORM CRISIS (1517-1648)

*And Jesus went into the temple of God,
and cast out all them that sold and bought
in the temple, and overthrew the tables
of the moneychangers, and the seats of
them that sold doves. And said unto them,
It is written, My house shall be called
the house of prayer;
but ye have made it a den of thieves.*

MATTHEW 21:12,13

A. Prelude to Reform
1. Political Conditions
2. Ximenes in Spain
3. Indulgence Controversy
B. Reform in Germany
1. Martin Luther
2. The Ninety-Five Theses
3. The Gathering Storm
4. The Break with Rome
5. The Diet of Worms
6. The Continuing Struggle
7. Developing Lutheranism
8. The Peasants' Revolt
9. From Speyer to Augsburg
10. The Death of Luther and the Survival of Lutheranism
11. Lutheranism Beyond Germany
C. Reform in Switzerland
1. Zwingli and Zurich
2. Calvin and Geneva
a. Calvin's Institutes   b. A Model Christian Community   c. Opposition and Control
3. The Spread of Calvinism
a. Huguenots in France   b. Insurrection in the Netherlands   c. Reform in Scotland
D. Anabaptists and Radical Reformation
1. Thomas Muntzer and the Zwickau Prophets
2. The Swiss Brethren
3. The Hutterites in Moravia
4. Melchior Hoffman and Chaliasm
5. Jan Matthys and the Munster Episode
6. The Mennonites and the Amish
E. Reform in England
1. Preparation and Causes
2. Supremacy Under Henry VIII
3. Protestantism Under Edward VI
4. Catholicism Under Mary
5. Settlement Under Elizabeth
a. Diplomacy and Force   b. Puritans and Separatists
6. Revolt Under the Stuarts
a. James I and the Baptists   b. Charles I and Oliver Cromwell
7. Restoration Under Parliament
F. Reform in Catholicism
1. Renewal of Piety
2. Society of Jesus
a. Ignatius Loyola   b. Combating Protestantism
c. Jesuit Education   d. Missionary Expansion
e. Fraternal Opposition
3. Council of Trent
a. Background and Sessions   b. Dogma and Authority   c. Reform and Retrenchment
4. Wars of Religion
a. Sixteenth-century Conflicts   b. The Thirty Years' War   c. Absolutism in France

hen Jesus of Nazareth boldly cleansed the temple and accused the moneychangers of making it a den of thieves, he was echoing the words of the prophet Jeremiah in his famous temple sermon against the idolatry and hypocrisy of Israel (Jeremiah 7:11). When the Apostle Paul admonished the Corinthians for their lax religion, he used the same temple metaphor: "And what agreement hath the temple of God with idols? for ye are the temple of the living God; as God hath said, I will dwell in them, and walk in them; and I will be their God, and they shall be my people" (2 Corinthians 6:16). Thus, when the sixteenth-century reformers rose up to cleanse the halls of Christendom, they felt themselves to be in line with the biblical affirmation that the church is the temple of God, and as such should be cleansed of all that is ungodly.

A. PRELUDE TO REFORM

While the issues of the Reformation did eventually center upon "cleansing the temple" of theological heresy and ecclesiastical abuses, it must be noted that many other factors prepared the European church for its greatest upheaval.

1. POLITICAL CONDITIONS

We have previously mentioned the clash between crown and papacy during the rising nationalism of the fifteenth century. This confrontation increased in number and intensity as rising national states demanded more control of church government. This alone, however, did not promote reformation. The kings involved were not concerned with reforming the church, only controlling it. The contribution of nationalism to the Reformation was that it curbed the power of the pope and weakened his ability to crush the Reformation.

England was the first country to become a distinct and solidified nationality. Since the time of William the Conqueror (1066) the English king had been the head of the English church, severely curtailing the strength of the pope. In 1265, the House of Commons was formed, providing the king with the additional support of the great middle class of England. The feudal lords had been ruined with the Wars of the Roses (1455-1495) and the succeeding kings ruled in great power under parliamentary forms. On the eve of the Reformation, England recognized the pope as the head of the Church of England only "insofar as the laws of the land permitted."

France was still reeling from the devastating Hundred Years' War (1338-1453) which had demolished the French nobility and consolidated the royal power. Charles VIII (1483-1498) had ambitions of making France instead of Germany the head of the Holy Roman Empire. In 1516, Francis I and Pope Leo X designed the Concordat of Bologna, which made the king the virtual head of the church in France.

Spain had been under Mohammedan rule for several centuries, but was finally able to drive out the Moors in 1492. The Spanish monarchy was born with the marriage of Ferdinand of Aragon and Isabella of Castile, who sought to reform the church and bring it under submission to the crown. In 1482 they were able to force such an agreement (Concordat) with the pope.

Germany was divided into about three hundred virtually independent states, but solidly organized under the Articles of Confederation. Since the time of Otto the Great (962), the head of the Germanic states was also emperor of the Holy Roman Empire. Although the pope was the nominal head of all the churches in this vast domain, consolidation in Germany provided the perfect organization for a national church under state control.

Elsewhere, the Scandinavian countries had been drained by the migrations of the ninth and tenth centuries, and consequently did not play a prominent role in the history of medieval Europe. Russia had emerged as a great world power, but since it was in the camp of the Greek Orthodox Church, it had no active part in the Reformation. Turkey was the most powerful Moslem country in Europe and threatened to conquer all of Europe in the name of Mohammed. Bajazet I (1347-1403) vowed that his horse "should eat oats on the high altar of St. Peter's in Rome." The Turkish menace, which almost conquered Vienna in 1529, occupied so much attention from Emperor Charles V and the Catholic princes that they were unable to concentrate on the sweeping threat of the Reformation.

Thus the prevailing political conditions afforded a favorable climate for the growing demand for reform. In fact, in Spain the political situation provided the arena for the first national reform movement.

2. XIMENES IN SPAIN

The great Spanish reformer Cardinal Francisco Ximenes was archbishop of Toledo and personal confessor to Queen Isabella. As the primate of all Spain, he had a burning zeal to purge the church of unworthy and undisciplined clergy and monks. He unleashed a remarkable upsurge of piety and learning, setting the example himself by an austere life-style of discipline and devotion. In a rare combination of force, education, and moral severity, he sought to purify the ecclesiastical orders of Spain. He eliminated many monastic abuses, stopped clerical irregularities, and fought heresy with great passion. As a humanist scholar, he promoted biblical and medical studies and founded the University of Alcala. He published the famous Complutensian Polyglot, the Bible in original languages. The first printing of the New Testament in Greek is accredited to Ximenes.

In this strange and remarkable man resided all the native skills and public power to execute a thoroughgoing reform of the church. His energies, however, became increasingly directed toward stamping out heresy, and he launched campaigns of preaching and violence against infidels and deviators from the faith. In 1507 he became head of the Spanish Inquisition, and during his ten-year administration as Grand Inquisitor, he put to death more than 2,500, imprisoned and tortured more than 40,000, and burned in effigy 1,300 who could not be apprehended. The man who had begun church reform aborted it with cruelty and oppression. Yet it was Ximenes who set the pace for the inner reform and counter revolutionary measures of Ignatius Loyola and the Jesuits yet to come.

3. INDULGENCE CONTROVERSY

While far-off Spain was cowing under the double-edged sword of Ximenes' reform and inquisition, central Europe was seething for revolt against a corrupt church and an unjust society. Without a doubt, the underlying causes of the eventual revolt were political, social, and economic as well as religious. The practical occasion which brought these disparate issues into clear focus was the profligate sale of indulgences by church officials. An indulgence was the means by which the church alleviated an individual's temporal penalties in purgatory because of special merit earned or exceptional contributions made. In the eleventh and twelfth centuries, popes promised soldiers indulgences for fighting against the Moslems in the crusades. Then indulgence was extended to those who could not go on the crusades, but financially sponsored someone who could. The practice was broadened to include many specified good works. To undergird the practice of granting indulgences, there developed the theological principle of the "treasury of the church," supported by leading school men such as Thomas Aquinas, Albertus Magnus, and Alexander of Hales. The idea of the "treasury of the church" was simply that the apostles and saints had done far more than was necessary to assure themselves of heaven, thus providing a surplus of merit. This, added to the great work accomplished by Christ, gave the church a rich treasury of merit which could be transferred to penitent sinners in satisfaction for their offenses. In 1343 Clement VI gave official papal endorsement to this principle, and trade in indulgences increased dramatically, developing into a business enterprise to raise money for the papacy.

In 1476, Pope Sixtus IV introduced the idea of allowing the living to buy indulgences for those already dead and in purgatory. By 1517, the practice of selling indulgences had become so commercial that a Dominican named Johann Tetzel was literally hawking indulgences throughout Germany by clever promotional methods, promising that as soon as the money fell into the coffer, a soul was released from purgatory. Tetzel and his co-workers told the people that the money they contributed to the indulgence fund was going to rebuild St. Peter's Church in Rome. The truth, however, was that only half the money was to go to the pope, and the other half was secretly pledged to pay off a personal ecclesiastical debt. Albert of Brandenburg, a prince-bishop, coveted the archbishopric of Mainz, but he already held two bishoprics and it was against canon law to hold more than one—and besides, he was too young to have any. To circumvent canon law and secure such privileges required large bribes and fees. Albert borrowed the needed money from the Fugger bankers, using as security the promise of an indulgence campaign in his territory, with half the proceeds going to the Fuggers and half to the pope.

At first, Luther was ignorant of this covert arrangement, and his celebrated attack on indulgences had already been launched on theological grounds. In several sermons in 1516, he had openly questioned the effectiveness and ethics of indulgences, declaring that the pope had no power to release souls from purgatory. Later, Luther pointed out that while others before him had merely attacked papal morals, he had gone to the theological roots of the problem: the perversion of the doctrine of grace, the externalizing of the sacrament of penance, and the ensnaring of conscience in a legalism contrary to the gospel of Christ. The indulgence controversy provided the tangible expression of these intangible issues, and when Luther posted his Ninety-Five Theses calling for a theological discussion on the efficacy of indulgences, he literally threw open the gate which had been straining for centuries against ecclesiastical abuses and theological heresies.

B. REFORM IN GERMANY

The Reformation as a religious movement was grounded in, and most fully supported by, the people of Germanic stock in northern and western Europe. The people of Germany had begun to resent papal efforts to drain the wealth of Germany's developing mines and to subject the middle classes to harsh financial abuses. The presence of Christian humanists in Germany had also stirred the fires of reform. The Germans' spiritual nature and strong nationalism thus prepared them to readily accept Luther as their champion and spokesman.

1. MARTIN LUTHER (1483-1546)

The founder of the German Reformation was born in the little town of Eisleben on November 10, 1483, the eldest of seven children. His father was a miner who eventually gained considerable wealth through shares he held in copper mines and smelters. The peasant traits of spirituality and superstition, however, remained in the family and left an indelible imprint on young Martin. He attended a school of the Brethren of the Common Life in Magdeburg for a brief period, and then was sent to school at Eisenach where he received advanced instruction in Latin to prepare him for university studies. Eventually, Luther received a bachelor's degree in 1502 from the University of Erfurt. According to his father's wishes, he planned to study law, but these plans were abruptly interrupted by an acute religious crisis. Always in the background of the Medieval Catholic there hovered the specter of purgatory and the wrath of God, with escape from such wrath being best found in the monasteries. Luther's childhood exposure to excessive superstition and his natural sensitivity to spiritual meanings led him to interpret several incidents as warnings that he must get right with God. Then a climactic event occurred on July 2, 1505. While walking near Stotternheim in a severe thunderstorm, Luther was almost struck by a bolt of lightning. He screamed out in fear, and vowed to Saint Anne (his father's patron saint) that if spared from death, he would become a monk. His father tried to restrain him from keeping his vow, suggesting that the experience was a "trick of the devil." Nevertheless, Luther kept his vow and two weeks later he entered the Augustinian monastery at Erfurt.

Life and training in the monastery did not bring Luther the peace he sought. When he performed his first Mass in May of 1507, he was overwhelmed with his unworthiness and fear of God, and was left with a terrible sense of loneliness and depression. He sought relief through the performance of good works and self-denial. He sought the merits of the saints, engaging in excessive confession of every type of sin. On a visit to Rome in 1510-11, he hoped to find forgiveness and release from his despair. He was, however, deeply shocked and disappointed by the superficial and worldly leaders in the very center of the Catholic world. (He later said that he had carried onions to Rome and brought back garlic.) Upon his return to Germany, he began preparing diligently for an appointment as professor of theology at the University of Wittenberg. He received his doctorate on October 19, 1512, and became lecturer in biblical theology, the position which he held until his death.

Luther began to lecture on various books of the Bible. From 1513 to 1516, he lectured on Psalms, Romans, Galatians, and Hebrews, studying personally from the original languages. From his intensive study and dedication to Scripture there developed his concept of *sola scriptura*, the idea that the Scriptures are the only authority for sinful men in seeking salvation. This concept formed one of the two main themes of his theological system. The other was *sola fide*, justification by faith alone. He arrived at the latter theme through the famous "tower experience," while studying the book of Romans in the tower room of the Augustinian friary at Wittenberg. The words of Romans 1:17, "The just shall live by faith," seemed to literally leap out at him, and the watchword of the Protestant Reformation was born. Writing about the experience thirty years later, Luther said, "Thereupon I felt as if I had been born again and had entered Paradise through wide-open gates. Immediately the whole of Scripture took on a new meaning for me. I raced through the Scriptures, so far as my memory went, and found analogies in other expressions."

In the place of an angry God, Luther had discovered a merciful God. He had been trying to appease the wrath of a God of justice, and now he encountered the forgiveness of a God of grace. He now knew that this forgiveness occurs by *sola fide*. Man is justified before God by faith alone, by accepting God's forgiveness in faith, not by achieving acceptance through good works. The difference between his old faith and his new faith was the difference between achieving and receiving. He soon developed the attending idea that man does good works not to earn his way into heaven but to express his joy and gratitude for what God has already done. His twin themes of *sola scriptura* and *sola fide* led to clear and distinctive affirmations which rocked the Catholic world: (1) Salvation is by faith alone, and not by works. (2) God is accessible to every Christian without the mediation of priest or church, hence the priesthood of all believers. (3) The Bible is the only source and standard for faith and life. (4) The Bible must be interpreted by the aid of the Holy Spirit. The individual man with his Bible (like Luther in his tower) came to symbolize the Protestant Christian.

With these revolutionary ideas, Luther undercut the dominant claims and practices of the church for the previous thousand years. Yet he did not immediately break with Rome. He was still a good, pious Catholic who did not feel that he was in opposition to the true doctrine of the church. He attacked only the evils and the abuses, most of which were not actually sanctioned by the church. The sacraments and the church always remained important to Luther. In the four years from 1513 to 1517, Luther's theological development was greatly influenced by (1) Occam's School of Theology, (2) the writings of Augustine, (3) the epistles of the Apostle Paul, and (4) German mysticism. Occam helped him to rely upon positive revelation and to mistrust reason. The writings of Augustine and Paul helped him to understand the doctrines of human sin, the righteousness of the law, and the true righteousness of God. German mysticism enabled him to acquire full certainty of God's grace and his salvation, a certainty which the medieval church had never been able to give.

One who had particularly helped Luther in arriving at the joyous

The posting of Martin Luther's Ninety-five Theses sounded the opening challenge to Rome which set off the Protestant Reformation. (The Bettmann Archive)

certainty of his salvation was his mentor and predecessor in the theological professorship, Johann von Staupitz. A sensitive and sympathetic spiritual advisor, Staupitz had encouraged Luther as early as 1505 when he was still a guilt-ridden monastic and while Staupitz headed the Augustinian community at Erfurt. Staupitz's insights into the gospel meant love and laughter as well as learning, and his gentle counseling with the troubled Luther undoubtedly had a decisive bearing on the latter's turning from cringing terror before a punishing Deity. Staupitz was faithful to medieval theology and the mystical piety of the middle ages.

It is little wonder that Luther still considered himself in mainstream Catholicism, for he seemed to be following the coaching of his honored Staupitz. To his surprise, however, Luther was seen in a singular light. His religious pilgrimage and his often-told experience of justification by faith soon made him a person of importance in Germany and eventually in all western Europe. Indeed, on May 8, 1517, he wrote to a friend at Erfurt that the lectures (at Wittenberg) on scholastic theology were deserted, "and no one can be sure of an audience who does not teach our theology." It appeared at the outset that Luther's reforms would be confined to theological curriculum. But he was a parish priest as well as a professor of theology; and when current abuses in the church threatened to imperil the souls of his parishioners, he was compelled to speak out. Thus, when the indulgence controversy reached Wittenberg, it came face to face with its indomitable foe, Martin Luther.

2. THE NINETY-FIVE THESES

October 31, 1517, is generally considered the birth date of the Protestant Reformation. It was on that fateful day that Dr. Martin Luther posted his famous Ninety-Five Theses on the Wittenberg Castle Church door in protest of the flagrant hawking of indulgences by Johann Tetzel. When Tetzel made the extravagant claims that indulgences would grant full pardon of all sins, even for the dead in purgatory, and even if one had violated the Virgin Mary, Luther felt compelled to protest the whole business.

The Castle Church, which served as the university chapel, housed almost eighteen thousand relics which had been collected by the Elector Frederick of Saxony (Luther's prince) and his predecessors. Offerings from religious pilgrims who came to view the relics were used as revenue for the university. The revered relics purportedly included bones from many saints, a twig from Moses' burning bush, pieces of Mary's girdle, feathers dropped by angels, and a tear shed by Jesus as he wept over Jerusalem. Payment to see the relics also served as indulgences, and it was possible to purchase as much as 2,000,000 years of release from purgatory. As early as 1516, Luther had spoken out against such obvious fraud. To do so was professionally precarious since his own salary depended in part on such income to the university's coffers. When Tetzel came hawking the new papal indulgences, Frederick forbade him to enter electoral Saxony for fear that Tetzel's wares would detract from his own. The people poured across the nearby border to buy Tetzel's indulgences, and Luther decided that it was time someone brought the whole issue into open debate.

Thus, on October 31, 1517, Luther nailed his ninety-five statements (theses) on the door of the Castle Church, which customarily served as a sort of university bulletin board. In academic circles this was a normal procedure for calling for debate or discussion on controversial issues, and Luther accordingly expected to have a normal academic and theological debate on the issue. In his preface he explains, "In the desire and with the purpose of elucidating the truth, a disputation will be held on the underwritten propositions. . . . He [Luther] therefore asks those who cannot be present and discuss the subject with us orally, to do so by letter in their absence." In his formal "Protestation" he says, "I implore all men, by the faith of Christ, either to point out to me a better way, if such a way has been divinely revealed to any, or at least to submit their opinion to the judgment of God and of the church."

The Ninety-Five Theses invited debate on three general subjects: (1) the traffic in indulgences, which Luther insisted was unscriptural, ineffective, and dangerous; (2) the power of the pope in forgiveness of sins, which Luther rejected; and (3) the treasury of the church, which Luther contended was the gospel and not the merits of Christ and the saints. The tone of the theses can be discerned through these representative charges: "(5) The pope has neither the will nor the power to remit any penalties. . . . (6) The pope has no power to remit any guilt, except declaring and warranting it to have been remitted by God. . . . (27) They preach man, who say that the soul flies out of purgatory as soon as the money thrown into the chest rattles. (28) It is certain that, when the money rattles in the chest, avarice and gain may be increased, but the suffrage of the church depends on the will of God alone. . . . (32) Those who believe that, through letters of pardon, they are made sure of their own salvation, will be eternally damned along with their teachers. . . . (56) The treasures of the church, whence the pope grants indulgences, are neither sufficiently named nor known among the people of Christ. . . . (62) The true treasure of the church is the holy gospel of the glory and grace of God. . . . (79) To say that the cross set up among the insignia of the papal arms is of equal power with the cross of Christ, is blasphemy. . . . (86) Why does not the pope, whose riches are at this day more ample than those of the wealthiest of the wealthy, build the one Basilica of St. Peter with his own money, rather than with that of poor believers?"

Luther had struck at the vital nerves of the Catholic system. He had forthrightly named as a fraud the whole indulgence business, which was the church's best means of acquiring funds. He had declared that the gospel itself supersedes the claims of the pope. He had impugned the integrity and authority of the pope. His theses were translated from Latin into vernacular German and, by means of the recently invented printing press, were circulated widely, causing others to come forth with their own grievances against the church. A furor erupted in every hamlet and village and Luther became a national hero overnight. The obscure professor-priest of Wittenberg had opened the floodgates of pent-up resentments, and the people felt at last they had a spokesman.

Tetzel and a group of Dominicans did accept Luther's challenge to debate, countering with their own set of theses. In effect, the Tetzel party reaffirmed hard-line Catholicism, upholding papal supremacy and infallibility, declaring that Catholic truth contains no falsehood, and that dissenters are heretics. Luther did not bother to refute Tetzel, as he had sent a copy of his theses to Archbishop Albert of Mainz, who had sent it on to the pope. Luther was confident that he would receive a just and fair hearing at the highest levels of the ecclesiastical hierarchy. Pope Leo X, however, was deeply involved in Italian and European politics and took only casual notice of what he thought was a minor squabble among monks. He did order the head of the Augustinians to quiet the noisy Luther, but at a chapter meeting of the Augustinians in April of 1518, Luther received substantial support from his peers, and one of those present, Martin Bucer, was to become a Reformation leader in his own right.

3. THE GATHERING STORM

The support of his peers and the German population gave Luther additional courage and incentive, and he became even bolder in his teaching and preaching. In July of 1518, Silvester Prierias, Master of the Sacred Palace and Papal Inquisitor, persuaded the pope to summon Luther to Rome for examination on suspicion of heresy. In the summons citation, Prierias declared that the pope is virtually the universal church, that he is infallible, and anyone who questions the pope on indulgences or any other matter is a heretic. Luther could not believe the document was from the pope, for all Christians, even the pope, know that Christ, not the pope, is the embodiment of the church. He further retorted that it is the Bible which is infallible and that popes and councils are fallible.

Through the influence of Frederick, Luther's prince, the summons to Rome was changed to a consultation at Augsburg with Cardinal Cajetan, which occurred in October, 1518. Luther soon discovered that Cardinal Cajetan did not want a discussion of the issues, but demanded an immediate retraction and submission from Luther, who replied that he could not submit without being shown his error either by Scripture or reason. In his replies to both Prierias and Cajetan, Luther stressed the authority of Scripture, shifting the controversy from the issue of indulgences to the issue of authority, the very issue which to this day remains the greatest dividing line between Protestants and Roman Catholics. Fearing arrest, and perhaps execution, Luther appealed to a general council as the ultimate earthly authority in Christianity. To ask for a council to judge him rather than the pope was a direct act of hostility against the papal office since such appeals had been seen as open heresy for over a century. It seemed that Luther was progressively "tightening the noose around his own neck," when he received unexpected relief from the intricate machinations of politics.

The emperor of the Holy Roman Empire Maximilian died early in 1519, and his successor was to be elected from among the reigning monarchs of Europe. Pope Leo X desperately wanted to block the election of a strong ruler who would dominate the papacy, such as Francis I of France or Charles I of Spain. He preferred a minor prince such as Frederick, and since Frederick was also one of the electors for the new emperor, it did not seem politically wise for the pope to press action against Frederick's most famous professor and protege, Martin Luther. Thus, a strange reversal of papal attitude toward Luther brought a brief reprieve.

To begin with, a papal bull was issued to clarify (modify) the position of the Roman Catholic Church on indulgences. It stated that indulgences could only reduce the temporal penalties on earth and in purgatory but could not release a soul from hell. Even then, they could not be applied until the sacrament of penance had been adequately observed. Concerning papal authority, the bull explained that the pope could remit penalties on earth but, for those in purgatory, he could only petition God, using the surplus merits of Christ and the saints as petitionary collateral.

Karl von Miltitz was sent as papal representative to conciliate Luther until after a new emperor was chosen. Miltitz disowned Tetzel, who soon died in distress and frustration, and got Luther to promise that he would refrain from debate if his opponents would do likewise. Miltitz had exceeded his authority from the pope and also erroneously reported back that Luther was ready to recant. Although Luther saw through Miltitz's duplicity, he refrained from further debate until provoked by the attacks of the renowned Johann Eck.

A distinguished professor of theology at the University of Ingolstadt, Johann Eck was also a humanist and a former friend of Luther. His continued attacks upon Luther's position provoked public demand for a formal debate between the two. This debate was arranged and took place in Leipzig in July of 1519, and became known as the Leipzig Disputation. It was an elaborate affair which lasted three weeks and attracted wide attention, even outside Germany. With his incessant prodding and skills of debate, Eck was able to draw Luther out to definitive positions which had heretofore been vague and embryonic. These critical and decisive positions included: (1) Luther's support of the ideas of John Hus, who had been condemned and burned by the Council of Constance a century ago; (2) Luther's belief that general councils are fallible, that they had erred, might err again, and often contradicted one another; (3) Luther's affirmation that articles of faith must come from Scripture and could not be established by the pope or the church.

Eck was jubilant over the debate, seeing himself as the clear winner. He had forced Luther's hand, and had revealed the plain "heresies" of the Wittenberg agitator. It was, indeed, an open revelation of what Luther really did believe. He had clearly denied the authority of the Roman Catholic Church, insisting that ultimate authority rests in the Bible as interpreted by the individual. The storm had reached its apex. Issues were now in the open, and churchmen, politicians, and the general population began to line up on one side or the other. Eck and most orthodox churchmen branded Luther as an avowed heretic. Many humanists, however, supported him, and practically all of his colleagues at Wittenberg stood solidly with him. Elector Frederick shrewdly protected his prize professor. Charles V had won enough votes to be chosen emperor, but he had no desire to create opposition in Germany, so he initially backed away from the controversy. An ultimate confrontation between Luther and the pope himself was becoming obvious and imminent.

4. THE BREAK WITH ROME

Luther was rapidly becoming an international figure. His collected Latin works were published in Basel and quickly sold out, with copies going throughout Germany, England, France, Switzerland, Spain, and Rome. The northern humanists hailed him as another Johann Reuchlin, and Erasmus called him a good man whose arguments should be met by reasoning rather than persecution. The year 1520 was a year of prolific writing for Luther. He seemed obsessed with articulating and circulating the ideas which now characterized his theology and personality. His writings that year took the form of essays known as tracts. In May he completed his *Sermon on Good Works*; in June he wrote *The Papacy at Rome*; in August, *The Address to the German Nobility*; in September, *The Babylonian Captivity of the Church*, and in November, *The Freedom of the Christian Man*. These were all written in terse German vernacular. They exuded burning conviction and displayed obvious scholarship. The tracts received an extensive reception and people throughout Europe were able to read what Luther actually believed.

In his *Sermon on Good Works*, he declared that the "noblest of all good works is to believe in Christ." He held that good works are to be done gladly and freely, not to attain salvation, but to please and serve God without thought of reward. He also insisted that good works are not limited to "religious" works such as praying, fasting, and giving alms, but include the normal activities of daily life. Obviously drawing from his own background of disappointment in pilgrimages, fasting, and confessing, he considered such exercises as evidence of spiritual immaturity and insecurity.

In *The Address to the German Nobility*, Luther attacked the three "walls" which the Roman church had built to protect itself. The first wall he named as the superiority of popes, bishops, and priests over the laity. He stated that all Christians are priests by baptism and that the clergy is not exempt from the jurisdiction of civil authorities. He described the second wall as the papal claim to the exclusive right to interpret Scripture. He repeated that every true believer is a priest and therefore competent to discern the Scriptures. Luther said the third wall was the claim that only the pope could summon a council and confirm its acts. He pointed out that Nicaea, the most famous of all councils, was called by the Emperor Constantine. He attacked the pomp and luxury of the pope and cardinals and called upon civil authorities to forbid the constant "milking" that the church committed against the people. He advocated the freedom of priests to marry, the abolishment of processions, festivals, masses for the dead, and all the various saints-days. He called for the expulsion of papal legates from Germany, the reform of the universities, and the teaching of the Bible in the schools.

In *The Babylonian Captivity of the Church,* Luther dealt with the sacraments and drastically departed from Catholic doctrine. He portrayed the papacy as the kingdom of Babylon which had carried the church into captivity. One form of the captivity was the denial of the cup to the laity. Luther insisted that communion should be given "in both kinds" to all believers who sought it and as often as they sought it. Another bondage Luther exposed was that of transubstantiation. He held that the bread and wine remain such and do not become the flesh and blood of Christ. He did believe, however, that the real presence of Christ abides in the real bread and wine, issuing in the view called consubstantiation. Luther also denied that the mass is a good work and a sacrifice, holding instead that it is a gift from God which can only be received in faith and thanksgiving. He expressed a high regard for baptism and did not deny it to infants, believing they are aided by the faith of those who bring them to baptism (a point which would later cause the Anabaptists to part with Luther). Although he did not practice it, he expressed preference for total immersion as the proper symbol of death and resurrection. Except for penance, Luther saw no scriptural grounds for the other sacraments. He saw the value of confession, but believed it need not be to an ordained priest. He acknowledged confirmation as a ceremony of the church but saw no grounds for regarding it as a sacrament. He upheld matrimony and denounced divorce, but again he knew of no scriptural basis for making matrimony a sacrament. He did not condemn ordination, but since all believers are priests, ordination simply designates a leader but has no sacramental value. He also did not condemn extreme unction, but he rejected any claims to a scriptural basis for it, and insisted that the faith of the recipient was the real issue. Again, he could not find biblical grounds for vows, and he contended that a farmer in his fields or a woman in her household duties were just as sacred in the sight of God as members of a religious order living by ecclesiastical vows.

In *The Freedom of the Christian Man*, Luther declared: "A Christian man is the most free lord of all, and subject to none; a Christian man is the most dutiful servant of all and subject to everyone." This was his definitive essay on justification by faith alone and the servanthood of the believer. He carefully explained that his doctrine of salvation by faith does not permit immorality, but promotes morality and good works. "It is not from works that we are set free by the faith of Christ but from foolishly presuming to seek justification through works." This essay was addressed to the pope after the latter had already issued his primary bull against Luther.

The essays of Luther were read avidly throughout Europe, and many disparate groups were finding a common champion in the bold German professor. Those who sought reform on a biblical basis found Luther more than adequate as a Bible scholar who obviously intended to fashion his reform around the Bible. The mystics who insisted that man could approach God without the mediation of priest and church heard Luther speaking their kind of language. Humanists who were working for reform on the intellectual level welcomed the open and erudite Luther. Patriotic Germans who dreamed of a reform to restore their beloved land to the people took Luther to their hearts as one of them. Luther also exhibited the deliberate and methodical life-style of the Germanic people, which caused them to trust him. He moved slowly step by step from protest to disputation to condemnation to separation, clear steps the people could follow and understand.

The step of separation was first provoked by Pope Leo X before Luther had finished writing his bold essays of that summer and fall. On June 15, 1520, Leo issued his famous *Exsurge Domine*, which began: "Arise, Lord, and judge thy cause. . . . A wild boar has invaded thy vineyard." In the papal bull, forty-one alleged errors of Luther were condemned, his books were ordered burned, and Luther himself was ordered to recant and submit within sixty days after the bull was placed in his hands. Widespread opposition to the bull caused three months to elapse before the document was delivered to Luther on October 10, 1520. Luther issued a blast against the bull and, on December 10, 1520, before an assembly of the students, teachers, and populace of Wittenberg, he burned the bull, along with works of his opponents and writings which supported papal claims. On January 3, 1521, the pope carried out his threat and issued a bull of excommunication against Dr. Martin Luther.

5. THE DIET OF WORMS
It was the desire and intention of the Church of Rome to have Luther publicly excommunicated as a heretic and turned over to the secular authorities to be burned at the stake. The newly elected emperor of the

Holy Roman Empire was Charles V from Spain, the grandson of Ferdinand and Isabella, who shared his grandmother's desire for reforming the church, but also had a strong loyalty to the pope and the Roman Catholic faith. He probably would have proceeded with Luther's execution had it not been for his own novice status as emperor and the sensitive political situation in Germany. Thus, he assembled imperial and ecclesiastical dignitaries to the Diet of Worms on April 18, 1521, and summoned Luther to come for a hearing.

The moderate Catholics who followed Erasmus worked to avert the schism and possible war that would erupt if Luther were burned. They tried to get Luther to compromise on the question of the sacraments, which would have made it possible to negotiate many other points. Their hopes for reconciliation, however, were crushed when Luther, called before the diet, acknowledged his authorship of a stack of books and writings, including the critical essay on sacraments. When asked if he still stood by all that he had written, Luther asked for time to reflect on his reply, and the next day he strongly affirmed that he did, indeed, still believe and stand by all that he had written. His famous statement of conviction centered on the principle of authority, rather than on sacraments or any other particular doctrine: "Since then your majesty and your lordships desire a simple reply, I will answer without horns and without teeth. Unless I am convicted by the Scriptures and plain reason—I do not accept the authority of popes and councils, for they have contradicted each other—my conscience is captive to the Word of God. I cannot and I will not recant anything, for to go against conscience is neither right nor safe. Here I stand. I cannot do otherwise. God help me. Amen."

Following his appearance before the full diet, Luther was summoned to a committee which tried to persuade him to compromise on some point, warning him that his obstinacy could provoke insurrection, division, and war. His reply was that truth is not open to negotiation. Then, still under the safe-conduct order of the emperor, Luther left Worms. On his way home, he was "kidnapped" by a band of his supporters, and taken, by order of Elector Frederick, to Wartburg Castle, near Eisenach. He remained there in disguise under an assumed name for eleven months.

The Emperor Charles V had hoped to negotiate with Luther, for he desired the same unity which the Erasmus party pursued. When, however, he saw that Luther was impenitent and immovable, he had no recourse but to take positive action against him. A month after the diet, in May of 1521, Charles issued the Edict of Worms, declaring Luther to be "a limb cut off from the Church of God, an obstinate schismatic and manifest heretic." The imperial edict commanded all subjects of the empire to refuse Luther hospitality, lodging, food, or drink, to take him prisoner and turn him over to the emperor. The decree also prohibited the printing, buying, or selling of Luther's works, and even called for the arrest of his friends and the confiscation of their property. Although it was never enforced, Luther lived out his days under the shadow of this edict. By the middle of 1521, Luther had been excommunicated by the Roman Catholic Church, and banned as an outlaw by the empire.

6. THE CONTINUING STRUGGLE

Although Luther was safe from his enemies at Wartburg, he was besieged by depression, insomnia, and various physical ailments. He turned his attention to arduous intellectual labor, and in nine months he wrote a dozen books and translated the entire New Testament from Greek into German. A powerful translation in popular German language, Luther's New Testament made the Bible a dominant influence in German life and contributed largely to the formation of the modern German language. In later years he also translated the Old Testament into German.

While Luther was at Wartburg, two of his colleagues at the University of Wittenberg assumed leadership of the Reformation. Philipp Melanchthon, the twenty-five-year-old grandnephew of the humanist Reuchlin, was a prodigy of classical learning who formulated the fundamental concepts and doctrines of the Bible in a work called *Loci Communes, rerum Theologicarum* which was in effect the first systematic theology of the new movement. Luther was so pleased with this work that he said it deserved a place in the scriptural canon. Concerning Melanchthon himself, Luther said, "I am rough, boisterous, stormy, and altogether warlike. I must remove the stumps, cut away the thistles and thorns, and clear the wild forests; but Master Philip comes along, softly and gently, sowing and watering with joy." History was yet to record that Melanchthon's softness and gentleness made him eager to compromise with Reformed and Catholic views, and contributed greatly to the doctrinal controversies within the Lutheran church in the sixteenth century.

The other colleague of Luther's to come to the front at this time was Andreas Carlstadt, an erratic and radical professor who tried to turn Luther's reform efforts into a full-scale revolution. He advocated the abolition of confession, priestly garb, and clerical celibacy (he himself married in 1522). He used German rather than Latin in the Mass, gave both bread and wine to the laity, and denounced the use of pictures and images. Mainly because of his influence, riots broke out against the Mass, with much destruction of church art and property. Appealing to the principle of the priesthood of all believers, Carlstadt dressed like a peasant and insisted on being called Brother Andreas rather than Doctor. He also denounced the use of music and music instruments in church services. When Luther returned to Wittenberg, he rejected Carlstadt's radicalism, and Carlstadt left in disgrace, living in obscurity and poverty most of the rest of his life. He finally settled in Switzerland in 1530 and worked with the Zwinglian reformers until his death.

The town council of Wittenberg, alarmed at the radical measures of Carlstadt and others, appealed to Luther to return and resume leadership of the movement which he had started. Luther did so, at grave risk to himself, for the imperial edict still condemned and banned him. Once in Wittenberg, however, Luther openly took charge and exerted all the force of his natural leadership. He advocated moderation rather than extremism, urging love and freedom of choice on controversial issues. His firm control and forthright sermons soon suppressed the radicals, such as the "Zwickau prophets" who espoused most of the views of the Anabaptists, also teaching that the kingdom of God would soon appear on earth and that their followers would receive special revelations.

Luther was now entrenched as the undisputed leader of the Reformation with Wittenberg as its center. Although Luther's return to Wittenberg had been fraught with danger, that danger never materialized. For twenty-five years he lived and worked untouched, mainly because his chief opponent, the Emperor Charles V, was constantly involved in fighting the French or a confederation of smaller powers, which at different times included England, Venice, the German Protestants, the Turks, and even the popes. This does not mean that Luther worked in peace and solitude. He was forever the center of controversy and occasionally the excuse for war. Some of his colleagues became his competitors and some of his friends became his enemies.

One of the first breaks was with the leading humanist, Erasmus. At the outset of the Reformation movement, Erasmus had sympathized with Luther, insisting that he was not a heretic. In fact, the two men were so much alike in their thoughts on church reform that their writings were often confused one with the other. But while Erasmus worked for moral reform within the church, he was passionately loyal to the structure and unity of the church. His hope that the church could work out its problems obviously stemmed from his humanistic philosophy that tended toward an optimistic view of human nature with the resulting concept that man is competent to work out his own salvation.

It was thus inevitable that Luther and Erasmus would clash over the doctrine of salvation as it touched on the free will of man. Because of his personal experience, his study of Augustine, and his reliance on biblical authority, Luther held that man is absolutely corrupt, incapable of earning anything from God, and can be saved only by the undeserved grace of God. Because of Erasmus' humanism, his exposures to Scholasticism, and his recognition of the supreme authority of the church, he staunchly upheld the ability and responsibility of man to participate in affecting his own salvation. In 1524 and 1526, Luther and Erasmus aired their differences in a series of pamphlets. When Erasmus wrote "On the Freedom of the Will," he stated that he could not accept Luther's view of the impotence of human will and the worthlessness of human works. Luther replied with a tract,

"On the Bound Will," in which he developed the theme of justification by faith alone and strongly attacked Erasmus' moralism. And so the controversy raged back and forth, until many humanists, including Erasmus, withdrew completely from the new movement, fearing that Luther was leading it toward social barbarism. Luther, on the other hand, felt the humanists had placed their trust in education and reason and did not even understand what the message of the Reformation was all about. Philipp Melanchthon was one of the young humanists who remained loyal to Luther and active in the cause of the Reformation.

7. DEVELOPING LUTHERANISM

The Luther who had furnished the dynamic catalyst for reform and revolt was now faced with the necessity of providing order and organization to the new movement. His energy which had been used to arouse the people must now be used to teach and train them. Theologically, Luther's position never wavered from his basic principles of *sola fide* and *sola scriptura*. He built his whole system on justification by faith and the primacy of the Word of God.

Holding to the priesthood of all believers, Luther taught that all Christians should view their occupations as vocations, callings of God, and that everyone had direct access to God through Christ without the mediation of priests or saints. He did not, however, advocate abolition of the priesthood, as did some of the radical reformers. He contended that the clergy was necessary for the equipping of the saints to perform their ministries in daily life. For guidance of the clergy and congregation he wrote *Ordering of Worship* and a booklet on baptism with a baptismal service in German. In 1526 he wrote a German Mass, in which he stressed the Eucharist as worship, fellowship, and thanksgiving.

Luther held the Christian sermon in highest esteem, elevating it to a place of unprecedented prominence in worship. He continued to be a popular preacher himself throughout his lifetime, and the place of preaching in Protestantism owes its origins to Luther's conviction and practice. He also made much of music in worship. Congregational singing was one of his great joys, and he contributed to this growing phenomenon both materially and inspirationally. He issued a hymnal and wrote some of the hymns himself. The most famous hymn from the pen of Luther was "A Mighty Fortress Is Our God," composed about 1528 when Charles V was trying to suppress the Reformation.

Education was another of Luther's major concerns. As a corollary to his belief in the priesthood of all believers, he sought the education of all, with the teaching of the Scriptures given prominence. He stimulated the publication of religious literature, taking upon himself to write a Small Catechism for children and a Large Catechism for adults. He wanted the entire body of Christian believers to be intelligent in their faith.

A significant departure from Catholic teaching and practice came about when Luther abolished monastic vows and obligatory clerical celibacy. Mendicant monasticism was no longer considered a virtue or a way of salvation. City ordinances in Protestant towns forbade begging, and monks and nuns who could were required to work. As they began to leave their monasteries and convents in large numbers, Luther told them they were free to marry. Although he had not intended to marry, Luther became a participant in one of his own projects. In 1525 all the nuns of one convent had escaped to Wittenberg in a disguised wagon, and Luther undertook to place them all safely in homes. The last remaining nun, Katharina von Bora, was favorably disposed toward Luther himself, and the untamed "boar" became a domesticated husband and father. Luther rationalized his marriage by saying that it would please his father and displease the pope. Besides, he noted, since Christ would return soon, there might never be another opportunity. Luther and his beloved "Herr Kathe" (Lord Katie) became the parents of six children and established the archetype of the Protestant parsonage. Their home was always open to friends, clergy, and students, the latter group recording for historical posterity Luther's scintillating "Table Talk."

Luther believed that the civil government should not impede the gospel, but that it was responsible for the maintenance of the true faith. He proposed a system of state visitation by which "visitors" appointed by the Elector (who was now John Frederick, succeeding his uncle Frederick the Wise who died in 1525) would investigate all the parishes in Saxony. Those priests found to be irrevocably ignorant and immoral were deposed. Those who were reputable but still committed to the old church were given instruction in the new faith. Gradually, the territory became uniformly Protestant, and the ministers became dependent on the state for their salaries, paid from the income of the confiscated properties of the Catholic Church.

Thus, with deliberate speed, Luther fashioned new forms of worship, church government, family life-styles, and civil government. By 1530, Lutheranism had taken a definitive shape, but it was not a universally popular shape, nor one carved out without dissension and even bloodshed.

8. THE PEASANTS' REVOLT

Even as Lutheranism developed and spread, it lost many of the class from which it had sprung, the peasants. This was always a deep grief to Luther, whose church in Wittenberg remained largely a peasant congregation. The uprising of the peasants climaxed in a series of revolts known to history as the Peasants' War. For centuries the peasants throughout medieval Europe had been complaining and revolting. Their complaints had been against the economic and social oppressions under which they suffered. They wanted relief from burdensome taxes, tithes, rents, labor services, and flagrant violations of their privileges. At first, the issues were not primarily religious, but soon the peasants realized that their national champion, Luther, had provided theological bases for their demands.

They began to apply his words on freedom and faith to social issues rather than theological propositions. In 1525, they published their *Twelve Articles* in which they said that since people are free to be Christians, they should also be free from serfdom. Luther's view of the priesthood of all believers provided ground for a society of equality, and his denunciation of corruption in monasticism gave them excuse to confiscate and plunder monasteries and convents. In the *Twelve Articles* the peasants claimed the right to choose and depose their own pastors, hunting and fishing rights, communal ownership of forests and meadows, and payment for extra services. They demanded the withdrawal of the cattle tax and the hated death tax. They swore to obey Scripture and believed their demands were in accord with God's Word.

At first, Luther was sympathetic with the peasants' demands, and some Catholics even accused him of starting the revolt. In April of 1525, he published a pamphlet, *Admonition to Peace: A Reply to the Twelve Articles of the Peasants,* in which he tried to act as conciliator between the princes and peasants. He admonished the princes for their tyranny, intolerance, cruelty, and unjust demands. He agreed that peasants should have the right to choose their own pastors, and that their social demands were also just. At the same time, he rebuked the peasants for misinterpreting the gospel and using its message of spiritual freedom to apply to social conditions. He objected to making all men equal and trying to translate the kingdom of heaven into a physical kingdom in this world. He also deplored insurrection, advised arbitration, and insisted that civil authorities should be respected and obeyed as the servants of God.

Instead of heeding Luther's advice to be patient and compromise, the peasants erupted in violence, plundering and ravaging the land. On April 16, peasants stormed Weinsberg, massacring its inhabitants and burning castles and cloisters. At Muhlhausen, Thomas Muntzer, a radical reformer, led other fiery preachers in calling for the slaughter of the oppressors in the name of God. Luther was appalled by this violent turn of events and issued his scathing essay *Against the Robbing and Murdering Hordes of Peasants.* In this unfortunate publication, Luther called on the princes to use any means to suppress the rebels: "Smite, slay, and stab, secretly or openly . . . as if among mad dogs, lest the whole land be ruined." Luther contended that the peasants deserved death since they had broken their oaths, had become robbers and murderers, and had done it all in the name of the gospel.

Such an exhortation was not needed; the German nobility, both Lutheran and Catholic, had united to crush the uprising. On May 15, at Frankenhausen, 50,000 peasants armed with clubs and pitchforks were overwhelmed and butchered. Lightning swift reprisals throughout the country left the peasants defeated and demoralized. An estimated 100,000 were killed, and many more severely wounded and mangled. This time Luther was horrified by the brutality of the princes, and came out with a third pamphlet asking for mercy to the captives. He declared that the devils, having left the peasants, had not returned to hell, but instead had entered the nobles. Nonetheless, the peasant revolt was crushed and the territorial princes had increased their power in all areas, including the affairs of the church. Luther had opted for the ruling powers, and demonstrated that he was committed to the sovereignty of the state. The peasants in south Germany, where the uprising had centered, felt that Luther had betrayed them, and, on his part, Luther henceforth had a deep distrust of the common man and a growing fear of chaos.

This fear also led him to sever his relations with the more radical reformers, especially Thomas Muntzer and his former colleague Andreas Carlstadt. Luther urged the princes to prevent the radicals from executing the ungodly and those who honored images. He campaigned tenaciously for sanity and peace. It often seemed that he had created a monster he could no longer control. This internal turmoil among the Reformers was enough to exhaust his time and energy, but there was yet to come the final showdown with Rome.

9. FROM SPEYER TO AUGSBURG

The imperial Edict of Worms, issued in 1521 against Luther and his followers, was still in effect. Although Charles V had not forgotten Luther and the edict against him, he had been too occupied with wars against France and threats by the Turks to enforce the edict. Now he began to move in that direction and was successful in getting the Diet of Nuremberg to decree in 1524 that the Edict of Worms should be enforced "insofar as might be possible." The princes in south Germany were remaining loyal to Rome and supporting the emperor, but the princes in the North were lining up with Luther. The Diet of Speyer was convened in 1526 to consider the emperor's demand that the Edict of Worms be enforced and the northerners won a temporary victory. It was decreed that each of the princes was "so to live, govern, and carry himself as he hopes and trusts to answer it to God and his imperial majesty." This appeared to be a suspension of the Edict of Worms, and the evangelicals felt free to regulate their religious affairs as they pleased.

The diet met again in Speyer in 1529, and this time it had a Roman Catholic majority, and ordered that no further changes in religion be made. It also decreed that Catholic minorities must be allowed in Lutheran areas, but that Lutheran minorities would not be tolerated in Catholic areas. The Lutherans in the diet entered a formal protest against this decree, and it is from this protest that the term Protestant is derived. At first limited to

Lutherans, the term was eventually applied to all those movements which broke from the Catholic Church in the sixteenth century.

By 1530, Charles V had repulsed the Turks in their drive toward Vienna and was able to give his personal attention to the devisive religious issue of the empire. In an effort to restore unity, he called a meeting of the Diet at Augsburg and invited all parties to present their beliefs. Melanchthon was commissioned to draw up the statement of Lutheran beliefs. In consultation with Luther (who remained at Coburg since he was still under the imperial ban) Melanchthon produced the famous Augsburg Confession, a lengthy document which became regarded as the official statement of the Lutheran position. Its main tenet is justification by faith, which is elevated over meritorious works. It places authority in the biblical Word of God as interpreted by conscience. Among other things, it rejects transubstantiation, propitiatory Mass, and invocation of the saints. It upholds civil government and the duty of Christians to hold office. The first part of the confession, however, enumerates the ways in which the Lutheran position is in harmony with the universal church, and even the church of Rome, insofar as that church has not strayed from the early Fathers. The Augsburg Confession was heartily endorsed by Luther and the Lutheran princes who knew they were in danger of losing their titles, lands, and perhaps their lives. On June 25, 1530, the northern princes and representatives from the cities stood boldly for two hours while the Augsburg Confession was read before the imperial diet.

All of the Reformers who were present, however, did not subscribe to the confession. Divisions had been growing among them on theological issues, especially the matter of the Lord's Supper. Zwingli regarded the Lord's Supper basically as a memorial, and the Reformers of Strassburg maintained a position between Zwingli and Luther, who still believed in consubstantiation (that the real presence of Christ was in the Supper) though he repudiated Catholic transubstantiation (that the bread and wine are transformed into the body and blood of Christ). In October of 1529, Philip of Hesse, a Reformation prince, had succeeded in getting Luther, Zwingli, Melanchthon and Bucer (the Reformer of Strassburg), to come together at his castle at Marburg to resolve their differences. Known as the Marburg Colloquy, the meeting extended over several days and at times appeared profitable, but they parted still divided on basic issues. So, a year later at Augsburg, Zwingli and the Strassburgers refused to sign the Lutheran confession and each presented his position in a separate document on July 3 and 11.

The Roman Catholic *Confutation* was presented on July 13, but the emperor considered it too long (351 pages) and too abusive, so it was rewritten and submitted on August 3. Then the emperor attempted to reconcile the differences of the various positions through committee conferences and negotiations, but to no avail. The diet, dominated by a

Catholic majority, held that the Protestants had been refuted and should recant. The emperor gave the Protestants until April 1531 to surrender their positions and submit to the authority of the Roman church.

Fearing military action, the Protestant princes met in Schmalkalden and formed a defensive coalition called the Schmalkaldic (Smalcald) League. The Strassburg Reformers also accepted the Augsburg Confession and joined the league. The Turks entered the picture again, however, and in July of 1532, the emperor and the Schmalkaldic League agreed upon a truce while united against the Turkish invasion, a truce which lasted for some sixteen years. At the emperor's insistence repeated conferences of Protestants and Catholics were held in 1540 and 1541, but failed to bring accord.

10. THE DEATH OF LUTHER AND THE SURVIVAL OF LUTHERANISM

Luther's later years were marked by complications, some of which were physical illnesses and some emotional distresses. He found himself constantly at the center of controversy and having to take a stand for and against a vast array of complex issues. He had earlier opposed the burning of Anabaptists by Lutherans, but now he reluctantly agreed that the death penalty was just, for they were guilty of sedition and blasphemy. He also became a vigorous enemy of the Jews, denouncing them for their rejection of Christ, and insisting that their synagogues be burned, their books taken from them, and that all Jews who could not be deported to Palestine should be forced to earn their living by tilling the soil. Of course, he continued to rail against the pope, and his railings became more explicit and crude. To the end of his life, he kept busy preaching, teaching, and revising his translation of the Bible. In all, he produced over four hundred works and 125 hymns. Toward the end he majored on spiritual counseling, giving special guidance to Melanchthon, who took up the leadership of Lutheranism. On February 18, 1546, Martin Luther died in Eisleben where he had been born sixty-three years earlier.

Luther had been spared the pain of seeing Protestants and Catholics in open warfare, but the next year, in April of 1547, hostilities began. The Lutherans suffered initial defeat by imperial forces. Philip of Hesse and the Elector John Frederick of Saxony were defeated and imprisoned. It appeared that thirty years after the posting of Luther's Ninety-Five Theses that Protestantism had been crushed in Germany. The general populace, however, refused to be suppressed, and war broke out again, with the king of France coming to the aid of the Protestant princes. The emperor was defeated and almost captured in 1552.

The diet met again at Augsburg to affect a peaceful settlement, and after months of debate the Peace of Augsburg was formulated on September 25, 1555. The settlement was a compromise, centered around the principle of *cujus regio, ejus religio* (whose region, his religion). Each prince was to determine the kind of religion for his territory. Lutheran princes were allowed to remain so, and Roman Catholic princes were not to be disturbed. Neither group of princes was to molest the other. If either Protestants or Catholics wished to emigrate, they were to be allowed to sell their property and move. No forms of Protestantism other than Lutheranism were to be tolerated. With the Peace of Augsburg, Lutheranism had at last gained a legal status within the empire.

11. LUTHERANISM BEYOND GERMANY

From the first days of the Reformation, Lutheranism spread quickly from Germany to other countries. The most significant converts to Lutheranism were the people of the Scandinavian countries. At the beginning of the sixteenth century, Denmark, Norway, and Sweden were ruled by the monarchs of Denmark, where the church was powerful and wealthy. Along with the power and wealth had come corruption and worldliness, and early in the sixteenth century Paul Helgesen began to urge reform. He was followed by Hans Tausen, a professor of theology at Copenhagen, who had heard Luther preach at Wittenberg. Tausen's powerful sermons on reform aroused the people of Denmark and moved them toward Lutheranism. Under the monarchy of Christian III (1534-1559) Denmark became fully Lutheran. Luther himself approved the proposed administrative structure of the new church. A liturgy was compiled, the Augsburg Confession was adopted, and the Bible was translated into Danish by Christiern Pederson, the first writer of importance to use Danish. The entire kingdom became Lutheran with a national church which had the monarch as its executive head.

The development of Lutheranism in Norway was not as popular nor successful as it was in Denmark. When the Roman Catholic Archbishop of Tronhjem opposed the monarchy of Christian III, the king drove him from the country, leaving the Catholics without an official leader. All but two of their bishops were turned out and those two became Lutherans and remained. A few Lutheran pastors came to minister to the people, but it was not until the beginning of the seventeenth century that religious conditions in Norway began to improve.

In Sweden, Lutheranism was adopted in connection with a political revolution led by a young nobleman, Gustavus Ericksson, who became known as Gustavus Vasa, from the *Vasa*, or sheaf, which was on his coat of arms. With an army of peasants, he drove the Danes out of Sweden and was crowned king in 1528. The new kingdom was in desperate need of financial resources, and the new king found these in the wealthy church of Sweden. State and church were welded together as two in one, making a convenient vehicle for Reformation methods.

The chief preacher of the Swedish Reformation was Olaf Petersson, who had taken his master's degree at Wittenberg, and was, in fact, present there when Luther nailed his Ninety-Five Theses on the church door. He returned to Sweden before the Reformation reached its radical stages, and his stand was for moderate reform and not wholesale changes.

The break of the Swedish church from Rome was thus instigated not by doctrinal differences but by administrative disputes over the confirmation of bishops and the paying of customary annates to Rome. In November of 1523, the king declared that he recognized "Christ the only and highest pontiff," and the tie with Rome was severed. Changes in the Church of Sweden were not as drastic as they were in Lutheran Germany; the marriage of priests, and former monks and nuns, was permitted, preaching was elevated, and the Bible was translated into Swedish.

Olaf Petersson continued to be the leading theologian, translator, hymn-writer, and spokesman of the Swedish Reformation. He was joined in his work by his brother, Lars Petersson, Archbishop of Uppsala, who became a strong influence in helping the church regain partial autonomy from the state. In the latter part of the sixteenth century several attempts were made to introduce Calvinism into Sweden, but Sweden remained staunchly Lutheran.

The island of Iceland was also ruled from Denmark, and under Christian III it was forcibly brought into the Lutheran camp. Later, the peaceable and scholarly bishop, Gudbrand Thorlaksson, gave Lutheranism its permanent foothold through literature: a Norse translation of the Bible, hymnals, and catechisms. A similar procedure was followed in Finland, which had been subject to Sweden for centuries. Gustavus Vasa introduced the Reformation to Finland, but it was Isaac Rothovius, Bishop of Abo from 1627 to 1652, who raised the level of Christianity by improving the quality of the clergy, advancing education, founding a university, and translating the Bible into Finnish.

Lutheranism also spread eastward toward central Europe. By the end of the sixteenth century, nine-tenths of the population of Bohemia was Protestant. In an unusual confederation of unity, Lutherans and Calvinists had formulated a common confession of faith (1575) to withstand aggressive Catholic attempts to retake the country. Hungarians who had studied at Wittenberg brought back the teachings of Luther and Melanchthon, and were in a strategic position to move into power when Catholic leaders were overthrown by the Turks in 1526. A great preacher, Matthias Biro of Deva (also known as Devoy), came to be called the Hungarian Luther, and Stephen Kis of Szeged became the country's leading Protestant theologian. By 1568, equal rights had been granted to Catholics, Lutherans, Reformed, and Unitarians in the country of Transylvania. Luther's writings were being circulated in Great Britain, Italy, and Spain. He had become the catalyst for church reform, and the worldwide chain reaction of his movement continues to the present day.

C. REFORM IN SWITZERLAND

Although Luther was unquestionably the strongest voice of the Reformation, he was by no means its only voice. As Lutheranism was developing in Germany, another kind of Protestantism was emerging, usually known as the Reformed Church. There are many varieties of the Reformed Church continuing in the worldwide association to this day. The two outstanding leaders of the Reformed movement were Zwingli and Calvin, and the small, beautiful country of Switzerland was the vineyard in which they labored.

1. ZWINGLI AND ZURICH

About six weeks after Martin Luther was born in Germany, Ulrich Zwingli was born January 1, 1484, at Wildhaus, an obscure town in the district of Toggenburg, Switzerland. Ulrich was a brilliant student and was sponsored in his education by his uncle, a parish priest. He was first educated in the schools of Basel and Bern, and later at the universities of Vienna and Basel. He was particularly influenced by the ancient works of Augustine and the contemporary writings of Erasmus. In 1506, he was appointed parish priest at Glarus, where he served for ten years. His pastorate there was terminated when he began to preach unpopular sermons against mercenary service, with which he had become disenchanted while serving as field chaplain. He took a post as priest at Einsiedeln in 1516, the year before Luther nailed his theses on the Wittenberg chapel door. He became extremely well-known as a strong preacher and in 1519 he was made priest of the Great Minster in Zurich, a small but wealthy and influential city. At the time of his appointment to Zurich, he was investigated for alleged heresy and seduction of a young girl. He denied both charges, but admitted sexual incontinence, insisting that celibacy vows did not include chastity. The city council acquitted him on both charges, and officially supported his ministry.

Zwingli was already acquainted with Luther's writings and endorsed them, but he later denied that he was a product of the Wittenberg Reformer. Indeed, he was an individualist, in his thinking, preaching, and reforming. His religious experience was also different from Luther's. Whereas the latter had undergone a dramatic conversion while wrestling with guilt and discovering that the "just shall live by faith," Zwingli's decisive commitment occurred as an expression of gratitude for providential mercy. The city of Zurich was ravaged by the plague in 1519 and Zwingli was stricken and almost died. He promised that if God spared him he would consecrate his life fully to the service of Christ wherever that might lead him. Luther had struggled with sin and grace, while Zwingli had submitted clearly and logically to the will of God. Both, however, arrived at the same theological positions of *sola fide* and *sola scriptura*.

In 1520 Zwingli surrendered his papal pension in order to be a free man and to practice what he had been preaching. The authority of the Scriptures became increasingly paramount to Zwingli, and he led the civil rulers of Zurich to decree that priests should be free to preach directly from the Scriptures according to their consciences. He demonstrated his own preaching and exegetical skills in a masterful series of studies from the Gospel of Matthew. Thereafter, he began to expound Scripture verse by verse, book by book, and by 1525, he had preached through the entire New Testament. Great crowds attended his preaching, and to reach more people, he began preaching in the markets.

In 1522 Zwingli precipitated a critical encounter with the bishop of Constance by his vigorous preaching against Lenten fasts and rules. When the bishop insisted that Zwingli cease his attacks upon these Catholic traditions, the city council of Zurich backed Zwingli and ruled that all religious customs should be based on the pure Word of God. The authority of the bishop of Constance had been replaced with civil rule in accordance with the Word, which became the reform motif of Zurich. This open conflict with church authorities brought about several public debates over the next two years. The first of these was held in January of 1523 at the Town Hall of Zurich, where Zwingli presented his famous *Sixty-seven Articles*, in which he substituted the authority of the Scriptures for the authority of the church, and attacked the primacy of the pope, the worship of saints, the merit of good works, fasts, festivals, pilgrimages, monastic orders, celibacy of the clergy, auricular confession, absolution, indulgences, penances, and purgatory. He declared them all to be of human invention, with no foundation in Scripture. The city government of Zurich endorsed Zwingli's ideas and promptly set up new regulations to enforce them. Also, priests and nuns began to forsake their monasteries and convents and to marry. Zwingli himself officially married Anna Reinhart, a wealthy widow, in April of 1524. They had been living together for some two years, with various reports that it had been a secret marriage, a common-law marriage, or an irregular liaison.

A second public debate was held in October of 1523 to discuss the use of images in the churches and the Catholic doctrine of the Mass. Zwingli called for the removal of all statues and pictures in the churches, which was soon accomplished. He eventually removed all ornaments, clerical robes, tapestries, frescoes, relics, crucifixes, candles, and images. Bell-ringing, chanting, and organ playing were ceased, and the great organ in Zurich was dismantled. The Mass was declared to be a memorial of the death of Christ and not a sacrifice. Thus, Zwingli rejected transubstantiation in favor of a symbolic and commemorative view. The elaborate rite of the Mass was abolished and the first evangelical communion service was held in the Great Minster Church of Zurich on April 13, 1525.

The Zwinglian Reformation had made a complete break from the Roman Catholic Church, and the Swiss Reformer began the process of building a new church. His best theological work, a *Commentary on True and False Religion,* appeared in 1525. He contended that the Bible alone was authoritative for faith, and that Christians should reject anything not expressly given in Scripture. He stated his belief in an omnipotent God who directs men and foreordains the elect, an election made known through a faith experience. He believed that the Spirit operates outside the sacraments, even inspiring non-Christians such as Socrates and Cato. His philosophical humanism obviously influenced his theological positions. It also led him to be a champion of Christian education, forming elementary schools, and translating the Bible into the vernacular. Zwingli's intellectual and moral approach to reform was in obvious contrast to Luther's tempestuous struggle for assurance of justification by faith.

The two Reformers actually differed on several major points and finally came to an irreparable break over the issue of the Lord's Supper. Luther maintained that Christ is actually present in the consecrated elements, although he was never able to explain exactly how that happens. Zwingli regarded the rite primarily as a memorial, and accused Luther of perpetuating Roman Catholic superstition. Martin Bucer, who had won Strassburg to the evangelical cause, tried repeatedly to unite Luther and Zwingli and was instrumental in setting up the Marburg Colloquy in 1529. The meeting was hosted by Philip of Hesse who also desired to see unity between the German and the Swiss Reformers. It met in the Castle at Marburg-on-the-Lahn on October 1-3, 1529. Martin Luther and Philipp Melanchthon represented the Saxons, and Ulrich Zwingli, Martin Bucer, and Johann Oecolampadius (who had won Basel) represented the Swiss. Agreement was reached on fourteen of the fifteen "Marburg Articles" which Luther (or Melanchthon) had drawn up, but the conference failed with Zwingli's refusal to accept the Lutheran doctrine of consubstantiation. The articles eventually became the first of the Lutheran Symbolical Books and incorporated into the Augsburg Confession of 1530, against which Zwingli presented a separate confession of faith.

While Zwingli had trouble with Luther's attitude toward the Supper, he was also experiencing difficulty with the Anabaptists over infant baptism. Conrad Grebel, Felix Manz, and many of Zwingli's early supporters began to insist that he abolish infant baptism, and there are several indications that he leaned in that direction himself. Always politically minded, however, he knew that to do so would "unchurch" the whole Zurich city council which had put through his reform measures. Thus, he retained infant baptism; but he carefully explained that he did not consider it necessary for salvation but only as a means of identifying the child with the Christian covenant. This was not good enough for the Anabaptists, and they began to go their own way.

Zwingli also had his troubles with the surrounding cantons in Switzerland, trouble which ended in his death. For some three hundred

years, the Swiss republic had been organized around independent small
countylike states called cantons, with each canton having one vote in the
diet or congress. Zwingli had been successful in bringing several strong city
cantons, such as St. Gall, Basel, Bern, and Strassburg, into the Reform
movement. Most rural cantons, however, were satisfied with the old
Roman Catholic relationship, and they formed a league with Lucerne to
withstand the reform. The city cantons and some southern German cities
confederated in a Reform league, and by 1529 civil war seemed imminent.
Hostilities were restrained for a while, and Zwingli worked fervently to
secure acceptance of his reform in all the thirteen cantons of Switzerland.
This infuriated the five Forest Cantons (Catholic) who made a sudden and
unexpected attack on Zurich. They were met by a small force at Kappel,
where Zwingli, who as chaplain carried the banner, was killed on October
11, 1531.

Henry Bullinger succeeded Zwingli in Zurich, respecting the treaty
signed with the Catholics, and limiting his work to his own canton. In less
than a generation the Zwinglian movement was swallowed up by the larger
and more influential movement of John Calvin.

2. CALVIN AND GENEVA

He who has been called "the greatest theologian and disciplinarian of the
great race of the Reformers" and "the only international Reformer," John
Calvin, was born in 1509 at Noyon, France. His father was secretary and
attorney to the bishop of Noyon, and provided his family with comfortable
circumstances. Young John Calvin was reared in aristocratic society and
always bore the manners of that class. His father intended him to enter an
ecclesiastical career and sent him to study theology at the University of
Paris when he was only fourteen. By coincidence, he was in the university
at the same time Francis Xavier and Ignatius Loyola, leaders of the Catholic
Reformation, were enrolled; but there is no evidence that he ever met them.
Calvin appeared to have doubts about his priestly vocation and his own
faith, and left Paris in 1527. He went to Orleans to study law when he was
nineteen, and was strongly attracted to current humanism, Latin, Greek,
and Hebrew. In 1532, at the age of twenty-three, he published an erudite
humanist book, *Commentary on Seneca's Treatise on Clemency*.

Sometime within the next year, Calvin experienced what he called a
"sudden conversion." He always refused to elaborate on this experience,
saying only that God had spoken to him through the Bible and had to be
obeyed. "God subdued and brought my heart to docility. It was more
hardened against such matters than was to be expected in such a young
man." Later, he adopted as his crest a flaming heart on an outstretched
hand with the inscription, "My heart I give Thee, wholly and freely."

Although the sincere and sensitive young Calvin saw the deep need for
reform within Catholicism, he had no desire or plans to break with the

Roman church. Very soon after his conversion, however, he became involved in a singular incident which precipitated the break. His close associate, Nicholas Cop, was installed as rector of the University of Paris, and in his inaugural address Cop called for church reform, stirring up a storm of protest. Since Calvin was so closely associated with Cop, he was identified immediately with the call for reform. In fact, he was often accused of being the ghostwriter for Cop's address. Calvin and Cop were forced to flee Paris, but were captured and imprisoned briefly at Noyon, from whence they fled France and sought safety in Basel, Switzerland. Thus, Calvin felt compelled to break with Rome and took his stand henceforth with the Reformers.

a. Calvin's Institutes. At Basel, while he was still only twenty-six years old, Calvin published in 1536 the first edition of what became the most influential single book of the Protestant Reformation, *The Institutes of the Christian Religion.* Originally writing it in Latin, he soon translated it into French. Then and thereafter Calvin did more than any other person in making French the great world vehicle for philosophical and theological discussion. He revised the *Institutes* many times, giving it its final form in 1559, only a few years before his death.

The *Institutes* was originally and formally addressed to King Francis I of France, who had been persecuting the French Protestants on spurious charges of sedition and anarchy. Calvin's book was a comprehensive and orderly summary of Christian Reformed doctrine, in which he made a systematic presentation of the Protestant position. The work was not particularly original, for many others had already stated the Protestant position, but it was immediately successful and widely read because of its clarity, comprehensiveness, and orderly arrangement. The *Institutes* was the most inclusive and systematic presentation of the Christian faith as held by Protestants which had thus far appeared. In the final edition of the *Institutes* there were four books, conforming to the order of the Apostles' Creed. The first dealt with God the Father as creator, preserver, and governor of the universe; the second outlined the redemption of man by God through Christ; the third examined the work of the Holy Spirit; and the fourth discussed the church and its relation to civil governments.

Calvin's key thoughts were clearly and forcefully spelled out in the *Institutes.* God is absolute sovereign in his creation, and thus foreknows and foreordains all things, including man's destiny. Although originally pure, man has fallen through Adam's disobedience and is sinful. Man can be saved only by the undeserved grace of God, as mediated through Jesus Christ; man cannot earn his own salvation through good works. Those predestined to be saved by God will not be able to resist his grace. Calvin's position on predestination was intended as a source of comfort during persecution, and Calvinism produced strong, confident men by assuring

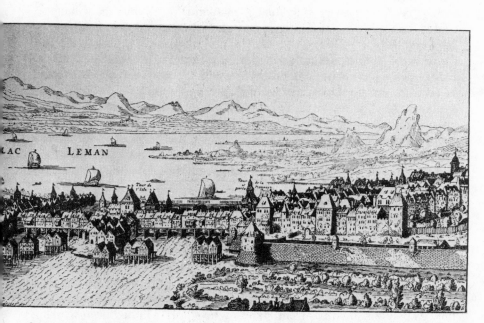

Geneva at the time of the Reformation, from an engraving by Visscher (1641). (The Bettmann Archive)

them that God had a plan of salvation, that he had called them to be his fellow workers, that he would stand by them in the midst of opposition, and that they would ultimately prevail.

Election or predestination became the dominant theme of Calvinism, with God always in the role of sovereign. Why does God elect some to be saved and some to be lost? Because it pleases him to do so. For Calvin, God does not have to explain himself to man nor satisfy human rationalism. Everything is as God ordains: "He governs heaven and earth by his providence, and regulates all things in such a manner that nothing happens but according to his counsel. . . . Predestination we call the eternal decree of God, by which he has determined himself, what he would have to become of every individual of mankind. . . . While the will of God is the supreme and primary cause of all things, and God holds the devil and the godless subject to his will, nevertheless God cannot be called the cause of sin, nor the author of evil, nor subject of any guilt. . . . Man falls as God's providence ordains, but he falls by his own fault." Men are saved by God's gratuitous mercy, but they are damned by their own depravity. Also, although God's grace is irresistible, it may also be unknown to the recipient. Those who are elected will manifest the presence of the Spirit in disciplined morality and calling, a concept which prompted some later Calvinists to do good works to convince themselves of election, and which made Calvin's experiment of a controlled community possible.

b. A Model Christian Community. Because he had championed the cause of the persecuted Protestants in France and had articulated their beliefs so clearly and forcefully, Calvin became an overnight hero and a sought-after leader. Soon after the *Institutes* was published, he was on his way to Strassburg where he intended to settle down in a quiet library and devote his life to scholarly studies. He was forced to detour through Geneva because of heavy fighting, and became acquainted with William Farel, a fiery, impetuous Reformer from France, who since 1533 had been working to bring Geneva solidly into the evangelical camp. Farel convinced Calvin that it was God's will for him to stay in Geneva and help develop that city into a model Christian community. Calvin remained, and except for three years' banishment at Strassburg (1538-1541), he spent the rest of his life at Geneva.

The city was ruled by a bishop and an administrator, both of whom were controlled by the duke of Savoy. The citizens shared in local government through a general assembly and an elected committee known as the Little Council. This appeared to be an ideal arrangement for the reform which Farel and Calvin proposed for the city. In January of 1537, Calvin presented to the Little Council of Geneva a series of articles calling for reform. His ideal was that of a Puritan society of trained and conscientious Christians, needing no restraint by civil authorities except for those who abandoned the church.

There were three basic steps in organizing Calvin's model community. First and foremost, the Lord's Supper was to be of central importance. Instead of a daily Mass, he proposed that the Supper be observed monthly, with the unworthy being excluded. In order to identify and discipline the unworthy, Calvin asked the Council to appoint "certain persons of upright life and good reputation among all the faithful, who being divided and distributed in all quarters of the city, shall have an eye to the life and conduct of each one." Those who refused to repent of their moral infractions were to be excommunicated, "rejected from the company of Christians."

The second step was to impose a confession of faith on the citizenry. The whole population was required to choose between Romanism and Protestantism. The members of the council were asked to profess publicly the Reformed faith, and then to appoint representatives who would work with the pastors to receive a profession of faith from all persons in Geneva, "that it may be understood who of them agree with the Gospel, and who love to be of the kingdom of the Pope rather than the kingdom of Jesus Christ."

A necessary third step to facilitate the first two was a systematic program of teaching and training. For the adult population, Calvin prepared a Confession of Faith (1536) and for the children a Catechism (1537). Each contained an orderly and lucid outline of Christianity, a sort of pocket edition of the *Institutes*. The Council was asked to order parents to see that their children learned the catechism and present themselves to the ministers at appointed times. The future of Protestantism in Geneva would thus be assured.

c. Opposition and Control. Tension and controversy swirled around Calvin's proposals. The Little Council adopted the articles with modifications. It set the observance of the Lord's Supper at only four times a year, and expressed preference for the system of discipline at Bern where the church was under the control of the state. While supporting the Confession of Faith, the Council refused to withhold the Supper from those who did not. Farel and Calvin were adamant in their demands and refused to compromise. They were forbidden to preach and preached in defiance. Thus the Little Council and General Assembly commanded the two Reformers to leave Geneva in April, 1538. They went to Bern and to Zurich, gaining support for their articles of reform but criticism for their unbending rigidity on discipline. Finally, in Strassburg, Calvin was to enjoy three happy and productive years.

He became pastor of the French refugees in Strassburg, and lectured to advanced classes in the schools. He began his famous expositions of biblical works and prepared an enlarged version of the *Institutes*. In August, 1540, he was married to Idelette de Bure, the widow of an Anabaptist convert. Their only child, born in 1542, lived only a few days, and Calvin's wife died in 1549. He always spoke in highest terms of his wife and their happiness.

While Calvin was absent from Geneva, Cardinal Sadoleto appealed to the city to return to the Catholic fold, and Calvin's *Reply to Sadoleto* (1539) justified the evangelical position, enhanced his reputation, and prepared the way for his return to Geneva.

The party which had opposed Calvin was overthrown in the elections of 1540, and Calvin's friends prevailed upon him to return to Geneva to restore order and stave off the drift back to Rome. Calvin returned with the assurance that he would be allowed to institute his reforms. He insisted that the Council adopt his *Ordonnances,* a thoroughgoing constitution built on the Articles of 1537, which completely directed the civil and religious affairs of Geneva. For twenty-three years, from 1541 until his death, Calvin molded Geneva. The instrument of control was a Consistory of twelve elders who received and judged reports of moral infractions. Penalties included fines, imprisonment, excommunication, banishment, and death, with adulterers, witches, blasphemers, and traitors being sentenced to death. Practically every human activity was branded as either holy or unholy, and houses could be checked without notice at any time. In addition to regulating community morals, Calvin developed the commercial part of Geneva into a prosperous economy, and encouraged education, founding what eventually became the University of Geneva. He made Geneva a haven for Protestant refugees. As many as 5,000 (about 30 percent of the population of Geneva) sought refuge under Calvin and formed a substantial part of his power.

Calvin continued, however, to have his dissenters and enemies. Many of the old families of Geneva resented an outsider controlling their lives and city, and many of the younger people chafed under his bitter bit of discipline. Some, such as Sebastian Castellio, parted with him over doctrinal disputes. The most serious test of his control was occasioned by Michael Servetus, a Spanish scholar, physician, scientist, and radical Reformer. In 1531, Servetus published *On Errors of the Trinity,* in which he attacked the doctrine of the Trinity as being extrabiblical. He also rejected infant baptism, and exhibited disgust for self-serving orthodoxy and ecclesiasticism. He was forced to live in France under an assumed name for twenty-two years. In 1533, Servetus produced his masterpiece, the *Restitution of Christianity,* aimed at refuting Calvin's *Institutes.* At Calvin's instigation, Servetus was arrested in France but escaped and fled for Naples. He stopped, however, in Geneva, where he was recognized and arrested. The Genevan Council found him guilty of spreading heresy and sentenced him to death by burning. In spite of Calvin's plea for a more merciful form of execution, Servetus was burned at the stake on October 27, 1553. He was not the first nor the last to be executed in Calvin's Geneva, but the most famous.

Calvin's opponents erupted with bitter criticism of Servetus' execution. Castellio wrote a brilliant attack titled *Concerning Heretics,* in which he said that the burning of heretics is far removed from the spirit of Christ and that "to kill a heretic is not to defend a doctrine, but to kill a man." Other Reformers, however, defended Calvin, including Melanchthon and Bullinger and the governments of Wittenberg, Basel, Bern, and Zurich. They contended that heresy threatened the Body of Christ like a rotten limb that had to be amputated. Harsh immediate action was deemed necessary. Although the execution of Servetus became a shameful blot on Calvin's record, it served to establish him once and for all as the unchallenged power at Geneva. Until his death, Calvin dominated Geneva—like a tyrant according to his enemies, and like an emissary from God according to his friends. Calvin died May 27, 1564, in the arms of Theodore Beza, who became Calvin's biographer and successor at Geneva.

3. THE SPREAD OF CALVINISM

After the death of Zwingli in 1531, his reform spread no farther, but it was just the opposite with Calvin. In fact by 1566, Calvinism had thoroughly conquered the Zwinglian cantons, and Zwinglianism virtually disappeared within Calvinism, which also spread to other countries.

a. Huguenots in France. It will be remembered that Calvin addressed his first edition of the *Institutes* to King Francis I who had been persecuting the Protestants. In subsequent years, Francis was intermittently at war with Spain, and extending the persecutions was not to his advantage or main interest. French preachers by the score began attending Calvin's school at Geneva and returning to France to preach the Huguenot (Protestant) gospel. By 1559 there were forty-nine Huguenot congregations in France, and a synod was held in Paris which formed a national organization and adopted a Calvinistic confession of faith. Within two years the number of congregations increased to 2,150, but a series of wars broke out between the Huguenots and Catholics, known as the Wars of Religions, and lasting intermittently from 1562 until 1594. The infamous incident remembered as the Massacre of St. Bartholomew's Day occurred in August, 1572, when many Huguenots were killed while attending the wedding of Henry of Navarre, a Protestant, to Marguerite, daughter of Catherine d'Medici, the mother of ten-year-old King Charles IX. Catherine, serving as regent, had ordered the massacre, which spread the war to other parts of France. This same Henry of Navarre became King Henry IV of France in 1594, converted to Catholicism, and promised to protect the Huguenots. The promise was crystallized in the form of the Edict of Nantes in 1598, which guaranteed freedom of public worship to the Huguenots.

Nevertheless, the Huguenots continued to be a disruptive force in France until their fortress of La Rochelle was destroyed in 1628. Under Louis XIV, persistent efforts were made to nullify the Edict of Nantes, and it was finally revoked on October 18, 1685. Many Huguenots apostatized under persecution and hundreds of thousands fled to Holland, Switzerland, England, Prussia, and America. Marriages performed by Huguenot ministers were not recognized by the state until 1787, and it was not until 1802 that the legal standing of the Huguenot Church was established. In 1907, there came into being the National Union of Reformed (Calvinist) Churches of France, a body which combined with non-Calvinistic bodies to form the Protestant Federation of France.

b. Insurrection in the Netherlands. The Netherlands consisted of about seventeen Spanish provinces in what is now Belgium and Holland. Lutheranism had found an eager response in this land which had produced Erasmus; . . . the Waldenses, the Brethren of the Common Life, mysticism, and humanism were well represented. The Mennonites had made real inroads also until about 1540, when many left the Mennonite ranks to become Calvinists because the Mennonites were pacifists and Calvinists were not. Spain was waging war against the Netherlands, and pacifism was not a practical concept of the day. By 1550 the Calvinists began organizing churches in homes, and in 1571 the first national synod was held, and the Dutch Reformed Church (Calvinistic) was organized.

Emperor Charles V had always favored the Netherlands, where he had been reared. But when he abdicated in 1555, his son and successor, Philip II, subjected the Netherlands to the dreaded Spanish Inquisition. Armed rebellion broke out and the leader of the resistance, William of Orange, once the closest friend of Charles, was now the bitterest enemy of Philip. Also known as William the Silent, the Prince of Orange was originally a Roman Catholic but out of deep conviction joined the Reformed church in 1573. He led in the forming of the United Provinces (the Protestant North) which eventually became the United Netherlands. Assassinated in 1584 at the age of fifty-one, William did not see full independence, but in 1609 hostilities stopped and the United Netherlands won their freedom. Their independence, however, was not recognized by Spain until 1648.

During the struggle, the Dutch Reformed Church had taken shape, adopting a Presbyterian government, the Heidelberg catechism, and the Belgic Confession. The church was closely tied with the government, but religious tolerance was also granted to others, even Roman Catholics and Anabaptists. After the political wars subsided, doctrinal battles broke out within the Dutch Reformed Church. Theologians divided over the question of whether God absolutely decreed that certain men should be lost and others saved. Those who rejected this position were known as Remonstrants, and were led by Jacob Arminius, professor of theology in the University of Leiden. Since the, the Remonstrant position has been known as Arminianism, which rejects unconditional election, limited atonement (that Christ died only for the elect), irresistible grace, and the perseverance of the saints. Arminianism was condemned at a synod held at Dort in 1618 and 1619, and the Remonstrants continued in Holland as a distinct church.

c. Reformation in Scotland. Calvinism eventually had its strongest expression in Scotland, where it took the form of Presbyterianism and became the faith of the overwhelming majority and the official religion of the state. At the turn of the sixteenth century the Catholic Church in Scotland was in desperate need of reform and the country was permeated with lawlessness. There was an openness that resembled a plea for help. By 1525 Luther's writings were being circulated and the English Bible was introduced in 1527. Patrick Hamilton, once a student at Wittenberg, began to preach Lutheranism in the streets and at the University of St. Andrews, for which he was burned at the stake in 1528. John Knox was a student at St. Andrews at the time and was profoundly shaken by the event but nevertheless proceeded to be ordained to the Catholic priesthood in 1540.

Another advocate of reform, George Wishart, was burned at the stake in 1546. John Knox had defended Wishart theologically and physically and thus jeopardized his own position. A few weeks later, Cardinal Beaton, archbishop of St. Andrews, who had tried and condemned Wishart, was assassinated by Wishart's disciples, who then fortified themselves in the Castle of St. Andrews. John Knox joined them in 1547 and became minister of the castle congregation. He became well known for his powerful preaching and Scripture exposition, but was captured, imprisoned for nineteen months, and then banished to the continent, where he became thoroughly confirmed in Calvinism.

From the continent, he returned to England where the Reformation was in full stride under Edward VI. He was appointed minister at Berwick on the Scottish border, and declined the bishopric of Rochester in order to return to his beloved Scotland. The accession of Mary Tudor, however, reversed the Reform movement in England, and Knox again became a refugee on the continent. He spent three years as minister of a congregation of English refugees in Geneva. Calvin was at the height of his influence and Knox worked side by side with the father of Calvinism himself. He also married Margaret Bowes, to whom he had become betrothed while in England.

Knox returned to Scotland in 1559, and became the leader of the Reforming party, preaching and procuring money and troops from England. Scottish Protestantism and Scottish independence were in danger of being exterminated by the marriage of Mary Queen of Scots to Francis II of France. While Mary was in France, her mother, Mary of Lorraine, served as regent and forbade Reformed preaching. Knox aroused the masses and in the civil war which erupted, French troops supported Mary, and English forces sent by Queen Elizabeth aided the Protestants. In 1560 the regent died, and the French troops sailed for home. That same year Knox established a Presbyterian system throughout the kingdom, adopted a Calvinistic confession, abolished the pope's jurisdiction, and called the first General Assembly.

In 1561, however, Mary Queen of Scots returned to Scotland, her husband Francis II of France having died in December, 1560. The lovely and charming young widow aroused widespread popular sympathy and divided Knox's supporters, especially among the Scottish Protestant nobility. Mary reinstituted the saying of Mass in her private chapel, married her cousin Darnley, a Roman Catholic, and set about to wrest the English throne from Elizabeth. Knox preached daily and forcefully against the revival of the Mass and the immorality of Mary's court. He had frequent audiences with Mary, with neither giving ground and tension constantly mounting. Mary, however, proved to be her own worst enemy, overplaying her hand in an unwise matrimonial venture, intrigues, murder, and civil strife. She was finally driven to England in 1568, and executed there in 1587 on the charge of plotting to assassinate Elizabeth. Her son, James VI, came to the throne upon her abdication, and Knox preached at the coronation of the infant, who was to become James I of England after the death of Elizabeth. Thus, John Knox lived to see the triumph of Presbyterianism and Scottish independence, his two great loves. From Scotland, Calvinism was literally exported around the world through the strong influence of Presbyterianism on English Puritanism, extensive migrations, and ambitious mission enterprises.

D. ANABAPTISTS AND RADICAL REFORMATION

The two dominant expressions of the Protestant Reformation were Lutheranism and Calvinism. The record thus far reviewed portrays these two groups as being drastically opposed to, and eventually separated from, all that Rome stood for. Yet, in comparison with another militant group, they appear extremely conservative. The truth is that the Lutherans and Calvinists were conservative in breaking with Rome, retaining many Roman practices and creeds. Lutheran churches rejected only those Catholic features they believed were forbidden by Scripture, and Reformed churches retained from Catholicism only what they believed justified by Scripture. Both continued to practice infant baptism, and to attempt to bring every person in the community into the church by that means. Also, like the Catholics, Luther, Calvin, and their followers believed in working through the close relationship of church and state.

Another expression, commonly called the left wing of the Reformation, was much more radical than Lutheranism and Calvinism, as well as determined to exclude everything not in Scripture, dedicated to returning to primitive Christianity, and constituted of "believers only." Those radical Reformers insisted that the true church was the "gathered" church of believers and not the whole community. They rejected infant baptism as

Some of the bitterest persecutions of the Inquisition fell upon the Anabaptists and Huguenots of Western Europe. (Historical Pictures Service, Chicago)

being unscriptural and as a great deterrent in maintaining churches of the regenerate only. They "rebaptized" those who professed adult conversion, thus obtaining the derogatory nickname of Anabaptist. Besides the mockery involved, they disowned the name because they did not consider infant baptism valid, and therefore the adult baptism was the first, not a rebaptism. But the name has survived historically.

The Anabaptists repudiated any sort of connection between church and state and upheld the doctrine of absolute liberty of conscience. Many of them opposed the swearing of oaths, the bearing of arms, and capital punishment. There was a strong movement among them of chiliastic anticipation, believing that the millennial reign of Christ was imminent. All of them placed the observance of the Lord's Supper as a high and solemn act of worship, and a high standard of morality prevailed among them. Their rapid growth and diverse backgrounds made it impossible to consolidate into a definitive organization such as the Lutherans and Calvinists had accomplished. Some of them were able, however, to convene in 1527 at Schleitheim on the Swiss-German border in what was the first "synod" of the Protestant Reformation. They adopted a statement of beliefs known as the "Brotherly Union" to which most Anabaptists in all of Europe agreed.

Ironically, the Anabaptists were the common enemies of Catholics and other Protestants. The Anabaptists were spread over such a broad area it was feared they would displace the established churches. At the Diet of Speyer, in 1529, both Catholics and Lutherans agreed to subject them to the death penalty throughout the Holy Roman Empire. Luther would not consent to this extreme measure at first, but by 1531, his fear of anarchy persuaded him to approve the death penalty for blasphemy and sedition. In the late 1520s and the early 1530s thousands of Anabaptists were killed, some by beheading (by the state), some by drowning (by the Protestants), and some by burning (by the Catholics). Popular support of the persecutions was gained by reminding the people that the Anabaptists had been greatly responsible for the bloody peasant uprisings of 1524-1525. Fear of rebellion and anarchy almost exterminated the Anabaptists on the continent, but they survived and exerted influence on other groups, notably in Britain in the movements of the Independents, Baptists, and Quakers. There were about a half dozen main groups of Anabaptists which need to be distinguished.

1. THOMAS MUNTZER AND THE ZWICKAU PROPHETS

As noted earlier, these appeared in Wittenberg in 1521. Muntzer sympathized with the Peasants' Revolt, and taught a doctrine of the Inner Light which reappeared later in the Quakers. Muntzer did reject infant baptism, which identified him as an Anabaptist, but his main concern was with political and social action, not theological issues. He became disgusted with Luther's type of reform as not being radical enough. Claiming direct instruction by the Holy Spirit, he seized control of Mulhausen and set up a theocracy, outraging Protestants and Catholics alike by his senseless destruction of church property and preaching civil turmoil. He was executed, having given Anabaptists a bad name in many parts of Europe.

2. THE SWISS BRETHREN

In Zurich, Conrad Grebel and Felix Manz attracted a group known as the Swiss Brethren. At first warm friends and followers of Zwingli, Grebel and Manz became impatient with the Reform movement in their native Zurich. Unwilling to wait for the city council to act (as was Zwingli's approach), they undertook a thoroughgoing reform to abolish the Mass and the use of images. In 1524 they came out against infant baptism, rebaptized adult believers, and observed the Lord's Supper with simple rites. Grebel was a brilliant humanist scholar, able to debate on equal terms with Zwingli. He was also a fervent missionary, taking his radical ideas to other cities. He and Manz were eventually arrested in Zurich, were condemned to life imprisonment, escaped, and were recaptured. Manz was executed by drowning on January 25, 1527, the first martyr to the Anabaptist cause. Grebel had died a few months earlier.

Balthasar Hubmaier was also associated with the Swiss Brethren. A former pupil of Johann Eck, Luther's early opponent, Hubmaier was a professor at Ingolstadt, preacher at Regensburg cathedral, and parish priest at Waldshut. It was in Waldshut that he came in contact with the Swiss Reformers and allied himself openly with Zwingli in 1523. Soon, however, he abandoned Zwinglian doctrines for those of the Anabaptists. He rejected infant baptism, rebaptized converted adults, began serving the Lord's Supper, and instituted foot washing. He became involved in the Peasants' Revolt and may have been the author of the Twelve Articles. When Waldshut was occupied by government troops, he fled to Zurich, and from there to Moravia, where he worked for the Anabaptist cause by writing pamphlets on theological questions. In 1527, the Austrian authorities demanded his extradition, and he was taken to Vienna where he was burned at the stake on March 10, 1528.

Others in this group included Hans Denck, a humanist scholar, proficient in Greek and Hebrew, who called for an inner reformation by heeding the voice of the Spirit within, the indwelling Christ, and the Scripture. He renounced violence, worked in several different cities, and died of the plague in his early thirties. His close friend, Ludwig Hetzer, assisted him in translating the prophetical books of the Old Testament into German, and led the radical movement in Augsburg. Hetzer was executed in Constance in 1529.

3. THE HUTTERITES IN MORAVIA

The relentless persecution of the Anabaptists' in Austria caused many of them to seek refuge in Moravia, which had shared with Bohemia in the

Hussite revolt against Rome and in the Taborite and Bohemian Brethren movements. Thus Jakob Hutter, one of the leading Anabaptists in Tyrol, came to Moravia and assumed a leading position there. He was first associated with the congregation at Austerlitz in 1529, but later (in 1531) broke off with a radical group, which found refuge in the small settlement of Auspitz. Here Hutter established the small community settlements, known as Bruderhofe, and based on the common ownership of property. Soon there developed a series of Brethren villages in Moravia, fed by the influx of refugees. The movement received the designation of "Hutterian Brethren" or Hutterites, and was characterized by pacifism and communal households, called Houses of the Brethren.

Because of their great reputation in agriculture and handicraft, the Hutterites were in demand by the nobility and country barons. This friendly treatment of the refugee Anabaptists incited King Ferdinand I and the government in Vienna to enforce obedience to the edicts of the emperor, and persecution was pressed into Moravia. Fleeing for his life, Hutter was captured, cruelly tortured, and on February 25, 1536, burned at the stake. His wife was executed a short time later. Although he was not a theologian or teacher, Hutter's practical and social applications of the Christian principles earned him a lasting place in Christian history, and the story of his martyrdom became a legend among Anabaptists.

4. MELCHIOR HOFFMANN AND CHILIASM

A radical Anabaptist and fanatical chiliast, Hoffmann began as a Lutheran lay preacher, being a leather dresser by profession. He came in conflict with the authorities in Livonia in 1523 and left for Stockholm in 1526, where he became obsessed with eschatological ideas and prophesied the approaching end of the world. In a debate with Johann Bugenhagen (pastor at Wittenberg) in 1529 he denied the Lutheran doctrine of the Lord's Supper, was later banished to Denmark, but went to Strassburg where he joined the Anabaptists. He traveled extensively, attracting a large following in the Netherlands. Hoffmann believed himself to be divinely appointed to lead the faithful to Strassburg, which would become the "New Jerusalem," when Christ returned on the Last Day in 1533. He prophesied that all who opposed him would be destroyed. Thus, he went confidently to Strassburg, where he was arrested and kept in his dungeon prison until his death in 1543. He remained unshaken in his eschatological beliefs, and his influence was so strong that the "Melchiorites" or "Hoffmannites" survived him as a distinct party among the Anabaptists.

5. JAN MATTHYS AND THE MUNSTER EPISODE

One of Hoffmann's ardent disciples was Jan Matthys, a baker from Holland, who announced in 1533 that he was the prophet Enoch who had been promised by Hoffmann. He assumed leadership of the fanatical party while Hoffmann was in prison. Matthys was not dismayed when Hoffmann's prophecy of the end of the world in 1533 was unfulfilled. He merely announced that Hoffmann had been mistaken, that Munster was to be the "New Jerusalem," not Strassburg. Munster, a city of Westphalia, not far from the Dutch border, had become Protestant and enrolled in the Schmalkaldic League under the influence of a popular young humanist chaplain named Bernhard Rothmann. When Rothmann denounced infant baptism, word spread that Munster had become Anabaptist, and many followers of Melchior Hoffmann flocked there for refuge.

Jan Matthys, one of these immigrants, led the movement to take Munster by armed force and sought to establish a Kingdom of the Saints. Convinced that Munster would be the "New Jerusalem," the radicals attempted to organize a Christian society, but the enterprise was aborted by the siege laid to the city by the Bishop of Munster. Aided by both Lutherans and Catholics, the bishop recaptured the city in June, 1535. Jan Matthys was killed in the battle, and was succeeded by Jan Bockelson, who was captured, tortured, and killed. Stories began to circulate about odious practices of the Anabaptists during the siege, including polygamy and the ruthless suppression of opposition. The Munster episode left a dark stain on the reputation of Anabaptists everywhere, leading many people to believe that all Anabaptists fomented chaos in government, society, morals, and religion.

6. MENNONITES AND THE AMISH

The great majority of Anabaptists were appalled and ashamed at the Munster episode, and a respected moderate by the name of Menno Simons was especially outspoken in decrying that sort of fanaticism. Menno was a Roman Catholic priest whose studies of the Scripture led him to break with Rome to become an evangelical preacher in 1530. He joined the Anabaptists in 1536 because he felt that Luther, Zwingli, and Calvin were wrong in continuing the practice of infant baptism. Although he strongly disapproved of the errors of the Anabaptists at Munster, he admired their courage under persecution, and expected such persecution for himself. This expectation was fulfilled, as he also had to live like a fugitive and an outlaw. He continued, however, to extend his missionary efforts, married, and had children. His missionary work took him throughout Germany where he was always harassed by both Catholics and Germans. He eventually found refuge on a nobleman's estate in Denmark where he remained for the rest of his life, writing, teaching, and venturing forth to organize and strengthen congregations. He became the outstanding leader of the Anabaptists in the Netherlands and north Germany, and his followers became known as Mennonites.

Menno's views were similar to those of the Swiss Brethren, including the stress on believers' baptism, the responsibilities and rights of local congregations, pacifism, and a rejection of Christian participation in the magistracy (he refused to allow civil authorities to belong to his church). There are over 500,000 Mennonites in the world today, with about half of them in the United States. Although each Mennonite community is different, common beliefs include the rejection of church organization, infant baptism, and the real presence of Christ at the Lord's Supper. Every congregation is independent, and both men and women may preach. Most Mennonites refuse military service and the taking of the oath and any public office. There is, however, no official doctrine for the Mennonites.

In the latter part of the sixteenth century, an Anabaptist-Mennonite elder named Jakob Amman brought about a serious split in the German speaking Mennonite community. Contentious and ultraconservative, Amman demanded that Mennonite congregations shun all nonbelievers and ostracize lapsed members. He excommunicated all who disagreed with him, and his followers became a close-knit sect with rigid rules regarding uniformity of dress, untrimmed beards, and foot washing as an element of worship. They became known as Amish after their founder Jakob Amman. Severe persecution drove them from the continent, and they emigrated to William Penn's colony of Pennsylvania, where their descendants remain to this day, preserving the Anabaptist-Mennonite-Amish practices of 1700.

The radicals and Anabaptists who formed the "left wing" of the Reformation were the most hated and persecuted religious groups on the continent in the sixteenth century. Ironically, twentieth-century Protestantism often expresses more keenly the ideas of the radical Reformers than the traditional Reformers. Whereas Luther and Calvin had their hands tied by political and social commitments in a state church, the radical Reformers were free to reject nonscriptural concepts and practices. They especially insisted that the world or community cannot make Christians, which for them undermined the whole premise of infant baptism. They contended for a "gathered" church in which only believers with a faith baptism could participate. This led to a strong stance for the separation of church and state. Above all, the Anabaptists believed in the competency of the soul, the ability and responsibility of each individual to experience the presence and salvation of God for himself. One can readily see how these ideas have prevailed and entrenched themselves in some of the great evangelical movements of the present day.

E. REFORM IN ENGLAND

While the Protestant Reformation was exploding on the continent, the British Isles were experiencing a similar phenomenon. The English Reformation, however, was decidedly English in character. Even though it was influenced by the issues and events on the continent, the reasons for its occurrence and the directions of its course were uniquely English.

1. PREPARATION AND CAUSES

The reform which came to England, Wales, and Ireland was a long time in developing, and that development came essentially from within Britain rather than simply overflowing from Europe. There were at least a half dozen distinct causes which precipitated the Reform movement and the break with Rome.

First, there was the rising trend of nationalism, as strong in England as anywhere on the continent. There was widespread resentment over interference from a foreign pope and the sending of money to the papal treasury while much of England was impoverished. The English tendency toward independence had been encouraged by the famous *Magna Carta* of 1215, in which the barons of England had won fundamental freedom from papal authority. The law of *Praemunire*, 1353, was also a powerful weapon in the hands of those desiring independence from Rome. During the "Babylonian Captivity" when the popes were residing at Avignon, the English parliament passed the law of *Praemunire*, which forbade appeals to Rome. Henry VIII revived this old law and used it for his personal benefit.

Another factor was the growing anticlericalism which Wycliffe had inspired with his translation for the common man, and his primitive concept of the priesthood of all believers. The Peasants' Uprising in 1381 was greatly influenced by Wycliffe's insistence that unworthy clergymen should be deprived of their soft living. The anticlerical attitude was kept alive by the followers of Wycliffe, known as Lollards, who based their teaching on personal faith, divine election, and the Bible. The Scriptures were the sole authority in religion and every man had the right to read and interpret them for himself. The Lollards became an influential cause of the English Reformation through their attacks on clerical celibacy, transubstantiation, indulgences, and pilgrimages. They held that the validity of priestly acts was determined by the priest's moral character and that endowments, the pope, and the hierarchy were all unscriptural.

Although the Lollards were persistently persecuted and condemned, they could not be stamped out, and the anticlerical feelings fanned by them ran deep in England. The abusive and excessive life-style of many English prelates did nothing to relieve the tension. For example, Cardinal Thomas Wolsey, papal legate, minister of state, and archbishop of York virtually ran England from 1515 to 1529. He held four bishoprics, was enormously wealthy, had over five hundred persons in his household, and two of his residences eventually became royal palaces—Hampton Court and York Place (Whitehall). In his absolute control of clerical appointments, he flagrantly favored relatives, friends, and political cronies. Thus, both the preaching of the Lollards and the practices of the clergy kept anticlericalism as a major force in English attitudes.

The humanistic renaissance in England could be given as a major factor in spawning the English Reformation. Oxford and Cambridge had become strongholds of humanism after Erasmus had visited and taught there from 1510 to 1513. John Colet (1467-1519) had already left his mark on religion and education in England through his profound lectures and sermons at St. Paul's cathedral and his attempts to reform the clergy and eliminate corruption and superstition. A close friend of Colet and Erasmus was Sir Thomas More, a brilliant humanist who was destined to play a tragic role in the drama of Henry VIII versus Rome. More remained a faithful Catholic until his death, but he led the battle against ignorance, strife, and injustice. In his classic satire *Utopia* he called for a religion based on the dictates of reason and the laws of nature. Humanism, while being patronized by the papacy, was making inroads against that institution with its theme of "back to the sources," which subtly suggests the circumventing of current ecclesiastical establishment.

Luther himself provided a significant element to the fomenting conditions in England. Luther's writings poured into England and quickly found acceptance at Oxford and Cambridge. The leader of a group of humanist "heretics" at Cambridge was Thomas Bilney, who was burned at the stake in 1531, becoming the first English martyr for espousing Lutheran ideas. One of Bilney's proteges was Hugh Latimer, a popular preacher who supported Henry VIII in his break with Rome and was martyred under Queen Mary. Luther's popularity in England provoked a papal ban on his books and a massive crusade to burn all his writings. Cardinal Wolsey personally conducted the first burning of Luther's works at St. Paul's Cathedral in 1521. Although Henry VIII later broke with Rome, he denounced Luther as a calumniator, a schismatic, and a menace to society. His rebuttal of Lutheran doctrines, *Assertion of the Seven Sacraments*, earned Henry the title "Defender of the Faith."

While Henry was defending the faith against the likes of Martin Luther, he was providing the decisive cause of the English Reformation. The personal desires and ambitions of Henry VIII became the final fuel for the kindling fire. His personal desire to divorce Catherine and marry Anne Boleyn, and his ambition to attain total supremacy, even in religious matters, made Henry the catalyst for one of the major splits in Christendom, bringing about the birth of the Church of England. Although reform had been brewing for centuries, it was Henry's personal obsession and obstinance that brought it to a head.

2. SUPREMACY UNDER HENRY VIII
His father, Henry VII, was the first in a new line of English kings, the Tudors. The politically shrewd monarch arranged a marriage for his fourteen-year-old son Arthur to sixteen-year-old Catherine, the daughter of Ferdinand and Isabella of Spain in 1501. Less than six months later, Arthur died, and Henry VII gained special papal dispensation to have his younger son Henry marry the widowed Catherine in order to preserve the

advantageous ties with Spain. Henry VIII ascended the throne in 1509 upon the death of his father and consummated the marriage to Catherine. Of the six children born to Henry and Catherine, only one survived, a daughter named Mary. Henry became deeply concerned over not having a male heir, for England had never been ruled by a woman except in one short fiasco in the twelfth century. He became obsessed with the idea that his marriage to his brother's wife had incurred divine wrath. Then he became obsessed with the beautiful Anne Boleyn, who refused to share his bed without sharing his crown. Thus Henry began his long and weary battle to dissolve his marriage with Catherine.

At first he sought a simple annulment, but Catherine closed this door by solemnly swearing that the marriage between her and Arthur had never been consummated and that there was no legal impediment to her marriage to Henry. Next the king pushed for papal permission for a divorce, but Pope Clement VII was not in a position to cooperate. In 1527, Rome had been sacked and the pope captured by Emperor Charles V, the grandson of Ferdinand and Isabella and the nephew of Catherine. The pope dared not incur the wrath of the emperor, but neither could he bring himself to flatly reject Henry's request and thereby lose the lucrative and powerful English support. The issue was, therefore, dragged out for more than four years, with Henry losing patience over the obvious ploys and subterfuges. Cardinal Wolsey, acting as Henry's emissary, had failed to please his sovereign and was summarily stripped of his positions. He finally died in disgrace in 1530.

Henry was at his wit's end as to how to resolve his dilemma when Thomas Cranmer, Archbishop of Canterbury, suggested that the king should seek the opinions of the theologians in the universities. Henry quickly acted on Cranmer's suggestion, applying pressure, negotiations, and intrigues. Oxford and Cambridge decided in favor of Henry, followed by the French universities and even Bologna in Italy. Essentially, the scholars decreed that Henry's marriage to Catherine was contrary to divine law and was never a valid marriage. So Henry was free to marry without need of dispensation from Rome. In 1533, Henry married Anne Boleyn and forced the pope to name Thomas Cranmer Archbishop of Canterbury.

Infuriated with Henry's highhandedness, Pope Clement threatened to excommunicate him. Henry's reaction to the threat was to get parliament to legalize the supremacy of the king. In the Restraint of Appeals, the legal principle of the English Reformation, parliament declared that all cases having to do with religion "shall be from henceforth heard, examined, discussed, clearly, finally, and definitively judged and determined within the king's jurisdiction and authority, and not elsewhere . . . from the see of Rome, or any other foreign courts or potentates of the world." This was followed the next year by the ecclesiastical principle of the English Reformation, the Act of Forbidding Papal Dispensations, which took from the pope all rights of nomination and dispensation and severed all payment of money to the pope. Also in 1534, the Supremacy Act confirmed Henry as "supreme head" of the Church of England. Then the Act of Succession declared Princess Mary, daughter of Catherine, illegitimate, and named the infant daughter of Anne Boleyn, Elizabeth (born September 7, 1533) as heir to the throne. Pope Clement reaffirmed the validity of Catherine's marriage to Henry and excommunicated the King of England. Henry, therefore, set up an independent national English Church, with the king as the supreme head. A royal proclamation erased the pope's name from all the service books, and the breach with Rome was complete.

Several of the church leaders who refused to accept Henry's supremacy were executed. Among them was John Fisher, cardinal, Bishop of Rochester, former chancellor of Cambridge University, friend of Erasmus, and confessor to Catherine. The humanist scholar and once close friend of Henry, Thomas More, was also beheaded because he would not sanction Henry's marriage to Anne Boleyn.

Although severely criticized on the continent for these executions, Henry had made himself the undisputed master of both state and church. He obviously, however, was never able to master his own personal passions and problems. He eventually executed Anne Boleyn for alleged infidelity and for failure to give him a male heir, and married four more times. Of his six wives, two were executed (Anne Boleyn and Catherine Howard), two were divorced by him (Catherine of Aragon and Anne of Cleves), one died in childbirth (Jane Seymour), and one managed to outlive him (Catherine Parr).

The English Reformation had not culminated in a great theological schism as had the German and Swiss movements. Henry had, in fact, opposed the theological heresies of Luther and prided himself on being the "Defender of the Faith." In basic beliefs, Henry was a Catholic, and breaking from Rome did not make him a Protestant in theology. Catholic dogma and rites were still upheld, and Lutheranism was still outlawed as a "pernicious poison." John Frith, who had assisted Tyndale in translating the New Testament, was burned in London in 1533 for denying transubstantiation and purgatory. In 1535 twenty-five Anabaptists were burned in a single day. Henry had not given Protestantism to England in exchange for Catholicism. He had merely given England a new authority, exchanging the supremacy of the pope for that of the king.

In 1535, Henry appointed Thomas Cromwell, Earl of Essex, as Vicar General of the English Church, and Cromwell became the chief adviser and instrument of the king in all ecclesiastical affairs. Presiding at Convocation, he even took precedence over the Archbishop of Canterbury. It was Cromwell who dissolved the monasteries in a sweeping visitation crusade between 1536 and 1539. Monasticism virtually disappeared from England, the most drastic change in England's religious life under Henry VIII besides the separation from Rome itself. Cromwell also ordered that a Bible should be provided in every church and that the clergy should perform certain definite duties. He overstepped his usefulness to Henry, however, when he arranged a marriage between the king and Anne of Cleves, in a diplomatic effort to bring about an alliance of England with the Protestant princes of Germany. Henry was disgusted with the marriage and with Cromwell, who was arrested, sentenced for treason, and beheaded on July 28, 1540.

Although it appeared for a while that Cromwell had been promoted over him, the real ecclesiastical power behind Henry was still Thomas Cranmer, Archbishop of Canterbury. Cranmer remained at the king's side in his personal battles. It was he who annulled Henry's marriage to Catherine; then when Henry wished to rid himself of Anne Boleyn, he pronounced that marriage null and void; and again at the king's behest, he declared his marriage to Anne of Cleves to be invalid. Besides his obvious subservience to the crown, Cranmer was a profound theologian who eventually was largely responsible for shaping the Protestant Church of England. He was greatly involved in two successive statements of doctrine issued by Henry, supporting the first and opposing the second.

The Ten Articles of 1536, drafted by Henry with the help of Cranmer, indicated that Henry was leaning toward Protestantism. They named only three sacraments—baptism, penance, and the eucharist; stressed the importance of teaching the people the Bible and the early creeds; and declared that justification is by faith and by confession, absolution, and good works. But the articles also held that Christ is physically present in the eucharist, and that Masses for the dead, the invocation of the saints, and the use of images are desirable. Henry was obviously attempting to mix Catholic and Protestant doctrines together in a compromise religion. Three years later he reversed himself and pushed through parliament, over the opposition of Cranmer, the Six Articles which reaffirmed basic Catholic doctrine under the threat of severe penalty. Called the "Whip with Six Stings," the famous Six Articles declared as law of the land: (1) transubstantiation, (2) withholding the cup from the laity, (3) celibacy for priests, (4) vows of chastity, (5) private Masses, and (6) the necessity of auricular confession. During the next seven years, scores of people were executed for violating one or more of the articles, with the article on transubstantiation being the most serious.

At the same time, however, he encouraged the publication of the Bible in the vernacular, a distinctly Protestant stance. Miles Coverdale, a graduate of Cambridge and a member of the circle of which the martyred Thomas Bilney had been the leader, made a full translation of the entire Bible into English. Known as the Great Bible, it was placed in the churches with the approval of both Cranmer and Cromwell. By the order of the king, Cranmer prepared forms of worship, including a litany which was to be sung in English.

Henry attempted in his last years to promote some religious reforms while maintaining the substance of traditional Catholicism. As a symbol of his repudiation of Protestantism, he married Catherine Howard, a Roman Catholic, in 1540, and entered into a military alliance with Charles V. The alliance was unsuccessful, as was his marriage. In 1542 Catherine Howard was beheaded for adultery, and the following year Henry married Catherine Parr, who outlived him. Henry VIII died on January 28, 1547, with Cranmer at his side. The archbishop who had supported the king in his personal affairs and in his break with Rome, but who had opposed him in his doctrinal positions, was now left to guide the nation into accepting Protestantism as the official ecclesiastical policy of England.

3. PROTESTANTISM UNDER EDWARD VI

Henry VIII was succeeded by his son Edward, who was born to Henry and his third wife Jane Seymour. Edward was only nine years old when he came to the throne, and died in 1553 when he was only fifteen. Yet, during his six-and-a-half-year reign, England was carried with strong strides toward Protestantism. This was not due, however, to Edward's personal efforts; for while he was a serious and deeply religious boy, the policies of his reign were determined by a council of regency which had been appointed by his father in his will. Thomas Cranmer and Edward Seymour (the new king's uncle) emerged as the dominant leaders of the council, encouraging Protestantism and writing evangelical tenets into the laws and customs of the land.

The first parliament of the new reign repealed the Six Articles, laws which had restricted the printing of Scriptures, and laws which had promoted the trial and persecution of heretics. Images were removed from the churches, communion was given to the laity, and a general confession took the place of private confession to the priest. Leading continental reformers were welcomed to England, especially by Cranmer. Martin Bucer came from Strassburg to Cambridge, Peter Martyr from Florence to Oxford, and Jan Laski from Poland to London. Along with many others they went throughout England, strengthening Protestant views and training the clergy who would later be so obstinate during the reigns of Mary and Elizabeth.

Cranmer also increased the Protestant hold with his own literary contributions. His *Book of Homilies* and *Book of Common Prayer* were published for public worship. In 1549, Parliament enacted the Act of Uniformity which required all clergy to use the *Book of Common Prayer*, which has endured and united the diverse elements of the Church of England. It should be noted that the *Book of Common Prayer* was imposed on the nation by parliament, the governing body of state, rather than the convocation, the body through which the church spoke. In 1553, the Forty-two Articles of Religion, written by six theologians led by Cranmer, were issued under the authority of the king. These articles gave the doctrinal position of the Church of England, and although they were abrogated by Mary, they later became the Thirty-nine Articles of the Church of England.

In the political arena, Edward Seymour, who had been named as Lord Protector, did not fare so well as Cranmer in the theological arena. He failed in attempts to contract a marriage between Edward VI and the young Scottish Princess Mary, in domestic agricultural reforms, and in controlling an uprising of restless farmers. In 1552 the Earl of Warwick had Seymour beheaded and took his place as titular head of the government, becoming the Duke of Northumberland. Although he was unscrupulous and ruthless, he did favor the Protestant program because it suited his plans of tyranny and greed. Thus he supported the Act of Uniformity and eliminated many objectionable papal influences from the realm. Warwick attempted to place Lady Jane Grey in succession to the throne in case of Edward's death, but was decidedly unsuccessful. Lady Jane Grey was the granddaughter of Henry VIII's sister Mary and the wife of Warwick's fourth son. Warwick was so unpopular with the people that even some Protestants supported Mary Tudor when Edward died in 1553.

4. CATHOLICISM UNDER MARY

In Henry VIII's will, he had provided that in case Edward died without leaving an heir to the throne of England, he should be succeeded by Henry's two daughters, Mary and Elizabeth, in the order of their birth. At the age of thirty-seven and in ill health, Mary Tudor became Queen of England and reigned for five years until her death in 1558. She was intensely loyal to the memory of her mother, Catherine of Aragon, and it was a foregone conclusion that she would attempt to bring England back into the Catholic fold. She began her reign with a show of force, beheading both Warwick and Lady Jane Grey, and imprisoning Cranmer, Hugh Latimer, and Nicholas Ridley.

Mary began immediately to reverse the religious changes brought in under Edward. She abolished the *Book of Common Prayer*, reinstated clerical celibacy, restored the Mass, and appointed as her chief counselor Bishop Gardiner of Winchester, who had helped Henry frame the Six Articles and had advocated a return to papal authority. This return to papalism was symbolized by the return of Cardinal Legate Reginald Pole, who had fled the country rather than accept Henry's supremacy. On St. Andrew's Day, 1554, the queen knelt with parliament while Cardinal Pole absolved the nation of heresy and received it back into communion with the church of Rome. Roman Catholicism had reasserted itself, but the English spirit of nationalism was growing, as was the general desire for political stability and economic security.

When Mary married Philip II, son of Charles V of Spain, many Englishmen feared foreign domination, and uprisings occurred throughout the land. Still, Mary pressed her return to Catholicism with fanatical zeal. She executed about three hundred Protestant leaders, including Cranmer, Latimer, and Ridley. So numerous were the beheadings and burnings during her reign that she became known as "Bloody Mary." When Latimer and Ridley were burned at the stake together, it was reported that Latimer encouraged his comrade with the words: "Be of good comfort, Master Ridley, we shall this day light such a candle by God's grace in England as, I trust, shall never be put out." The words proved to be prophetic, for Mary was not able to extinguish the light of reform which was now sweeping more forcefully than ever across England. She died a bitter, unhappy, and childless woman. She had lost most of her friends and alienated the affections of many of her subjects. The five-year revival of Catholicism ended with her pathetic death in 1558, with England poised on the verge of rebellion.

5. SETTLEMENT UNDER ELIZABETH
Mary was succeeded by her half-sister Elizabeth, daughter of Henry VIII and Anne Boleyn.

a. Diplomacy and Force. Elizabeth inherited a kingdom torn by religious strife and weary of persecution by fanatics from both camps. Fortunately, Elizabeth was wise and diplomatic, and chose to favor neither extreme papalism nor extreme Protestantism. She correctly assessed the public mood and gained the people's support of a policy of moderation. She reformed the Prayer Book to make it less offensive to Roman Catholics, but she reinstituted the liturgy of Edward VI. She kept the episcopal form of church government, but lessened the power of the bishops. In 1559, parliament passed the Act of Supremacy, which acknowledged her highness' supremacy in all matters spiritual or ecclesiastical, as well as temporal. In the Act, however, she was not called the "Supreme Head" of the church and realm, but the "Supreme Governor." Most of the parish clergy subscribed to the Act of Supremacy, but 2,000 Catholic priests refused to sign and all but one of the Catholic bishops from Mary's reign resigned.

This strong Catholic resistance caused Elizabeth to lean toward the Protestants. Matthew Parker, who had been removed from ecclesiastical office under Mary, was appointed the new Archbishop of Canterbury. Other bishops were chosen and consecrated, and the Church of England has contended to this day that the apostolic succession of the episcopate was preserved despite the break with Rome. Centuries later, Pope Leo XIII declared in 1896 that Anglican orders were invalid and not in the apostolic succession. Although the Elizabethan Settlement met bitter Catholic opposition, Elizabeth was tactful enough to avoid excommunication for eleven years; but she was eventually excommunicated as a heretic by Pope Pius V in 1570.

In the meantime she had revised the Forty-two Articles of 1553, which became the official Thirty-nine Articles of the Church of England. In the same year (1563), parliament passed the Test Act which required an oath of obedience to the queen as the supreme governor of the realm, and excluded Catholics from the House of Commons. Also in 1563, John Foxe published his famous *Book of Martyrs*, which inflamed prejudice against the Catholics because of its vivid portrayal of Catholics slaughtering and murdering thousands who would not bow to the pope.

Angry Catholic reaction to these events exploded in the northern revolt of 1569, and Rome began a series of intrigues to unseat Elizabeth and place Mary Queen of Scots on the English throne. Mary had been ousted from power in Scotland and sought refuge in England, but because she posed a threat to Elizabeth, she was imprisoned. In 1571, a plot to start an insurrection and unseat Elizabeth involved the Duke of Alva, Philip II, Pope Pius V, and the Duke of Norfolk. Catholic priests were trained and sent to England secretly as missionaries and subversives, and many Jesuits conspired to overthrow the Elizabethan government by force. In 1585 parliament passed the Act of Association which called for Mary's execution if she conspired against Elizabeth; and when she became involved in the Babington conspiracy of 1586, Mary was executed on February 8, 1587.

Philip II of Spain and Pope Sixtus V had dreamed of uniting Europe again under one emperor and one church, but had thus far failed, and their failure at bringing England back to the Catholic fold was especially bitter. When Philip determined to take England by force with the "Invincible Armada" of 132 ships, the pope helped plan and finance the ambitious campaign. Elizabeth appealed to the patriotism of her subjects, who sent two hundred smaller and faster ships to encounter the great Armada. Under the brilliant leadership of Sir Francis Drake, the mighty Spanish fleet was totally destroyed in 1588. This astounding defeat of the Spanish Armada enhanced Elizabeth's prestige everywhere and ushered in a golden age known as the Elizabethan Period, renowned for its literature, its commerce and growth in wealth, and its exploits on the sea. England appeared to have survived the threat of foreign interference, but some of Elizabeth's most disturbing problems were at home among extreme Protestants who did not feel she had gone far enough in breaking with Catholicism.

b. Puritans and Separatists. Elizabeth's settlement of a compromise religion had engendered opposition from orthodox Catholics, and now it faced obstinate criticism from radical Protestants. Throughout the land there had risen a large and vocal group known as Puritans, for their insistence that the Church of England be "purified" from all traces of Roman Catholicism. Many of them, especially the leaders, had been refugees on the continent during the persecution of Mary Tudor and were known as the Marian exiles. They became closely connected with and influenced by the continental reformers, especially the Calvinists. So when they returned to England under the Elizabethan Settlement, strong sentiments of total reform came with them. Their position was strengthened by the fact that Calvin's *Institutes* had become the recognized theological textbook in the universities of England.

There were three main types of Puritanism: the Episcopal Puritans, the Presbyterian Puritans, and the Separatist Puritans. The Puritan opposition within the remodeled Anglican church (Episcopal Puritans) was directed mainly against the clerical vestments and the details of liturgy. The decade of 1560 was characterized by controversy over the order of worship services. The Puritans protested the bowing of the knee at the observance of communion, the sign of the cross at baptism, and above all else, the altar robes. The opposition to the vestments, known as the Vestiarian Controversy, was based on the Protestant concept of the priesthood of believers, that clergy and laity are the same before God. Some Puritans, however, were willing to conform to the state church when the archbishop gave in on a few points. These were known as Conformists, and those who refused to compromise and refused to serve in the state church were known as Nonconformists. From about 1560 until 1689, the conflict between the Church of England and Nonconformity was of great significance.

Elizabeth was taking her nation down the road toward Protestantism, but she feared, as Luther had in Germany, that the entire cause of the Reformation was in danger of being wrecked by some radicals. Also, her Renaissance interests made her naturally react against those who wanted to do away with church music, paintings, sculpture, and beautiful stained glass windows. Thus, radical Puritanism was unacceptable to Elizabeth, and she fought constantly to control it if not eliminate it. Yet she found herself depending on the support of the Puritans in the decade of 1570 when she had been excommunicated, Catholic uprisings were occurring in the North, and plots to unseat her were seething.

During the 1570s when Puritanism was enjoying growth and popularity, a devout professor at Cambridge, Thomas Cartwright, came forth demanding that all ministers be on an equal level, since he could find no graduated organization of hierarchies in the New Testament. This challenge to episcopal church administration gained a wide hearing, and Cartwright became the theoretical father of English Presbyterianism. He was removed as professor and banished from the university, but he and other strong Puritan leaders privately organized classes and synods. In this way the Presbyterian church began in England, and its supporters were determined that it would eventually become the dominant church.

When Archbishop Parker died in 1575, Edmund Grindal was appointed to replace him. The new Archbishop of Canterbury had been a Marian exile, was deeply committed to Calvinism, and was sympathetic to

Presbyterian Puritanism. Because of his leanings in that direction, he was relieved of his official duties in 1577 and remained without authority or influence until his death in 1583.

Grindal was replaced by a hard line Episcopalian, John Whitgift, whose love of pomp and position was diametrically opposed to the plainness and simplicity of the Puritans. Whitgift denounced Cartwright, supported the queen's Renaissance style, and led the battle in parliament to crush the effort to introduce the Presbyterian system into the Church of England. To enforce the queen's policy of uniformity, Whitgift created a Commission for Causes Ecclesiastical for the purpose of repressing the Puritans. In 1593 he and Elizabeth pressured parliament to pass acts against the Puritans and Recusants (Catholics who wanted the papacy to dominate), which ordered all such seditions and disloyal persons to either conform to the services of the Church of England or leave the realm. Cartwright was imprisoned in 1590, but escaped to Holland, where he became a preacher in the Mercantile church in Middleburg.

Even more radical than the Puritans of this period were the Separatists or Independents. While the Puritans wanted to remain with the Church of England and purify it from within, the Separatists, like the Anabaptists on the continent, believed in "gathered" churches, made up of those who were freely and consciously Christian, not simply all the population of a given area. They were concerned not over vestments and liturgy, as were the Puritans, but over the structure and administration of the congregation. This was the beginning of Congregationalism, which first appeared in England in the 1580s. An early pioneer in embryonic Congregationalism was Robert Browne, a graduate of Cambridge, where he had been influenced by Cartwright. Browne organized the first free church practicing infant baptism in the post-Reformation period. In 1581 in Norwich he established a congregational type church, constituted of believers, bound together in a covenant relationship. It was autonomous, with no other ecclesiastical body having authority over it. Browne was arrested and imprisoned and his congregation forced to emigrate to Holland, where he joined them in 1582. His church remained in Holland for ten years, but Browne left for Scotland, where he was again imprisoned and finally returned to England, where he surrendered to the Archbishop of Canterbury in 1585 and was reinstated as a priest in the Anglican church. The early Independents were often called Brownists; but, ironically, he departed from them at the end of his life. These spiritual ancestors of the later Congregationalists were Separatists in that they withdrew from the Church of England; and they were Independents in that they believed in the full autonomy of each local church.

Despite the protests of ardent Catholics and radical Protestants, such as the Puritans and Separatists, Queen Elizabeth's Anglicanism prevailed and her *via media* succeeded in establishing the Church of England as a settlement religion halfway between Rome and Geneva, between popery and dissent. It was largely through her genius that England became the foremost Protestant power in Europe to which continental Protestantism was to look for support during the centuries to come. Elizabeth died in 1603, and except for the political revolt and beheading of Lord Essex, the last decade of her reign was quiet. However, stability was not a permanent legacy of the Elizabethan Era. Revolt and long conflicts loomed on the horizon.

6. REVOLT UNDER THE STUARTS
With the death of Elizabeth, the English monarchy passed from the house of Tudor to the house of Stuart.

a. James I and the Baptists. The son of Mary Queen of Scots and Lord Darnley (Henry Stuart) had reigned as James VI in Scotland since his mother's abdication in 1567. James was also the great-great-grandson of Henry VII, and as such ascended to the English throne as James I upon the death of Elizabeth (1603). All three factions in England had reason to believe that the new king would favor them. The Catholics felt that their cause would be close to his heart because his mother had been executed by Elizabeth and he had married a Roman Catholic, Anne of Denmark, in 1589. The Puritans, however, were encouraged because of his experience with Scottish Presbyterianism. The Church of England felt confident because of its subservient stance toward royal supremacy, for his exalted opinion of his station as supreme ruler was already well known. The Anglican confidence was justified, and the Church of England won the battle for the new king's support.

At the outset, however, the Puritans made the first move to gain favor and concessions. While he was on his way to London to assume the monarchy, James was met by a group of Puritans, who presented him with the Millenary Petition, so called because it bore a thousand signatures. The petition called for amendments in the Church of England, especially in rites and ceremonies. James was noncommital about the petition, but did promise to hold a conference with the Puritans. This promise was kept by the Hampton Court Conference in 1604, a conference of bishops and Puritans which produced only one significant result, the initiation of a fresh translation of the Bible. James appointed fifty-four scholars who worked from 1607 to 1611 to produce the "Authorized Version" which came to be known as the King James Version, the most popular and widely read version of the Bible ever printed.

James, however, did not revise the Prayer Book which the Puritans considered too popish. Neither did he revise or repeal the Thirty-nine Articles or the authorized catechism. He also maintained the episcopal form of church government, and Puritan ministers who objected lost their pulpits. In 1618, James issued the *Book of Sports*, which approved lawful sports on Sunday, and ordered the reading of the book and the announcement of sporting events to be made from the pulpits of the land. The Puritans had especially stressed reverent observance of Sunday and were infuriated at this royal command to approve and announce dancing, athletics, and May games on the Lord's Day. The Puritans had also emphasized Bible reading, devotional services in their homes, and purity in all moral issues; and thus the emphases of the king were in opposition to all they stood for. In addition, royal edicts were issued (in 1622) to instruct ministers as to sermon topics that were permissible and those which were not to be discussed. The Puritan conviction that the minister must be free to preach God's Word as led by the Spirit was thus openly defied by the king. Puritans throughout England were displeased and restless, but they were not yet agitated enough nor organized enough to revolt. Those who could not tolerate Anglican restrictions and requirements began to emigrate.

A small but significant group of emigrants was led to Holland in 1608 by John Smyth and John Robinson. Smyth was a Cambridge graduate and a rector of the Church of England. From 1600 to 1602 he was city preacher at Lincoln, but by 1603 he had developed distinctive Puritan leanings. He gathered a congregation in Gainsborough, where he renounced his episcopal ordination in 1606. The Gainsborough congregation became a full Separatist church, but it soon split and from it another congregation was organized in Scrooby. The pastor of the Scrooby church was John Robinson. In 1608, both Smyth and Robinson led their congregations to emigrate to Amsterdam. Robinson's followers moved on to Leyden, eventually joining the Mayflower group which came to Plymouth in 1620. Robinson himself was not able to sail on the *Mayflower*, but he assisted the Pilgrims in the preparations, and became known as the pastor of the Pilgrim Fathers. He died in Holland in 1625.

John Smyth's group at Amsterdam began debating the meaning of church membership and the question of baptism. Smyth came to the conclusion that, if the Separatist contention that "the church of the apostolic constitution consisted of saints only" was correct, baptism should be restricted to believers only. He insisted that he could find no scriptural support for the baptizing of infants. And since the Scriptures must be the sole guide for faith, he firmly announced his position for the baptism of believers only. In 1609 he put his conviction into action by baptizing first himself and then thirty-six others who joined him in forming a Baptist church. The baptism, however, was administered by pouring, not by immersion, which later Baptists insisted on.

Smyth had baptized himself on the principle that such an act was justified if no true church existed from which a valid baptism could be obtained. He soon, however, learned of the existence of a Mennonite

(Anabaptist) community in Amsterdam, concluded that it was a true church, and recommended union with it. This union was opposed by Thomas Helwys and other members of the group, who also disagreed with Smyth's doubts about his authority and procedure in baptizing them.

Thomas Helwys and John Murton led many of Smyth's congregation back to England where they established the first permanent Baptist Church on English soil about 1611-12. Helwys was an outspoken champion of religious liberty and his book *Declaration of the Mystery of Iniquity* was one of the first outright calls for religious liberty and a complete separation of church and state. For this stand he was imprisoned and later died there. But the movement he had started flourished, and by 1648 there were at least fifty General Baptist Churches in England with as many as fifteen thousand members. They were called General Baptist because of their Arminian doctrine of "general atonement," that Christ died for all men, not just the elect. General Baptists were the first English group to champion complete religious freedom. After 1644, they began to be called by the single name Baptist. Another group, known as the Particular Baptists, held to the Calvinistic doctrine of election—that Christ died only for the elect. The Particular Baptists, who practiced immersion rather than sprinkling or pouring, emerged about 1638 out of the first Congregational Church in England (which had been established by Henry Jacob at Southwark in 1616).

All those who had emigrated to Holland did not return to England. Many stayed in their new home, and others emigrated to the new world called America. On September 6, 1620, 101 Pilgrim venturers sailed on the *Mayflower* for America. Their leaders were William Bradford and William Brewster. During the next twenty years, more than forty thousand sought refuge in America. Those Baptists who remained in England constituted, along with other so-called "sectaries," the revolutionary core for Oliver Cromwell's army during the English Civil War.

The Puritans were not the only thorn in James' side. From the beginning of his reign, he had been vigorously opposed by devout Catholics. Jesuits advocated that any means, even assassination, were justified in advancing Roman Catholicism. Many assassination plots were uncovered, the most famous being the Gunpowder Plot of 1605. A small band of Roman Catholic conspirators hired a cellar under the Houses of Parliament, stored it with gunpowder, and arranged for Guy Fawkes to start the explosion intended to destroy the king, the lords, and the commons all together, in the hope that the Roman Catholics could then seize the government. The plot was exposed, the leading conspirators executed, all seminarians and Jesuits ordered to leave England, and Catholics were barred from such vocations as trustees, lawyers, doctors, and guardianships. James became even more adamant in Anglicanism and his own royal supremacy. Parliament grew weary of his frequent lectures on his divine attributes and prerogatives, and began to diminish his supremacy by denying him money for his domestic and foreign policies. He died in 1625, disliked and distrusted by the people whom he had tried to win over.

b. *Charles I and Oliver Cromwell.* James I was succeeded by his son Charles I, a deeply religious and morally pure monarch who was also a haughty, autocratic believer in the divine right of kings. From the beginning he quarreled with parliament, which was constantly denying his unexplained demands for money. In 1629 he dismissed parliament and ruled without it for eleven years.

Charles' mother had been a Catholic and he was married to a Catholic, Henrietta Maria, daughter of Henry IV of France. Although he remained a staunch Anglican, he decidedly favored the Catholic faction over the Puritans. In 1633 he appointed as Archbishop of Canterbury one William Laud, who introduced the Anglo-Catholic tradition. Anglo-Catholics view the Roman Catholic Church as a true church, not apostate as the Puritans viewed it; but at the same time, the Church of England is seen as preserving more faithfully the Catholic faith. Laud transformed communion tables back into altars, opposed Calvinistic theology, suppressed Puritan lectureships, restored church fabrics, and enforced uniformity against both Catholics and Puritans. He was extremely unpopular and personally symbolized all that the Puritans hated in ecclesiasticism. During Laud's oppressive administration, John Winthrop led 1,500 Puritans to Massachusetts in 1630, and 20,000 more followed during the next ten years.

Laud finally overstepped himself when he led the campaign to force episcopacy upon Scotland. Since James I had begun his reign as sovereign of both kingdoms, he and the Church of England had been trying by subtle diplomacy to lead Scotland away from Presbyterianism, and some progress was made in that direction. Now his son Charles joined Archbishop Laud in trying to force Anglicanism on Scotland. They insisted that Scotland adopt the Anglican Prayer Book and that the government and policy of the Church of Scotland be dependent upon Canterbury or Scottish bishops controlled by the king and Laud. The result was explosive. The Scots entered into a covenant with each other, known as the National Covenant of 1638, a covenant to die if necessary to keep their religious and political liberties. When Charles tried ineffectively to suppress the rebellion, the Scots replied by invading northern England in 1640.

Charles had managed for over a decade without a parliament, but now he was forced to summon parliament to raise money and an army. Parliament, however, was hostile to the king and demanded political and religious reforms if he expected their help. Charles responded by dissolving the body. It had met for just three weeks and is known as the Short Parliament. Archbishop Laud then directed a number of canons declaring that the king had divine right over his subjects with or without their consent, and the clergy was required to sign an oath never to change the government of the English church. Rather than gathering support for the crown, these actions created a furor among Englishmen everywhere. The Scots were advancing, and Charles was forced to summon parliament again. Known as the Long Parliament, it sat from 1640 to 1653, and became a greater center of revolt than the Scots.

The Long Parliament impeached Laud for high treason and imprisoned him in the Tower of London until he was beheaded on January 10, 1645. Then it set about to accomplish revolutionary changes in the Church of England. The Catholic features introduced by Laud were swept aside, and the king's devious tax schemes were declared illegal as was the king's right to dismiss parliament without its consent. Charles retaliated by attempting a military coup against the House of Commons in January, 1642. Public outcry and mob action forced the king to leave London, but he set about to assemble an army, and within months the troops of the king and the troops of parliament were locked in civil war.

Parliament needed Scottish aid in its fight with Charles and agreed to oppose episcopacy and work for uniformity in church organization throughout England, Scotland, and Ireland. The Westminster Assembly was set up to advise parliament on religious questions. The Assembly was composed of both clergy and laity, mostly Puritans, with a few Episcopalians and Independents. The Westminster Assembly produced three landmarks of Presbyterianism: the *Directory of Worship,* which replaced the Anglican Prayer Book; the *Shorter Catechism,* a concise statement of Calvinism; and the *Westminster Confession,* the definitive statement of Presbyterian doctrine in the English-speaking world. The Assembly also recommended a Presbyterian type of church government, which was established in 1646, and Anglicanism was outlawed for fifteen years.

The English Civil War brought to prominence a unique leader, Oliver Cromwell, who was to lead England into a most unusual kind of ecclesiastical government. Cromwell was a member of parliament during both the Short and Long Parliaments, and emerged as the military commander of parliament's troops. He built up a magnificently trained and disciplined fighting force known as the "New Model Army," which he led in overwhelming victories such as that at Marston Moor in 1644 and at Naseby in 1645. Cromwell held the religious and political views of the Puritans and evidenced the fervent spirituality of the Independents. To him, as to Charles I, the civil war was a religious struggle, and the Old Testament supplied the ethics for this holy war. All of Cromwell's battles were preceded by prayer meetings, and all his victories were ascribed to the Lord. During this period he wrote, "We desire only to fear our great God, that we do nothing against his will." To parliament he wrote, "We that serve you beg you not to own us, but God alone."

Indeed, Cromwell not only was unwilling to be owned by parliament, but in 1648 he purged parliament of those members who refused to back the army's intention to dispose of the king. These purged members were Presbyterians who were caught in the middle of political intrigue and military conflict. King Charles had been defeated and captured by the Scots, whom he convinced that he would favor Presbyterianism if they would support him against Cromwell. The ensuing battle resulted in a decisive victory of Cromwell over the Scots, the purging of parliament, and the trial and beheading of Charles I, the only English monarch ever to be executed.

In the occasion of a vacant throne, Cromwell became the military dictator of England, using his army to repress any attempts at insurrection. When Cromwell saw the embodiment of Roman Catholicism in the Irish revolt, he crushed that nation in bloody ruthlessness. When the Scots attempted a resurgence of hostilities against England he overpowered them with awesome strength at Dunbar in 1650 and a year later at Worcester. He had long been dissatisfied with the inefficient and factious Long Parliament and forcibly dismissed it on April 20, 1653. He also made himself Lord Protector with a standing army of 50,000 men. When he was later offered the title of king by the parliament of 1656, he declined, preferring to retain the title of Lord Protector.

Under Cromwell, the government was called the Commonwealth, and was a kind of republic. During the Cromwellian period, England was ruled by a series of constitutional experiments, from the "Bare-bones" parliament of 140 "saints" to the Major-Generals, none of which was really successful. As a benevolent dictator, Cromwell was firm, efficient, and tolerant. Attempts were made to improve the morals of the country, to reform the law, further education, and instill "true godliness." Cromwell gave to England the nearest approach to religious liberty that it had thus far known. As early as 1648 Cromwell had issued an order against forcing religion into one mold. Even then, however, Catholics and Unitarians were not to be tolerated. Cromwell abandoned a state church in favor of a national religion, built mainly on the Presbyterian, Independent, and Baptist faiths.

There were several Puritan groups which were not pleased with Cromwell's mediating stance in religion and contended for extremist measures. The Levellers believed that there is a natural law written in the hearts and consciences of men, and that sovereignty resides in the nation at large. The Diggers protested against private ownership of land. The Fifth Monarchy Men preached that Christ was to return soon to establish the "Fifth Monarchy" to succeed the Assyrian, Persian, Greek, and Roman empires. The Quakers sought to follow the Inner Light, and enjoyed religious freedom, but were imprisoned when they refused to pay tithes.

The Quakers (known also as the Society of Friends since 1800) were founded by George Fox who discovered in 1646 that moral victory is possible through the Inner Light of the living Christ. He henceforth abandoned church attendance and began preaching that truth is to be found in the inner voice of God speaking to the soul. He was frequently imprisoned, but his enthusiasm and moral earnestness soon attracted followers whom he formed into a stable organization. The nickname Quaker was first given by Justice Bennet in 1650 when George Fox bade the justice to tremble at the Word of the Lord. Early Quakers also explained it by the spiritual trembling sometimes experienced at their religious meetings. Cromwell had a great respect for George Fox personally, and felt drawn to his ideas. But the obstinacy and the openness of the Quakers (they refused to go underground as other groups did) were a constant irritation to him. An especially exasperating case was that of James Nayler, who after a long imprisonment was met by some women singing "Hosanna, blessed is he that cometh in the name of the Lord," as he rode into Bristol. Parliament spent an entire session trying Nayler for blasphemy on the charge that he had staged a triumphal entry in imitation of Christ. Although severely punished, he was not executed, and the Protectorate of Cromwell had won a significant victory, that henceforth neither heresy nor blasphemy would be subject to the death penalty.

At times ruthless and at other times magnanimous, Cromwell was unquestionably the genius of the Commonwealth. He believed that he was the instrument of divine providence: "I have not sought these things; truly I have been called unto them by the Lord." He also believed that that same providence was more important than human instruments. In his last prayer, the dying Lord Protector uttered, "Teach those who look too much on Thy instruments, to depend more upon Thyself." Cromwell died on September 3, 1658, the anniversary of the battles of Dunbar and Worcester, and was buried in Westminster Abbey. During the Restoration his body was disinterred and hung at Tyburn.

7. RESTORATION UNDER PARLIAMENT

Cromwell was succeeded by his son Richard, who was too weak to continue the military-ecclesiastical-political rule inaugurated by his commanding father. Under the sponsorship of George Monck, Cromwell's strongest general, the son of the executed Charles I returned from exile as Charles II in 1660. He was installed as a constitutional monarch, taking office under an agreement, and paid as a civil servant by parliament. This particular parliament was overwhelmingly and ardently Anglican, and immediately set about the restoration of Anglican government, worship, and practices. The Church of England was back in control and Puritans were dismissed and persecuted under a series of acts called the Clarendon Code.

When Charles II first came to the throne, he had promised religious freedom in his Breda Declaration of 1660, but in 1661 parliament passed

Oliver Cromwell, a member of parliament, led the "new model army" to victory in 1644 and 1645 against the Scots. He championed the cause of the Puritans and Independents. His purges resulted in the trial and beheading of Charles I, the only English monarch ever to be executed. (The Bettmann Archive)

the Corporation Act, which, among other things, stated that holy communion must be kept according to the Anglican rite. And in 1662 it passed the Act of Uniformity, requiring all ministers to have episcopal ordination, use the Anglican Prayer Book, and swear loyalty to the king. (In fact, the first Restoration Parliament was so thoroughly royalist that the pleased and obligated Charles kept it in session for eighteen years.) In 1664, parliament passed the First Conventicle Act prohibiting the assembling of more than five Nonconformists. The Five Mile Act of 1665 forbade Nonconformist ministers or teachers to live within five miles of an incorporated town or their former parishes. The Conventicle Act of 1670 increased fines for attending Nonconformist services and provided that anyone connected with the group could be forced to pay the fines of the entire group.

The restoration of Anglicanism was the clear intent of parliament, and as titular head of the Church of England, Charles II tried to cooperate with parliament's intention. His real devotion, however, leaned toward Roman Catholicism. His exile in France had impelled him toward the Catholicism and absolutism of Louis XIV. In 1670 Charles made a secret agreement with Louis XIV, known as the Treaty of Dover, to eventually restore England to Catholicism. Then, in 1672, Charles issued the Declaration of Indulgence, which permitted public worship for Catholics and Protestant dissenters; but parliament forced its withdrawal and passed the Test Act which required all civil and military officers to take the oath of allegiance to supremacy and receive the Lord's Supper according to Anglican doctrine. From then on, Charles abandoned his scheme with Louis XIV and stayed in the Anglican camp throughout his reign; but on his deathbed he confessed his Catholicism.

Charles II had no legitimate male heirs, and his brother James was next in line to become king. James was an avowed Roman Catholic, and in 1678 one Titus Oates had testified of a papal plot to assassinate Charles, massacre the English Protestants, and put James on the throne. In the resulting hysteria many Catholics were wrongly executed and three Puritan parliaments elected. Although parliament tried to pass an Exclusion Bill to keep James from succeeding Charles, it was unsuccessful. James ascended the throne upon the death of his brother in 1685.

James II tried openly to reinstitute Catholicism. He brought in Jesuits and monks and appointed Catholics to military commands, and religious and teaching posts. In 1687, in a Declaration of Indulgence, he openly avowed his Catholicism and stated his wish that all his subjects might also be Catholic. The populace was deeply resentful of James' efforts in this direction, and the birth of a son justified their fears that a Roman Catholic successor would be in the wings. In 1688 the two political parties in parliament, the Tories (Anglicans) and Whigs (Puritans) united in issuing an invitation to Mary, the Protestant daughter of James, and her husband

William of Orange, to invade England and restore liberty and religion. James fled to France and parliament offered the throne to William and Mary, ushering in the "Glorious Revolution" of 1688, which signaled the final victory of Protestantism in England.

In 1689 parliament enacted the Bill of Rights, which declared many of the actions of James II as illegal, and stipulated that no Roman Catholic could ever be king in England. That same year, parliament passed the Act of Toleration, which is regarded as one of the milestones in the struggle for religious liberty. This act suspended the laws against Protestant dissenters who did not attend services in the Church of England, but the toleration was limited in many cases. Presbyterians and Independents had to subscribe to all the Thirty-nine Articles, except those on polity and liturgy. The Baptists were excused from the article on infant baptism. The Quakers were relieved from the obligation to take an oath. Catholics and Unitarians, however, were excluded from the benefits of the act. Complete toleration for Catholics did not come until 1829. Although limited and incomplete, the Act of Toleration had come a long way from the days of Inquisition, wars, imprisonments, exiles, and executions. It was a transition attitude on the threshold of the age of Enlightenment. The Glorious Revolution had succeeded in stablilizing Anglicanism as the official religion of England, but royal supremacy had given way to constitutional limits on the monarchy.

This period also produced some of the great literature of civilization. The immortal William Shakespeare (1564-1616) was at the height of his dramatic power at the opening of the seventeenth century. At the close of the century, some of the richest writing in English literature was produced by such men as John Donne, Jeremy Taylor, John Bunyan, and John Milton. Bunyan (1628-88) was a Particular Baptist who was arrested for his Puritan views and spent twelve years in prison, where he wrote *The Holy City* in 1665 and *Grace Abounding* in 1666. In a second imprisonment he wrote *Pilgrim's Progress* in 1678, which made him one of the most popular and influential religious writers in all of English history. In all his works Bunyan pictured life as a spiritual warfare and salvation as man's chief concern. Milton (1608-74) wrote the two great masterpieces, *Paradise Lost* in 1667 and *Paradise Regained* in 1671, to expound the themes of the fall and redemption of man. He also became involved in the political scene, defending the execution of Charles I but later becoming a critic of Cromwell, and finally landing in jail for opposing the divine-right rule of Charles II.

The Reformation in England was dominated by the issue of royal supremacy and was often more political than religious. Roman Catholicism, Puritanism, and the free church movements were considered subversive, not primarily because of theological views but because they threatened royal supremacy. The Act of Toleration in 1689 greatly diminished that royal supremacy and acknowledged the legal rights of free church dissenters. The victors in the almost two-hundred-year struggle were the power of the state and the spirit of nationalism, which rapidly filled the vacuum of broken church authority.

F. REFORM IN CATHOLICISM

The term Reformation is usually associated with the Protestant movement, but reform efforts within the Roman Catholic Church delineated a very distinct period of Catholic Reformation. It is often referred to as the Counter-Reformation, implying that it was a reaction to the Protestant initiative. Most Catholics, however, insist that history abundantly testifies to a revival within the Catholic Church in Europe before, during, and even after the launching of Protestantism. The Catholic Reformation is usually considered as extending from about the middle of the sixteenth century (1555) to the period of the Thirty Years War (1618-48). There were, however, definite stirrings of renewal long before Luther posted his theses at Wittenberg.

1. RENEWAL OF PIETY

Martin Luther was not the first nor the only Catholic priest burdened about the spiritual and moral condition of the church at the beginning of the sixteenth century. In fact, there seemed to be a grass roots demand for a religious awakening and many attempts were made to accomplish this throughout Catholicism. Why, then, did Luther and others feel it necessary to break with Rome, and how was the Protestant Reformation different from the Catholic Reformation? The answer to both questions is the same: the Catholic reform was ascetic, not theological. The concern was for moral purity and for organizational integrity, but the theological foundations of medieval Christianity remained intact. This was not enough for the Protestants, who contended that theology (the root) must be right before activity (the fruit) can be reformed. The Catholics, on the other hand, insisted that their theology was right, but admitted that many abuses did need correction. Thus the Catholic expression of internal reform was essentially a renewal of piety.

In the section on the critical-reform movement, we surveyed the call for reform by John Wycliffe, and John Hus, and the mystics, Meister Eckhart and John Ruysbroeck, and the saintly Thomas à Kempis. We heard the humanists such as Colet and Erasmus advocate a return to the Bible and the early Church Fathers. In the prelude to reform, immediately preceding the Protestant break, we noted that Ximenes and wielded a powerful sword in the name of reform in Spain. All of the early Reformers were originally Catholic. Even Luther was a devout priest who merely wanted to make some things right in his beloved church.

The same year that Luther nailed his theses to the chapel door in

Wittenberg (1517), there was founded in Rome the Oratory of Divine Love, a close-knit group of some sixty Catholic leaders who met for worship and mutual edification. They dedicated themselves to reform their own lives and the lives of those about them. In the expression of this dedication, they established orphanages and hospitals, cared for the sick, fasted, gave alms, went on pilgrimages, and continued to meet frequently for prayer, discussion, and preaching. The Oratory of Divine Love was dispersed when Charles V sacked Rome in 1527, but its influence extended to many later reforms. When Pope Paul III appointed the Commission of Nine to investigate the state of the church and recommend reforms, most of the commission had belonged to the Oratory. The commission made its report in 1537, revealing many scandalous conditions in the church, and emphasizing the urgent need for radical reform.

Two members of the commission who had also been founding members of the Oratory of Divine Love were Giovanni Caraffa and Gaspar Contarini. These men represented the two disparate methods of attempting reform, for while all members of the commission advocated administrative and moral reforms, they did not all agree as to the method of procedure. Contarini represented the group which sought reform through humanism. He earnestly believed that reconciliation between Protestants and Catholics was possible and worked with Melanchthon to that end. Although the two finally agreed on a statement on justification by faith, and were both excited about the possibility of reconciliation, their statement and proposals were rejected by both Luther and the pope. Contarini died a disappointed man, his dream shattered.

Caraffa, who later became Pope Paul IV, represented those who advocated reform through force. He was fiercely loyal to the church and recommended establishing the Holy Office of the Inquisition to discover and punish heretics, thereby hoping to stop the defections to Protestantism. Caraffa himself headed the office of the Inquisition, which set about to imprison, confiscate property, torture, and execute. As pope, Caraffa made up a list of forbidden writings and directed the burning of thousands of books. He advocated extreme asceticism and sought to force his standards of morality on the people. While Contarini had worked for conciliation with the Protestants, Caraffa urged a stern repression of all doctrinal divergences. Pope Paul III appeared at first to favor Contarini's method, but eventually adopted the repressive methods of Caraffa, a policy followed by later popes of that period.

Coming out of the Oratory of Divine Love were other organizations dedicated to various expressions of reform. The Theatines, named after the bishopric of Theate, where the group started, was an association of pious clergymen devoted to preaching, to the care of the sick, and the salvation of criminals. The Theatines were also forerunners of the Jesuits in their fervor to suppress heresy (Caraffa was one of their founders). The Barnabites or

Clerks Regular of St. Paul were organized in 1533 to combat the rank immorality of the day by preaching and example. The Sommaschi, started in 1527, were concerned with relieving any kind of misery among the living and burying the unwanted dead.

Another organization which spawned renewal groups was the Franciscan Order, which was undergoing reform tensions. The Capuchins, formally recognized in 1528, was an order of ascetic Franciscan hermits devoted to humility, simplicity, and charity. They suffered attacks from other jealous friars, but survived and grew. The Ursulines were organized in 1535 for the purpose of teaching and caring for children. The Brothers of Mercy were begun in 1540 to care for the sick in hospitals and asylums. The Brothers of Good Death was founded to care for those with incurable diseases. The Angelicals of St. Paul were devoted to work with orphans and penitent girls. The Daughters of Mary were committed to improving education.

Scores of associations and orders emerged and flourished in the early part of the sixteenth century. Itinerant monks preached revival and reform throughout towns and villages. Laity and clergy alike read books of prayer and devotions. Devout scholars and church leaders sought to bring about a religious seriousness in lieu of a formal ecclesiasticism. Underneath it all, however, it must be remembered that the reform consciousness in Roman Catholicism was motivated by the conviction not to reform doctrine but to reform lives. The most obvious and enduring result of this motivation was to harden rather than soften the tenets of mainline Catholicism.

2. SOCIETY OF JESUS

The most influential order which was born in this period was the Society of Jesus, also known as the Jesuits, which became the spearhead for the Counter-Reformation, and remains today one of the most prominent orders of the Catholic Church.

a. Ignatius Loyola. The founder of the Jesuits was a Spanish nobleman-soldier named Inigo Lopez de Recalde, better known to the world as Ignatius of Loyola. Born between 1491 and 1495 at the castle of Loyola near the Pyrenees, Ignatius served as a page at the court of Ferdinand and Isabella, and envisioned a great army career for himself. His days as a professional soldier, however, were ended when he sustained a severe leg wound in 1521 during an attack on the French on Pampeluna. During a long and painful convalescence he read provocative accounts of the life of Christ and the early saints. He vowed to become a soldier for Jesus Christ and to use the same military qualities of discipline and obedience with which he had served Ferdinand. Following his recuperation, he journeyed to the Benedictine abbey at Montserrat, where he hung his sword and armor on the Virgin's altar and dedicated himself to chastity, poverty, and service. From Montserrat, Loyola went to the nearby town of Manresa where he

Ignatius Loyola and his first companions, taking the pledge in the Church of Montmartre in Paris on Ascension Sunday, 1534. (The Bettmann Archive)

lived the life of an ascetic, fasting, praying, begging his food, and caring for the sick. He read many works of devotion, and began writing his famous *Spiritual Exercises,*which was to become one of the most influential religious books in the world.

The exercises were intended to serve as an examination of conscience and a guide for meditation, contemplation, and prayer. The exercises were designed to cover four weeks, the first week concentrating on sin, the second focusing on the life of Christ, the third revolving around the passion of Christ, the fourth centering on the triumph of the resurrection. The meditations and rules developed under these four major themes were intended to lead souls to conquer their passions and give themselves totally to God. The *Exercises* skillfully employed a combination of sense impressions, imagination, and understanding in actuating the will toward the pursuit of perfection. After the Society of Jesus was organized, all Jesuit candidates were required to go on retreat for the four-week exercises; and even to this day, the *Spiritual Exercises* of Ignatius Loyola are prescribed by the Roman Catholic Church for all candidates for orders and are widely used by many others.

After about a year at Manresa, Loyola went first to Rome and then to Jerusalem, where he planned to witness to Moslems. The Franciscans in the holy city discouraged his missionary efforts; so he returned to Spain, where he began his formal education (although he was already over thirty years of age) and attended school in Barcelona with mere boys. Next he went to the University of Alcala, which had been founded by Ximenes as a center of reform. There he began the practice of putting others through his regimen of the *Spiritual Exercises,* came under suspicion of the Inquisition, was briefly imprisoned and commanded not to teach without express permission. From Alcala, he went to the University of Salamanca, where he was also imprisoned and told he must study four more years before he could preach. Then he went directly to the University of Paris to continue his studies in the most famous center of Christian theological learning of the day.

Loyola was a student at the University of Paris the same time as John Calvin, but there is no evidence that they ever met. From the same educational setting, these two great minds of the sixteeenth century went in opposite directions: Calvin to be a leader of the Protestant Reformation, and Loyola to be the strident force of the Catholic Reformation. In 1533, Calvin renounced his benefices and fled to Protestant Basel; and in the same year Loyola banded together with six other close companions to form the nucleus of what eventually became the Society of Jesus. One of the seven was a roommate of Loyola's, Francis Xavier, destined to become one of the greatest missionaries of all time.

On August 15, 1534, the group of seven made an oath to poverty, chastity, missionary work, and absolute obedience to the pope. The group ventured a pilgrimage to Jerusalem, which was never completed. While detained in Venice, Loyola met Giovanni Caraffa, the future Pope Paul IV, and was impressed with his zeal to suppress heresy. Loyola and the others in his group, which had grown in number, were ordained in Venice. A year later Loyola proceeded to Rome. There he placed the services of the new band at the complete disposal of the pope, and they sought permission to constitute themselves into an order. After considerable opposition and some hesitation, Pope Paul III approved the Society of Jesus on September 27, 1540.

Loyola became the first general of the "Regimini militantis Ecclesiae," and drew up the constitutions of the Society between 1547 and 1550, constantly improving on them. Loyola was a curious mixture of soldier, mystic, and monk. But on one thing he was clear and positive: the ultimate authority of the church. Whereas Luther had found his peace by rejecting the traditions of the medieval church in favor of the biblical basics of primitive Christianity, Loyola found his peace by rededicating himself to the conventions of the medieval church.

In his *Spiritual Exercises,* Loyola wrote, "Laying aside all private judgment, we ought to hold our minds prepared and prompt to obey in all things the true Spouse of Christ our Lord, which is our holy Mother, the hierarchical Church," and "To arrive at truth in all things, we ought always to be ready to believe that what seems to us white is black, if the hierarchical Church so defines it." Loyola also stood diametrically opposed to Luther's doctrine of justification by faith, declaring in the *Exercises* that "man was created to praise, reverence, and serve God our Lord, and by this means to save his soul." He also opposed Calvin's doctrine of election, believing that man's free will enables him to serve or not to serve, as he chooses. So, although he appeared on the scene with his Jesuits some fifteen years after the Reformation had exploded, Ignatius Loyola became the Catholic answer to the Protestant challenge.

b. Combating Protestantism. The Jesuits' work centered on three main tasks: counteracting the Protestants, providing high quality education, and promoting missionary expansion. The Jesuits' motto was, "All to the greater glory of God." This sounds as though it would be a motto understood and accepted by Christians anywhere, but to the Jesuits it meant very explicitly the extension of God's kingdom on earth, and this kingdom was condensed in the Roman church and was represented by the pope. All doctrines and organizations which deviated from the papal church were heresies. Luther, Zwingli, and Calvin were emissaries of Satan whose influence had to be destroyed by any means. This obsession led the Jesuits to develop two infamous ethical doctrines known as *probabilism* and *mental reservation.*

Probabilism allowed Jesuits to declare any act to be perfectly acceptable to Christ if there was any probability that it might be all right. *Mental reservation* allowed them to withhold part of the truth, even under oath, or leave a wrong impression if the end for such action seemed good. Both concepts led to the overriding principle that the end justifies the means. Thus, any means was justifiable in stamping out the satanic Protestantism.

In France, in what is today Belgium, in southern Germany, and in eastern Europe, the Jesuits led the counterattack against the Protestants. Using almost any means at their disposal, they recaptured large areas for the church of Rome. They earned the reputation as "the feared and formidable storm-troops of the Counter-Reformation." About the only place they were unsuccessful was in England. They were the most loyal advocates of the papacy, holding that the pope had the right to excommunicate and depose sovereigns and that excommunicated sovereigns might be assassinated.

The Roman church backed up the work of the Jesuits with the dreaded Inquisition, which was applied most severely by Torquemada, Ximenes, and Caraffa. When he became pope, Caraffa developed another weapon against heresy, the Index, a list of books that the faithful were not permitted to read. The books of Erasmus and some Protestant editions of the Bible were on the list. The Inquisition forced many to recant their Protestant views, and the Index kept many Catholics from reading Protestant literature. The Index was not abolished until 1966.

Force and persecution were not the only weapons of the Jesuits. They understood well the importance of preaching to the Protestant congregation, and some of them became masterful preachers. Under their ethical banner that the end justifies the means, they often modified Catholic worship services to be less offensive to Protestants in order gradually to win the dissenters back into the fold. Marked by absolute obedience to the pope, and determined to restore the Catholic Church to its previous dominance, the Jesuits swept across Europe with every available means of spiritual, intellectual, and physical warfare. Although the original Society had been limited to sixty members, by 1626 the Jesuits had 15,000 members and 803 houses, and by 1750 they had 22,000 members.

c. Jesuit Education. In their efforts to reclaim Europe for Catholicism, the Jesuits concentrated heavily on education, believing that man's reason should be cultivated so that he would choose right. Jesuit schools became famous for high standards and attainments, and many of society's elite and many of the world's opinionmakers were won to Roman Catholicism through the excellency of Jesuit education. Children were given special attention, and the now familiar Jesuit saying was coined: "Give me a child until he is seven, and he will remain a Catholic the rest of his life."

Before Loyola's death in 1556, Roman, German, Greek, Hungarian, and English colleges were established by the Jesuits at Rome. In addition they had colleges at Vienna, Bavaria, and Munich. By 1626, the Jesuits had 476 colleges and 36 seminaries; by 1750 they had 669 colleges, 176 seminaries, and 700 lower schools in France alone. Latin, the official language of the church, was used in instruction, and no modern languages were allowed until 1832. All books were carefully censored to eliminate the possibility of heresy, and a system of spying was methodically executed. The schools were grounded in rationalism and discipline, and instant, blind obedience was demanded. Under the leadership of dedicated scholars such as Robert Bellarmine and Peter Canisius, the Jesuit schools helped reclaim many territories that had fallen to the Protestants. Today, the educational ministry of the Jesuits continues to make its impact in the world. The Jesuits are responsible for the Gregorian University of Rome and have nine universities among their eastern missions. They also support and control many schools and academies in all parts of the world and edit several important periodicals.

d. Missionary Expansion. The third avowed aim of the Jesuits was missionary expansion in new areas, and they excelled in this as much, if not more, than in their educational system. Because of the Jesuits, the sixteenth century was the great century of Roman Catholic missions. Jesuit priests traveled to America, Africa, and Asia in search of converts, which they left with a fanatical brand of Catholicism. They also produced scholarly accounts of the history and geography of the places they visited. Jesuit missionaries went with Spanish colonists to Mexico and South America, playing a leading role in the conversion of Brazil and Paraguay. They were not as successful in Africa, but they were exceedingly successful in the Orient. By the end of the century they had made great gains in India, Indochina, the Philippines, China, and Japan, led and inspired by Francis Xavier, "the apostle to the Indies and to Japan."

Xavier was born into Portuguese nobility and taught philosophy at Beauvais until meeting Ignatius Loyola, who induced him to study theology. He was one of the original members of the Society of Jesus, and Loyola realized that this handsome, brilliant, and cheerful young man would make a powerful servant of the Lord. Ordained a priest in 1537, Xavier heard the appeal of King John III of Portugal for missionaries to India and walked from France to Portugal to answer the call. He was appointed the pope's ambassador and sent to evangelize Goa (in East India) in 1542. After laboring there for three years, he went to what is now Malaysia and Vietnam, and finally to Japan. In ten years he covered enormous distances, traveling through Ceylon, Hindustan, the Malaccas, parts of China, and Japan. His most remarkable mission was in Japan, where he established a flourishing church which has survived to the present time.

Altogether, Xavier preached in fifty-two different kingdoms and baptized a million converts. Although his ministry was limited to perfunctory baptism, the Mass, ceremonies, memorized prayers, and catechism, he did sow the seeds of Catholicism which continued to grow after his death at the age of forty-six in 1552.

The Jesuit missionary enterprise was carried on by such devoted men as Matteo Ricci, the apostle to China. Between 1550 and 1650, the Jesuits, Dominicans, Franciscans, and Augustinians led the Catholic Church in a new period of rapid overseas expansion. Nearly all of Mexico, Central America, the Philippines, and smaller numbers in Africa, India, the East Indies, and the Far East, became adherents of the church of Rome.

e. Fraternal Opposition. The success abroad, however, was offset by opposition closer to home. The unscrupulous methods of the Jesuits and their interference in European politics gained them much enmity among Catholics and Protestants alike. Neither was their outspoken theology on the freedom of the will and the saving power of good works compatible with all Catholics.

In the early years of the seventeenth century the University of Louvain was in the throes of a violent conflict between the Jesuits and the Augustinians. A young divinity student by the name of Cornelius Jansen joined the Augustinian party and began a lifetime of opposing the theologians of the Counter-Reformation. With his close friend Jean Duvergier de Hauranne, he laid plans for a reformation of the church from within, on principles radically different from the Jesuits. His antipathy to the Jesuits, however, did not bring Jansen nearer the Protestants. He wanted to prove that Catholics could interpret the Bible just as mystically and pietistically as the Protestants.

In 1617 Jansen became director of a Dutch theological school at Louvain, where the Jesuits were still fomenting conflict. In his writings and his lectures he accused the Jesuits of Pelagianism, the heresy that teaches that man chooses to save himself by his own efforts. His *Augustinus,* a treatise on the theology of Augustine, was published posthumously in 1640, and it launched a vigorous reform movement known as Jansenism. Pope Urban VIII condemned the *Augustinus* in 1642, but the condemnation had little effect.

Jansen's friend Duvergier had become abbe of St. Cyran where he led his followers to support the doctrines of the *Augustinus.* After St. Cyran's death in 1643, Antoine Arnauld (the "Great Arnauld"), priest and theologian at the Sorbonne, became leader of the Jansenist movement. Arnauld was outspoken concerning the need for thorough internal preparation for communion, and the Jesuit abuses of the confessional. He was supported by the Dominicans and by Blaise Pascal, who wrote his *Provincial Letters* of 1656 to attack the Jesuits for their ruthlessness, unscrupulousness, and untrustworthiness. Arnauld was censured by the Sorbonne and was forced into retirement until he was restored by the "Peace of the Church" in 1668.

One of Arnauld's collaborators was Pierre Nicole, a French philosopher and theologian who wrote a number of works against the teachings of the Jesuits. He was also, however, very strongly opposed to the Calvinists. Biased against mysticism, Nicole began to move farther away from Jansenism, and eventually defended the universal saving will of God and the sufficiency of grace for all men. In 1713 a papal bull again condemned all the substantive tenets of Jansenism, and the Jansenists suffered persecution in France during most of the eighteenth century. After Napoleon's Concordat in 1801, French Jansenism survived only as a secret conviction of a few Catholics.

The Jesuits had also continued to be a foreign irritation in France and were expelled in 1764, largely because of the work of the Jansenists. Trouble was brewing for the Jesuits elsewhere, and in 1759 they were banished from Portugal, and in 1767 from Spain. Under extreme pressure the pope suppressed the Society in 1773 with the bull *"Dominus ac Redemptor."* Suppression did not mean, however, that the Jesuits were exterminated. They were allowed to teach in Austria and Germany, and were protected in both Prussia and Russia. Gradually the Jesuits managed to reestablish themselves, and in 1814 the Society was formally restored by Pope Pius VII.

3. COUNCIL OF TRENT

Among the enduring contributions of the Jesuits was their involvement in the pivotal Council of Trent, the most definitive embodiment of the ideals of the Catholic Reformation. In fact, the Council of Trent stands as an epoch turning point in the history of the Roman Catholic Church, shaping the structure and doctrine of the church for the next four hundred years. The decisions and decrees of the Council of Trent were not significantly questioned until Vatican Council II (1962-65), and even then the extent of actual change is debatable.

a. Background and Sessions. Since the early centuries of Christendom, the church had sought to settle its problems and theological differences with the convening of general councils, a number of which we have already reviewed. It will be remembered that the last great council had been the Council of Constance (1414-18), designed to end the Great Schism, to bring about the reform of the church, and to deal with various heresies. This council made the momentous declaration that a general council derived its authority directly from God, and that every Christian, even the pope, was bound to obey it (the famous *Sacrosancta* decree). In succeeding papacies, however, the decree was ignored with varying degrees of antipathy, until finally in 1460, Pope Pius II issued his *Execrabilis*, which negated the supremacy of councils, and even made the call for a council a cause for excommunication. In spite of this, calls for reforming councils continued to be heard, especially in the first half of the sixteenth century.

Protestantism was in full bloom and spreading across the continent. England had declared the supremacy of the king over the pope. Catholicism was losing ground practically everywhere, and the basic causes of the Reformation still had not been seriously addressed within the official ranks of the Roman church. Fundamental doctrinal beliefs and ecclesiastical morality comprised the two chief complaints of the reformers. Serious and sincere Catholic leaders began to insist that the church must convene a council to consider its basic dogma and to honestly investigate reputed immorality and ecclesiastical abuses. The Protestant Reformation was no longer a minor irritation, it was a major challenge, threatening to destroy the centuries-old Holy Roman Empire and the Roman Catholic Church. The cry for a reform council came at first from the lower clergy and then from the universities, and finally from Emperor Charles V, who was determined to get the religious issue settled.

Yielding finally to the imperial pressure, Pope Paul III decided to convoke a general council. He had already shown great concern over conditions within the church, appointing the commission which drew up the startling report of 1537, clamping down hard on clerical graft and concubinage, approving the Society of Jesus, and reviving the office of the Inquisition. It was only natural that Paul III should be the one to convoke the reform council which would become the famous Council of Trent.

The pope issued several summonses, one in 1537, another in 1538, and still another in 1542, which were not consummated for various reasons. It was not until December 13, 1545, that the first session of the council began. The council subsequently went through twenty-five sessions, ending on December 4, 1563, almost exactly eighteen years after it had begun. However, the revolt of the princes against Charles V led to the suspension of the council in 1552, and under the violent anti-Protestant papacy of Paul IV (Caraffa) there was no hope for it to reassemble. So there was actually a ten-year lapse before it met again under Pope Pius IV in 1562. The twenty-five sessions were convened in three designated "periods." Period I was in 1545-7 and conducted sessions 1-8. Period II was in 1551-2 and conducted sessions 9-14. Period III was in 1562-3 and conducted sessions 15-25.

An attempt was made for general representation in the sessions. Ironically, however, those who had heralded the call for the council, the middle and lower clergy and university representatives, were not even invited. Prominent theologians and canonists served as consultants, but had no vote. Protestant leaders were invited; but, of course, they had no vote, and only a few attended. Luther said he would participate in a general council only if it were not dominated by the papacy, and if it took Scripture as its final authority. As expected, his conditions were immediately denied. It was decided at the outset that voting should be on an individual basis, rather than by nations as at Constance, giving the propapal Italian bishops a preponderating influence. It was also decided at the outset that the two main issues at hand, the discussion of dogma and the need for disciplinary reform, should be treated equally and concurrently.

b. Dogma and Authority. The council was dedicated to discussing fully and deciding firmly all the disputed and challenged points of Catholic dogma. In each and every session, and over the long and turbulent years of its convocation, the council discussed, debated (often with intense fervor), and consistently reaffirmed the traditional Catholic positions. Every dogma which had been challenged by the Protestants was investigated in detail and reaffirmed unequivocally. Not a single concession was made to the Protestant perspective.

One of the first issues settled, after vigorous debate, was the question of authority, the very question Luther had placed before them by refusing to attend unless Scripture was recognized as ultimate authority. The decision of the council has had far-reaching impact and consequences upon all that Catholicism has preached and promoted in the subsequent four hundred years. The council decisively affirmed that tradition is as equally inspired and as equally binding as Scripture. Conflicting interpretations of either Scripture or tradition are left to the ultimate authority of the pope. The church was certified as the sole authority for interpreting Scripture, and all individuals had to submit to the opinion of the church. The council also sanctioned the Apocrypha as having canonical standing, a retaliation against Luther's challenge of the Apocrypha in 1534. The Latin Vulgate translation by Jerome was adopted by the council as the Catholic Church's official translation of the Bible. In compact summary, the council established religious authority as residing in the Old Testament, the Apocrypha, the New Testament, and the unwritten traditions, all equally inspired, as translated by Jerome, and as interpreted by the church, with the final voice residing in the pope.

The council then, with this perspective of authority, began to confront and dispose of every significant Protestant challenge. While it used Protestant language in speaking of justification by faith, it clearly specified that faith does not save unless it is given reality by love and good works, thus a principle of "faith cooperating with good works." The council also affirmed (1) that one can never know with certainty that he has obtained the grace of God except by special revelation, and (2) that there is no such thing as predestined, irresistible grace. It came out strongly in defense of the doctrine of purgatory and for merits earned by good works.

Protestants had discarded all of the seven sacraments except two, baptism and the Lord's Supper, and the council addressed itself forthrightly to this challenge. It declared that grace is conferred through all seven of the Catholic Church's traditional sacraments: baptism, eucharist, confirmation, penance, extreme unction, holy orders, and matrimony. The council reaffirmed the doctrine of transubstantiation, holding that the bread and the wine become the body and blood of Christ, and rejecting any weakening of that position, even the moderate view of consubstantiation. It also asserted that it was unnecessary to give the cup to the laity, another demand of the Reformers.

The council rejected the Protestant idea of the priesthood of believers, insisting that only bishops and priests have the power to pronounce the forgiveness or retention of sins. It came out emphatically in favor of invocation of the saints, for the veneration of the relics of the saints, for the use of sacred images and paintings, and for the efficacy of indulgences. Celibacy and virginity were extolled and underscored. Marriage was declared valid only when performed by a priest before two witnesses. Divorce was condemned and remarriage prohibited as long as the other partner lived. The council clarified and reasserted most of the doctrines of the medieval Roman church. The first great issue of the Reformation, doctrine and authority, had been met head-on with a rejection of all Protestant views and a tightening of all substantive Catholic dogma.

c. *Reform and Retrenchment.* The second great issue, discipline and reform, met with more admission for the need for change. Even the most ardent Catholic, theologically speaking, knew that the name of Christianity was suffering from excesses and abuses within the church. The implementing of change, however, was a delicate matter, and the Reformers were never satisfied with what they considered surface changes that were more symbolic than substantive. Major reform proposals which failed were attempts to limit the use of excommunication, allow the Mass in the vernacular, and encourage Scripture reading in the ethnic language. Excessive abuses of indulgences were discouraged, but the central issue of buying and selling indulgences (which had precipitated Luther's revolt) was practically bypassed. The papacy was left in control of appointing bishops, eliminating any possibility of a ministry of equals. Regardless of what a priest or bishop individually felt was God's will for his place or program of service, he had to always defer to the pope, the vicar of Christ and final voice of God's authority on earth.

The reform measures which did succeed were closely associated with an improved preparation of the clergy and a better structured hierarchy. The holding of several cathedral churches by one man was forbidden, and those who received income from several benefices were restricted. It was decided that no one could be ordained to the diaconate until he was twenty-three years old, or to the priesthood until he was twenty-five. Every cathedral and metropolitan church was required to have a college or seminary for training boys for the clergy. Every ordained clergyman was to have a definite post, to abolish the wandering and begging clerics. Bishops were directed to visit their entire diocese regularly, to preach and encourage their priests to preach. Bishops were admonished to live frugally and to refrain from using church property to enrich themselves or their relatives. The bishops' authority was greatly strengthened, with decrees directing that no one could preach in a diocese without that bishop's permission, that all candidates for benefices must be approved by the bishop, that only bishops could confer ordinations, and that all monasteries were to be under the jurisdiction of a bishop. The administrative machinery of the Roman Catholic Church was reworked and tightened, with more explicit power than ever being placed in the papacy. The council left the confirmation of its decrees to the pope, but the pope made it clear that the council had acted in the first place only with his permission.

In 1564 Pope Pius IV ratified the actions of the council and issued his creedal summary known as the Tridentine Faith, or the Creed of Pius IV. This was a formal recapitulation and brief summary of the doctrinal statements and reform policies of the Council of Trent. It was couched in personal terms, each paragraph beginning with "I believe and profess," as though each precept had personally come from the pope, and since the council had deemed the pope to be the only valid interpreter of Scripture and tradition, this form conveyed the spirit of Trent. In 1870, Vatican Council I confirmed the spirit of Trent with its explicit statement of papal infallibility. The Council of Trent and the resulting Tridentine creed entrenched medieval Catholicism and especially strengthened the papacy. All Catholic history since then has been called post-Tridentine. It was not until Vatican Council II met in 1962 that the adequacy of Tridentism was challenged.

4. WARS OF RELIGION

While theologians and ecclesiastics were hammering out the doctrinal positions of Catholicism at Trent, the Counter-Reformation also continued to employ force in its attempt to bring defectors back into the fold. The sword had been recognized as a legitimate instrument of the church ever since Constantine had used military force to bring the empire into the embrace of Christianity. Succeeding centuries had witnessed varying degrees of the use of political methods and weapons for the suppression of religious dissent. The medieval period was especially punctuated with the sword of the crusades and the tortures of the Inquisition. The burning of heretics was a common practice which stubbornly persisted through several centuries. The Hussite Wars of the fifteenth century foreshadowed the coming conflict between Catholics and Protestants that was to span two centuries and keep Europe bathed in blood for almost a hundred and fifty years.

a. Sixteenth Century Conflicts. Although we have already reviewed the confrontations of the sixteenth century under other headings, it will be helpful to see them in the light of their relationship to the Catholic

Reformation. The use of secular power was not a coincidental reaction to dissension; it was a deliberate and integral part of the church's effort to retain its solidarity and extinguish the threat of heresy. Neither was the use of force new and unexpected to the dissenters. The sixteenth century opened with the pontificate of Julius II, the warrior pope who boasted of his prowess with the sword. For ten years (1503-13) Julius reigned in such a military fashion as to have his warlike character scathingly attacked by Erasmus. With his mighty papal army, Julius drove Caesar Borgia from Italy in 1504, forced Perugia and Bologna to submit to his sovereignty in 1506, crushed Venice in 1509 for violating papal claims, and in 1511 founded the Holy League including England, Spain, Venice, and Switzerland for the purpose of defeating France. Julius was also the pope who instigated the selling of indulgences for rebuilding St. Peter's, the occasion for Martin Luther's Ninety-Five Theses. Luther and the other Reformers knew that they were challenging the military might of Rome as well as its theological claims.

The Roman Catholic Church tried every means at its disposal to suppress the growing Protestant threat. Debates were held, diets were convened, edicts were declared, and excommunications were issued. After the Diet of Augsburg in 1530, it was clear that none of these methods would assuage the Reformers. In a united stand they had made their statements of faith and subsequently formed the Schmalkaldic League to withstand the expected Catholic attack. Invasion of the Turks caused both Catholics and Protestants to delay confrontations for some sixteen years, but eventually they did clash in the brief but ferocious Schmalkaldic War (1546-47). The Emperor Charles V was determined to restore Catholic unity in the Holy Roman Empire, even if he had to do it with force. Sporadic fighting continued for several years, with the advantage alternating between Protestants and Catholics. The turmoil finally ended in the Peace of Augsburg in 1555, which we have already noted established the principle of *cuius regio, eius religio* (whose region, his religion). This arrangement lasted uneasily until the outbreak of the Thirty Years' War in 1618.

With a compromise peace settled with the Lutherans, the next major military action of the Catholics was against the Calvinists (Huguenots) in France. In our previous review of the spread of Calvinism we noted the rapid growth of Huguenot congregations in France. So many nobles joined the Huguenots that they became a political threat, and the Catholic House of Guise led the persecution of the Protestants (who were led by the House of Bourbon). The resulting series of wars lasted from 1561 to 1593. The infamous massacre of St. Bartholomew's Day occurred in the midst of these wars on August 24, 1572. The planned marriage of Henry of Navarre to the sister of King Charles IX posed the possibility of a Protestant inheriting the throne of France. Queen Mother Catherine d'Medici plotted with various Catholic leaders to prevent the marriage by striking the Protestant nobles assembled for the wedding. On a given signal the Catholics killed all the Protestants they could find in the city, and extended the massacre to outlying provinces. Some 8,000 Protestants were murdered in Paris and 20,000 in the provinces. The severed head of Admiral Coligny was sent as a trophy to the Cardinal of Lorraine. Pope Gregory XIII thanked God for the event, proclaimed a jubilee, and struck a medal commemorating the slaughter.

Henry of Navarre had escaped death even though he was captured by the Roman Catholics. He later became the head of the Protestant party, and a new series of wars began in 1576, which dragged on until 1593, when Henry professed Catholicism to secure his claim to the throne upon the death of Henry III. As Henry IV, he remembered his former religious compatriots, and issued the Edict of Nantes (1598), granting religious toleration and certain political rights to the Huguenots. This edict was eventually revoked by Louis XIV in 1685, causing tens of thousand of Huguenots to "convert" to Catholicism and hundreds of thousands to flee to England, Prussia, and America.

The third major military assault against Protestantism was launched in the Netherlands, where Philip II of Spain was determined to stop the growth of Protestantism in his subject provinces. Employing the hated Spanish Inquisition, Philip provoked the people to rebellion, and then sent the Duke of Alva to quell the rebellion. Alva terrorized the territory for six years, executing hundreds and imprisoning thousands. He was so ruthless and oppressive that Catholics joined with Protestants in driving him from the territory. The wars, however, continued until 1609, with William of Orange as the early leader of the Protestant forces. He sought to lead all seventeen provinces to proclaim their independence from Spain but ultimately only the seven northern provinces set up an independent state, The United Provinces (Dutch Republic), in 1581. William was assassinated in 1584, and Jan van Oldenbarneveldt assumed his place of leadership. Calvinism became the official state religion of the United Provinces, whose independence was officially recognized by Spain in the Peace of Westphalia in 1648.

b. The Thirty Years' War. The last of the so-called wars of religion was the Thirty Years' War, 1618-48. This seemingly futile conflict ravaged and devastated Germany, involved practically all of Europe, and ended with religious lines drawn much as they were back in 1529, and much as they remain to this day. While the war seems, in retrospect, to have been futile and senseless, it also appears to have been inevitable. Tension had been building up between Protestants and Catholics in Germany ever since the Peace of Augsburg in 1555. The vitality of the Catholic Reformation added to the tension. Ardent Jesuits were never satisfied with the compromise treaty of Augsburg, and in 1608 some of them pressed for restitution of ecclesiastical property that had fallen to the Protestants, causing old animosities to form new alliances.

Calvinists were also unhappy with the Peace of Augsburg because it provided only for Lutheranism and Catholicism, while practically outlawing Calvinism. In Bohemia, Calvinism was particularly strong, and when Ferdinand II, a Jesuit-trained Catholic, was made king of Bohemia, the Bohemian Protestants refused to accept Ferdinand, claimed the right to choose their own king, and offered the Bohemian crown to Frederick, the Calvinist ruler of the Palatinate, one of the major German states. In May of 1618, a group of armed Bohemian noblemen tossed two of Ferdinand's regents from a high window in Prague. Although they survived, the incident signaled the beginning of physical hostilities, and the war began.

The first phase of the war, 1618-23, concerned the status of Protestantism in Bohemia, Moravia, Austria, and the Palatinate. Frederick V, the Protestant king of Bohemia and Elector of the Palatinate, was not able to get the necessary Protestant support to oust the Catholics. Ferdinand, the Catholic king, had, in the meantime, also been elected Emperor Ferdinand II, and as emperor was able to make tempting promises in return for support. Maximilian of Bavaria and Philip III of Spain were enticed to join the emperor's forces against Frederick, and even the Lutheran elector of Saxony was finally persuaded to send an army for the emperor's use. In the battle of White Hill in 1620, the Bohemian rebels were crushed by the imperial armies under General Tilly. Ferdinand took his vengeance by confiscating Protestant property, executing leading rebels, and imposing strict Catholicism under Jesuit supervision. All Lutheran and Reformed churches and schools were closed in Bohemia, Moravia, and Austria. The Palatinate itself was conquered in 1621-23.

The second phase of the war, 1623-29, was marked by an all-European character. The Lutheran princes of North Germany decided to mobilize their forces in defense of Protestantism. In 1625 Christian IV of Denmark sent an army to oppose the Catholics, and England and Holland sent some help. The prime minister of France tried to form a defensive league of Protestant nations. But in spite of the renewed fervor and additional support, the Protestants were defeated time and again in a succession of battles. In 1629, Ferdinand issued his Edict of Restitution, demanding the restoration of all Roman Catholic property confiscated by Protestants since the Peace of Passau in 1552, and the expulsion of all Protestants from Catholic territory.

The third phase of the war, 1630-32, began with quarrels and jealousies within the Catholic camp. Members of the Catholic League argued over the spoils of the war, and over the enforcement of the Edict of Restitution. Albrecht von Wallenstein, a plundering soldier of fortune, had been given the task of enforcing the edict, and he was so ruthless with his burning and looting that Catholic leaders demanded his dismissal. That same year,

Gustavus Adolphus, the "Lion of the North," landed a Swedish army in Germany. With financial backing from France, and military support from Brandenburg and Saxony, Adolphus smashed Tilly's troops at Breitenfeld in 1631. Then the Saxons captured the city of Prague, and Adolphus captured the Bavarian capital in 1632, the battle in which Tilly was slain. Wallenstein, who had been recalled by the emperor, met Adolphus in a fierce battle at Lutzen near Leipzig. Adolphus was slain, but the Protestants won a decisive victory at Lutzen. Two years later Wallenstein was murdered by his own soldiers.

The fourth and final phase of the war, 1635-48, was violent and savage. Catholic France openly joined Protestant Sweden, but some Protestant states fought on the imperial side. What had begun as a religious war with political overtones became a political war with religious overtones. Mercenary troops ransacked and devastated Germany. It became obvious that no one was winning this senseless war, and the weary and exhausted opponents finally began negotiations for peace. The Peace of Westphalia (1648) was the treaty terminating the Thirty Years' War. Actually, it was a pair of treaties, one with France at Munster in Westphalia and the other with Sweden and the Protestant states at Osnabruck. Many territorial boundaries were decided, and the Augsburg formula of *cuius regio, eius religio* was accepted as the basis of ecclesiastical settlement. The main difference was that the formula was to apply now to the Calvinists as well as the Lutherans and Catholics. Princes were restrained from changing their religion, and the Roman see was restricted from interference in religious matters in Germany. Because of these two provisions, Pope Innocent X strongly denounced the treaty, but the treaty stood and its constitutional, territorial, and ecclesiastical changes helped to facilitate the dissolution of the Holy Roman Empire in the early nineteenth century. Anabaptists and other sects were excluded from the treaty, and they suffered renewed persecution, but otherwise Protestantism and Catholicism had arrived at a balanced stalemate.

c. Absolutism in France. After the war, the continent experienced a phenomenal growth of political absolutism. Spain's prestige had been diminished abroad, especially since the defeat of its fabled Armada in 1588, but it became even more absolutist at home. The German states were incapable of political unification, since there were over three hundred small sovereign principalities, many which had built up despotic regimes within their own territories. The most notable example of absolutism was France, which had emerged from the Thirty Years' War as the most brilliant and most powerful of the European states.

Henry IV, the former Huguenot leader who had turned Catholic to secure the throne, started France down the road toward monarchical absolutism. When he issued the Edict of Nantes he established the principle of a monarch granting religious toleration and political rights to minorities. During his reign, Henry IV weakened papal power with the French clergy, stabilized national finances so that he could afford to be independent, and actively opposed the Catholic house of Hapsburg in order to expand France's territory. Under the reign of Henry's son, Louis XIII (1610-43), Cardinal Richelieu became chief minister and virtual ruler of the country. His loyalty was neither to Catholic nor Protestant, but to the monarchy of France. He outraged the papacy by going to the support of the Lutherans in the Thirty Years' War. On the other hand, when the Huguenots became rebellious, he subdued them, as typified in his siege and capture of the Huguenot fortress at La Rochelle. He deprived them of their military and political privileges, but reaffirmed the religious clauses of the Edict of Nantes. Tolerance for the Huguenots was to depend henceforth on the good will of the crown, and when the Huguenots realized their religion was confirmed, they became utterly loyal to the crown.

Monarchical absolutism reached its zenith in the reign of the *Grand Monarque*, Louis XIV (1643-1715). The Catholic Reformation also reached its peak in France during Louis XIV, for he demolished the Huguenot schools and churches and revoked their religious privileges. Gallicanism, the doctrine which asserted the freedom of the Roman Catholic Church from the ecclesiastical authority of the papacy, was effectively suppressed. The Edict of Nantes was revoked, and hundreds of thousands of Protestants emigrated from France. The Catholic Reformation enjoyed new vigor with the revival of the old maxim that the state can prosper if supported by the true religion, and the true religion can be but one. Thus, monarchical absolutism was joined with religious absolutism in France, which now was the land of *un roi, une loi, une foi* (one king, one Lord, one faith).

The Reformation was indeed a crisis, a crossroads, for Christianity. After the smoke and heat of battle had settled, it was apparent that Christianity had irrevocably chosen two roads, not one, to travel. On both sides of the great controversy there had been leaders of heroic proportions, who also displayed very human traits. They fought and died for the freedom to practice what they believed, and persecuted others for wanting that same freedom. The period produced some great men, but no perfect saints. The church at Rome reasserted its authority and doctrine; the Reformers proclaimed liberty and preached salvation by faith. The first-century gospel was still intact, Christianity was still in business, but the "cleansing of the temple" had started a whole new chain of events for civilization. The stage was set for the age of reason and piety.

THE FOOLISHNESS OF GOD AND THE WISDOM OF MEN: FAITH AND REASON (1648-1776)

*Because the foolishness of God
is wiser than men;
and the weakness of God
is stronger than men.*

1 CORINTHIANS 1:25

A. Enlightenment—The Age of Reason
   1. Rationalism
      a. Francis Bacon
      b. Thomas Hobbes
      c. René Descartes
      d. Sir Isaac Newton
   2. Deism
      a. Forerunners
      b. John Locke
      c. John Toland
      d. Matthew Tindal
      e. Francois-Marie Arouet de Voltaire
      f. Jean-Jacques Rousseau
      g. Hermann Samuel Reimarus
      h. Gotthold Ephraim Lessing
   3. Reactions to Deism
      a. The Spiritualism of Blaise Pascal
      b. The Moralism of Joseph Butler
      c. The Skepticism of David Hume
      d. The Subjectivism of Immanuel Kant
B. Enrichment—The Age of Faith
   1. Pietism
      a. Philip Jacob Spener
      b. August Hermann Francke
      c. Count von Zinzendorf
   2. Methodism
      a. The Wesley Family
      b. The Holy Club
      c. The Georgia Mission
      d. The Aldersgate Experience
      e. The Methodist Societies
      f. The Inevitable Departures
   3. Revivalism
      a. The Evangelical Revival in England
      b. The Revival in Wales and Scotland
      c. The Great Awakening in America
         (1) The New World
         (2) The New England Colonies
         (3) The Awakening and Results
             (a) Beginnings
             (b) Jonathan Edwards
             (c) Whitefield's Impact
             (d) Definitive Results

I f definite dates were required, the start of the Reformation could be set at 1517, when Luther posted his theses at Wittenberg; and the Peace of Westphalia in 1648 would mark the close of the physical and political struggles. Yet there were numerous preludes to reform long before Luther's time, and the postludes continue to unfold. In fact, all of world history has been profoundly affected by the 150-year period known as the Reformation. Practically all western philosophies are somehow related to the Reformation either as extensions of or reactions against the principles of the Reformers. It is not an accident of time that the Age of Reason followed immediately on the heels of the age of reform.

A. ENLIGHTENMENT—THE AGE OF REASON

The great intellectual awakening of the seventeenth and eighteenth centuries, commonly called the Enlightenment, was built upon the conviction that right reasoning could find true knowledge and could lead mankind to happiness.

The Enlightenment was the revolution of man's autonomous potentialities against heteronomous authority which he could no longer accept. The authoritative claims of the Roman Catholic Church had been broken, as symbolized by the way the general populace ignored Pope Innocent X when he invalidated the Peace of Westphalia. Yet the people also felt that the Protestant claims of dogmatic revelations had no more authoritative substantiation than those of Roman orthodoxy.

After 1648, the church was no longer in the center of national affairs. In fact, as early as 1625, Hugo Grotius, the great Dutch jurist, had said that since natural law is the basis of government, the church has no reason for meddling in state affairs.

1. RATIONALISM
In the new expression of thought in the eighteenth century, reason superseded revelation as the supreme court of appeal. It was a rationalism,

or reason, based on the spirit of autonomy, compatible with observed nature, optimistic about future progress, and tolerant of other ideas. These facets of the Age of Reason were the concepts and products of the great minds at work in that period.

a. Francis Bacon (1561-1626). One of the forerunners of the Enlightenment was Francis Bacon, an English philosopher, essayist, orator, lawyer, and member of parliament. In 1605 he published his *Proficience and Advancement of Learning*, in which he summed up the deficiencies of human knowledge, and insisted that man's power to control nature was in his own hands, and that success rested on applying the right methods. His most famous work was *Novum Organum* (1620), in which he made a systematic presentation of the inductive method of reasoning. Bacon contended that by inductions from the simplest facts of experience, man could reach forward to the discovery of fundamental principles which in turn would issue in beneficial, practical results.

Bacon carried his empiricism (philosophy of experience) into the realm of morals. Although he was a member of the Church of England, he denied the existence of absolute rules of conduct.

In all his works, Bacon stressed the importance of the observation of facts as the basis for conclusions. Although this may sound elementary today, it was revolutionary in Bacon's day, establishing him in the eyes of many as the father of modern thought.

b. Thomas Hobbes (1588-1679) was the son of an Anglican clergyman and conformed outwardly to the Church of England, but revolted against scholastic philosophy. He had met and was greatly influenced by Francis Bacon and was a close friend of René Descartes. Hobbes was perhaps the first philosopher to attempt seriously to base a theory of human conduct on natural science. His early work *De cive* (1642) has often caused him to be called the founder of modern social science. His greatest work, *Leviathan*, was published in 1651 and censured by the House of Commons in 1666 as being atheistic. In it he developed the doctrine of political absolutism which had replaced the supremacy of the medieval church and which, in Hobbes' exposition, leaves no genuine moral distinction between good and bad. He was a pioneer in psychology and in 1656 he published *Questions Concerning Liberty, Necessity, and Chance*, in which he expounded a doctrine of psychological determinism. Although extremely controversial, and generally regarded as an atheist, Hobbes stimulated thought on ethics and the study of society and government.

c. René Descartes (1596-1650), a French Catholic who spent most of his life in the Netherlands, is usually credited with heralding the new age of reason. At first when we hear him say (in his *Discourse of Method*) that we must "abstain from accepting the false for the true and always preserve in our thoughts the order necessary for the deduction of one truth from another," he sounds like the philosophical counterpart of Luther in his theological stand before the Diet of Worms a hundred years earlier. Closer examination, however, reveals how Descartes differed from Luther, and thereby did typify a new approach to discovering truth. While Luther insisted that his conscience must bear witness to the truth, the basis of that truth was the authority of the Word of God. For Descartes, the basic authority was a self-evident idea which any rational thinker could see was true.

In his quest for rationality, Descartes based his philosophical reasoning upon the principles and methods of mathematics. A brilliant mathematician, Descartes applied algebraic formulas to geometric figures and solids and founded analytic geometry. He then proceeded to demonstrate that, in experience as in mathematics, whatever is clearly and distinctly conceived as part of a logical and coherent whole is true. In his effort to develop rationality from first principles, he encountered the elementary question: how do we know our senses can be relied upon? His answer, which became the starting point of all his subsequent philosophy, was his famous formula, *Cogito, ergo sum*, "I think, therefore I am." He arrived at this premise by first doubting everything—revelations, concepts about God, the world of values, all physical things, and the opinions of the ages which had been passed on as knowledge. One can readily see how such a position threatened the domains of church and state.

Yet Descartes' assumptions led to a rational faith in God, not a rejection of faith. He said that the first "clear and distinct idea" which a thinking ego finds outside itself is the idea of God, and that this idea is unaccountable except on the assumption that God exists. In his arguments for the existence of God, he relied on and revived the ontological argument of Anselm, and adapted Aquinas' cosmological argument which argued back to a first cause. But his adaptation of the latter was heavily influenced by his own insistence that God must be held to exist as the cause of our idea of him. The significance of Descartes' philosophy was not the details of it, but the very fact that someone living in the sixteenth and seventeenth centuries was saying that men must doubt if they are to establish certitude in place of skepticism. When doubt was asserted as the beginning of knowledge, modern science was born, and profound consequences for orthodox religion began.

Following Descartes' mathematical rationalism, several outstanding philosophers left their mark on theology. Baruch Spinoza was an intense Jew who used Descartes' geometrical principles to present a pantheistic universe, asserting that all reality is the manifestation of God. The German Protestant, G. W. Leibniz, held a different view of reality. He said that the universe is made up of an infinite number of *monads*, or simple substances without parts and which are eternally active. The *monads* form an ascending series, from the lowest which is next to nothing, to the highest which is God.

d. *Sir Isaac Newton* (1642-1727) was a mathematics professor at Cambridge, which he represented in the House of Commons. He was the most eminent physicist of his day and is still renowned for his formulation of the law of gravitation, the discovery of the differential calculus, and the first correct analysis of white light. He was appointed Master of the Mint in 1699 and knighted by Queen Anne in 1705. He had been a member of the Royal Society since 1672 and was its president from 1703 until his death.

Newton was a conforming member of the Church of England, but he was not orthodox in his theological views. In his famous work, *Mathematical Principles of Natural Philosophy* (1687), he outlines his religious convictions, acknowledging divine transcendence, omnipotence, and perfection, and rejecting the pantheistic idea of a world soul. For Newton, belief in God rests on the admirable order of the universe. God is the Supreme Being with complete authority over the material universe as well as over human souls. In his Four Rules of Reasoning, he underscored that man lives in an orderly, cause-and-effect universe, a premise which became the model for future scientific investigations. Newton also developed a mechanical view of the universe which God created and set in motion to run by fixed laws. The way was thus paved for a whole new school of philosophical and theological thought, and Deism burst upon the scene.

2. DEISM
The new philosophy which married rationalism to religion was known as Deism, and generally regarded God as the intelligent creator of an independent and law-abiding world, but denied that he providentially guides it or intervenes in any way with its course of destiny. Deists were not atheists; they believed in God, but they believed that reason is the sole instrument through which God's existence and nature can be deduced from the perfectly rational workings of the universe. They sought to strip religion of its claim that God acts supernaturally and miraculously in history.

a. *Forerunners.* Among the forerunners of Deism was Pierre Charron, a popular Catholic preacher-priest, who distinguished three kinds of wisdom: the evil wisdom of the world, the theological wisdom produced by reflection and grace, and human wisdom which stood between the two. His treatise *De la Sagesse* opened the way for the secularization of morals, for free thought, and for Deism.

An English philosopher and poet who laid foundations for future Deists was Lord Herbert of Cherbury. In *De Veritate* (1624) he maintained that common to all religions were five innate laws: (1) that there is a God; (2) that he ought to be worshiped; (3) that virtue is the chief element of this worship; (4) that repentance for sin is a duty; and (5) that there is another life of rewards and punishments. His insistence that the essence of religion consists of these laws and his denial of revelation caused Archbishop Ussher to refuse Lord Herbert communion as he was dying, and the Deists to acknowledge him as one of the great forerunners of reasonable, universal, natural religion.

b. John Locke (1632-1704), who profoundly affected politics, philosophy, and religion, was himself greatly affected by the works of Lord Herbert and René Descartes. Locke was the foremost defender of free inquiry and toleration in the later seventeenth century. His ideas on human liberty were embodied in the Glorious Revolution and the Act of Toleration of 1689. His thoughts on religion comprised a system that was a combination of Christian rationalism (reason) and empiricism (experience). In his famous *Essay Concerning Human Understanding,* he attacked the Platonist concept of innate ideas, holding that the human mind is a *tabula rasa*, a blank slate, and all our knowledge comes from experience. Knowledge through the senses, however, is never absolute or final, but is probable and reasonable. Neither is the spirituality of the soul certain, but it is at least probable. The existence of God, on the other hand, can be discovered with certainty by reason.

In his *Reasonableness of Christianity* (1695), Locke maintained that the only secure basis of Christianity is its reasonableness, and that the excellence of Christianity as a religion consists precisely in the fact that it coincides with the findings of reason unassisted by revelation. On the other hand, Locke did not dispense with the corroboration of revelation. Although he admitted that dogma cannot be proved, he contended that Christianity is simple, harmonious, and reasonable in what it calls men to believe and do. Locke received the following of the moderate clergy and the majority of the laity by asserting that the ethics of Christianity, the revelation of Christ as Messiah, and the miracles of the New Testament are in harmony with reason.

Archbishop Tillotson, the most famous preacher of the day, agreed and maintained that virtually all the substance of Christianity was identical with natural religion except the two sacraments and praying in Christ's name. Tillotson also agreed with Locke that revelation does not have to be discarded in favor of reason. In fact, revelation clarifies the truths discerned by natural reason and makes for their more effective reception. "Natural religion is the foundation of all revealed religion and revelation is designed simply to establish its duties." Both Locke and Tillotson were rational supernaturalists, and both Locke's writing and Tillotson's preaching provided a bridge to the natural religion of Deism.

c. *John Toland* (1670-1722) did not agree with Locke and Tillotson on the point of revelation. A Roman Catholic Irishman, Toland was converted to Protestantism at age sixteen, graduated from Edinburgh, and studied at Leyden and Oxford. While at Oxford he wrote his first and most important book, *Christianity Not Mysterious* (1696), in which he proposed to show "that there is nothing in the gospel contrary to reason, nor above it, and that no Christian doctrine can be properly called a mystery." He accused self-interested professionals of introducing mysteries into Christianity. He rejected the idea of revelatory truths which are above reason. He argued that reasonable facts or truths may be discovered by us for ourselves or may be made known to us by the testimony of others which may be given by revelation. But, in either case, revelation is never mysterious or incomprehensible once it is known.

John Locke sharply repudiated Toland. Toland's book aroused great indignation and was condemned and burned by the Irish Parliament in 1697. Toland was the first to use the term "pantheism" in 1705, and was constantly involved in philosophical and theological controversies. His books made a significant contribution to later discussions on the relations between reason and revelation and the genuineness of the New Testament books.

d. *Matthew Tindal* (1655-1733), an English philosopher who called himself a Christian Deist, declared that natural religion is God's original gift to man, and that man can discover in nature all that is required of him. In 1706, he wrote *The Rights of the Christian Church*, in defense of a rationalistic and Erastian position. The book created quite a furor. Author, publisher, and printer were prosecuted, but four editions were printed. Tindal then wrote *A Defence of the Rights of the Christian Church* (1709), which was burned in 1710 by order of the House of Commons. He replied at the end of his life, at age seventy-three, by writing his monumental *Christianity as Old as the Creation* (1730), which became the "Bible" of Deism. It sought to show that, common to all rational creatures, "there's a law of nature or reason, absolutely perfect, eternal, and unchangeable; and that the design of the gospel was not to add to, or take from this law, but to free men from superstition."

Tindal especially attacked superstition, discarding the miracles of the Bible, and the priestly crafts of the Roman Catholic Church. Concerning revelation, he contended that all men are equal and that doctrines not revealed to all cannot be doctrines imposed by God. For Tindal, the end of religion is morality, and he called everything in religion superstitious and dangerous which is not directly conducive to morality. Matthew Tindal articulated classical Deism: God established an orderly universe, he gave man reason to discern and live by what he had done, and he made no further revelation. He stands in a pivotal position between the rational supernaturalism of John Locke and the skepticism of David Hume.

e. Francois-Marie Arouet de Voltaire (1694-1778). It is often said that the religion of reason had its origins in England but was made popular in France. The French philosophers were not formal philosophers but were literary men and zealous disseminators of the new knowledge. French Deism was much less theoretical and constructive than English Deism, but it was clear and crisp and exuded a self-evident authority. The man who best exemplifies French Deism and who exerted the most important influence on European thought and life for over half a century was not a philosopher but a poet, a dramatist, a critic, and a sage.

Voltaire, educated by Paris Jesuits, embarked upon a literary career in which his brilliant and malicious wit gained him both admirers and enemies. He was constantly engaged in striking out against oppressive authority, which gained him two imprisonments in the Bastille and an exile to London where he was exposed to Deism and the English Enlightenment. In 1734 he published philosophical papers which contrasted the rationalistic currents in England (which he favored) to the reactionary outlook of France, and which made a violent attack on Blaise Pascal. In 1734, he wrote a recommendation of Deism and completed several plays, including the blasphemous epic of Ste. Joan of Arc. In 1759, he wrote *Candide*, which was filled with hatred of orthodox Christianity and marked by a pessimism which, in the face of the presence of evil in the world, denies the Christian conception of a good and omnipotent God.

Voltaire was not, however, an atheist. He argued against atheism from the evidence of design, and recommended a deistic religion. He regarded belief in the existence of God and personal immortality as necessary for the government of the masses. Yet he was a bitter and merciless critic of institutionalized Christianity, and especially Roman Catholicism. With the weapon of cruel sarcasm he lashed out against the deceit, superstition, and fanaticism he saw in organized religion. In the place of Christianity, Voltaire envisioned a new religion—a rather vague, popular form of Deism. Doctrine would be reduced to the belief in one just God, whose service was the practice of virtue. In spite of his violent attacks on Christianity, to the end of his life Voltaire held to his rational faith in God.

Voltaire's major philosophical work was his *Philosophical Dictionary*, which consisted largely of articles he had written for Denis Diderot's *Encyclopedia*, a work that was intended to be a complete review of the arts and sciences of the day. Between 1751 and 1780, thirty-five volumes of the *Encyclopedia* appeared, voicing free thought, Enlightenment, and revolutionary change. Many of the articles were anti-Catholic and antiaristocratic, and the *Encyclopedia* was among the principal disruptive intellectual elements which encouraged the French Revolution.

f. Jean-Jacques Rousseau (1712-78) has been called the father of the French Revolution, for it was his principles of natural reason which encouraged and enflamed the spirit of revolution. Rousseau was the son of a French refugee family at Geneva, was brought up a Calvinist, later became a Catholic, and finally embraced Deism. In Paris Diderot introduced him to the circle of Encyclopedists, for whom he wrote several articles. He wrote his first major work in 1750, presenting the thesis that progress in art and science corrupts human morals. In 1760, he wrote a passionate love story *(Julie)* in which he condemned society for its hypocrisy about marriage and suggested an undogmatic personal interpretation of the Gospels. In 1762, he developed a utopian program of education in accordance with nature, and uncorrupted by the influence of society *(Emile, ou de l'Education)*. He advocated a kind of sentimental Deism, consisting in belief in the existence of God, the soul, a future life, and the necessity of following one's conscience.

Rousseau's monumental work, *The Social Contract*, was also written in 1762, and set out his theory of the just state, resting on the general will of the people, the expression of which are the laws. Although the divine right of kings had been overthrown in England by those who believed that kings were bound by law and were not above the law, in France and other European countries, the divine right of kings was still upheld. Rousseau dropped a veritable bombshell into all this with a radical and secular theory of government which has influenced the world ever since. He said that neither laws nor the government of a state is appointed by God. Both are based on the general will of the people who are governed. Society is based on a social contract to which its members consent. The contract is designed to combine individual freedom with just government in the interests of the majority. Thus, Rousseau paved the way for the American Declaration of Independence in 1776 and the French Revolution in 1789.

g. Hermann Samuel Reimarus (1694-1768). The German *Aufklarung* (Enlightenment) was different from the movements in England and France. The German movement was rooted in the Leibniz-Wolff tradition of rationalism rather than the Anglo-French empirical tradition of John Locke. The most prominent German Deist was H. S. Reimarus, professor of Hebrew and Oriental languages at Hamburg. In his *Wolfenbuttel Fragments*, he rejected miracles and revelation, and sought to convict the biblical writers of conscious fraud, innumerable contradictions, and fanaticism. Reimarus also published two works in defense of natural religion. Reimarus subjected the whole biblical history, and thus Christianity, to critical analysis, making him a forerunner of later biblical criticism. The *Fragments* of Reimarus, which were not published until after his death, created a sensation in Germany. The man who published them, G. E. Lessing, became one of the most influential figures in the German Enlightenment.

h. Gotthold Ephraim Lessing (1729-1781). Although he was the son of a Lutheran pastor and was intended to study theology, Lessing took up a literary career and became well known as a dramatist and art critic. In his later years he was occupied with theological and philosophical problems. His influence on modern theology has been significant. In his play *Nathan the Wise* (1779) Lessing transmits his views through the principal character, an ideal Jew who through enlightened rationalism has become extremely tolerant, benevolent, and generous, and who sees the essence of religion as humanitarian morality independent of historical revelation.

In *The Education of the Human Race* (1780), he laid the foundations for the Protestant liberalism that was to dominate Germany throughout the nineteenth century. He pictured mankind as passing through three stages of education: the childhood stage was the Old Testament, the youth stage was the New Testament, and the manhood stage is the present world of reason.

Critics of Lessing have seen him as teaching that Christianity belonged to a past, inferior period of human development. Actually, Lessing taught that all religions are relative, that they will one day be superseded by a universal religion, and that the truth of religion cannot be settled by appeals to history but by the employment of reason. The enlightened person realizes all this, and lives according to good sense, and in tolerance and harmony. Lessing seemed to sum up the deistic philosophy which subordinated Scripture and tradition to reason, and emphasized a reasonable ethic as the end product of religion.

3. REACTIONS TO DEISM

While Deism was popular, it was by no means unanimous. Bitter controversies boiled throughout the eighteenth century. Some men of piety vigorously fought the reduction of everything to the primacy of reason. Some men of science ridiculed the notion that religion could be proved by reason. Both factions left their marks on future Christian theology and philosophical thought.

a. The Spiritualism of Blaise Pascal (1623-62). The noted French theologian, mathematician, and philosopher, Blaise Pascal, was not at all convinced by the rational arguments of Deism. In 1646, he came in contact with and strongly supported the Jansenists, the so-called Calvinist Catholics, because of their acceptance of the doctrine of predestination.

Pascal called his experience with the Jansenists his "first conversion." On November 23, 1654, his "definitive conversion" took place when he discovered the "God of Abraham, the God of Isaac, and the God of Jacob, and not of philosophers and men of science."

Pascal's religion was centered on the person of Christ as Savior, and was based on his personal experience. In theology he employed the same tool of experimental knowledge that he used in scientific investigations. He held that faith is essential because human existence is confronted with the necessity of making a decision for or against God. He recognized the element of risk in the life of faith and emphasized the importance of the will. He did not exclude the use of reason from demonstrating the truth of faith, but he insisted that "the heart has its reasons of which reason knows not."

His most famous work, *Pensées* (Thoughts) was published eight years after his death, and was designed as a vindication of the truth of Christianity against the indifference of the *libertines*, whom Pascal hoped to convince by the presentation of facts, the fulfillment of prophecy, and by an appeal to the heart.

b. The Moralism of Joseph Butler (1692-1752). The Deists of England found a worthy opponent in Joseph Butler, preacher at Rolls Chapel in London. The publication of *Fifteen Sermons Preached at Rolls Chapel* in 1726 established Butler as one of the prominent English moralists. In 1736, he published *The Analogy of Religion*, which was addressed to those Deists who would concede the existence of God as moral governor of the world, but were skeptical of the claims of Christianity. He challenged the Deists to admit honestly that the world of nature in which they found God had just as many ambiguities and contradictions as the Bible. Butler used a firm grasp of principle, sustained reasoning, caution, moral force, and irony to counter the attacks on the Christian world view and the fundamental grounds of morality. To him, the principles of morality were self-evident and errors of moral judgment arose only from superstition and self-deception. His belief in God convinced Butler that conscience, benevolence, and self-love were the primary constituent principles of human nature.

Other Englishmen joined Butler in his stand against the Deists. Jonathan Swift (1667-1745), known most commonly as the author of *Gulliver's Travels* (1726), was Dean of St. Patrick's in Dublin and an English satirist. In 1708 he published his *Argument to Prove the Inconvenience of Abolishing Christianity*, in which he called attention to the primordial selfishness of man, which the rationalists tended to ignore. William Law (1688-1761) wrote the splendid devotional book, *A Serious Call to a Devout and Holy Life* (1728), which has probably had more influence than any other post-Reformation spiritual book except *Pilgrim's Progress*. Law also wrote *The Case of Reason* (1732) as a rebuttal to Matthew Tindal in which he

Blaise Pascal (1623-63) Theologian, mathematician, and philosopher. He supported the so-called Calvinist Catholics in their reaction to the deism of the seventeenth century. (Historical Pictures Service, Chicago)

enumerated the incongruities and shortcomings of the rationalists. He especially argued that man cannot comprehend the whole of religion by rational processes because God is above reason. William Paley (1743-1805) was a mathematician, lecturer, and clergyman, who sought to prove the existence of God from the argument of design, and the authenticity of the New Testament from internal evidence. His chief works were *Evidences of Christianity* (1794) and *Natural Theology* (1802). Deism had its opponents and orthodoxy had its champions even in the days of Enlightenment, but both Deism and orthodoxy were to be dealt a severe blow.

c. The Skepticism of David Hume (1711-76). Ironically, the man who did the most damage to Deism and the religion of reason was one who based his philosophy on the experimental method of John Locke and the subjective idealism of George Berkeley. David Hume, Scottish philosopher and historian, became the foremost British philosopher of his century through such writings as *Treatise of Human Nature* (1739), *Philosophical Essays* (1748), and *Natural History of Religion* (1779, published posthumously). Hume reduced reason to a product of experience, thereby destroying its claim to sole validity, which had been the battle cry of the *Aufklarung*. He said that all perceptions of the human mind are either impressions of experience, or ideas—which are faded copies of these impressions. He ridiculed the theory of cause-and-effect, saying that such an approach is not a concept of logic but a result of habit and association. Belief in the existence of God cannot be proved by reason, and the immortality of the soul is doubtful.

Hume taught pure skepticism. His scathing attack on miracles appealed to experience: "It is contrary to experience that a miracle should be true, but not contrary to experience that testimony should be false." Hume's keen reasoning demolished traditional popular reliance on the miracles as prime proofs of Christianity and encouraged skepticism among thinkers. But he also devastated the deistic ideal of a simple, rational religion of nature by pointing out that primitive, polytheistic nature cults preceded monotheism. In spite of Hume's skeptical pessimism, he was remarkably calm and apparently at peace with himself. His indifference to the "religious hypothesis" is typical of the agnosticism of the modern secular man, and his part in producing that modern secular man is considerable.

d. The Subjectivism of Immanuel Kant (1724-1804). The climax as well as the termination of rationalism was marked by the life and philosophy of Immanuel Kant, professor of logic at Konigsberg University. Kant took his followers to the very summit of pure reason to point out its marvelous possibilities as well as its definite limitations. Kant was not willing to leave science and religion in the shambles of skepticism which Hume had produced, but neither was he willing to defend the natural theology which the Deists had promoted. Although Kant has been called the ultimate Enlightenment man, his critique of reason was so fundamental and radical that he has also been called the destroyer of the whole rational theology of the Enlightenment. The development of this paradoxical phenomenon is one of the most fascinating epics in Christian theology.

In 1781 (at the age of fifty-seven) Kant published his *Critique of Pure Reason*, which startled scholars around the world. From Locke to Hume, the empiricists had been saying that there are no innate ideas in the mind, which is an empty vessel *(tabula rasa)*, "collecting" ideas, and thus all ideas come from empirical experience. Kant began with a new hypothesis: that the mind is active. In fact, the mind has cognitive forms which are imposed upon the material of experience. Basically, all knowledge is confined to the realm of space and time and twelve categories which Kant identified. Man cannot have knowledge of anything beyond space and time, that is, beyond pure reason. The categories of human understanding are limited to empirical experience, and, therefore, we cannot know *noumena*, things-in-themselves, or supersensible objects. Objective knowledge is thwarted when it is applied to a sphere which transcends that of space, time, and perception. Thus, such metaphysical concepts as God's existence are not matters of experience and cannot be known as such.

Kant sought to demonstrate that the attempt of natural theology to prove the existence and attributes of God by reason is completely fruitless. But he also made it clear that neither can God's nonexistence be proven by pure reason alone. He acknowledged the value of the concept of God as a supreme intelligence for scientific investigation of a united and systematic world, but denied any knowledge of the attributes of God in himself. He accepted the classical central ideas of metaphysics as being God, freedom, and immortality, but believed that the validity of the ideas would have to be established in a way other than the rationalism of natural theology. Thus, Kant said that he "found it necessary to deny knowledge in order to make room for faith."

The way in which he proposed to make room for faith is discussed at length in his second major critique, *The Critique of Practical Reason* (1788). His fundamental theme here is the moral order or realm of value constituted by certain *a priori* propositions. The very fact that our empirical knowledge is limited points to a pure reason operative in our practical life. Our knowledge of what we ought to do is prior to and more certain than any scientific findings. Kant noted that we live in a moral world, that moral "oughtness" is universal, and that moral law is a "fact of reason," not an empirical fact. It is the original legislative principle which Kant calls the categorical imperative, simply stated: one should "act only on that maxim whereby thou canst at the same time will that it should become a universal law." But moral law cannot be derived from external sources, such as the Bible or the church. Morality is not based on knowledge of God, but rather the knowledge of God is the result of moral reason. Kant calls this moral autonomy, and he refers to his whole philosophy as the "Copernican Revolution" of philosophy. It will be remembered that Copernicus taught that the sun, and not the earth is the center of the universe. Kant was right in comparing the shock effect of his philosophy with the sensation created by Copernicus, but perhaps he was ill-advised in the choice of his comparison. The irony is that Kant was doing the opposite of Copernicus; he was placing man in the center of his universe and making everything else revolve around him.

In his third critique, *The Critique of Judgment* (1709), Kant elaborated his theory of the human value system, and tried to help man escape the finitude in which he had previously imprisoned him. He actually ended up developing a theory of nature which fairly establishes him as the father of the modern *Gestalt* theory. He supported the judgment that nature is an organism as a whole, and the judgment that in art there is an inner aim in every representation of meaning.

In 1793, Kant published his *Religion Within the Limits of Reason Alone*, written expressly to demonstrate two things: (1) how the free will, though radically evil, can regenerate itself, and (2) how Christianity, rationally interpreted, exemplifies this process of moral regeneration. Kant was willing to think of Jesus Christ as the historical exemplification of man well-pleasing to God and no more. The historical question neither can be nor need be answered, for the real object of faith is the ideal of the Son of God well-pleasing to God. The rightness of one's moral imperative atones for the imperfection of his previous evil deeds. This new man in us is our Redeemer who accepts the punishment of the old man's sins as a vicarious punishment. We can readily see how this view of Kant's as to the atoning work of the Son of God created great controversy within orthodox Christianity, and spawned a whole new era of thinking. It was Kant who established new insights into man's finitude, and laid the groundwork for modern discussions of man's existential situation. Every theologian since Kant has been forced to deal with the gauntlet which he threw down to philosophy and theology.

All of Kant's disciples did not agree with his conclusions. For instance, G. W. F. Hegel (1770-1831) rejected Kant's idea that things-in-themselves are not knowable. Instead, he taught that behind reality is the Absolute Spirit or Reason, which is in the process of coming to be. He used a scheme of thesis, antithesis, and synthesis to demonstrate how the process works. No expression of the Absolute Spirit is complete yet, but will be finally. In the meantime, every new thesis results in an antithesis, and the synthesis of the two becomes a new thesis. Hegel believed that the Absolute Spirit received a figurative expression in the religious language of Father (thesis), the incarnate Son (antithesis) and Holy Spirit (synthesis).

Another Kantian disciple, Arthur Schopenhauer (1788-1860), was a notorious pessimist who maintained that the thing-in-itself, the reality behind everything, is a great irrational Will, and that this empirical world is an illusion. Things, animals, even people do not really exist, and the best achievement is to cease to be and become one again with the indiscriminate Will.

Ludwig Feuerbach (1804-72) came under the personal influence of Hegel, rejected all belief in transcendence, and insisted that Christianity is but an illusion, the very "dominance of subjectivity." Feuerbach was extremely influential upon the thinking of Karl Marx (1818-83) and the whole Communist school in Germany.

Friedrich Nietzsche (1844-1900), who proclaimed the death of God and articulated the meaninglessness of modern life, was also influenced by Feuerbach, Hegel, and Kant. Immanuel Kant had obviously opened a Pandora's box with his subjective, categorical imperatives, and his relentless attack upon traditional religion.

Deism—the religion of reason—left its indelible mark upon Christianity in all subsequent centuries and in all lands where the message of Christ was preached. Immigration of English Deists, deistic writings, and deistic soldiers of the English army in America during the war of 1756-63 helped to spread Deism in the colonies. Benjamin Franklin, Thomas Jefferson, Ethan Allen, and Thomas Paine were among the leading Deists in America. Paine was an English-born radical political and religious thinker who encouraged and supported the American revolution with such publications as *Common Sense* (1776). He wrote his controversial *Age of Reason* from 1794 to 1807, and was subsequently attacked as an atheist. He did not espouse atheism, as charged, but he did defend the deistic position, and helped open the way for biblical criticism.

It must not be supposed that Deism was the only important expression of thought and action during the seventeenth and eighteenth centuries. Numerous spiritual movements on the Continent, in England, and in America arose concurrently with the development of Deism and rationalism. These movements also left indelible marks on subsequent Christianity, and many of them endure until today.

B. ENRICHMENT—THE AGE OF FAITH

The Enlightenment had made some positive contributions to Christendom and the world in general. The campaign against superstition put an end to witchcraft trials; the ideal of humanity advanced democracy over totalitarianism; the slogan of *liberté, égalité, fraternité* raised a banner against slavery; the idea of progress challenged the mood of despair; and moral consciousness experienced a general awakening. Yet the Enlightenment threatened the very citadels of Christianity: the Scriptures, the miracles, conversion, prayer, the deity of Christ, the Trinity, the visible church, and above all, an immanent God involved with his creatures. It is likely that Christianity could not have survived with these integral elements intact had it not been for the spiritual enrichment of Pietism, Methodism, and Revivalism. From the perspective of these movements, and their lasting effect, the same period of time known as the Age of Reason could be known also as the Age of Faith.

1. PIETISM

It should be clearly understood that Pietism and the other spiritual enrichment movements were not reactions or answers to Deism. In fact, the pietistic movement preceded the deistic emphasis. Pietism was a reaction to the cold formalism that was developing in Lutheranism. Luther had carried out a revolution against the objectivism of the Roman church with his explosive experience and message of a personal relation to God. A hundred years later that revolution had begun to develop into Protestant scholasticism. The vital insights of the Reformers had hardened into rigid formulas. A deep concern began to spread throughout Protestantism, expressed vividly by the mystic Jacob Boehme, the shoemaker, who asked what it would profit a man to know the Bible by heart if he knew not the spirit which had inspired the book. The widespread concern resulted in the spiritual Pietist revival which reemphasized the importance of the new birth, personal faith, and the warmth of Christian experience as the motive to effective mission. The movement was led by some exceptionally strong and able men.

a. Philip Jacob Spener (1635-1705). The great leader and teacher of Pietism was Philip Jacob Spener, son of devout Protestant parents, a student of history and philosophy, and minister at Strassburg and Frankfurt. On a visit to Switzerland, Spener was influenced by the Labadists, a communal Protestant sect which believed that the Bible could be understood only by the immediate inspiration of the Holy Spirit. From this time his religion took a personal and internal turn, and he became increasingly aware of a call to revive the Lutheran church with evangelical fervor. In many ways the church needed reviving. It had become engrossed in detailed controversy over every kind of doctrine, and church services had become formal and sterile. The long Thirty Years' War had left its profound effect on both clergy and laity, with drunkenness and immorality widespread. The state had also begun to interfere excessively in church affairs.

Spener had no desire to withdraw from Lutheranism, and he remained one of its most prominent ministers until his death. He did, however, have an intense desire to reform the church of the Reformers. He called for a deep personal awareness of Christ's presence and careful devotional habits. He discounted the importance of doctrine, but strongly emphasized the importance of the new birth. He advocated a self-discipline which included abstinence from cards, dancing, and the theater, and moderation in food, drink, and dress. He proclaimed the universal priesthood of all the faithful, but remained true to the Lutheran structure of the church and clergy. He began small group gatherings in his home for the purpose of Bible study, prayer, and discussion of sermons. This practice spread and the groups became known as *collegia pietatis*, which gave the name of Pietism to the movement.

In 1675, Spener published his *Pia Desideria* (variously called *Pious Wishes* or *Devout Wishes*, or by the longer title, *Earnest Desires for Reform of the True Evangelical Church*). In this book, which aroused a storm of criticism, he made six proposals for reviving or reforming Lutheranism: intense Bible study for personal devotion, practical expressions of the priesthood of all believers, an emphasis on love as well as intellectualism, a seeking of truth rather than victory in theological arguments, a reorganization of the universities with higher standards of morality, and a revival of evangelical preaching. Two years later, in a separate tract, he urged all Christians to study the Bible and test the preached word by the Scriptures. This emphasis, along with his other calls for reform, appeared to many Lutheran churchmen as a threat of schism, and he was severely attacked.

In 1686 Spener left Frankfurt and became court preacher at Dresden, where he continued to encounter opposition from the clergy and the universities of Leipzig and Wittenberg. He was received more warmly at Berlin where he was appointed in 1691 by the future King of Prussia, but in 1695 he was publicly charged by the theological faculty at Wittenberg (where Luther had begun the Reformation) with 284 theological "errors" in his writings, for slighting dogma in favor of devotionalism. Nevertheless, Spener continued his campaign to breathe new life into the lifeless official Protestantism of his day by stressing personal morality and pietist methods. His close friends and disciples assisted him and carried on his work after his death. The famous German hymnwriter, Paul Gerhardt, was closely associated with Spener, and his hymns helped to spread the ideals of Pietism.

b. August Hermann Francke (1633-1727). While Spener was the pioneer and founder of Pietism, his friend and disciple, August Francke, carried the movement to its greatest success. Francke was a gifted and influential educator and theologian at Leipzig University, where he founded a Bible study group of university professors known as the *Collegium Philobiblicum*. In 1687, he experienced what he described as a "new birth," and moved to Dresden, where he became associated with Spener and the German Pietist movement. He returned to Leipzig, caused great division in the university with his popular lectures, moved then to Erfurt where he again stirred up controversy, and finally settled at Halle in 1692, where he exercised a powerful ministry.

The University of Halle was just being established through the influence of Spener and the sponsorship of the Elector of Brandenburg. Francke became a professor at Halle and the pastor of a neighboring village, Glauchau, where his sermons and pastoral activities soon attracted a large congregation. Because of his pastoral ministry, he brought to the lecture room not only theory but practical experience.

For three decades Francke dominated the University of Halle and made it the center of the Pietist movement. He founded schools with innovative educational programs, which had a significant part in shaping the future educational system of Prussia. He engineered a tremendously successful educational program for underprivileged children, founded an orphanage, a Bible institute, a Latin school, a publishing house, a dispensary, and many related enterprises. His vast venture was financed almost entirely by contributions which came from all over Europe, in what Francke insisted was direct answer to prayer. Thousands of children were taught in Francke's schools, and some six thousand priest clergy were trained in the Halle theological faculty, which was the largest divinity school in Germany.

From the Halle center of Pietism came the first foregleams of the modern mission movement. In 1705, Halle supplied the first missionaries for the Danish mission in India. The most noted missionary from Halle to India was Christian Friedrich Schwartz, who labored in India for forty-eight years. Henry M. Muhlenberg, probably the most outstanding early American Lutheran, came from Halle in 1742. The immense success of Francke, combined with his stress on the personal nature of Christianity, made him many enemies among the clergy at Halle. Opposition against him diminished after he was visited in 1713 by the Prussian king Frederick William I, who studied and incorporated Francke's educational ideas into Prussia's system. August Francke was a successful pioneer in the application of Christian philosophy to specific social programs, and the University of Halle continued to be a powerful influence until the last half of the century.

c. *Count von Zinzendorf* (1700-60). The Pietism of both Spener and Francke was the dominating influence in the life of Nikolaus Ludwig, Count von Zinzendorf, a Lutheran nobleman who became the key figure in the renewal of Moravianism in the eighteenth century. His father, a cabinet minister in Saxony, died when Zinzendorf was only six weeks old. The Count was brought up by his grandmother, Baroness von Gersdorf, a devotee of Pietism and a personal friend of Spener, who became Zinzendorf's godfather. At the age of ten, Zinzendorf was sent to Francke's grammar school at Halle, where he had intense religious experiences. He subsequently studied law at the universities of Wittenberg and Utrecht, and entered the civil service in 1721.

The next year, 1722, Count von Zinzendorf allowed refugees from the persecutions of Protestants in Bohemia and Moravia to settle on his large estate near Berthelsdorf, about seventy miles from Dresden. The refugees established the village of Herrnhut ("Lord's Watch"), which resembled a monastery in its religious focus, good works, strict morals, and industry. By 1727, Zinzendorf relinquished his court responsibilities to serve as spiritual leader of the Herrnhut community. He tried to keep the Moravians tied to the state Lutheran Church, but the Lutheran leaders were very suspicious of the newcomers. When they accused Zinzendorf of starting an independent sect on his estate, he had himself ordained as a Lutheran pastor (1734) to soften criticism. Two years later, however, he was expelled from Saxony for creating a separate church.

In 1727, a great "moving of the Holy Spirit" came to the Herrnhut community, and the Moravian Brethren became intensely evangelistic and missionary. They joined the Halle Pietists in inaugurating the modern missionary movement, sending missionaries to the West Indies, Greenland, North America, Guiana, Egypt, South Africa, Labrador, Holland, England, and the Baltic States. A group of Herrnhuter Moravians migrated to Pennsylvania and founded the city of Bethlehem. They are known today as the Unity of the Brethren (not to be confused with the United Brethren) or, more commonly, the Moravian Church.

In 1737, Zinzendorf was consecrated a bishop in the Moravian Church; in 1738-39, he toured the West Indies; in 1741 he visited England; and in 1741-43, he spent two years superintending Moravian mission efforts in the American colonies. He returned to Germany in 1743, and spent the rest of his life in pastoral oversight of Moravian congregations.

Count von Zinzendorf placed great stress on the emotional importance of the religious experience. Although he was a thoroughgoing Protestant in his doctrine, much of his pietistic expressions were modeled after the Catholic Quietism of the seventeenth century. The fundamental element of Quietism was the condemnation of all human effort, and thus it received the denunciation of most of official Catholicism. Miguel de Molinos (1640-97) was a Spanish Quietist who taught that the state of perfection in perpetual union with and complete transformation into God was hindered by all external observances. Madame Guyon (1648-1717) was a French Quietist who taught complete indifference, even to eternal salvation, and that in contemplation all distinct ideas should be repulsed in order for the soul to experience illumination. François Fénelon (1651-1715) was Archbishop of Cambrai, friend and defender of Mme. Guyon, who tried to keep the benefits of Quietism and the orthodoxy of Catholicism both intact and cooperative. Zinzendorf was widely ecumenical in his attitude toward other denominations. In fact, he was the first to use the word "ecumenical" in its modern meaning. His "religion of the heart" had a profound impact upon John Wesley, the founder of Methodism, and his emphasis on feeling found strong expression in the theology of Friedrich Schleiermacher in the late eighteenth and early nineteenth centuries.

Although Pietism was not a direct reaction to rationalism, it presented a distinct alternative and a historical challenge to the Age of Reason. Pietism knew no national or denominational boundaries. It was an integral part of Lutheranism, Moravianism, Quakerism, Methodism, and even Catholicism. It suggested a universal need that neither orthodoxy nor rationalism satisfied. It was characterized by a scriptural morality, a sense of guilt and forgiveness, the holiness of prayer and devotion, compassion for human needs, and emotional expressions of feelings and aspirations in sermon and song. Pietism's call for the living presence of Christ within endeavored to make religion intensely personal and individualistic. Pietism was contagious, spreading rapidly throughout Lutheran churches in Germany, Prussia, and in the Scandinavian countries; and in England it was vividly expressed in the Inner Light of the Quakers and the evangelical awakening of Methodism, which became a large and significant movement of itself.

2. METHODISM

Although influenced by Pietism, the great Methodist revival in England stands separately as a modern phenomenon of Christianity. It was the third religious awakening in England, coming after the sixteenth century Reformation and the seventeenth century Puritanism. Methodism ranks with the French Revolution and the Industrial Revolution as one of the great historical events of the eighteenth century. Politically, some say that Wesley's preaching saved England from a revolution similar to that of France. Religiously, Methodism was to Anglicanism what Pietism was to Lutheranism.

a. The Wesley Family. Four men were significantly prominent in founding Methodism. John Wesley (1703-91) was the great organizer of the movement; Charles Wesley (1708-88) was the great hymnwriter; George Whitefield (1714-70) was the great pulpit orator; and John William Fletcher (1729-85) was the great theologian. The two Wesley brothers, John and Charles, came from a rich religious background and a strong spiritual heritage. Their father was Samuel Wesley, a priest of the Church of England and a long-time minister of the rural parish of Epworth. Samuel's father had been a Nonconformist clergyman. Samuel's wife was Susanna, whose father Samuel Annesley had also been a Nonconformist clergyman. Susanna was to become an exceptionally strong influence in the religious devotions of John and Charles.

Samuel and Susanna Wesley had nineteen children, eight of whom died in infancy. John was the fifteenth child and Charles was the eighteenth. Their serious and hard-working father organized one of the religious societies then in vogue, and their mother exercised methodical discipline, exacting regularity and obedience. These early examples produced obvious fruit in the later ministries of the Wesley brothers. In 1709, the family home, the rectory at Epworth, burned and John and Charles were barely

John and Charles Wesley during their stormy voyage across the Atlantic in the company of Moravian missionaries who appear completely unafraid of the storm. (The Bettmann Archive)

rescued, causing John to refer to himself in later years as "a brand snatched from the burning."

John attended Charterhouse School in London and then Christ Church College, Oxford. He was a diligent student and became adept in several languages. He was vigorously healthy and athletically active. He was also deeply religious and an avid reader of spiritual writings. He was ordained a deacon in 1725 and a priest in 1728 in the Church of England. He became a fellow of Lincoln College, but was given periodical leaves, between 1726 to 1729 to serve as his father's assistant. Charles went to Oxford the same year that John left (1726) for the first time to assist their father.

b. The Holy Club. While John was away from Oxford, Charles and two other undergraduates, Robert Kirkham and William Morgan, began their own "Oxford group," emphasizing high church Anglicanism. It was a small club dedicated to aiding one another in their studies, to reading helpful books, and participating in frequent communion. The club never grew very large (about twenty-five members) but it attracted wide interest because of the stringent, joyless, rule-keeping its members observed in order to save their own souls. For this they were derisively called the "Holy Club," or the "Godly Club," or the "Bible Moths," and finally the "Methodists" because of their strict methods and regularity of rules and studies. The club was also dedicated to social issues such as improving schools and jails. John Wesley assumed leadership of the Holy Club when he returned to Oxford, and he later called the work of this group the first rise of Methodism.

Yet the Holy Club, for all its methodical morality, experienced little peace and joy in the enterprise. One of the books studied by the club was William Law's *Serious Call to a Devout and Holy Life,* which was published the same year the Holy Club was formed. An interesting event transpired when John and Charles traveled across England to visit William Law in person. They shared with him the work of the Holy Club and their burden about its seeming failure. Law told them that they were trying to make something complicated and burdensome out of Christianity. "Religion is the plainest and simplest thing in the world," he said. "It is just this: We love, because he first loved us." Although the brothers were profoundly moved by the meeting, it would be several years before they would discover personally the essence of Law's observation.

c. The Georgia Mission. The year 1735 was an important one in the spiritual development of the Wesleys. At this stage of his Oxford career, John began intensive reading of the Greek New Testament, fasted on Wednesdays and Fridays, received communion weekly, and ministered to the prisoners in the local jail. Yet he was still dissatisfied with his lack of emotional involvement and peace of heart. Also, in 1735, twenty-year-old George Whitefield joined the Holy Club and soon demonstrated the powerful preaching ability that was to establish him as one of the greatest orators in Christian history. Then, later in that same year, John and Charles Wesley sailed for Georgia as missionaries of the Society for the Propagation of the Gospel in Foreign Parts.

The mission to Georgia was at the invitation of Governor James Oglethorpe. Although they were ostensibly going to minister to the colonists and to the Indians, John frankly admitted later that he had gone in "hope of saving my own soul." The experience, however, brought him even less satisfaction than the Holy Club. During the Atlantic crossing, a severe storm created panic and terror in John, who felt ashamed and perplexed when he observed the cheerful confidence of the twenty-six Moravians on board. In Georgia, John was a joyless bore. He worked strenuously to be the proper parson, but he was tactless and unpopular with the colonists. He became romantically attracted to a young girl, Sophie Hopkey, who gave him an opportunity to propose. When he proposed that they sing Psalms, she married someone else. He, thereafter, refused to give communion to the young lady and aroused further resentment from the colonists.

It was in Georgia, however, that John Wesley had his famous encounter with the Moravian leader Augustus Spangenberg, an encounter from which he could not escape as he wrestled with his soul's discontent. Spangenberg pointedly asked Wesley, "Do you know Jesus Christ?" John could only reply, "I know he is the savior of the world." Spangenberg countered with, "True, but do you know that he has saved you?" This emphasis on inner assurance of salvation was to become one of the great cardinal features of English Methodism. Charles became ill and returned to England in 1736, but John remained and gathered a small society of serious Christians, which he later called the second rise of Methodism. Yet he himself still felt frustrated and unfilled. Disheartened by the colonists' hostility and his own lack of assurance, he finally returned to England in early 1738.

d. The Aldersgate Experience. Soon after he arrived in London, John Wesley had the profound experience which sent him out as preacher and organizer of the Methodist movement. John and Charles had both been deeply impressed by the Moravians in their Georgia mission, and back in London they sought out the fellowship of this group. Peter Bohler, the charismatic leader of the Moravians, led the brothers to see that it was impossible to save their souls by legalistic righteousness and precise self-discipline. On Whitsunday, May 21, 1738, Charles had a profound, satisfying conversion experience which produced quiet confidence and inner peace. Three days later, on May 24, 1738, John reluctantly attended an Anglican "society" in Aldersgate Street, London. While listening to a reading of Luther's preface to the *Commentary on Romans,* John had a sudden and illuminating understanding of the Reformation doctrine of justification by faith. He vividly and exultantly described the experience in his journal: "About a quarter before nine, while he [Luther] was describing the change which God works in the heart through faith in Christ, I felt my heart strangely warmed. I felt I did trust in Christ, Christ alone, for salvation; and an assurance was given me that he had taken away my sins, even mine, and saved me from the law of sin and death."

After his Aldersgate experience, John Wesley sought to learn more from the Moravians, and was an original member of the Moravian Fetter Lane Society. He went to Germany and spent several days at Herrnhut with Count von Zinzendorf, the great Moravian leader. Back in England, John and Charles began to preach extensively, but they encountered severe opposition from the orthodox Anglican churches. Their main themes were conscious acceptance by God and daily growth in holiness. They were especially criticized for preaching such an intensely personal gospel. As the doors of the churches were closed to them more and more, they went to the marketplaces, where great crowds thronged to hear them. They also spoke tirelessly in the "societies" in the vicinity of London. Their friend George Whitefield had experienced remarkable success in preaching to the miners of Bristol, and he encouraged John to do likewise. At first reluctant, John eventually became enthusiastic and astounded at the response of the crowds as he gathered them in open fields. According to the regulations of the Church of England, John was forbidden to preach in the boundaries of a parish until the clergyman in charge gave his permission. When that permission was refused, as it usually was, John preached without it, declaring, "The world is my parish" (which became an enduring Methodist slogan).

e. *The Methodist Societies.* Although Wesley did not possess the oratorical eloquence of Whitefield, he still commanded respect and rapt attention wherever he spoke. It soon became apparent, however, that his greatest talent lay in the realm of practical organization and administration, and he began to exercise his gift for organization in the far-flung fields of the preaching missions. He gathered his converts into "societies," which he patterned after those at Oxford, in Georgia, and at Fetter Lane. The societies were divided into "classes" with "class leaders" to aid members in the nourishment of the Christian life. Eventually, "stewards" were introduced to care for the property of the societies. When laymen began preaching in some of the societies, Wesley was at first reluctant to endorse this innovation. His mother, however, convinced him that this may well be the work of the Holy Spirit in reviving the church, and lay preachers became, and remain, an outstanding feature in Methodism.

Wesley traveled almost incessantly, visiting each of the societies to supervise them and enforce discipline. Naturally, as they increased in number, this became impossible, and he began to assemble his preachers in "annual conference," the first of which met in London in 1744. As the movement grew, Wesley established "circuits" with traveling preachers. And as an assistant to himself, he placed a "superintendent" in charge of each circuit.

Wesley always thought of himself as a loyal Anglican and never left the Church of England. He intended his societies to be an order within the established church. In spite of his intentions, however, an independent organization developed, with its own network of chapels or congregations and separate institutional machinery. Wesley refused to permit the sacraments to be administered by unordained men, but this posed a serious problem where few episcopally ordained men were available. So he began ordaining his own ministers, an action which caused severe disagreement with his brother Charles.

John's younger brother was opposed to many of the innovations of Methodism, and was more faithfully attached to Anglicanism than John. Lacking his brother's ruggedness, Charles was forced to stop traveling after 1756. The greatest contribution which Charles Wesley made was his hymn-writing. He penned over six thousand pieces, including: "Hark, the Herald Angels Sing," "Ye Servants of God, Your Master Proclaim," "O for a Thousand Tongues to Sing," "Love Divine, All Loves Excelling," "Soldiers of Christ, Arise," "Christ, Whose Glory Fills the Sky," and "Rejoice, the Lord Is King." From the very outset the Methodist movement was characterized by enthusiastic song. John contributed some notable translations of German hymns, but it was Charles who really gave Methodism, and all of Christendom, some of its finest music.

f. The Inevitable Departures. Charles was not the only one to disagree with John's innovations, but more serious were disagreements over basic doctrines. Although Methodism has been aptly described as the greatest expression of Pietism in the eighteenth century, John Wesley found himself growing away from some of his earliest pietistic influences. The Moravians, who had been instrumental in his conversion and early development, became too mystical for him with their "stillness" theology. Under the leadership of Philip Molther, the Fetter Lane Moravians began to teach that a person should wait in perfect stillness for God to do his work of grace, and that good works should not be preached either before or after salvation. John Wesley strongly disagreed, believing that justification by faith was to be accompanied by a newness of life evident in acts of love toward others. He contended that freedom of faith was from sin, not from works of God. He wrote many tracts directly opposing the Moravian antinomianism of the day (which they also later rejected). In 1745 the Moravians announced that they had no connection with John and Charles Wesley. John continued his crusade against the antinomian stance, and in one of his most powerful publications, *A Blow at the Root* (1762), he pointedly attacked them with the insistence that Christians must live for God and walk as Christ walked. He also found himself rejecting the mystical elements in William Law and Count von Zinzendorf, fearing that these also could lead to antinomianism.

The same fear of antinomianism caused a breach in his friendship with George Whitefield, who had been in the original Holy Club at Oxford and had encouraged Wesley in field preaching. Whitefield, however, was a strong Calvinist, a position which John Wesley could not accept. He believed in the sovereignty of God, but he could not accept a doctrine of extreme election and predestination. He was afraid that antinomianism could be the possible end result of such a stance, and also that the work of Christ offered salvation to all, not just a select few; and in 1770 he openly denounced Calvinism as a "poison to faith." In 1778 he published *The Arminian Magazine* to make clear his stand on antipredestination.

The break with Whitefield came as early as 1740 with the publication of Wesley's sermon on "Free Grace." Although they were reconciled in friendship and supported each other's ministry, Whitefield and Wesley traveled different paths doctrinally and organizationally. Whitefield's evangelistic fervor and Calvinistic doctrine attracted the interest of the wealthy widow, Selina, Countess of Huntingdon, who formed what came to be known as the Countess of Huntingdon's Connection and later as the Calvinistic Methodists. She built chapels and appointed chaplains over them, one of whom was George Whitefield. The supervisor of Lady Huntingdon's college at Trevecca for the training of ministers was John William Fletcher, the Swiss theologian. He eventually, however, took his stand with Wesley against Calvinism and for Arminianism, and became one of the prominent theologians of the Methodist movement.

The departure of the Methodists from the Church of England came gradually in degrees. Although Wesley's opponents charged him with dissension, disobedience, and disruption, he never separated from the Church of England, and to his death he considered himself a faithful Anglican. He had, however, sown all the seed and provided all the organization necessary to launch a vast new Christian enterprise. In 1743 Wesley drew up distinctive rules for his Methodist societies; in 1744 they held their first conference; and by 1759 the movement was referred to as the Methodist Church. In 1763, Wesley provided doctrinal standards for his preachers, and in 1784 he provided for the legal continuation of the societies with the Deed of Declaration. In the same year (1784) Wesley, though he was not a bishop himself, ordained Thomas Coke and Francis Asbury, who became America's first ordained bishops. The formal break with the Church of England did not come until after Wesley's death, but the Methodist organization and influence were widespread and considerable by then.

Wesley was personally a tireless campaigner who traveled over 250,000 miles the last fifty years of his life, delivering over 40,000 sermons. His journeys took him to Ireland, Scotland, Wales, Germany, and Holland. He made some twenty visits to Ireland where he was enthusiastically received. When he died, his followers in England numbered about 80,000 with 1,300 preachers. The Methodists in America numbered 60,000 with 200 preachers. Today, the Methodist Church is the largest free Protestant body in England with over one million members. In the United States, the Methodist Church, with more than ten million members, is the second largest Protestant body. Unofficial membership or constituency in association with the World Methodist conference is over forty million today. Active almost to the end, John Wesley died in 1791, at the age of eighty-eight, "leaving behind nothing but a good library of books, a well-worn clergyman's gown, a much-abused reputation, and—the Methodist Church."

3. REVIVALISM

Methodism was but one expression of the larger revivalism of the period from 1726 to 1815. The rapid expansion of Protestantism into one of the most powerful forms of religion mankind has ever known owes its source to those years of spiritual awakening. While Methodism was one of the outstanding forces of revivalism, the awakening was not confined to any one branch of Protestantism. It began with the Pietist movement in Germany, blossomed in the Evangelical awakening in England, swept across America in the Great Awakening, and penetrated into Wales and Scotland. It produced the movement of Methodism, but also rejuvenated the Church of England and the Church of Scotland. It gave birth to new denominations and strengthened existing ones, especially affecting Methodists, Baptists, Congregationalists, and Christians or Disciples of Christ. Later it spread to the Reformed Churches on the continent of Europe. The impact of the awakening was most noticeably felt in the British Isles, the United States, Canada, Australia, and New Zealand.

The Protestant awakenings had distinctive features, such as the authority of the Scriptures, salvation by faith alone, and the priesthood of all believers. The last emphasis led to an unusually strong involvement of the laity, as opposed to Roman Catholicism, where the clergy was emphatically in control. The movement made much of a personal religious experience, of a new birth through trust in Christ, of the cross, and of the resurrection. It was "evangelistic" and emphasized "evangelism." Those who promoted these views and activities, regardless of their denomination or church membership, came to be known as "Evangelicals," and they labored to take the gospel to all mankind, initiating a thrust that still has not diminished in Christendom.

a. The Evangelical Revival in England. We have already noted the vast influence of Wesley and the Methodists, but the eighteenth-century awakening in England was certainly not confined to the societies associated with Methodism. The Protestant element which had been in the Church of England since the Reformation was especially responsive to the revival. In fact, there developed a strong party of Anglican Evangelicals, devoted to seeking spiritual renewal within the Church of England. Cornwall was the center of Anglican Evangelicalism, and Samuel Walker of Truro was the leader of the party until his death in 1763. James Hervey, who ministered in the west of England, wrote books designed to bring the evangelical message to polite society. The scholarly William Romaine was the first evangelical to have a parish in London, and the evangelical stalwarts in the north included Henry Venn at Huddersfield and William Grimshaw at Haworth. Venn was a graduate of Cambridge and a distinguished evangelical clergyman, whose son, John Venn, was one of the founders of the Church Missionary Society. Hannah Moore was a prolific writer who deeply influenced the literary and artistic circles of England with her warm evangelical piety. Charles Simeon was pastor of Trinity Church in Cambridge and exerted a powerful evangelical influence on the university. John Newton, a converted slave-trader, became an outstanding Anglican rector, and wrote such popular hymns as "Amazing Grace" and "How Sweet the Name of Jesus Sounds."

Many far-reaching missionary organizations developed within the evangelical revival of England. Foremost among these were the Baptist Missionary Society (1792), the London Missionary Society, an interdenominational venture (1795), and the Church Missionary Society (1799). In 1786 the Wesleyan Conference approved the plan of Thomas Coke to take the gospel to India. In 1792 the Baptist Missionary Society was organized, primarily as the result of the efforts of William Carey. The British Foreign Bible Society was born in 1804, and in 1799 there came into existence the Religious Tract Society, still continued today as the United Society for Christian Literature.

The evangelical awakening gave a new dimension to Christian education with the introduction of Sunday schools. They were started in 1769 by Hannah Ball, a Methodist, and developed and popularized by Robert Raikes, an Anglican layman. The Church of England Sunday School Society was founded in 1786, and the Sunday School Union was formed in 1803. The Sunday School Movement was a significant step in procuring a general free education for everyone.

One of the most prominent features of the Evangelical revival was involvement in social issues. With a determination to end many of the decadent practices and social injustices in British and American life, the evangelicals created a new social conscience in England. The campaign to banish slavery from British colonies was led by evangelical revivalists. Granville Sharp, a wealthy philanthropist, founded, in 1787, a home for freed Negroes; and Thomas Clarkson, a son of a clergyman of the Church of England, gave up his plans to follow his father's profession to devote full time to the antislavery cause. The most renowned antislavery crusader was William Wilberforce, who led in parliament the campaign which in 1807 put on the statute books an act abolishing the slave trade in the British Empire. Wilberforce had been converted by Isaac Milner, an outstanding evangelical who went on to become president of Queen's College, Cambridge. John Wesley had been a serious source of encouragement to Wilberforce in his antislavery activities. Wesley also advocated prison reform and encouraged John Howard in his crusade for reforming the appalling conditions in the prisons. The evangelicals also advocated stricter observance of Sunday; sought to curb gambling, dueling, and cruel sports; fought for better laws to regulate child labor; promoted the education of the masses; and took a stand against the immorality in eighteenth-century literature.

Wesley's Methodist societies set the example for the evangelicals in their practical concern for the poor, distributing clothing and food to the needy. Dispensaries were set up to treat the sick. Jobs were created for the unemployed. A lending bank was opened by some Christians in 1746 to assist those unable to borrow elsewhere. Legal advice and aid was made available, and widows and orphans were provided for. To aid the underprivileged, the Benevolent or Strangers' Friend Societies began in 1787, and brought immeasurable relief until the state finally assumed responsibility. The evangelical revival made all of England aware of its social obligations. Within the churches, many nominal members experienced the new birth and became dynamic witnesses. Thousands who had never claimed religion were converted. The clergy was reformed, setting new and higher standards for pastoral care. Anglicans and Nonconformists alike shared in the refreshing breath of revival that swept over England.

b. The Revival in Wales and Scotland. The winds of revival were also blowing in the rest of the British Isles. The early signs of the revival in Wales appeared almost simultaneously at both Talgarth and Llangeitho in the summer of 1735. Griffith Jones, the founder of the Welsh circulating schools, had been preaching the evangelical message in Llandowror for over twenty years. Jones had dedicated himself to further social and religious reforms, and to that end he made several successful preaching tours. He was also a prominent leader in the Society for Promoting Christian Knowledge. In the summer of 1735, a schoolmaster in Talgarth named Howell Harris was deeply moved by reading books published by that society; and on Whitsunday, he was converted at a communion service. His heart was filled with "the fire of the love of God," and he soon began witnessing and gathering a small society of fellow believers. They were the beginnings of the Welsh Calvinistic Methodist Church. Harris resolved to enter the Anglican ministry, but after being refused ordination four times, he remained a lay preacher for the rest of his life. His preaching inspired revivals throughout South Wales, and in 1739 he moved to North Wales, and carried out a work of evangelism comparable to that of Whitefield and Wesley in England. In 1752 he established a religious community at Trevecca, where the Countess of Huntingdon supported him in the training of students for the ministry.

In the same year that Harris was converted (1735) Daniel Rowlands was spiritually awakened in Llangeitho through a sermon by Griffith Jones. His subsequent preaching brought about a spiritual awakening in his own parish, and he soon joined Harris in working for an awakening throughout all of Wales.

The revival in Scotland is usually attributed to George Whitefield, who was invited there in 1741; but as he did in America, Whitefield sowed the seed on prepared soil. The religious condition in Scotland had caused the eighteenth century to be described as "the dark age of the Scottish Church." Heretical views about the person of Christ, similar to those voiced by the Deists in England, were being taught. A watered-down system of morality called "Moderatism" was being developed. Ministers were more concerned about culture than conversion, and not at all interested in their rich heritage of persecuted forefathers. Out of this depressing condition came a small group of spiritually concerned objectors, led by Ebenezer Erskine of Stirling. When they set up an independent presbytery, they were forced to leave the national church in 1740. Known as the "Seceders," they gained considerable support, and invited Whitefield to Scotland to lead revival efforts.

Ironically, Whitefield accepted the invitation of the Seceders, but refused to confine his activities to their churches, and they disowned him. He immediately found an opportunity to work within the Church of Scotland, and brought great revival results to the establishment church which the Seceders had left. Under the leadership of William McCullough, the revival spread to Cambuslang, which Whitefield visited during his second Scottish tour. The surrounding area was soon engulfed in revival, with outstanding results in Kilsyth. The evangelical party which led the Scottish revival were mocked as "Zealots" or "High-flyers," but they left an indelible mark on Scotland and literally changed the outlook of the Church of Scotland.

c. The Great Awakening in America. The richest and most extensive development of revivalism was in the American colonies. In fact, the character of American Protestantism remains, two hundred years later, a fairly accurate reflection of the mood and methods of that influential, though brief, period. One must be acquainted with the background drama of America's discovery and development to appreciate the significance of the revival.

(1) The New World. The discovery of America was not by chance or accident. European kings and merchants were diligently and persistently seeking a new trade route to the Far East. When the Turks seized

Constantinople in 1453, they closed the profitable trade which had been flourishing with the East. Explorers from various maritime nations were sent westward to see if it might, indeed, be true that the earth was round, and that the Far East could be reached by sailing westward. Prince Henry of Portugal sent out explorers from Portugal until Vasco de Gama discovered the way to India around the southern tip of Africa. But Christopher Columbus was obsessed with the great dream of reaching the East by a voyage due west, and, with the patronage of Ferdinand and Isabella of Spain, he sailed on August 3, 1492, arriving on October 12 at what is probably one of the Bahama Islands. Martin Luther was nine years old at the time, making the beginning of Protestantism and the beginning of American colonization contemporaneous events.

Upon the return of Columbus, King Ferdinand requested Pope Alexander VI to confirm his title to the newly discovered lands. The subsequent papal bull, which delineated the rights of Spain and Portugal, anticipated conquests for Christianity and gains for the church as well as territory and revenues for the kings. Spanish explorers swarmed to the southern coast of the United States, to Mexico, Central America, and the northern part of South America. In 1519, Hernando Cortez led a band of conquistadors from Cuba to Mexico to seek the fabled gold of that land. He captured Mexico City and took Montezuma captive. Every Spanish expedition of discovery, invasion, and colonization was accompanied by priests, as chaplains to the Spaniards and missionaries to the Indians. The first Spanish missions were established in the West Indies and in Mexico. A bishopric was established at Santo Domingo in 1512, at Santiago de Cuba in 1522, and at Mexico City in 1530. The University of Mexico was established in 1551, and the University of Lima was begun in 1557. Spanish missionaries went from Mexico to South America, and by 1553 they had extended to Chile. The first Spanish settlement in Argentina came in 1580 at Buenos Aires, but the Portuguese had begun settling Brazil as early as 1510. Soon all of South America was conquered, and Roman Catholicism was established as the official religion.

Within the territory which was to become the United States, the first Spanish missions were established in Florida (Flowerland) when Ponce de Leon went there in 1521 in search of gold and the fountain of youth. De Soto discovered the Mississippi in 1541, and Francisco de Coronado swept across Texas, Colorado, and New Mexico in 1541-42 looking for alleged cities of gold. By 1630, missionaries from Mexico had planted twenty-five missions in New Mexico. Although explorers scouted the coastlands of California as early as 1542, the enduring settlements of the famous California missions did not come until Father Junipero Serra accomplished his legendary work in the last half of the eighteenth century. Hostile resistance and bloody uprisings by the native Indians discouraged permanent settlements in the Southwest in the latter part of the seventeenth century, and Spain concentrated most of her efforts at colonization and missionizing in Mexico and South America.

The northern part of North America was opened by French explorers, traders, and missionaries. The first permanent French colony was established in Quebec in 1608, and the French began to unfold a grand plan to establish a splendid French empire in the New World. French explorers and soldiers of fortune flocked to the regions which appeared to abound in the immediate wealth of furs and fish. Shiploads of emigrants were sent at the expense of the French government to establish colonies, which enjoyed royal patronage, endowment, and protection. Explorers and colonists were always accompanied by Jesuit priests and Recollet missionaries who established Roman Catholic missionary stations and built churches, convents, and schools. A typical example of the double-interest of the French occurred in 1682 when the famous soldier of fortune, La Salle, reached the mouth of the Mississippi, while Father Louis Hennepin, a Recollet priest, explored the river northward to Minneapolis. French claims in North America soon included Canada, Louisiana, half of New York, half of Maine, and half of Vermont. From Quebec to New Orleans, the French maintained a line of scattered forts and missions, and it appeared that their grand dream would become a reality. But the dream experienced a sudden and permanent collapse. The French government practically destroyed its own dream by subordinating colonial interests to ambitious European politics, smothering individual enterprise among the colonists, restricting the emigrants to Catholics, emphasizing trade over settlement, and causing irreconcilable hostility between the Huron and Iroquois Indians. The final death of the French dream came at the close of the Seven Years' War (1756-63), known in America as the French and Indian Wars. Canada and all French possessions in North America east of the Mississippi except New Orleans were ceded to England, and Louisiana west of the Mississippi was ceded to Spain. The French Catholic church was almost completely removed from North America, except in eastern Canada, in parts of Maine, and in some western areas. France and Spain had both failed in their efforts to build magnificent colonial empires in North America. Only the colonization efforts of England remained as Europe's hope of conquering the New World.

(2) The New England Colonies. Soon after Columbus' successful voyages, Henry VII of England commissioned John Cabot and sons to explore the western and northern seas. In 1497, the Cabots took possession of Newfoundland in the name of the King of England. A later expedition went as far south as the capes off North Carolina, and the English subsequently claimed the American coast from Labrador to Florida. During the long reign of Queen Elizabeth (1558-1603), efforts were begun to colonize the American continent. Sir Walter Raleigh explored the central coast of North America and named it Virginia in honor of the virgin queen;

and in 1607 came the first permanent colony of Virginia, named Jamestown after James I, now king of England.

The Jamestown settlement was essentially a commercial venture, but it did have its religious character. The settlers were English cavaliers, and all were members of the Church of England, which remained as the established church of Virginia by law until 1776. The College of William and Mary was founded in 1693 for the purpose of training American ministers to serve the Church of England congregations in the colonies. North and South Carolina also established the Church of England by law, and many Anglican congregations were found among the early settlers of Georgia, New York, and New Jersey. Only one of the original thirteen colonies was founded by English Roman Catholics, led by George Calvert (Lord Baltimore) and his son Cecil. Originally established as a colony for refugee Roman Catholics, Maryland withstood bitter battles over its religious and legal status until it was made a crown colony in 1691, and the following year the Anglican church was established by law. By 1704 Catholic priests were legally forbidden to say Mass or baptize children of non-Catholic parents, and in 1718 Catholics were deprived of their right to vote.

Meanwhile, Congregationalism was flourishing in the colony of Massachusetts. Some of the English Separatists who had fled to Holland in 1608 sailed for the New World in 1620. The ship of these Pilgrims, the *Mayflower*, landed in November of 1620 and founded the settlement of Plymouth. In the next decade, Puritans and others, seeking to escape the oppressive measures of Charles I and Archbishop Laud, made extensive settlements around Massachusetts Bay. In 1628 John Endicott led a band of followers to Salem, and more than twenty thousand flowed into the area in the next few years. In 1636, a group from Massachusetts Bay was led by their pastor, Thomas Hooker, to found both Hartford and Connecticut. In 1638 a band of Puritans, led by Theophilus Eaton and John Davenport, founded New Haven, which was later united with Connecticut. At first the great influx of Puritans caused dissension and distrust with the Pilgrim Separatists who had arrived first. Eventually, the hostility and misunderstanding between the Separatists and Puritans were removed, and the two groups united into a single church system in which the authority resided in the congregation. The new Congregational churches were banded together by a covenant, pastored and taught by ministers whom they set apart, and maintained as part of a theocratic government. In 1631 the Massachusetts Bay Colony enacted a regulation that only members of the established Congregational churches could be freemen. Ironically, those who had been Separatist dissenters in England were now intolerant of separatism. In fact, Congregationalism became the established church in New England, and the Anglicans were seen as dissenters.

When Roger Williams arrived in the colony in 1631, he was quickly labeled as a troublemaker for his strong stand for religious liberty. Williams was London-born and Cambridge-educated, and was ordained a Puritan minister in 1629. He displeased his intolerant congregations with sermons on religious liberty, and had to flee to Boston to escape arrest in England. He declined a position to teach in the Boston church because it was connected with the Church of England, and the Boston congregation controlled the civil affairs of the town. He denounced the community leaders of Salem for not paying the Indians for lands they had appropriated, creating more problems for himself. In 1635 the General Court tried Williams for heresy and ordered him deported to England. He escaped, however, and fled south where he survived the rigorous winter living with the Narraganset Indians. The following year, he established the town of Providence on land secured from the Indians. Roger Williams' colony became the first to grant freedom of worship, separation of church and state, and equality to all citizens. He journeyed to England in 1644 and secured a charter for his Rhode Island colony, which became a haven for the persecuted, and a prototype of a working democracy. A prolific writer, Williams produced many pamphlets which had great influence on the founders of the American Republic. Williams' church was the first duly constituted Baptist church in America, but the evangelizing Baptists soon exported their ideas to other settlements. Also, other Baptists came from England to the middle colonies.

The English were not the only settlers on the eastern seaboard. In 1609, under the flag of the Dutch Republic, Henry Hudson explored the river that bears his name, and in 1626 Peter Minuit purchased Manhattan from the Indians to begin the city of New Amsterdam, which was renamed New York when the British navy took it over in 1664. The Dutch Reformed Church (Calvinistic) was organized there in 1628, and there was general religious tolerance until Peter Stuyvesant became governor in 1647. Calvinism in the form of English and Scotch-Irish Presbyterianism also began to infiltrate the colonies, encountering considerable opposition from the Congregationalists, but strong reception from the Dutch Reformed leaders in New Amsterdam.

Also included among the early colonists of New Amsterdam were Dutch Lutherans who came about 1623. Swedish Lutherans founded New Wilmington, Delaware, in 1638, and established the first Lutheran congregation in America. By 1655, the Dutch had eliminated Swedish rule, but enough Swedes remained to continue to receive aid and clergymen from the Church of Sweden until 1791. Eventually, however, the Swedish Lutheran churches became Episcopalian. The outstanding Lutheran leader in America's colonial days was Henry Melchior Muhlenberg, who brought the Pietism of Halle to the New World. Muhlenberg became pastor of German Lutheran churches in Philadelphia, traveled widely, and in 1748 brought together the first Lutheran synod in the colonies. Michael Schlatter

Driven from the Massachusetts Bay Colony, Baptist Roger Williams escaped to Rhode Island, made friends with the Narragansett Indians, and later established a chartered Colony at Providence. (Historical Pictures Service, Chicago)

was the outstanding missionary and organizer for the Germans of the Reformed church.

The settlement of Pennsylvania was the fulfillment of the dream of William Penn, a convert to the Society of Quakers in 1667. Penn desired a colony where everyone could find political and religious freedom, and in 1681 he was granted a charter to begin his "holy experiment." Two thousand settlers from England, Germany, Holland, and France responded to Penn's offer of religious freedom, self-government, fifty acres of free land, and 5,000 acres for 100 pounds. In the pivotal year of 1682, Penn arrived at the forest which would become Pennsylvania, wrote his controversial *Frame of Government*, established Quaker meetings, and founded Philadelphia, the city of brotherly love. Although Penn's policies included treating the Indians as equals, they did not exclude slavery, which became a thorny issue for him. The colony thrived, but Penn's personal fortune declined and he spent some of the time before his death in 1718 in a debtor's prison in England. Delaware, which had been part of Penn's colony, obtained an independent status in 1702.

In New Jersey, Lord John Berkeley and Sir George Carteret attracted settlers by promising complete freedom of conscience and a popular assembly. In the Carolinas, large numbers of Quakers and Presbyterians were able to delay the establishment of Anglicanism until 1704 in South Carolina and 1715 in North Carolina. In Georgia, James Oglethorpe founded Savannah in 1733, and granted religious freedom to all except Roman Catholics. The Moravians had an extremely successful settlement, led by Augustus Spangenberg, who encountered John Wesley during his ill-fated mission to Georgia. Anglicanism was established as the official religion in 1755, three years after Georgia became a royal province.

Thus, the American colonies were populated by immigrants from many different countries who had come to the New World for a great variety of reasons. Several different religious bodies were represented, the principal ones being the Church of England, Congregationalists, Calvinists, Lutherans, Roman Catholics, and Baptists. Ironically, although the spirit of the people and the rules of government were the direct result of the ever-present religious consciousness, the large majority of the population actually had no formal church connection. In the early 1700s, only about five out of a hundred were members of churches. Concern for the religious welfare of the colonists was evidenced in the Church of England as the Bishop of London sent commissaries to the colonies. One of these, Thomas Bray, organized the Society for Promoting Christian Knowledge and the Society for the Propagation of the Gospel in Foreign Parts, which greatly increased the number of churches and clergymen in America. Still, the large majority of the colonial population was unregenerate, and spiritual clergymen became intensely concerned and prayerful that a season of revival would come to the land. The answer to their prayers was far beyond their expectations.

(3) The Awakening and Results. The First Great Awakening in America was practically contemporaneous with the Pietism of Germany and the Methodism of England, and exhibited many of the traits of those movements. It was, however, distinctively American in many features which were hitherto unknown in mainline Christianity. The emphasis in America was on the "gathered" concept of church, which meant that all members were required to testify of a definite experience of conversion or of being "saved." Those who could not do so were considered "unconverted" or "unsaved." The efforts of concerned clergy and laity to win the unsaved often resulted in special seasons when many were converted in the same period of time. Soon, there evolved a deliberate planning of meetings, which came to be known as "revivals," for the purpose of "evangelistic" preaching especially to convert the unsaved. This early version of frontier evangelism, later translated into camp meetings, became a distinctive and permanent feature of the Christianity of the United States.

(a) Beginnings. The first known stirrings of the Great Awakening began in the 1720s among German Mennonites, Dunkers, and Moravians in Pennsylvania. But the first notable revivalist preacher was Theodore J. Frelinghuysen, a German Pietist minister to the Dutch Reformed of northern New Jersey in the Raritan Valley. He began proclaiming with impassioned conviction the necessity of having a deep inner experience of transformation rather than the mere outward performance of religious ceremony. He also began conducting private prayer meetings for the conversion of the unsaved. Although other ministers criticized him, he attracted a wide following, and by 1726 his preaching had resulted in numerous conversions and the ingathering of many new members. Vast numbers were baptized, and many church members began to make evident their commitment in changed lives. In 1737, Frelinghuysen began moves which brought about the formal creation of the Dutch Reformed Church in America.

A young Presbyterian minister in New Brunswick, also in the Raritan Valley, was deeply impressed by Frelinghuysen. He was Gilbert Tennent, son of the distinguished Presbyterian pastor William Tennent, founder of the first "Log College" in Neshaminy, Pennsylvania, for the purpose of training new ministers. Gilbert Tennent carried the revival to the English and Scotch Presbyterians, and attracted large crowds with his eloquence, scholarship, and flair for imaginative figures of speech. Tennent pled for a genuine change of heart, and compared nonevangelical Presbyterians to Scribes and Pharisees. When colonial Presbyterians split into New Light and Old Light factions over the revival issue from 1741 to 1750, Tennent emerged as the leading spokesman for the evangelical New Light group, yet he worked effectively to reunite the two groups. He also served for many years as a trustee of the College of New Jersey (now Princeton).

(b) Jonathan Edwards (1703-58). The best known and most influential expression of the Great Awakening occurred in 1734 among the people of Northampton, Massachusetts. Jonathan Edwards, minister of the Congregational Church at Northampton, was deeply concerned for the spiritual condition of the citizens of Northampton. He was also fearful of the current drift toward Arminianism. Edwards had a distinguished background and a fine education. The grandson of the formidable Solomon Stoddard, he had succeeded his famous grandfather at Northampton after graduating from and teaching at Yale. In 1734 he preached a series of sermons on justification by faith alone, creating a sensational interest in personal conversion throughout the Northampton community. Within a year more than three hundred persons, nearly all the people in town above sixteen years of age, professed conversion.

In his detailed account in *Faithful Narrative of the Surprising Works of God* (1737), Jonathan Edwards minutely analyzed the causes and results of the Northampton revival. The book became an instant best-seller in America and England, stirred new expressions of revival practically everywhere it was read, and established Edwards' fame. His succeeding books and powerful sermons continued to fan the flames of revival. When emotional excesses began to mar the Great Awakening, Edwards forthrightly denounced them, and called for the evidence of a responsible moral life as opposed to emotionalism as the test for genuine conversion. He abhorred shallow revivalism deeply and tightened the requirements for church membership. He excluded all "unconverted" from communion, an action that stirred a controversy which resulted in his having to resign the Northampton church in 1750. For the next several years, America's first great theologian humbly served as a missionary to Massachusetts Indians while serving a small parish in Stockbridge. During that time he wrote his most important works on freedom of the will (1754), and original sin (1758). He was invited in 1758 to serve as president of Princeton, but he died from the effects of a smallpox inoculation shortly after taking office. Jonathan Edwards, besides being the leader of the Great Awakening, was the first great formative figure in what has been called New England theology. This was a modification of the Reformed faith, which remained true to the Calvinistic sovereignty of God and election to salvation, but allowed for action of the sinner in accepting divine forgiveness.

The effect of the Northampton revival was felt in the surrounding areas, and "souls did as it were come by floods to Jesus Christ." Within the next three years, the Awakening swept throughout New England, New York, New Jersey, Pennsylvania, Maryland, and Virginia. Under the outstanding preaching and leadership of Samuel Davies, revivalistic Presbyterian churches were built in Virginia. Uneducated but zealous preachers such as Shubal Stearns and Daniel Marshall revived and expanded the Baptists throughout Virginia and the Carolinas.

Everywhere the revival movement appeared it gained strong support or provoked adamant opposition. It created temporary schisms in almost every denomination in the American colonies, but it also stimulated the churches to vigorous new growth. From 1740 to 1742 the Awakening swept 25,000 to 50,000 members into the New England churches. Between 1750 and 1760, 150 new Congregational churches were formed, and it was almost impossible to keep count of the new Baptist congregations.

(c) Whitefield's Impact. The high tide of the Great Awakening came in 1740-41 when George Whitefield came to assist the effort with his incomparable eloquence and commanding personality. Whitefield had originally intended to be an actor. He had a voice which could reach thousands in the open air and an expressive and dramatic style which could sway audiences as few men have ever done. He had been in the original Holy Club with the Wesleys at Oxford, and had also accompanied them on their Georgia mission; but now he returned as a seasoned and prominent preacher. Before the close of his ministry he would make six preaching tours to America. In his first tour, he began in Delaware and spoke in major centers of population. In Boston, thirty thousand heard him at one time on the common. Even a man so practical and religiously unorthodox as Benjamin Franklin was moved by him and recorded his impressions of his sermons. He was warmly welcomed by Frelinghuysen, Tennent, Edwards, and other revival leaders. Together they organized an itinerant evangelistic work which greatly aided in bringing the various colonies closer together. Whitefield was uncommonly free from denominational bias, and cheerfully preached in all pulpits. His remarkable voice and compelling presence moved vast audiences and increased membership in all Protestant groups. He found, however, a greater following among the Presbyterians and Congregationalists than among his fellow Anglicans.

(d) Definitive Results. The results of the Great Awakening were many and obvious. Most importantly, there was a general quickening of religious life, a renewed emphasis on personal conversion, a large increase in church membership, and a higher standard of morality. The Baptists began the rapid growth that was to be their hallmark for the next two centuries. They attracted many with their stand against infant baptism, their insistence upon a regenerate church membership, and baptism by immersion only. Divisions occurred in some denominations, especially the Presbyterians and Congregationalists, over the legitimacy of the revival and its methods.

The Great Awakening provided a new impetus for education. With many young men entering the ministry, the churches were concerned about their training. To this end, the Presbyterian synod of New York, in 1745, established the College of New Jersey, which became Princeton University. The University of Pennsylvania was founded in 1753 on a nondenominational basis. King's College (now Columbia University) was started in 1754 as an Anglican institution. Rhode Island College (Brown University) was established by the Baptists in 1764. The Dutch Reformed opened Rutgers College in New Jersey in 1766, and the Congregationalists founded Dartmouth College in New Hampshire in 1769. Numerous parochial schools were established, the common (public) school was upgraded, and the English Latin grammar school was replaced by the American academy with its more practical studies.

Another result of the Great Awakening was its stimulation of missions to the Indians and Negroes. The Indian population had become sparse, and they found it difficult to adapt to the white man's agricultural economy, and to survive the diseases and strong liquors of the whites. In most of the colonies, Indian churches were organized and through them the natives were assisted in adjusting to their new cultural environment. One of the most notable missionaries to the Indians was David Brainerd, who was engaged to marry the daughter of Jonathan Edwards. Obsessed with the plight of the Indians, Brainerd rode horseback for endless days and nights taking the gospel to the most remote tribes, until his journeys took their toll and he died before he could marry or fulfill the promise of a brilliant career in the ministry. The personal journals of his work among the Indians were published and widely read, exerting a profound influence on young people both in America and England.

The most dominant "nonreligious" result of the Great Awakening was its influence upon the thinking of the founders of the new republic which was about to be born. The spirit of religious liberty was stronger than ever as practically every denomination had learned new strength in flexing new spiritual muscles. Independence of thought and personal religious experience were the rule, not the exception. Ideas and institutions were being molded by people who believed ardently in democracy. In Massachusetts, a Baptist preacher named Isaac Backus, who was converted in the Great Awakening, formulated and publicized the evangelical position of separation of church and state. Throughout New England, clergymen began preaching in their pulpits that all persons are born free, and all are accountable unto God. Some even went so far as to preach the duty of resistance to encroachments upon personal rights and freedom. In short, two distinctive principles of the Reformation, salvation by the faith of the individual and the priesthood of all believers, characterized the Great Awakening and undergirded the principles of democracy which would be incorporated in the coming new republic, the United States of America.

X

THE WORLD-SHAKERS: REVOLUTIONS AND REPERCUSSIONS (1776-1900)

*These that have turned the world
upside down are come hither also.*

A C T S   1 7 : 6

A. The American Revolution
   1. Conditions and Causes
   2. The War and the Churches
   3. Decline and Revival
   4. Nationalism and Protestantism
B. The French Revolution
   1. The Reign of Terror
   2. The Napoleonic Empire
   3. The Reassertion of Ultramontanism
   4. The Rise of Romanticism
      a. Romanticism and the Arts
      b. Romanticism in Philosophy
      c. Romanticism in Theology
   5. The Appearance of Liberalism
      a. Biblical Criticism
      b. The Ritschlian School
      c. Nietzsche's Atheism
      d. Kierkegaard's Existential Dialectics
      e. Catholic Modernism
C. The Industrial Revolution
   1. Technological Features
   2. Sociological Problems
   3. Theological Response
      a. The Churches
      b. The Chapels
      c. The Salvation Army
      d. The Reformers
      e. The Evangelists

he American and French Revolutions ushered in the nineteenth century. These were violent rejections of old forms of oppression and exploitation, and Christianity was both involved in and affected by these military revolutions. There were also other nonviolent developments which affected the church, notably rapid industrialization and progressive secularism. Because these are not as easily related to a time frame as a war, they might be called evolutions, but because of their dramatic influence upon the world in general and Christianity in particular, they were truly revolutionary. These major revolutions, and reactions to them, have shaped the world as it is today.

A. THE AMERICAN REVOLUTION

Our last chapter contrasted the Age of Reason and the Age of Faith, which appeared to be antithetical at every turn. Yet, it was the strange mixture of revivalism and Deism which contributed greatly to the momentous occasion of the American Revolution. Some of the basic ideals of the Revolution came from the Reformed faith and the strident sermons of the Great Awakening. The leaders who translated these ideals into political realities, however, were Deists such as Thomas Jefferson, Benjamin Franklin, and Thomas Paine. Thinking men and praying men had come together in a consensus that all men should be free to govern themselves and believe for themselves. The American Revolution was neither totally Christian nor anti-Christian. It was born of both the Spirit of God and the spirit of man.

1. CONDITIONS AND CAUSES

There were many religious and philosophical moods and issues which prepared the colonists for the Revolution. The humanistic idea of the dignity of man, the interest on life here and now, and the rising tide of individualism provided philosophical underpinnings for those about to challenge the old authorities. The vast majority of the early colonists were Protestants, dedicated to the Protestant ideas of active participation of all citizens in government and religion and the divine right of the people as against the divine right of kings. About 83 percent of the colonists were English, and had brought with them the English traditions of representative government and liberty. But their spirit of independence soon went far beyond anything known in England. One of the first tangible steps of opposition occurred when the Church of England proposed an Anglican bishop in America. The colonists, especially the Congregationalists and Presbyterians, strongly opposed this attempt to curb religious independence. John Adams explained, "The objection was not only to the office of a bishop, though that was dreaded, but to the authority of parliament on which it must be founded. The reasoning was this: There is no power less than parliament which can create bishops in America. But if parliament can erect dioceses and appoint bishops, they may introduce the whole hierarchy, establish titles, establish religion, forbid dissenters, make schism heresy, impose penalties extending to life and limb as well as to liberty and property." In a very real sense, the American Revolution had religious as well as political and economic causes.

The political and military clash between England and America started when England tried to make the colonists pay for some of the expenses of the Seven Years' War (French and Indian Wars) and for some of the expenses of colonial administration. To increase the necessary colonial revenue for these purposes, parliament enforced the Sugar Act in 1764, which hurt American trade with the West Indies and the Azores. In 1765 parliament passed the Stamp Act, which required stamps on all legal documents, and in 1767 it passed the irritating Paint, Glass, and Paper Act. All of these acts raised the all-important question of taxation without representation. Resentment soon turned to open revolt as "Patriots" asserted that taxation without representation was tyranny. Angry mobs gathered in Massachusetts and Virginia, active resistance was organized in groups such as the Sons of Liberty, and tax collectors were forced from their districts. In 1765 nine colonies sent representatives to the Stamp Act Congress in New York, which sent a list of grievances to the authorities in England, especially declaring that taxation without consent was a violation of every Englishman's right. Repeal of the acts in 1770 came too late; there had already been armed clashes in Manhattan and Boston, the latter producing the infamous Boston Massacre. In 1773 a group of patriots destroyed British tea in the famous Boston tea party to protest British monopoly of the tea trade. As a consequence, parliament passed four intolerable acts against Massachusetts in 1774, closing the Boston harbor and replacing American governmental officials with British. In response, the colonies assembled the Continental Congress at Philadelphia in September, 1774, to prepare for armed resistance. The first hostilities began in April, 1775, at Lexington-

Concord, Massachusetts. The first major battle was fought at Bunker Hill near Charlestown, Massachusetts, on June 17, 1775. Soon after, the Second Continental Congress appointed George Washington general of the army.

On July 4, 1776, the colonies declared their independence. The influences of both the Enlightenment and the Awakening were obvious in the Declaration of Independence: "We hold these truths to be self-evident, that all men are created equal; that they are endowed by their Creator with certain inalienable rights; that among these are life, liberty, and the pursuit of happiness. That, to secure these rights, governments are instituted among men, deriving their just powers from the consent of the governed; that, whenever any form of government becomes destructive of these ends, it is the right of the people to alter or to abolish it, and to institute a new government. . . ." The inevitable had happened and a new chapter was about to be written in the progress of civilization and the history of Christianity.

2. THE WAR AND THE CHURCHES

The American Revolutionary War lasted until 1783, when the colonies finally forced the British to negotiate favorable peace terms. As already indicated, the war had religious causes as strong as the political and economic, and churches were active in arousing and informing public opinion, stirring the people to action, and physically giving of their men and means in combat. The established church, the Church of England, was caught in a no-win situation. To the colonists, it was the church which had oppressed their fathers, and its English ministry was largely sympathetic to the mother country. Anglicans in New England were the most loyal to England; the middle colonies were about equally divided; and the southern colonies were largely pro-American. It is noteworthy that George Washington, James Madison, John Marshall, Patrick Henry, Alexander Hamilton, and two-thirds of the signers of the Declaration of Independence were members of the Church of England. With the close of the war, it was obvious that the Church of England could not exist as such in free America, and in 1789 William White and Samuel Seabury, Jr., led in reorganizing the Anglican congregations into the Protestant Episcopal Church in the United States.

The Congregational churches were the most outstanding in leading the fight for liberty. Their Puritan ministers effectively used their pulpits to reach the masses, and numerous Puritan sermons, often used for political instruction, were published in pamphlet form by acts of legislature. The Puritan clergy articulated in part the political philosophy of the American Revolution. The most influential Presbyterian leader was John Witherspoon. A prominent Scotch preacher, Witherspoon had become president of the College of New Jersey (Princeton) in 1768, was elected a member of the Continental Congress, and was the only clergyman among the signers of the Declaration of Independence. Many other distinguished Presbyterian ministers and elders took an active part in the struggle for independence.

The American Lutherans gave almost unanimous support to the cause. John Peter Gabriel Muhlenberg, son of Henry Melchior Muhlenberg, left his pastorate and took some three hundred of his parishioners with him into battle. His outstanding military service earned him the rank of Major General, and at the close of the war he served in several positions of honor in the government and never returned to the pastorate. On March 19, 1776, the Lutheran German newspaper printed an appeal to colonial Lutherans: "Remember that your forefathers immigrated to America to escape bondage and to enjoy liberty." Two Lutherans were members of the Continental Congress, Christopher Ludwig and Michael Hillegas, who became the first treasurer of the United States. The most prominent Lutheran layman was John Adams Treutlen, who as Governor of Georgia, thwarted the efforts of the British in that area.

Roman Catholics, who were very small in number, were overwhelmingly in support of the revolution. Among the signers of the Declaration of Independence, the Articles of Confederation, and the Constitution were three Catholics, Thomas Fitzsimmons, Daniel Carroll, and Charles Carroll. Numerous Catholic officers came from Europe, especially France, to aid the inexperienced colonists. In 1780 the Catholic bishops and priests of France gave six million dollars to the new Republic. At the close of the Revolution, the American Catholics, who had been under the jurisdiction of the Vicar Apostolic of London, formed an American Roman Catholic organization, and the Reverend John Carroll became the first Roman Catholic bishop, with Baltimore as the first American see.

Baptists, who had been among the first champions of religious freedom and separation of church and state, took a prominent part in the Revolution. Baptist grievances had been presented to the First Continental Congress by President Manning of Rhode Island College, Isaac Backus, John Gano, and others. Influential Baptist leaders included John Leland in Virginia and Richard Furman in South Carolina. Many Baptists rose to high responsibilities in the chaplaincy and throughout the army. By the close of the war, Baptist churches were active and growing in all the colonies.

The Methodists were still a part of the Church of England, and therefore divided among themselves and held in suspicion by their fellow Americans. John Wesley added to the suspicion with the publication of *A Calm Address to the American Colonies*, advising submission to the king. When the war began, he instructed the Methodist preachers in America to remain neutral. All of the English-born preachers returned to England except Francis Asbury, who believed in America's future as an independent nation. The American-born preachers supported the Revolution, and after the war, they led Methodism to become one of the first religious groups to form a national organization. The Quakers, Mennonites, and Moravians as pacifists were against combat, and were consequently subjected to considerable animosity from their patriot neighbors. The Quakers who joined the army were expelled from the regular Quaker Society, and organized into a society called the Free Quakers. Every religious group in America was involved to some degree in the Revolution, which ushered in a whole new era of religious liberty for mankind.

3. DECLINE AND REVIVAL

Ironically, although the Revolution owed its inception to religious motives and forces, the war for independence had an immediate adverse effect on Christianity in the United States. All of the denominations had suffered severely, with churches destroyed, congregations scattered, ministers and members slain, and very few new ministers trained. Spiritual religion had been neglected, with the resulting increase of crime and immorality. Excessive debts were threatening and demoralizing to individuals and churches, as well as the government. Added to these negative internal conditions was the imported influence of popular agnosticism. The bitterness and cynicism which always accompany a war prepared the way for English Deism, French naturalism, and the growing fad of atheism. Skepticism and infidelity were encouraged by the anti-Christian writings of Voltaire and Thomas Paine. At the close of the Revolution, less than 10 percent of the American population professed to be Christians. Atheism was especially fashionable among students and educated men. Rationalistic and atheistic societies flourished everywhere except in the lower South, where the effects of the First Great Awakening had persisted. Then, in the opening years of the nineteenth century, a Second Great Awakening, also known as the Great Revival, swept throughout the nation.

The Second Great Awakening, which dates approximately from 1795 to 1835, actually had three phases: The first phase (1795-1810) was associated with the frontier camp meetings conducted by James McGready, John McGee, and Barton W. Stone in Kentucky and Tennessee. The second phase (1810-25) centered in the Congregational churches of New England under the leadership of Timothy Dwight, Lyman Beecher, Nathaniel W. Taylor, and Samuel Hopkins. The third phase (1825-35) was largely involved with the activities of Charles G. Finney, who began his revival work in small towns in western New York in the 1820s but eventually conducted revival meetings in the largest cities in America and Britain.

The camp meeting phase of the Awakening began when James McGready, a Presbyterian hell-fire and brimstone preacher, took his inflammatory style of evangelism to congregations along the Gasper, Muddy, and Red rivers in southwestern Kentucky. As the name implies, those who attended McGready's meetings came prepared to camp out, gathering from as far as thirty or forty miles away. As many as 10,000 to 20,000 were reported at some meetings. Often ministers from different denominations preached simultaneously in various parts of the campgrounds. The meetings featured preaching, hymn singing, prayer meetings, anxious benches, weddings, and baptisms.

The camp meetings filled a definite need in the unchurched settlements of the West, but they also caused strife and dissension. The meetings, which usually lasted for several days, were often accompanied by great emotional and physical excitement. Scenes of wild enthusiasm and hysteria gave the camp meetings a bad reputation among conservative churchmen. The Presbyterian Church refused to approve them after 1805, and as a corollary action, refused to ordain new men for evangelistic work without proper prerequisite training. A group of Presbyterians on the Kentucky-Tennessee frontier disagreed with the high educational requirements for a frontier ministry and became agitated over excessive ecclesiastical authority. Out of the resulting schism came the Cumberland Presbyterian Church, which stressed evangelism, repudiated predestination, and avoided a highly centralized authority.

The Disciples of Christ (which will be discussed more thoroughly later) also came out of the camp meetings. The Disciples, Cumberland Presbyterians, Methodists, Baptists, and Shakers carried the camp meetings westward with the frontier, emphasizing sudden conversion experience, breaking down old creedal standards, and undermining the tradition of an educated pastoral ministry. In spite of occasional fanaticism and excess emotion, the camp meetings helped to bring the stabilizing and humanitarian elements of religion to the raw wilderness settlements.

The second phase of the Second Great Awakening was more conservative and less emotional than the first phase. Lyman Beecher, Presbyterian pastor in Boston and later president of Lane Seminary in Cincinnati, was one of the most distinguished preachers of "revivals" in the first half of the nineteenth century. His daughter, Harriet Beecher Stowe, echoed her father's strong conviction against slavery in *Uncle Tom's Cabin*. His son, Henry Ward Beecher, became one of the greatest pulpit orators America has produced. Beecher called for Christians to realize the "religious and political destiny of the nation" by preaching the gospel, distributing Bibles, planting churches, establishing schools, and reforming American morals. Presbyterians, Congregationalists, Baptists, Methodists, and Episcopalians rallied to his call and launched deliberate efforts of evangelism and education across the country.

Beecher was a graduate of Yale where he had come under the influence of the new president, Timothy Dwight. As the grandson of the noted revivalist Jonathan Edwards, Dwight energetically promoted the theology of his famous grandfather. He was a popular speaker and writer and literally molded several generations of students at Yale, making that institution a spiritual and intellectual center during the Second Awakening. Dwight also left a large legacy in his many hymns, including "I Love Thy Kingdom,

Beginning with the Great Awakening in America, the Gospel was carried throughout the east coast regions through itinerant evangelists and the preaching at camp meetings. The drawing from Harper's Weekly *shows a camp meeting in progress at Sing Sing, New York in 1859. (Courtesy of the Billy Graham Center Museum)*

Lord." His older contemporary, Samuel Hopkins, had studied under Dwight's grandfather and while pastor in Rhode Island he stirred up what became known as the Hopkinsian Controversy. Hopkinsianism opposed the traditional ideas of original sin and the atonement. Although conversion was a central belief, no one could know for sure this side of the grave if he was among the elect. Atonement was expressed as a "governmental" theory because Christ's death was a satisfaction of "general justice" rather than of specific sins. Theology was a critical issue during this phase of the Awakening. Eventually, the revivalistic theology in all denominations shifted from Calvinism to Arminianism as preachers emphasized the ability of sinners to make an immediate decision to save their own souls. Controversy ran deep within Congregationalism over the issue of natural depravity and free will. Nathaniel W. Taylor, head of the Yale Divinity School, championed the moderate Calvinist position, which maintained that moral depravity was man's own act, consisting in a free choice of something other than God. Taylor's precise, intellectual appeals to logic, ignoring witness and emotion, caused a fervent group of his opponents to found Hartford Seminary in 1834.

The third and final phase of the Second Great Awakening stemmed from the aggressive evangelism of Charles G. Finney. First a school teacher, then a lawyer, Finney was dramatically converted in 1821 and was immediately convinced that he had been given a "retainer from the Lord Jesus Christ to plead his cause." He left his law practice to become an evangelist, and was licensed by the Presbyterian Church. Finney preached colorful, but well-planned sermons, addressing his congregations as he used to plead with juries. He also adopted the use of the "anxious seat" from the frontier revivals. These and other methods employed by Finney in his revivals were called "new measures" and aroused intense opposition, especially from ministers trained in the New England schools and at Princeton. As his methods became more polished, Finney was more accepted in the established churches. In 1827 Lyman Beecher gave Finney fair warning to keep out of his territory: "Finney, I know your plan, and you know I do; you mean to come into Connecticut and carry a streak of fire to Boston. But if you attempt it, as the Lord liveth, I'll meet you at the State line, and call out all the artillerymen, and fight every inch of the way to Boston, and then I'll fight you there." Four years later, however, Beecher invited Finney to his Boston pulpit, and admitted that he did very well.

The opposition against Finney lessened for several reasons. The obvious success of his revivals could not be denied. Revival fires burst into flame when he crusaded through upstate New York. In 1830-31 an incredibly successful revival broke out in Rochester. Yet Finney's meetings did not feature the emotional excesses of the frontier revivals. Also, he moved into the realm of benevolent action, giving special attention to the temperance and abolition movements. The wider acceptance of Finney also reflected the development of revivalism from raw frontier villages to the growing urban centers. Revivals were no longer characterized by spontaneous emotional outbursts but rather by carefully designed meetings. Finney and his associates, however, maintained the same emphasis of all revivalists during the Awakening, that man has the ability to make himself a new heart by his own choice, and should take the initiative in seeking his conversion.

In 1832 Finney became pastor of the Second Free Presbyterian Church in New York and launched an almost continuous revival there. His theological differences led him away from Presbyterianism and into Congregationalism, and he built his Broadway tabernacle. In 1835 he became professor of theology at Oberlin in Ohio, and from 1851 to 1866 he served as president of the college as well as minister of the First Congregational Church in Oberlin. The carefully contrived revival techniques which have survived unto the present owe their inception to many of Finney's innovations.

In summary, the Second Great Awakening produced a large increase in church membership, made soul-winning the primary function of the ministry, and stimulated many moral and philanthropic reforms. Soon thereafter, in 1857-58, a "prayer meeting revival" swept the cities of the United States, and crossed the Atlantic to Northern Ireland and England in 1859-61.

4. NATIONALISM AND PROTESTANTISM

Although the Revolutionary War ended in 1783, the United States did not begin as a nation until 1789, with the adoption of the Constitution. In 1791 the first ten amendments guaranteeing basic individual rights were approved. The first of these amendments addressed the religious issue: "Congress shall make no law respecting an establishment of religion, or prohibiting the free exercise thereof. . . ." No church had been powerful enough to demand establishment, and, as Thomas Jefferson observed, no one religion was essential to peace and order, but national sovereignty and morality were. Even though Deists, rationalists, and traditionalists disagreed on theological matters, there was general agreement that sociopolitical morality was a necessary foundation for government. Regardless of their doctrinal and ecclesiastical differences, all Protestant denominations were united in supporting a civil law which recognized that government, Christian morality, liberty, and safety were necessary to each other. The nation, rather than one particular church, became the vehicle for God's chosen people to realize their manifest destiny. Thus, Protestantism and Americanism were practically consolidated, and churches and denominations were identified with nationalism even to the extent of the nation's political and economic systems.

The identification of nationalism and Protestantism increased the anti-Catholic mood in the country. Dislike and distrust of Catholics and foreigners had been building in the United States since the seventeenth century. In the nineteenth century popular Protestantism joined with patriotic nationalism to produce "Native Americanism." The pope was regarded as a foreigner and Catholics often viewed as subversive agents. During the American war with Mexico (1846) it was rumored that there were papal plots to poison United States soldiers. In 1830 the American Bible Society urged Protestants to unite against Catholic influence in the West. In 1837, Horace Mann developed a system of public education for Massachusetts, which included nonsectarian teaching of the Bible. Protestants immediately approved and supported the system, while Catholics, led by Bishop John Hughes of New York, opposed public education and sought to gain public funds for Catholic parochial schools. Instead, state after state banned aid to sectarian schools and set up the public school system. The tension between Catholics and Protestants was greatly agitated by the large number of Catholic immigrants during this period. Also, the French Revolution had caused the papacy to reaffirm the right of the pope to dictate to secular governments, causing American Protestants to fear any appearance of Catholic strength in America. The new nation was not only shaped by the events of the American Revolution, but by other revolutions as well, and from the standpoint of worldwide Christianity the French Revolution was more serious and far-reaching.

B. THE FRENCH REVOLUTION

In our discussion of the Age of Reason, we observed that the history of Christianity shifted from the arena of politics and force to that of ideas and movements. Yet some of the ideas emanating from Christianity inspired a series of political revolutions which spread across the earth, beginning with the English Civil War, the Commonwealth, and Glorious Revolution of the seventeenth century, continuing in the American Revolution and French Revolution, and expanding in the nineteenth and twentieth centuries into Japan, China, India, and Russia. The French Revolution was of major importance to the world and to Christianity, not only because it overthrew an old system but also because it demonstrated that rationalism could and would use violence to achieve its ends. It was not a struggle for religious power as Christendom had experienced up through the Thirty Years' War. Nor was it a crusade for religious freedom as England and American had witnessed. It was, rather, a revolt to overthrow religion and enthrone the very worship of reason itself. Yet many phases of the Revolution were at times irrational and uncontrollable.

1. THE REIGN OF TERROR

Toward the end of the eighteenth century, complex conditions and seething discontent pushed against the thin and brittle facade of France's monarchy.

With twenty-six million people, France had the largest population in Europe, and could not feed it adequately. French participation in the American Revolutionary War had completed the ruin of the nation's finances. Most of the population lived in dire poverty, while the richest class was the ecclesiastical hierarchy—cardinals, archbishops, bishops, and abbots. The lower clergy were among the poorest, and in the Revolution they joined the common people against their own superiors. While the French government neared bankruptcy, the French church, which owned about 20 percent of the property in France, hoarded its wealth, earning the resentment of the impoverished masses.

The people of France were divided into three classes (estates): the clergy, some 130,000; the nobility, some 400,000; and the Third Estate, which included everybody else. In a pamphlet published in January, 1789, the Abbe Emmanuel-Joseph Sieyes asked and answered three questions: "What is the Third Estate? Everything. What has it been till now? Nothing. What does it want to be? Something." It was truly nearly everything, including the *bourgeoise* or middle class of bankers, brokers, manufacturers, merchants, managers, lawyers, physicians, scientists, teachers, artists, authors, journalists; and the "people," consisting of the proletariat and tradesmen of the towns, the transport workers on land or sea, and the peasants. The "people" were easily identified because they wore ankle-length trousers rather than the knee breeches *(culottes)* and stockings of the upper class, giving them the nickname of "sansculottes" (without culottes). Under that name they played a dramatic part in the Revolution.

The taxes, tithes, and feudal dues, always difficult to pay, brought unrelieved misery in the year 1788 when France was deluged with devastating weather, crop failure, famine, unemployment, and rampant fear. Louis XVI was a good man, but a terrible administrator. Overwhelmed by the crises of weather, famine, bread riots, revolt against taxes, and the growing deficit in the treasury, he issued, on August 8, 1788, a call to the communities of France to elect and send to Versailles their leading nobles, clerics, and commoners (representing all three classes) to form an Estates-General that would give him advice and support in meeting the problems of the realm. Optimism swept throughout the land; never before, in the memory of Frenchmen, had any of their kings asked advice of the people. Ironically, the "people," the sansculottes, were left out of the voting process.

The Estates-General began with pomp, pageantry, and celebration, but serious confrontation developed quickly. The king and the nobility were merely wanting some workable suggestions for relieving the country's fiscal woes. The Third Estate wanted to replace the parasitic royalty and clergy with a representative government. When the other two classes refused to join them, the delegates of the Third Estate declared themselves the representatives of the French nation, and formed the National Assembly on June 17, 1789. Two days later the clerical order voted to join them, with the exception of the ecclesiastical hierarchy which joined the nobility in appealing to the king to dismiss the Estates-General. Finding the doors locked, the deputies of the Third Estate gathered in a nearby tennis court and pledged to persevere until a national constitution was firmly established (the famous Tennis Court Oath). The king grudgingly gave in and appealed to the three classes to unite and form the National Constituent Assembly; but at the same time he began gathering troops to dissolve it.

With troops surrounding Paris, the population panicked, and insurrection erupted. An armed and unruly mob seized and destroyed the Bastille, an old fortress used since 1370 to imprison victims of royal or noble vengeance, on July 14, which was to become the national holiday of France. Across the land, peasants rose against their lords; and on August 4, the National Assembly decreed the abolition of the feudal regime and of the tithe. Next it followed the example of the American revolutionaries and produced the *Declaration of the Rights of Man, and of the Citizen* on August 26. It proclaimed liberty, equality, the inviolability of property, and the right to resist oppression. The king refused to sanction the decrees or the declaration, but the assembly continued its revolutionary work. On November 2, it seized the property of the church in France, and declared that the clergy would be functionaries of the state, which would pay their salaries.

Early in 1790 all monasteries were ordered dissolved, and the parish priests and bishops were to be chosen by elections in which all citizens, Protestants and Jews as well as Roman Catholics, were to vote. The pope could still define the doctrines of the church, but could have no administrative control in France. On July 12, 1790, the Assembly authorized the Civil Constitution of the Clergy, which completely subordinated the church to the state. Pope Pius VI condemned the actions of the Revolution, and about two-thirds of the Roman Catholic clergy in France stood with their pontiff in opposing the Revolution. Papalists, along with royalists, were now identified as counterrevolutionaries.

When the National Assembly proclaimed a revolutionary principle of international law, that a people had the right of self-determination, rulers of neighboring countries stepped up their criticism of the Revolution, and the gulf widened between France and the rest of Europe. Jacobins, supporters of the Revolution, were persecuted in many European countries. On April 20, 1792, France declared war on Austria and Prussia. At first, France suffered defeat, and the Austro-Prussian army advanced rapidly toward Paris. The French revolutionaries stormed the residence of the king, imprisoned the royal family, broke into the prisons and massacred the nobles and clergy (counterrevolutionaries) imprisoned there. The French stopped the Prussians on September 20, 1792, at Valmy, causing Goethe (who was present at the battle) to write, "This place and day marks the beginning of a new era in the history of the world." The next day a new assembly, the National Convention, met and proclaimed the establishment of the republic and the abolition of the monarchy. In January, 1793, the Convention ordered the king beheaded, ushering in the infamous Reign of Terror, 1793-94, with its mob rule and wholesale executions with the guillotine terrifying the land.

The Convention was accused of being antireligious and lawless, and many foreign nations appeared poised to invade France and stop the spread of terror. In an attempt to allay the charges and deter invasion, the Convention formally inaugurated a new religion on June 8, 1794. Following Deism, the Convention decreed that the people of France recognized the existence of a Supreme Being and the immortality of the soul; but Christianity was denounced as a superstition. The seven-day Christian calendar week was exchanged for a ten-day week, and the worship of the new religion was ordered to be on festival days celebrating great events of the Revolution. Political heroes replaced saints, and churches were designated "temples of reason." Goddesses of Reason appeared in Notre Dame and churches throughout France. Salaries to Catholic clergy were stopped and priests were forbidden to teach in public schools. Reason's Festival of the Supreme Being was celebrated on June 8, 1794, with the raising of a Statue of Wisdom. It was the avowed intention of the revolutionaries that Liberty, Equality, and Fraternity would replace God, the Son, and the Holy Ghost, and that the furtherance of the new Trinity would be the chief aim of society and the final test of morality.

The dream of the revolutionaries was never realized. The attempt to replace Christianity with rationalism began to turn the country against the Revolution. The guillotine bloodbath made the people suspicious of their new republic's "justice," and the continuing riots for food were proof that its economics were not working. The workers, who had inaugurated the Terror, began to rise against the Revolutionary troops, with more slaughter ensuing. After more than three years of political and economic disruption, religious division, constant war, and uncertainty of work, food, and life, a weary and fearful nation began to rebel against the Revolution. On October 26, 1795, the National Convention was dissolved, and on November 2, a new government was constituted. The executive part of the government was the Directory, which proclaimed religious freedom but remained anti-Christian in its posture. During its brief existence (four years) the Directory's most significant accomplishment was the introduction of Napoleon Bonaparte to the world.

2. THE NAPOLEONIC EMPIRE
Napoleon was born at Ajaccio in Corsica on August 15, 1769, fifteen months after Genoa had sold Corsica to France. Although he became the leader of the French Revolution and Emperor of the French Empire,

Napoleon was of Italian stock, sharing neither the traditions nor prejudices of his new country. Napoleon's father, Carlo Buonaparte (the family changed the spelling of their name in 1796) died in 1785, leaving Napoleon as head of the family at age sixteen. He was able, however, to complete his studies at the military academy in Paris and was made second lieutenant in the artillery. He vigorously supported the Jacobins and the Convention. He first distinguished himself in the battle for Toulon (1793). Having been made adjutant general in charge of bombardment, he drove the British from the town, and was promoted to brigadier general. On February 7, 1794, he was appointed commandant of the artillery in the army of Italy. When he crushed a left-wing group (the Pantheon club) in 1796 for promoting a new revolution to install a communist regime, he was rewarded for his loyalty by being made commander-in-chief of the army of Italy. A week later he married Josephine de Beauharnais, and two days later left to lead the army in brilliant victories over Sardinia and Austria, and established the Republic of Lombardy. The next three years were filled with triumph after triumph which elevated him to become the national hero of France.

Meanwhile, confusion mounted in the new government of France. Great Britain, Austria, Russia, and Turkey had formed a new coalition against France, while French royalists were clamoring for a return of the monarchy. Emmanuel Sieyes and Napoleon planned and executed a *coup d'etat* on November 9-10, 1799. The directors were forced to resign, the members of the legislative councils were dispersed, and a new government, the consulate, was set up.

The consulate government was virtually run by three consuls: Napoleon, Sieyes, and Roger-Ducos. As the first consul, Napoleon Bonaparte became, at the age of thirty, the master of France. The new constitution gave sweeping powers to the first consul which made it possible for Napoleon to impose a military dictatorship on France.

Although he was personally indifferent to religion, Napoleon shared Voltaire's belief that the people needed a religion. In 1796 he had invaded Italy and wrung from the pope a retraction of all antirevolutionary bulls and encyclicals. When the pope appealed to Austria, Napoleon marched on Rome, forcing the abdication and exile of Pope Pius VI. The pope's successor, Pius VII, was more agreeable to negotiating with Napoleon, and they soon produced a concordat reconciling the Roman Catholic Church with the Revolution. The pope recognized the French republic and called for the resignation of all former bishops; new prelates were to be designated by the first consul and instituted by the pope. Papal acts were not to be published in France or catechisms drawn up without the state's authorization.

By 1802 Napoleon had defeated every effort to overthrow France, and general peace prevailed in Europe for the first time in ten years. The French people voted overwhelmingly to elect Napoleon as first consul for life, and

Years of glory and military triumph ended for Napoleon Bonaparte and his French patriots at the Battle of Waterloo, shown here. (Historical Pictures Service, Chicago)

he began grandiose expansion plans for France. These ambitions for expansion caused the British to declare war on France again in 1803, and Napoleon was convinced that his only hope of maintaining stability and power was to transform the life consulate into a hereditary empire. The senate and the tribunate acquiesced and the empire was proclaimed on May 18, 1804. Napoleon wanted to be consecrated by the pope, who agreed to come to Paris for the coronation ceremony. At the last moment, however, the emperor took the crown from the pope and set it on his own head (recalling the same act from Charlemagne). Pius VII and Napoleon subsequently had a complete break. The pope refused to join in a blockade against England, and in retaliation Napoleon occupied Rome in 1808 and merged the Papal States into the French Empire. Pius excommunicated Napoleon, and the emperor put the pope in prison, where he languished for five years. The pope repudiated the earlier concordat, and Napoleon again retaliated by suppressing monasteries throughout the empire.

Napoleon reached his zenith of power in 1810, but the disastrous defeat by the Russian winter came in 1812, followed by the cataclysmic "Battle of the Nations" at Leipzig (1813), when the Grande Armee was torn to shreds. By January, 1814, France was being attacked on all its frontiers, and by March 30, the combined armies of Russia, Prussia, Austria, and England had pressed to the gate of Paris. The senate proclaimed the deposition of the emperor, instituted a provisional government, and elected Talleyrand as president.

After a year in exile on the island of Elba, Napoleon returned to lead the army again, this time to be decisively defeated at Waterloo by Wellington, and forced to abdicate by the legislative chambers. From 1815 to 1821, Napoleon lived in exile on the island of St. Helena, dying at the age of fifty-one. His last will requested, "I wish my ashes to rest on the banks of the Seine, in the midst of that French people which I have loved so much." After the fall of Napoleon, Pius VII returned to Rome with great popular acclaim. All the papal territories were returned to the pontiff except Avignon, and the papacy regained the highest prestige it had known since the sixteenth century.

3. THE REASSERTION OF ULTRAMONTANISM

One of the first acts by Pope Pius VII when he was freed from prison in 1814 was to reconstitute the Society of Jesus (Jesuits), which was correctly understood as a reassertion of the orthodoxies of the past. It signaled a revival of Ultramontanism which did not diminish until Vatican II (1962-65). The word Ultramontanism is from *"ultra montes,"* beyond the mountains, and indicates that, from the French and German viewpoints, the rule of the church was coming from beyond the mountains, from the papacy at Rome. The term had been used as early as the eleventh century, and revived in the seventeenth century with the rise of Gallicanism in

France. Now that the French Revolution had been branded as the natural
outcome of such heresies as Gallicanism, Jansenism, and Josephism,
Ultramontanism began to reassert its basic tenet and regain its power
in Europe. Simply stated, Ultramontanism favors the centralization
of authority in the papal curia as opposed to national or diocesan
independence. The Jesuit Order which Pius VII revived had always been
a mainstay of curial authority as opposed to local authority.

With the fall of the Napoleonic Empire, the Roman Catholic Church set a
course diametrically opposed to the secularizing, democratic, rationalistic
forces in western Europe. It asserted that it alone had the divine right to
control and guide all aspects of culture. After reviving the Jesuits, Pius VII
repossessed the papal states through the Congress of Vienna in 1815, and
negotiated concordats with Bavaria, Sardinia, Naples, Russia, and Prussia.
In 1829, Pope Pius VIII continued the promotion of Ultramontanism with
an encyclical which prohibited unauthorized, heretical, biblical translations.
He declared that only the clergy could interpret Scripture, condemned
marriages of Catholics to non-Catholics, denied the principle of national
sovereignty, and affirmed that the church is divinely instituted and not
subject to any human power.

The Catholic revival of Ultramontanism was theologically expressed in
traditionalism and fideism, which were closely allied with the spirit of
Romanticism. Some of the great Catholic traditionalists were also listed
among the Romanticists. Three years after Schleiermacher published his
Speeches on Religion, Francois Chateaubriand (1768-1848) published *The
Genius of Christianity,* a brilliant rhetorical defense of Catholic Christianity.
Like Schleiermacher, he sought to defend Christianity by shifting the
discussion from rationalist argument to aesthetic feeling. He argued that the
study of history proves that the Christian faith had been the main source
of art and civilization in Europe, and for Chateaubriand, Catholic
Christianity is the universal symbolization of all human aspiration.

Another Catholic traditionalist of this period was the popular Abbe
Felicite de Lamennais (1782-1854) of France. Lamennais argued that men
long for belief in order to avoid the nagging emptiness of skepticism. But
certitude can never be reached by individual reason, only by general reason
or universal consent. Thus, certitude is a matter of faith in the testimony of
others, and since the Catholic faith is the tradition with the largest number
of witnesses, it is only in the Catholic Church that one can experience
universal reason and spiritual peace.

In 1823 Lamennais advocated a theocracy of man with the pope as its
supreme leader, which won the approval of Pope Leo XII. However, when
he came out for universal suffrage, freedom of the press, worship, assembly,
education, and speech, he was rebuffed by Pope Gregory XVI (1831-46). In
1832 Gregory specifically censured the idea that a religion of humanity
ought to prevail over the Word of God, and attacked the "unbridled

license" which comes with the loss of authority. Lamennais retaliated by denouncing papal political tyranny and praising democratic socialism. The pope condemned Lamennais personally and attacked freedom of opinions and speech and "absolute liberty of conscience." Lamennais separated from the church, denied the whole supernatural order, and died a Deist, inspiring many of the sociopolitical ideas of the later nineteenth century. Although he eventually left the church, Lamennais was very important in securing Ultramontanism in his early years.

One of the leading theorists of Ultramontanism was Joseph Marie Comte de Maistre (1753-1821). The French Revolution turned de Maistre against rationalism and liberalism, and he found in the Catholic Church a safeguard against both intellectual and political instability. In his book *Du Pape* (1819) he argued that the only foundation of society lay in authority, which he found best exemplified in monarchy and in the papacy. He insisted, however, that papal authority was supreme over national monarchy, and since the decisions of the pope are not subject to appeal, he is infallible in decisions regarding faith and morals. The Ultramontanists presented their theory of infallibility with the following reasoning: without an infallible pope there can be no church; without a church there can be no Christianity; without Christianity there can be no religion; and without religion there can be no civilized society. Ultramontanism also received bolstering from unexpected quarters. The "Catholic Emancipation Act" of 1829 gave Catholics and Protestant dissenters in England equal privileges. Frederick William IV made the Catholic Church independent of Prussian state control in 1850, and Austria followed suit in 1855. The Church of Ireland (Anglican) was disestablished in 1869. With these changes in government policies, the pope was able to gain more and more direct control of the Catholic Church in all lands.

Ultramontanism won its greatest victories during the pontificate of Pius IX (1846-78). In 1854, Pius proclaimed the dogma of the Immaculate Conception of the Blessed Virgin Mary, a clear victory for Mariologists, traditionalists, and Ultramontanists. In 1864, he issued his "Syllabus of Errors," a sweeping antimodern, antiliberal document, in which he censored eighty errors and trends which threatened papal supremacy, including freedom of conscience, freedom of the press, Protestantism, Communism, rationalism, Bible societies, civil marriage, free scientific investigation, separation of church and state, nonsectarian schools, and religious toleration. The Ultramontanist drive of Pius IX climaxed in the dogma of papal infallibility, pronounced on July 18, 1870, at Vatican Council I (the first ecumenical council since the Council of Trent, 1545-63). This dogma declared that the Roman church has supremacy over all other churches, and that all must submit to the Roman pontiff, who when he speaks *ex cathedra*, "that is, when exercising the office of pastor and teacher of all Christians," when defining "a doctrine regarding faith or morals to be held by the universal Church, by the divine assistance promised to him in blessed Peter, is possessed of that infallibility with which the divine Redeemer willed that his Church should be endowed for defining doctrine regarding faith or morals."

Although Pius had won a significant ecclesiastical victory, he was losing political ground during this same period of time. A new Kingdom of Italy had been formed in 1861 and Victor Emmanuel whom Pius refused to recognize, was proclaimed king. Rome was captured on September 30, 1870, and made the capital of Italy. The pope became a voluntary prisoner in the Vatican. The new state passed the Law of Guarantees in 1871, guaranteeing the papacy privileges and immunities equal to those of the king, amounting to "a free church in a free state." The papacy was never satisfied with this arrangement although it lived under it for fifty-nine years. The situation was not resolved until Benito Mussolini's Fascist government canceled the Law of Guarantees and negotiated the 1929 Lateran Treaty, in which the pope received sovereignty over Vatican City in return for recognizing the regime of Mussolini.

The successor to Pius IX was Leo XIII (1878-1903), who implemented many of Pius' Ultramontanist policies. Over a period of twenty-five years, he issued eighty-six encyclicals, the largest papal corpus since the Middle Ages. In 1881, Leo rejected the idea that authority comes from the people, condemned the free spirit in Protestantism, and proclaimed that political power must be guided by Christian (Catholic) doctrine. In 1884, he attacked naturalism and Freemasonry. In 1885, in his *Christian Constitution of States*, he condemned the separation of church and state, and insisted that while the state may have different forms, it must publicly profess Roman Catholicism as the only true religion. In 1888, his encyclical *On Human Liberty* declared that liberty consists in doing what the church dictates, that man's highest duty is to submit to the authority and law of the church, and that there must be no freedom of worship. His most famous encyclical, *Rights and Duties of Capital and Labor,* 1891, was one of the first major statements from a Christian body that recognized the injustice of the plight of laborers. In 1893 he attacked modernism and historical and literary criticism, upheld biblical inerrancy, and reiterated the church as the teacher, guide, and interpreter of Scripture. In 1902 he established the Biblical Commission to enforce traditionalism against the findings of literary criticism. The battle between Ultramontanism and modernism continued into the twentieth century and was one of many confrontations the Catholic Church faced in its efforts to maintain control of Christendom. Catholicism had been deeply humiliated and severely wounded by the French Revolution. It was determined never to be put in that vulnerable position again.

Catholics were not the only ones who had been frightened and repulsed by the excesses of the French Revolution. All of Europe had been shocked and awakened to the power of ideas and the possible disaster of unrestrained rationalism. The Revolution turned Europeans to seek less violence and more idealism, leading to an age of religious and literary romanticism.

4. THE RISE OF ROMANTICISM

Longing for the beauty and tranquility of the past, a war-weary continent began to express renewed interest in the supernatural and the idealism of nature. The result was the Romantic Movement, which flourished from 1760 to 1870, and which reasserted passion and imagination in reaction from the classicism and rationalism which marked the eighteenth century. Actually, Romanticism strove for an inclusiveness, which cherished both experience and tradition, both emotion and reason, both religion and science, both order and freedom, both man and nature. The Romanticists insisted that experience includes more than analytical reasoning and scientific experiment—that it also includes imagination, feeling, and intuition. They also expressed a new concern for the rich diversity of human life, and they pointed to nature's insatiable creative process of diversification. Whereas rationalism had called for a unity of man because of the basic similarities in all men, Romanticism emphasized the individuality of man because of universal diversity. The Deists searched for a universal creed, while the Romanticists espoused variety as the very essence of religious experience. Yet, for all the evidence of nature's diversity, the Romanticists saw a fundamental kinship between man and nature. They also believed that behind nature some Spirit or Vital Force was at work, whether called God or by some other name.

Ironically, the greatest pre-Romantic influence was Rousseau, the "father of the French Revolution." While his political theories and civil religion appealed to the revolutionaries, Rousseau's emphasis on nature and the emotional nature of man inspired the Romanticists. They also found much to emulate in Rousseau's assertion of man's natural goodness, social equality, and sentimental idealism.

The Romantic Movement was not a precise system so much as a mood and a tendency, yet it was very explicit in the works of this period. Literature, art, philosophy, and theology often overlapped in the quest for a new concept of experience that would transcend the rationalism and moralism of the eighteenth century.

a. Romanticism and the Arts. The diversification which characterized Romanticism was especially evident in the arts. There is no common Romantic style to be compared with, for instance, Classical or Baroque style. The poets, musicians, painters, and novelists of the time exhibited abundant local and personal variations of Romanticism, making a definition or identification practically impossible. Hugo identified Romanticism with liberalism and revolt; Delacroix with a metaphysical interpretation of the world; Blake with imagination; Berlioz with heroicism; Gautier with youth; Nerval and Holderlin with dream; Musset with disenchantment; Herder with magic; Schlegel with yearning or nostalgia; Coleridge with imagination; and Wordsworth with illumination or intuition.

William Wordsworth (1770-1850) was directly influenced by Rousseau's view of nature, and by the plight of man as exposed by the French Revolution. He saw God in nature, and chaos in human society. In moving poetry, he lamented man's artificial achievements in contrast to the harmony of nature. Sir Walter Scott (1771-1832) used the romantic pageantry of medievalism in his novels, and thereby provided imaginative escape from rationalism. Different expressions of Romanticism are also found in the works of John Keats, Lord Byron, William Cullen Bryant, Herman Melville, Beethoven, and Chopin. The brilliant literary creations of Johann Wolfgang von Goethe (1749-1832) reflect Romanticism's concept of opening up the literary treasures of the world through translation and criticism. This great German poet and dramatist was a classic example of Romanticism's diversification; Goethe was a critic, journalist, painter, theater manager, statesman, educationalist, and natural philosopher. He was encouraged to complete his monumental *Faust* by another of Germany's great dramatists, poets, and literary theorists, Friedrich von Schiller (1759-1805), who exemplified in his own life and work the triumph of man's spirit over adverse circumstances.

b. Romanticism in Philosophy. While the poets and artists dramatically demonstrated the philosophy of Romanticism, there were a few who systematically taught its principles as a legitimate academic pursuit. Friedrich von Schelling (1775-1854) was a German philosopher who formulated a system of metaphysics based on the philosophy of nature. He taught that nature is a reality of its own which speculative or intellectual intuition has to interpret. In his system of transcendental idealism, Schelling tried to unite his philosophy of nature with epistemology and ethics. He viewed the human mind as working like nature does, but consciously and intentionally; and, nature, on the other hand, works as the mind does, but unconsciously and unintentionally. This effort to reconcile nature and mind to one another was a typical example of the Romantic spirit.

Friedrich von Schlegel (1772-1829) was a German writer and critic who originated many of the philosophical ideas that inspired the early German Romantic movement. He maintained that poetry should be at the same time philosophical and mythological, ironic and religious. His semiautobiographical novel *Lucinde* (1799) gives a religious significance to love as a physical and spiritual unity. His original work as a writer was small, but his influence as a critic and aesthetic philosopher was (and still is) considerable.

He has profoundly influenced modern literature with his theories of creative criticism, his definitions of Romanticism, of irony, of the myth, and of the novel. In 1808 he became a Roman Catholic and united his concept of Romanticism with medieval Christianity. He turned against his earlier stand for the unconditional freedom of the individual, and became the ideological spokesman of the anti-Napoleonic movement for German liberation.

c. Romanticism in Theology. Although he was a poet, philosopher, and literary critic, Samuel Taylor Coleridge (1772-1834) had a lasting impact on English theology and became known as the "father of the Broad Church Movement." In 1795, he made the acquaintance of William Wordsworth, and in 1798 they published together the *Lyrical Ballads,* Coleridge's most famous contribution being "The Rime of the Ancient Mariner," in which he refers to the God who "made and loveth all." In 1816 he published a volume of poems containing "Christabel" and "Kubla Khan." His most important religious publications include *Lay Sermons* (1816), *On the Constitution of Church and State* (1830), *Aids to Reflection* (1825), and *Confessions of an Enquiring Spirit* (1840, posthumously).

Coleridge was not limited to any one school or party, and his broad base enabled him to become responsible for the rebirth of a vital English theology out of the orthodoxy and rationalism of the late eighteenth century. Through Coleridge, German Romanticism and Idealistic philosophy were introduced into British intellectual life. He insisted that the mind is active and not merely a passive receptacle of sensations. He taught that the Bible's spiritual authority lies "in its fitness to our nature and our needs." He contended that divine revelation is neither a wholly objective or subjective reality but requires both poles, objective fact and existential appropriation. Coleridge is the purest example in England of the Romantic protest against rationalism, which he believed to be a deadening "mechanical philosophy."

While Coleridge was making his stamp on English theology, Germany was being notably influenced by the brilliant Friedrich Daniel Ernst Schleiermacher (1768-1834), who is generally considered to be the dominant Protestant theologian between John Calvin and Karl Barth. His theology is the most forceful and systematic statement of the Romantic and liberal understanding of the Christian religion. As Barth said, "Schleiermacher is the watershed of modern theology." The son of a Reformed army chaplain, Schleiermacher was educated at a Herrnhuter Brethren college and seminary, but found the teaching too narrow for his independent intellect, and entered the University of Halle in 1787. He was ordained to the ministry in 1794 and appointed a Reformed preacher at Berlin, where he came into close contact with representatives of the Romantic Movement, especially Friedrich Schlegel. While serving as a hospital chaplain in Berlin, he wrote his epochal *On Religion: Speeches to Its*

Cultured Despisers (1799). It was an attempt to win the educated classes back to religion, which he defines, in Romantic language, as "a sense and taste for the infinite." He proposed feeling, rather than intellect or dogma, as the base of religion. The next year (1800) he published *Soliloquies*, his "confessions," which represents the quintessence of the Romantic spirit. In this book he calls upon every man to accept his unique place in humanity and to develop his own individuality to the fullest.

In 1811, Schleiermacher was offered the chair of theology at the University of Berlin, which marked a new era in his life. From this position he played an influential part in the Prussian war against Napoleon, especially through his stirring sermons. From 1819 he became occupied with developing his system of dogmatics, which he published in his theological masterpiece, *The Christian Faith* (1821-22). He began, not with dogmas of the past as most classical theologians did, but with an inward analysis of himself. In his probing, he became aware of a sense of dependence on something beyond himself, and he felt that the awareness of this dependence was God-consciousness, the source of all religion. From this God-consciousness, Schleiermacher developed his theory of the feeling of Absolute Dependence. For him, the claims of faith do not represent objective knowledge, but expressions of devout self-consciousness or the Christian's inner experience. The ceremonies and doctrines of religion are always preceded by devout self-consciousness, God-consciousness, and the absolute feeling of dependence. It was Christ's perfect God-consciousness that constituted his divinity, and he redeems men by inspiring God-consciousness in them. Thus, we are dependent on Jesus, but orthodox doctrines such as the resurrection and second coming of Christ are not essential. Schleiermacher's strong emphasis on feeling as the basis of religion was a reaction against both rationalism and formal orthodoxy. His influence on Protestant thought has been enormous, and his introduction of psychology into systematic theology has influenced all of modern religion. It has often been said that in the theological expression of Romanticism, Goethe was its divinity, Schlegel was its high priest, and Schleiermacher was its prophet.

5. THE APPEARANCE OF LIBERALISM

Schleiermacher is also credited with being the father of Liberal Protestantism, which originated in the nineteenth century and achieved its zenith in the decades preceding the Second World War. It may seem strange to link Schleiermacher with Liberalism since his theology was definitely in the vein of Romanticism, a reaction against rationalism; and Liberalism was a continuance of rationalism. Yet it was his thesis that all doctrines must be shown to be directly related to the religious self-consciousness that opened the way for radical examination of previously uncontested orthodox doctrines.

Liberalism was characterized by an eagerness to discard old orthodox forms if they were judged to be irrational in the light of modern knowledge or irrelevant to what was regarded as the central core of religious experience. The second criterion (the central core of religious experience) came directly from Schleiermacher. The first criterion (the light of modern knowledge) came indirectly from G. W. F. Hegel, whom we have already discussed in the section on rationalism. Hegel's dialectical process of thesis, antithesis, and synthesis was postulated on an essentially evolutionary view of the universe. His system involved not only the natural sciences but also such disciplines as history, law, aesthetics, and religion. To Hegel, truth lay not in individual truths or in individual disciplines, but in the whole. He did away with rigid distinctions between the world of things and the world of the spirit, insisting rather that all things are the result of the growth of spirit toward the ideal. His reasoning method opened the way for analyzing how things are evolved, even the Scriptures. Hegel was a contemporary of Schleiermacher and Coleridge, and his disciples in the same period began to develop definite schools of thought from his premise that Absolute Spirit is manifesting itself in the historical process.

a. Biblical Criticism. F. C. Baur (1792-1860) used Hegel's methodology to develop his methods of biblical criticism. He saw Peter's portrayal of Jesus as the thesis and Paul's as the antithesis, with the early church creeds becoming the synthesis. He proceeded, from this basis, to attempt to determine which New Testament books were written by Paul, and which were not. His conclusions are not as important as the fact that he opened the way for careful and scientific research on the Bible. He was also a pioneer in the method of treating his subject historically rather than systematically. Baur founded the Tubingen School, a school of German New Testament theologians, whose principal endeavor was to apply Hegel's conception of development to primitive Christianity.

David Friedrich Strauss (1808-74) was a pupil of Baur, and was strongly influenced by Schleiermacher and Hegel. In 1832, he became a lecturer on Hegelian philosophy at Tubingen University. Applying Hegelianism to the New Testament, Strauss wrote his *Life of Jesus* in 1835, portraying Jesus as simply a man who was raised to the mythical status of Christ by the messianic expectations of his time. He denied the historical validity of many of the Gospel narratives, and set the pace for others to work on the New Testament books in an effort to establish their historical value. His book aroused a storm of indignation and led to his dismissal from Tubingen. He turned his attention to politics, and declared his preference for scientific materialism over Christianity.

Another *Life of Jesus* was written in 1863 by Ernest Renan (1823-92), who presented Jesus as the enlightened modern man of rationalism as opposed to the orthodox Christ which the world had known for seventeen centuries.

Renan repudiated the supernatural element in Jesus' life and saw him as a charming and amiable Galilean preacher who taught a high system of ethics. He rejected the accounts of the miracles as being unscientific and untenable. His book created an immediate sensation throughout Europe, and he was removed from his professorship of Hebrew at the College of France.

Baur, Strauss, and Renan represented an era of biblical studies in which serious theologians were applying general historical principles to the Bible. These principles presupposed that the biblical documents are human, and that it is possible to ask if the reported events in the documents are true.

The historical inquiry also led to other kinds of questions: What are the most reliable and trustworthy biblical texts? What are the relationships between the various books? When and by whom were the texts written, and for what purpose? What are the sources the authors used? What is the relationship of these sources to other oral and written materials of the time? What seems to be the author's purpose and intention? Protestant conservatives attacked the "higher criticism," and the Roman Catholic Church established the Biblical Commission (1902) to make sure that no Roman Catholic scholar advocated historical views alien to church dogma.

b. The Ritschlian School. The new Liberalism of the nineteenth century agreed with Schleiermacher that religious faith must be grounded in experience, but it pointed out that Schleiermacher failed to see that Christian experience is only appropriated through the existence of particular, objective events in history. The new call, therefore, was "back to the historical sources," and the theological response to that call was the Ritschlian school of theology whose influence dominated Protestant thought in Germany from 1875 to World War I and in America from 1900 to as late as 1930. Basically, the Ritschlian school excluded metaphysics from theology, rejected speculative theism, condemned ecclesiastical dogma, emphasized the practical side of religion, revealed the contrast between religious and theoretical knowledge, contended for the historical revelation of God in Christ as opposed to any natural revelation, espoused the idea of the kingdom of God as the regulative principle of Christian dogmatics, and limited theological investigation to the contents of religious consciousness. The Ritschlian school was a perfect expression of Protestant Liberal theology because of its skepticism concerning metaphysics, its rejection of church dogma and natural theology, its concentration on the historical Jesus and his moral teachings, and the idea of the kingdom of God as the communion of spiritually free persons.

The Ritschlian school was named after Albert Ritschl (1822-89), son of a prominent Lutheran preacher, disciple of Baur, and professor of theology at Bonn and at Gottingen. His outstanding publications included *Theology and Metaphysics* (1881), *History of Pietism* (1880-86, three volumes), and his magnum opus, *The Christian Doctrine of Justification and Reconciliation* (1870-74, three volumes). Ritschl agreed with Schleiermacher that religion is a matter of experience, but he disagreed with him on the nature of religious experience. He believed the Schleiermacher came dangerously close to subjectivism. As a historian, Ritschl held that the proper object of theology is not man's consciousness but the historical reality of the gospel as given in the New Testament. For Ritschl, religion is not located in feelings, as with Schleiermacher, nor in metaphysical knowledge, as with Hegel—but in the practical experience of moral freedom. We apprehend by faith, not by reason, and this faith rests not on the intellectual apprehension of a series of facts but on the making of value-judgment. Ritschl also insisted that it was to a community, not to individuals, that the gospel was, and still is, committed. He taught that the final purpose of God for redeemed man is the moral integration of humanity into the kingdom of God. Among the many outstanding disciples of Ritschl was Adolf von Harnack (1851-1930), German historian and the greatest Patristic scholar of his generation. Harnack applied Ritschl's critical methodology to the field of church history, maintaining that the metaphysics which came into Christian theology was an alien intrusion from Greek sources. In his later years, he stressed the moral side of Christianity, especially the claims of human brotherhood, to the exclusion of all that was doctrinal. In summary, the Ritschlian school was characterized by its stress on ethics and on the "community," and its repudiation of metaphysics and religious experience.

c. Nietzsche's Atheism. The student of Ritschl who became the most extreme in his rejection of traditional religious doctrine and values was Friedrich Nietzsche (1844-1900), frequently called the archenemy of Christianity. Many believe that Nietzsche's attacks on Christianity were the most merciless ever waged against the faith, but some of his ardent followers called him the restorer of primitive Christianity. Friend and foe alike acknowledge his overpowering influence in the philosophy and theology of the twentieth century, for it was long after his death that movements developed which could be traced in part to Nietzsche's seminal ideas. The Nazism of Hitler's Germany is often referred to as a product, or at least a by-product, of Nietzsche's philosophy. The Nihilism of the twentieth century (with which we will deal in the section on that period) definitely had roots in Nietzsche, as did the "Death of God" theologians of the 1960s.

Friedrich Nietzsche was the child of a Lutheran pastor, and his mother's father and grandfather were also Lutheran pastors. As a young boy he was serious and introspective, and was known by his companions as "the little pastor." Indeed, he intended to enter the ministry and studied briefly for that purpose. However, after only a year at the University of Bonn, he moved to Leipzig where he became an ardent pupil of Friedrich Ritschl.

While in Leipzig, he also came under the influence of the works of the atheistic philosopher Schopenhauer. In 1869, on the recommendation of Ritschl, Nietzsche was appointed to the Chair of Philology at the University of Basel, where he became a close friend of the composer Richard Wagner. During his early years at Basel he wrote *The Birth of Tragedy*, which reflected his attachment to Wagner, *Thoughts Out of Season*, which attacked D. F. Strauss, and essays extolling Schopenhauer and Wagner. Because of ill health he resigned from Basel in 1879, and spent ten years as a wanderer. In this period he produced *Human—All Too Human*, *The Dawn of Day*, and *Joyful Wisdom*. By now, he was making definitive attacks on metaphysics, traditional morality, self-renunciation, and Christianity, which he called "the one great curse, the one immortal blemish of mankind."

Nietzsche's most famous work, *Thus Spake Zarathustra*, appeared in four parts between 1883 and 1885. In this visionary and poetical work he presents two of his most significant ideas: the transvaluation of values and the *Ubermensch* (Superman). The term Superman is often associated with something supernatural, and has often been identified with Nazi racial theories. Nietzche's own translation of *Ubermensch* would probably be "Overman" or superior man. Nietzsche denounced the Christian values of pity, humility, kindness, and gentleness as weakness and herd morality. He contended that these "slave" values must be abolished for they hinder the creative manifestations of the Superman. He extolled the "will to power" as being life's dominant force—not the power of the masses, but the power of the great individual, disciplined and perfected in mental and physical strength, serene and pitiless, ruthlessly pursuing success without moral scruples. One can readily see how the charge of being a protofascist has clung to Nietzche.

The reevaluation of values was necessary for Nietzsche because of the "death of God," which he was the first to announce. He saw the modern world in a state of cultural decline, a condition he called nihilism, nothingness, or meaninglessness. The "death of God" was not the result of philosophical investigation but of cultural fact; and when we step out of the shadow of the dead God and realize that he is truly dead, madness will erupt. This is true because the death of God means the death of the ultimate ground and support of all traditional values. Strangely and ironically, Nietzsche says that this atheistic posture is the ultimate result of applied Christianity. It is the truth-seeking which is encouraged by Christianity which leads to its own death, making atheism the last evolutionary phase of the Christian ideal of divine truth. As though intent upon fulfilling his own prophetic utterance about madness resulting from the death of God, his last works revealed a hostile, frenzied, though brilliant mind—*Nietzsche contra Wagner*, *The Twilight of the Idols*, *The Antichrist*, and *Ecce Homo*, all written in 1888. Soon thereafter he plunged into a state of total insanity from which he never recovered. Christianity has not yet fully recovered nor fully dealt with the devastating blows that came from the powerful and pathetic mind of Nietzsche.

d. Kierkegaard's Existential Dialectics. Another man whose influence increased even more in the twentieth century was Soren Kierkegaard (1813-55), a Danish theologian whose work was a conscious effort to overthrow the rational pretensions of Hegelianism, which was the reigning philosophy in the Denmark of Kierkegaard's day. Kierkegaard was a curious recluse who never married after breaking his engagement to Regina Olsen in 1841; nor was he ever ordained after studying theology at the University of Copenhagen. From 1846 until a year before his death, Kierkegaard's life was outwardly uneventful, being spent almost entirely in writing. Although well known in Denmark, he was generally shunned as an eccentric because he demanded such a radical Christianity in nineteenth-century Europe. Yet his influence was monumental in Europe after World War I, and he is known today as the "father" of Christian existentialism. He is also considered the spiritual founder of the dialectical theology associated with Karl Barth and Neoorthodoxy. Among his notable works were *The Concept of Dread* (1844), *Sickness unto Death* (1849), *Christian Discourses* (1850), and *Training in Christianity* (1850).

Whereas the Ritschlian school emphasized the concept of community, Kierkegaard laid stress on the relation of the individual soul with God almost to the exclusion of the idea of a Christian community. He lambasted the hypocrisy of conventional Christianity and the institutional church, especially the state church of Denmark. He said that where everyone is considered Christian by the conventional act of baptism, Christianity as such does not exist.

In his well-known doctrine, "Truth is subjectivity," he insists that it is wrong to think of religious truth, or faith, as acquired in the same way one acquires other knowledge. In Christianity, the issue is not objective truth, but the relationship of the existing individual to Christianity. In true existential form, he held that only a faith which exhibits passionate appropriation of its object is a true faith. Since its object cannot be certainly known, faith involves a risk, which Kierkegaard calls the "leap of faith." Man, in his finitude and sin, is in no position to resolve his own predicament. Salvation can come only from God himself, the Wholly Other, a description which occupied the attention of Neoorthodoxy in the twentieth century. In dialectical fashion, Kierkegaard argued that the self is a unity of radical freedom and limitation and faith is the acceptance of this paradoxical unity. Faith, however, is not the acceptance of a creed or doctrine; it is the decision to be oneself as this person in this situation (existentially). From Kierkegaard's Christian perspective, this decision is possible only by the gracious and unconditional acceptance of man by

God, which we know by the proclamation and acceptance of the gospel.

Kierkegaard accepted the biblical traditions and was uninterested in the historical criticism of men like D. F. Strauss; but he opposed Hegel's idea that absolute knowledge is possible and rational, contending instead that man must decide to take the "leap of faith" without proofs of God's existence.

e. Catholic Modernism. The counterpart to Protestant Liberalism is usually referred to as Modernism in the Roman Catholic Church. Beginning in the later years of the nineteenth century, Modernism was a movement aimed at bringing the tradition of Catholic belief into closer relation with the modern outlook in philosophy, the historical, and other sciences and social ideas. The Catholic Modernists wholeheartedly adopted the critical view of the Bible, and accepted that the biblical writers were subject to many of the limitations of other historians. Often they were even more skeptical than the Protestant scholars.

The Catholic Modernists were also characterized by a philosophy of action. They sought the essence of Christianity in life rather than in an intellectual system or creed. They especially welcomed the pragmatism of William James and the intuitionism of Henri Bergson. The Modernists possessed a teleological attitude of history, believing that the meaning of the historic process is to be found in its issue rather than in its origins. Thus, the essence of the gospel will lie in its full and final expansion rather than in its primitive historic kernel.

One of the leading figures of Catholic Modernism was Alfred Firmin Loisy (1857-1940), a French professor who was excommunicated in 1908 for his liberal treatment of the Gospels. In reply to Harnack's *What Is Christianity?*, Loisy wrote *The Gospel and the Church* in 1902, maintaining that the essence of Christianity is to be found in the faith of the developed church. To Loisy it was not necessary to prove that Christ founded a church or established the sacraments. The important fact is the present existence of both. He also concluded that the Gospels do not report reliably the teachings of Jesus but express the faith of the early church. The Roman Catholic Church condemned all of Loisy's works and finally excommunicated him.

Another Catholic Modernist of note was George Tyrrell (1861-1909), an Irishman who was converted to Catholicism from high Anglicanism. Tyrrell accepted the apocalyptical interpretation of Jesus and his message as set forth by Loisy, Weiss, and Schweitzer. He held that the important thing about Jesus' apocalyptic message was its spiritual truth. That Jesus was mistaken in his literal belief in a coming new age is not significant; Jesus was possessed by the truth of a great idea and had to embody it in the limited thought forms of his day. For his Modernist views, Tyrrell was dismissed from the Society of Jesus and then deprived of the sacraments.

Catholic Modernism was most systematically formulated by the Frenchman Edouard Le Roy (1870-1954), a distinguished mathematician turned philosopher. His book *Dogma and Criticism* (1907) is the clearest philosophical expression of French Catholic Modernism. Le Roy rejected the scholastic conception of dogma, claiming it would lead either to anthropomorphism or agnosticism. Instead, he saw dogma as having a simple twofold purpose of excluding certain false notions and guiding us in our religious life. The resurrection of Christ, for instance, is not to be understood as a historical fact but as a guiding principle of Christ's continuing activity in the world. Le Roy's work was condemned the same year it was published.

Leo XIII (Pope, 1878-1903) at first gave considerable encouragement to the Modernists but, in his later years, he became increasingly critical of the movement. His successor, Pius X (1903-14), distrusted Modernism from the first and condemned it in 1907. In 1910 he imposed an anti-Modernist oath on all suspect clergy, and most of the clergy identified with the movement were excommunicated. The Modernists were totally defeated, and the result of their efforts was a church more deeply committed to entrenched positions. Critical scholarship was severely limited, and Catholic biblical scholarship did not recover any real vitality until after World War II. The Modernist crisis led to zealous heresy-hunting and persecution. Although Modernism was almost completely eradicated in the Roman Catholic Church, the more recent doctrines of men like Emmanuel Mournier and Teilhard de Chardin reflect vestiges of the earlier Modernism.

Thus, both Protestant Liberalism and Catholic Modernism reflected the cultural climate at the turn of the century. Traditional metaphysics was under fire, and the Bible and church dogma were undergoing historical and analytical scrutiny. There was a real concern to simplify Christianity, which for many liberal theologians meant a recovery of the ethical message of Jesus. Religious authority resided in personal experience rather than in canonical Scripture or church dogma, and salvation was interpreted in moral, social, and progressive terms. Many of the new emphases came not only as reactions to the French Revolution, but also from the so-called Industrial Revolution of the nineteenth century.

C. THE INDUSTRIAL REVOLUTION

Although used earlier by French writers, the term Industrial Revolution was first popularized by the English economic historian Arnold Toynbee (1852-83) to describe England's economic development from 1760 to 1840. Since then it has been broadened to include practically the entire process of industrialization which has dramatically transformed society throughout the entire world. Simply stated, this transformation of society occurred by taking large numbers of people from the agricultural life that had formed

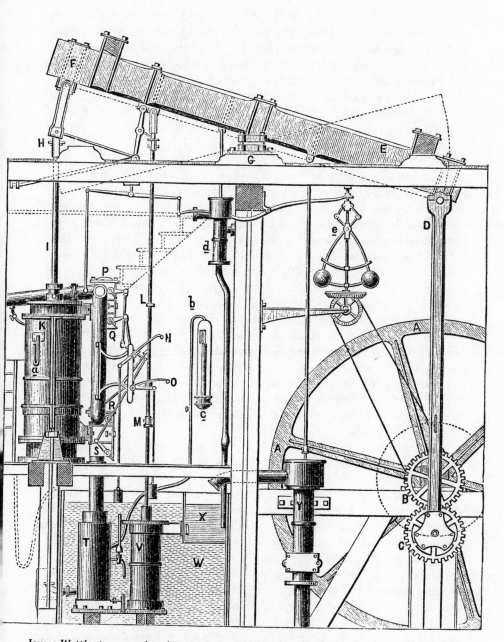

James Watt's steam engine, invented in 1781, marked the beginning of the Industrial Revolution. (Historical Pictures Service, Chicago)

man's main occupation since the beginning of civilization and introducing them to new ways of working and living. It would be naive to think that such a drastic change would not affect society or the churches within that society. So, while people were striving to survive the crush of wars, such as the American and French Revolutions, and while they were trying to assimilate the ramifications of new philosophies and theologies, they were also called upon to adjust to sudden physical and psychological shocks brought on by rapid industrialization.

1. TECHNOLOGICAL FEATURES

In the popular understanding of the term, the Industrial Revolution is generally regarded as referring to the development of improved spinning and weaving machines, James Watt's steam engine, the railway locomotive, and the factory system. But these are merely the best known of many features of this revolutionary movement. The use of new basic materials, such as iron and steel, opened up many new industries and skills. New energy sources included not only the steam engine but also coal, electricity, petroleum, and the internal combustion engine. The spinning jenny and power loom increased production with a smaller expenditure of human energy. The factory system was a new way of organizing work, involving division of labor and specialization of function. The steam locomotive was just a prelude to the expanding developments in transportation and communication, which would eventually include the steamship, automobile, airplane, telegraph, and radio. Science increasingly became a partner with industry, and the technological results made possible a tremendously increased use of natural resources and the mass production of manufactured goods.

Although France was the wealthiest and most powerful nation in Europe, the Industrial Revolution occurred first in Great Britain because the British were more able to meet the prerequisites of industrialization. France's capital was being diverted to war expenditures, upkeep of the wasteful court and bureaucracy, and forced loans to the state, while British capital was more available and at much lower interest rates. Also, the labor supply in England was more mobile and adaptable since serfdom and the guild system had virtually disappeared. Although France had a larger population than England, the English had a larger market because of her growing colonies and world empire, and the British had a greater merchant marine for overseas trade. With the development of the canal system and later the railway system, England had more flexibility in the geographical location of industry. So, Great Britain was the first industrial nation and the first to realize that the price of progress can often be a bitter burden.

2. SOCIOLOGICAL PROBLEMS

Industrialization brought many social changes to humanity. Agricultural improvements made possible the provision of food for a larger population.

The decline of land as a source of wealth, rising industrial production, and increased international trade resulted in a wider distribution of wealth. The shift in economic power brought about political changes corresponding to the needs of an industrialized society. The growth of cities, the development of working-class movements, and the emergence of new patterns of authority caused broad cultural changes. Some of these changes were instantly and obviously beneficial, but some were dehumanizing and retrogressive rather than progressive.

While the Industrial Revolution enabled some men to produce more, travel faster, communicate more rapidly, and acquire more material conveniences, it also deepened the poverty and misery of many people. Workers labored long hours for miserable wages and lived in ugly, unsanitary tenements. The workers seldom saw daylight, with gas illumination enabling them to work all hours of the day and night. The rhythm of nature was exchanged for the rhythm of the machine, and God's sun was replaced with the factory clock and bell. The factory's precision and discipline caused drunkenness to be a major problem as men sought to escape the tyranny of industry. Child labor was so widespread and generally accepted that a bill introduced in parliament in 1833 seemed radical for stipulating that children under nine should be excluded from factories, and that those under thirteen should not work more than nine hours. The conditions of labor encouraged crime, which was punished by death or imprisonment. Prisons were without sanitary facilities, and prisoners were exploited by jailers.

Overpopulation and unemployment were burgeoning problems of industrialization. Between 1811 and 1851, England's population increased from twelve to twenty-one million. Large cities began to develop, all of them with disgraceful slums, filled, in part, by those displaced by industrialization. In the early years of the Industrial Revolution some machines were wrecked by the men they were putting out of work. In 1779, many textile mills were destroyed during riots in Lancashire. Chronic mass unemployment was a prevailing problem because of the influx of workers from overpopulated rural areas, the employment of women and children, temporary shutdowns, depressions, and business failures. Some could not work because of old age or disability, and others lost their jobs because technological improvements enabled one machine to do the work of many men.

Capitalism, private enterprise, and open competition brought in a new economic system. Wealth grew by leaps and bounds, and as always there were great extremes in the possession or absence of wealth. Huge fortunes were accumulated by a few, moderate comfort achieved by some, but in many places the majority endured extreme labor, sordid poverty, and moral and physical degradation.

It is true, of course, that not all the workers suffered under the factory system, and in some cases their conditions were improved. But it was tragically obvious that human gains were small in comparison with the great strides made in technology. The sufferings of the nineteenth-century factory worker have attracted the interests of historians and sociologists for decades. The conditions also attracted the attention of the churches of that day.

3. THEOLOGICAL RESPONSE

Christianity faced one of its greatest challenges in the intolerable social conditions caused by the Industrial Revolution. What would, and could, the church do for the masses who yearned for relief? Two overwhelming needs cried for attention: spiritual conversion of the thousands of souls who packed the cities and physical assistance to the oppressed and destitute. The response of the religious community came in wide variety, both in the kind and the amount of help.

a. The Churches. As a whole, the established churches of the nineteenth century were not able to accommodate the radical changes brought on by industrialization and swelling cities. The Church of England had great difficulty in responding to the new situation. Its organizational structure made it virtually impossible for it to be flexible enough and expedient enough to meet the demands. An act of parliament was required for a new parish to be created, which was both time-consuming and costly. Consequently, the new urban masses found that there was not room for them in church, and there usually was no clergyman to care for their spiritual needs. The parish church was often referred to as "the Tory Party at prayer," while a whole generation grew up outside the church. Christianity was viewed in contempt as "the bulwark and refuge of privilege" by many who were burdened for the betterment of the conditions of the masses. Then, in the 1830s and 1840s, an awareness of responsibility seemed to take hold of both parliament and the Church of England, resulting in acts to correct the more flagrant abuses and to enable the church to meet the conditions of the day. Larger parishes were reduced to more manageable size and new parishes were created. Revenues of the wealthy bishoprics and archbishoprics were shared with the poorer sees. The compulsory payment of local parish rates was abolished and made voluntary. Several societies were formed to sponsor the erection of new church buildings and the remodeling and expansion of older ones, augmented by substantial government grants. In 1836 the Pastoral Aid Society was organized to increase the number of clergy. At last, the venerable old Church of England was rising to meet the needs of the people, and in consequence experienced a striking awakening and transformation in the last half of the century.

The Methodists were much quicker to respond to the new industrial society. With their itinerant and local preachers, it was easier for them to go where the people were. Their simple, barnlike preaching places made the poor feel comfortable in church. Their lack of ecclesiastical machinery made it possible for them to act quickly and decisively as needs arose. Since a small group is usually able to take a more radical stand than a larger group, the Methodists were in the forefront of many social reforms. A particular branch of Methodism called the Primitive Methodists had a special interest in those who were displaced by the looms. While Methodists would not condone violence, great numbers of them joined Workingmen's Associations, although labor unions were illegal until the middle of the century. Thereafter, one-third of the Methodists entered the labor unions, taking with them their zeal, their Christian ideology, and their experience as lay preachers.

The concept of class imposed itself on the character of the churches. The Wesleyans (Methodists) and the Congregationalists tended to attract the middle class, while the Baptist "Tabernacle" and the Primitive Methodist "Bethel" usually had a working-class congregation. As already noted, the Church of England was mainly the church of the privileged. There developed a very distinct difference between the "chapel working class" and the "brute working class" of the back alleys. The Pleasant Sunday Afternoon (PSA) Movement was organized in 1880 for the express purpose of ministering to the working classes. Men were assembled on Sunday afternoons, in their working clothes, for a program that was entertaining, religious, and patriotic. In the twentieth century the PSA became the basis of the international Brotherhood Movement. Churches were trying desperately to minister to the hordes of workers, but it was obvious that new and faster methods were needed to "get at the masses."

b. The Chapels. Beginning in the 1840s the city churches of England established satellite missions in the poorer areas of the city. More than just preaching stations, these missions were all-purpose relief stations, with clothing societies, penny banks, soup kitchens, and other benevolent agencies. The concept of church as a covenant community gathered for worship gave way to the idea of church as a bustling organization engaged in various aspects of the missionary task. Ministers became organizational men, running vast programs of evangelism and social redemption. These missions were known as chapels.

The identification of chapel, however, was not reserved for the small satellite mission stations. It became the accepted distinction between the established Church of England and the Nonconformist evangelicals. Some of the great free churches of this time were called chapels. Charles Haddon Spurgeon was the most popular preacher of his age and is today still referred to as the "prince of preachers." In 1854 he became pastor of the Park Street Chapel (Baptist) in London, where the power of his sermons led to many conversions. His chapel was expanded into the specially erected

Metropolitan Tabernacle which seated six thousand. Commensurate with the chapels of that day, the Metropolitan Tabernacle also supported a large orphanage, a Pastor's College for training young ministers, a Colportage Society for distributing Christian literature, and a monthly magazine *The Sword and the Trowel.* The title of the magazine symbolized the spirit of the day, the sword (Bible) of the church united with the trowel of service and work.

In the latter part of the nineteenth century "Church" came to mean bishops, parishes, the *Book of Common Prayer,* and deference to "the Establishment" in both church and state. "Chapel" stood for two forms of dissent: the older, more loosely organized groups, such as the Baptists and Congregationalists, and the newer, more centrally organized brands of evangelicalism such as the Methodists. Chapel religion made great strides and produced deep rifts in English Christianity. The chapels of the Industrial Revolution gave encouragement to the rural dissent against urban Anglicanism, and Nonconformists pushed to secure equal rights with Anglicans. It became obvious that more unity among the free churches was needed to accomplish this equality and greater power in preaching the gospel. In 1856 a number of Methodist groups came together in the United Methodist Free Church. Presbyterian union was achieved in 1876, and in 1891 the New Connection of General Baptists united with the Particular Baptists.

c. The Salvation Army. One of the most effective and enduring efforts to offset the problems of an industrialized society was the formation of the Salvation Army, which still exists today as an international religious and charitable movement. William Booth (1829-1912) was the founder and first general of the Salvation Army. Booth was an ordained minister in the Methodist New Connection. He went to London in 1849, and in 1855 he married Catherine Munford, who shared his aspirations and became a famous preacher herself. In 1861 the Booths left the Methodist Church and established a revivalist movement of their own. In 1865 Booth began his ministry among the poverty-stricken, unchurched masses in the East End of London. At first he sought to make his work supplementary to the churches, but this was impractical because most of the converts did not want to go to the churches where they were sent, and they often were not accepted when they did go. Thus, Booth began to organize his work under the name of the Christian Mission, giving his followers a place to worship and grow in their new faith. Aware that needy souls could not be cared for if the body were hungry or in distress, Booth started his social scheme to feed and house even the most depraved, and then to try to uplift them spiritually.

In a short time, Booth's mission stations were spread throughout London and beyond. In 1878 the name was changed to the Salvation Army, with an explicit military theme, including uniforms, corps, citadels, and the magazine *The War Cry*. The organization followed a military pattern, which provided a direct line of authority and a system of training personnel. The style of government was autocratic, and unquestioning obedience was required throughout the ranks. The oversight, direction, and control of the Army was vested in one person, the general superintendent, commonly called the general. Booth was secured in the office of general for life, and had power to appoint his successor and to exercise complete control of all the property and money of the Army. Upon his death, Booth was succeeded by his son William Bramwell Booth on his father's nomination, but since 1931 the general has been elected by the High Council.

The work spread quickly over England, Scotland, and Wales. Overseas expansion followed, and the first Army pioneers reached the United States in 1880. The first headquarters were established at Philadelphia, and the work advanced rapidly against opposition and misunderstanding from mainline churches. Today the Army is generally accepted and widely supported. Following its original emphases of salvation and service, its ministry includes treatment centers, maternity homes and hospitals, camps, boys' and girls' clubs, community recreation centers, clubs for servicemen, mobile canteens, hotels and lodges, nurseries and settlements, missing persons' bureau, care for alcoholics, work with prisoners, and community centers for the aged. All services are given without respect to race, color, creed, or condition. The Army also conducts regular worship services and regularly proclaims the gospel on the streets. It uses aggressive evangelistic methods, well-trained bands, and mass communication techniques. In its preaching, it stresses the need for conversion, preceded by repentance and followed by growth in holiness. One of the great principles of the Army is that women have absolute parity of privilege, position, and dignity with men. The international headquarters are still in London, and the American headquarters are now in New York City.

d. The Reformers. Booth was only one of many who became impatient with the church's slow response to the needs of the masses, and who took individual initiative to correct social evils of the day. Anthony Ashley Cooper, Earl of Shaftesbury, was a dedicated reformer who championed many causes. As a member of the Conservative Party in parliament, he worked tirelessly to relieve the oppression of the working classes. His personal investigation of the London slums in 1846 led to the passing of the Ten Hours' Bill in 1847 and the Factory Act of 1874. He also took up the cause of women and children in the mines and collieries. In behalf of the young chimney sweeps, he secured passage of the Climbing Boys Act. He was long time chairman of the Ragged School Union, and in 1872 he founded Shaftesbury Park Estate at Battersea. He was for many years president of the British and Foreign Bible Society, and took great interest in the work of the London City Mission, the C.M.S., and the Y.M.C.A. He was a fervent evangelical, who hated ritualism and fought rationalism. A friend of all oppressed peoples, the Earl of Shaftesbury also worked for the abolition of slavery, the reformation of juvenile delinquents, the education of poor children, improved housing, and even the protection of animals.

Two outstanding Brethren who came to the aid of homeless children were Thomas Barnardo, who set up a huge institution for them in London, and George Muller, who operated his famous orphanage in Bristol.

The abolition of slavery had been the consuming passion of William Wilberforce in the late eighteenth century. Although the slave trade was abolished in the British Isles in 1807, the emancipation of slaves with the British Empire did not come until 1833, after a long campaign led by Fowell Buxton, who was supported by outraged missionaries describing the dehumanizing degradation of slavery upon the life of blacks in Africa and America. Many others were also concerned about the "white slavery" in the factories of England, and complained that the ineffective Factory Acts of 1802 and 1818 did not go far enough. Yorkshire evangelicals prevailed upon Richard Oastler, the administrator of a Yorkshire estate, to turn his well-known antislavery efforts to the slavery in the factories of his own area. Oastler spent the rest of his life championing shorter hours and better conditions for the workers. His famous letter to the *Leeds Mercury* entitled "Yorkshire Slavery" caused repercussions throughout England.

The Christian Socialists was a group of men dedicated to applying Christian principles to social reform. In the main they were of the Church of England but had become disenchanted with the slow response of the establishment to the needs of the day. J. F. D. Maurice (1805-72), an ordained Anglican minister and professor, was the principal thinker of the group. Writing in defense of social reforms and criticizing materialism, Maurice greatly influenced Anglican thought about the secular world in the twentieth century. One of his colleagues was the eminent novelist, Charles Kingsley, who also started as an Anglican clergyman but soon dedicated his life to educational and sanitary reform for the relief of the masses. The Christian Socialist workshops were weak in organization and too idealistic to last long. The "Working Men's College," started in 1854, was somewhat more successful. The group's periodical, *Politics of the People*, and its *Tracts on Christian Socialism* met with much hostility. The movement was shortlived but marked the beginning of the modern social movement in the Church of England.

e. The Evangelists. While some were interested primarily in the physical plight of the oppressed, there were others during the Industrial Revolution who were concerned about the spiritual needs and eternal destination of the souls who packed the cities. They were also advocates of social reform, but they saw their primary calling as that of spiritual ministry. Within the Church of England, the minority strain of evangelicals continued to thrive, preaching the necessity of conversion, stressing family prayers and the observance of Sunday, studying the Bible fervently, producing religious literature, and giving sacrificially to charity. The evangelicals of this period produced a wealth of hymns for Christendom, the words of some which we sing today: "Come, ye thankful people, come" (1844), "Ten thousand times ten thousand" (1867), "In heavenly love abiding," (1850), "O God the Rock of Ages," (1860), "I love to tell the story" (1866), and "Take my life and let it be consecrated, Lord, to thee" (1874).

The fervor of the evangelicals and the commitment of the Methodists were greatly strengthened by the introduction of American evangelism to the British Isles. Throughout the United States itinerant "evangelists" were devoting themselves to "personal work" and "revivals," especially in the cities. The two most prominent evangelists of this period were Charles G. Finney and Dwight Lyman Moody. Finney was the outstanding leader of the religious revivals which swept across the northern part of America in the second quarter of the century. He made several preaching tours in the cities of the British Isles in the middle of the century, and the Salvation Army copied many of his methods.

Dwight L. Moody was a drastic contrast to the erudite Finney. He was neither a scholar nor an ordained clergyman. Converted in a Congregational church in his late teens, he went to Chicago and became a successful shoe salesman. He devoted most of his time, however, to voluntary religious work, organizing a Sunday school, home visitation, welfare activities, and personal "soul-winning." In 1860, he gave up his business and became an independent city missionary. During the Civil and Spanish Wars (1861-65) he worked with the Y.M.C.A. ministering to the wounded. He returned to Chicago in 1865, and organized several state and international Sunday school teachers' conventions. Ira David Sankey (1840-1908) joined Moody in 1870, accompanying his preaching with singing and organ-playing. Moody first visited England in 1867, and returned with Sankey on a preaching tour from 1872 to 1875, in the course of which the *Sankey and Moody Hymn Book* was published. The tour through England, Scotland, and Ireland was supported by clergy of all denominations, and had a wide and enthusiastic response.

Moody conducted a similar mission to Brooklyn, Philadelphia, New York, and Boston, 1875-77. He founded a girls' school, Northfield Seminary, in 1879, a boys' school, Mt. Hermon, in 1881, and a Bible institute, Moody Bible Institute, in 1889. He made a second tour of Great Britain from 1881 to 1884, during which he made his first appeal to the academic world. He subsequently began organizing student conferences for Bible study. In 1891-92, he made another successful visit to England. Moody's wide success as an evangelistic preacher was due to his courage in pursuing converts in spite of opposition, the frankness, vigor, and urgency of his appeal, and the use of the inquiry room and other revivalist methods. Christianity had produced men and methods who knew how to reach the masses, and tens of thousands were converted; but still the "field was white unto harvest" and the harvest was great but the laborers were few.

X I

THE WITNESSES: MISSIONS AND MOVEMENTS (1792-1914)

Ye shall be witnesses unto me both in Jerusalem, and in all Judea, and in Samaria, and unto the uttermost part of the earth.

ACTS 1 : 8

A. Missions: Foreign and Domestic
   1. Protestant Missions
      a. William Carey
      b. Missionary Societies
      c. The Bible Societies
      d. Beginning of American Missions
      e. David Livingstone
      f. Hudson Taylor
      g. The Impact of Missions
   2. Catholic Missions
      a. Orders and Organizations
      b. Countries and Continents
B. Movements: Friendly and Unfriendly
   1. The Oxford Movement
      a. Causes for Concern
      b. John Henry Newman
      c. After Newman
   2. The Youth Movement
   3. The Ecumenical Movement
   4. Evolution and Agnosticism
      a. Charles Darwin
      b. Outrage and Enthusiasm
   5. Communism and Socialism
      a. Karl Marx
      b. The Attack on Religion
   6. The Social Gospel
      a. Walter Rauschenbusch
      b. The Gospel of Wealth
   7. The Abolition Movement
      a. Antislavery Reformers
      b. Slavery and Abolition in the United States
      c. The American Civil War
      d. The Role of the Churches
   8. Denominationalism
      a. Older Denominations
         (1) The Roman Catholic Church
         (2) The Eastern Orthodox Church
         (3) Lutheranism   (4) Anglicanism
         (5) Congregationalists
         (6) Unitarianism   (7) Calvinism
         (8) Methodism   (9) Baptists
         (10) Quakers
      b. New Denominations
         (1) The Catholic Apostolic Church
         (2) The Plymouth Brethren   (3) The
         United Brethren   (4) The Disciples
         of Christ   (5) The Seventh-day
         Adventists   (6) The Church of
         Christ, Scientist   (7) Jehovah's
         Witnesses   (8) The Church of Jesus
         Christ of Latter-day Saints   (9) The
         Pentecostal Movement

he nineteenth century was the great century for Christianity, as it began to encircle the globe in a dedicated determination to carry out Christ's commission to "make disciples of all nations." Modern inventions and far-flung explorations opened new frontiers in practically every human situation and location. This creative vitality and geographic expansion gave Christianity its opportunity to fulfill its potential and responsibility in the world.

A. MISSIONS: FOREIGN AND DOMESTIC

There have been four great missionary periods in the history of Christianity. The first was the spread of the gospel among the Jews, Greeks, Romans, and barbarians by the apostles and other early Christians. The second period was the conversion of the barbarian tribes in Europe during the Middle Ages. The third was the Roman Catholic period of missions during the Counter-Reformation in the seventeenth century. The fourth period is the modern mission movement in all parts of the world.

1. PROTESTANT MISSIONS

The first extensive Protestant missionary activity began in the early part of the eighteenth century. The German Pietists founded the Halle-Danish mission in 1705, and Halle University furnished at least sixty missionaries during the eighteenth century. Moravian missions started in 1732, and Quaker missionaries soon went to Europe, Asia, Africa, and America. Several English organizations developed for the purpose of evangelizing the colonies: the Society for Propagation of the Gospel in New England (1649), the Society for Promoting Christian Knowledge (1699), and the Society for the Propagation of the Gospel in Foreign Parts (1701). The big push for Protestant missions did not come, however, until Jonathan Edwards published a biography of David Brainerd. The story of young Brainerd's work among the Indians and his untimely death moved many to consider a similar calling. Among those directly inspired by Brainerd's story was William Carey, destined to become the "father" of modern missions.

a. William Carey (1761-1834) was a British cobbler who had taught himself Latin, Greek, Hebrew, Dutch, and French. After a conversion experience in 1779, he left the Anglican church and became a Baptist preacher. In 1792 he wrote *Inquiry into the Obligation of Christians to Use Means for the Conversion of the Heathens*. In that same year he preached a powerful sermon on missions at a ministers' meeting in 1792, stating the famous watchword, "Expect great things from God; attempt great things for God." The result was the founding of the Baptist Missionary Society, and as the first missionary of that society, Carey sailed with his family for India in 1793. Although he lost all his equipment in the Hugli River, he resourcefully took charge of an indigo factory at Malda, learned Bengali, and began the first of numerous translations of the Bible into Indian dialects. In 1799 he moved his operations to Serampore, and established a church, a school, and a printing shop. By 1809 he had printed the entire Bible in Bengali and parts of it in twenty-six other languages and dialects. For thirty years he served as professor of Oriental languages at the Fort William College at Calcutta. During his lifetime he produced more than 200,000 Bibles and Scripture tracts in forty different languages and dialects. He literally gave his all to missions, with his wife and children all dying of diseases in India. Carey's reports from India had a great effect in promoting interest in the overseas mission of Christendom. His work stimulated the formation of missionary societies and boards in nearly every denomination in Britain and America.

b. Missionary Societies. The voluntary societies of the nineteenth century literally reshaped Christianity. They circumvented all the established forms of church government, making ecumenical activity possible. By encouraging lay leadership, the power base of the church was altered, and a broad base of support was enlisted. The London Missionary Society was organized in 1795 by a group of Congregationalists, Anglicans, Presbyterians, and Wesleyans, who united to promote Christian missions to the heathen. Its first twenty-nine missionaries sailed to Tahiti in 1796. Robert Morrison was sent to China in 1807, the first Protestant missionary to that country. One of the basic principles of the society was that individual missionaries should be left free to choose whatever form of church government they wished to introduce to the heathen. Despite its ecumenical intentions, the L.M.S. soon became maintained almost exclusively by Congregationalists. The society still carries on extensive work in China, India, Southeast Asia, South and East Africa, and the South Sea Islands.

The Church Missionary Society, originally called the Society for Missions in Africa and the East, was founded in 1799 with John Venn as president.

Hudson Taylor, founder of the China Inland Mission (now Overseas Missionary Fellowship), shown at a tea party in his honor at Chang-Shan, China, June 1905, on the day of his death. (Courtesy of the Billy Graham Center Museum)

It was the first really effective organization of the Church of England for missions to the heathen. It had a struggling and difficult time during the early part of the nineteenth century. In the first ten years it sent out only five missionaries. However, by the middle of the twentieth century it had missionaries at work in Africa, Palestine, Iran, India, Pakistan, Ceylon, and the Far East.

John Wesley was intensely interested in transatlantic Methodist work, and by 1790 the West Indies had been made a separate Methodist province. Thomas Coke was anxious to expand Methodism on a world scale and began as early as 1784 to attempt to get a missionary society approved. Local missionary auxiliaries were recognized in 1814, and in 1818 the Methodist conference brought the auxiliaries together in the Methodist Missionary Society. Similar organizations were soon springing up in America, Germany, France, Scandinavia, and Holland. Practically every denomination had numerous missionary societies specializing in various spheres of activity. The Church of Scotland Mission Boards came into being in 1825, and Alexander Duff was its first missionary to India (1829). Among the larger societies in England were the South American Missionary Society (1844), the Melanesain Mission (1846), and the Universities' Mission to Central Africa (1859), the last being the response to the challenge sent out by David Livingstone. The largest interdenominational missionary society, the China Inland Mission, was founded by J. Hudson Taylor in 1865.

During the nineteenth century, the missionary societies were reluctant to commission women with status equal to that of men; and they failed to give sufficient emphasis to special work for women and children. Therefore some strong-willed women stepped forward to organize both denominational and nondenominational boards and societies. The Woman's Union Missionary Society of America was organized in 1860, the Zenana Bible and Medical Mission in 1861, and the Church of England Zenana Missionary Society in 1880. After the general missionary societies gave attention to such work, the women's societies merged with the general agencies or became auxiliary to them.

c. *The Bible Societies.* Concurrent with the establishing of missionary societies was the rise of Bible societies, which became a definite arm of Christian missions. In 1802 Thomas Charles, a noted Calvinist minister of North Wales, asked the Religious Tract Society in London to produce a Welsh Bible. The Tract Society decided that Bible distribution was not a part of its responsibility, so a movement was begun to establish a separate Bible society.

Joseph Hughes, a Baptist from Battersea, wrote a moving essay urging that an agency be formed to provide Bibles for all of Britain and for other countries throughout the world. On March 7, 1804, the British and Foreign Bible Society was formed in London. The purpose of the organization was to "encourage the wider circulation of the Holy Scriptures, without note or comment." Most of the well-known evangelicals of the day associated themselves with the project. Soon similar societies began to appear throughout the United Kingdom, with the Glasgow Bible Society formed in 1805, the Edinburgh committee in 1809, the Hibernian Bible Society of Dublin in 1806, the Canadian Bible Society in 1807, the Australian society in 1817, and the New Zealand society in 1837.

The British and Foreign Bible Society also suggested and led in the establishment of the Russian Bible Society in 1813. In rapid succession the British group then assisted in establishing Bible societies in Amsterdam, Hanover, Berlin, and Dresden, followed by Norway, Sweden, and Denmark. Even Roman Catholics joined in support of the work. The B.F.B.S. did have growing problems which centered around such issues as whether to include the Apocrypha and whether to require a doctrinal test of those on the managing committee. It continued to expand, however, and by 1906 there were 5,800 auxiliaries and branch societies in the United Kingdom, with 2,200 outside the United Kingdom. Meanwhile an American Bible Society had been formed. The British society began as a central unit which expanded into branch units, whereas the American society began as individual local committees which eventually combined into a national organization. One of the leading organizers was Samuel Mills of the "haystack group." The American Bible Society was officially founded on May 8, 1816, in New York, and most of the early effort was devoted to providing Bibles for the pioneers opening up the West, for European immigrants who were flooding into the United States, and for various tribes of American Indians. The American society, like the British, soon became involved in foreign translations and distributions.

Wherever missionaries worked Bible societies appeared, encouraging the young churches with native translations of the Word. An ecumenical spirit has characterized the Bible societies since their inception. In 1946 the major Bible societies of the world met at Haywards Heath in England and formed a cooperative organization, the United Bible Societies, which has significantly increased the translation, production, and distribution of the Bible.

d. Beginning of American Missions. The American missionary societies were initially inspired by the presence of the neighboring American Indians. Following the example of British societies, Americans organized in an effort to reach the non-Christian Indians. The first American society was the New York Missionary Society, organized in 1796. In the early part of the nineteenth century Samuel J. Mills kindled a missionary fire at Williams College at Williamstown, Massachusetts. Mills and several fellow students were caught in a rainstorm in 1806 and took refuge in a haystack where they held an impromptu prayer meeting. This famous "haystack prayer meeting" produced a dedicated group of young men, known as "the haystack group," who began to meet regularly to pray, ponder, and plan for some mission to the heathen. The original group consisted of Samuel Mills, Luther Rice, James Richards, Francis Robbins, Harvey Loomis, Gordon Hall, and Byron Green. Later they were joined by Adoniram Judson, Samuel Newell, and Samuel Nott. Out of this group's efforts was born, in 1810, the American Board of Commissioners for Foreign Missionaries, the first American society specifically designed for worldwide missions.

In 1812 Adoniram Judson and Samuel Newell sailed with their brides for India, followed nine days later by Gordon Hall, Luther Rice, and Mr. and Mrs. Samuel Nott. Five months later the little band reached Calcutta and began their separate ministries. At the time of departure from America, Judson had been a Congregationalist, but during the voyage his study of baptism in the New Testament convinced him that immersion was the only proper baptism. Upon arriving in Calcutta, he was baptized by William Carey, joined the Baptists, and helped form the Baptist Missionary Union. He settled at Rangoon in Burma in 1813 and began a long missionary service to the Burmese, enduring hostility, imprisonment, and ill health. He produced a translation of the Bible in Burmese, prepared a Burmese grammar and dictionary, and contributed immeasurably to the spirit of toleration and good will toward Christians among the suspicious Burmese.

Luther Rice had also arrived at the same conclusion as Judson concerning baptism, and he also became a Baptist, returning to America in September of 1813 to organize Baptists for support of foreign missions. Largely because of his efforts there was organized in Philadelphia, on May 18, 1814, the General Missionary Convention of the Baptist Denomination in the United States for Foreign Missions. One of the first orders of business for the convention was to establish support for Adoniram Judson, Rice's colleague who was already on the mission field in service. Thus, the impetus of foreign missionary work brought the scattered Baptist churches across America into a Baptist denomination. The Methodist Episcopal Church created its Board of Foreign Missions in 1819, and other denominations soon took a similar step.

The Baptist convention (called the Triennial Convention because it met only every third year) expanded its mission activity significantly until the crisis of slavery. Meeting at Philadelphia in 1844, the convention voted neutrality on the question of slavery, but the "acting Board of Boston" ruled that it would not appoint a slaveholder as a missionary. The Virginia Baptist Mission Society called for a consultative convention to consider the organization of a foreign mission society "to do any sort of denominational work that seemed wise." At that meeting in Augusta, Georgia, May 8, 1845, the Southern Baptist Convention was born. Baptists outside the South continued to operate their several societies until they organized the Northern Baptist Convention in 1907. The name was changed to the

American Baptist Convention in 1950. When the Southern Baptist Convention was organized in 1845, two boards were established: the Foreign Mission Board at Richmond, Virginia, and the Board of Domestic Missions at Marion, Alabama. In 1874 the latter's name was changed to the Home Mission Board, and it was moved to Atlanta, Georgia, in 1882.

e. *David Livingstone* (1813-73). A name that is synonymous with missions and exploration is that of David Livingstone, the famous Scottish missionary doctor and explorer of Africa. Livingstone was born in the industrial west of Scotland, his parents being poor but godly members of an independent church. He had to begin work in a cotton mill at age ten, but he read constantly, taught himself, and attended night school when possible. After his conversion, he professed a strong call to missions and began studies of medicine and theology, finally graduating with degrees in both from Glasgow. He was commissioned by the London Missionary Society in 1840, starting his service in South Africa with the famous Dr. Robert Moffat, whose daughter he married. Livingstone combined his medical missionary work with exploration, discovering Lake Ngami in 1849 and penetrating the upper reaches of the Zambesi River in 1853. His walk across Africa between 1851 and 1856 was recorded in his *Missionary Travels and Researches in South Africa* (1857). This book was immensely popular and began the legend of David Livingstone. In 1857 he broke from the London Missionary Society and led government expeditions into the interior of Africa. After 1866 he continued to explore and minister independently. Presumed lost and dead after total silence for three years, he was located by New York newsman Henry Stanley in 1871, following a sensational search. He died two years later in the African bush. His African companions carried his body back to the coast, and he was buried in Westminster Abbey as one of Britain's revered heroes. Livingstone is still for many the epitome of the dedicated missionary and has retained his place as one of the world's foremost explorers. His greatest contribution, however, may have been in discovering and exposing the horrors of the African slave trade.

f. *Hudson Taylor* (1832-1905) was a Yorkshireman who went to China in 1853 as a missionary with the Chinese Evangelization Society. Because of the weak support system of that organization and his leanings toward Brethren thinking, he became an independent missionary until ill health forced him home in 1860. He completed his medical training, and in 1865 he founded the China Inland Mission. This was the first truly interdenominational foreign mission, and it became the prototype of the "faith" missions that played a prominent part in world evangelization in the nineteenth century.

Hudson Taylor introduced several innovations into the mission enterprise. He determined at the beginning that he would never ask for financial support from anyone but the Lord. His writings on prayer and faith at this point have become Christian classics. He also accepted missionary candidates who had no college training, something no other group had ever done. Then, he insisted that all his missionaries identify completely with the national peoples, even to the use of Chinese clothing and customs. He refused to let the control of mission operations be located back home, insisting instead that the work be directed on the spot. He did, however, keep the people back home thoroughly informed of his work with volumes of reports and inspirational writings. His biography, written by his son and daughter-in-law, Dr. and Mrs. Howard Taylor, rapidly became a classic addition to Christian literature and missions.

g. The Impact of Missions. The far-flung efforts to Christianize the world touched and affected practically every part of the globe during the nineteenth century. The missionary societies and boards were not study groups but dynamic activist organizations. The Leipzig Society, founded in 1836, had thriving missions in India and Africa. The Gossner Society, 1836, also shared the burden of India. The Swedish Missionary Society, 1835, established orphan homes and schools in Lapland. The Norwegian Missionary Society, 1842, sent missionaries to South Africa and Madagascar. The Hermannsburg Missionary Society, founded in 1849 by Louis Harms, had missions in India, Africa, New Zealand, and Persia. The Evangelical Fatherland Association (Swedish), 1856, became involved in the mission work of East Africa and Central India. The Finnish Missionary Society, 1859, was active in Africa and China. In addition to the energetic activity of the societies, practically every mainline denomination established mission boards and sent ambassadors for Christ throughout the world.

Even commercial enterprises became arms of missionary concerns. The early missionary ventures in Southeast Asia were associated with the Dutch East India company, whose chaplains founded many congregations now more than three hundred years old. The Dutch missionary societies concentrated exclusively on Indonesia. The German Rhenish mission developed the renowned Batak church in Sumatra and the church among the Dayaks of Borneo. The American Methodists did outstanding pioneer work among the Chinese and the animists of Borneo. The Presbyterian Church in the United States maintained the chief work in Thailand, and the Christian and Missionary Alliance worked almost alone in Indochina. The work in the Philippines was originally begun with a cooperative effort of several American denominations, but later became mainly associated with the Episcopal Church. Although Robert Morrison had begun his work in Canton in 1807, the greater part of China was not open to missionary work until the treaties of 1842-44. Japan was subsequently opened, and mission work began there in 1859 but was curtailed in 1900 by a strong reassertion of nationalism. The first heroic attempts to introduce Christianity into Korea ended in martyrdom, and it was 1884 before a continuing mission work was established. The Korean churches, however, became rapidly self-supporting and renowned for their Bible study and evangelistic zeal.

Protestant efforts in the Near East and North Africa were mainly directed toward converting the Jews and reviving the ancient eastern churches. Education, medicine, and literature received the strongest emphases. The work was weak, producing very few converts from Islam, and after World War I the Armenian and Nestorian evangelicals who had gained a foothold in Turkey and Iran were destroyed or expelled. The Moravians began work in South Africa in 1737, and some West African missions were founded in the first half of the nineteenth century. The principal work in the vast continent of Africa did not begin, however, until the twentieth century. The problems of working under colonial governments and with the rising new African republics limited the mission in Africa, and the main contribution of the African work was to furnish inspiration for the whole missionary cause through men like David Livingstone and Robert Moffat. In Latin America, the evangelical churches were started largely by groups from the United States. Brazil has the largest number of evangelicals, and Pentecostals form the largest group in Chile.

Besides making converts to Christianity, the bustling missionary activity of the nineteenth century wrought significant cultural changes throughout the world. Hundreds of languages were given a written form for the first time. Western type schools were established, and many governments were led to begin an organized educational system. Orphanages were opened practically everywhere missionaries went. Famine relief and agricultural improvements became standard mission work. Hospitals were founded and public health education inaugurated. Efforts were persistently made to raise the status of women. Missionaries did more to awaken the conscience of the world and abolish Negro slavery than any other group. They also fought the production and sale of opium and any form of forced labor. The presence of Christian missionaries greatly affected and changed the policies and practices of white businessmen who had taken their ventures to foreign countries.

The new missionary fervor also produced marked results back home. It became the stimulus for prison reform, better care for the insane, legislation to improve labor conditions, protection of women and children, and upgrading of housing. One of the most dominant features was the escalation of education, which produced hundreds of new colleges, universities, and seminaries. The political scene was drastically affected as mission-minded Christians encouraged international cooperation to eliminate war and alleviate suffering. The Red Cross came into being in 1863 through the efforts of a Protestant layman of Geneva, Henri Dunant, and bore all the marks of its Christian origin. New hospitals sprang up and flourished, and the new profession of nursing appeared on the scene, largely from Protestant sources. The devout Roman Catholic, Louis Pasteur, made dramatic advance against disease. Benevolence and philanthropic giving became a big business as wealthy Christians were moved to dedicate their money and services for the public good. Of course, the basic result of all mission effort, at home or abroad, was individual religious experience of a vital faith. Men and women were being converted to the Christian faith by the thousands in every part of the world, with far-reaching results in every endeavor of human relationships. The churches had begun to discover the dynamics of Jesus' teaching on dying to self, for the more they gave away and sent to foreign lands, the more their own churches and homelands were enriched both spiritually and materially.

2. CATHOLIC MISSIONS

Roman Catholic missionary efforts had never ceased, but they had reached a low ebb by 1800 in the very throes of the French Revolution. Slowly these efforts began to revive and again became vigorous and expansive.

a. Orders and Organizations. The counterpart of the Protestant missionary societies was the establishment of new orders and organizations for evangelism and missions. The Sacred Heart Congregation for the Propagation of the Faith directed a worldwide mission effort, supported by An Institute for the Propagation of the Faith, formed in Lyons in 1822 for the purpose of raising money for the total mission effort. Eventually the National Society for the Propagation of the Faith was established in most countries where Catholicism was strong.

In 1815 three priests founded the Society of the Missionaries of France with the purpose of reviving the religious life in the parishes. That same year saw the inauguration of the Marianists, who directed schools and workshops. In 1816 the Oblates of the Immaculate Virgin Mary began with the express design of being missionaries among the de-Christianized population (those who had fallen away during the revolution). The Society of Mary (or Little Brothers of Mary) was also begun that year, originally to carry on missions among the de-Christianized people of France, but by 1836 it had obtained papal approval and had expanded its operations to the islands of the Pacific. The Congregation of the Most Precious Blood was founded in 1815 to upgrade the quality of Christianity in the papal states, but it spread throughout Italy and eventually to North America. In 1835 Vincent Mary Pallotti began the Catholic Apostolate, a name soon changed to the Pious Society of Missions, which included laymen, priests, and sisters. It spread throughout Italy, Germany, the Americas, and Africa. In 1841, a converted Jew, Jacob Libermann (baptized Franz Maria Paul) started the Congregation of the Immaculate Heart of Mary with the objective of doing missions among the Negroes of Africa and America. It was joined in 1848 by the Society of the Holy Ghost, which had been working chiefly in the French colonies.

The Society of Missionaries of Our Lady of Africa (the White Fathers) was begun in 1868 to witness to the Moslems of North Africa. The congregation of the Immaculate Heart of Mary which was founded in Belgium in the 1860s had extensive missions in Inner Mongolia and the Belgian Congo. The Society of the Divine Word was a German order, started in 1875 for training and sending Germans to non-Christians, with its first mission being in China. Many communities of women were instituted for foreign missions, the largest being the Franciscan Missionaries of Mary, which was begun by "Mary of the Passion," a popular missionary to India. The Society of St. Vincent de Paul was organized in 1833 to enlist laymen for the care of the sick and the poor. Many novel and supportive orders appeared as the desire to be involved in mission causes spread throughout the church.

b. Countries and Continents. In the sixteenth and seventeenth centuries the Catholic Church had accomplished a major missionary endeavor in the Far East. The eighteenth century was a period of crisis for Catholic missions, with the suppression of the Society of Jesus in 1773, the French Revolution in 1789, and the Napoleonic era. The nineteenth century, however, witnessed a revitalized mission thrust around the world. In 1825, the Picpus Fathers were given the responsibility for Oceania, the costal areas of central and southern Africa, which had received Catholic missions as early as the sixteenth century. In 1836, the Marists assumed the work in central Oceania and New Zealand. In Australia, Irish immigrants began to introduce Catholicism. The West African mission was entrusted to the Holy Ghost Fathers in 1845; the evangelization of Central Africa was begun in 1846, and that of East Africa in 1878 by the Jesuits and the Society of Missionaries of Africa. At the close of the nineteenth century there were a half million Catholics in Africa south of the Sahara.

Japan opened its doors to Christian missions in 1858, after being closed for 250 years. Freedom of religion was proclaimed in 1889, and in 1891 an archbishopric was established at Tokyo, with Japanese Catholics numbering 50,000. Missionaries returned to Korea in 1881, but persecution had severely reduced the number of Catholics there. Persecution had also decimated the church in China, but work was renewed in 1844, and by the end of the century there were more than 800,000 Catholics in China. However, the antiforeign Boxer Rebellion of 1900 led to a general massacre of Chinese Christians and of the missionaries. In Vietnam, Christianity was relatively free from 1802 to 1825, and Catholics baptized 316,000. But persecutions from 1833 to 1862 claimed at least 90,000 victims. The establishment of French rule in 1883 brought religious peace and at the end of the century there were more than 700,000 Vietnamese Catholics. In Thailand, mission work which had been halted by persecution was resumed in 1826, and mission activity began in Cambodia in 1850 and in Laos in 1899. The work was revived in India in 1832, and by 1896 there were three Indian bishops for the Syro-Malabar communities.

Also, in the nineteenth century, Catholic missionaries and clergy were very influential in the shaping of Central and South America. In Argentina, sixteen of the twenty-nine who signed the declaration of independence in 1816 were clergymen. In Peru, the constituent assembly of 1822 had fifty-one members, twenty-six of whom were priests. The president was Francisco Javier Luna Pizarro, later archbishop of Lima. Independent Mexico did not get its first archbishop until 1840. Brazil had gained independence in 1822, and the Catholic Church was relegated to a subordinate position. With the establishment of the republic in 1889, the new government disestablished the church. Yet, despite the many setbacks to the church in Brazil, by the mid-1960s Catholics numbered more than sixty million.

In the United States, the Roman Catholic Church experienced phenomenal growth during the nineteenth century. In 1800 it was a small denomination of fewer than 50,000 members, and by 1860 it had become the largest single denomination in America with more than three million members. A Catholic press appeared, and Catholic schools increased rapidly. The church in Europe sent over a constant stream of priests and missionaries to assist the American churches. Financial subsidies came from the French Society for the Propagation of the Faith and other organizations. The main contribution from Europe, however, was immigrants by the hundreds of thousands, the large majority being Irish and German Catholics until the 1890s. Then many came from central Europe. The new world had become a new stronghold for the oldest denomination in Christendom.

Catholic missions among the American Indians had been launched as early as 1565 at St. Augustine in Florida, 1598 in New Mexico, and 1691 in Arizona. In 1769, Franciscans under the inspired leadership of "Father Juniper" Serra moved into California and created a series of twenty-one missions along the coast. By 1820 they had reported the baptism of over 50,000 American Indians.

The Catholic Church in the United States did very little in sending missionaries or funds to foreign missions until the twentieth century. It was itself a recipient of substantial financial aid from European mission societies, and was not able to start contributing to the Society for the Propagation of the Faith until after the Civil War. The American church officially entered foreign mission service in 1893, when overseas mission territories were first assigned to United States religious orders. In 1911 there was established the Catholic Foreign Mission Society of America, the

Maryknoll Fathers, sending missionaries from the United States and Canada to Asia, Africa, and Latin America. With the church in Europe devastated by depression and two world wars, the American church emerged in the second half of the twentieth century as the chief source of financial support for Roman Catholic foreign missions.

In summary, the nineteenth century saw the Roman Catholic Church making a strong recovery after the storm of the French Revolution. Old religious orders were revived and new orders established, many of them for the purpose of fostering mission activities. A large portion of the laity was stirred to give financial support to the worldwide extension of the faith. Roman Catholic missions attained a greater geographical and numerical expansion than ever before. Catholics were represented in more and more lands, knit together and directed by the central authority in Rome. Missions had become a way of life for both Protestants and Catholics.

C. MOVEMENTS: FRIENDLY AND UNFRIENDLY

The nineteenth century saw the birth of numerous movements which affected the shape and ministry of Christianity. Some of the movements were supportive of traditional Christianity and strengthened the base and field of the churches. There were several strong movements, however, which posed a threat for orthodoxy and traditionalism. Then, there appeared movements and causes which carried both a bane and a blessing for religion, making some aspects of Christianity stronger and virtually destroying other traditional practices. All of these movements made churchmen realize that religious issues can be addressed, even created, outside the official church body, and that the church was no longer insulated and isolated from independent movements, friendly or unfriendly.

1. THE OXFORD MOVEMENT
The movement which did more than any other to revitalize religion in England in the mid-nineteenth century was the Oxford Movement, so called because most of its original founders were associated with Oxford University. The movement was also known as the Tractarian Revival, because of the powerful influence of the published tracts; as the Anglo-Catholic revival, because of its tendencies back toward Rome; and as "Puseyism" after Dr. E. B. Pusey, one of its most dominant leaders.

a. Causes for Concern. The Oxford Movement was a reaction against the French Revolution, the Age of Reason, and the reforming tendencies of Liberalism in both church and state. The Oxford Movement was actually part of the larger spiritual and cultural movement known as Romanticism. The Oxford men abhorred the concept of "reason alone," and reflected the characteristics of the Romantic poets and novelists. Toleration and Liberalism had combined to produce conditions which were alarming to many Anglican churchmen. The Unitarians, who had been established in London by Theophilus Lindsey in 1772, were excused by parliament in 1813 from subscribing to belief in the Trinity. On the other hand, many groups which subscribed to most of Anglican dogma rebelled at the imposition of any human standard. The Congregational Union of England and Wales declared in 1833 that it "reserved to everyone the most perfect liberty of conscience." A prominent English poet, Lord Byron, condemned bondage to institutions, and the newly founded London University required no religious tests. Anglican church leaders began to be deeply concerned. Their reasoning was that either the Church of England was the established church or it was not, and if established, it should be honored as such.

The matter came to a head in 1833 when parliament passed the Church Temporalities Bill which sought to reform the Irish church by reducing the number of bishoprics and redistributing the rich, ecclesiastical incomes. Although the bill was really a moderate and reasonable measure, it was seen as one more move to transform the church into a dutiful servant of a secular state.

On July 14, 1833, John Keble, a gifted poet, a brilliant scholar and Anglican minister, preached a sermon on the subject before His Majesty's Judges of Assize at Oxford. Keble entitled his sermon "National Apostasy," and expressed alarm that the state had taken upon itself, without the church's consent, to determine episcopal authority, even episcopal existence. This sermon was considered by Newman and others to be the beginning of the Oxford Movement. Before the end of the month a group of like-minded scholars and clergymen, all of Oxford, began to meet, first to organize an Association of Friends of the Church, and then to prepare the way for the famous *Tracts for the Times,* which contained the fundamental principles of the Movement.

b. John Henry Newman (1801-90) wrote the first tract, and became the inspirational leader of the Oxford Movement, eventually writing twenty-four of its tracts. Newman was a brilliant classics scholar and don at Oriel College, Oxford, and was greatly influenced by the Anglo-Catholic ideas of Hurrell Froude, a young Anglican clergyman, who insisted that the church must recover ancient practices dropped by the Reformers, such as fasting, celibacy, confession, and reverence for the saints. Froude's sentiments were succinctly stated in his assertion that "the Reformation was a limb badly set; it must be broken again to be righted." Froude died at the age of thirty-three, but left indelible impressions on Newman, Keble, and their colleagues. In 1832 Newman experienced a near fatal fever and deep spiritual crisis during a Mediterranean tour, out of which came his famous hymn "Lead, Kindly Light." He returned to England just in time to hear

Oxford University, a 1923 aerial view. Oxford has been called the Cradle of England's Culture. The Oxford Movement, a reaction to the state's assumption of ecclesiastical powers, began, according to John Henry Newman, with a sermon preached at Oxford by John Keble. (The Bettmann Archive)

Keble's sermon, and immediately identified himself with the Oxford Movement.

He became vicar of St. Mary's, Oxford, and his sermons (published as *Parochial and Plain Sermons*) had a profound influence on the religious life not only of Oxford but of the whole country. In his tracts, Newman asserted the thesis of the "via media," the belief that the Church of England held an intermediate position between Romanism on one hand and Protestantism on the other. He developed this thesis more fully in *Lectures on the Prophetical Office of the Church* (1837) and in his *Lectures on Justification* (1838). Many of Newman's colleagues, however, were not satisfied with the "middle way" and moved more and more toward Rome.

Tract Eighty, written by Isaac Williams and titled *On Reserve in Communicating Religious Knowledge*, incited the clergy and brought charges of Jesuit leanings. Williams was subsequently denied the Poetry Professorship at Oxford because of his Tractarian affiliation.

The Bishop of Oxford began to accuse openly the Tractarians of Romish practices, and Newman constantly clashed with him over such matters as the Oxford memorial to Reformation martyrs and the establishment of an Anglo-Prussian Protestant Bishop of Jerusalem. These blatant recognitions of Protestant heretics were against all that the Oxford Movement was fighting for.

Newman began to move more and more toward Rome as possessing the marks of the true church. He was not willing to abandon the Church of England, but it became necessary for him to demonstrate that Anglicanism was compatible with Romanism. The stumbling block was the Thirty-nine Articles, the foundation of Anglicanism. In 1841, in his famous Tract Ninety, entitled *Remarks on Certain Passages in the Thirty-nine Articles*, Newman attempted to show that the Articles were compatible with the doctrine of the old church, and especially with the doctrines of the Council of Trent. The tract produced an uproar and was condemned by the Heads of Houses at Oxford. The Bishop of Oxford imposed silence on Newman, forbidding him to write any more tracts. Newman resigned his position at St. Mary's and retired to the village of Littlemore. Completely disillusioned with the "via media" of Anglicanism, he joined the Roman Catholic Church on October 9, 1845. Soon after, he published his *Essay on the Development of Christian Doctrine* in defense of his change of allegiance. He was ordained a Catholic priest in 1847 and was appointed rector of Dublin University in Ireland. He became involved in several Catholic publications, and in 1864 a controversy with Charles Kingsley resulted in his *Apologia pro Vita Sua*, explaining his theological position and gaining him great favor throughout Catholicism. In 1870 he published the *Grammar of Assent*, the work which contains much of his finest and best developed thought. In 1877 he was elected an Honorary Fellow of Trinity College, and two years later he became a cardinal. A brilliant master of English, Newman published works in theology, philosophy, patristics, church history, poetry, and novels.

c. *After Newman.* Following Newman's example, the defections to Rome
were numerous. Henry Manning, Archbishop of Chichester and a
prominent tract writer, joined the Roman Catholic Church in 1851, became
Archbishop of Westminster, and in 1875 was made a cardinal. William G.
Ward, a zealous newcomer to the Anglo-Catholic cause, wrote an
intemperate outburst against the Church of England in his book *The Ideal
of a Christian Church.* He was stripped of his university degrees and
demoted from his Oxford position. In 1845 he joined the Roman Catholic
Church, taught at St. Edmund's at Ware, and edited the *Dublin Review.*
Others joining the Catholic Church included Robert Wilberforce and
Frederick William Faber, the noted hymn writer, who founded the Order of
the Brothers of the Will of God, popularly known as the Wilfridians.

Newman's secession had been a severe blow to the Anglo-Catholic
movement, but two of its strongest leaders, John Keble and Edward B.
Pusey, remained. Pusey was the Regius Professor of Hebrew at Oxford
and a man of vast influence in the University and in the world outside
clerical Oxford. Pusey's scholarly tracts gave a theological erudition and
responsibility to the Oxford Movement but also cost him dearly professionally. In 1844, Dr. Pusey was suspended from preaching at the
University under charges of teaching transubstantiation and other heretical
doctrines. With Newman gone, Pusey became the dominant leader of the
Oxford Movement, so much so that contemporaries referred to the
movement as "Puseyism." He continued to defend the doctrine that the
Church of England had the power of the keys and the authority of priestly
absolution. In 1860 he wrote his famous letter to Keble on *The Church of
England a Portion of Christ's One Holy Catholic Church, and a Means of
Restoring Visible Unity.* In it he expressed his belief that union with Rome
was not prevented by the official teachings of the Catholic Church, but by
unofficial devotions to Mary and by the popular ideas of purgatory and
indulgences. Although constantly attacked by other Anglicans, Pusey
remained staunch in his advocacy of high church Anglicanism and had a
lasting effect on the ceremonial and worship aspects of the Church of
England.

2. THE YOUTH MOVEMENT

While the scholars and ecclesiastics were debating high church Anglicanism,
evangelicals and independents were assuring the future of their causes
with programs for and education of their youth. We have already noted
that the Sunday school movement was a direct product of the evangelical
revival in England, and it was almost exclusively directed toward the
young. The Sunday schools were originally set up to give religious and
moral instruction to the poor and to teach the illiterate to read and write;
but they proved adaptable to the children of other classes, and soon spread
to various denominations as a means of religious education. They flourished
among Protestants in the English-speaking world, and were especially

successful in the United States. Sunday schools were put to use by missionaries in Asia, Africa, and the Americas, and in 1889 the first of a series of World's Sunday School Conventions assembled in London. In 1907, the World's Sunday School Association was organized at the convention in Rome. The Sunday school movement depended chiefly on laymen and women as voluntary unsalaried teachers, but was generally supported by the clergy.

Another movement which focused on youth was the Young Men's Christian Association, begun in 1844 by George Williams, a London draper. Deeply influenced by the books of Charles G. Finney, Williams began to witness to his fellow clerks at work. During a prayer meeting in William's room, twelve young men banded together to win other young men to the Christian faith. They called themselves the Young Men's Christian Association, a name which has remained to this day. Similar groups began to spring up in the British Isles, Canada, and the United States. In 1855 the World's Alliance of the Young Men's Christian Association was established. The Y.M.C.A. began with emphasis on evangelism, prayer meetings, and Bible study, but soon added educational, social, and athletic facilities to promote wholesome activities for young men and boys. The stated object of the Y.M.C.A. is to win young men and boys for Jesus Christ by uniting them in fellowship through activities designed to develop and train their powers of the body, mind, and spirit, and to enable them to serve God and others. The greatest growth of the Y.M.C.A. has been in the United States where many large plants have been built. Its sister organization, the Young Women's Christian Association, first appeared in Germany and Great Britain in the 1850s, but like the Y.M.C.A., its greatest growth has also been in the United States. The World's Young Women's Christian Association was organized in 1894.

The Y.M.C.A. movement in the United States produced one of the most remarkable men in the entire history of Christianity, John R. Mott (1865-1955). Soon after graduation from Cornell University, he became a traveling secretary of the student department of the Y.M.C.A. He became one of the original founders of the Student Volunteer Movement and was the chairman of its executive committee from 1888 until 1920. From 1920 he served as General Secretary of the International Council of the Y.M.C.A. While associated with the Student Volunteer Movement, Mott, a Methodist layman, inspired thousands of youth to become evangelists and missionaries under the watchword, "the evangelization of the world in our generation." In 1895, he joined Karl Fries of Sweden in founding the World's Student Christian Federation. Countries from around the world invited Mott to organize their youth, the Anglican Church made him a canon, the Russian Orthodox Church granted him a doctor's degree, and in 1946 he received the Nobel Peace Prize. Mott's primary interests were youth, evangelism, and church unity. It seems significant that the man who united the young people of the churches to Christianize the world gave the last of his years to efforts to unite the churches.

3. THE ECUMENICAL MOVEMENT
Although John Mott became the spearhead of the ecumenical movement of the twentieth century, he was not its fountainhead. The spirit of ecumenism had been brewing since the founding of the missionary societies and Bible societies in the late eighteenth and early nineteenth centuries. An organization known as the Evangelical Alliance was put together in 1846 in a collective effort of several denominations to counteract the Tractarian or Oxford Movement and to strengthen Protestantism. The Alliance formed branches in several countries and quickly became an international organization. It met in Berlin in 1857, in Geneva in 1861, in Amsterdam in 1867, and in New York in 1873. The Congregational clergyman Josiah Strong was the general secretary of the American branch, but when his efforts to lead the Alliance into social action programs failed, he organized the Federal Council of Churches of Christ in America in 1908. By 1950 the Federal Council of Churches represented 144,000 local congregations with 32 million members in three dozen different denominations. That year it merged with other interdenominational groups to establish the National Council of Churches of Christ in the United States. Similar federations had also developed in France, Switzerland, Germany, New Zealand, Great Britain, Canada, and Australia.

Several denominations developed organizations to unite the many branches of their particular faith. The Church of England accomplished this through its Lambeth Conferences, the most notable occurring in 1888. The Presbyterians united in the World Alliance of the Reformed Churches in 1875. The International Congregational Council met for the first time in 1891. The Ecumenical Methodist Conference first convened in 1901, and the Baptist World Alliance was organized in 1905.

Missionaries of the various denominations had early begun to see the need and results of cooperating with other communions on the mission field and urged cooperative efforts on the part of the churches back home. As early as 1819 the secretaries of several foreign mission boards formed an association for "mutual counsel and fellowship." In 1866 the first of a series of Continental Missions Conferences was held, and in 1885 a standing committee representing all the Protestant missionary societies of Germany was constituted. A general Dutch missionary conference met for the first time in 1887, and the Foreign Missions Conference of North America first convened in 1895.

On a worldwide scale, the first of a series of missionary conferences met in Liverpool in 1860, followed by meetings in London in 1878 and 1888. The meeting in New York in 1900 was attended by delegates from 162 mission boards from America, the British Isles, and Europe. The most notable assembly was the World Missionary Conference, held in Edinburgh in 1910. This assembly became a landmark in the history of the ecumenical movement. John R. Mott had been one of the key figures in calling and organizing the Edinburgh conference, and presided at most of its sessions. He became chairman of the Continuation Committee and then of the International Missionary Council. Other prominent leaders at the 1910 conference were Joseph H. Oldham, Charles H. Brent, William Temple, V. S. Azariah, and Cheng Ching-yi. In addition to the Continuation Committee and the International Missionary Council, "Edinburgh 1910" produced the World Conference on Faith and Order and the Universal Christian Council for Life and Work. The latter two bodies merged to form the World Council of Churches in 1948, the progress of which will be followed in our section on Christianity in the twentieth century.

4. EVOLUTION AND AGNOSTICISM

While dedicated missionaries were carrying the gospel around the world, and while diligent churchmen were strengthening and uniting the home bases, there were other movements abroad which threatened the very essence of the religion which the missionaries and churchmen preached and defended. A new militant secularism raised many questions about the validity and value of religion. Even some religious writers assailed traditional theories which seemed to be at variance with the new findings of science. In 1838, Charles Hennell, an English disciple of D. F. Strauss, published *Inquiry Concerning the Origin of Christianity*, using scientific methods to question the inerrancy of the Scriptures. In 1860, Benjamin Jowett of Oxford published an essay on "The Interpretation of Scripture," suggesting a science of hermeneutics which allowed, among other things, a place for progressive revelation. These assaults on traditional views of inspiration and revelation had an immediate emotional impact on church leaders and Christian scholars, but the most lasting impact on the entire civilized world was the bombshell known as the theory of evolution.

a. Charles Darwin (1809-82) published his *Origin of Species* in 1859 and his *Descent of Man* in 1871, in which his theory of evolution challenged the Bible as a source of truth and also questioned the claim of human moral uniqueness. Darwin, a naturalist who had also studied medicine at Edinburgh and theology at Cambridge, had been preceded in his thinking by others. In 1795 James Hutton published his *Theory of the Earth* which raised doubts about the creation account in Genesis. In the 1830s Charles Lyell published *The Principles of Geology*, in which he argued that the present state of the earth's surface had been brought about by a long and gradual development. In 1844 this idea of evolution was extended from geology to all of animal life in Robert Chamber's *The Vestiges of the Natural History of Creation*. Chambers paved the way for Darwin as he connected

Charles Darwin (1809-1882) Author of The Origin of Species, *a work which set in motion the evolution controversy.* (Religious News Service Photo)

the idea of creation according to natural law with the idea of evolutionary development. He was, however, theistic, maintaining that the uniform law of natural development was the very expression of God's mind and plan. While Darwin was impressed by Chambers' book, the work which suggested to him the idea of natural selection as an explanation for the origin of the species was Malthus' *Essay on Population.*

Darwin first read Malthus' essay in 1838 and worked for the next twenty years on his theory of natural selection, or the survival of the fittest. Intending to write a multivolume presentation of the thesis, he was stopped abruptly in his research when he received an essay from the biologist A. R. Wallace, expressing ideas very similar to Darwin's. He immediately agreed to publish a joint paper with Wallace on the subject. Darwin gave up his plan for a massive work, and in late 1859 he published *On the Origin of Species by Means of Natural Selection, or the Preservation of Favored Races in the Struggle for Life.* What disturbed Darwin's critics most was the inference that man was not different in kind from other members of the animal class. Darwin did not deny the extraordinary difference between man and the brutes, but he was convinced that the differences were of degree and not kind. In 1871 Darwin wrote *The Descent of Man* specifically to make plain his views on the place of man in natural history. As most people feared he would, Darwin concluded that man and apes had a common ancestor. The die was cast, and the religious and intellectual world exploded.

b. Outrage and Enthusiasm. Public reaction to the theory of evolution ranged from open hostility to supportive enthusiasm. Among Christian leaders, Charles Haddon Spurgeon pronounced the theory a monstrous error which would be ridiculed within twenty years. In the United States, eleven states passed laws against the teaching of evolution. Eleven thousand clergymen and 137,000 laymen signed statements reaffirming their belief in the inerrancy of Scripture. The issue became creation versus evolution, an issue which has not yet died down. The issue eventuated in the famous Scopes trial of 1925, when a Tennessee teacher was tried for breaking the law by teaching evolution. The trial attracted worldwide attention, especially since the prosecuting attorney was William Jennings Bryan, former Democratic nominee for the presidency of the United States and at one time Secretary of State. The state supreme court eventually reversed Scopes' conviction.

There were some clergymen who were cautiously in favor of Darwinism when it first appeared. Frederick Temple, who later became Archbishop of Canterbury, saw evolution as a way of strengthening the Christian idea that the world is not just a series of accidents. Henry Drummond, a science professor at the Free Church College in Glasgow, renowned for his sermon on the thirteenth chapter of 1 Corinthians, applied the idea of the survival of the fittest in a unique way, demonstrating that care and compassion such as one finds in the gospel are essential to human survival. He also wrote the popular *Natural Laws in the Spiritual World* (1883) in an effort to bridge the gap between science and religion. John Fiske's *Cosmic Philosophy* of 1874 accepted evolution "as God's way of doing things." Henry Ward Beecher referred to himself as a "cordial Christian evolutionist." Lyman Abbott's *Theology of an Evolutionist*, 1897, portrayed evolution as God's providence and progress in history. Herbert Spencer came out strongly for evolution, declaring it as a manifestation of the Absolute on which all knowledge is dependent. Evolution and historical progress became linked together in the theological works of Brook F. Westcott, Joseph B. Lightfoot, Fenton John A. Hart, and Julius Wellhausen. In 1889, a group of English scholars led by Charles Gore published *Lux Mundi*, a tremendously popular book which attempted to reconcile science and religion by accepting both the Bible and Darwin.

Thomas Henry Huxley, the renowned biologist, not only agreed with Darwin but published many of his own works which gave the evolutionary theory the stamp of scientific orthodoxy. In 1863 there appeared his *Zoological Evidences as to Man's Place in Nature*, a defense of man's descent from the lower animal world, and in 1868 he delivered a lecture on "The Physical Basis of Life" in which he expounded on "agnosticism," a word which he coined to express the state of not knowing. Rather than denying God outright as did the atheist, Huxley said that he just did not know and was not in a position to know. His concept of neutrality—agnosticism— appealed to many intellectuals and became a popular fad. As Darwinism increased in its expression and popularity, all kinds of people tried to jump on the bandwagon. Capitalists such as Andrew Carnegie and J. D. Rockefeller appealed to evolution to justify the growth of big business. The most profound and far-reaching interpretation of the theory came when Karl Marx declared that Darwin had provided the biological basis for communism.

5. COMMUNISM AND SOCIALISM

Among the many upheavals, revolutions, expansions, and movements of the nineteenth century was the appearance of revolutionary theories for the social organization of mankind. After 1815 the old order had been partly restored, but the revolutionary tide surged forward again in the 1830s and 1840s. This time the expression was not in violence as with the French Revolution, but in ideology. "Democracy" became the key word of the new sociology, sometimes being in harmony with prevailing governments and sometimes hostile to them. Most of the theories which attacked the status quo were known as socialism, which in general stood for economic and political equality for all. Early advocates of communities where all things were distributed equally included Robert Owen, Comte Henri de Saint-Simon, and Louis Blanc.

a. Karl Marx (1818-83). The most outstanding socialist of all was Karl
Marx, who became the architect of world communism. Karl's father was
Herschel Marx, a German Jew, a brilliant lawyer, political liberal,
philosophical rationalist, and admirer of Voltaire and Kant. Nevertheless, for
prudent reasons, he was baptized a Protestant Christian in 1816, and
young Karl was baptized in 1824. At seventeen Karl entered the University
of Bonn to study law but transferred the next year to Berlin, where he
came under the influence of Strauss, Bauer, and Feuerbach. He became a
radical new Hegelian before moving on to the University of Jena where he
received his doctor's degree in 1841. The following year he began his long
and stormy career as a journalist. When the Prussian government
suppressed the daily paper of which he was editor-in-chief, he went to Paris
and joined a group of fellow radicals. It was in Paris that Marx met his
friend and collaborator, Friedrich Engels, the son of a wealthy industrialist,
who had come under the influence of the English socialists and the radical
Hegelians in Germany. In 1845, Marx and his friends were expelled from
France, at which time he moved to Brussels where he wrote eleven "Theses
on Feuerbach." Although Marx acknowledged that he received his view of
naturalistic humanism from Feuerbach, he signaled a break with Feuerbach
and the emergence of his own socioeconomic critique of religion with "The
German Ideology," written with Engels in 1845-46.

In 1847 Marx joined the International Communist League and was
commissioned with Engels to write a declaration of aims for the League's
Congress held in London. The result was *The Communist Manifesto*,
published in 1848, which came to be regarded as the birth-cry of modern
socialism. In 1864 Marx founded the International Working Men's
Association, and in 1867 he published the first volume of *Das Kapital*,
which was called "the Bible of the working class." The second and third
volumes were published posthumously by Engels in 1885 and 1894. With
the publication of *Das Kapital*, it was clear that Marx had rejected both
Hegel and Feuerbach. Neither the Absolute Spirit nor nature was the basis
of reality, which was to be found only in matter. The history of mankind,
then, is simply the history of how men are related to material things.
According to Marx, that history is moving in the direction of the communist
society, when private property will be a thing of the past and the state will
manage everything. The political program had already been articulated by
Marx and Engels in *The Communist Manifesto*. They called upon the
downtrodden masses to unite in revolution to overthrow the existing order
and usher in a new society. The *Manifesto* climaxed with this ringing
challenge: "The Communists disdain to conceal their views and their aims.
They openly declare that their ends can be attained only by the forcible
overthrow of all existing conditions. Let the ruling classes tremble at a
communist revolution. The proletarians have nothing to lose but their
chains. They have a world to win. Working men of all countries, unite!"

Karl Marx (1818-1883) the architect of world communism. (Historical Pictures Service, Inc.)

b. The Attack on Religion. For Marx, religion, especially the Christian religion, was one of the central problems in the hated capitalist system. In *Das Kapital,* he contends that Christianity and capitalism go hand in hand. In his view, they are the theoretical and practical forms of man's egoistic alienation. Religion is not only "the opiate of the people" (one of his most famous statements), but it is also "the illusory sun which revolves round man as long as he does not revolve around himself." This, to Marx, is the destructive thing about religion, in that it keeps a man from his real self. As early as his doctoral dissertation he had written about "the consciousness of man as the supreme divinity," and later he asserted that "man makes religion, religion does not make man . . . religion is the self-consciousness and self-feeling of man who has either not yet found himself or has already lost himself." The only way to free man from the bondage of religion is to change his social conditions which produced the religion. In the *Manifesto,* he insists that "man's consciousness changes with every change in the conditions of his material existence, in his social relations and in his social life." Thus, "intellectual production changes its character in proportion as material production is changed." It is not enough to simply criticize religion. It must be decisively overthrown. Marx very clearly called for an overthrow of all social and economic relations that so debase and enslave men that he requires the solace of religious illusions. His thesis was simple: take away the social conditions that produce illusions about another world, and the religious need for such otherworldly illusions will wither away. In his eleventh thesis on Feuerbach, he said, "The philosophers have only interpreted the world, in various ways; the point, however, is to change it!"

Of course, all socialists were not anti-Christian, and some were frankly Christian. J. F. D. Maurice (1805-72), one of the period's most influential theologians, founded the Christian Socialist Movement, and the Working Men's College, with support from Charles Kingsley, the noted author and rector at Eversley. However, even when socialism did not attack Christianity, it tended either to ignore it or drift away from any Christian roots it once had. The philosopher Auguste Comte (1785-1857) introduced the philosophy of "positivism" which built upon Marx's idea of material or economic determinism. Comte formulated the famous Law of Three Stages to describe how the mind of man progresses from a theological to a metaphysical stage before arriving at the last and final positive stage. A thoroughgoing empiricism, positivism holds that all true knowledge consists either of matters of fact or logic and mathematics. The economist John Stuart Mill (1806-73) translated Comte's ideas into a utilitarian religion of humanity, advocating utilitarian (only what is useful for relieving human need) programs as the means of realizing a truly democratic society. In America Henry George (1839-97) recommended public ownership of lands to protect the rights of the laborers on the land. In 1888 Edward

Bellamy wrote about a utopian society in *Looking Backward, 2000-1887*. Socialist parties were formed throughout the world, and in the second half of the nineteenth century they became prominent in the politics of several European countries.

The influence of Marx's ideas upon world history is epochal, and it is yet unpredictable what final effect Marxist materialism will have on Christianity. Our chapter on the twentieth century will trace the ongoing communist revolution as it impinges on Christian history. Suffice it to say here that its effect has been immense on the institutional church in Russia, China, and parts of Europe and Africa. Although Christianity has by no means been stamped out in those Communist dominated countries, Marx's critique of Christianity has been the most devastating attack the faith has suffered in the modern world.

6. THE SOCIAL GOSPEL

During the 1880s, the American clergy almost unanimously opposed socialism. After 1890, however, many Protestant leaders adopted ideas from socialism. The Society of Christian Socialists was organized in 1889, accepting many of the ideas of socialism, but repudiating its antireligious bias. George D. Herron (1862-1925), professor at Iowa College, was a popular lecturer on the subject of transforming society into the kingdom of God. His popularity waned when he became fanatical in insisting that the institution of private property was un-Christian. He had, however, opened the discussion of the possibility of the kingdom of God being this-worldly rather than other-worldly. The exponents of social Christianity offered a social doctrine of the kingdom of God, which was not redefined as the community which includes all who are ethically interested, whereas the church had long been more exclusively defined as the community of the redeemed. The man who gave classic formulation to this new concept of the kingdom of God was Walter Rauschenbusch, the leading theologian of social Christianity.

a. Walter Rauschenbusch (1861-1918). Rauschenbusch was the son of a German Baptist professor in the Rochester Theological Seminary. When his plans to go to India as a missionary were thwarted, Walter took the pastorate of the Second German Baptist Church in New York City, on the edge of Hell's Kitchen, one of the city's infamous slums. After eleven years of facing the horrors of poverty and economic insecurity, Rauschenbusch emerged to become the founder of social Christianity in America. From 1897 he served on the faculty of the Rochester Theological Seminary, but his primary role was as the leader of the "Social Gospel" movement. Like Ritschl, he was disinterested in metaphysics and dogma and stressed the historical Jesus as the initiator of the divine community, the kingdom of

God. This kingdom, as preached by Jesus, was not a purely internal, spiritual possession of the individual, but was involved with relationships and responsibilities for our fellowman. Among Rauschenbusch's works are *Christianity and the Social Gospel* (1907), *Christianizing the Social Order* (1912), and *A Theology for the Social Gospel* (1917).

In formulating his theology for the social gospel, Rauschenbusch stressed that the kingdom of God is always both present and future, that the kingdom of God is humanity organized according to the will of God, that the kingdom must be the purpose for which the church exists, that all problems of personal salvation must be considered from the point of view of the kingdom, and that the kingdom is not confined within the limits of the church.

Rauschenbusch led a host of outstanding thinkers and activists who sought to make ethics central in religion. Washington Gladden joined him in calling for unions, cooperatives, profit sharing, and socialization of railroads and utilities. Josiah Strong contended that greed for money was corrupting the nation. Harry F. Ward led the successful effort to get a social creed stated in the purposes of the Federal Council of Churches. Ernst Troeltsch published his monumental *Social Thinking of the Christian Churches*. These and many others contended that Christianity had deep ethical obligations to society, and they sought to state these obligations in terms of the theology of their day. They denounced concentration of wealth, unrestrained competition, and the policy of "laissez faire." The social gospel was not a revolutionary attack on capitalistic society from the outside, but a reforming effort from within.

b. The Gospel of Wealth. On the other hand, there was a strong movement of individualism which appeared to be the very antithesis of the social gospel. The Industrial Revolution had brought a burgeoning economy and made many wealthy overnight. Some Christians interpreted this as God's way of equipping certain individuals to do great good in the name of Christ. Few moved as far up the scale of wealth and power as did the Scottish immigrant, Andrew Carnegie (1835-1919). In 1889, Carnegie wrote his famous essay "Wealth," in which he formulated the gospel of wealth, which rested on the doctrines of the free individual, unfettered competition, the acquisition of wealth by industry and thrift, and the stewardship of the strong. He expressed the view that a man's life should fall into two periods—the first, that of acquiring wealth; the second, that of distributing it in such a way that the surplus would be used for the general welfare. Carnegie led the way, and many financial giants followed in setting up charitable foundations, endowing churches and other institutions, and establishing new universities and colleges. Philanthropy enjoyed an unprecedented boom, and by the end of the century hundreds of millions of dollars were being given annually. John D. Rockefeller (1839-1937) became one of the nation's leading philanthropists, setting up a vast network of charitable organizations. The Dodge family and Arthur and Lewis Tappan were only a few of the wealthy who became legends for their generosity.

Philanthropy, however, was not the acceptable remedy for many crusaders. In his *Progress and Poverty* (1879), Henry George protested the fact that many Americans were growing poorer while others were becoming fantastically wealthy. The period saw labor strikes, reform movements, the agrarian revolt, the Populist movement, and the Progressive movement, all with the motivation of restructuring society along the lines of Christian socialism. It was a time of transition and tension for the churches, which seemed faced with an endless variety of conflicting ideologies and theologies. The greatest conflicts occurred when the church was called upon to reevaluate its temporal positions in the light of the spiritual truths it preached. The most severe test was encountered when the church realized it was an integral part of the society which must resolve the seething issue of human slavery.

7. THE ABOLITION MOVEMENT

Slavery had been a thorn in the side of civilization since the middle of the fifteenth century. After Roman slavery was converted into serfdom, slavery was virtually unknown in western Europe until 1442, when the Portuguese began to bring back Negro slaves from their explorations along the west coast of Africa. Soon after, the need for labor in the colonies of North and South America created a large market for slaves. For more than three centuries, a vast trade market flourished, dominated in turn by Portugal, Spain, Holland, France, and England. Prior to 1800, more slaves (in excess of fifteen million) than English or European colonists crossed the Atlantic, mostly to the West Indies and South America.

a. Antislavery Reformers. Although it was known to be cruel and inhuman, the slave system strangely aroused little protest until the eighteenth century. The rationalists of the Enlightenment criticized slavery for its violation of the rights of man, and Pietists and evangelicals condemned it for its brutality and un-Christian principles. The dynamics of the antislavery movement were mainly religious, with the Quakers making the first significant protest (as early as 1671). The first American antislavery tract was written by the Quaker George Keith in 1693. The New Jersey Quaker John Woolman led a quiet but persistent personal crusade against slavery, and by 1800 all Quakers had ceased to hold slaves.

In Britain, Granville Sharp won a decision in the Somerset case (1772) that West Indian planters could not hold slaves in England, since slavery was contrary to English law. Between 1777 and 1804, all of the states north of Maryland abolished slavery. In the South, vigorous antislavery societies persuaded owners to free their slaves voluntarily. These victories, however, had little effect on the centers of slavery, the great plantations of the deep South, the West Indies, and South America. It became apparent that the major thrust to abolish slavery would have to be the prohibition of importing African slaves into the British colonies and the United States. English Quakers began to campaign for such a prohibition in 1783, and by 1787 had formed the Abolition Society.

The man who led the antislavery movement for more than thirty years in England was the tenacious Anglican evangelical William Wilberforce. As a member of parliament from 1780 to 1825, he persistently presented parliamentary resolutions against the British slave trade. He influenced prominent politicians, especially his close friend William Pitt, who was prime minister (1783-1801 and 1804-06). After two decades of fighting against extremely powerful opposition, Wilberforce, Thomas Clarkson, and the abolition forces succeeded in 1807 in passing a bill to abolish the importation of slaves to the British Colonies. A distinct influence in the passing of the bill was the Clapham Sect, a group of evangelicals who met informally in Clapham Commons to caucus and discuss means of effecting social reform. Wilberforce was a ringleader of the Clapham Sect, which gained much of its insight and evidence against slavery from its involvement in mission enterprises.

One of the mission enterprises of the Clapham Sect was a colony in Sierra Leone in West Africa. The colony had three aims: to provide a haven for freed slaves, to prove that economics did not dictate the need for the slave trade, and to be a base for missionary operations in Africa. After the abolition of the British slave trade in 1807, the colony became a haven for intercepted slave ships from all over West Africa. The capital of Sierra Leone was appropriately named Freetown. The spread of Christianity in West Africa began chiefly with the freed slaves of Sierra Leone. Inevitably the causes of mission and abolition of slavery marched together. By the end of the eighteenth century, opposition to slavery and interest in missions had become the twin identifying marks of the evangelical Christian. Throughout the mission field there developed the doctrine of the "Three Cs"— Christianity, commerce, and civilization, which held that the interests of all three lay in the same direction. Christianity and slavery were irreconcilably opposed. The most effective way of stopping the slave trade was to provide an attractive commercial substitute, agriculture and the accompanying technologies, which in turn ushered in "civilization." The Church Missionary Society proved the effectiveness of the "Three Cs" in its Yoruba mission, and old chiefs admitted that the mission-sponsored cotton industry brought more benefits than all the slave trade. The greatest promoter and prophet of the "Three Cs" was the legendary missionary, David Livingstone, who insisted that the Arab slave trade could be strangled by alternative commerce. As expected, the slave owners were deeply hostile to missionary

One of the good effects of the so-called "social gospel" was the advent of numerous antislavery movements. Shown is a Virginia slave auction before the time of the Civil War. (The Bettmann Archive)

activities and precipitated prosecution and maltreatment for many missionaries of various denominations.

Although parliament had abolished the importation of slaves in 1807, nothing had been done about the emancipation of those already in slavery. So, abolitionists began to concentrate on this problem, and the Antislavery society was formed in 1823, with Thomas Fowell Buxton taking the leadership in place of the aging Wilberforce. After another long and dramatic contest, parliament finally passed a law in 1833, freeing all slaves in the British colonies after a six-year period of apprenticeship, with compensation to their owners. In 1848, France also abolished slavery in its West Indian colonies. The French revolutionists had proclaimed emancipation in 1794, but the proclamation led to bloody and violent uprisings in Haiti, and Napoleon had reestablished slavery in 1802. Now, in the middle of the nineteenth century, the nations of Europe had removed the blight of slavery once and for all, and moral, political, and economic factors had united in the victory.

b. Slavery and Abolition in the United States. Across the Atlantic, the slavery question was yet to have its most severe impact as it tore a nation apart and sent Christianity reeling in distress. The Constitutional Convention of 1787 had almost placed a prohibition of the slave trade in the Constitution, but in a conciliatory move with the southern states, the convention agreed to a provision that congress could prohibit the trade after twenty years. So in 1807, the same year that Britain passed its prohibition, the United States also outlawed the importation of slaves. But, also like Britain, nothing had been done about the slaves already in America. The total population of America in 1790 was about four million, about one-eighth of which were slaves. The invention of the cotton gin by Eli Whitney in 1793 multiplied cotton exports by 200 percent within the next ten years, and the number of slaves was doubled. By 1860 there were more than four million slaves in America, the number of the total population seventy years earlier.

The abolition movement in America began in earnest in the 1820s with the tactics of gradualism and persuasion. When these approaches reaped little results, the antislavery forces turned to a more militant policy in about 1830, denouncing all slaveholders and demanding immediate abolition by law. The most extreme and conspicuous leader of the aggressive approach was William Lloyd Garrison, editor of the *Liberator* and founder of the American Antislavery society (1833). Theodore Dwight Weld was a burning evangelist, who with his "seventy apostles" carried the gospel of antislavery to pulpits throughout the North. The activity of free Negroes, such as Frederick Douglass, were significant and influential on the movement. The abolitionists ran James G. Birney for president on the Liberty Party ticket in 1840 and 1844. Harriet Beecher Stowe, daughter of the noted Preacher Lyman Beecher, and wife of Lane Seminary professor, Calvin Ellis Stowe, expressed her avid abolitionist views in one of the most influential novels of all time, *Uncle Tom's Cabin* (1852). The book by the "crusader in crinoline" sold over 500,000 copies and hardened Americans in the North against slaveholders.

In 1859 John Brown, a fanatical abolitionist, led a small armed band into Harpers Ferry, the site of a federal armory in northeastern West Virginia, in the first step of his plan to establish a stronghold where escaping slaves might gather and defend themselves. He attacked and took the armory, held sixty leading men of the area hostage, and held off the local militia before being overpowered by a force of U.S. Marines under Col. Robert E. Lee. Brown was tried for murder, slave insurrection, and treason to the Commonwealth of Virginia, and was hanged on December 2. Although the Harpers Ferry raid was a total failure for Brown, it heightened the sectional feelings that were already brewing toward war. Southerners paid little attention when Abraham Lincoln expressed disapproval of the raid, but they reacted violently when New England intellectuals such as Ralph Waldo Emerson and Henry David Thoreau spoke of Brown as a hero and a saint. After the war started, Union soldiers took up the song "John Brown's Body," and his soul went "marching on," making him a legendary martyr to the cause of freedom.

c. The American Civil War. While the issue of slavery was a religious issue at heart (which we will discuss later), abolition presented practical and political problems. Most important politically, it threatened the harmony of North and South in the Union, and it ran counter to the Constitution, which left the question of slavery to the individual states. In the practical arena, the South was convinced that its economy was fundamentally dependent upon slave labor. Three-fourths of the four million slaves in 1860 were employed in cotton growing in the lower South. Slaves outnumbered whites in both Mississippi and Georgia, and 50 percent of the white population of Mississippi owned slaves. Many Northerners shared southern apprehension about total abolition, but they opposed the spread of slavery into new territories. It was this issue of the new territories remaining free that sparked the famous debates between Abraham Lincoln and Stephen A. Douglas in their contest for the U.S. Senate. It was also the issue which gave birth to the Republican party, which Lincoln joined. During his debates with Douglas, Lincoln declared in 1858 that "A House divided against itself cannot stand. I believe this government cannot endure permanently half slave and half free." He insisted that the civil liberties of every U.S. citizen, white as well as black, were at stake. Lincoln lost the election for the senate seat, but became the frontrunner for the presidential election of 1860. With the Republicans solidly united and the Democrats drastically divided, Lincoln was elected President of the United States on November 6.

Six weeks after the election of Lincoln, the state of South Carolina seceded from the Union (December 20, 1860), and claimed possession of the forts in Charleston harbor and all other U.S. property in the state. Between January 9 and February 1, six other states followed South Carolina's example. Delegates from the seceding states met at Montgomery, Alabama, organized the Confederate States of America, and set up a provisional government with Jefferson Davis as president. On April 12, 1861, Confederate batteries in Charleston harbor opened fire on Ft. Sumter, which had refused to surrender to South Carolina's demands. "Then, and thereby," Lincoln informed Congress, "the assailants of the Government began the conflict of arms." Shortly thereafter, three more states seceded from the Union. The total population of the eleven seceding states was less than half the population of the nineteen states that remained in the Union.

The Civil War was fought savagely for four years, ending with the surrender of Gen. Robert E. Lee at Appomattox Court House, Virginia, on April 9, 1865. Approximately four million troops took part in the war. Total casualties exceeded 617 thousand dead (359 thousand from the North and 258 thousand from the South), and 375 thousand wounded. The war resulted in the preservation of the Union, important alterations in the Constitution, far-reaching social and economic changes, and the abolition of slavery. Before the end of the war, Lincoln freed the slaves in the rebellious states with the Emancipation Proclamation of 1863, and after the war the thirteenth amendment to the Constitution abolished slavery completely throughout the nation. Lincoln had saved the Union and freed the slaves, but he did not live to execute his plans for reconstruction. On Good Friday evening, April 14, 1865, just five days after Lee had surrendered, John Wilkes Booth shot Lincoln as he sat in Ford's theater in Washington. Early the next morning, Lincoln died.

d. The Role of the Churches. As already indicated, economics and states' rights were major issues in the Civil War, but as we have also already indicated, the religious and moral question of slavery became the core issue over which the abolitionists were willing to risk the very life of the Union. There was no doubt in anyone's mind that the battle centered around the validity of religion, and especially the Christian religion. But it was not a case of Christians fighting barbarians or infidels. It was a tragic instance of committed Christians on both sides convinced of the righteousness of their respective stands, employing Scriptures from the same Bible to justify their cause, and praying to the same God for victory. The churches played a major role in dividing the nation, and ministers were among the most fanatical on both sides. This was the period of revivalism and the evangelical movement, and both sides claimed large numbers of "conversions" among their troops. There was a tremendous increase in churchgoing and prayerfulness. Each side was inspired by some of the greatest preachers and finest theologians in America's history. This great divergence of spirit did not come instantly with the war; it had been building for years.

Charles G. Finney, the great revivalist, was an early abolitionist, and had fired many young preachers with the cause, including T. D. Weld, mentioned earlier, and Charles Stuart, who backed Weld financially. In 1832, Weld was influenced by the president of Western Reserve College, Charles B. Storrs, and two professors who were staunch abolitionists. He enrolled in Lane Seminary in Cincinnati in 1833, where the famed Lyman Beecher was president. In that same year the Christian philanthropists, Arthur and Lewis Tappan, were assisting W. L. Garrison in setting up the American Antislavery Society and pouring their money into militant efforts for immediate emancipation. In a letter to the American Colonization Society, Arthur Tappan charged that colonization was "a device of Satan, with a single motive to perpetuate slavery." This was indicative of the attitude of many outstanding laymen and clergymen, especially in the North.

Southern Christians began to close ranks after the black preacher Nat Turner led the Virginia slave revolt of 1831, in which fifty-seven whites were killed. Preachers and prominent churchmen in all denominations held slaves, such as Richard Furman (Baptist), William Capers (Methodist), Robert L. Dabney (Presbyterian), and Leonidas Polk (Episcopalian). An estimated two-fifths of all the Baptist clergymen in South Carolina owned slaves. In 1822, the South Carolina Baptist Association had produced a biblical defense of slavery, and in 1844 John England, Bishop of Charleston, provided a similar one for southern white Catholics. In 1843, over 1,200 Methodist clergy owned 12 thousand slaves, and 25 thousand Methodist church members owned more than 200 thousand slaves. In 1836, the General Conference of the Methodist Episcopal Church met at Cincinnati and censured George Storrs and Samuel Norris for their antislavery activities, and expressed unqualified opposition to "modern abolitionism." The New Hampshire and New England Conferences, however, were thoroughly infiltrated with abolitionism. After several splinter groups had formed, the Methodists split over the issue in 1844. After severe internal conflicts the Baptists split in 1845, and the Presbyterians suffered a series of splits from the mid-1840s to the outbreak of the war. Congregationalists and Unitarians, most of whom were in the North, did not split, and the Quakers, who were almost unanimously against slavery, did not split. For various reasons other major church bodies did not take a stand. The American hierarchy of the Roman Catholic Church, for example, never did pronounce slavery as an inherent evil.

Those churches which did split went to battle on opposing sides, like the feudal bishops of old. Leonidas Polk, the Episcopal bishop of Louisiana, immediately entered the Confederate army as a major-general. Thomas March, bishop of Rhode Island, told Union soldiers, "It is a holy and righteous cause in which you enlist. God is with us. The Lord of hosts is on our side." The Southern Presbyterian Church resolved, 1864: "We hesitate not to affirm that it is the peculiar mission of the Southern Church to conserve the institution of slavery, and to make it a blessing both to master and slave." The astute Southern Presbyterian theologian, Robert Lewis Dabney, called on God for a "retributive providence" which would demolish the North, and he called on the southern clergy to arm themselves with Scripture to uphold the theological validity of slavery. Benjamin Morgan Palmer, minister of the First Presbyterian Church of New Orleans, exclaimed, "We defend the cause of God and religion, for the abolition spirit is undeniably atheistic." But the New Haven theologian Theodore Thornton Munger declared that it was the Confederacy that was "in league with hell." Henry Ward Beecher said that the southern leaders "shall be whirled aloft and plunged downward forever and ever in an endless retribution." Thus, Christians on one side were saying that Negro slavery was divinely ordained, and Christians on the other side were contending that it was contrary to the Christian gospel.

After the war, the world was curious to see how the divided churches would relate to each other again. Some northern churchmen wanted to destroy the dissident southern branches. An influential church paper, the *Independent*, wrote: "The apostate church is buried beneath a flow of divine wrath; its hideous dogmas shine on its brow like flaming fiends; the whole world stands aghast at its wickedness and ruin. The Northern church beholds its mission." The historical fact, however, is that nothing really drastic happened in the postwar relationship between the churches. As in the Middle Ages, once peace had come, the rival churchmen came together again. Southern Methodists, Baptists, Presbyterians, and Lutherans continued to proclaim loyalty to the lost cause, but otherwise they resumed standard Christian attitudes and activities. The liberated slaves formed their own churches, usually Baptist and Methodist, which encompassed a third of the black population by 1900. In summary, it can be said that the Civil War was the most religious episode in all of American history, and in the process Christianity was placed under an almost intolerable strain. Yet, Christianity not only survived but actually flourished. One surprising development was that the fundamental denominational organizations of Christian life had not been seriously affected, even among those denominations which had split.

8. DENOMINATIONALISM
For nineteen hundred years the various expressions of Christianity had been weaving variegated patterns of theology and ecclesiology, of doctrine and organization. The nineteenth century is usually referred to as the "great

century" of Christianity because of its worldwide expansion. But it was also a great century in the final coalescing of many strains into definitive and identifiable bodies.

a. Older Denominations. Denominationalism had its most active period of organization and recognition, as emerging groups began to believe that their beliefs and programs were distinctive enough to warrant an entirely new religious body. At the same time, the old mainline denominations enjoyed renewed vigor and expanded growth.

(1) The Roman Catholic Church experienced marked contrasts throughout the world. While it was the century of great expansion, it was also a time when Catholic control was losing ground in some of its traditional strongholds. More new religious orders arose between 1815 and 1914 than in any previous hundred year period, but at the same time thousands of monastic houses were dissolved and their properties confiscated in what had been strong Catholic countries. In the New World, Catholic schools multiplied and flourished, but in western Europe the education of youth by the church was greatly reduced. The distinction between church and state became sharper and produced contrasting results. In some countries it meant more freedom for the church, as the state was forbidden to regulate religious affairs such as the appointment of bishops. In others, it meant the loss of territory and prestige for the church.

Ultramontanism, which was already discussed, strengthened the power of the pope and underscored orthodox positions. But this only served to cause many involved in the new political, economic, social, and intellectual movements to regard the church as their enemy. The popes of this period were typical of the contrasting (sometimes contradicting) status of the church. Leo XII (1821-29) negotiated favorable concordats with most of the important nations, including Protestant states. Catholics were given complete freedom in England. Yet Leo XII widened the theological breach with Protestants by his strong denunciation of Bible societies, calling their translations the "devil's gospel." Then in 1826 he announced that "everyone separated from the Roman Catholic Church, however unblamable in other respects his life may be, because of this sole offense, that he is sundered from the unity of Christ, has no part in eternal life; God's wrath hangs over him."

Pius IX ruled the church for almost a quarter of a century, and at first he instituted reform measures that made him appear liberal. He soon, however, took a hard-line stand against the trends of change and pronounced his severe *Syllabus of Errors.* He also proclaimed as dogma the immaculate conception of Mary, called the Vatican Council, and affirmed papal infallibility. Leo XIII, pope from 1878 to 1903, brought the office to the highest prestige it had known since the Reformation. In his efforts to reconcile the church with civilization he established and improved relations with many world governments. He upheld the dignity and rights of the state, whether monarchy or republic, and emphasized the compatibility of Catholic teaching with a moderate democracy. Leo XIII became known as "the workingman's pope" because of his stand for the right of workmen to organize labor unions and for the state to assume responsibility for the welfare of workingmen. At the same time he rejected the idea that public education is the duty of the state. He also denounced freedom of the press and the attitude that all religions are equal. He insistently blamed the Protestant Reformation for the deplorable aspects of the political and intellectual life of Europe.

Pius X (pope from 1903 to 1914) was the first pontiff in several hundred years to be deemed worthy of sainthood. He took a leading part in the social issues of the time, especially the labor problem. He took a strong stand against theological modernism and attempted a series of difficult reforms within the church. He was venerated as a saint during his lifetime, beatified in 1951 and canonized in 1954. None of the popes of the century were corrupt and two or three were exceptional leaders.

At the outset of the nineteenth century, Roman Catholics were a small minority in the United States, but by 1914 they had become the largest single Christian body, counting between fifteen and seventeen million in their fold. This rapid growth was due mainly to the flood of immigrants that poured into America during the nineteenth century. At first, the exploding Catholic population was ministered to by priests and missionaries trained in Europe, but by 1900 there were thirty-seven Catholic theological seminaries in the United States. The Catholic University of America was opened in the nation's capital in 1889. For the training of children, the church erected and maintained its own schools, separate from the public school system; and by 1910 there were a million and a quarter pupils in these parochial schools. The American Catholic Church was united as one ecclesiastical body loyal to Rome, which exercised control through the congregation for the Propagation of the Faith. In 1908, the United States was removed from that status, indicating that the Catholic Church in America had come of age and was no longer considered a mission enterprise. The vast growth of Catholicism in America resulted in the building of great numbers of churches, schools, monasteries, seminaries, colleges, universities, hospitals, and orphanages. A Catholic fraternal order, the Knights of Columbus, was born, and Catholic periodicals were numerous. Although no great Catholic theologians emerged during this period, there were some outstanding bishops, the most eminent being James Gibbons, who became Archbishop of Baltimore in 1877 and was made a cardinal in 1886, the second from the United States to gain that position.

(2) The Eastern Orthodox Church. After the great schism of 1054, the eastern division took the official name of the Holy Orthodox Catholic

Apostolic Eastern Church, usually referred to as the Eastern Church or the Greek Orthodox Church. Its present membership embraces about 7 percent of the world's population. The basic doctrines of the Eastern Church are practically the same as those of the Roman Catholic Church except, of course, the Eastern Church does not recognize the supremacy of the pope but is governed by patriarchs. In 1589 the Russian Orthodox Church had been made a national church with its head having an equal role with other patriarchs in the Eastern Church. In 1650 a new patriarch, Nikon, sought to reform certain rituals and was opposed by Avvakum and a group known as "Old Believers," who formed a separate church after Avvakum was burned at the stake in 1682. Under the reign of Peter the Great, the patriarchate was abolished and the Russian church was completely subjugated to the imperial power and placed under the control of a lay synod, whose members did not even need to be Christians.

Although the church was a virtual department of state until 1917, a revival within this state church began soon after 1800. Church schools were developed, and the Russian Bible Society was organized in 1813. The czar himself, Alexander I, had a profound religious experience through the influence of Swedenborg's writings. When Russia expanded its territory to include a large part of Poland, many Uniates (eastern churches in communion with Rome) became thoroughly Orthodox, and when Russia extended its authority over the Aleutians and Alaska, eastern missionaries followed this advance, baptizing many aborigines. In 1811 the historian Karamzin published the slogan, "one God, one czar, one people," supporting a policy similar to the Ultramontanism of the Roman Catholic Church. The Russian Orthodox Church began a policy of ruthless suppression and persecution. It banished to Siberia a sect called the Doukhobors, who believe that Jesus Christ is not God but a man possessing divine reason in the highest degree. The Stundists ("devotional hour") and Baptists were severely persecuted. The Lutherans in Estonia and Lithuania were systematically suppressed, and millions of white Russians and Ukranians were forcefully absorbed into the church. About 1880 a strong reaction began on the part of students returning from German universities where they had been introduced to the socialist ideas of Karl Marx. A social religion began to form which had a strong appeal to the industrial workers in Russia. A different reaction was that of a Gnostic-Spiritualistic Christianity, expressed in the books of Leo Tolstoy (1828-1910), who severed relations with the Orthodox Church and promoted his own brand of Christianity which opposed state, church, and nationality.

In the United States, thousands of immigrants were members of some branch of the Orthodox Church. Greeks, Romanians, Bulgars, Serbs, Syrians, and Albanians were among them. Following the Armenian massacre by the Turks in the 1890s, many of them fled to America, along with Jacobites and Nestorians. Congregations were organized and clergy obtained to minister to all of these. When the United States purchased Alaska in 1867, the Orthodox Church continued but without the financial support of the Russian government, and the bishop moved his residence to San Francisco in 1872. New York City became the headquarters of the archiepiscopate in 1905, and until 1914 it had jurisdiction over all the Orthodox in the United States.

(3) Lutheranism was caught up in controversy during most of the nineteenth century. Since the Reformation, many efforts had been made to unite the Lutheran and Reformed churches, but without success. Between 1815 and 1830 unions of the two confessions were achieved in several German states, mainly in Prussia. The unions were enforced by the state which also introduced a new liturgy, which led to dissension and secession. Restraint on the seceders was lifted by the new king, and in 1841 the Lutheran congregations came together and constituted the Evangelical Lutheran Church in Prussia. Eventually, there evolved the Lutheran Free or Old Lutheran churches of Germany.

Lutheranism also underwent a theological controversy in the middle of the nineteenth century, dividing the participants into "New Lutheranism" and "Old Lutheranism." As a reaction against the liberalism of the day, "New Lutheranism" was a confessional conservatism which emphasized the sacraments, and held that purity of doctrine is the sign of the true church, that there can only be one true church, and that since the Lutheran Church has the full truth in its confessions of faith, it is therefore the one true church. They also tended to identify the kingdom of God with the church. "Old Lutheranism" was a revival of Pietism which had similarities to the evangelical awakenings. It stressed personal commitment, evangelism, and foreign missions.

The conflicts between confessionalism and evangelicalism thwarted the attempts to unite Lutheranism in America. Before 1820 American Lutherans did not have a general body, but in that year the General Synod was formed. During the Civil War, the Lutherans in the southern states separated and formed the United Synod of the South. In 1867, the General Council was constituted, and the Synodical Conference was organized in 1872 for conservative or "strict" Lutherans, its largest constituent body being the Missouri Synod. Carl Ferdinand Wilhelm Walther was the leader in creating the Missouri Synod in 1847. This strong synod was shaped by the strict Lutheranism of the prerationalistic period. It emphasized the autonomy of the congregation and built a network of parochial schools. Its Concordia Seminary in St. Louis became a bastion for conservative Lutheranism. By the time of Walther's death (1887), the Missouri Synod had more than fifteen hundred congregations, reached from the Pacific to the Atlantic, and supported many foreign missions.

In 1918 dozens of once-autonomous synods formed the United Lutheran Church in America. Trends toward union have continued, resulting in three approximately equal-sized groups: (1) the American Lutheran Church, formed in 1961 by amalgamation of American Lutheran Church, Evangelical Lutheran Church, United Evangelical Lutheran Church, and Lutheran Free Church; (2) the Lutheran Church in America, formed in 1962 and made up largely of United Lutheran Church in America, Augustana Evangelical Lutheran Church, Finnish Evangelical Lutheran Church, and American Evangelical Lutheran Church; and (3) the Evangelical Lutheran Synodical Conference of North America, the old Synodical Conference which was formed in 1872 and includes the Missouri Synod and the Synod of Evangelical Lutheran Churches.

(4) Anglicanism in the British Isles went through the evangelical awakenings, the Oxford Movement, the rise of Liberalism, and Christian socialism during the nineteenth century. The many controversies, however, gave new life to the Church of England, bringing about the erection of hundreds of new churches and the plunging of clergy and laity alike into social problems caused by industrialization and urbanization. The Church of England also entered a vast foreign mission program, supported by some of the most successful missionary societies in Christendom. The average quality of the clergy in education and devotion was higher than ever, and bishops around the world were knit together in a close fellowship through the Lambeth Conferences.

In the United States, the Church of England became the Episcopalian Church with the advent of the American Revolution. Episcopalianism got off to a slow start because of its ties to England, its formal type of worship, and the shock of disestablishment. Generally representing the educated and upper economic groups, the Episcopalians had little interest in the revival movements but did organize seminaries and missionary societies in the second and third decades of the nineteenth century. After 1835, a new zeal for evangelism and expansion resulted in a new spurt of growth. The High Church, Low Church, and Broad Church parties of England had their counterparts in America, and the Oxford Movement decisively involved some American Episcopalians. There was no schism in Episcopalianism during the Civil War. The southern bishops were simply marked absent at the meeting of the General Convention in 1862, and after the war they were seated again.

(5) Congregationalists were the spiritual descendants of the Independents of the seventeenth and eighteenth centuries, but they had suffered from the spiritual lethargy of the eighteenth century. Then they surged forward in the nineteenth century on the rising tide of the evangelical revival. They gained thousands of new members, many from the Church of England, through their stirring revival preaching. Midweek prayer meetings were begun, and lay preaching increased. New academies and colleges were established, and in 1832 a national organization, known as the Congregational Union of England, was formed. The famed and highly

successful London Missionary Society was supported chiefly by Congregationalists. Some of England's most outstanding clergymen were Congregationalists.

The fate of Congregationalism in America did not run as smoothly. Although it had been in the forefront of the fight for independence, it was the object of resentment for obtaining state support of its clergy in Massachusetts, Connecticut, and New Hampshire, a practice that was not completely eliminated until 1833. Skepticism and liberalism took its toll on Congregationalism, with entire churches becoming Unitarian. With the appointment of Henry Ware as professor of theology in 1805, Harvard University became sympathetic to Unitarianism. However, Congregationalism received new life with the Second Great Awakening early in the century. Many new churches were founded, schools and seminaries were begun, and missionary societies were formed. The Civil War did not affect the fellowship of the Congregationalists because they had no churches in the South and were all strongly opposed to slavery. They were, however, affected by the renewed rationalism that followed the war, and many clergymen became liberal theologically and emphasized almost exclusively the social aspect of the gospel. Congregationalists were leaders in the ecumenical movement and united with the Evangelical Protestant Church in 1925 and the small body known as the Christian Church in 1931, changing their name to Congregational Christian Churches. In 1961, the United Church of Christ was established by the union of the Congregational Christian Churches with the Evangelical and Reformed Church.

(6) Unitarianism, which severely weakened the Congregationalists, rejects the doctrines of the Trinity and the divinity of Christ and teaches the impersonality of God. Unitarians became organized communities in the sixteenth and seventeenth centuries in Poland, Hungary, and England. John Biddle (1615-62) is generally considered the father of Unitarianism in England, but Theophilus Lindsey formed the first Unitarian denomination in 1773 when he seceded from the Church of England. In 1844 the Unitarians received a large boost with the Nonconformist Chapels Act, which allowed the Unitarians to keep chapels where twenty-five years' usage could be proved. In America the first definitely Unitarian congregation was formed in 1785 and the Unitarian denomination was organized in 1825. In the nineteenth century, Unitarianism's greatest advance was the inroads it made in Congregationalism. The ethical and philosophical aspects of Unitarianism were articulated eloquently by the renowned writer and lecturer, Ralph Waldo Emerson (1803-82).

(7) Calvinism, the Reformation theology of John Calvin, produced the Reformed and Presbyterian churches. The name Presbyterian refers to the form of government used by Reformed churches and came to be the name used by all Reformed churches of British background. During the

nineteenth century, Prussia united the Reformed and Lutheran churches in its territories. Generally, the Lutherans overshadowed the Reformed churches; but after 1861 there was a revival of Reformed strength with the rise of inner mission work, foreign missions, youth work, and other social activities. In 1798 the Dutch Reformed Church was disestablished, but in 1816 King William I reorganized the church and renamed it the Netherlands Reformed Church. Several splits led to the formation of the Christian Reformed Church (split in 1834, renamed in 1869) and the Reformed Churches of the Netherlands in 1892. The first Reformed church of continental European background to be established in North America was the Dutch Reformed Church. After the Revolutionary War, the church became wholly independent, and by 1820 the Dutch language had ceased to be used. The name Reformed Protestant Dutch Church was changed in 1867 to Reformed Church in America. Large migrations of Dutch people to the United States in the nineteenth century added greatly to the church. Several unsuccessful attempts have been made since the early nineteenth century to unite the Reformed Church in America with other Reformed and Presbyterian bodies in the United States.

Scotland has been thoroughly Presbyterian since 1689 when William and Mary came to the throne. Several different bodies formed during the eighteenth and early nineteenth century. The most severe inner struggle came in 1833-43 between the moderates and the evangelical group, which had been greatly strengthened by the revivals and the Sunday school movement. When the government in London supported the moderates on legal grounds, the disruption led by Thomas Chalmers took place. Chalmers (1780-1847) was a professor of divinity at Edinburgh and chairman of the church extension committee of the Church of Scotland. He and 474 ministers and thousands of lay people formed the Free Church of Scotland, free of state control, free of patronage, and zealously evangelistic. All but one of the missionaries of the Church of Scotland, and most of its best scholars, joined the Free Church. In 1876 the majority of the Reformed Presbyterians joined with the Free Church, and in 1900 the Free Church and the United Presbyterians merged to form the United Free Church of Scotland. In spite of severe doctrinal controversies, Presbyterianism solidified and grew during the century in Ireland, Wales, Canada, Australia, and New Zealand.

The first Presbyterian synod in the United States was formed in 1716. The revivals of the Great Awakening split the Presbyterians in 1741 but they were reunited in 1758. In a dispute, which began in 1801 over a Plan of Union with the Congregationalists, they split again into the New School (for union) and the Old School (against union). The Congregationalists then decided not to consummate the union in 1852. The New School was extremely active in frontier missions, education, and benevolent work. Union Theological Seminary in New York became their great center. During the Civil War the New School was active on the side of the North. The Old School Presbyterians built a well-organized denomination, with Princeton Seminary as its focal point. They made great strides in missions, colleges, and Sunday schools before being torn asunder by the Civil War. After the war, the Presbyterian Church in the United States was formed in the South, and the Presbyterian Church in the U.S.A. was formed in the North.

(8) Methodism as such was relatively new in the nineteenth century but had deep roots in Anglicanism. While still a minister of the Church of England, John Wesley had called his preachers together for the first Methodist conference in 1744. After Wesley's death in 1791, discussions and negotiations began which eventuated in the complete separation of Methodists from the Church of England in 1836. The new denomination grew rapidly, with churches, schools, academies, and children's homes springing up throughout England. Methodism was a strong leader in the social consciousness of the century, tackling such evils as unfair treatment of laborers, poverty, slavery, and alcoholism. A serious split occurred in 1811 with the formation of the Primitive Methodist Church, and in 1857 the Wesleyan Reformers and the Wesleyan Methodist association joined to form the United Methodist Free Churches. In 1907, the Bible Christians, the Methodist New Connection, and the United Methodist Free Churches combined to form the United Methodist Church. Throughout the nineteenth century Methodism spread to Canada, Australia, the West Indies, Ceylon, India, West Africa, South Africa, Burma, Canton, Hong Kong, and China.

In the United States the Methodist Episcopal Church was organized at Baltimore, Maryland, in 1784. Francis Asbury and Thomas Coke were chosen joint superintendents (bishops). In 1792 a general conference was formed which became a delegated body in 1808. Several schisms occurred in American Methodism. One early dissenting group formed the small Christian Church, which in turn united with the Congregationalists in 1931. Another group pulled out and joined the movement which later became the Disciples of Christ. In 1830, the Methodist Protestant Church was formed as a nonepiscopal body. Prior to the Civil War, an extreme abolitionist wing organized the Wesleyan Methodist Church of America in 1843. The most serious division over slavery came in 1845 when the Methodist Episcopal Church, South, was organized after Bishop James O. Andrew had been suspended for marrying a slaveholding wife. Steps toward reuniting the North and South began in 1870 and continued arduously and tenaciously, until finally in 1939 the two Episcopal Methodisms and the Methodist Protestants united to form the Methodist Church.

(9) Baptists took the forefront of the mission movement of the late eighteenth century, and their mission and evangelistic thrust has continued unabated to the present day. On the home fronts, unity and organization have needed and received focused attention. In England, Baptists were

sharply divided between Particular Baptists (Calvinist views of election) and General Baptists (Arminian views of universalism), who were finally brought together in 1891 to form the Baptist Union of Great Britain and Ireland. A leader in that merger was John Clifford who was also prominent in the founding of the Baptist World Alliance in 1905. Outstanding English Baptist preachers included Charles Haddon Spurgeon and Alexander Maclaren. Baptist churches were first established in Australia (1831) and New Zealand (1854) by missionaries of the English Baptist Missionary Society, but Baptist work had begun as early as 1763 in Canada.

The first Baptist church in the American colonies was established by Roger Williams in 1639 at Providence, Rhode Island. Baptists have been strong leaders for religious freedom throughout America's history. The General Convention of Baptists was formed in 1814 to support the missionary work of Adoniram Judson. Primarily as a result of the slavery controversy, the Southern Baptist Convention was organized in 1845, devoting most of its energies to foreign missions. The Northern Baptist Convention was formalized in 1907, changing its name to the American Baptist Convention in 1950. Today there are more than fifty Baptist bodies in the United States with more than thirty million members. The four major conventions are the Southern Baptist Convention, the National Baptist Convention, U.S.A., Inc., the National Baptist Convention of America, and the American Baptist churches. The multiplicity of Baptist groups in the United States is accounted for by the nineteenth-century controversy over slavery, by racial and national differences, and by differences of opinion on questions of doctrine and organization. Baptists are found throughout the world, with major communities especially in the British Isles, Russia, India, Burma, Zaire, Brazil, and Canada.

(10) Quakers had the distinction of being the first Christian body officially and actively to campaign against slavery, so naturally the abolition movement and the resulting Civil War were not problems for the fellowship of the Society of Friends. There was, however, a split within American Quakerism during the nineteenth century over the debate between Quietism and the evangelical tradition. In the eighteenth century, Quakers in both Great Britain and America were dominated by Quietism, which stressed passive spirituality and condemned all human effort. The influence of Wesleyanism, however, brought the energy and theology of the evangelical movement within the society. In Great Britain, tension prevailed between Quietism and evangelicalism throughout the nineteenth century, with the Quietists representing their conservative posture by maintaining the society's peculiarities of speech and dress. A group of ultraevangelicals known as the Beaconites organized their own society for a time before joining the Plymouth Brethren.

In the United States, the scene was even more complex. The "liberal" evangelicals were vigorously opposed by the Quietist conservatives led by

Elias Hicks, whose emphasis on the "Christ within" seemed to set aside the authority of the Scriptures and the historical person of Christ. The Hicksites created considerable controversy both in England and America and eventually brought about the schism of 1827. Ironically, the evangelicals became known as the "orthodox" group and the Hicksites became known as the "Liberal Branch." Although Hicks had supported the methods of Quietism, he had become doctrinally unorthodox when he rejected the doctrine of the person of Christ and the atonement. The "orthodox" and "liberal" groups began to have separate annual meetings with various types of organizations and purposes. Finally, in 1936, the differences appeared to be resolved and most American Quakers participated in forming the American Friends Fellowship.

b. New Denominations. In addition to the growth and structuring of the older groups, a great host of new denominations sprang up during the nineteenth century. Some of them were in the mainstream of normative Christianity, and some of them reflected radical tendencies, which caused many to question their right to be ranked with Christian bodies. We are able to review here only a few of the more prominent new denominations.

(1) The Catholic Apostolic Church was begun in 1832 mainly through the efforts of Edward Irving; hence members of this group are often called Irvingites. A Scottish Presbyterian clergyman, Irving came to believe that the second coming of Christ was near at hand, and that the early apostolic gifts of prophesying, speaking in tongues, and healing by faith were being revived. His work brought him into the circle of Henry Drummond, who was devoted to eschatological speculations. In 1828, Irving lectured in Edinburgh on the Book of Revelation. In 1830 he was excommunicated by the London presbytery for declaring Christ's human nature to be sinful. He continued to minister at his church at Regent Square until he was removed in 1832, after the outbreak of an emotional revival. His followers constituted themselves into the Catholic Apostolic Church, and the first "Apostle" was appointed by Henry Drummond. In 1835, the full "College of Apostles," numbering twelve, held its first "council" in London. Shortly thereafter they undertook missionary journeys to the continent and to America. The Oxford Movement influenced this group which showed increasing inclination toward Catholic doctrines and practices. Their service book, published in 1842, contained a mixture of Roman Catholic, Anglican, and Greek rites. Several Catholic priests in Holland and Germany joined them, and they were favored by the Prussian nobility. Their influence in Britain diminished considerably after 1901 when their last apostle, who had been expected to survive until the second advent, died. They still have a number of adherents in Germany and in the United States.

(2) The Plymouth Brethren were so named because their first center in England was established at Plymouth in 1830. They had been founded two

Among the many small religious groups which fled Europe for haven in the United States were the Amish. Despite a rapidly changing industrialized world around them, "the plain people" have held to their life-style of simplicity. (Grant Heilman Photography)

or three years earlier in Ireland by a former Anglican priest, J. N. Darby, and were popularly called the Darbyites. The Brethren, as they preferred to call themselves, endeavored to take the Bible literally and to model their churches after the New Testament patterns. They believed in personal conversion, held that social reform is useless, and taught that the mission of Christians is saving men and women out of the world. They practiced baptism by immersion and observed the Lord's Supper every Sunday. They did not have an ordained minister but used lay evangelists. One of the most prominent members of the Plymouth Brethren was George Muller (1805-98), who began and maintained orphanages at Bristol, relying entirely on faith and prayer for the necessary material needs. The Brethren were zealous missionaries and eventually were on every continent. Their teaching combines elements of Calvinism and Pietism, and strong emphasis is placed on the imminent return of Christ and the expected millennium. Their moral outlook is puritanical and their church government resides in the autonomy of the local church. They are still very active in missionary work, especially in India, East Asia, Central Africa, and South America.

(3) The United Brethren are often confused with the Plymouth Brethren, but are distinctly different. Organized by Philip William Otterbein and Martin Boehm, the United Brethren in Christ was constituted in 1799, and held its first annual meeting in 1800. Otterbein was a minister of the Reformed church who had a profound religious experience in Pennsylvania, and Boehm was a Mennonite who also had a marked conversion. Both of them became stirring and compelling preachers. The new denomination they formed originally preached only in German and was modeled after the Methodist Episcopal Church, both in spirit and organization. In 1946 the United Brethren joined the Evangelical Church to establish the Evangelical United Brethren Church. Then in 1968, this body united with the Methodist Church to form the United Methodist Church.

(4) The Disciples of Christ represented a new breed of churchmen who were dissatisfied with inherited denominational divisions and attempted to go back to the New Testament model for organization, forms, worship, and ceremony. The two outstanding leaders of this movement were Barton W. Stone (1772-1844) and Alexander Campbell (1788-1866). Stone was a Presbyterian pastor in Kentucky who became dissatisfied with the doctrines of total depravity and unconditional election in the Westminster Confession. After he was expelled by the synod, Stone and his friends formed an independent presbytery but dissolved it in 1804 to "sink into union with the Body of Christ at large." They called themselves simply Christians, and their churches simply Churches of Christ. They proclaimed the Bible "as the only sure guide to heaven," rejected ordinations and infant baptism, and baptized by immersion only.

A Scottish Presbyterian, Thomas Campbell, came to western Pennsylvania in 1807 and soon thereafter withdrew from his presbytery when they censured him for admitting Presbyterians of various beliefs to the Lord's Supper. He and his followers formed the Christian Association of Washington (Pennsylvania), adopting as a slogan, "where the Scriptures speak, we speak; where the Scriptures are silent, we are silent." In 1809, Alexander Campbell came from the British Isles to join his father in America. The younger Campbell had already been strongly influenced by John Glas and the Sandemanians, who believed much like the followers of Stone and Campbell. As a forceful, willing, and able debater, Alexander soon took over the leadership of the movement and exerted such influence over its formation that its adherents are still often referred to as Campbellites. For a short time after 1813, he and his group found fellowship with the Baptists, but obvious doctrinal and practical differences brought that to a halt. They became known as the Reformers or Disciples, and after Barton Stone and Alexander Campbell met, their groups united in the formation of the Disciples of Christ in 1827. The churches of this fellowship are congregationally organized, all credal formulae are rejected, baptism is essential and by immersion, and the Lord's Supper is the main act of worship every Sunday. They have always taken a prominent part in education and have founded a number of universities. About the middle of the nineteenth century, a large group of the Disciples opposed organized missionary societies and instrumental music in worship. They broke off and organized Churches of Christ, a movement which grew substantially and rapidly. The Churches of Christ today have more than three million members, operate twenty liberal arts colleges, and support direct mission work in 100 foreign fields.

(5) The Seventh-day Adventists were started by William Miller (1782-1849), a converted New York farmer who attracted a large following with his predictions of the second coming of Christ. In 1831, he began preaching that Christ would return in 1843, and by the time that year arrived a national movement known as the Adventists, or "Millerites," had come into existence. When 1843 passed without incident, Miller simply announced a new date for the "Eschaton," October 22, 1844. As the fateful day drew near, thousands of terrified people abandoned jobs and responsibilities, and on October 22, the faithful by the droves gathered on hilltops throughout the land, many in white robes, anticipating the last day, the dramatic climax to history. Many disillusioned followers forsook the movement, but Miller continued to maintain that the time was still soon. After prolonged conflict with other Protestant groups, the Millerites became a separate denomination in 1844. In deference to the views of Mrs. Rachel D. Preston, who had been a Seventh-day-Baptist before joining the Adventists, they began to observe the Old Testament Sabbath as the weekly day of rest and praise instead of Sunday, thus becoming the Seventh-day Adventists. The work was organized in England through a mission started at Southampton by W. Ing in 1878.

The Adventists are a staunchly Protestant body, believing that the Scriptures provide the unerring rule of faith and practice. The imminent return of Christ remains a central doctrine. They also require their members to live a life of strict temperance, including abstinence from alcohol, tobacco, and in some communities, tea and coffee also. They observe the Sabbath from Friday sunset to Saturday sunset, and observe adult baptism only, which is by immersion. Although they numbered only 80,000 in 1916, they were already well organized, actively missionary, and propagating their views throughout the world.

(6) The Church of Christ, Scientist (known generally as Christian Science) was founded by Mary Baker Eddy (1821-1910). She was reared in a devout Congregationalist home, but was a frail and sick girl, suffering from nervous disorders and hysteria. In 1843, she married George Glover who died before the birth of their son. She then married Daniel Patterson, a dentist whom she soon divorced. Still chronically ill, Mary Baker Glover Patterson encountered a flamboyant faith healer named Phineas P. Quimby, from whom she claimed to receive healing. She claimed that Quimby had rediscovered the healing techniques of Jesus Christ, but after Quimby died she became ill again. After a bad fall in 1866, she began to study the New Testament intensively, seeking a remedy for her "hopeless" condition. During this study she claimed to have been given an understanding of what she labeled as "Christian Science." She began to gather students for private instruction, and in 1875 she wrote *Science and Health,* which went through many revisions and eventually became *Science and Health with the Key to the Scriptures.* At her insistence, adherents to her movement hold that this book has equal authority with the Bible. It teaches that there is one Reality: Mind, God, and Good, and that matter, evil, and illness are unreal.

In 1877, she married Asa G. Eddy, one of her disciples, and in 1879 she founded the First Church of Christ, Scientist, Boston, which, as the Mother Church, was carefully supervised by her until her death in 1910. The movement has had a steady growth, and is still governed by the Mother Church, Boston, through a board of directors who hold their office for life and appoint their successors. One of the principal assets of the church is the *Christian Science Monitor,* a well-informed newspaper. "Christian Science" has never been accepted as a normative Christian movement by most Christian churches because its teaching on the unreality of matter, sin, and suffering conflicts with the fundamental biblical doctrines of the creation, fall, and redemption.

(7) Jehovah's Witnesses is a sect which has never been recognized as a normative Christian denomination, but it has had a spectacular publishing history and rapid growth. In the 1870s Charles Taze Russell, a Pittsburgh haberdasher, built up a fanatical following calling itself the Watch Tower Bible and Tract Society, but generally called Russellites by others. Russell had been at different times a Presbyterian, a congrega-

tionalist, an Adventist, and a dabbler in Oriental faiths. He finally
turned away from all religion, saying that "religion is against God." He
rejected belief in hell, the Trinity, and the divinity of Christ, reducing Jesus
to merely the greatest "witness." He became obsessed with the second
coming, and began predicting in 1872 that Jesus would return secretly and
invisibly in 1874, and that the end of the world would come in 1914 and
the millennium would begin. By 1874 he had a congregation, by 1879 he
had founded the *Watchtower* magazine, and by 1884 he had a large group
officially known as the Watch Tower Bible and Tract Society, which became
a flourishing business, publishing innumerable pamphlets and books. In
1909, his wife gained a divorce on the grounds of his immoral conduct with
members of his congregation. In 1911 another scandal involved his
fraudulent sale of "miracle wheat" alleged to have marvelous agricultural
powers. Despite these scandals, the sect continued to flourish, and even
when the millennium did not start in 1914, Russell enjoyed an outbreak of
fresh popularity when World War I began.

When Russell died in 1916, Joseph Franklin Rutherford, a Missouri
lawyer, took over the Watch Tower Bible and Tract Society, changing its
name to Jehovah's Witnesses. Rutherford developed the society on lines that
were openly subversive of civil authority. He held the theory of a
"theocratic kingdom," membership in which prevented allegiance to any
country. He carried on a vigorous propaganda against the British Empire
and all institutional religion. Rutherford was an authoritarian leader who
caused the spawning of several breakaway groups such as the Dawn Bible
Students Association. Even after his death in 1942, *The Watchtower* and
Consolation periodicals have continued to deny most of the fundamental
Christian doctrines, and to attack constantly the Roman Catholic Church,
and Church of England, and the Free Churches.

(8) The Church of Jesus Christ of Latter-day Saints, commonly miscalled
"Mormons," was founded by Joseph Smith (1805-44) in Seneca County,
New York, in 1830. Smith had been profoundly affected by the revivals of
that period, but was impatient with the existing denominational
differences. He reported that he had visions in which God told him that no
existing religious body represented the divine will, and that God had
chosen him to restore the true church. In 1823, Smith testified that a
heavenly messenger named Moroni, a resurrected ancient American
prophet, revealed to him the existence of a record engraved upon gold
plates hidden in a hill between Palmyra and Manchester, New York. Four
years later, Smith said, these plates were delivered to him with instruments
of interpretation called "Urim" and "Thummim." Smith's translation of the
plates became the *Book of Mormon,* named after Mormon, one of the later
prophets who served the ancestors of some American Indians about 600 BC
to AD 420. Latter-day Saints regard the Bible as "the stick" of Judah and the
Book of Mormon as "the stick" of Joseph (Ezekiel 37:16-19). Other books

accepted as scriptures are *Doctrine and Covenants,* a collection of revelations given directly through Joseph Smith, and *The Pearl of Great Price,* revelations given to Moses and revealed to Smith along with writings of Abraham translated by Smith.

The first temple built by Smith and his followers was at Kirtland, Ohio, in 1836, but because of adverse economic conditions and public pressure, they moved on to Jackson County, Missouri, where they were received well at first. Hostilities soon developed, however, and they were driven out of Missouri. They settled on the Mississippi River in Hancock County, Illinois, and soon built the largest city in Illinois. A strong political base was built by Smith until he had another revelation in 1843 sanctioning polygamy, which he was practicing. Rioting broke out and Smith was killed by a mob on June 27, 1844. He was succeeded by Brigham Young (1801-77), who moved the headquarters of the sect to Salt Lake City, Utah, in 1847. The practice of polygamy (Young himself had twenty-seven wives) brought them into conflict with the federal government until 1890 when the President of the Mormons advised his followers to conform to the law.

Some distinguishing doctrines and practices of the Latter-day Saints include the continuation of sanctioned marriages into eternity, baptism by the living for the dead, enforced tithing and a thoroughly organized welfare program, no professional clergy, but all males over twelve considered priests, a law of health which forbids alcohol, tobacco, tea, and coffee, and a strong emphasis on education. Intensely missionary, the Latter-day Saints have spread across the world and today number more than two million.

(9) The Pentecostal Movement blossomed in the early years of the twentieth century among those who sought a baptism in the Holy Spirit accompanied by speaking in tongues, based on the experience on the day of Pentecost in Acts 2:1-13. Manifestations of this nature occurred in Los Angeles in April, 1906, attracting worldwide attention. The movement spread rapidly, beginning in Britain in September, 1907, causing small Pentecostal meetings to spring up all over the British Isles, emphasizing charismatic Christianity, and led mostly by laymen. Between 1925 and 1935 the fervent preaching of the Welsh evangelists, Stephen and George Jeffreys, filled the largest halls in the land and featured great "Evangelistic and Divine Healing" campaigns. George Jeffreys organized a group of Pentecostals into the Elim Foursquare Gospel Alliance in 1915. The "Assemblies of God in Great Britain and Ireland" was constituted in 1924, and has become the largest Pentecostal denomination in Britain. Outside Britain, the Pentecostal movement has attained its greatest dimensions in North America, Scandinavia, and Brazil, where some churches have as many as 6,000 members.

The largest single Pentecostal group in the world is "Assemblies of God, U.S.A." which was formed at Hot Springs, Arkansas, in 1914. In 1916 its

Leaving New York, Joseph Smith journeyed on to Kirtland, Ohio, and later to Jackson County, Missouri. After Smith's death, Brigham Young took the main contingency of Mormons to Salt Lake City, Utah, now headquarters of the Church of Jesus Christ of Latter-day Saints. (Historical Pictures Service, Chicago)

headquarters were established at Springfield, Missouri. It teaches complete, but progressive sanctification (holiness or perfection) which is attested to by the bestowing of glossolalia (speaking in tongues). About forty different denominations in America practice glossolalia. The larger bodies are organized in the Pentecostal World Conference. Many of the Pentecostal churches in America trace their origin to the "Latter Rain" revival movement which began in the Great Smoky mountains in 1886 under the leadership of Baptist R. G. Spurling. It was taken over by A. J. Tomlinson, who established the Church of God in 1908. Many splits and schisms produced numerous branches of the Church of God, some of which repudiate speaking in tongues.

The Church of the Nazarene is the product of the merger of some fifteen bodies stemming from the nineteenth-century Wesleyan Holiness Movement. The first major merger came in 1907, uniting the Church of the Nazarene (organized in California in 1895) with the Association of Pentecostal Churches of America to form the Pentecostal Church of the Nazarene. The next year the Holiness Church of Christ joined the denomination. Other groups came in over the next several years from across America and England. "Speaking in tongues" was never a practice of the Nazarenes, and because of the association of that practice, the term "Pentecostal" was dropped from the name of the denomination in 1919. In doctrine, the church is in the tradition of Arminian Methodism, and regards its unique mission to be the promotion of complete sanctification as a work of grace subsequent to salvation.

By the early part of the twentieth century, Christianity had sorted and organized itself into a vast array of denominations, offering almost every imaginable variety of church and doctrine. In reflecting upon the cataclysmic events of the preceding hundred years, it is a wonder that Christianity remains intact and recognizable. The faith has survived revolutionary fanatics, greedy industrialists, unscrupulous promoters, slave-owning churchmen, agnostics, atheists, socialists, evolutionists, and unrelieved hostility on foreign soil. Now as the church moves into the twentieth century, it faces the sunrise of a new day and the promise of a brighter future.

XII

ABOUNDING SIN, ABOUNDING GRACE: THE PARADOX OF RECESSION AND ADVANCE (1914-81)

But where sin abounded,
grace did much more abound.

ROMANS 5:20

A. Ideologies: Freedom and Bondage
   1. Nihilism
   2. Secularism
   3. Racism
   4. Totalitarianism
      a. Communism
      b. Fascism
B. Encounters: War and Peace
   1. Dawn of a New Age
   2. The First Total War
   3. An Uncertain Interlude
   4. The Second World War
   5. Cold Wars and Hot Wars
C. Theologies: Conventional and Variant
   1. Liberalism
   2. Fundamentalism
   3. Neoorthodoxy
      a. Karl Barth
      b. Other Neoorthodox Theologians
   4. Existentialism
      a. Existential Philosophy
      b. Existential Theology
   5. Divergent Trends
   6. Biblical Scholarship
D. Endeavors: Consolidation and Expansion
   1. Ecumenism
      a. World Council of Churches
      b. Vatican II
      c. Other Ecumenical Movements
   2. Social Activism
      a. Alcoholism and Prohibition
      b. Civil Liberties
         (1) Civil Rights Movement
         (2) Martin Luther King, Jr.
      c. Fear, Hate, and Terrorism
   3. Evangelism
      a. Old-fashioned Revivals
      b. Billy Graham
      c. Nondenominational and Parachurch Ventures
   4. Worldwide Christianity
      a. Christianity and Culture
      b. Expansion and Opposition

Charles Dickens began his novel, *A Tale of Two Cities,* with the observation that "It was the best of times; it was the worst of times." Dickens' novel was set in the French Revolution, but it seems that his famous paradox could be more appropriately applied to the twentieth century. In Bonhoeffer's words, it was a "world come of age." Industrial technology and scientific discoveries catapulted man literally from the earth to the moon. Vast worlds and unlimited opportunities were opened up by inventions, transportation, and communication that would have staggered even Leonardo da Vinci.

On many fronts Christianity appeared to be on the verge of winning the world, and Christian principles were becoming the norm in various cultures. Yet, for all the dynamic advance in some areas, there was deadening recession in others. The most devastating wars ever fought, economic disaster and revolution, fanatical peddlers of hate, and discordant ideologies and theologies openly challenged the teachings and churches of Jesus Christ. Never had the world seen so much corruption and sin abounding, but neither had it ever experienced such abounding grace. While it is often easy to characterize a particular century or period, the twentieth century must be characterized by its pluralism and multiplicity; it is virtually the "age of everything."

A. IDEOLOGIES: FREEDOM AND BONDAGE

Civilization entered the twentieth century with the excitement of leaving the old world behind and discovering the new. There was a sense of challenge and adventure at every turn. The intellectual world formed the vanguard in search for new and better ways, going off in many directions and arriving at sundry ideologies, offering freedom from the old concepts, but introducing new kinds of bondage.

1. NIHILISM
For many, the turn of the century signaled the time to cut loose from the superstitions of religion and the fantasies of a hereafter. Although the Christian denominations had grouped and regrouped, expanded and

fortified, there were those who believed with Nietzsche that life has no meaning except what man gives to it. Although most could not bring themselves to his brazenness and profess atheism, many spoke of a sense of meaninglessness and uncertainty. The result was a pervading nihilism, which has not yet run its course. Nihilism is derived from the Latin *nihil*, meaning "nothing," and Christianity, a religion that seemed to promise everything, was challenged to answer this nothingness.

The seedbed of nihilism in the nineteenth century was Russia, where men were reacting violently to the injustices and opulence of Czar Alexander II. Although the Frenchman Pierre Joseph Proudhom, who had coined the word "anarchist," denounced violence while rejecting government, a Russian named Bakunin took the spirit of anarchy into the realm of terrorism and strikes. In the 1850s, Dmitri Pisarev, a literary critic, and his followers advocated smashing everything and using violence to destroy all forms of social organization and control. Ivan Turgenev wrote in *Fathers and Sons* (1862) of those turbulent days of unrestrained personal freedom and popularized the term nihilism. Prince Petr Kropotkin, the leading Russian anarchist, defined nihilism as a struggle against all forms of tyranny, hypocrisy, and artificiality in favor of individual freedom.

In the twentieth century, nihilism came to be associated with despair more than revolution. World War I increased the feelings of disillusionment and frustration for many. T. S. Eliot voiced these feelings in "The Love Song of J. Alfred Prufrock" (1917), "Gerontion" (1920), *The Waste Land* (1922), and *The Hollow Men* (1925). Nihilism was expressed deliberately in the Dada art of the 1920s, which was "an embodiment of nothingness, uselessness, and disgust." In *The Trial* (1925), Franz Kafka dealt with absurdity, frustration, and loss of values as man tries to relate to the institutions of culture. Edna St. Vincent Millay's poetry portrayed life as fruitless and absurd, with death as the final no. Martin Heidegger, the German philosopher, wrote in *Being and Time* (1927), that life is care and dread brought to nothingness in death. The French existentialist Jean-Paul Sartre popularized his disgust with the emptiness of routine living in *Nausea* (1938), *No Exit*, and *The Flies* (1943). In *Being and Nothingness* (1943), he spoke of ultimate nothingness, and insisted that all of life is meaningless except for what man invests it with. Throughout this long span, nihilism has had an eroding effect on the traditional bases for Christian morality and has called the supernatural and transcendent into question.

2. SECULARISM
The practical expression of the philosophy of nihilism is secularism, a term which was first used in about 1850 by G. J. Holyoake. Secularism denotes a system which seeks to interpret and order life on principles taken solely from this world, without consideration to belief in God and a future life.

Nude Descending a Staircase *(1911) Marcel Duchamp. Nihilism philosophy soon
began to be reflected in poetry and other literature and art.*
(Philadelphia Museum of Art: The Louise and Walter Arensberg Collection)

Holyoake's ideas were developed into a logical form of extreme atheism by Charles Bradlaugh (1833-91), notorious freethinker and member of parliament from London. Bradlaugh was a widely known lecturer and president of the London Secular Society. In his last years he was actively interested in promoting social and political reform in India. On the positive side of the this-worldly philosophy of secularism has been its active involvement in social progress and the improvement of material conditions for the working classes.

In the twentieth century, the term secularism came to be used in a more general sense for the modern tendency to ignore, if not to deny, the principles of supernatural religion in the interpretation of the world and existence. Many adherents of secularism may assert their belief in God or their acceptance of the idea that there is a god, but beyond that they have no need for such an hypothesis. They often possess a strong system of ethics and are religiously committed to positive progress, but they deny the need for a personal, significant relationship to the divine. The modern obsession with materialism, pleasure, and success are resulting expressions of secularism, although those caught up in these pursuits may also profess religion, even Christianity. By the middle of the twentieth century, secularism was wielding a strong influence in politics and economics throughout the world. Russian Communism, frankly antireligious, had taken over East Germany, Poland, Bulgaria, Romania, Czechoslovakia, China, North Korea, and was threatening the rest of Asia and Africa. In Turkey, secularism was in control of the government; and in India, Nehru was calling for a secular state. In the 1960s there developed a radical secular Christian theology, with a this-worldly, empirical, responsible attitude toward history and society. This secular theology, however, should not be confused with secularism, which is an antireligious, scientifically positivist ideology. Secular theology (which we will consider more fully later), on the other hand, is traditional Christian theology calling for more Christian participation in this world's needs.

3. RACISM
One of the most insidious problems to cripple the church in the twentieth century has been that of racism. Although not an organized and systematic philosophy or ideology, it has been an overpowering force in major confrontations throughout the world. One of the first racialist thinkers to formalize his views was Comte Joseph de Gobineau, who published his four-volume *Essay on the Inequality of Human Races* in the middle of the nineteenth century. He taught the superiority of the white race over all others, and among the whites, of the Aryans as having reached the heights of civilization, and the Teutons the purest of the Aryans. Gobineau societies sprang up in Germany and elsewhere, glorifying the Aryans and Teutons, and dedicated to keeping them "pure." Gobineau's most important follower

was H. S. Chamberlain, who published *The Foundations of the 19th Century* (1899), in which Jews were said to be especially alien in spirit. Gobineau and Chamberlain are generally regarded as the intellectual forerunners of the racial theories of the German Nazis. Racialism functioned as one of the most effective techniques of Nazi propaganda for achieving and maintaining power over the German people.

Early colonialism often laid the foundation for racism as explorers and missionaries emphasized their superiority over the heathen. When the Spaniards came to America, they were equipped with the theory that the Indians had an entirely different origin and were not human in the same sense as the Spaniards. There was, therefore, no conscience about taking their land and treating them other than as fellow human beings. The "white man's burden" became a familiar refrain in British literature, as imperialism was depicted as a noble activity destined to bring civilization to the unfortunate members of other races. This attitude is especially noticeable in the works of Thomas Carlyle, James A. Froude, Charles Kingsley, and Rudyard Kipling. The French also justified their colonial empire on the basis of their *mission civilisatrice*, their duty to bring civilization to the backward peoples of the world. Again, the twentieth century inherited a paradox from missions and colonization. Even though non-Christians around the world had been converted thereby, they were also often the victims of racial prejudice and injustice by the very people who had converted them. The fruit of this duplicity had to be gathered by the twentieth-century church as it sought to maintain integrity and solidarity.

Missions to the American Indians became a big concern in the nineteenth century. Although they probably never totaled as many as half a million, there were Indians in every state, and Christian missions were sent to almost every tribe. The Indians were being constantly subjected to exploitation and frustration, and they retaliated with raids and wars. Many conscientious Christian leaders took the lead in peaceful negotiations and in pressuring the government for fair treatment and education for the Indians. Christian missions continued among them, sent by both Protestant and Catholic groups. In fact, Protestants spent more on Indians per capita than upon any other racial group.

A greater challenge than the Indian's plight was that of the Negro. After the Civil War and emancipation, both whites and blacks were faced with adjustment to the new status, and in the process of adjustment, Christianity took some giant strides. In 1859 the Negro church members in the South numbered about half a million. By 1916, Negro membership throughout the country was almost five million, nearly half the entire black population, and almost exactly the same number as that of white church members. The overwhelming majority of Negro churches were Baptist and Methodist, and entirely under Negro control. The involvement of whites with blacks after emancipation was almost completely limited to education. The American Missionary Association, a nondenominational agency founded in 1846, established Negro schools for all grades and provided theological education for black ministers. Hampton Institute, Atlanta University, and Fisk University were established by this association. Several private foundations also contributed to Negro education, the foremost being that of John D. Rockefeller.

All of the relations between blacks and whites were not good. Misunderstanding and misinformation created tension and hostility on both sides. The Ku Klux Klan was organized in 1867 as the "Invisible Empire of the South" for the stated purpose of protecting the white people from obstreperous Negroes and to reassert the political and social superiority of the whites. Although disbanded a few years later, the Klan was reorganized near Atlanta, Georgia, in 1915 by Col. William J. Simmons, a preacher and promoter of fraternal orders. The new Klan was proclaimed as a high-class, mystical, social, patriotic society devoted to the protection of womanhood and the supremacy of white Protestantism. Now added to the targets for hostility were Catholics, Jews, foreigners, and organized labor. Membership rose to almost five million, and the Klan controlled politicians in both parties. Fiery crosses, a symbol of the K.K.K., were burned in all parts of the country. When Alfred E. Smith, a Catholic, ran for president in 1928, the Klan energetically worked against him under the slogan, "Keep the pope out of the White House." Scandals, corruption, and associations with American fascism caused the disintegration of the Klan, but it experienced a resurgence in the 1960s during the Civil Rights movement (which will be detailed later). Although the vast majority of Americans were repulsed by such extremes as the K.K.K., racism still continued to be evident in segregated schools, churches, and society in general. Prejudice and fear persisted even when physical hostility was absent. American churches were yet to face great inner turmoil and dissension on the racial issue.

4. TOTALITARIANISM
The most deadly challenge to democracy and Christianity in the twentieth century was totalitarianism, a political system in which all vital aspects of human existence are included in a single all-powerful state striving for a perfect order of mankind. A totalitarian state consists of a single, mass party, led either by a dictator or by a small group dedicated to the ideology, which controls every aspect of life. Right-wing versions of totalitarianism are generally known as fascism, and the left-wing versions as communism. In the twentieth century, it was communism which came first and lasted the longest.

a. *Communism.* In the Communist Manifesto of Marx and Engels, the word communism was used interchangeably with socialism. However, communist leaders and writers continue to use the word socialism to denote the type of social order known as communism in English-speaking countries. Marx did not find the basis for communism in religious assumptions, but in the new social sciences. He regarded the changing economic structure as the foundation of social life, but also advocated the forcible overthrow of any impediment to that change. By 1900, there were two types of communist revolutionaries in Russia, the Mensheviks and the Bolsheviks. The former were moderates who sought reform by law. They led a moderate revolution in 1905, which resulted in the czar ceasing to be the head of the church, and the patriarchate being restored.

In November 1917, Bolshevik Vladimir Ilyich Ulyanov, known as Lenin, seized power in war-devastated Russia, changed the Social Democratic Party to the Communist Party, and established the "dictatorship of the proletariat." The militant, disciplined, and purposeful Bolsheviks were in complete control. The Bolsheviks were the party of a new religion, which perverted many Christian ideas into communist concepts. Whereas Christians have often renounced private property voluntarily, Bolshevik communism forced renunciation. While Christians anticipate a new heaven and a new earth, communism is dedicated to creating a new earth only. Christians believe that God is the Lord of history, but communists believe in dialectical materialism as the determinism of history. Christians have been willing to die and to kill for their faith, and communists are utterly dedicated to exterminating any opposition or dissent.

The Bolsheviks who led the Revolution of 1917 were as fanatical and dedicated as any religious group has ever been, and their dedication was to the goal of converting Russia from a feudal state to a modern industrialized state in a single generation. To achieve this goal, they believed they must destroy not only the church but religion itself, "the opiate of the people." In one year (1918-19), twenty-eight bishops and 1,215 priests were shot, 687 monasteries (out of 1,026) were liquidated. The Bolsheviks confiscated church lands, canceled state subsidies for the church, decreed civil marriage, and nationalized schools.

How did the Russian Orthodox Church respond? Patriarch Tikhon excommunicated the revolutionary leaders. Church officials organized demonstrations and armed resistance, and called for restoration of the monarchy. In retaliation, the Council of People's Commissars ordered the separation of church and state, which completely disestablished the Orthodox Church, and banished every vestige of religion from state and public schools. When famine spread through Russia in 1922, the government confiscated church treasures for relief purposes. When Patriarch Tikhon urged the faithful to resist, he was arrested and released only after recanting his "anti-Soviet actions" and declaring himself loyal to the regime. A schism occurred with the Orthodox Church in 1923 when a group of parish clergy formed the "Living Church" (Renovationists), opposed the patriarchal church, and pledged allegiance to the communist government. In 1925, the government sponsored the League of Militant Godless, for the express purpose of promoting atheism through cultural media. In 1929, the Law on Religious Associations placed strict limits on the activities of churches, allowing public worship only to groups which could prove their loyalty to the regime. The Russian constitution was amended in 1936 to exclude the right of religious propaganda.

Pursuing Leon Trotsky's theory of "permanent revolution"—that revolution had to occur in other countries if the Russian venture were to succeed—the Bolsheviks created the Communist International in 1919 to coordinate the world revolutionary movement. A few communist regimes appeared briefly, but the time was not right. World communism had to wait until after World War II. When Lenin died in 1924, he was succeeded by Joseph Stalin after a bitter struggle for power with Trotsky. Stalin had attended the Orthodox seminary, but he abandoned religion for Marxism before completing his studies for the priesthood. He renounced Trotsky's theory of "permanent revolution" and introduced his own doctrine of "socialism in one country." Thus he began laying the foundation for the totalitarian control of the country's economic and social life. Prosperous peasants who resisted were wiped out as a class. Stalin concentrated heavily on education and youth organizations to win over the younger generation. By 1922, the Communist party exercised a dictatorship over all aspects of life and thought in the Soviet Union, as the country had been renamed. Some of the country's most outstanding thinkers were deported, including Nikolai Berdyaev, who lived in Paris from 1922, writing his classic *Freedom and the Spirit* (1935) and the *Destiny of Man* (1937).

The 1930s were years of intense persecution, with thousands of clergymen imprisoned or liquidated. Surviving clergy were rated as second-class citizens and constantly harassed by the secret police as "clerico-fascists." The Russian Orthodox Church was on the verge of disintegration by 1939. The Lutherans, Baptists, and evangelical Christian denominations were almost wiped out. Large numbers of Russian Mennonites emigrated to the Americas. Extensive persecution was carried out against Catholics, Jews, Muslims, and Old Believers. In 1930, Pope Pius XI called for a worldwide day of prayer in behalf of suffering Christians in Russia, heightening international concern. The Soviets responded by forming a Militant Atheists International to combat the Vatican. In 1937, the pope issued an encyclical condemning the "errors of communism," coming only four days after his encyclical criticizing Nazi Germany. In 1939 Stalin formalized a nonaggression pact with Hitler that opened the way for the German invasion of Poland and the launching of World War II; but two years later Hitler turned on Stalin. The loyal support given to the state by all Russian churches during World War II eased the tension and relieved the brutal persecutions. The policy has become one of propaganda and harassment, but persecutions and imprisonments are still employed to repress threats of dissension. Although the Orthodox cathedrals and the Baptist churches are crowded, one reason is that most churches have been closed and so many believers have had to consolidate in one place. Also, most sects and evangelical groups have been officially classed together as Baptists. Government control, propaganda, and constant harassment persist as the official posture toward religion in communist countries throughout the world.

b. Fascism. The right-wing version of totalitarianism was fascism, which stressed class unity, reaffirmed traditional values, and glorified the national unity. Fascism puts the nation-state or race, its power and growth, in the center of life and history. It disregards the individual and his rights, as well as humanity, in the exclusive interest of the nation. The Italian word *fascismo* is derived from the Latin *fasces,* "bundles," denoting in ancient Rome a bundle of rods with an axe, carried before Roman magistrates as a symbol of authority. Fascism permits some private property and capitalist enterprise, but retains state control. In many ways, fascism is a civil religion, extolling the values of struggle, action, violence, courage, and self-sacrifice. The principles of fascism come from several origins, including Darwin's "survival of the fittest," Gobineau's "superiority of the Aryans," and Nietzsche's "Superman."

Among the intellectual forerunners of fascism were two Frenchmen and an Italian. Georges Sorel emphasized the creative role of violence in history, Charles Maurras was the father of "integral nationalism" in France, and Vilfredo Pareto developed a cyclical theory of social change and of the rise of new elites.

The rise of the fascist movement in Italy was due to the economic crisis, frustration, and disillusionment which followed World War I. Also, a heightened sense of nationalism contributed. Benito Mussolini was the architect of Italian fascism from 1919 onward. Before 1914, he had been a leading member and editor of the Italian Social Democratic Party, but he was always more in favor of violent action than most in the party. So he founded his own newspaper, which carried the revolutionary motto, "Who has steel has bread," and Napoleon's saying, "The revolution is an idea which has found bayonets." Mussolini's first famous editorial bore the characteristic title "Audacity." Fired with a fierce nationalism and by the love of violence and adventure, he organized squads of violent young men to give the impression of strength and security in a day of weakness and insecurity. Mussolini formed the National Fascist Party in 1921, staged his mythical "March on Rome" in 1922, and was invited by the king to form a new government. He proceeded to establish a full dictatorship, outlawing all other parties, suppressing all civil liberties and constitutional guarantees, and subordinating all questions of program to the one question of power. Two of his slogans were "have faith, obey, fight," and "Mussolini is always right."

At first Mussolini ended the antagonism between the Roman Catholic Church and the Italian government, which had existed since 1870. In the Lateran Agreements of 1929, the papacy gave up its territorial claims in Italy, recognized the ruling Italian government, agreed to stay out of politics, and acquiesced in the state's approval of bishops. In return, fascist Italy recognized the Vatican City as an independent, sovereign state and the pope as its ruler, established Catholicism as the "sole religion of the state," allowed religious instruction in secondary schools, and gave legal standing to Catholic religious orders and associations. Pope Pius XI was a bitter foe of communism and traditional liberalism, and saw Mussolini's strength as the answer to suppressing both. He went so far as to praise the Italian dictator as a "man sent by providence." Ties also existed between Roman Catholicism and fascist-type movements in other parts of Europe, such as the "clerical-fascist" state in Austria, the *Falangist* regime in Spain, the "New State" in Portugal, and the "Arrow-Cross" party in Hungary. However, the pope began to have serious clashes with Mussolini over his unmovable state-supremacy and his cynical attitude toward the church. In a papal encyclical in 1931, Pius denounced Mussolini for absorbing the church youth organizations into the fascist structure and dissolving the Catholic Action groups. When Italy invaded Ethiopia in 1935, the pope suggested that wars of conquest are unjust, but used the occasion to extend papal authority over the Ethiopian church. This state of tension and uncertainty between church and state existed up to and throughout World War II.

The German brand of fascism, known as National Socialism, also fed upon disillusionment with the war, resentment over the peace and the economic crisis. Adolf Hitler, an Austrian-born exsoldier who served in World War I with enthusiasm, guided the fascist rise to power and engulfed the world in the horrible nightmare of World War II. In 1920, he joined the German Workers' Party, which was renamed *Nationalsozialistische Deutsche Arbeiterpartei* (of which "Nazi" was an abbreviation). He became president of the party within one year and was given unlimited power. He soon gathered around him several of the Nazi leaders who later became infamous—Alfred Rosenberg, Rudolf Hess, Hermann Göring, and Julius Streicher. As the result of an abortive attempt to seize power in Munich, he was sentenced to five years' imprisonment, during which time he wrote his first volume of *Mein Kampf.* He developed the concept of the superiority of the *Volk,* as represented by the Aryan race, and especially the German People. The unity of the *Volk* found its incarnation in the *Führer* (leader), endowed with absolute authority. In his view the greatest enemy of Nazism was not democracy but communism, and behind communism was the greatest enemy of all, the Jew, who was for Hitler the very incarnation of evil, a mythical figure into which he projected all that he feared and hated.

Plunging back into Germany's political scene, Hitler attracted many magnates of business and industry who supported his plan for a strong right-wing, antiworking-class government. Using the financial base of these supporters, he then appealed to the lower middle class and unemployed to trust him for Germany's recovery. Thus, with an unprecedented mass following, Hitler was invited to be Chancellor of Germany in 1933. Once in power, he proceeded to establish an absolute dictatorship. State capitalism replaced personal capital and industry, and all competing classes and interest groups were formed into an ideal supercommunity. Concern with race was central to Nazi ideology, and the emphasis was on "people, soil, and blood." Jews were seen as a "culture-destroying race" which gave the world capitalism and Marxism. Carrying out their barbaric doctrine of anti-Semitism, the Nazis deprived German Jews of their rights as citizens, expelled them from their jobs, constantly harassed them, and liquidated them by the thousands with their Nazi death squads. In 1940 the concentration camps became death camps for the Jews, the largest being Auschwitz in Poland. In these camps, the Nazis put into operation the "final solution," the extermination of the entire Jewish population of Europe. Men, women, and children were slaughtered in these "death factories" until six million, out of the total world population of eleven million Jews, were exterminated. The repercussions of this "holocaust" continue to be felt throughout civilization.

Christianity was also a target, because as Hitler explained, "The heaviest blow that ever struck humanity was the coming of Christianity. Bolshevism is Christianity's illegitimate child. Both are inventions of the Jew." Born and reared a Catholic, Hitler never formally broke from the church, nor was he ever excommunicated. Yet he abandoned all Christian principles in favor of the secular philosophies of the day. National Socialism itself was a new faith, which promised national regeneration. Many church leaders overlooked the anti-Semitic and pagan side of Nazism, and praised Hitler's anticommunism. In 1930, a strong coalition of Protestants formed the "German Christians," a pro-Nazi party within the church. They reconstructed their churches along Nazi lines, introduced the Führer principle into church government, and dismissed all people of Jewish origin from church staffs. Hitler, however, was cool toward the "German Christians," and virtually dismissed them with the creation of the Ministry of Church Affairs in 1935. The Catholic bishops also endorsed the new regime, the Catholic trade unions "voluntarily" dissolved themselves, and the Catholic Center Party voted for the measure to allow Hitler to rule by decree. In return, Hitler agreed to a concordat with the Vatican which guaranteed the freedom and independence of Catholics, and protected the Catholic educational system, but forbade all political activities by the clergy and regulated the appointing of bishops. From the very beginning, the

Nazis violated every part of the concordat that favored freedom, and tightened every part that suppressed the church.

In November 1933, Dr. Martin Niemoller, an outstanding Lutheran pastor, led in the formation of the Pastors' Emergency League to combat the ideas of the "German Christians." In the following year, this group repudiated Ludwig Muller, the head of the "German Christians," and set up an alternative body known as the Confessional Church, so named to emphasize that its opposition to the Nazis was primarily religious (based on confessions of faith), not political. Later, however, the group came to prefer the name Confessing Church, with the sense of being a church of confessors of the faith rather than those who owed allegiance to a formal dogmatic confession. The theological position of the Confessing Church was spelled out in the Barmen Declaration of May 1934, largely written by Karl Barth. The Barmen Declaration called the German church back to the central truths of Christianity, and rejected the totalitarian claims of the state in religious and political matters. The Confessing Church led a perilous existence, and was finally forced to work underground. Niemoller was arrested in 1937 and placed in a concentration camp. Rejecting all offers of compromise, he became the symbolical figure of the Protestant opposition to National Socialism. A few members of the Confessing Church, such as Bonhoeffer, became involved in the anti-Hitler resistance and paid with their lives. German Catholics were also drawn into the church struggle, as Hitler violated the concordat with Rome, and destroyed the network of Catholic organizations in Germany. Catholic churchmen appealed to the Vatican for help against the "new heathenism," and on March 14, 1937, Pius XI's encyclical was the first major church document to criticize Nazism. It called upon Catholics to resist the idolatrous cult of race and state, and to maintain their loyalty to Christ, his church, and Rome. Hitler responded by stepping up the pressure on church activities and clergy, heading off the possibility of organized resistance.

Fascism began in the early 1920s as a purely Italian movement, but at the beginning of the 1940s it had initiated the struggle for world domination. But its plans miscarried. World War II, started by the fascists, ended in complete defeat for them. Fascism survived after the war only in Spain and Argentina. In the 1950s fascist ideas gained in France in connection with the war in Algeria, and some fascist attitudes were reflected in the racial policy (known as apartheid) of South Africa. When Juan Peron was overthrown by the armed forces in Argentina in 1955, he left a legacy similar to that which Mussolini had left in Italy—widespread corruption, political chaos, and a profoundly shaken economy. Although the fascists never accomplished their goal of making the twentieth century a fascist century as they invisioned, the twentieth century was, indeed, shaped by fascism through the devastation which it rained upon the world.

B. ENCOUNTERS: WAR AND PEACE

The ideologies which opposed Christianity and democracy were not content with philosophical speculation. They meant business and they wanted action. Confrontation was inevitable, and the twentieth century became the stage for the dramatic encounters which engulfed the entire world.

1. DAWN OF A NEW AGE

On the night of December 31, 1900, vast crowds gathered in London's Trafalgar Square to celebrate the arrival of the new century. London was the center of the world trade, and the heart of an empire which covered a quarter of the earth. Imperialism was at its zenith, especially in Britain, where Queen Victoria had celebrated "sixty glorious years" at her diamond jubilee in 1897. The whole world was drastically different from the world of 1815. Great progress had been made for mankind in the areas of health, longevity, wealth, literature, and knowledge. New continents had been peopled and developed. The accomplishments of science and technology anticipated unlimited future progress. Men who could build Trans-Siberian and Canadian Pacific railways, dig Suez, Kiel, and Panama canals, construct skyscrapers and oceanic liners, could surely master the world.

Scientific learning was bursting at the seams. In 1904, Ernest Rutherford published his book on *Radioactivity,* and in 1905, a German-born physicist, Albert Einstein, an obscure official in a Swiss patents office, published his revolutionary paper on relativity. His complex mathematical ideas challenged Newton's system of physics, won speedy recognition among scientists, and eventually led to the creation of the atomic bomb in World War II. Also, at the turn of the century, Sigmund Freud and his Austrian associates gave new understanding to the working of the human mind and of the subconscious impulses in man. Although creating an outrage at first, the founder of psychoanalysis was to have a radical influence on western thought and behavior from the 1920s onward. The arts of this period were also in a state of ferment. Music, painting, and literature were all changing. The abstract music of Schoenberg shattered the conventional musical system of the Romantic composers. Picasso and Braque were experimenting with cubism in Paris, while the American-born poet T. S. Eliot was developing in Paris a technique known as "free verse."

For the rich and privileged, the first decade of the twentieth century was a time of pleasure and luxury; but the great mass of people lived in poverty. City slums were a reminder of the gulf between rich and poor. In these squalid conditions, international socialism found fertile soil in which to plant its seed. The trade union movement asserted its demand for radical reform, erupting in repeated strikes. Early in the century, many western governments began to implement variations of Bismarck's "state socialism" in Germany in the late nineteenth century.

Queen Victoria lived only a few months into the twentieth century, being replaced by Edward VII, who presided over an ostentatious period of European opulence. The ornate pageant of opera houses, fashionable race courses, and military parades was fostered by emperors, kings, and princes, most of whom were related. Britain's king-emperor, Edward VII, was known as the "Uncle of Europe." One of Edward's nephews, however, loathed him. Kaiser Wilhelm II of Germany was convinced that his uncle was plotting with France and Russia to encircle Germany. Although Germany had emerged as the dominant economic and military power on the continent, it was still bitter with memories of its defeat in the Franco-Prussian War of 1870-71. Germany now had the largest and most efficient army in the world, a driving economy, industrial genius, and superlative education, concentrating on science and technology. For over a century Britain had been the unchallenged mistress of the seas, but was now alarmed by Germany's growing naval power. Germany, on the other hand, was apprehensive about a concerted attack from France and Russia. Thus, intensive nationalistic rivalries and suspicions that had been building up for years brought Germany and Austria-Hungary to an ultimate confrontation with France, Britain, and Russia.

2. THE FIRST TOTAL WAR
Whereas other wars had been limited in purpose and scope, World War I was as complex in purpose as it was unlimited in involvement. It was the first war between nation-states that commanded the energies of all their subjects and the resources of modern industrial technology. It was also the first war on a scale large enough to disrupt the world economy. The strain on the financial and industrial national resources was immense. A new concept of "total war" emerged, as governments controlled supplies, trade, credit, transport, and manpower more fully than ever before. Centralized power and widespread government activities became the norm. Civil rights were curtailed, censorship was invoked, and the people were instilled with a sense of solidarity. This, the first war to be fought on land, sea, and air, became a righteous crusade. Church leaders reinforced the idea that it was a "holy war" against tyranny, despotism, and militarism.

The spark which exploded the powder keg of Europe occurred on June 28, 1914, in the Bosnian town of Sarajevo. The Balkans had been seething in rebellion against the once-mighty empire of the Hapsburgs, and on that fateful day in June, a Serbian nationalist, Gavrilo Princip, assassinated the Archduke Franz Ferdinand, heir to the Austro-Hungarian throne. Austria immediately declared war on Serbia, and Russia mobilized to protect Serbia. Germany stood by Austria, and France mobilized to stand by Russia and to protect itself. Then Britain declared war when Germany refused to

The Archduke Francis-Ferdinand and his wife coming out of the Hotel de Ville in Sarajevo, about to enter a car, a few minutes before his assassination, June 28, 1914, an act which helped trigger the start of World War I. (The Bettmann Archive)

respect the neutrality of Belgium. Britain's foreign secretary, Sir Edward Grey, remarked prophetically, "The lamps are going out all over Europe. We shall not see them lit again in our lifetime."

Everyone involved thought the war would be over in a few short months. Millions of men were cheered as they marched joyously to the front. But by the autumn of 1914, it became obvious that the war was stalemated and would drag on with vast casualties. The war could not be confined to Europe, and in April of 1917, the United States entered the war against Germany. Later that same year, the czarist regime in Russia collapsed, and the Lenin-led Bolsheviks took over in November, pulling Russia out of the war. Now the war became more truly a struggle between the western, democratic, maritime powers and the autocracies of central Europe. President Woodrow Wilson's Fourteen Points in 1918 enunciated the ideology of national self-determination and sovereignty, which became the aim for winning the war and the pattern of postwar Europe. Germany's allies were the first to crumble, then on November 9, 1918, Kaiser Wilhelm II abdicated, and the recently formed liberal government signed an armistice on November 11.

The Roman Catholic Church was severely shaken by World War I, which destroyed what had long been a bulwark of Catholicism, the Hapsburg-ruled Austria-Hungarian Empire. Belgium, a solidly Catholic country, had received serious damage. France, which had sent out more Catholic missionaries in the nineteenth century than any country, was drained. Italy, the headquarters of Catholicism, had subsequently joined the Allies, but was critically weakened by the war effort. The defeat of Germany was a blow to the resurgent Catholicism in that country. During the war, Pope Benedict XV (1914-22) addressed the world repeatedly, calling for peace and urging the antagonists to resolve their differences. He used the facilities of his church to alleviate the sufferings from the war and to promote the relief of devastated areas. More than any other time in history, Christian groups of all denominations worked to relieve suffering in the war-torn areas, and to aid prisoners of war and wounded soldiers. The first "total war" had demanded total commitment from everyone, even the churches.

3. AN UNCERTAIN INTERLUDE

The two decades between the two world wars was a period of nervous uncertainty. The war of 1914-18 had been the "war to end all wars," and international institutions based on goodwill, such as the League of Nations, were dedicated to the idea that no generation would ever have to fight again. The chief architect of the League of Nations was President Woodrow Wilson, a Presbyterian minister's son, who brought to bear his Christian idealism upon the international plan for peace. The covenant of the League of Nations was one of the first items of business at the Paris peace conference in January 1919, and it was quickly adopted. The basic idea behind such an organization was that aggressive war is a crime against not only the immediate victim but against the whole human community. Thus it is the right and duty of all states to join in preventing it, and if it is certain that they will so act, no aggression is likely to take place. General propositions for effectively implementing the League included collective security, arbitration, economic and social cooperation, reduction of armaments, and open diplomacy. Ironically, Wilson's own government, the United States congress, failed to approve the League by the necessary two-thirds majority, thus drastically weakening the strength of the movement by the absence of the world's greatest economic power. Also, the Soviet Union was not admitted to membership until 1934, and by then Japan and Germany had ceased to be members. The League had a very active, if not always successful, existence of twenty years, ending with the outbreak of World War II in 1939. Although the League was unable to fulfill the hopes of its founders, its very existence was an event of decisive importance in the history of international relations.

Immediately following the war there was a revival of interest in the pacifist movement which had been active at the beginning of the century. During World War I the word pacifism became especially associated with conscientious objectors who refused military service, but became more generally identified with the antiwar philosophy which has continued to prevail. Rufus M. Jones, an outstanding Quaker educator and theologian, set forth "The Quaker Peace Position," stating that Quakers stand unconditionally for peace. Yet, during portions of both world wars, Jones was chairman of the American Friends Service Committee for European Relief. In 1936 an Anglican clergyman, H. R. L. Sheppard, founded the Peace Pledge union, aimed at getting as many persons as possible to sign a solemn pledge to refuse to take part in any war. The pacifist movement was strongest in Great Britain and the United States, less strong in the British dominions, and fairly weak on the European continent. In India, Mohandas Gandhi, with his creed of nonviolence, was an inspiration to pacifist movements all over the world.

The greatest threat to peace and stability during the interwar period was the worsening economy. Inflation, unemployment, and acute social unrest dominated much of Europe during the 1920s. Germany was gripped by an inflation which reduced its currency, the mark, to worthlessness, and destroyed its middle class. In Britain, workers' discontent led to a general strike in 1926. France was haunted by instability of currency and severe unemployment. Low standards of living and unemployment prevailed throughout Europe. In contrast, America was riding on a wave of prosperity, its standard of living the admiration and envy of the world. Henry Ford's mass production methods brought the motor car within the ordinary citizen's reach, and the "Jazz" age produced a culture and entertainment symbolized by the cinema. Novelists such as F. Scott Fitzgerald, Sinclair

Lewis, and Ernest Hemingway gave American literature a new status at home and abroad. The bubble of America's unparalleled prosperity burst in October-November, 1929, with the Wall Street crash of the New York Stock Exchange. The collapse of America's economy brought Europe's economy down with it. The worst hit country was Germany, with six million out of work. In the United States, the churches were confronted on every side with suffering and social anxiety. The older denominations went into a decline, but the new Holiness and Pentecostal churches effectively ministered to the victims of unemployment and poverty, and achieved phenomenal growth. The disaster of world economic depression provided the perfect setting for ripening socialism, and the universal instability made governments eager to turn to the strong-arm tactics of the Nazis.

At the end of World War I, democracy was in vogue, but the economic crisis and social unrest gave new vigor to extremist political movements. By the end of 1926, Hungary, Italy, Portugal, Poland, and Lithuania were all under authoritarian or dictatorial regimes. In 1933, Hitler came to power in Germany. Democracy had been shortlived in Europe, and in Russia the dictatorship of Stalin became increasingly savage and tyrannical. The postwar era began to give place to a prewar era. The western powers refused to believe that it was happening. Although Hitler had nullified all the peace treaties of World War I, they refused to accept that Germany was prepared to plunge the world into another war, and so they embarked upon a policy of appeasement. In 1931, Japan had attacked Manchuria and left the League of Nations, along with Germany, in 1933. In 1935, Italy attacked Ethiopia, a fellow member of the League. In 1936, Hitler reoccupied the Rhineland with German troops, and made a pact with Mussolini that became the basis for the Rome-Berlin axis. Germany and Italy then supported General Francisco Franco in his successful bid to gain power in the civil war in Spain. Then Hitler stunned the western powers by making a pact with the Soviet Union, hitherto presented by Nazi propaganda as Germany's deadliest enemy. With Russia thus held at bay, Hitler attacked Poland on September 1, 1939, and launched the Second World War.

4. THE SECOND WORLD WAR

There were many parallels between the two great wars, both beginning in eastern Europe, both engaging virtually the same original antagonists, and ending in similar victory, leaving similar problems in the aftermath. Yet, the second was truly more a world war than the first, for it involved prolonged fighting in the Pacific as well as the Atlantic, and in Asia and Africa as well as Europe. Eventually it led to the defeat of Japan as well as Germany. Poland surrendered less than a month after being attacked by Hitler. Russia attacked Finland and was expelled from the League of Nations for that action. In the spring of 1940, Germany struck with lightning speed, invading Norway, Denmark, the Netherlands, and France. She then began a

The failure of the League of Nations, and growing worldwide political pressures brought on renewed hostilities. The U.S.S. Arizona, the U.S.S. Tennessee, and the U.S.S. West Virginia, left burning in Pearl Harbor following the surprise attack by the Japanese on December 7, 1941. (The Bettmann Archive)

concentrated air bombardment of Britain. Italy declared war on already defeated France and attacked Greece. Germany also declared war on Greece and Yugoslavia, the latter retaliating with a courageous guerrilla force which became legendary. In June of 1941, Germany turned on her recent ally and invaded Russia. On December 7, Japan attacked Pearl Harbor, provoking the United States to declare war, and three days later Germany and Italy declared war on the United States. With dramatic suddenness the war was transformed from a war in Europe and the Atlantic to a world war involving all the great powers on all the oceans of the world.

In late 1942 the tide of war began to run in favor of the western Allies. In the summer of 1943, Italy underwent an internal revolution, Mussolini was overthrown, the Fascist Party disbanded, and Italy surrendered on September 8 and declared war on Germany on October 13. The western air forces launched concentrated bombing attacks on Germany, landed at Normandy on June 6, 1944, and liberated Paris on August 25. The Allies converged upon Germany—Russia from the east, and Anglo-U.S. forces from the south and west. On May 7, the German high command surrendered unconditionally, Hitler having committed suicide when the Russians reached the heart of Berlin. The extensive campaigns against Japan continued until the first atomic bomb was dropped on Hiroshima, August 6, 1945, and the Japanese surrendered on August 14. It was now obvious that any peace settlement would have to be as global in character as war itself had been. To facilitate such an aim, a new international organization, the United Nations, was established. Its charter was signed by representatives of fifty nation-states.

Fifty-seven nations had participated as belligerents in World War II. The high cost of the war on such a scale is incalculable. The number of casualties is only a part of the overall destruction. The battle dead from the United States numbered 292,131, about one in every 450 of the 1940 population. The killed and missing from the British Commonwealth totaled 544,596, about one of every 110 of Britain's population. The Soviet Union reported 7,500,000 military personnel killed and missing, about one in every 22 of its 1940 population. France had 210,671 servicemen killed, one in every 200 of its 1940 population. Germany lost 2,850,000 military personnel, one in every 25 of its 1940 population. Italy had about 300,000 casualties, one in every 150 of its population. China's battle losses numbered 2,200,000 or one in every 200 of its population. Japan lost 1,506,000, or one in every 46 of the population of its home islands. The total number of military personnel killed and missing was about 10,650,000 for the Allied powers, and about 4,650,000 for the Axis powers, for a total exceeding 15,000,000. Added to this was the vast amount of destruction to cities and industries, and the uncounted loss of civilian lives. Because of the bombing raids and widespread invasions, the war cost

Europe alone more than thirty million lives. The worldwide financial and social loss was beyond calculation. Although Nazism was ultimately defeated, the unspeakable record of its concentration camps and "death factories" left a deep scar on the conscience of the civilized world. Before one can review, let alone evaluate, the religious activity during World War II, it is essential to be aware of the immensity of the universal horrors and astronomical casualties that touched every nation and practically every family on the face of the earth.

When World War II broke out in 1939, churchmen in the various countries pledged loyalty to their respective governments. The peace movement in the West soon collapsed, with notable theologians such as Reinhold Niebuhr advocating the rejection of neutralism and the acceptance of intervention as necessary. Some clergymen did oppose the war, especially condemning the obliteration-bombing of Germany and Japan. In Germany, Protestant and Catholic leaders in general urged the people to back the war effort. We have already discussed the formation of the Confessing Church in opposition to the Nazi-supporting German Christians. A more aggressive defection was the Kreisau Circle, a small minority of laymen from both Protestants and Catholics who openly opposed the Nazis. Most of them were tried and condemned in the assassination attempt on Hitler on July 20, 1944. Count Klaus von Stauffenburg, who planted the bomb, was a Catholic layman. Also executed was Father Alfred Delp, a Jesuit member of the Kreisau group, and Dietrich Bonhoeffer, a brilliant young Lutheran theologian.

Generally, the churches' resistance was very meager, as they preferred to accept the Nazis' claim to be the only alternative to communism. Hitler's policy toward the churches was to let them suffer a "natural death" by subordinating them to the new order and stripping the clergy of all privileges. In occupied areas of eastern Europe, priests, pastors, and devout laymen were treated as common criminals, with thousands being executed or sent to concentration camps. In March 1939, the Roman Catholic Church chose Cardinal Pacelli, an accomplished diplomat, to be pope. As Pius XII, he was deeply committed to bringing peace to the world. Although he personally detested both communism and Nazism, his efforts to stem the tide against them were ineffective. The influence of the papal voice was considerably weakened when Pius XII remained strangely silent about German aggression, especially the murder of millions of Jews. Critics have maintained that the Jewish massacre might have been avoided if the pope had spoken out and threatened to excommunicate German Catholics involved in carrying out the "final solution." Defenders of the pope have argued that he would have lost the allegiance of the German Catholics and perhaps brought about the annihilation of the church throughout all of occupied Europe. World War II presented the papacy with a crisis of conscience without historical precedent.

The Protestant ecumenical movement was also caught in the middle of the war. The 1938 Madras conference of the International Missionary Council noted that a militant "new paganism" had arisen which demanded religious devotion from its followers. However, no specific nations or acts were condemned, in fear that believers in the Axis countries would suffer retaliation. After 1939, the council assisted churches and missions throughout the world which had been "orphaned" by the war. Other ecumenical groups were involved in relief efforts, caring for war prisoners and refugees, and maintaining contacts between churches on both sides. Overall, World War II had a devastating effect on Christianity. Thousands of churches were destroyed, clergymen killed, and faithful believers persecuted. Beyond the physical destruction, the faith of many was destroyed, turning vast numbers away from God in anger, bitterness, and cynicism. The seeds of nihilism and secularism found rich and ready soil in which to grow. In addition, Christianity was faced with the unpleasant task of responding to critical moral issues which the war presented. Paramount among these were: (1) the direction of the war against civilian populations, (2) indifference to the sufferings of Jews and other minorities, (3) development of a military-industrial society, and (4) the alliance of the western democracies with the totalitarian Soviet Union.

5. COLD WARS AND HOT WARS

The immediate political results of World War II centered around the obvious fact that the world was left with two great political forces, Soviet communism and western democracy in its various forms. The psychological warfare, or the war of nerves, which had its inception with the extensive use of propaganda in the war, continued to complicate and retard the terms for peace settlements. However, postwar Europe soon rose from the ashes; the problem of millions of "displaced persons"—refugees—was settled; and economic recovery was almost immediate. The United States emerged from the Second World War as the unquestioned leader of the western world. Along with Soviet Russia, the United States had become a "superpower," possessing a strength without precedent in history. The ideological struggles between these two superpowers have been spread across the entire globe. After China was lost to communism in 1949, the United States was committed to resisting communism almost everywhere.

The "cold war" which developed between international communism and western democracy had the support of Christian churches on both sides. Russian Orthodox leaders, for instance, were openly active in the Soviet-sponsored peace campaigns. Following Stalin's death in 1953, the "peaceful coexistence" emphasis led the Orthodox church to participate in ecumenical affairs, and finally join the World Council of Churches in 1961. The Soviets preached the doctrines of communism and the necessity of freeing peoples oppressed by "imperialists." The West reacted with a strong movement of anticommunism. The Vatican was extremely critical of communism, with Pius XII excommunicating Catholics involved in communistic activities, and backing resistance efforts by East European Catholics. In America, many Catholics held the same strong anticommunist position, and in conservative Protestant pulpits throughout America communism was regularly condemned. The interdenominational National Association of Evangelicals and American Council of Churches urged forceful action to halt the spread of communism. When Mao Tse-tung overthrew Chiang Kai-shek in 1949, and established the People's Republic of China, he expelled foreign missionaries, liquidated church organizations, and subjected believers to intense persecution. In communist Europe, Albania rooted out all religion, and churches in Bulgaria and Romania worked under severe restraints. Poland, Yugoslavia, Hungary, and Czechoslovakia permitted a moderate amount of religious activity, but beginning in 1959, the Soviet Union intensified its level of religious persecution. The (East) German Democratic Republic permitted university theological faculties and a large number of churches to exist, but discriminated against practicing Christians and actively worked to win the young people away from the churches.

Two oriental "hot wars" threatened global peace over the issue of communist domination. In 1948, South and North Korea were established as separate states. Determined to unify Korea under communist rule, North Korean forces invaded South Korea in June 1950. The United Nations came to the aid of South Korea, and sixteen member nations sent troops. Communist China entered the conflict on the side of North Korea in 1951. A cease-fire was agreed upon in July 1953, and Korea remained divided at the thirty-eighth parallel. In 1972, the two sides began talks on eventual reunification.

The other conflict was longer and provoked bitter controversy among Christian groups throughout the world. Vietnam was also divided into North and South, with the North being communist controlled. From the early 1960s, the North Vietnamese sent arms and troops in support of a communist uprising in the south, hoping to bring about the overthrow of the South Vietnamese government. In 1965 United States forces were committed to the fighting to save the South Vietnamese regime from collapse. By 1968 there were over half a million American troops in Vietnam, with U.S. planes bombing the North. Peace talks opened in Paris in 1968, but the conflict dragged on for another four years before terms were finally agreed on in January 1973. The United States withdrew its troops from Vietnam, but hostilities between North and South Vietnam continued. The ruthless conduct of the war on both sides and the hardship it brought to the civilian population aroused tense and bitter controversy throughout the world. Christian solidarity in America was thoroughly shaken as churches and individuals sided with "doves" and "hawks" during the long controversial war. Draft evasion reached an all-time high on conscientious objection to the "immoral" war in Vietnam. Most Christian denominations have preferred to shelve and forget the tragedy of Vietnam rather than trying to resolve the rightness or wrongness of the protagonists.

In the Middle East and Northern Ireland both ethnic and religious differences contributed to tensions after World War II. After thirty years of strife between Palestinian Arabs, Jewish immigrants, and the British, the state of Israel was founded by the United Nations in 1948. West European and North American Christians solidly supported Israel, while Orthodox Christians sided with the Palestinian Muslims against Israel. However, Greek Orthodox and Turkish Muslims clashed in Cyprus when Archbishop Makarios was chosen president in 1960. A six-day war erupted in 1967, in which Israel regained all of Jerusalem from Arab control. In 1973 another Arab-Israeli war broke out, with massive Egyptian and Syrian armies attacking Israel. The Israelis counterattacked and days later an inconclusive ceasefire was agreed on. The Middle East continues to be involved in military skirmishes and international legal battles over the rights to Palestine. Christian fundamentalists, especially dispensational premillenialists, have generally taken a strong stand for Israel's unequivocal biblical right to the land.

Ireland has been involved in a virtual civil war since the South was made the Irish Free State in 1922. The six northern counties, which were largely Protestant, remained in the United Kingdom as Northern Ireland. In 1937 the Irish Free State was renamed Eire, and in 1949 it became the Republic of Ireland. Demands for the reunification of Ireland persisted into the 1950s and violence broke out in the North between Catholics and Protestants in 1969. The campaign of violence in the North has been conducted mainly by the illegal IRA (Irish Republican Army). After the British embassy was burned in Dublin in 1971, "direct rule" by Britain was introduced. The hostilities have continued, however, and neither a religious nor a political solution has come forward.

C. THEOLOGIES: CONVENTIONAL AND VARIANT

The turbulent events and the secular ideologies of the twentieth century were dramatically answered by creative theologies that were often themselves turbulent and secular. Openness and frankness became the order of the day, whether in liberalism or fundamentalism. The brutal frankness of the wars and the open challenge of secularism demanded that spokesmen of the faith be candid and clear.

1. LIBERALISM
The modern phase of theological Liberalism dates from the mid-nineteenth century through the 1920s. It is marked by emphases upon the significance of historical time and the notion of progress. Decisive influences on

Liberalism were the Industrial Revolution and Darwin's *Origin of Species*. In the same vein of historical and biological development, there arose studies in the history of religions, in religious doctrine, of social and religious institutions, morals, and customs. The overriding stress was on the primacy of the present. The foundations for Liberalism had been laid by Schleiermacher's religious self-consciousness, Ritschl's judgments of values, and Kant's empirical objectivism. At the turn of the century, Protestant Liberalism was characterized by an emphasis on the fatherhood of God, the supreme moral and religious example of Jesus, the essential goodness of man, and the duty of doing something to correct the conditions which denigrated mankind.

The most influential theologian in the first decade of the twentieth century was Adolf von Harnack (1851-1930), a leading German church historian who stressed the history of dogma. In the winter of 1899-1900, Harnack delivered a series of lectures in Berlin, in which he sought to present a summary of what he considered the essence of the gospel. This series was later published under the title *What Is Christianity?* and is considered the finest and most influential statement of liberal Protestant theology. For Harnack, the essence of Christianity lay in three central truths: the fatherhood of God, the brotherhood of man, and the infinite value of the individual human soul. He depicted Jesus as a liberator who released men from legalism and showed them the presence of God and the way of love. A practical application of these ideas was attempted during this same period of time by the "social gospel movement" led by Walter Rauschenbusch (who has already been discussed).

The "History of Religion School" was an influential group of German biblical scholars between 1880 and 1920, who advocated extensive use of data from the comparative study of religions in the interpretation of Christianity. Dogmatic considerations were reduced to a minimum, as the School concentrated on tracing historical developments inside Judaism and Christianity. Then it began to search for parallels in Egyptian, Babylonian, and various Hellenistic religious systems. It subsequently concluded that many biblical passages were based on the ancient myths not only of the Hebrews, but also of Babylon, Egypt, and others. Among the leading proponents of this school of thought was Hermann Gunkel (1862-1932), one of the first to develop the method of form-criticism, especially in relation to the Old Testament. Another developer of form-criticism was Johannes Weiss, the first to attempt a consistent eschatological interpretation of the gospel, maintaining that the eschatological ideas underlying the terms "Messiah" and "Kingdom of God" were largely of non-Jewish origin.

Albert Schweitzer (1875-1965), the renowned philosopher, theologian, musician, and medical doctor is perhaps best known for his sacrificial missionary work in a jungle hospital on the Lambarene River in steamy

French Equatorial Africa. By the middle of the twentieth century, Schweitzer had become the best known and most admired Christian in the world, and he was showered with honors, including the Nobel Peace Prize. Less known to most of the world, however, was Schweitzer's contribution to Liberal theology in the early part of the century. His *Quest of the Historical Jesus* (1910) became a classic in a field already crowded with great scholars attempting to interpret the life of Christ (e.g., D. F. Strauss, J. E. Renan, O. Pfleiderer, and W. Wrede). Schweitzer held that Christ shared the contemporary expectation of a speedy end of the world, and when this proved a mistake, he concluded that he himself must suffer in order to save his people from the tribulations preceding the last days. Schweitzer's liberal view of the limited person and knowledge of Christ aroused opposition not only among conservative, but also among liberal Protestant theologians.

A significant scholar of this period was Max Weber (1864-1920), a German sociologist who interpreted the relation of thought to social reality. For instance, he contended that Calvinism had a tremendous influence on the way the capitalistic rulers gained their fortunes and ran their factories by a personal inner-worldly asceticism as called for by the Calvinist ethic. This view from the sociologist's perspective was repeated and amplified in the theological field by Ernst Troeltsch (1865-1923), Professor at Berlin. One of the first to note the close connection between faith and culture, Troeltsch concluded that all religions, including Christianity, grew not out of revelation but out of inner feelings. In his book *The Absoluteness of Christianity and the History of Religions* (1902), Troeltsch criticized Harnack's attempt to define the essence of Christianity in *What Is Christianity?* For Troeltsch, there is no essence of Christianity, for Christianity is an open-ended historical development and in such a historical process there is no essence. Christianity is its history, its totality.

Form-criticism received its strongest advocates immediately after World War I. The basic idea of form-criticism is to assess the historicity of particular biblical passages by a close analysis of their structural forms. Gunkel had applied this method to the narratives of Genesis. In 1919, Martin Dibelius published *From Tradition to Gospel*, in which he attempted to trace the various oral traditions that lay behind the written Gospels, and to seek out the influences which determined the different forms. He concluded that the *Sitz im Leben*, or life situation, out of which the Gospel traditions arose was principally traceable to the preaching and worship of the early church. The most radical approach to form-criticism was by Rudolf Bultmann (1884-1976), who introduced the concept of "demythologizing" the Bible. By this expression, he means that we must liberate the biblical message from the mythological language in which it is expressed so that the modern man who does not share the biblical world view can honestly accept the biblical message. Bultmann was hesitant, however, in recognizing material that could with certainty give historical information about Jesus. He did not make a distinction between "legend" and "historical narrative," and thereby created a great deal of confusion and opposition. Much of form-criticism's methodology had been laid down by Julius Wellhausen (1844-1918) in his *Prolegomena to the History of Israel* in 1885. Wellhausen maintained that the books of the Pentateuch were the combination of four documents, labeled J for Yahwist, E for Elohist, D for Deuteronomist, and P for Priestly. He held that the study of the sequence of JEDP revealed the evolutionary development of the faith and culture of Israel.

In America, Protestant Liberalism was expressed more in practical application rather than in theological dogma, Walter Rauschenbusch's "social gospel" being the most notable example. Early in the century, William James (1842-1910), professor of psychology and philosophy at Harvard University, published *The Varieties of Religious Experience* (1902), making a scientific analysis of conversion. Although widely criticized, the book remains a classic in the study of the psychology of religion. Harry Emerson Fosdick (1878-1969) was a Baptist minister and professor at Union Theological Seminary who was forced by conservatives to leave a Presbyterian Church he was supplying. He became a popular liberal preacher in the Riverside Church in New York City, a church that John D. Rockefeller helped to build. His practical application of liberal theology is evidenced in his books *The Manhood of the Master* (1913), *The Meaning of Prayer* (1915), *The Modern Use of the Bible* (1924), *Successful Christian Living* (1937), *Living Under Tension* (1941), and *A Faith for Tough Times* (1952).

The great majority of Protestant liberals were "evangelical liberals," who did not break so radically with traditional Christianity. Another group developed, however, which has been termed "liberal modernists," because they are basically determined in their thinking by a twentieth-century outlook. The American variety of this approach is frequently referred to as the "Chicago School," with most of the leaders coming from the Divinity School or other divisions of the University of Chicago. Typical of the "Chicago School" is Henry Nelson Wieman (b. 1884), who represented the farthest extreme of Christian Modernism. Wieman is a religious naturalist, rejecting all beliefs that cannot be verified in human experience. For him, the Christian theological tradition is not an adequate guide for men. He maintains that scientific inquiry and not tradition is the principle and power that will shape our lives in this modern technological age. Wieman is convinced that of all the factors obstructing the creative advance of human life, theologies based on faith in a transcendent, supernatural God are among the most dangerous to man's future. While his stance is an extreme minority, it illustrates the ultimate progress of twentieth-century Liberalism.

2. FUNDAMENTALISM

The exponents and tenets of modern Liberalism did not go unchallenged. The advent of literary analysis ("higher criticism"), the concept of evolution, and the general prestige of the scientific method alarmed many conservative churchmen. The reaction of these conservatives against liberalizing tendencies of modern thought launched a movement which came to be known as Fundamentalism. The basic content of fundamentalist teaching was identical with that of classical Protestant orthodoxy. It sought to preserve the nature of Christianity as a redemption religion, the place of the supernatural and the miraculous in Christianity, and the nature of the Bible as the authoritative revelation of the mind and purposes of God.

There are four rather distinct periods in the life of twentieth-century Fundamentalism. From the 1870s to 1920, Bible conferences, Bible schools, and conservative publications established the issues involved. The decade following World War I (approximately 1920-30) witnessed a militant conflict commonly known as the fundamentalist-modernist controversy. From 1930 to 1950, Neoorthodoxy took center stage while Fundamentalism lost its thrust in the large denominations and survived mainly in independent fundamentalist churches, many of which were loosely united in the Independent Fundamental Churches of America, organized in 1930.

The first stage, from the 1870s to 1920, was characterized by a series of conferences in which the views of biblical inerrancy and literal interpretation were applied to emphasize the premillennial second coming of Christ. One of the earliest such Bible conferences was held at Swampscott, Massachusetts, in 1876, and was followed in 1877 by a prophetic conference in New York City. Then the notable Niagara Bible Conferences met annually for several years. Out of these conferences came the so-called Five Points of Fundamentalism. Although there were actually fourteen points, the hard core of fundamentalist doctrine was expressed in the Five Points: the plenary inspiration and inerrancy of Scripture; the deity of Jesus; the virgin birth of Jesus; substitutionary blood atonement; and the bodily resurrection and premillennial second coming of Christ. The Bible conference movement was strongly prophetic and vigorously evangelistic.

Some of the leaders of the Bible conferences founded Bible schools to provide biblical training for lay people. Nyack Missionary College in New York began in 1882. Moody Bible Institute opened in 1886, followed by Toronto Bible College in 1894 and the Bible Institute of Los Angeles in 1908. Wheaton College, one of the nation's foremost evangelical schools, predated all of these with its formation in 1860. The explosive decade of the fundamentalist-modernist controversy saw the establishment of more nondenominational schools, such as Columbia Bible College (1923), Dallas Seminary (1924), and Bob Jones University (1926).

In addition to conferences and schools, the pulpit and the press were used to champion the cause of conservative theology. In 1909, C. I. Scofield published his Scofield Bible, which supported dispensational premillennialism in the footnotes. It became the unofficial text of the Bible for many Bible schools. Also in 1909, the preaching of A. C. Dixon inspired oilmen Lyman and Milton Stewart to underwrite the publication of a series of twelve volumes under the general title *The Fundamentals*. Sixty-four distinguished authors from both denominational and nondenominational evangelicals contributed to this extremely influential series. The Stewart brothers also established and endowed the Bible Institute of Los Angeles. W. E. Blackstone's popular book *Jesus Is Coming* and periodicals such as *The Sunday School Times, Moody Monthly,* and *The Christian Herald* helped to promote the early work of Fundamentalism.

World War I delayed the outbreak of open controversy between the fundamentalists and the modernists, but soon thereafter several mainline denominations plunged into conflict over liberal theology. Among the Baptists the Divinity School of the University of Chicago was a focal point of the controversy. The dean of the school was Shailer Matthews, an outstanding Protestant leader who had served as president of the Northern Baptist Convention and of the Federal Council of Churches of Christ in America. In his book *The Faith of Modernism* (1924), Matthews contended the modern man's view of the Bible must be based on "scientific investigations." He also applied the evolutionary philosophy to religion, revealed an optimistic view of man, and indicated that God could be "found" by man. In defending his position, Matthews attempted to demonstrate that the Modernism of the twentieth century was to the theological right of nineteenth-century Liberalism. He was not able to convince many of his fellow Baptists that the University of Chicago was either evangelical or on the theological right. In 1913 the Northern Baptist Theological seminary was founded as a split from the Chicago school.

The Rochester Theological Seminary was also under suspicion as being liberal, and when A. H. Strong, president emeritus of Rochester, visited Baptist foreign mission stations in 1918, he reported his alarm at the presence of liberal tendencies among missionaries who had been trained at the seminary. In 1920 Curtis Lee Laws, editor of the *Watchman-Examiner,* called for a conference of "fundamentalists" within the Northern Baptist Convention. Some historians record this as the first use of the term "fundamentalist" which gave the movement its name. Others point to *The Fundamentals* series as the origin of the name. It is clear that those convened by editor Laws were the first to call themselves fundamentalists. This group worked energetically to stem the tide of liberalism within the denomination, but some more militant Baptists did not think enough had been accomplished and pulled out to form the fundamentalist General Association of Regular Baptists.

In 1923 the fundamentalists formally organized their forces in the Baptist Bible Union of America. Its triple presidency was J. Frank Norris in the South, W. B. Riley in the North, and T. T. Shields in Canada. The union centered its attacks mainly on the boards of missions, and although it was a Baptist union it recommended nondenominational Bible institutes run by fundamentalists. The Baptist Bible Union phased out as an organization in the late 1920s, but active fundamentalists in the North continued their efforts until the Conservative Baptist Association of America separated from the Northern Baptist Convention in 1947.

Presbyterians encountered the fundamentalist-modernist conflict as tensions built over the infiltration of biblical criticism, resulting in a long controversy over the revision of the Confession of Faith. The ablest theological exponent of the fundamentalist position was J. Gresham Machen of Princeton Theological Seminary. In his book *Christianity and Liberalism* (1923) Machen identified all forms of Liberalism with radical naturalism, and called for a division of the church which would separate "Liberalism" from "Christianity." Under Machen's leadership a highly conservative group withdrew from Princeton and organized Westminster Seminary in Philadelphia in 1929. This led to an Independent Board for Presbyterian Foreign Missions in 1933, and to a separate denomination, the Presbyterian Church in America, in 1936. It renamed itself the Orthodox Presbyterian Church in 1939, and remained a small body.

Another controversy within Presbyterianism was precipitated by the liberal Baptist Harry Emerson Fosdick. In 1922 he preached a sermon entitled "Shall the Fundamentalists Win?" in the First Presbyterian Church of New York where he had been preaching regularly as guest minister. The widely published sermon angered the fundamentalists because he was too liberal and the liberals because he was too conservative. The general assembly of 1923 directed the New York presbytery to see that the pulpit of First Church conform to the Presbyterian Confession of Faith. Fosdick was pressured to leave the pulpit and take the pastorate of the prestigious Riverside Church in New York City. In 1927, however, the general assembly denied itself the right to set up tests of orthodoxy, leaving room for a considerable degree of liberalism in the church.

In Methodism, a tendency toward a more liberal view of the Bible and toward emphasis on the "social gospel" was seen in the church's publications and in seminary training. An organized group of "essentialists" opposed but could not stop the tendency. The question of "sinful amusements" became an issue, as did biblical criticism, but the antagonisms of the fundamentalist controversy did not leave deep scars in Methodism. Fundamentalism in the Protestant Episcopal Church appeared mainly as an issue between those who insist on rigid adherence to the Thirty-nine Articles, and those who do not. The Lutheran Churches in the United States mostly escaped the modernist-fundamentalist controversy of the 1920s. Their confessionalism and theological conservatism since the middle of the nineteenth century reduced the crisis for them. The powerful Missouri Synod helped to hold the line with its emphasis on biblical literalism and an almost Calvinistic position on predestination.

In the Disciples of Christ there has consistently been strong resistance to the liberal movement. The denomination has never taken much interest in the doctrines of the atonement or the premillennial second coming but has instead majored upon baptism as essential for salvation, and that by immersion only. Many conservative Bible colleges and universities have been established by the Disciples, who oppose cooperation with other bodies through missionary and benevolent agencies. Most of the Disciples do not cooperate with the International Convention of Christian Churches because they hold that that agency does not properly exemplify their slogans of "restoration of primitive Christianity" and "loyalty to the New Testament."

Interdenominational Fundamentalism flourished when a huge World Bible Conference in Philadelphia in 1919 led to the organization of the World Christian Fundamentals Association. In 1930, a group of independent churches united in Independent Fundamental Churches of America, requiring member Churches to sever every connection with any denomination. Strong conservative organizations in the second half of the twentieth century include the National Association of Evangelicals and the American Council of Christian Churches, both of which were organized to offset the efforts of the World Council of Churches to create an ecumenical church. The N.A.E. was formed in 1942 with members from more than forty denominations, including the Assemblies of God, National Association of Free Will Baptists, Church of God, Pentecostal Church of God, International Church of the Foursquare Gospel, Free Methodist Church of North America, and Pentecostal Holiness Church. The A.C.C.C. was organized in 1941, and admits into its membership only those who are separated from the National Council of Churches in the U.S.A. Although sometimes confused with the N.C.C., the A.C.C.C. has only fourteen member denominations with a total membership of only 300,000, and the constituent churches of the N.C.C. have a membership of over forty million. The largest groups in the A.C.C.C. are the General Association of Regular Baptist Churches, World Baptist Fellowship, and Evangelical Methodist Church of America.

During the years from about 1930 to 1950, Fundamentalism as a movement prevailed largely in independent churches and interdenominational fellowships. In the mainline denominations theological conservatism remained strong, but was often expressed in "Neoorthodox" terms, which many regarded as a scholarly middle way between Liberalism and Fundamentalism. As the century neared midpoint a new Fundamentalism began to emerge. Many Christians had become distressed that Fundamentalism had been allowed to drift in the period between the two world wars, and some blamed the situation on Fundamentalism's lack of concern over social issues. In 1947, in his *Uneasy Conscience of Modern Fundamentalism*, Carl F. H. Henry expressed concern over Fundamentalism's failure to apply Christian truths to the problems of modern man. In 1956

Henry was persuaded to leave the faculty of Fuller Theological Seminary to become editor of *Christianity Today,* a new periodical launched by Billy Graham and other evangelicals. Under Henry's direction the journal became a tool to advance an enlightened fundamentalism and to present the implications of the gospel for every area of life.

Such men as Carl Henry, Harold Lindsell, and Francis Schaeffer became known as the "Evangelical Establishment," emphasizing the verbal inspiration and inerrancy of the Scriptures, without excluding social action by Christians. An expression of the older Fundamentalism came from the right-wing separatism of such groups as those led by Bob Jones, Carl McIntire, and John R. Rice. To the left of the theological center appeared the "neoevangelicals," a term coined by Harold J. Ockenga, president of Fuller Seminary. This group holds the Bible to be an infallible authority for faith and practice, but believes that biblical criticism can be used profitably. In the 1970s and 1980s verbal inspiration and inerrancy became critical issues again in many major denominations. Fundamentalism proved itself to be alive and thriving.

3. NEOORTHODOXY

At the beginning of World War I, Liberalism was holding sway in the theological world, and one of the main tenets of Liberalism was the progressive realization of the kingdom of God on earth. The devastation and terrors of battle profoundly shook the confidence of the young men who returned to the theological seminaries. The crisis of disintegration for the whole liberal culture was accentuated by the sweeping privations of the great Depression, the diabolic nature of right and left wing totalitarianism, and finally another destructive global war. Between 1930 and 1950, declining Liberalism was seriously challenged and almost thoroughly replaced by Neoorthodoxy, also called crisis theology, or dialectical theology. The term "crisis theology" indicates that the movement began as a Protestant response to the crisis of Christendom after World War I. "Crisis theology" is also taken from the Greek, meaning separation, judgment, and catastrophe. The phrase "dialectical theology" refers to the method of paradox employed by the theologians of this movement.

Neoorthodoxy is the name most used in America, and it recognizes that these theologians speak the traditional language of the Christian church as found in the Bible, the creeds, and the main line of orthodox theology. Yet the language has undergone radical changes, repudiating much of the literalism of later orthodoxy. The movement is sometimes called neo-Reformed theology as reflected in the effort to return to the essentials of the Reformers. Soren Kierkegaard, the great theologian of the nineteenth century (whom we have already considered), can rightfully be called the father of Neoorthodoxy. It was Kierkegaard who insisted that man must take the "leap of faith," because there are no historical or natural "proofs" of

Christianity. Kierkegaard had broken the ground for Neoorthodoxy's Wholly Other, by insisting that man, in his finitude and sin, is in no position to resolve his own predicament. This truth came crashing home as the world surveyed its war-torn cities and depressed economy. It knew it faced a crisis and needed a crisis theology.

a. Karl Barth (1886-1968) was the great Swiss theologian around whom the Neoorthodoxy movement took shape, and it is in his early writings that the major themes of the movement are most forcefully expressed. Karl Barth was born in Basel, Switzerland, and his father, Fritz Barth, was a professor of church history and New Testament at Berne. Karl began his theological studies under his father at age eighteen, but soon moved on to study under many of the great liberal theologians of the day, Adolf Harnack, Hermann Gunkel, Johannes Weiss, and Wilhelm Herrmann, a leading Ritschian who exerted the greatest influence over young Barth. In 1909 Barth became the pastor of a Swiss Reformed church in Geneva where he served for two years. In 1911 he became pastor at Safenwil where he remained for ten formative years. At Safenwil, Barth heard the distant thunder of the guns of World War I, and became acutely aware of sin as man's desire to be independent of God. The liberal messages which he was preaching did not satisfy either him or his congregation in this time of critical need. He and a fellow pastor, Eduard Thurneysen, covenanted together to begin a reevaluation of their whole theological position. During this period of intense study, Barth discovered what he called "the strange new world within the Bible" which his liberal professors had never showed him. He saw in the Bible the world of God which is utterly different from man's world, and he began studying one particular book in the Bible, Romans, which was to launch him and Christian theology into a new era.

Karl Barth's *Commentary on Romans* was published in 1919, and like Luther's work in Romans, it led to a theological revolution. An instant bombshell, the book divided the theological world of Germany into advocates and bitter detractors. The originality, critical power, and actuality of its message gave him a wide hearing, especially in the pessimism of the postwar situation. In 1922, Barth, Thurneysen, George Merz, and Friedrich Gogarten started a journal titled *Zwischen den Zeiten* (Between the Times) to become the organ of a new "theology of crisis," or as they preferred, the "theology of the Word of God." In 1921, Barth was invited to become Honorary Professor of Reformed Theology at Gottingen. In 1925, he moved to the University of Munster as Professor of Dogmatics and New Testament Exegesis. In 1930 he became Professor of Systematic Theology at Bonn. During all this time he was writing, producing *The Word of God and the Word of Man* (1924), *Theology and Church* (1928), and his beginning *Prolegomena of a Christian Dogmatics*. He abandoned this latter work, and began a few years later on a vast scale. The first volume of his *Church*

Dogmatics appeared in 1932, and he worked on it for more than twenty years, producing twelve massive volumes which contain over six million words on seven thousand pages.

When Hitler came to power in 1933, Barth joined Martin Niemoller in forming the German Confessing Church to oppose the pro-Nazi German Christians. In May of 1934, representatives of the Confessing Church met at Barmen where they fashioned the famous Barmen Declaration, which was essentially the work of Barth. It affirmed the sovereignty of the Word of God in Christ over against all idolatrous political ideologies. In December of 1934, Barth was suspended from his teaching post at Bonn when he refused to take an oath of unconditional allegiance to the Führer. The next spring he was forced out of Germany by the Nazis, but the Basel City Council had already elected him to the chair of theology, and he lived and taught there from that time forward, retiring in 1962. Long before his death in 1978, Barth was being classed in the same company of Christendom's great theologians, Augustine, Anselm, Aquinas, Luther, and Calvin. Without question, he has been the greatest Protestant theologian of this century, and every theological movement of the past fifty years has had to defend itself in the light of Barth's theology. Like the Reformers and Schleiermacher, Karl Barth was a genuine watershed in the history of Christian theology.

Simply stated, Barth's theology was a refutal of all "natural theology." God's sole revelation is in Jesus Christ and the Word of God is his one and only means of communication with man. Since man is utterly dependent on divine grace, all his boasted cultural achievements are rooted in sin. Barth deliberately provoked a crisis in Christian thinking by stabbing at the subjectivism which confused man with God, demanding that God be allowed to be God. Barth analyzed sin as man's continual attempt to twist truth even in religion to suit his own ends. Barth sought to force man into a confrontation with the holy, transcendent God of the Bible. His theology came to be called dialectical because of the profound contrasts between Holy God and sinful man, Creator and creature, grace and judgment, God's *Yes* and *No*. He insisted that it is not important what man thinks about God, but what God thinks about man. This led Barth to a renewed emphasis on the Christ who addresses men out of the Bible. In the preface to his 1922 edition of *Romans,* he wrote, "God is in heaven, and thou art on earth." His concept of God as Wholly Other left no way from man to God, but there is a way from God to man, the way of God's gracious self-revelation. Barth has often been called the theologian of the Good News, because the central theme of his *Church Dogmatics* is the gospel of God's gracious election. After 1935, Barth's whole theology became focused on Christology, with every doctrine defined in the person and work of Christ, in whom God has declared himself for man, for all men. Barth's theology

Theologian Karl Barth, who joined Martin Niemuller in forming what came to be known as the Confessing Church. The courageous Barmen Declaration, largely Barth's work, affirmed the sovereignty of the Word of God over political ideologies. Barth was suspended from his teaching and preaching for refusing an oath of allegiance to Hitler's Nazi party. (Religious News Service Photo)

has also been referred to as the "triumph of grace," and the theological scene of the mid-twentieth century could be referred to as the "triumph of Barth."

b. Other Neoorthodox Theologians. Although his was the strongest voice, Barth was not the only churchman concerned about the inability of Liberalism to answer the despair of the twentieth century. A number of outstanding thinkers assumed the stance of crisis theology and employed the language of orthodox Christianity. Some of these were closely associated with Barth, but some could be only moderately called neoorthodox. Emil Brunner (1889-1966) was at the beginning Barth's friend and collaborator, but later they parted over the question of natural theology. Brunner lived and taught in his native Zurich, in Berlin, and in the United States. In *The Theology of Crisis,* a series of lectures given in the United States in 1928, he repudiated modern European culture by attacking idealism, scientism, rationalism, evolutionism, romanticism, immanentism, and Liberalism. What he saw in all this was man's pride and self-deification, which he regarded as the root of all evil in the modern world. Yet he did believe that there is something in man as man which makes it possible for God to be recognized as God by man. This was the point which estranged him from Barth, who countered with *Nein!* (1934), his explosive insistence that the image of God in man is totally destroyed. Brunner also accused Barth of being blind to the responsibility of making theology relevant to modern man's situation. Brunner had a flair for accenting Reformation doctrines in meaningful terms and published influential studies on Christ (*The Mediator,* 1927), ethics (*The Divine Imperative,* 1932), man (*Man in Revolt,* 1937), the Bible (*Revelation and Reason,* 1941), and then later his carefully written *Dogmatics.*

Rudolf Bultmann is often listed as a neoorthodox scholar because he combined the Barthian tendencies of crisis theology with the existentialism of Heidegger. Yet, it is for his demythologization that Bultmann is best remembered. Friedrich Gogarten was one of Barth's earliest collaborators, who formulated a fresh interpretation of culture and civilization in the spirit of dialectical theology. Eduard Thurneysen, Barth's fellow pastor in the critical years of World War I, continued to be his closest friend, and developed the pastoral and social application of dialectical theology.

Dietrich Bonhoeffer (1906-45) was a brilliant young German Lutheran clergyman who was imprisoned and hanged by the Nazis for his participation in the anti-Hitler resistance movement. His tragic martyrdom prevented the full development of Bonhoeffer's theology, and it is difficult to classify him. Yet he is often grouped with neoorthodox thought because of the influence Barth and Bultmann had on him, and his early association with the Confessing Church. Although only thirty-nine when killed, Bonhoeffer left a rich legacy of books, *Sanctorum Communio, Act and Being,*

The Cost of Discipleship, and *Life Together,* as well as letters, papers, and notes published after his death. His *Letters and Papers from Prison* have become classics in confronting a world "come of age." When he calls for men to reject the way of "religion" he echoes the Wholly Other of Barth, and when he speaks of Christ as the "Man for others" he anticipates Tillich's cultural involvement. Bonhoeffer's ideas have sparked and shaped diverse movements, including ecumenism, death of God theology, liberation theology, Christian resistance to war and to oppressive political regimes, and traditional tributes to Christian discipleship, heroism, and martyrdom.

Neoorthodoxy blossomed in the United States in 1932 with the publication of Reinhold Niebuhr's *Moral Man and Immoral Society.* An activist pastor in Detroit, Niebuhr followed Barth and Brunner in attacking the idealism, rationalism, and optimism of the old Liberalism. Yet he criticized Barth, and even Kierkegaard, for their failure to talk adequately about ethics. Particularly concerned with social and political ethics, Niebuhr himself took an active part in politics and founded the Fellowship of Socialist Christians. His was one of the first voices to urge America to help stop Hitler. When Tillich was blacklisted by the Nazis in 1933, Niebuhr arranged refuge for him in America. Although he was often criticized for his socialist emphases, Niebuhr opposed the optimistic humanism of the social gospel movement, and turned to the Bible and Augustinian theology for his insights into human nature and destiny. He criticized both the Marxist and liberal views of human nature in *The Nature and Destiny of Man* (1941-43), insisting that the final answer to the human problem lay beyond history, in the love of God and the cross of Christ. Reinhold's younger brother, Richard Niebuhr, professor of Christian ethics at Yale Divinity School, was also an influential neoorthodox theologian who made important contributions to the study of Christianity and culture. Thus, Neoorthodoxy can be seen as the catalyst for a number of philosophies and theologies, but it was not the only new strand of thought developing after the First World War.

4. EXISTENTIALISM
Neoorthodoxy opposed Liberalism by appealing to transcendent truths, but another movement was on foot which opposed Liberalism by emphasizing the reality of the human situation, rather than idealism. The modern movement of existentialism had its roots in Kierkegaard as did Neoorthodoxy, but began in earnest in Germany following World War I, spread to France and America, and reached its zenith in the late 1940s and 1950s.

a. Existential Philosophy. Although existentialism has varied and diverse expressions, there are common concerns, motifs, and emphases. Basically, existentialism is a reaction against the Greek idea of the general and universal essence of things. The chief doctrine of existentialism is that existence precedes essence, thus the concrete comes before the abstract. The existentialist begins his philosophizing with problems that arise from his own personal existence as a human being. All significant knowledge must pose the question, "What does this knowledge mean for me?" It is not enough that a man know the objective truth, but that he make it existentially his own. Existentialism is profoundly concerned about authentic and inauthentic existence, about being-in-the-world, about anxiety, about depersonalization, and about limit-situations. Existentialism criticizes traditional western philosophy for being intellectualistic and rationalistic, and offers instead a philosophy of change, consciousness, process, movement, passion, and decision.

As already indicated, Kierkegaard was the father of existentialism with his avowal that truth is subjectivity, that God is not discovered by abstract demonstration or in nature but by the leap of faith, and that the life of decision-making man is constantly in a state of anxiety and despair. In the twentieth century, the philosophy of existence received ample development in the writings of Karl Jaspers, who elaborates Kierkegaard's teaching of the inadequacy of general rules and the necessity for crucial and critical decisions. Jaspers pointed out the inability of science to reach the self, which is the ground of all existence.

Existentialism was also linked with the work of Edmund Husserl, the founder of phenomenology. Husserl said that philosophers should turn their attention away from the natural world and toward the inner experiences, which are basic for our apprehension of the natural world. Husserl's famous pupil and successor, Martin Heidegger, moved far beyond Husserl and developed the first part of a theory of being as a whole (ontology). Heidegger saw man cast into an unsympathetic world and condemned to an inescapable fate. Thus, man can be true to himself only by living constantly with the thought of his eventual death. Heidegger's *Sein und Zeit* (1927) had a profound effect on subsequent existentialist writers. Associated with Heidegger is the most influential modern French existentialist, Jean-Paul Sartre, who also studied under Husserl. Sartre is openly atheistic and holds that the problems of life and morality belong not to the world of intellectual theorizing but to concrete human experience. Hence, Sartre believes that the best vehicles for conveying existential principles are not philosophical treatises but the drama, the novel, and personal diaries.

The most prominent exponent of a Christian existentialism in France is Gabriel Marcel, a converted Catholic. Originally an idealist, Marcel came to a "melancholy assurance" that he would never reach a philosophy which was metaphysically satisfying. He concluded that religious faith consists not in adherence to a dogmatic formula, but in trust in a Person. He found, however, the genesis of religion to be in hope, not in despair like

Kierkegaard. A prominent Jewish existentialist who has had considerable impact on Christian thought was Martin Buber (1878-1965). In his book, *I and Thou* (1923), Buber emphasizes the primacy of relation. What really determines the being of a man lies not in the objects which stand over-against him, but in the way he relates himself to the beings and events in the world. Buber says it is the nature of the relation that constitutes the person.

b. Existential Theology. It was only natural that existential philosophy should be of interest to Christian theologians, for the themes of man's freedom, fallenness, evil, alienation, and authentic existence have been integral parts of Christian concern from the Apostle Paul to the present.

Rudolf Bultmann, whom we have already associated with Liberalism and Neoorthodoxy, wears yet another hat in his own self-identification as a follower of existential philosophy. He insists that his demythologizing is an existential analysis of the Scriptures, working through the existential significance of mythical imagery. Bultmann contends that man is the central figure of history, and cannot remove himself from it. Meaning is to be found not in the totality of history but in the personal history of each man himself, which is shaped by his responsible decisions. With this clearly existential posture, Bultmann goes on to reinterpret Jesus' message in light of the personal element of history. Existential self-understanding of that personal element comes only in encounter with that which is other than self. To understand that "other" it becomes necessary to employ myth, that form of thought which represents the transcendent reality to which it refers in terms of the world—the divine in terms of human life.

Paul Tillich (1886-1965) is usually ranked along with Karl Barth as one of the great theologians of the twentieth century. He is also often ranked as neoorthodox because he shared so much of Barth's language and concerns. Yet his methodology was drastically different, and it is this methodology which puts him in the camp of the existentialists. In *Perspectives on Protestant Theology*, he explained it like this: "Karl Barth starts from above, from the Trinity, from the revelation which is given, and then proceeds to man. Whereas, on the other hand, I start with man, not deriving the divine answer from man, but starting with the question which is present in man and to which the divine revelation comes as the answer." In this same volume, Tillich discusses his being called an existentialist: "Often I have been asked if I am an existentialist theologian, and my answer is always short. I say, fifty-fifty. This means that for me essentialism and existentialism belong together. A pure existentialism is impossible because to describe existence one must use language. Now language deals with universals. In using universals, language is by its very nature essentialist." Thus, Tillich stands as a monumental bridge between Neoorthodoxy and existentialism.

Paul Tillich was born in Starzeddel, Germany, the son of a Lutheran pastor. He studied at several universities, including Berlin, Tubingen, and Halle. He received his Doctor of Philosophy from Breslau in 1911. He served as an army chaplain for four years during World War I, and then began his teaching career at Berlin. Next he served as professor of theology at Marburg, Dresden, and Leipzig. In 1929 he became professor of philosophy at the University of Frankfurt, where he became involved in the Religious-Socialist movement. Because of his political activity and opposition to Hitler and National Socialism, he was dismissed from Frankfurt in 1933. Reinhold Niebuhr urged him to come to America, where he became professor of philosophical theology at Union Theological Seminary in New York, until his retirement in 1955. He was then made university professor at Harvard, but in 1962 he went to the University of Chicago where a special chair of theology was created for him. Between 1951 and 1964, Tillich published the five parts of his *Systematic Theology*, which ranks with Barth's *Church Dogmatics* as one of the most significant theological works of this century. After World War II, Tillich wrote several popular books, including *The Courage to Be, The Shaking of the Foundations, The New Being,* and *Dynamics of Faith.*

Tillich's main aim was to relate Christian faith to secular thought. He wanted to make connections between theology and philosophy, religion and culture, Lutheranism and socialism, and between German and American thought. His *Systematic Theology* attempts to offer theological answers to secular questions. In his "method of correlation" he demonstrates the mutual interdependence of existential questions and theological answers. The questions affect the answer, and in the light of the answer the questions are asked. Tillich holds the traditional idea of revelation as that which is spoken to man and not by man to himself. But he also asserts that men cannot receive answers to questions they never ask. He affirms that God is the answer to the question implied in human finitude, for God is "the ground of all being." Indeed, God is being-itself: "the being of God cannot be understood as the existence of a being alongside others or above others." For Tillich, "it is as atheistic to affirm the existence of God as it is to deny it. God is being-itself, not *a* being." He then proceeds to develop a creative reconception of Jesus Christ as the New Being, who is "the ultimate criterion for every healing and saving process." Paul Tillich covers more than a categorized system of philosophy, such as existentialism. In the vast scope of his work, he must be accepted and studied as a master theologian of our time.

5. DIVERGENT TRENDS

The twentieth century has witnessed an unbelievable plethora of theologies. Some have been radical, secular, and humanistic, while others have retained orthodox or traditional traits. The latter have been exceptionally prominent in the Neo-Scholasticism or Neo-Thomism within the Catholic Church. It will be remembered that Pius X condemned and effectively suppressed Modernism, and in 1914 he made it explicitly clear that Thomas Aquinas was the official guideline for Catholic orthodoxy: "All teachers of philosophy and sacred theology should be warned that if they deviate so much as a step from Aquinas, they expose themselves to grave risk." In 1917, Benedict XV required all professors of philosophy and theology to hold and teach the doctrines of Thomas Aquinas. In 1923, Pius XI declared, "St. Thomas should be called the Common or Universal Doctor of the Church: for the Church has adopted his philosophy for her very own." In 1950, Pius XII defended Thomism against the thread of a new Modernism in men such as Teilhard de Chardin. With the reign of John XXIII, beginning in 1958, the rigid adherence to Aquinas was relaxed, but the neo-Thomism had taken a strong hold. Among the earliest leaders of the Thomist revival were Desire Cardinal Mercier, Maurice de Wulf, Ambroise Gardeil, Antonin Sertillanges, and Reginald Garrigou-Lagrange. The two greatest and most influential Thomists of the twentieth century are Jacques Maritain and Etienne Gilson. Briefly stated, neo-Thomism is an attempt to bring the traditional teachings of Thomas Aquinas into the very different twentieth century and show that his doctrines are as relevant to modern problems as they were in the thirteenth century. The theme of the movement is "continuity and adaptation."

As previously indicated, Dietrich Bonhoeffer spawned a great diversity of new trends, including a new radical, secular Christian theology. A number of radical theologians have followed Bonhoeffer's lead in announcing the death of God as father-image. Among these are Bishop John A. T. Robinson, William Hamilton, Paul van Buren, J. J. Altizer, and Harvey Cox. Van Buren explained that what is meant by the "death of God" is that the *word* "God" is dead, and that language about God has no meaning. Altizer, however, asserts that God died when Christ died on the cross. In *The Secular City* (1966), Harvey Cox says that "God comes to us today in the event of social change." In his explosive little book *Honest to God* (1963), Bishop Robinson rejected the notion of a God "up there."

Alfred North Whitehead (1861-1947), distinguished professor of philosophy at Harvard, introduced in *Process and Reality* (1929) the concepts of "creative advance" and "unity of life" to build his "philosophy of wholeness." To Whitehead, the nature of reality is becoming rather than being, and both God and his universe are becoming rather than being. In this process philosophy, which has been developed into several brands of process theology, God is not independent, immutable, and impassable, but is like other entities, dependent, changing, and in process. Charles Hartshorne has devoted himself to the formulation of a natural theology on the foundations of Whitehead's metaphysics. Other contemporary theologians who are developing theologies along the lines set out by Whitehead and Hartshorne are Norman Pittenger, Daniel Day Williams, John B. Cobb, Jr., and Schubert Ogden. Pierre Teilhard de Chardin (1881-

1955) was a Jesuit scientist-theologian who related the Christian vision of God and the world to a scheme of evolutionary process. He saw the cosmos as a fundamental energy in the process of development, with Christ as the "Omega Point." So, God and his world are together evolving to a new, or more perfect order. Teilhard is thus in the camp of process or evolutionary thought.

In *Theology of Hope* (1965), Jurgen Moltmann of Tubingen strikes a note of triumph as he constructs a theology on the premise that the people of God are a pilgrim people who are pulled from the future eschatological hope which has already been revealed in Jesus Christ. Wolfhart Pannenberg of Munich has refuted the Bultmannian school, and has constructed a theology of liberation on God's deeds in the context of history as a whole, with special emphasis on the importance of Jesus' resurrection. Liberation theology emerged in Latin America in *A Theology of Liberation* (1973) by the Roman Catholic Peruvian Gustavo Gutierrez and in Roger Shaull in North America. Black theology and feminist theology have also joined the classification of liberation theology, the main thesis of which is that authentic revelation occurs where the oppressed are being liberated. Salvation means to struggle against misery and exploitation and involves all men and the whole man. Because of the multiplicity of problems in the twentieth century, a multiplicity of theologies developed, attempting to solve those problems through the efforts of autonomous man and an immanent deity in a human Christ.

6. BIBLICAL SCHOLARSHIP

Between the early 1940s and the early 1960s there arose the Biblical Theology movement, which stressed a basic single message in the Bible, a message known as *heilsgeschichte*, or "salvation-history." The thrust of this movement was that the biblical material is a record of God's saving acts in the history of Israel and the church. Oscar Cullman is a noted New Testament scholar who holds that the central theme in the Christian proclamation is that the key to all history lies in the salvation-history of Israel, Christ, and the church. This theme views history not as cyclical, but as linear, pointing to God's unrepeatable acts and to history's future goal. Old Testament scholars who have supported the Biblical Theology idea with outstanding works have included Martin Noth, A. Weisser, and Gerhard von Rad. New Testament commentaries on the theme have come from Vincent Taylor, C. K. Barrett, and F. F. Bruce. Old Testament archaeology and history have been treated together in the works of W. F. Albright, John Bright, and G. Ernest Wright, who made popular the term "theology of recital," indicating that biblical theology is really just reciting what God has done in history.

There were many scholars who were not willing to accept the "single message" theory of *heilsgeschichte* for many reasons. There was the question of interpretation or "hermeneutics," which treats the relation between the ancient text and the modern reader. There was the appearance of a new technique known as "redaction criticism," which analyzes how each Gospel-editor ("redactor") shaped the material toward his own special theological interest. Redaction criticism soon became a serious and accepted tool along with form-criticism and literary criticism. Out of these currents of study came the tendency to see the Bible as containing not one but many theologies. Also, there arose a "new quest of the historical Jesus," which paid more attention to Jesus as a historical figure than Bultmann did. Leaders of this movement include E. Kasemann, G. Bornkamm, and E. Fuchs. All of these new approaches in biblical scholarship have opened up new questions about biblical authority, and the relation between the Bible and tradition.

Archaeological discoveries have made significant contributions in answering some of these questions. From 1929 onward a series of discoveries was made at Ras Shamra in Syria, which shed new light on the myths and religious practices of the Canaanites. Also, excavations at Mari, on the River Euphrates, revealed new facts about the history of the Near East from the time of the early patriarchs to the conquest of Canaan. These relatively recent finds have given strong support to the reliability of the biblical narratives. In 1947 the famous Dead Sea Scrolls were accidentally discovered by a Bedouin shepherd boy among the caves of Qumran, just northwest of the Dead Sea. The scrolls, which contained portions of every book of the Old Testament except Esther, date from the first or second century BC, making them about 1,000 years older than texts previously known. These and other discoveries have encouraged a biblical scholarship which uses the Bible itself as a source-document of historical evidence. Since Christianity is a religion of the "revealed Word" it is impossible for any history of Christianity to ignore developments which relate to the interpretation and application of its sacred Scriptures.

D. ENDEAVORS: CONSOLIDATION AND EXPANSION

As evidenced by the vast profusion of theologies and scholarship, twentieth-century Christianity has not been all heat and no light. On the other hand, neither has it been all light and no heat. Intellectual activity has been more than matched by practical activity. In fact, no century, including the "great" nineteenth century, has witnessed more bustling activity and pragmatic ventures in the name of Christ. Like the rest of the century's developments, this activism has been paradoxical, characterized by both unity and diversity, consolidation and expansion.

1. ECUMENISM
Since its inception, the "scandal" of Christianity has been its fragmentation. Throughout its long history there have been varying degrees of efforts to

overcome this scandal and to bring about unity and cooperation within Christendom. From any historical standpoint, one of the big stories of the twentieth century has been the worldwide ecumenical movement, the offspring of the missionary activity of the nineteenth century. Living as small minorities among vast populations of non-Christians, Protestant missionaries and their converts were driven into alliance with one another. This worldwide sense of fellowship found expression in a series of conferences at Liverpool in 1860, at London in 1888, and at New York in 1900.

a. World Council of Churches. The first World Missionary Conference held at Edinburgh in 1910 is generally regarded as the starting point of the modern ecumenical movement. Through the continuation committee of the conference, there was established the first permanent instrument for international Christian work outside the Roman Catholic Church. Three main movements came out of the Edinburgh conference: the International Missionary Council, the Faith and Order movement, and the Life and Work activity.

The International Missionary Council was formed in 1921, with John R. Mott as its first chairman. The council contributed greatly to the development of ecumenical confidence and mutual trust, particularly in the formation of national Christian councils in many parts of Asia and Africa. The council met at Jerusalem in 1928, Madras in 1938, Whitby in 1947, Willingen in 1952, and Ghana in 1958. By common consent nothing had been said at Edinburgh (1910) about problems of faith and order, but they eventually had to be discussed. Under the inspiration of Bishop Charles H. Brent, the Episcopal Church in the United States called for a world conference on faith and order, at which the churches would meet precisely to discuss the things about which they differed. Planning was delayed by World War I, but eventually the first World Conference on Faith and Order was held at Lausanne in 1927. It appointed a continuation committee and began a process of joint theological study. Further world conferences on faith and order were held at Edinburgh (1937), Lund (1952), and Montreal (1963). The Roman Catholic Church declined to have anything to do with the Lausanne conference, but the Orthodox churches (Constantinople, Greece, and others), which had not been present at Edinburgh in 1910, were well represented. The third movement to come out of Edinburgh was the Life and Work conferences which took shape in the period after World War I. During the war, Archbishop Nathan Soderblom of Uppsala made extensive but ineffective efforts to mobilize the churches in the cause for peace. After the war, he and others continued to press for a united Christian stand on social issues, and under Soderblom's chairmanship, the first Universal Conference on Life and Work met at Stockholm in 1925. The next meeting was at Oxford in 1937, the same year the Faith and Order

The World Council of Churches, meeting in the Concertgebouw of Amsterdam, came into being in August 1948. The historical session was presided over by Geoffrey Francis Fisher, Archbishop of Canterbury. (Religious News Service Photo)

conference was meeting at Edinburgh. The continuation committee of Life and Work accomplished much in the education of all the churches as to the social responsibilities implicit in the gospel.

There were now three ecumenical bodies which had come out of Edinburgh 1910, often overlapping in emphases and personnel. At the meetings of Faith and Order and Life and Work in 1937 and at the meeting of the International Missionary Council in 1938, the question was raised of the formation of a World Council of Churches. The proposal was readily accepted by all three conferences, and William Temple, Archbishop of Canterbury, and W. A. Visser 't Hooft, general secretary of the World Student Christian Federation, were appointed to head the founding committee. The first meeting of the council, planned for 1941, was postponed by the outbreak of the World War II. During the war the World Council of Churches, still only in process of formation, stayed in contact with churches on both sides, and through its service to prisoners of war, refugees, and devastated countries made itself a living reality to the world.

The official formation of the World Council of Churches came on August 23, 1948, at Amsterdam. The council has held five full assemblies: at Amsterdam (1948), Evanston (1954), New Delhi (1961), Uppsala (1968), and Nairobi (1975). At the New Delhi meeting in 1961, the World Council and the International Missionary Council were integrated into one great ecumenical body. Also, at that meeting, the Orthodox Churches of Russia, Bulgaria, Romania, and Poland were admitted to membership in the World Council. The Serbian Orthodox Church was admitted in 1965. The World Council also includes representatives from the separated eastern churches, from the Orthodox Churches of Greek, Arabic, and Slavonic speech, from the Old Catholics, from all the Anglican churches, from the older churches which stem from the Reformation—Lutheran (not all), Reformed (not all), Congregationalist, Baptist (not all), from many of the churches of more recent development, such as the Methodists, the Disciples of Christ, the Society of Friends, and the Salvation Army. The more recently formed churches in Africa and the East have been especially enthusiastic about membership in the Council. Three of the largest Christian bodies in the world, however, do not belong: the Roman Catholic Church, the Southern Baptist Convention, and the Lutheran Missouri Synod.

Since its fourth assembly at Uppsala, Sweden, in 1968, the World Council has turned more and more to the left politically, theologically, and socially. Salvation has been viewed as an earthly and physical experience rather than spiritual. The themes of liberation theology have become central. A commission meeting in Bangkok, Thailand, in 1973 interpreted its theme "Salvation Today" as being the "humanizing of society" to free man from all forms of oppression and to create a new society on earth. The fifth assembly at Nairobi, Kenya, in 1975 adopted a stance of liberation theology oriented toward socialism.

The trend toward socialism in the Council has caused grave concern in governmental as well as ecclesiastical bodies. Church unity had been the original goal of the Council, but the organization has become characterized by "secular ecumenism." Council leaders have argued that unity can best be furthered by overcoming mankind's economic, racial, educational, and other social ills and problems. But the Council's increasingly aggressive involvement in politics and its financial support of violence have caused division rather than unity among the member churches. The United Presbyterian Church, which gives more per capita than any other American W.C.C. affiliate, lost more than one million members in the 1970s, and deep resentment about the World Council's leftist ideology was one clearly expressed reason. Lutheran theologian Richard John Neuhaus has observed that the Council's social and political activities have created "much sharper divisions in the church than any of the old denominational and doctrinal problems did."

One obvious reason for the Council's new leftist image is its altered composition. At the Council's founding in Amsterdam only a small percentage of the delegates were from Third World countries. At the Nairobi assembly in 1975 almost half the delegates were from the Third World. Of the 301 member churches, only twenty-eight are American. A militant anti-western mood dominated the Nairobi meeting, with a strident call for peoples' democracies to replace capitalist states. The head of the Council's Commission on World Mission and Evangelism stated that "the philosophical basis of capitalism is evil, totally contrary to the gospel." Marxist governments, especially the Soviet Union, are practically never criticized by the W.C.C. These and other liberal tendencies have caused the W.C.C. to lose much of its previous support. West Germany's Peter Beyerhaus, head of the International Christian Network, said, "If we don't succeed in bringing the W.C.C. back onto a course that represents its true calling, it would be far better to simply dissolve it."

b. Vatican II. Although the Roman Catholic Church considers itself to be the one true church of Christ, it is deeply concerned about unity and pursues its own way toward it. The annual week of prayer was begun by a Catholic priest and spread worldwide, being officially adopted by the Faith and Order section of the World Council of Churches in 1951. In 1960, the pope established a Secretariat for Promoting Christian Unity, the first official recognition of the existence of the ecumenical movement. It was not expected, however, that the Church of Rome would hold an ecumenical council of its own. The last such council, Vatican I, had been held in 1870 and had declared the infallibility of the pope, increasing even more the distance between Rome and other churches. The whole world was caught by surprise when Pope John XXIII (1958-63) announced that he was calling a council.

Born Angelo Giuseppe Roncalli, John XXIII was elected pope at the age of seventy-six, and most thought he would merely be a caretaker pope. Instead, he began a new age in the Roman Catholic Church, issuing eight encyclicals and updating papal social teaching. He called for cooperation between individuals and social groups, stressed the duty of developed nations to aid emerging nations, argued that peace flows from right order, urged reconciliation during the world political crisis over Berlin, and revised canon law in a sweeping move to update the church. The peak of his achievement was the Second Vatican Council (1963-65), which he called to improve the pastoral work of the church.

Vatican II inaugurated numerous reforms in traditions and customs and made significant strides in the ecumenical pilgrimage. It was the intention of John XXIII that Vatican II was not only to restore the church's energies and seek the forms best adapted to present-day needs, but also to invite the "separated brethren" of East and West to join in a search for reunion. He expressed the hope that the council would be a new Pentecost and a means of spiritual renewal for the church as well as an evident sign of its internal unity.

The decree of ecumenism which the council adopted on November 21, 1964, extols the growth of the ecumenical movement and sets forth ways and means for Catholics to respond to the divine call to unity. It admits that Christians on both sides were often to blame for dissensions, and it recognizes that all who believe in Christ and are baptized are in communion, although imperfectly, with the Catholic Church. It also admits that many of the elements that give life to the church can exist outside the Catholic Church, and that the spirit of Christ has used the separated churches for the salvation of their adherents. It allows Catholics to join in prayer with their separated brethren in certain circumstances, but forbids indiscriminate common worship. It then points out what the Catholic Church has in common with the separated eastern churches and the separated churches and ecclesiastical communities of the West.

As the council was ending (December 1965) the eastern and western anathemas of 1054 (the Great Schism) were withdrawn by a papal mission and by the patriarch of Constantinople. In March 1966, the pope and the archbishop of Canterbury met formally in the Vatican and pledged themselves jointly to work for the reunion of the churches. Vatican II did not change the official position of the Roman Catholic Church toward other churches, but its openness in the decree of ecumenism considerably changed the climate of interchurch relations. The Roman Catholic Church now takes an active part in almost every form of ecumenical activity.

c. *Other Ecumenical Movements.* Efforts toward church union and/or unity have not been limited to the World Council of Churches and Vatican II.

There has been a rather successful effort toward actual organic union in some communions. Between 1910 and 1966, at least forty-six mergers took place in various parts of the world. The Faith and Order conferences directly influenced one of these, the union of the French Protestant churches in 1938. The Consultation on Church Union in the United States began in the early 1960s and has drawn in ten Protestant confessions, affecting some thirty million members; but no extensive agreement has yet been reached.

Each of the main denominations now has its own international organization, such as the World Alliance of Reformed Churches (or Presbyterian World Alliance) which is the earliest (1875), and the Baptist World Alliance (1905). In 1966, the World Alliance of Reformed Churches and the International Congregational Council each passed a resolution in favor of union with the other, the first proposal for union between two worldwide confessions. On the national scale, the union of three branches of Methodism in 1939 brought into being the largest single Protestant denomination in America (until surpassed by the Southern Baptist Convention in the 1960s). In 1957, the Congregational Christian Churches, the Reformed Church in the United States, and the Evangelical Synod of North America united to form the eight major interdenominational agencies merged to form the National Council of Churches of Christ in the United States of America, representing a constituency of more than thirty million Christians.

Evangelical ecumenism has also been a recent development on the part of many who are dubious about the value of the wider ecumenical movement. The first World Congress on Evangelism was held in West Berlin in 1966 under the theme of "one race, one gospel, one task." Thus, Berlin 1966 spoke of an interdenominational, international, and interracial unity that evangelical evangelism inspired. A clear emphasis was the image of apostolic unity under the authority of the Scriptures rather than under ecclesiological or denominational traditions. Subsequently four congresses met on four different continents as regional expressions of Berlin, at Singapore (1968), Minneapolis (1969), Bogota (1969), and Amsterdam (1971). In July of 1974, 2,700 participants from more than 150 nations convened the International Congress on World Evangelization at Lausanne, Switzerland. Evangelist Billy Graham was one of the chief architects of the congress. The interdenominational nature of his ministry was characteristic of Lausanne. The outstanding document of the congress was the Lausanne Covenant which, although not a doctrinal statement, is in the best traditions of Pietism, revivalism, and evangelicalism. The World Council of Churches brought the Lausanne Covenant to the attention of the Fifth Assembly delegates at Nairobi in 1975. More and more, the various ecumenical, missionary, and evangelization conferences are beginning to recognize each other's work, a prerequisite for any further dialogue on Christian unity.

2. SOCIAL ACTIVISM

The domestic and world crises which have confronted Americans during the twentieth century have contributed to a considerable reshaping of the patterns of Christian social thought and action. The earlier social gospel had focused largely, though not exclusively, on problems arising from the conflict of capital and labor. The Great Depression of the 1930s forced the social question upon the churches and extended it to nearly every area of life.

a. Alcoholism and Prohibition. One of the major social problems in America and England at the turn of the century was alcoholism, which received concentrated attention from a wide segment of the Christian churches. Under the leadership of Congregationalist and Presbyterian ministers, the first national temperance association, the American Society for the Promotion of Temperance, was founded in 1826 in Massachusetts. In 1838, the Massachusetts legislature passed the first temperance law. In 1846, the first state prohibition law was passed in Maine, and by the 1850s state prohibition was in effect in thirteen states. In 1869, the National Prohibition Party was founded, pledging in the 1872 presidential election to achieve nationwide prohibition. In 1874, the Woman's Christian Temperance Union (WCTU) was founded. Under the leadership of Frances Willard, it was the leading temperance organization in the United States during the 1880s and 1890s. It was also active in other social reforms, including women's rights, the labor movement, and the Americanization of immigrants. By the end of the nineteenth century, fifteen states had had experience with state prohibition; but only five states still had prohibition by 1900.

In 1906, a renewed attack on the sale of liquor began in many states, with the support of churches, small towns, and rural political power. The drive was led by the Anti-Saloon League, founded in 1895, which applied intensive political pressure on candidates. Wide support was generated through the public opinion of church members. The League utilized the pulpit to spread its message, the ministry as a source of local leadership, and the congregation as a base of financial support. The major source of prohibitionist strength was in the Protestant middle-class segments of the American population, especially the more evangelical ones such as the Methodist and Baptist churches.

The drive from 1906 onward was extremely successful. In 1906, only three states still had prohibition in force, but by January, 1920, when the eighteenth amendment went into effect, prohibition was already in effect in thirty-three states covering 95 percent of the land area and 63 percent of the total population of the United States. The Prohibition Amendment was ratified on January 16, 1919, and went into effect on January 16, 1920. Gaining compliance proved to be a difficult problem. Prohibition was far from universally obeyed, nor was it energetically enforced. The support of

*Several other nations tried and failed at the prohibition of alcoholic beverages.
Despite the 18th Amendment and the efforts of many prohibition movements, the
movement failed with the passing of the 21st Amendment in 1931.* (Religious News
Service Photo)

the federal government to the enforcement of prohibition varied according to personnel, politics, and pressure. The illegal manufacture and sale of liquor continued on a large scale, with prohibition being enforced wherever the population was sympathetic to it. Prohibition introduced a new kind of criminal, the bootlegger, and the rise of bootlegging gangs led to a succession of gang wars and murders.

During the 1920s the temperance movement itself changed radically. The alliance between the progressive and social gospel wings of American Protestantism and the more fundamentalist groups was greatly weakened. The urban forces and the members of the Federal Council of Churches were inclined to withdraw from association with the more militant, rural fundamentalist leadership. The excessive zeal and political pressure of the Anti-Saloon League and the Methodist Board of Temperance alienated many former supporters. Further splits with the ranks came with the involvement of the Ku Klux Klan and the 1928 nomination of Alfred E. Smith as the Democratic candidate for the presidency. Smith repudiated his party's "dry" platform and the repeal of the eighteenth amendment became a major issue in the campaign. The Republicans won the 1928 election, but the Democrats, with a platform calling for repeal, won in 1932. In February 1933, the Senate and House adopted a joint resolution proposing the twenty-first amendment repealing the eighteenth. After repeal a few states continued statewide prohibition, but by 1966 all had abandoned it. In general, liquor control in the United States came to be determined more and more at local levels.

The United States is relatively unique in its attempt to legislate against the use of alcoholic beverages. Aztec society, ancient China, feudal Japan, the Polynesian Islands, Iceland, Finland, Norway, Sweden, Russia, Canada, and India have all attempted some system of prohibition, but only Finland and the United States have ever experimented with national prohibition. Finland adopted it in 1919 and repealed it in 1931. Unquestionably, the ascetic strain in American Protestantism has been the dominating force in the United States in the drive against alcoholism, which continues to be a serious problem. Since the 1960s an additional problem has arisen from the "drug culture," and the fight against drug abuse has received the attention of church groups, government agencies, and private foundations. New pressure has also been brought to bear on the tobacco industry with the dissemination of medical reports indicting tobacco as the cause of cancer and other medical problems.

b. *Civil Liberties.* Many of the basic principles of Christianity have been applied to constitutional governments throughout the world and are especially notable in the United States. The first ten amendments to the United States Constitution are generally called the Bill of Rights, of which the first and fifth amendments are the most far reaching. The first provides that "Congress shall make no law respecting an establishment of religion, or prohibiting the free exercise thereof; or abridging the freedom of speech or of the press; or the right of the people peaceably to assemble, and to petition the Government for a redress of grievances." The fifth amendment guarantees that no person shall be "deprived of life, liberty, or property, without due process of law; nor shall private property be taken for public use without just compensation." These two amendments have provided the background for various concerns within the religious life of America. Government support for parochial schools has been consistently opposed on the grounds of the first amendment. In 1962, the Supreme Court ruled that the organized recitation in public school classrooms of a nondenominational prayer composed by the New York State Board of Regents was unconstitutional. The repercussions have resulted in proposed legislation to legalize school prayers, the establishment of thousands of non-Catholic parochial schools, and a broadside charge of humanism in public education.

(1) Civil Rights Movement. Following the Civil War, three important amendments provided for the civil liberties of minority races. The thirteenth amendment prohibited slavery, the fourteenth provided full citizenship for Blacks and others, and the fifteenth guaranteed the right to vote regardless of race, color, or previous condition of servitude. Blacks continued, however, to be deprived of many rights and segregation remained a way of life, even in the churches. It was not until the Supreme Court's decisions of 1954 and 1955 that segregation was outlawed in public schools. It was also in 1955 that the Interstate Commerce Commission ruled that segregation was illegal on trains, buses, and in waiting rooms. There soon followed proposed bills in Congress to protect the civil and political rights of Blacks. Under President Eisenhower's leadership a Commission on Civil Rights was established in 1957, and in 1964 the twenty-fourth amendment to the Constitution outlawed the poll tax, which had kept many Blacks from voting. In 1964, Congress finally passed a civil rights bill which had been proposed by President Kennedy and strongly supported by President Johnson. The new law strengthened the guarantee of voting rights for Blacks, forbade racial discrimination in places of public accommodation, and encouraged further desegregation of schools.

Reaction to this emphasis on civil rights was highly emotional. Many Blacks were impatient with the slow progress, while many whites insisted it was happening too fast. Churches and denominations became embroiled in controversies over seating and admitting Blacks, and one's stand on the racial issue was often seen as a test of his theology in one direction or the other. Tension mounted throughout the nation with marches and riots erupting. In March 1965, a march on Selma, Alabama, to protest voting policies that denied Blacks was marked by violence and the intervention of federal troops. Nonviolence had been the official policy of the National

Association for the Advancement of Colored People (N.A.A.C.P.), and they organized student "sit-ins" and other methods of protest against segregation of public facilities.

(2) Martin Luther King, Jr., was the strongest advocate of nonviolence, and became the acknowledged leader of the civil rights movement. King was born in 1929 in Atlanta, Georgia, where his father and grandfather had been ministers of the Ebenezer Baptist Church. He also served the church as co-pastor with his father for a while. After attending Morehouse College, Crozer Theological Seminary, and Boston University, King became pastor of Dexter Avenue Baptist Church in Montgomery, Alabama. In 1955, a Black woman in Montgomery, Mrs. Rosa Parks, refused to move to the Black section of a racially segregated bus and was arrested. Young pastor King took up her cause and led a boycott of the public buses in Montgomery to protest racial segregation. A year of economic pressure resulted in the U.S. Supreme Court ruling that racial segregation in interstate as well as intrastate transportation was unlawful.

King was propelled into world prominence as a crusader for social justice. He organized and served as president of the Southern Christian Leadership Conference, which gave him a southwide base of operation and a national platform. He lectured in all parts of the country, conferred with heads of state, and discussed the problems of Blacks with civil rights and religious leaders in the United States and abroad. He played a major role in the civil rights march on Washington in 1963, and in the antidiscrimination and voter registration drives at Albany, Georgia, and Birmingham and Selma, Alabama. He combined direct mass action with a spirit of nonviolence. Basing his policies on the message of Jesus (love your enemies) and the method of Gandhi (nonviolence) he provided both the philosophy and the strategy for the civil rights movement. King was a powerful speaker whose voice rang with a revivalist's fervor. He endured arrests and jailings, was bombed from his home and church, stabbed by a deranged woman in New York, stoned by a Chicago mob, and criticized by "Black power" militants. During the thirteen years he led the civil rights movement, he won victory after victory without once resorting to violence. In 1964, he was awarded the Nobel Peace Prize. An assassin's bullet ended the life of Martin Luther King, Jr., in 1968 at the age of thirty-nine.

c. Fear, Hate, and Terrorism. The twentieth century has been a time of exceptionally great violence. The two world wars and the smaller conflicts seemed to set the scene for violent reactions. Tragically, some of the violence was the result of religious bigotry. The assassination of Martin Luther King, Jr., was clearly the result of his strong leadership in behalf of the civil rights of Blacks. Five years earlier, President John F. Kennedy had been assassinated by an unstable communist sympathizer, but the tragedy occurred within a national atmosphere of seething unrest over Kennedy's

Martin Luther King, Jr., led an estimated 10,000 civil rights marchers from Selma to Montgomery. King was assassinated in 1968. (United Press International Photo)

civil rights program and involvement in the Vietnam crisis. Kennedy's assassination was followed by that of his brother, Robert Kennedy, as he campaigned for the presidency. Robert was shot down by a fanatical young Muslim.

Violence and terrorism became an international phenomenon as men demanded their way. In 1979, a fanatical new regime of militant Muslims took over Iran and inaugurated a thoroughgoing religious Islamic state. The American diplomatic corps in Iran was held in hostage and the world held its breath for fear of an escalating war. That crisis was no sooner over when another American president, Ronald Reagan, was wounded in an assassination attempt. Only weeks later, Pope John Paul II was shot in Vatican Square. The prayers for his recovery by Christians in all the churches of the world demonstrated the strong feelings toward Christian unity and the revulsion against violence. Later that same year (1981), Anwar Sadat, the president of Egypt, was assassinated by a group of Arab loyalists who were angry at his attempts to make peace with Israel. Violence and sporadic raids continued to break out in the weary standoff between the Protestant and Catholic factions in Ireland. Missionaries were murdered indiscriminately when they appeared to hinder the political aims of terrorist groups in various countries where they served. Whereas churches had historically been able to address the issue of war and peace through government agencies which had the power of response, now they found themselves facing an unknown and unseen danger of terrorism, carried out by a handful of fanatics, feeding on the atmosphere of hatred and fear. The importance of converting individuals has become more obvious in the light of the limitations of social reforms, and evangelism has enjoyed increased popularity and success.

3. EVANGELISM
Every century since the Reformation has produced evangelists and revivalists of the stamp of Wesley, Whitehead, Edwards, Finney, Spurgeon, and Moody. The twentieth century has witnessed the evolution of evangelism from the "sawdust trail" tabernacle to international satellite television productions. The huge mass meetings have continued, but they have been augmented with sophisticated training of skills for personal witnessing. Evangelism has become big business for mainline churches and denominations, for independent nondenominational associations, and for the newer phenomenon of parachurch groups.

a. Old-fashioned Revivals. The twentieth century was born in the excitement of newness, but the revival meetings of the nineteenth century continued to be the style of evangelism. The interdenominationally supported revivals of D. L. Moody and his imitators in 1875-1915 were bolstered by a concern to alleviate the unrest of urban industrial society by "evangelizing the masses," and to counter the challenge to evangelical orthodoxy brought by higher criticism of the Bible and Darwin's *Origin of Species*. In the first half of the twentieth century, many educated evangelical churchmen lost interest in revivalism because of its association with Fundamentalism, and turned their attention to social reform. A notable exception was R. A. Torrey, distinguished among the other revivalists of the period by his educational background.

Reuben Archer Torrey (1856-1928) graduated from Yale University and from the Yale Divinity School, was ordained a minister in the Congregational Church, and studied at Leipzig and Erlangen. He joined Moody in his evangelistic work in Chicago in 1889, and later became dean of the Moody Bible Institute and pastor of the Moody Church. He was invited to conduct a series of meetings in Australia, and taking the musician Charles Alexander with him, he preached in Australia and Japan and other parts of the world for two and a half years. This was followed by an overwhelmingly successful campaign in Great Britain in 1903-05. He later conducted similar campaigns in the United States and Canada (1906-11), and in England, Scotland, and Ireland (1911). He then returned to Japan and China (1919). In 1912 he became dean of the Los Angeles Bible Institute and pastor of the Church of the Open Door. Among the thousands he trained was Charles E. Fuller, who became a world-renowned radio evangelist. Torrey became known as the "father of the Bible institutes" because of the foundation he gave Moody Bible Institute and the Los Angeles Bible Institute, from which the other institutes sprang. Yet in his day he was more widely recognized as the educated evangelist who had encircled the globe with the fires of revival.

Contemporary with Torrey, but dramatically opposite in style and education, was the sensational Billy Sunday, whose vivid sermons caused more than one million to "hit the sawdust trail" to confess their conversion. William Ashley Sunday (1862-1935) was the son of a brickmason who died in the Union Army. Billy spent four years in an orphan's home, grew up on a farm, completed high school, and worked as an undertaker's assistant before becoming a professional baseball player in 1883. While playing for the Chicago White Stockings (later the Chicago Cubs), Sunday was converted at the Pacific Garden Mission in Chicago. He joined the Jefferson Park Presbyterian Church, pastored by Frank Dewitt Talmage, son of the famous T. Dewitt Talmage. He played baseball for four more years before becoming secretary for the Chicago Y.M.C.A. During his third year at the "Y," he was asked to become assistant to J. Wilbur Chapman, a well-known evangelist. When Dr. Chapman accepted the pastorate of the Bethany Presbyterian Church in Philadelphia, Billy Sunday and his wife struck out on their own. Billy erected massive tabernacles, seating thousands, who flocked to hear his fiery, fundamentalist sermons. During his career he preached twenty thousand times, averaging seventy-five sermons a month.

He had an exceptionally strong body and voice which enabled him to carry on a vigorous coast-to-coast ministry. He also played a prominent part in the prohibition movement, often holding one-night conventions fighting against the liquor interests. The peak of his career came during a revival in New York City in 1917. Financially backed by John D. Rockefeller, the New York campaign attracted a million and a half people in ten days, resulting in 150,000 conversions. Homer Rodeheaver was Sunday's beloved song leader for many years, and together they gave old-fashioned revivalism a flair and a popularity which paved the way for the crusades of the last half of the century.

b. *Billy Graham* is unquestionably the most successful Christian mass evangelist in history. William Franklin Graham was born near Charlotte, North Carolina, on November 7, 1918. He was converted in an evangelistic campaign in 1934 conducted by an old-style, hell-and-damnation preacher named Mordecai Ham. Grady Wilson, Graham's longtime associate and close friend, was converted the same night with Billy and began preaching immediately. Billy, however, was not sure of his own future vocation. He attended Bob Jones College briefly, but soon left because of the religious rigidity. In the Florida Bible Institute he made his decision to preach, and while conducting a crusade for Southern Baptists in Florida, he decided to become one of them, leaving his parents' Associate Reformed Presbyterian Church. He graduated from Wheaton College in Illinois, where he received a bachelor's degree in 1943. The same year he married Ruth Bell, daughter of a veteran missionary in China. He pastored First Church, Western Springs, Illinois, in 1943-45, where he began his first radio program, "Songs in the Night." In 1946 he became first vice-president of Youth for Christ, International, and began his Crusades for Christ. He became a popular preacher overnight, and was offered the presidency of Northwestern College in Minneapolis, Minnesota, a post he held from 1947 to 1951.

Billy Graham was catapulted into national prominence by a highly successful and much publicized crusade in Los Angeles in 1949. The following year he brought together a talented team to form the Billy Graham Evangelistic Association, and to initiate the radio program, "The Hour of Decision." After resigning the college presidency, he devoted his time to holding evangelistic crusades throughout the world, many of which were televised to widen their impact. His first tour outside the United States took place in 1954-55, when he visited Great Britain and continental Europe. One million attended his revival in Glasgow. At his crusade in Ft. Worth, Texas (1951), Graham began his "follow-up" system of conserving the results of the crusades, and produced his first Billy Graham feature film. Conducting crusades in every state in the union and in more than sixty foreign countries, Graham has preached the gospel to more

Billy (William Franklin) Graham is unquestionably the most successful mass evangelist in history. Los Angeles Crusade, 1949. (Wide World Photo, Courtesy of the Billy Graham Center Museum)

people than any other person in history. He has become confidant and counselor to presidents and heads of state, and holds honorary degrees from more than two dozen colleges and universities.

Graham has published several best-selling books, produced a series of evangelistic films, started the magazine *Decision* in 1960, and played a leading role in founding the periodical *Christianity Today* in 1956. His organization has been constructed on the highest standards of big business, and his methods have won the support of a vast cross section of Christians in every denomination and country. Eager to develop an enduring program of evangelical unity, Graham was instrumental in setting up the World Congresses on Evangelism in Berlin (1966) and Lausanne (1974). He is also concerned that his crusades result in social ministries and change, recalling that "one of the greatest and most far-reaching social revolutions of history was directly related to, and grew out of, the great evangelical revivals of the eighteenth century. I believe that a great spiritual revival today would have social consequences around the world." In spite of his own interdenominational crusades, Graham has consistently emphasized the importance of the local church: "If all churches were engaged in perennial evangelism, I don't think there would ever be need for a person like me." Dr. W. A. Criswell, pastor of the 20,000-member First Baptist Church of Dallas, Texas, where Billy Graham is a member, says, "Billy Graham, beyond any minister of Christ in the world, speaks to his generation."

c. Nondenominational and Parachurch Ventures. Billy Graham's successful use of radio and television has encouraged a multimillion dollar business in media evangelism. Most of the "big time" electronic evangelists are fundamentalists in their theology, and some, like Oral Roberts of Tulsa, Oklahoma, have added the dimension of faith healing. City-wide and area-wide crusades have been styled after Graham's methods, and churches have started training counselors for converts on the same order as the Graham team. James Kennedy originated Evangelism Explosion in his Coral Ridge Presbyterian Church in Ft. Lauderdale, Florida. Through this program, now used in many denominations, the laity is trained through teaching and practice in the art of home visitation and presentation of the gospel.

One of the first parachurch groups was the Gideons, organized in 1898, and dedicated to placing Bibles in hotels, motels, and schools. They distributed copies of the New Testament throughout the armed services during World War II. The Christian Businessmen's Committee International began in 1931 to help businessmen in evangelizing their colleagues. Since 1954 the International Christian Leadership has sought to reach political leaders through prayer breakfasts. The Torchbearers, with headquarters in Capernwray, England, was formed after World War II to train for personal witnessing through shortterm Bible schools. The Navigators were founded during World War II to win sailors to Christ and to disciple them in the Christian life. Billy Graham enlisted the aid of the Navigators in developing a follow-up program for his converts.

A number of groups have specialized in reaching youth. In 1943 the first Youth for Christ rally was held in Indianapolis. Torrey Johnson was the first president and Billy Graham was the first traveling respresentative of Youth for Christ. Young Life was created in 1941 to reach high school students through Bible study groups. The Inter-Varsity Christian Fellowship was started in England in 1923 and incorporated in the United States in 1941, and the Student Foreign Missions Fellowship affiliated with it in 1945. Campus Crusade was organized in 1951 to present the gospel to students on college and university campuses.

Some of the ongoing parachurch groups have had goals and purposes other than specific evangelism, but have contributed to church growth and involvement. Elton Trueblood's Yokefellows has promoted church renewal through the study of Christian classics and personal discipline. Bob Pierce's World Vision International has become a multimillion-dollar benevolent organization, providing food, medicine and shelter for orphans and refugees from war and natural disasters. David Wilkerson's Teen Challenge has focused on helping young drug addicts, and Alcoholics Anonymous continues its long tradition of giving moral and spiritual support to reforming alcoholics. The support of parachurch groups by denominations and churches varies greatly, depending on locale and church leadership. Some denominations have offset the influence of these groups by establishing similar services within their own fellowships, but variety and experimentation continue to be the motif both inside and outside mainline denominations.

4. WORLDWIDE CHRISTIANITY

By the end of the nineteenth century, a worldwide Christian community had been created. The first World Missionary Conference, held in Edinburgh in 1910, heralded a new era of mission posture and strategy. The traditional center for Christianity had been Europe for centuries, but now it became increasingly difficult to speak of a "center" anywhere, for the dispersal of Christianity's strength was becoming worldwide. (Although this volume of the history of Christianity has tended to focus on European and American developments, one should realize that a vast history of innumerable names and movements could be written about any area where the gospel has made inroads and become a viable religion for the peoples of that country.)

a. Christianity and Culture. The modern mission movement cannot be isolated from political, economic, and cultural imperialism. Missionaries carried not only the message of Christianity but the values and perspectives of western man. Thus, while Christianity brought the gospel hope, it also caused disruption of morals, mores, and culture which were centuries old. One of the effects of this disruption has been the revolutionary demand for liberation from colonization, and the emerging of new nations. Christianity today faces the turmoil of an age of liberation that its missionary thrust has been largely responsible for ushering in.

Early mission efforts often included the westernizing of culture, and for many people in the Third World, Christianity became a symbol of modernity. Western missionaries assumed that new churches in the mission territory would have to be patterned after the models that they imported with them from back home. This lack of cultural sensitivity has led to an increased demand for indigenous leadership, and a syncretism of Christianity with indigenous culural patterns. Many countries are producing a "native" version of Christianity, strongly nationalistic and tolerating ancient ideas and customs. Some more traditional leaders are afraid that this is often no more than "baptized heathenism." In Africa, for instance, the practice of polygamy or witchcraft may accompany some forms of Christianity. Concerned African theologians say that the urgent task is to provide a theology which is both true to the gospel and free from western culture. They contend that Africans themselves can and should build bridges between the Christian gospel and African thought-forms. Christian theologians in India are also concerned about expressing the gospel in ways that relate to the Indian culture. Some agree that the concepts of Hinduism must be used to expound the doctrine of Christ to Indians, but others see this as compromising the gospel. The issue seems to be the same one which separated Barth and Tillich in their theology: should the starting-point in theology be our own present experience in life, or should we begin with the givenness of revealed truth?

b. Expansion and Opposition. It is overwhelmingly evident that Christianity has flourished and expanded greatly during the twentieth century. In 1910, 40 percent of the population in the United States held membership in the Christian churches. By 1976, that had increased to 77 percent. Concomitant with that figure, 70 percent of all Protestant missionaries, and an even higher proportion of the total cost of missionary operations, came from North America. In Canada, the Roman Catholic Church has enjoyed a huge growth and now embraces approximately 45 percent of the population. In 1925, the Methodists, Congregationalists, and a majority of the Presbyterians united to form the United Church of Canada. It and the Church of England are the largest non-Catholic bodies in the Dominion. However, in recent years evangelistic, fundamentalist, and enthusiastic churches have experienced a spectacular growth.

Latin America has been regarded as a Christian continent for several centuries, but up until World War II, the missionaries (Roman Catholic) were mainly from Europe. By 1950, the region had become the major foreign field of the Roman Catholics in the United States. Catholic missions in Latin America, however, have had numerous setbacks, especially in Mexico where some fourteen states had forbidden priests and made the saying of Mass and the giving of sacraments a criminal offense around 1935; but the condition had become more favorable in the 1940s. Catholicism also has had a difficult task of competing with positivism, theosophy, spiritualism, and communism among its adherents. On the other hand, Protestantism grew at an amazing rate during the first three-quarters of the twentieth century. In 1914 there were only about 500,000 in all of Latin America, and by 1970 they numbered over ten million, including nearly eight million in Brazil. Luis Palau, called the Billy Graham of South America, has had many successful urban mass crusades in leading Latin cities.

Since the latter half of the fifteenth century, Christianity had been in Asia and Africa south of the Sahara, but during the twentieth century it faced the test of survival over the burgeoning nationalism and the efforts to liquidate all occidental colonial rule. Not only did it meet the test, but in most places appeared to thrive on the challenge. In Madagascar, Christians comprised about one-fourth of the population in 1914, and by 1950 the ratio had risen to one third. A great boost to Christian solidarity came in 1934 when the majority of Protestants there formed the United Protestant Church of Madagascar. Catholic increase was largest in equatorial Africa, where they had four indigenous African bishops by 1952. In the Union of South Africa, Christians increased from about one-third of the population in 1914 to more than one-half by midcentury, the large majority being Protestants. There has been a large proliferation of Protestant divisions in Africa, with many new sects and churches branching off. Approximately one hundred new "independent" groups are founded every year. By 1975, there were some 100 million Christians in all of Africa. Thirty million are Catholics, 22 million Protestants, 8 million independent Protestants, and 5 million in the Ethiopian Coptic Church.

Although Christians still comprise a very small minority in India, their influence on the culture and politics there has been significant since 1914. Numerically, Christians rose from about 1 percent of the population in 1914 to about 2½ percent in 1950. Catholics and Protestants both have majored on developing Indian leadership which has influenced cultural trends, especially seen in education, medicine, rural life, and the position of women. Christianity in Indonesia underwent severe persecution during the Japanese occupation of World War II, but has had a recent resurgence. A revival which began there in 1965 resulted in 200,000 conversions in Timor in only two years. Church growth was strong in the Philippines from 1914 to 1942, but Japanese conquest disrupted everything throughout the islands. After the war, growth accelerated again, and in 1948 the Presbyterians, Congregational Christians, Evangelical United Brethren, and some Methodists and Disciples of Christ formed the United Church of Christ of the Philippines.

In China, Christianity made great strides after the revolution of 1911-12 and the disintegration of Confucianism, and by 1924 there were more than two million Catholics and half a million Protestants. In the late 1920s the communists spearheaded a strong anti-Christian movement, and many missionaries left the country. During World War II the sections of China under Japanese rule had severe restrictions placed on the churches. After the war, Christians multiplied. Sun Yat-sen, the most influential Chinese of the century until communism, was a Protestant, and Chiang Kai-shek was baptized by a Protestant, and became a Christian. For a brief time, the World Council of Churches had a Chinese as president. Then the triumph of communism dealt Christianity its most severe blow in a century and a half in China. By the end of 1950, practically all missionaries were gone from China. In that year, over four hundred thousand Chinese Protestants signed the *Christian Manifesto,* which condemned "all imperialism and aggressive design in China" and pledged "patriotic support of the Common Program." The Church of Christ in China and the National Christian Council came under communist control, and Protestants were constrained to join these groups.

From 1914 to the early 1930s, Christianity enjoyed a stable growth in Japan, producing some exceptional leaders, such as Toyohiko Kagawa (1888-1960), who rose to worldwide fame as a Christian social reformer, evangelist, and author. After Japan invaded Manchuria in 1931, it was condemned by the League of Nations and withdrew from that body in 1933. Then came the invasion of China in 1937 and the outbreak of war with the United States and the British Empire in 1941. Christians suffered greatly in Japan during the war, but after the defeat and occupation of Japan, the doors were opened again for Christianity. By 1970 there were about a million Protestants and about a half million Catholics in Japan. Christian work in Korea suffered greatly during the war between North and South Korea, but after the armistice of 1953, Christianity began to flourish in South Korea. Out of a population of 31 million there are three million Christians, and the number is increasing at the astonishing rate of 10 percent a year, more than four times as fast as the population growth. There are more than 1,600 churches in the capital, Seoul, one of which is the largest Christian church in the world with over 100,000 members.

No religion in history has spread as far and as quickly as Christianity has in the past few decades. Yet many countries do not welcome Christianity. The Muslim world is especially hostile to Christians, and communism works methodically and persistently to choke out all religion. Also, Christianity is not the only agressive and growing religion. In recent decades a general revival of religions has been witnessed throughout the world. Occultism and Asian religions have even flourished in the West.

Islam has had a resurgence in some areas of Africa, Malaysia, and Pakistan. Buddhism has experienced revival in Thailand, Vietnam, Cambodia, Burma, and Sri Lanka. Hinduism has felt new life stirring in India, and Japan has witnessed Shintoism's returning popularity. In spite of all its unparalleled growth and expansion, Christianity is still not a majority religion in the world. Out of a world of four billion people, there are about one billion Christians, but there are about 700 million Muslims and about 500 million Hindus.

In two thousand years, the dozen disciples of Jesus Christ have multiplied to embrace one-fourth of the world's people. The journey has been diverse and precarious. The detours have been confusing and threatening. The guides have been numerous and contradictory. But the essential message of Christianity has remained intact. Whether couched in the intellectual vocabulary of philosophy and theology or expressed simply in pietistic humility, the good news of the gospel continues to be that "the Word was made flesh, and dwelt among us, and we beheld his glory, the glory as of the only begotten of the Father, full of grace and truth" (John 1:14). Those who believe that Jesus of Nazareth was "truly God and truly man" continue to proclaim his message and perform his ministry.

As the "body of Christ" the church lives and serves in both simplicity and complexity, in poverty and wealth, in lowliness and greatness. In some places it holds sway in power and majesty; in others it gasps for breath under persecution and suffering. Some men marvel at what the church has accomplished, and some are disappointed that it has not done more. Some wonder if a better vehicle could have been chosen for such an awesome task as the transformation of the world, but the scriptural affirmation and the historical evidence still contend for the purposeful paradox: "We have this treasure in earthen vessels, that the excellency of the power may be of God, and not of us" (2 Corinthians 4:7).

I N D E X

Abbe Felicite de Lamennais 371
Abbott, Lyman 419
Abelard, Peter 175, 177, 191
A Blow at the Root 337
Abolition 425, 426, 428, 429, 431
Abraham, God's covenant 16
absenteeism 202
absolutism 309
Acacian Schism 111
Academics, the 102
A Calm Address to the American Colonies 358
Acre, fall of 173
Act of Association 279
Act of Forbidding Papal Dispensations 273
Act of Supremacy 278
Act of Toleration 291, 317
Act of Uniformity 290
Adams, John 356
A Defence of the Rights of the Christian Church 318
Admonition to Peace 246
Adolphus, Gustavus 309
Adoptionists (Monarchians) 77
Adrian IV, English pope 191
Against Heresies, Irenaeus 78
Against Marcion, Tertullian 78
Against Praxeaus, Tertullian 78
Age of Reason 314, 332, 364, 409
agnosticism 359
Alaric, king of Visigoths 96, 105
Albert of Brandenburg 230
Albert of Mainz, Archbishop 236
Albert of Vercelli, patriarch of Jerusalem 173
Albert the Great 172
Albertus Magnus 175, 179

Albigenses 192
Albright, W. F. 494
Alcoholics Anonymous 513
Alcuin 147
Aldersgate 335
Alexander I 435
Alexander II 164
Alexander III 191, 193
Alexander V 208
Alexander VI, pope 221, 222, 343
Alexander of Hales 229
Alexander of Rome 109
Alexander the Great 19
Alexandria 109, 134
Alexius Comnenus 186-187
Alfred the Great 147
Altizer, J.J. 493
Amalricians 194
Ambrose, Bishop of Milan 96, 100, 102
American Baptist Convention 403, 441
American Bible Society 364, 401
American Council of Churches 475, 483
American Missionary Association 458
American Revolution 359, 364
Amman, Amish 270
Anabaptists 243, 249, 254, 264, 266, 267, 268, 269, 274, 281, 309
Anacletus 109
Anastasius 97-98
Andrew, Bishop James O. 440
Anglicans 280, 284, 285, 390, 437
Anglo-Saxons 127, 128
Anne, Queen 316
Anselm 166, 174, 176-177
Anthony 90, 102
antinomianism 337
Antioch 109, 133, 134
Antioch, bishop of, 71, 77
Antiochus III 19
Antiochus IV 19-20

Apocrypha, the 303
Apostles, tradition about their deaths 54, 55
Apostles' Creed 194, 256
Apostolic fathers 66-71
Aquinas, Thomas 101, 172, 175, 179, 182, 229, 315, 493
Aramaic 18
Arcadius 96
Arianism 90, 92, 93, 95, 96, 97, 99, 100, 109, 111, 114, 115, 124, 126, 153
Armenia, Armenians 155, 184, 405
Arminius, Jacob, Arminianism 262, 263, 338, 362
Asbury, Francis 338, 358
asceticism 89, 91
Assemblies of God 448
Athanasius 93, 99, 100, 115, 157
Athenagoras 71
Atilla the Hun 97, 109
Augsburg Confession 248
Augustine of Canterbury 128
Augustine of Hippo 92, 96, 100-106, 128, 174, 213, 243
Augustinians 173, 231, 236
Avignon popes 199, 205

Backus, Isaac 352, 358
Bacon, Francis 314
Baldwin of Flanders 188
baptism 145, 239, 283
baptism, infant 136, 239, 267, 269, 270, 283, 291
Baptists 266, 283, 291, 340, 346, 360, 398, 431, 440-441, 445, 481, 482
Baptist World Alliance 415, 441
"Bare-bones" parliament 287
Barmen Declaration 464, 486

Baroque 374
Barth, Karl 376, 382, 464, 485, 486
Basil the Great 91
Basil II 157
Battle for Toulon 368
Battle of Bunker Hill 357
Battle of the Nations 370
Battle of Tours 134
Beaconites 441
Beecher, Henry Ward 360, 419, 432
Beecher, Lyman 359, 360, 362, 428, 431
Beethoven, Ludwig von 375
Belgic Confession 262
Benedict I 127
Benedict IX 149
Benedict X 164
Benedict XI 202
Benedict XIII 203
Benedict XV 468, 493
Benedict of Nursia 112-114
Bernard of Clairvaux 169, 177, 187, 190
Berthold (Carmelites) 173
Beza, Theodore 261
Biro, Matthias of Deva (Devoy) 251
Blackstone, W. E. 481
Bloody Mary 278
Boccaccio, Giovanni 213
Boehme, Jacob 328
Bogomile, Bogomiles 156, 194
Bohemund of Tarentum 187
Boleyn, Anne 272
Bolsheviks 459, 460, 463
Bonhoeffer, Dietrich 464, 473, 488, 493
Boniface 130, 142
Boniface VIII 201-202
Book of Common Prayer 276, 390
Book of Homilies, Cranmer 276
Book of Martyrs, Foxe, John 279
Book of Mormon 447
Book of Sports, James I 283
Booth, William 390
Borgia, Cesare 221, 306
Borgia, Lucrezia 221
Boston Massacre 356
Boston tea party 356
Boxer Rebellion 407
Bradford, William 284
Brainerd, David 352, 397
Bramante, Donato 218, 222
Breda Declaration of 1660 288
Brent, Charles H. 416, 496
Brethren of the Common Life 211, 215, 231, 262
Brewster, William 284
British and Foreign Bible Society 340, 400

Brude, king of the Picts 112
Bucer, Martin 254, 276
Bullinger, Henry 255
Bultmann, Rudolf 478, 488, 491
Bunyan, John 291
Burgundians 124, 126
Buxton, Thomas Fowell 392, 428
Byzantine art 124, 158
Byzantine Empire 94, 138, 153, 184

Cabot, John 344
caesar 22, 86
Caesaropapism 98, 138, 152, 154, 157
Calvert, George (Lord Baltimore) 345
Calvin, John 106, 255, 296, 376
Calvinism 251, 258, 264, 280, 285, 321, 362, 438, 444
canonization 52, 53, 191
Canute the Great 131
capitalism 387
Cappadocia 91, 111
Caraffe, Giovanni 293, 297, 298
Carey, William 340, 398, 402
Cartwright, Thomas 280
casualties of World Wars 472
Cathari 192-194
Catholics, Catholicism 158, 291, 294, 308, 332, 364, 372, 383, 408, 442, 463
Celestine III 189
celibacy of priesthood 159, 165, 271
Chalcedon 97, 153
Chardin, Teilhard de 384, 493
Charlemagne (Charles the Great) 142-146, 370
Charles I 287, 291, 345
Charles II 288, 290, 291
Charles V, Emperor 173, 228, 241, 243, 244, 247, 262, 273, 276, 293, 302, 306
Charles VIII 222, 228
Charles IX 261, 306
Charles Martel 134, 141
Children's Crusade 188
Christianity and the Social Gospel, Rauschenbusch 424
Christianity Today 484, 512
Christian Science 446
Christian Socialists 392, 422

Chrysostom, John 101
Church fathers 99
Church Missionary Society 340, 392, 398, 426
Church of England 228, 272, 274, 277, 279, 282, 288, 290, 291, 345, 356, 388, 410
Church of Jesus Christ of Latter-day Saints 447
Church of Scotland 285, 342, 400, 439
Cistercians 168, 183
City of God, The, Augustine 96, 105-106
Civil Rights movement 458, 504-508
Clarkson, Thomas 340, 426
Clement of Alexandria 79
Clement of Rome 68, 108, 109
Clement IV, pope 182
Clement V 174, 199, 202
Clement VI 229
Clement VII 273, 274
Clovis, king of the Franks 124, 126
Cluny, Cluniac Reformation 166, 167, 184
Coke, Thomas 338, 400, 440
Coleridge, Samuel Taylor 375, 376
Colet, John 215, 272
Communism 327, 372, 458-461
Communist Manifesto, The 420, 458
Concordat of Worms 166
Confederate States of America 430, 432
Confessing Church, The 464, 486
Confessions, Augustine 105
Conformists 280
Confutation, reply to Augsburg Confession 248
Congregationalism, Congregationalists 281, 284, 345, 346, 356, 360, 362, 363, 389, 390, 410, 437
Constantine 88, 92, 93, 94-95, 109, 110, 239
Constantinople 91, 94, 184, 187, 188, 191, 200
Constantinople, Council of 79, 91, 100, 115
consubstantiation, doctrine of 92, 239, 248, 254, 304
Consultation on Church Union 501
Council of Arles 92
Council of Basel 205, 206, 220

Council of Chalcedon 97, 110, 118, 153
Council of Constance 204, 205, 208, 237
Council of Constantinople 91, 100, 115, 116
Council of Ephesus 97, 117
Council of Nicaea 99, 108, 110, 114, 137, 153
Council of Pisa 203, 204
Council of Trent 301, 302, 305, 372, 412
Council of Verona 193, 194
Counter-Reformation 292, 298, 305
Coverdale, Miles 275
Cranmer, Thomas 273, 275, 276, 277, 278
Cromwell, Oliver 284, 286-288, 291
Crusades, the 172, 184-190
Cyprian 64, 81, 107-108, 110

Dabney, Robert Lewis 431, 432
Damasus 107, 110
Dante, Alighieri 212
Darwin, Charles, Darwinism 416, 419, 461
Das Kapital 420, 422
Dead Sea Scrolls 495
"death of God" theology 380, 381, 493
Declaration of Independence 320, 357, 358
Deism, Deists 316, 319, 320, 321, 322, 325, 327, 359, 363, 367, 374
"demythologizing" Scripture 478, 491
Descartes, René 314, 315, 317
Diet of Augsburg 248, 306
Diet of Worms 241, 315
Diocletian 61, 65, 81, 82, 85, 86, 90, 91
Dionysius 13, 75
Disciples of Christ 360, 440, 444, 445, 482
d'Medici, Catherine 261, 306
docetism 74, 75
Dominicans, monastic order 172, 173, 180, 195, 236
Donation of Constantine 110, 142, 205, 214
Donatus, Donatism, Donatists 91, 92, 97, 104, 129
Donne, John 291

Drummond, Henry 418, 442
Duke of Alva 279, 307
Duns Scotus 172, 175, 182
Durer, Albrecht 216
Dutch Reformed Church 262, 346, 349, 439
Dwight, Timothy 359, 360

Eastern Orthodox Church 150, 434
Eck, Johann 237, 238, 267
ecumenical movement 474, 495-499
Eddy, Mary Baker 446
Edict of Milan 88, 89
Edict of Nantes 261,262, 307, 309, 310
Edict of Worms 241, 247
Edward VI 263, 276, 278
Edwards, Jonathan 349, 350, 351, 360, 397
Eighth Ecumenical Council 155
Elizabethan Settlement 278, 280
emancipation 428, 430
Emerson, Ralph Waldo 429, 438
English Civil War 284, 364
Enlightenment 291, 319, 325, 327
Episcopalian 360, 431
Erasmus, Desiderius 211, 214-215, 222, 238, 241, 243, 262, 272, 298
Ethelbert, king of the Jutes 127, 128
Eugenius III, pope 169, 187, 190
Eugenius IV, pope 205, 206, 220
Eusebius of Caesarea 66, 86, 89, 107, 115
evangelicals 339, 393
evolution 416, 479
existentialism 488, 489, 490, 491, 492

Factory Acts 391, 392
Falangist of Spain 462
Familiar Colloquies, Erasmus 215
Farel, William 258
Fascism 461, 464, 472
Fawkes, Guy 284
Federal Council of Churches 415, 481, 504
Felix V 206, 220
filioque 145, 154, 155, 159
Finney, Charles G. 359, 362, 363, 393, 414, 431

First Conventicle Act 290
First Great Awakening 349, 359, 360
Five Mile Act 290
Flavian 117, 118
form-criticism 479
Forty-two Articles of Religion 276, 279
Fosdick, Harry Emerson 479, 482
Four Prague Articles, Hussite 210
Fourth Crusade 187, 188, 191, 192
Fourth Lateran Council 168, 172, 178, 188, 192, 195
Fox, George, Quaker 287, 288
Foxe, John, Book of Martyrs 279
Francis I 228, 237, 256
Franciscans, the 169, 183, 294, 408
Francis of Assisi 169-171, 193
Franklin, Benjamin 327, 351
Frederick I (Barbarossa) 187-188, 191
Frederick II 188, 191, 195
Frederick III 220
Frederick V 308
Frederick the Elector (Saxony) 234, 238, 241
French Revolution 320, 332, 364-367, 371, 374
Froude, Hurrell 410
Froude, James A. 457
Fugger bankers 230
Fuller, Charles E. 509
Fuller Theological Seminary 484
Fundamentalism 430, 479-484
Fundamentals, The 481
Furman, Richard 358, 431

Gaiseric 97, 109
Galerius 61, 85, 88
Gandhi, Mohandas 469, 506
Gardiner, Bishop of Winchester 277
Garrison, William Lloyd 428, 431
General Association of Regular Baptists 481
General Baptists (Arminian) 284, 441
George, Henry 422, 425
"German Christians" pro-Nazi 463
Gideons, International 512
glossolalia 450

Gnosticism 73, 76, 79, 107, 109
Gobineau, Joseph de 456, 461
Goethe, Johann Wolfgang von 366, 375, 377
Gogarten, Friedrich 485, 488
Göring, Hermann 462
Goths 98, 111
Grace Abounding, Bunyan 291
Graham, (William Franklin) Billy 501, 510
Gratian 96, 100
Great Awakening, The 339, 352, 439
Great Bible, The 275
Great Schism (East-West) 158, 184
Grebel, Conrad 254, 267
Gregory, Bishop of Nazianzus 91, 115
Gregory, Bishop of Nyssa 91, 115
Gregory I (the Great) 126, 146, 176
Gregory II 130
Gregory III 136, 137, 141
Gregory V 149
Gregory VI 149
Gregory VII 146, 165, 167
Gregory IX 195
Gregory XI 203
Gregory XII 204
Gregory XIII 307
Gregory XVI 371
Grey, Lady Jane 277
Grindal, Edmund 280, 281
Groot, Gerhard 211
Gunkel, Hermann 477, 485
Gunpowder Plot, Guy Fawkes 284
Gutenburg, Johann 219
Guyon, Madame 331

Hadrian I, Pope 137
Halle-Danish mission 397
Halle Pietists 331
Hamilton, Alexander 357
Hamilton, Patrick 263
Hamilton, William 493
Handbook of the Christian Soldier, Erasmus 215
Hanukkah, Feast of 20
Harnack, Adolf von 380, 477, 485
Harris, Howell 341
Hart, Fenton John A. 419
haystack prayer meeting 401
Hegel, G.W.F. 326, 327, 378, 382
Hegira 132

Heidegger, Martin 454, 490
Heidelberg catechism 262
Hellenism 95, 99
Helwys, Thomas 284
Hennepin, Father Louis 344
Henry I 166, 176
Henry II 188, 194
Henry III 164
Henry IV 166, 167, 184, 307, 309, 310
Henry IV (Navarre) of France 261, 306
Henry V (of Germany) 166
Henry VII 272
Henry VIII (of England) 168, 272, 273, 274, 278
Henry, Carl F. H. 483, 484
Heraclius, emperor 131
"hermeneutics" 495
Herrnhut 331
Hess, Rudolf 462
higher criticism 379, 479
Hildebrand, Gregory VII 164-168
Hitler, Adolf 462
Hoffmann, Melchior 268
Holy City, The, Bunyan 291
Holy Club, The 334
Holy League 222, 306
Holyoake, G. J. 454, 456
Holy Roman Empire 228, 266, 306, 309
homos-ousios 93, 115
Honorius 96, 110
Honorius III 170, 172, 175, 195
Hooker, Thomas 345
Hopkins, Samuel 359, 362
House of Commons 228, 279, 286
Houses of Parliament 284
Howard, Catherine 276
Hugh of Vermandois 187
Huguenots 261
humanism 212-215, 243, 262, 272
humanists 212-215
Hume, David 319, 324
Hus, John 208-210, 237
Hussite 268, 305
Hutterites 268
Huxley, Thomas Henry 419
hypostaseis 79, 115

iconoclasts 154
icons 136-138
Ignatius of Antioch 68, 77
Imitation of Christ, The 211, 212
immaculate conception 179, 372, 433
Independent Fundamental Churches of America 480, 483
Independents 266, 281, 291

Index, The (Caraffa) 298
indulgences 221, 222, 229, 230, 234, 235, 271
Industrial Revolution 332, 384, 386, 390, 424, 477
inerrancy of Scriptures 416, 418, 480, 484
infallibility of the pope 206, 372, 433, 499
Innocent I 101, 104, 110, 190
Innocent II 169
Innocent III 188, 189, 191, 194, 195
Innocent IV 195
Innocent VIII 221
Innocent X 309, 313
In Praise of Folly, Erasmus 215
Inquisition, The 194-195, 202, 229, 298, 305
Inquisitor's Manual 195
Institutes of the Christian Religion, The, Calvin 256
International Congregational Council, The 415, 501
International Missionary Council 416, 474
Irenaeus 107, 108
Irving, Edward, Irvingites 442
Islam 131-134, 158
Ivan III (the Great) 200

Jacob, Henry 284
Jacobins 366, 368
James I (of England) 282, 285
James II 290, 291
James VI of Scotland (James I) 264, 282
James, William 383, 479
Jansen, Cornelius 300
Jansenism 301, 322, 371
Jerome 59, 95, 100, 101, 110, 303
Jerusalem 51, 109, 133, 134, 186, 187
Jesuits (Society of Jesus) 293, 294, 297, 298, 299, 300, 407
Jews 366, 463
John of Damascus 136, 137
John VIII 131, 148
John XI 148
John XII 148
John XXII 211
John XXIII 204, 205, 210
Judaism 72, 158
Judson, Adoniram 402, 441
Julian the Apostate 95, 96, 100
Julius II 218, 222, 306
Justin Martyr 70

Kaaba, The 131
Kagawa Toyohiko 516
Kaiser Wilhelm II 466, 468
Kant, Immanuel 324, 327, 420, 477
Keats, John 375
Keble, John 410, 413
Keith, George 425
Kennedy, James 512
Kierkegaard, Soren 382, 484, 489
King James Bible (Authorized Version) 282
King, Martin Luther, Jr. 506
King's College (Columbia Univ.) 351
Kingsley, Charles 392, 412, 422, 457
Knights Hospitalers 173, 186
Knights of Columbus 434
Knights Templars 173, 174, 186, 202
Knox, John 263, 264
Koran, The 132
Kreisau Circle 473
Ku Klux Klan 458, 504

Labadists 328
labarum 86
laissez faire 424
Lambeth Conferences 415
Laoghaire, High King 112
Lapking, Olaf 131
lapsed 61
Large Catechism 244
Lateran Agreements 462
Lateran Synod 165
Latimer, Hugh 272, 277, 278
Laud, William 285, 345
Lausanne Covenant 501
Law of Three Stages 422
Laws of Guarantees 373
League of Militant Godless 460
League of Nations 468, 470
"leap of faith," Kierkegaard 382
lectio, Scholastics 174
Lee, Robert E. 430
Leibniz, G. W. 315
Leipzig Disputation 237
Leipzig Society, The 404
Lenin 459
Leo I, the first pope 97, 110, 117, 128
Leo III, the Iconoclast 136, 141, 144
Leo III, Emperor 154
Leo V, the Armenian 137
Leo IX 159, 163, 164
Leo X 222, 228, 237, 240
Leo XII 371, 433

Leo XIII 278, 373, 384, 433, 434
Leonardo da Vinci 216
Le Roy, Edouard 384
Lessing, Gotthold Ephraim 321
Levellers 287
libellatici 61
Liberalism 377, 409, 476–479, 482, 484
Liberation theology 494
Liberius, Bishop of Rome 95
Licinius 86, 88
Life of Constantine, Eusebius 89
light, particles of, tenet of Manichaeism 76
Linacre, Thomas 215
Lincoln, Abraham 429, 430
Lindsell, Harold 484
Lindsey, Theophilus 410, 438
Livingstone, David 400, 403, 405, 426
Locke, John 317, 318, 319
Log College, the 349
Lollards, Wycliffe's itinerant preachers 207, 208, 271
Lombard 97, 144
London Missionary Society 340, 398, 403, 438
Long Parliament 286, 287
Lord's Supper, the 60, 259, 266, 267, 290, 303
Lorenzo di Valla 142, 205
Louis VII, Crusade leader 187
Louis XII 222
Louis XIII 310
Louis XIV 261, 262, 290, 307
Louis XVI 365
Loyola, Ignatius 255, 294, 297, 299
Luther, Martin 101, 173, 219, 222, 230, 231, 249, 272, 292, 293
Lutheran 358, 482
Lutheran Church Missouri Synod 436–437, 482, 498
Lutheranism 250, 251, 264, 308, 328, 329, 436–437
Lyell, Charles 416

McCullough, William 342
McGee, John 359
McGready, James 359
McIntire, Carl 484
Maccabean Revolt 20
Macedonia 25, 50
Machen, J. Gresham 482
Maclaren, Alexander 441
Madison, James 357

Magna Carta 271
Magnentius 95
Magyars 146, 147
Major-Generals, Cromwell 287
Mandeville, Sir John 218
Manichaean 102, 104, 129
Manichaeus 76
Mann, Horace 364
Manz, Felix 254, 267
Mao Tse-tung 475
Marburg Colloquy 248, 254
Marcion, Marionism 75, 104, 107
Marco Polo 218
Marcus Aurelius 62
Marian exiles 279, 280
Marston Moor 286
Martin V 205
Martin of Tours 111–112
martyrs, martyrdom 46, 61, 90
Marx, Karl 327, 419, 420, 435
Marxism 463
Mary, daughter of Henry VIII 273
Mary Queen of Scots 263, 272, 279, 282
Mary Tudor 263, 277, 279
Mass, the 253, 267, 304
Massachusetts Bay Colony 345
Massacre of St. Bartholomew's Day 261
Matthys, Jan 268, 269
Maurice, J.F.D. 392, 422
Maxentius 86, 88
Maximian 86, 88
Maximilian, Emperor 214, 222, 237
Maximin Daza 65
Maximus Thrax 64
Mayflower 283, 345
Mein Kampf 462
Melanchthon, Philipp 242, 244, 248, 293
Mendicant monks 169–173
Menno Simons, Mennonites 262, 269, 270, 358
mental reservation, Jesuit doctrine 297–298
Methodism, Methodists 328, 332, 337, 360, 388, 389, 390, 431, 440, 482
Methodist Episcopal Church 440, 444
Methodius, 131, 138, 146
Metropolitan Tabernacle 390
Michelangelo 216, 218, 222
Miller, William 445
Mills, Samuel J. 401, 402
Milton, John 291

Minucius Felix 71
mission civilisatrice 457
Modalists 77
Moffat, Robert 403, 405
Mohammed 131, 146, 147
Moltmann, Jurgen 494
monads 315-316
Monarchianism 77
monasticism 89, 111-114, 155, 156, 274
Monologium, Anselm 176
Monophysites 97, 98, 137, 153
monotheism 77, 132
Montanus, Montanism 76, 107, 109
Montezuma 343
Moody, Dwight L. 393, 508
Moody Bible Institute 393, 480
Moral Men and Immoral Society, Niebuhr 489
Moravianism 146, 331, 332, 335, 348, 358, 405
More, Sir Thomas 215, 272
Morrison, Robert 404
Mott, John R. 414, 416, 496
Muhlenberg, Henry M. 330, 346, 358
Muller, George 392, 444
Muntzer, Thomas, Peasants' Revolt 246, 247, 266
Murton, John 284
Mussolini, Benito 461, 472
mysticism 210, 232, 262

Napoleon Bonaparte 367, 368
Napoleon's Concordat 301
National Assembly 365, 366
National Association of Evangelicals 475, 483
National Council of Churches of Christ 415, 501
National Covenant of 1638 285
Navigators, The 512
Nayler, James 288
Nazi, Nazi Party 457, 462
Nazism 380, 463, 473
Neoorthodoxy 382, 480, 484, 491
Nepos, Julius 97
Nero 61-62
Nestorians 117, 137, 155, 405, 435
Newell, Samuel 402
New Jersey College (Princeton) 349
New Light Presbyterians 349
Newman, John Henry 410

Newton, John 340
Newton, Sir Isaac 316
Nicaea 93, 239
Nicene-Constantinopolitan Creed 93, 95, 96, 115, 116
Nicholas of Cusa 142, 175, 205, 206, 211, 214
Nicholas V 206, 220
Nicole, Pierre 301
Niebuhr, Reinhold 473, 489, 492
Niebuhr, Richard 489
Niemoller, Martin 464, 486
Nietzsche, Friedrich 327, 380, 381, 454, 461
Nihilism 380, 381, 453, 454
Ninety-Five Theses 230, 234, 235, 306
nominalism 175
Nonconformists 280, 290, 389, 438
Northern Baptist Convention (American) 402, 441, 481, 482
Northfield Seminary 393
Novation 81
Novum Organum, Bacon 314

Oastler, Richard 392
Oates, Titus 290
Ockenga, Harold J. 484
Odoacer 97
Oecolampadius, Johann 254
Oglethorpe, Governor James 335
Old Light Presbyterians 349
Olga, Queen 158
"On the Bound Will," Luther 244
On Divine Lordship, Wycliffe 207
On the Education of a Christian Prince, Erasmus 215
"On the Freedom of the Will," Erasmus 243
On Monarchy, Dante 212
On Prayer, Origen 79
On the Unity of the Church, Cyprian 81
Ordering of Worship, Luther 244
Ordonnances, Calvin 260
Origen, 79, 92
Origin of Species, The, Darwin 416
Ostrogoths 124, 126
Oswy, Northumbrian king 128
Otto I, (the Great) 148, 149, 158, 228
Otto II 149
Ottoman Turks 199

Oxford Movement, The 409, 410, 413, 415, 442

Pacelli, Cardinal 473
Pachomius 90
Pacific Garden Mission 509
pacifism 270, 358, 359, 469
paganism 88
Paine, Thomas 327, 359
Palladius, in Ireland 112
Pannenberg, Wolfhart 494
Papacy at Rome, Luther 238
Papal states 142, 370
Papias 69
Paradise Lost, Milton 291
Paradise Regained, Milton 291
parish rates, compulsory 388
Parker, Matthew 278
Parr, Catherine, wife of Henry VIII 276
Particular Baptists (Calvinists) 284, 390, 441
Pascal, Blaise 101, 300, 319, 321, 322
Pasteur, Louis 406
Patripassians (Monarchians) 77, 78
Paul of Samosata, Paulicians 77, 155, 156
Paul II 220, 221
Paul III 293, 302
Paul IV 293
Peace of Augsburg 249, 307, 308
Peace of Westphalia 309, 313
Peasants' Revolt (or Uprising) 207, 245, 266, 267, 271
Pecham, John, Archbishop of Canterbury 201
Pelagius, Pelagianism 104, 105, 300
Penn, William 348
Pentecostal churches 450, 470
Pepin 141, 142
Persecutions, Rome 60-66
Peter, Simon 44, 81, 107
Peter the Hermit 187
Philip, King of France 201-202
Philip II 277, 279, 307
Philip III 308
Philo 92
Photius, Patriarch of Constantinople 146, 154, 155, 159
Picts 112
Pietism 328, 332, 337, 346, 349, 397, 436, 444, 501

Pilgrim's Progress,
  Bunyan 291, 322
Pius II 220
Pius IV 302
Pius V 278, 279
Pius VI 366, 368
Pius VII 368, 370
Pius VIII 371
Pius IX 372, 373, 433
Pius X 384, 434, 493
Pius XI 182, 460, 462, 464
Pius XII 473, 475
Pizarro, Francisco Javier
  Luna 408
Plato, Platonism 92, 95, 174
Pleasant Sunday Afternoon
  Movement 389
Plymouth Brethren 441,
  442-444
Polk, Leonidas 431
Polycarp 68, 107
Pompey 20
Pontifex Maximus 80
Populist Movement 425
positivism 422
Praemunire 271
Praxeaus 77
Prayer Book (Anglican) 282,
  285, 290
predestination 105, 258,
  360
Presbyterian,
  Presbyterianism 264, 280,
  285, 287, 291, 349, 360,
  363, 400, 404, 431, 440,
  482
Presbyterian Puritans 280,
  281
Presbyterianism,
  English 280
Pricillian of Spain 96
Prierias, Silvester 236
Primitive Methodists 389,
  440
Princeton Theological
  Seminary 440, 482
Princip, Gavrilo 466
probabilism, Jesuit
  doctrine 297, 298
*Proficience and Advancement
  of Learning,* Bacon 314
Prohibition 502, 504
proletariats
  (sansculottes) 365
Proslogium (a Discourse),
  Anselm 176
Protestants,
  Protestantism 247, 248,
  264, 279, 364, 366, 372
Proudhom, Pierre
  Joseph 454
Provincial Letters,
  Pascal 300
Pseudoclementines 73
psychology, Tertullian 78
Ptolemy 19

public schools 364
Punic Wars 21
purgatory, doctrine 229,
  230, 231, 235
Puritans, Puritanism 264,
  279, 280, 281, 282, 283,
  285, 288, 291, 332, 357
Pusey, Edward B. 409, 413

**Quakers, Quakerism 266,
  287, 288, 291, 332, 358, 397,
  425, 426, 431, 441, 442, 469**
Quatuor Libri Sententiarum
  (The Sentences) 178
Quest of the Historical Jesus,
  Schweitzer 478
Quietism 331, 441, 442

**Racism, discrimination
  456, 505**
Ragged School Union 391
Raikes, Robert 340
Raleigh, Sir Walter 344
Raphael 216, 218, 222
rationalism 313, 314, 363,
  372, 374
Rauschenbusch, Walter 423,
  477, 479
Raymond of Provence 173
Raymond of Toulouse,
  Crusade leader 187
Reagan, Ronald 508
Reasonableness of Christianity,
  Locke 317
recapitulation, doctrine of
  Irenaeus 78
Recared, King of Spain 126
Red Cross, The 405
Reformation 280, 292
Reformation, Catholic 304
Reformers, English 391
"Regula Primitiva" Francis of
  Assisi 170
Reign of Terror 1793-94
  367
Reimarus, Hermann
  Samuel 320
remanence, definition 207
Renaissance 145, 147, 212,
  215, 280, 281
Renaissance popes 220-222
Renan, Ernest 378
Restoration, The 288
Restoration Parliament 290
Reuchlin, Johann 214, 238
revival, revivalism 328, 339,
  349, 362
Revolution of 1917
  (Bolshevik) 459
Rhode Island College
  (Brown) 351

Rhodo, opposed
  Marcionism 75
Ricci, Matteo 300
Rice, Luther 402
Richard I 188
Ridley, Nicholas 277, 278
Rigorists 91
Riley, W. B. 481
Ritschl, Albert 379, 477
Ritschl, Friedrich 380
Ritschlian school
  (Liberalism) 379
Robert of Molesme 168
Robert of Normandy 187
Roberts, Oral 512
Robinson, John A. T. 493
Robinson, John 283
Rockefeller, John D. 419, 424,
  425, 479, 510
Rodeheaver, Homer 510
Romaine, William 340
Roman Catholic
  Church 292, 366, 431,
  433, 462, 496, 498
Roman Catholicism 291,
  343
Roman Empire 21, 25, 26-
  28
Romanticism 371, 374, 377,
  409
Rome, Fall of 96
Rome, preeminent
  church 80
Roncalli, Angelo Giuseppe
  (John XXIII) 500
Rothmann, Bernhard 269
Rousseau, Jean-Jacques 320,
  374, 375
Rowlands, Daniel 342
Rufas, King William 176
Rule of St. Augustine 173
Rule of St. Benedict 114
Russell, Charles Taze 446
Russia 158
Russian Bible Society 435
Russian Orthodox
  Church 414, 459, 460
Rutgers College 352
Ruysbroeck, John, Flemish
  priest 211

Sabellianism, Sabellius 77
*Sacramentis Fidei Christianae,
  De,* Hugo 178
sacraments 104, 136, 232,
  239
Sadat, Anwar 508
Sadoleto, Cardinal 260
saeculum obscurum (Dark
  Ages) 147
Saladin, Moslem
  leader 187, 188
Salvation Army 390, 391
Salvian 124

Sandemanians 445
Sankey, Ira David 393
Saracens 92, 134, 156, 157
Sartre, Jean-Paul 454, 490
Savonarola, Girolamo 222
Saxons 124, 144
Schaeffer, Francis 484
Schiller, Friedrich von 375
Schlatter, Michael 346, 348
Schlegel, Friedrich von 375, 376, 377
Schleiermacher, Friedrich Daniel Ernst 331, 371, 376, 377, 477, 486
Schleswig, Anskar's school 130
Schmalkaldic League 249, 269
Schoenberg 465
Scholasticism 174, 213, 215, 243
Schopenhauer, Arthur 326, 381
Schwartz, Friedrich 330
Schweitzer, Albert 383, 477, 478
Science and Health with the Key to the Scriptures 446
Scofield, C. I. (Bible) 480
Scopes trial 418
Scott, Sir Walter 375
Seabury, Samuel, Jr. 357
"Seceders" 342
Second Crusade, The 187, 190
Second Great Awakening 359, 362
Seleucus 19
Seljuk Turks 184, 186, 187
Separatists 280, 281, 283, 345
Septimius Severus 62
Sergius III, Pope 148
Serra, "Father Juniper" 343, 408
Seven Years' War 344, 356
Seventh-day Adventist 445
Seventh day Baptist 445
Severus 86, 88
Seymour, Edward 276, 277
Seymour, Jane 276
Shakespeare, William 291
Sharp, Granville 340, 425
Shields, T. T. 481
Shorter Catechism (Westminster) 286
Sigismund, emperor 204, 210
Simony 72
Six Articles, The, (Henry VIII) 275, 276
Six-Day War 476
Sixtus IV 221, 230
Sixtus V 279
Sixty-seven Articles, Zwingli 253

skepticism 324, 359
Smith, Alfred E. 458, 504
Smith, Joseph 447
"social gospel" movement 423, 477, 479, 482
socialism 419, 458
Society for Promoting Christian Knowledge 348
Society for the Propagation of the Gospel in Foreign Parts 335, 348, 397
Society of Jesus (Jesuits) 294, 296, 370
sola fide 232
sola scriptura 231
Sophronius 134
Southern Baptist Convention 402, 441, 498
Southern Christian Leadership Conference 506
Spangenberg, Augustus 335, 348
Spener, Philip Jacob 328
Spinoza, Baruch 315
Spirituals, order of monks 170, 183
Spurgeon, Charles Haddon 389, 418, 441
St. Peter's Basilica 230, 235
Stalin, Joseph 460, 474
Stamp Act 356
Stanley, Henry 403
Statute of Praemunire 201
Staupitz, Johann von 234
Stephen of Rome 107, 108
Stoics 92
Stone, Barton W. 359, 444
Stowe, Harriet Beecher 360, 428
Strauss, David Friedrich 378, 381, 383, 416, 420
Strong, Josiah 415, 424
Stuart, Henry (Lord Darnley) 282
Student Foreign Missions Fellowship 513
Stuyvesant, Peter 346
Summa Contra Gentiles, Aquinas 179
Summa Theologica, Aquinas 179
Sunday observance 89, 283
Sunday school movement 340, 413, 439
Sunday, William Ashley (Billy) 509
Sun Yat-sen 516
Swift, Jonathan 322
Syllabus of Errors, Pius IX 372, 433
Sylvester 110
Sylvester II 149
symphonia 98, 152
Synod of Dort 263
Synod of Hieria 137

Synod of Toulouse 195
Synod of Whitby 128
Synod of Worms 166

"Table Talks," Luther 245
tabula rasa 317, 325
Talmage, Frank Dewitt 509
Talmage, T. Dewitt 509
Tappan, Arthur and Lewis 425, 431
Tatian 71
Tauler, Johann 211
Tausen, Hans 250
Taylor, Jeremy 291
Taylor, J. Hudson 400, 403, 404
Taylor, Nathaniel W. 359, 362
Teen Challenge 513
Temple, Frederick 418
Temple, William 416
"temples of reason" (churches) 367
Ten Articles of 1536 275
Ten Hours' Bill 391
Tennis Court Oath 366
Teresa of Avila 173
Tertullian, Quintus Septimus Florens 59, 75, 77, 78, 80, 107, 108
Test Act 290
Tetzel, Johann 234, 236
Theodora 137, 138, 148
Theodosius I 96, 100, 106
Theodosius II 97, 117
Theodotus 77, 109
Theology of Liberation, A 494
Theophilus 71, 75, 101, 137
Theotokos 118
Third Estate 365, 366
Third Lateran Council 191, 193, 194
Thirty-nine Articles 277, 279, 282, 291, 482
Thirty Years War 292, 306, 309, 310, 328, 364
Thomas à Kempis 211
Thomas Becket 191
Thoreau, Henry David 429
Thorlaksson, Gudbrand 251
Thuringia 130
Thurneysen, Eduard 485, 488
Thus Spake Zarathustra 381
Tikhon, Patriarch 459
Tillich, Paul 491
Tindal, Matthew 318, 322
Tolstoy, Leo 435
Tome to Chalcedon, Christology 110, 118
Torah, The 19
Torquemada, Grand Inquisitor 195, 298
Torrey, Reuben A. 509
totalitarianism 458

Toynbee, Arnold 384
Tractarian Revival 409, 415
traditionalists 363
traditores 61, 91, 104
translations 242
transubstantiation 192, 207, 239, 248, 253, 271, 304
"treasury of the church," indulgences 229, 235
Treutlen, John Adams 358
Tridentine faith 305
Trinity, doctrine of the 78, 93, 97, 98, 115, 154, 155, 177, 192
triple sense in Scripture, Origen 79
Troeltsch, Ernst 424, 478
Trueblood, Elton 513
Tryggvason, Olaf 131
Turgenev, Ivan 454
Twelve Articles, (Peasants' Revolt) 246, 267
Tyrell, George 383

Ubermensch **(Superman), Nietzsche 381**
Ulphilas 111, 124
Ultramontanism 370, 372, 433, 435
Ulyanov, Vladimir Ilyich (Lenin) 459
Unam Sanctam 202
Uncle Tom's Cabin, Stowe 360, 429
Union Theological Seminary 439, 479, 492
Unitarians, Unitarianism 287, 291, 431, 438
United Brethren 444
United Methodist Church 440, 444
United Methodist Free Church 390, 440
United Nations, The 475
un roi, une loi, une foi 310
Urban II, Pope 184, 186
Urban V 203
Urban VI 203
Urban VIII 300
Ussher, Archbishop 317
Utopia, Thomas More 272

Valens 96
Valentian III 110
Valentinian I 96
Valentinus 78
Valerian 64
Valla, Lorenzo 214
van Buren, Paul 493
van Oldenbarneveldt, Jan 307

Vandals 97, 98, 110, 124, 126
Vasco de Gama 219, 343
Vatican, The 220, 373
Vatican Council I 372, 499
Vatican Council II 205, 301, 370, 499, 500
Venn, Henry 340
via media 281, 412
Victor Emmanuel 373
Victoria, Queen 465, 466
Voltaire, Francois-Marie Arouet de 319, 359, 368, 420
Vulgate, Latin 110, 303

Waldo, Peter; Waldenses 193, 194, 262
Wall Street 470
Wallace, A. R. 418
Wallenstein, Albrecht von 308, 309
War of the Roses 228
Watch Tower Bible and Tract Society (Jehovah's Witnesses) 446, 447
Watt, James 386
Weber, Max 478
Weiss, Johannes 477, 485
Weld, Theodore Dwight 428, 431
Wellhausen, Julius 419, 479
Welsh Revivals 341
Wescott, Brook F. 419
Wesley, Charles 332, 337
Wesley, John 331, 332, 358, 400
Wesleyans (Methodist) 389
Wesleyan Methodist Association 440
Westminster Abbey 159
Westminster Assembly 286
Westminster Confession 286
Westminster Seminary 482
Whigs (Puritans) 290
Whitefield, George 332, 334, 336, 342, 351
Whitehead, Alfred North 493
Whitgift, John 281
Whitney, Eli 428
"Wholly Other" 485
Wilberforce, William 341, 392, 426, 428
Wilkerson, David 513
William of Occam 172, 183
William of Orange 262, 291
William the Conqueror 228
William the Silent 262
Williams, Roger 345, 346, 441
Willibrord of Saxon Northumbria 129
Wilson, Grady 510

Wilson, Woodrow 468
Winifrid (Wynfrith) 130
Winthrop, John 285
Wishart, George 263
Witherspoon, John 357
Wolsey, Cardinal Thomas 271
Woman's Christian Temperance Union 502
Wordsworth, William 375, 376
Working Men's College 392, 422
World Conference on Faith and Order 416, 496
World Congress on Evangelism 501
World Council of Churches 416, 474, 483, 496, 498, 501
World Missionary Conference 416, 496, 513
World Vision International 513
World War I 466, 470
World War II 377, 469, 470
World's Sunday School Association 414
Wrede, W. 478
Wright, G. Ernest 494
Wycliffe, John 201, 207, 208, 271

Xavier, Frances 255, 296, 299
Ximenes, Cardinal Francisco 228, 229, 296, 298

Yaroslav 158
Yokefellows 513
Young, Brigham 448
Young Life 513
Young Men's Christian Association 392, 393, 414
Young Women's Christian Association 414
Youth for Christ, International 510, 513

Zacharias, Pope 142
Zealots 21
Zeno, Emperor 97
Zinzendorf, Count von 330, 336
Zwickau Prophets 243, 266, 267
Zwingli, Ulrich 248, 252-255, 267
Zwischen den Zeiten 485

DATE DUE

			HIGHSMITH #45230
NOV 1 3 2006			
MAR 0 5 2004			

Printed in USA